INVENTORY

OF

CHURCH ARCHIVES

SOCIETY OF FRIENDS

IN

PENNSYLVANIA

PREPARED BY

THE PENNSYLVANIA HISTORICAL SURVEY

DIVISION OF COMMUNITY SERVICE PROGRAMS

WORK PROJECTS ADMINISTRATION

CLEARFIELD

Originally published
Philadelphia, 1941

Reprinted for
Clearfield Company, Inc. by
Genealogical Publishing Co., Inc.
Baltimore, Maryland
1996

International Standard Book Number: 0-8063-4650-7
Made in the United States of America

FEDERAL WORKS AGENCY

WORK PROJECTS ADMINISTRATION

Howard O. Hunter, Commissioner
R. C. Branion, Regional Director
Philip Mathews, State Administrator

Division of Community Service Programs

Florence Kerr, Assistant Commissioner
Agnes S. Cronin, Chief Regional Supervisor
Anne M. Butler, State Director

Research and Records Programs

Harvey E. Becknell, Director
Edward J. Bennett, Regional Supervisor
Robert McCullough, State Chief

Pennsylvania Historical Survey

Sargent B. Child, National Director
J. Knox Milligan, State Supervisor

The Pennsylvania Historical Survey

is sponsored by the

Pennsylvania Historical Commission

Ross Pier Wright, Chairman
Edward R. Barnsley   Gregg L. Neal
Frances Dorrance   Roy F. Nichols

Donald A. Cadzow, Executive Secretary   S. K. Stevens, Historian
Francis B. Haas, Superintendent of Public Instruction, ex officio

This inventory of the archives of the Society of Friends in Pennsylvania supplies a long-felt need. It is both a historical description of the origin and development of Quaker meetings in the State, such as Ezra Michener attempted eighty years ago (A Retrospect of Early Quakerism, Philadelphia, 1860), and a check list of Quaker Meeting records, similar to that which Morgan Bunting published in 1906 (A List of the Records of the Meetings Constituting the Yearly Meeting of the Society of Friends, Held at Fifteenth and Race Streets, Philadelphia, Printed for the Representative Committee, 1906). But it is more complete than either of these. In combining the functions of a history and an archival catalogue it provides a handbook of inestimable value for the study of the Quaker contribution to the growth of the Commonwealth.

Both Michener and Bunting were members of the "Race Street," or "Hicksite" branch of the Friends. Their work was therefore limited to their own group for the period following the schism, or "Great Separation," of 1827-28. This present volume has the virtue of being partisan to no particular branch of the Society of Friends in Pennsylvania. It records with equal fidelity the history of "Orthodox," "Hicksite," "Primitive," and "Progressive" Friends, now happily tending toward unity, as the presence in these pages of various new "United" meetings show.

Pennsylvania Quakerism and "The Yearly Meeting for Pennsylvania, New Jersey, Delaware, and Parts Adjacent," as Philadelphia Yearly Meeting was at one time called, are not coterminous. The Yearly Meeting itself was first organized in Burlington, New Jersey, in 1681, and did not meet permanently in Philadelphia until after 1760. But the exigencies of the Research and Records Programs require a study of religious organizations by states. New Jersey, Delaware, Maryland and "Parts Adjacent" will also have their Inventories of Quaker Archives, which, when completed will tell the story of "Philadelphia Yearly Meeting," outside the boundaries of Pennsylvania. A list is provided, however, of these out-of-state meetings which could not be included in this volume.

In western Pennsylvania, however, there were during the last decades of the eighteenth century and the early part of the nineteenth century many Quaker meetings which had no formal connection with Philadelphia Yearly Meeting. They were settled during the westward movement of Friends from Maryland and Virginia, up the Potomac River and down the Monongahela to the Ohio, and were originally under the jurisdiction of Baltimore Yearly Meeting. In time the meetings which persisted after the tide of Quaker migration had passed on into the Ohio Valley, were transferred to the newly-established Ohio Yearly Meeting. Eventually all these meetings were, in Quaker terminology, "laid down," and of them hardly a memory now remains. One of the most useful sections of this present volume is that which describes in detail these obscure Quaker meetings on the western slopes of the Alleghenies, and traces the location of their scattered manuscript records.

There are two principal depositories of Quaker records in Pennsylvania, besides the safes and strong boxes owned by local meetings. The archives of Philadelphia Yearly Meeting (Orthodox) are in the hands of the Custodian of Records at the Friends' Book Store, 302 Arch Street,

Philadelphia. Those of Philadelphia Yearly Meeting (Hicksite) are deposited in the Friends Historical Library of Swarthmore College, Swarthmore, Pennsylvania. Yearly meeting records prior to the Separation of 1827-28 are at the Arch Street depository, as are many of the older records of quarterly, monthly, and preparative meetings. Some of the local records from the earlier period are at Swarthmore, however, where they are now being copied on film to facilitate their use and preservation. Subordinate meetings have been encouraged to place their noncurrent records in these central depositories, but some of them have as yet failed to do so. Current records are, of course, in the hands of meeting clerks, whose names and addresses are noted in the follcwing pages.

Since the history of a Quaker meeting involves not only the activities recorded in its minutes, but also data regarding its buildings, burial grounds, school, homes for the aged,and other institutionalized activities, this inventory includes these data as well. It also contains information relating to books of marriage certificates, registers of. births, deaths, disownments, and membership, for these records are integral parts of the meeting archives.

This inventory of the archives of Pennsylvania Quakerism will be useful in many ways. Students of Pennsylvania history, in its religious, social, and even political phases, will find it a most valuable handbook. Used in conjunction with the Pennsylvania volumes of William Wade Hinshaw's Encyclopedia of American Quaker Genealogy, it will be most helpful to local historians and to genealogists. It should also encourage Friends and others to preserve their records more carefully, and inspire them to emulate the virtues of Pennsylvania's Quaker citizens whose lives and works are recorded in their annals.

It is a pleasure to voice a feeling of gratitude to the Pennsylvania Historical Survey for compiling this valuable book. Particularly to J. Knox Milligan, State Supervisor and to Karl Goedecke, Eugene M. Braderman, and Lewis C. Moon, former Supervisors of the Survey, and to their staffs of workers throughout the State, should credit be given for instituting and carrying through to completion this exhaustive survey of the official records of Pennsylvania Quakerism.

Chairman of the Publications Committee   THOMAS E. DRAKE
Friends Historical Association
November 1941

Friends' Historical Association

Founded 1873   Incorporated 1924

Official Publication: BULLETIN OF FRIENDS' HISTORICAL ASSOCIATION

Secretary
ANNA B. HEWITT
Haverford College
Haverford, Pa.

Treasurer
I. THOMAS STEERE
30 Buck Lane
Haverford, Pa.

President
WILLIAM W. COMFORT
Haverford College
Haverford, Pa.

Editor
THOMAS K. BROWN, JR
226 Dickinson Avenue
Swarthmore, Pa.

Curator
LYDIA FLAGG GUMMERE
Shirley Court Apartments
Upper Darby, Pa.

Eleventh Month 15, 1941

TO CITIZENS OF THE COMMONWEALTH OF PENNSYLVANIA
AND MEMBERS OF THE SOCIETY OF FRIENDS

    Since this first volume in the Pennsylvania Inventory
of Church Archives concerns the Society of Friends, it is
appropriate that the Friends' Historical Association should
act as its local sponsor. The Association, like this Inventory
of Quaker Archives, includes all branches of the Society of
Friends in Pennsylvania, and is interested in promoting the
study of Quaker history regardless of ancient schism or
Separation.

    Individual members and organizations in the two
Philadelphia Yearly Meetings, as well as the treasury of the
Race Street Yearly Meeting, and that of The Book Association
of Friends, have generously contributed to the cost of printing
and binding the Inventory. The Pennsylvania Historical Survey,
while having facilities for gathering information, had no funds
available for the considerable amount needed to publish the
work.

    Certain members of Friends' Historical Association have
advised with the Editor, Lewis C. Moon, but the entire credit
for the research and editorial work belongs to the Pennsylvania
Historical Survey. It is my pleasure to sponsor this volume
on behalf of Friends' Historical Association, and, at the same
time, to thank the Pennsylvania Historical Survey for preparing
this valuable reference work on the history and archives of the
Society of Friends in Pennsylvania.

WW Comfort

President

PREFACE

One of the primary object: .s of the Pennsylvania Historical Survey
is to preserve and make accessible historical source material. In fulfillment of this aim is presented herewith the _Inventory of Church Ar-
chives_, Society of Friends in Pennsylvania, one in the series of inventories of the records of all denominations numbering approximately one
hundred and fifty religious denominations and sects which are being compiled by the Survey. The published volumes are intended to serve not
only the clergy and officials of religious organizations but also students of social and economic history and persons engaged in genealogical
research.

The church archives survey covers both living and defunct churches
and their records. The information presented in this inventory was gathered by qualified workers throughout the State and is based on a search
of Meeting records and local Quaker history supplemented by statements
of clergymen, church historians, and denominational officials. This information has been checked for accuracy with all known sources. If dis-
crepancies in dates or other such data occur, corrections based on authentic sources will be welcomed in order that these errors may be elim-
inated from further editions.

For cheerful and helpful assistance, the Survey is indebted to the
Custodians of the various Friends' Record Depositories and to many in-
dividuals from the Meetings listed herein. Colonel Philip Mathews, State
Administrator and the Research and Records Programs of the Work Projects
Administration in each district have given this endeavor their support
and approbation. The editorial staff has also profited by the construc-
tive criticism and advice of the National Office of the Historical Records
Survey.

The various units of the _Inventory of Church Archives_ will be published for distribution to the key libraries of the State, to a selected
list of libraries and depositories throughout the country, and to National
denominational offices. Requests for information concerning any of the
units of the Survey or suggestions covering data contained herein should
be addressed to the State Supervisor, 46 North Cameron Street, Harrisburg,
Pennsylvania.

Philadelphia, Pennsylvania
November 1941

J. KNOX MILLIGAN
State Supervisor

TABLE OF CONTENTS

Page

Part A. Introduction to History and Organization

I. Historical Sketch   3
     Polity and Organization. The Keithian Quakers
     (Quaker Baptists). The Free Quakers. The Great
     Separation of 1827-28. Progressive Friends. The
     Wilburite Controversy. The Primitive Friends.
     United and Independent Meetings.

II. Organizational Affiliations of Friends in North America . . .   33
     Friends World Committee for Consultation. Five
     Years Meeting of Friends in America. Friends
     General Conference. Independent Yearly Meetings.
     United and Independent Groups. Location and Ac-
     cessibility of Records.

Part B. Meetings and Their Records

I. Philadelphia Yearly Meeting (Orthodox)   37
     List of Quarterly Meetings Outside Pennsylvania.
     List of Quarterly Meetings in Pennsylvania: Phila-
     delphia Quarterly Meeting; Chester Quarterly Meet-
     ing; Bucks Quarterly Meeting; Western Quarterly
     Meeting; Warrington and Fairfax Quarterly Meeting;
     Abington Quarterly Meeting; Warrington Quarterly
     Meeting; Caln Quarterly Meeting; Concord Quarterly
     Meeting; Burlington and Bucks Quarterly Meeting.

II. Keithian or Christian Quakers 198
     Philadelphia Meeting. Oxford Meeting. Thomas
     Powell Meeting.

III. Philadelphia Yearly Meeting of Free Quakers 202

IV. Friends General Conference (Hicksite) 206
     List of Component Yearly Meetings. History and
     Records.

V. Philadelphia Yearly Meeting (Hicksite) 208
     List of Quarterly Meetings Outside Pennsylvania.
     List of Quarterly Meetings in Pennsylvania: Abing-
     ton Quarterly Meeting; Bucks Quarterly Meeting;
     Concord Quarterly Meeting; Western Quarterly Meet-
     ing; Caln Quarterly Meeting; Philadelphia Quarter-
     ly Meeting; Fishing Creek Half-Year Meeting; Mill-
     ville Half-Year Meeting.

VI. Pennsylvania Yearly Meetings of Progressive Friends 293

1

VII.   Primitive Friends   295
       Baltimore Yearly Meeting List. Fallsington Gen-
       eral Meeting List. Baltimore Yearly Meeting En-
       tries. Fallsington General Meeting Entries.

VIII. United Friends Meetings   302
       State College United Meeting. Chestnut Hill United
       Monthly Meeting. Concord United Monthly Meeting.
       Providence United Monthly Meeting. Radnor United
       Monthly Meeting. Upper Dublin United Monthly Meet-
       ing. Harrisburg United Monthly Meeting.

IX.   Independent Friends Meetings   306
       Pittsburgh. Buck Hill Falls.   Pocono Manor.
       Pocono Lake. Harrisburg. Lehigh Valley. Lake
       Shore.

X.   Friends Meetings with Extra-State Affiliations   309
       Baltimore Yearly Meeting (O). Baltimore Yearly
       Meeting (H). Ohio Yearly Meeting (O). Ohio Year-
       ly Meeting (H).

XI.   Friends Institutions in Pennsylvania   348

XII.   Glossary   355

       Explanatory Notes and Symbols   360

       Subordinate Meetings Outside of Pennsylvania   363

       Bibliography   367

       Alphabetic Index to Entries in the Quaker Volume   381

Maps and Charts

Family Tree of Quaker Groups in Pennsylvania . . . opposite   2

Early Friends Meetings in Old Philadelphia . . . . opposite   3

Meetings of Friends in Ohio Yearly Meetings . . . opposite 338

FAMILY TREE OF
QUAKER GROUPS IN PENNSYLVANIA

1941
TENDENCY

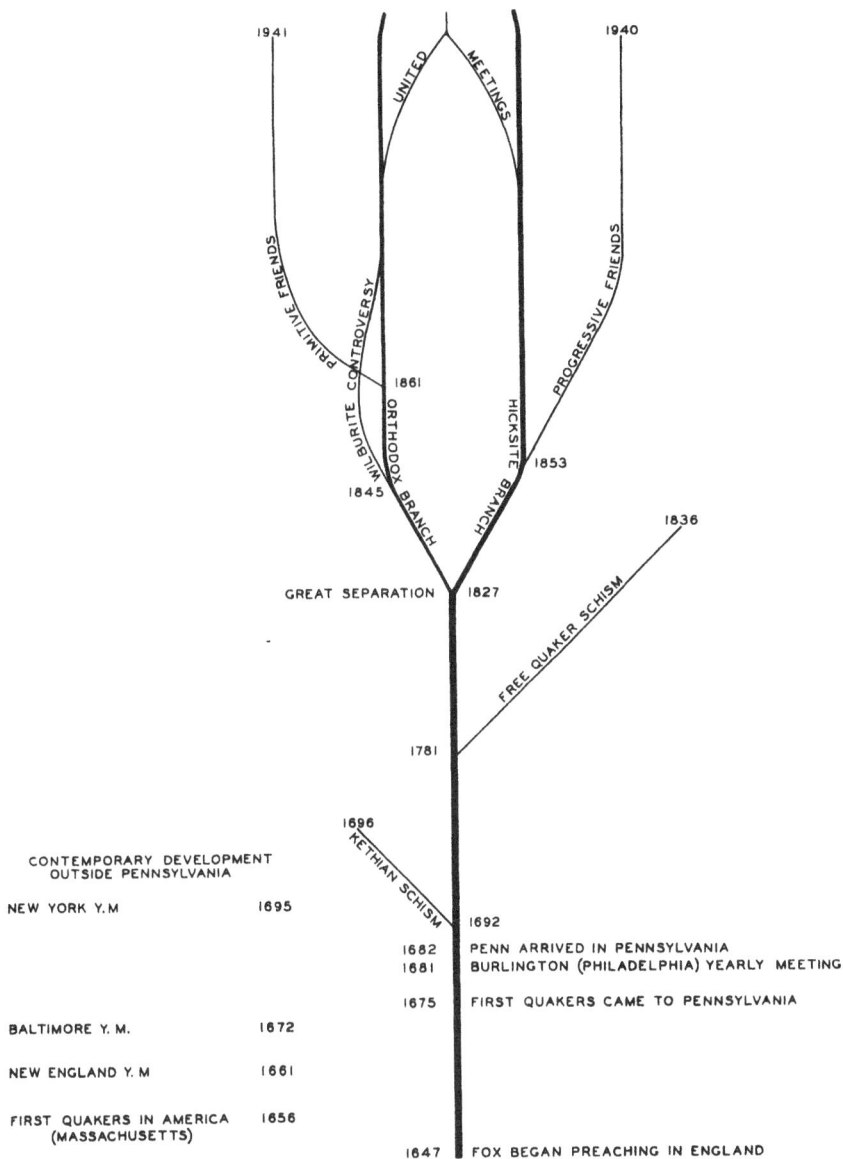

1941

UNITED   MEETINGS

1940

PRIMITIVE FRIENDS

PROGRESSIVE FRIENDS

WILBURITE CONTROVERSY

1861

ORTHODOX BRANCH

HICKSITE BRANCH

1853

1845

1836

GREAT SEPARATION   1827

FREE QUAKER SCHISM

1781

1696

CONTEMPORARY DEVELOPMENT
OUTSIDE PENNSYLVANIA

KETHIAN SCHISM

NEW YORK Y. M.   1695

1692

1682   PENN ARRIVED IN PENNSYLVANIA
1681   BURLINGTON (PHILADELPHIA) YEARLY MEETING

1675   FIRST QUAKERS CAME TO PENNSYLVANIA

BALTIMORE Y. M.   1672

NEW ENGLAND Y. M   1661

FIRST QUAKERS IN AMERICA   1656
    (MASSACHUSETTS)

1647   FOX BEGAN PREACHING IN ENGLAND

GEORGE FOX BORN 1624

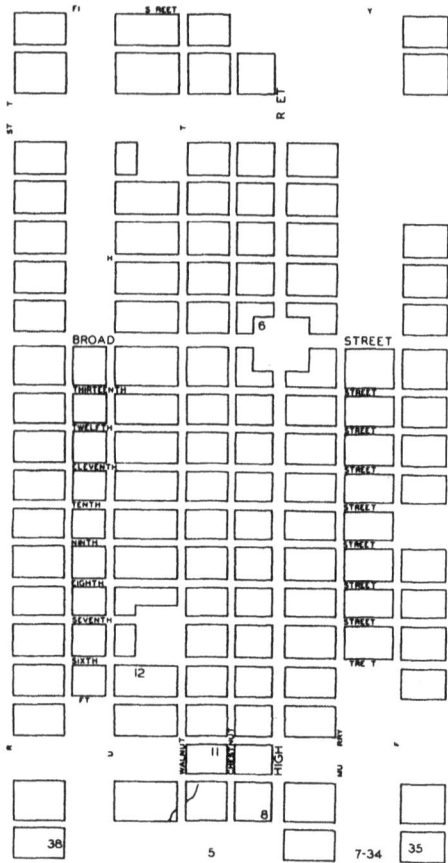

LEGEND

NUMBERS REFER TO ENTRY NUMBERS IN TEXT

4	SHACKAMAXON
5	BOARDED MEETING HOUSE
6	CENTER SQUARE MEETING HOUSE
7	FIRST BANK MEETING HOUSE
8	THE GREAT MEETING HOUSE
9	FAIR HILL MEETING HOUSE
11	FOURTH STREET MEETING HOUSE
12	ORANGE MEETING HOUSE
20	THOMAS DUCKETT'S MEETING HOUSE
34	SECOND BANK MEETING HOUSE
35	KEYS ALLEY MEETING HOUSE
38	PINE STREET MEETING HOUSE
54	GREEN STREET MEETING HOUSE

LOCATION OF EARLY FRIENDS MEETINGS
IN OLD PHILADELPHIA

PART A. INTRODUCTION TO HISTORY AND ORGANIZATION

I. HISTORICAL SKETCH

The Quaker influx to the early American Colonies has been recorded by many historians more fully than can be attempted in this brief sketch. The purpose of this essay is to provide a short introductory statement concerning their migration and effect upon the inception and development of religious life and organization in Pennsylvania.

This sect, early known as "Children of the Light" and "Friends in the Truth," later in derision called "Quakers," and now commonly called The Society of Friends, has as its background the revival of mysticism and the various mystical sects which arose in England and on the Continent during the seventeenth century.[1] It was founded by George Fox (1624-1691), who was born in Leicestershire, England. A thoughtful lad even in early years, Fox was given to lonely meditation of the Scriptures and deep searching of heart. Born in a turbulent time, both politically and spiritually, he sought spiritual communion more satisfying then that of the profession and formality of the religious leaders of his time to whom he went for help. Weighed down with the spiritual darkness of the world and his own search for God, he writes that one day a voice spoke to him, saying, "There is One, even Christ Jesus, that can speak to thy condition . . . and when I heard it my heart did leap for joy."[2] From this early revelation and subsequent spiritual "openings" Fox developed the doctrine of the Inward Light, which holds that there is "that of God" in every man, which, if heeded, will lead him to a correct spiritual state and right relationship with God and his fellow man. Growing directly out of this conception of man's relation to God is the Quaker ideal of worship, a silent inward communion with God without the need of intermediary priest or preacher. The office of preaching and testimony was developed as a means of accomplishing the ideal in group worship, and hence was never considered a necessity.

The history and development of American Quakerism is closely bound up not only with the wider religious movement which had its rise in the spiritual awakening of the sixteenth and seventeenth centuries, but is also bound up with the political and social development of early colonial America.[3] This type of religion, which took root in Massachusetts as early as 1656, grew to be a very significant influence in ten out of the thirteen original colonies. It was in some cases at first a disturbing element, later it became a shaping influence both of the religious and social life. In Pennsylvania, "The Holy Experiment" has become a synonym for Quaker influence on early colonial life. It is unnecessary to deal here with the spiritual urge or the principles of belief which motivated "the mighty work in the nations beyond the seas (America)." Al-

---

1. Rufus M. Jones, *The Quaker in the American Colonies*, Introduction, p. xiii-xxxii, hereinafter cited as Jones, *Quakers in Colonies; see also* William C. Braithwaite, *The Beginnings of Quakerism*, p. 132.
2. George Fox, *Journal*, I, 11.
3. Rufus M. Jones, *Spiritual Reformers of the Sixteenth and Seventeenth Centuries*, pp. 2-7.

though the Quaker experiment in Pennsylvania, and elsewhere among the
colonies, is closely linked with the westward march of world empire, the
Quaker urge was primarily a spiritual and not a political one.

A basic conception of the Society of Friends has always been that
the individual spirit partakes of the Divine. "I speak to that of God
in you" is an expression often used by early Friends. Many of the doctrines of the Society can be linked with this conception. Hence the
idea of the sacredness and equality of human personality. Since Quakers
held this doctrine, even in an age when women's position generally was
very inferior, it is, therefore, not strange that the first Friends to
arrive in America were women. Mary Fisher and Ann Austin came from England to Boston in 1656 and Elizabeth Harris arrived in Maryland the same
year.[1]   The earliest Quaker arrival in Pennsylvania dates back about
twenty years before the coming of William Penn. One Josiah Coale had
been instructed by George Fox to search out a home in the New World, and
on a second visit in 1660, his first being in 1657, he was definitely
commissioned by Quakers in England to purchase lands along the Susquehanna from the Indians. He returned home, however, without having accomplished his purpose.[2]   Prior to 1663 a few Quakers in search of a
more congenial religious atmosphere had settled among the Swedes near
Upland (Chester),[3] on the west bank of the Delaware. These Friends were
visited by George Fox a few years later, and in 1679 Dankers and Sluyter,
two Dutch travelers, narrate in no friendly tone their impressions of
those early Quaker settlers along the Delaware. Of Tinicum Island, below what is now Philadelphia, they say: "In the evening there arrived
three Quakers, of whom one was their great prophetess, who travels
through the whole country in order to quake. She lives in Maryland, and
forsakes home and children, plantation and all, and goes off for this
purpose. She had been to Boston and had been arrested by the authorities on account of her quakery."[4] At Upland they found two widows who
were at variance and whom the prophetess was trying to reconcile. One
of these widows named Anna Salters lived at Tokany (Tacony). The travelers, however, speak highly of Robert Wade and his wife, calling them
"the best Quakers we have seen." Wade has been called the pioneer Friend
of Pennsylvania.[5] He came to Upland in 1675 from Salem, New Jersey, and
it was to his home, the Essex House, formerly the residence of the Swed-
ish governors, that William Penn came immediately after landing from the
Welcome at New Castle on October 27, 1682.[6] It was here, too, that the
first Assembly of Pennsylvania met on December 4 to 7. A notation of the
first Quaker arrivals in Pennsylvania is not complete without mention of
a few Friends who, prior to William Penn's arrival, crossed the Delaware,
built homes, and established the Falls Meeting in what later became
Bucks County. This meeting which began meeting in private homes about

1. Jones, *Quakers in Colonies*, p. 266.
2. James Bowden, *The History of the Society of Friends in America*, I, 389.
3. Jones, *Quakers in Colonies*, p. 358.
4. Cited in *Ibid.* p. 419.
5. *Ibid.* p. 420.
6. For explanation of Old Style and New Style Calendar, *see* Explanatory Note 8.

1680[1] was not officially "set up" as a monthly meeting until 1683.

Long before Philadelphia became the Quaker metropolis of the New World it had existed as an Indian meeting place of primitive America. It was conveniently accessible from all directions. The Delaware and its tributaries, the Schuylkill, the Susquehanna and the Swatara, all of which, with the addition of a few short overland marches, provided easy means of travel; and the many Indian trails, one of which is followed by the present Germantown Avenue, leading to the high ground which overlooks the Delaware, point to its use by the Indians for their council fires and treaties with neighboring nations. "It was in recognition of this immemorial meeting place that Penn reserved a small plot of land on the east side of Second Street, near Walnut, to which the Indians could continue to resort and build their council fires," writes Fisher.[2] Philadelphia, like most of the great cities, of the Old World, was founded on a site of great importance in the religion and tradition of the primitive people who resorted to it perhaps centuries before the coming of Penn and the Quakers. With the founding of Pennsylvania the westward migration of Friends into the American colonies began in earnest.

Penn had entered the Quaker movement after it had passed through the early and somewhat fanatical phase of its inception. He did not adopt the peculiar forms of dress and conduct followed by Fox and others. His was a more business-like and practical attitude toward all doctrinal and controversial matters. Penn had his first contact with Quakers in Ireland, where his father went to live after his temporary retirement from the Royal Navy about 1656. It was in Ireland at the age of about fifteen that he came in contact with Thomas Loe, the Quaker itinerant preacher, who made a profound impression on young Penn. His two years at Christ Church, Oxford, and an equal period at the Huguenot College of Saumur in Anjou, followed by the study of law at Lincoln's Inn, constituted his formal academic training. At the age of twenty-two he was sent to manage his father's estate in Ireland, and it was from this experience and the many intimate contacts with men of affairs that he gained the fund of practical knowledge which so well fitted him for his part in the colonization of Pennsylvania which he received in payment of a debt of 16,000 pounds owed by the Crown to his father. His selection, through Markham his deputy, of the excellent site of the city to be built, his handling of boundary disputes and his dealing with the Indians attest his sound judgment. This and other personal qualities in Penn as well as his Quaker piety must have inspired confidence and respect for the youthful leader among all classes in England, for among those who followed his lead to Pennsylvania, many were from homes of wealth and refinement. Almost immediately after his landing in 1682 the wave of Quaker migration began. Penn reports that during the first nine months of his stay he had built 80 houses and that 50 ships had arrived bringing some 3,000

1. Ezra Michener, *A Retrospect of Early Quakerism*, p. 76. This date, 1680, given for the first settlers in Bucks county from New Jersey, is probably not too early. Michener himself places a question mark after it; but Bowden, *op. cit.*, II, 16, states that Quakers who arrived in Thomas Lurtin's ship in 1681 and settled at Burlington, crossed the Delaware early in 1682 and settled at Newtown. Why would these settlers pass over the fertile and more accessible lands immediately bordering the west bank of the river and settle 8 miles back in the wilderness, if these more desirable lands were not already occupied by earlier settlers.

2. Sidney Fisher, *The Making of Pennsylvania*, p. 30.

settlers, two-thirds of whom have been estimated to be Quakers.[1]

Penn's vision and plans of a New World colony were inextricably bound up with his desire to found a haven for his fellow believers. One of his first acts upon arrival at Philadelphia was to attend a monthly meeting held at the home of Thomas Fairman at Shackamaxon. An early Friend's meeting minute states; "At a Monthly Meeting the 8th of 9th month 1682 . . . . At this time Governor William Penn and a multitude of Friends arrived here and erected a city called Philadelphia, about half a mile from Shackamaxon."[2] We learn from a reference in a later minute of Abington Monthly Meeting that this monthly meeting at Fairman's had been appointed[3] in March of 1682 to be held in alternate months with one at the home of William Cooper at Pyne Point, N. J. By tradition and inference it is well established that the famous Treaty Elm, under which Penn met and established with Kings Metamaneen and Metanequan the lasting peace and brotherhood pact, was located near the Fairman home. Robert Fairman of London, in a letter dated in 1711, in mentioning the Fairman Mansion and its locality, speaks of the house at the Treaty Tree.

With the rapidly growing city and the increased stream of Quaker settlers the organization and development of the Society of Friends forged ahead. The Shackamaxon Meeting was moved within the limits of the new city. Other meetings sprang up immediately because of a demand for meeting places for the increased body of members, and also because of the numerous communities formed by the settlers which were isolated from the city by streams or lack of roads. Hundreds of newcomers joined the ranks of the young colony, many of whom were recently won over to the Quaker way of life. Church government and discipline must needs be attended to. This was not a great problem for the American Quakers. A system of church government and discipline was already well established in England, and George Fox during his visit to America in 1672 found many local meetings already in existence in Virginia, Maryland, and New Jersey. At West River, Maryland, he helped to establish the annual meeting which became Baltimore Yearly Meeting, and upon his visit to New England he found a yearly meeting already in existence, which had been founded by George Rofe at Newport, Rhode Island in 1661.[4] If Bowden is correct in his statement that the monthly meeting system was first proposed by Fox at Durham in 1653, but that the system was not generally established until 1666,[5] then many of the American monthly meetings, and also New England Yearly Meeting, were established and in operation a few years prior to the establishment of the system in England. The first monthly meeting established within the borders of Pennsylvania, of which we have record, is the meeting set up at the home of Robert Wade, at Upland (Chester) September 15, 1681. Meetings for worship had no doubt been held at the same place at least four or five years prior to this, since Wade had been living in Upland since 1675. As early as 1680 meetings for worship were also held in the homes of William Biles and others just

---

1. For family names, see William W. Hinshaw, *Encyclopedia of American Quaker Genealogy*, Vol. II and forthcoming Vol. III.
2. John F. Watson, *Annals of Philadelphia and Pennsylvania in the Olden Times*, I, 140.
3. *Ibid.*, p. 141.
4. *Inventory of the Church Archives of Rhode Island: Society of Friends*, p. 18.
5. Bowden, *op. cit.*, I, 209.

below the Falls in what became Bucks County.[1] This meeting was organized in 1683 into the Falls (Fallsington) Monthly Meeting.

The home of Thomas Gardiner in Burlington, New Jersey, is the birth-place of Philadelphia Yearly Meeting.[2] At a monthly meeting held there in third month 1681 it was decided to establish a yearly meeting to be held in the sixth month following. It was at this first yearly meeting that quarterly meetings were set up. The Friends on the west side of the river began holding annual meetings immediately after the arrival of William Penn, but since the yearly meeting at Burlington (first called New Beverley, later Bridlington) was already established and the two settlements were so near each other it was agreed in 1685 that in the future the yearly meetings would be held alternately between the two places. This arrangement continued until 1760 when the sessions removed permanently to Philadelphia. The time for holding the annual meeting was changed in 1755 from the sixth to the ninth month, and again in 1798 to the fourth month, which appointment it continues to the present time. By 1780 it is estimated that there were upwards of 25,000 Friends in Pennsylvania.

Polity and Organization

Having briefly considered the early beginnings of Quakerism together with the founding of the Pennsylvania colony it would seem well to note also something of the method and organization of the Society of Friends as it developed in the colony. It appears that by the beginning of 1683 there were three yearly meetings along the Delaware; one at Burlington and Salem, one at Shrewsbury, and one which met in Philadelphia probably only once, in third month of 1683. The following year these were offi-cially combined and met at Burlington, with the exception of Shrewsbury which seems to have been absorbed by the Burlington group.

Any discussion of the polity and method of the Religious Society of Friends will need to consider some of the fundamentals of the Friends' manner of thought, and the chief differences between their organization and that of most other religious denominations. From the very beginning,

---

1. Bowden, *op. cit.*, II, 20, quotes *in toto* a letter dated First month 17, 1683, and signed by William Penn and 25 others which states that there were 9 meetings for worship and 3 monthly meetings at that time. A minute of Philadelphia Quarterly Meeting dated Eleventh month 9, 1682 states the concern of the Quakers and their action in setting up these business meetings.

2. Philadelphia Yearly Meeting in reality had a triple origin. A letter signed by William Penn and others contains the following: "For our meetings, more especially of worship there are in West Jersey, one at the falls of the river Delaware, another at Burlington, one at Assisconck, one at Rancocas, one at Newtown, and one at Salem, and two Half-year meetings, one at Burlington and one at Salem, to which the Half-Yearly Meeting of Friends in East Jersey is joined, who also have a Yearly Meeting of themselves, a men and women's meeting, and a Yearly meeting at Shrewsbury. In Pennsylvania there is one at the Falls, one at the Governor's house, one at Colchester River, all in the county of Bucks; one at Tawsany (Trelawny), one at Philadelphia, both in that county; and at Darby at John Blunson's, one at Chester, one at Ridley at John Simcock's, and one at William Ruse's, in Chichester in Chesire. There be three Monthly Meetings of men and women for Truth's service: in the county of Chester one; in the county of Philadelphia another; and in the county of Bucks another; and intend a Yearly Meeting in the Third Month next." Bowden, *op. cit.*, II, 22.

down to the present, the polity of the Society of Friends has been democratic and congregational.   The local monthly meeting has full administrative authority and is the executive unit.[1] The yearly meeting
is the authority in matters of doctrine. In early times, theoretically
though not always in practice, down to the present, the Quaker was advised and guided in most of the conduct of his daily life by the wisdom
of his religious associates. Marriage, clothing, business dealing, type
of business, manner of speech, relation to political authority, even ar-
guments with neighbors, all were a definite part of his Christian conduct, and hence matters of concern to the monthly meeting of which he
was a part.[2]

Nevertheless the Friend was very individualistic; to an outsider he
must at times have seemed fanatically so. His individual conscience
was his guide. He recognized no law of man capable of compelling him to
act contrary to what he felt to be right. He submitted to the discipline
of his denomination because it conformed to his own concept of the truth,
for had not he himself had a vital part in shaping that discipline. He
was not a slave to meeting discipline but a participant in it. Therefore it is natural that he should have been adverse to delegating authority to others to speak for him. In his meetings for worship he needed
no minister to lead him in the ritual of worship. He not only appointed
delegates to attend quarterly or yearly meetings, but went himself, and
had the, same right of expression in the meeting. At the monthly meeting
there were no delegates. Each member's opinion carried weight according
to his experience and judgment. This was the basic method. However,
increasing numbers and distances made full attendance at yearly meetings
impossible. Other denominations solved the problem by conferences of
ministers with a limited number of lay delegates, each one elected and
authorized to speak and vote in behalf of his own local organization.
Friends preferred to select informally a few members to attend and speak
for them. Although referred to as representatives, technically they
were not. Any or all other members could attend and each had an equal
voice.

As the colony became larger and the monthly meetings increased in
number, the business of the quarterly and yearly meetings grew in volume.
A natural division of business evolved. Matters pertaining to the
strictly moral and spiritual affairs of the church were attended to by a
meeting of the ministers and elders of the superior bodies, while other
matters of current church organization and development, together with
some disciplinary questions were passed upon by the larger body of the
superior meetings.[3] In the main the function of the two superior meetings has become legislative and advisory. They are the co-ordinating
bodies of the Society's organization.

The sending of delegates is so common among other organizations
that admonitions on the part of a monthly meeting urging the particular
meetings to choose one or two of their numbers to attend the monthly

1. U.S. Bureau of the Census, *Census of Religious Bodies, 1936, Friends*, pp. 12, 20, hereinafter cited *Religious Bodies, 1936.*

2. *See* Glossary, for explanation of Yearly, quarterly, monthly, preparative, particular
and other types of meetings.

3. *Ibid.*

meeting are taken to mean that they should send them as delegates. In such cases the Friends chosen came as individuals, but by making sure of the attendance of at least one or two from each particular meeting at the monthly meeting, business was expedited. Cases sometimes occur, as for instance in the 1715 minutes of Falls Monthly Meeting, when due to bad weather or some such cause, there were four at the meeting, action was deferred because none but John Scarborough attended from his particular meeting.

With regard to ascertaining the will of the meeting, it must be remembered that parliamentary rules were not observed and votes were not taken. The meetings were not satisfied with action acceptable to a bare majority but endeavored to take action acceptable to the entire group. Hence the minutes contain no reference to a motion being carried. Instead, a suggestion or proposal was "united with" or sometimes "concurred with," or it was simply stated that "it is the sense of the Meeting." The idea was entirely one of mutual agreement. It is, no doubt, this dependence of a large and complicated organization upon the individual sense of right or wrong, instead of upon formalities, that makes the Friends' organization hard to understand and so thoroughly democratic.

All business meetings from the yearly meeting down to the Preparative meeting kept minutes and records of all transactions. The Friends were also very conscientious in keeping records of births, deaths, marriages, dismissals, transfers, property records, matters of finance, etc. Since marriage was considered a social contract, Friends early developed the custom of allowing the contracting parties to pledge their vows to each other in the presence of the monthly meeting and without the aid of priest or clergy. Before a marriage was allowed by the monthly meeting, a committee made a careful investigation of the two people and their fitness for the marriage state. The marriage certificate was signed by a large group of the members present, and the certificate and names of witnesses were recorded in the minutes of the monthly meeting. In reading the minutes it is necessary to keep in mind slight peculiarities of wording. The days of the week are numbered instead of named; also the months of the year.[1] The "first Fourth-day of the Eleventh month" is the first Wednesday in November. Motions or resolutions are not offered in the meetings, but subjects are "proposed for consideration" and the proposal is not voted upon but it is "approved" or "united with." A meeting is sometimes said to be "established" but usually it is "settled," "set up," or "erected." If it becomes defunct, it is "laid down." If a meeting for worship or a preparative meeting is laid down, its members may attend any other convenient meeting under the same monthly meeting. If a monthly meeting is laid down its members are "joined" to a definitely specified monthly meeting. This is because all records pertaining to individual Friends are kept by their respective monthly meetings. A change from one meeting of worship to another under the same Monthly meeting involves no changes in records but a transfer from one monthly meeting to another does.

With the rapid growth of the Quaker organization in Pennsylvania there was a concomitant growth of the province. Many persons of varied religious persuasions hastened to take advantage of the freedom for religious worship which the newly chartered colony offered. There were

---

1. *See* Explanatory Notes No. 8.

Germans from the Palatinate a few of whom became Quakers, and a large
company of Welsh immigrants who were already Quakers, who followed Penn
to the New World and some of the Welsh even preceeded him. Many Hugue-
nots, after the revocation of the Edict of Nantes in 1685, sought refuge
in the American colonies and a few of them came down the Wyoming Valley
from New York into Pennsylvania. Some of these groups who came to find
religious freedom in the Quaker colony later united with the Quaker meetings. Pennsylvania Quakerism grew stronger both in membership and in
leadership. By 1780 it is estimated that there were 75,000 Quakers in
the American colonies scattered from Maine to the Carolinas. One-third
of these were in Pennsylvania, members of approximately ten quarterly
meetings and about one hundred and fifty local meetings. Traveling ministers went and came on religious visits both to the other colonies and
also abroad. Quaker leaders from England came on religious concerns to
Pennsylvania.

Out of the ferment of religious thought of that period various sectarian doctrines were born, some of which made impact on Quaker ideas.
The political exigencies of the colonial situation in the matter of defense also had an influence in coloring the total picture of Quaker belief. During the first century and a half a few variations from the
root-stock of Quaker belief crystallized, and under the enthusiasm of
zealous leaders led to actual schisms in the church in a few cases. It
is the purpose of the following brief sketches to take up in chronological order the most important of these divisions in the Quaker body and
note them here as a part of the total historical development of Quakerism
in Pennsylvania.

The Keithian Quakers (Quaker Baptists)

Quakerism was about thirty-five years old when William Penn began
his "holy experiment" in Pennsylvania. In England religion and doctrine
were much discussed topics, in market place and stage coach. Public
discussions and debates on doctrines and creeds were indulged in both
for their dogmatic and pedagogic value, and also for the purpose of en-
tangling dissenters from the established church. The founders and a-
pologists of early Quakerism entered into many such disputes in order
to clear themselves of false accusations or to clarify the teachings of
the new movement. Among the ablest of the early Quaker apologists was
George Keith, a contemporary and companion of Robert Barclay, the logician and defender of the tenets of Quakerism set fourth by Fox and his
co-laborers. Barclay and Keith together defended the theses set forth
in a paper by Barclay at the well-known Aberdeen Dispute in 1675.[1]

George Keith was born in 1638 in Aberdeenshire. His formal education was obtained at Marischal College and Aberdeen University; and from
the latter school he received the M.A. degree in 1662.[2] His family had intended that young Keith should enter the ministry in the Scottish Kirk,
but in some way he was diverted from this profession and became a surveyor and mathematician, and later a schoolmaster. He was trained in
logic and much of his lifetime was spent in preaching, debating, and

1. Robert Barclay, *Truth Triumphant*, p. 5; *see also* Horace M. Lippincott, "The Keithian
Separation," *Bulletin of the Friends Historical Association*, XVI, (1927), No. 2, p. 49; hereinafter cited as Lippincott, *Keithian Separation.*

2. John Barclay, *Life of Alexander Jaffray*, p. 548.

religious controversy. He was a schoolmate of Bishop Burnet, who knew him at college and in later life, and who no doubt influenced Keith to return to the Established Church. It was Burnet who said of Keith, "he was the most learned man ever in the Quaker sect, well versed both in oriental tongues and in philosophy and in mathematics."[1]

About 1664, after he had completed his formal education at Aberdeen, Keith allied himself with the Quakers. For some years following this he was active in the Quaker controversies in England and was an able defender of their beliefs. He had traveled with Fox and Penn in Holland and Germany and was well grounded in the fundamental teachings set forth by the Founder. He had suffered for his convictions by imprisonment and persecution.[2]

In 1685 Keith emigrated to New Jersey where he was engaged to mark out the boundary line between East and West Jersey. He was called to Philadelphia in 1689 to become master of the grammar school which had been recently founded under the initiative of Penn, which later developed into the William Penn Charter School and the Friends Select School.

Contrary and speculative doctrines which Keith had acquired before he came to America[3] evidently lay heavy on his mind and he was not at ease in his Quaker associations in Philadelphia. He had not openly taught these opinions, but he had written upon them and promoted them privately. He was therefore restless in his new position as head master of the school and resigned at the end of the first year. He began traveling through the colonies, preaching and debating, often challenging religious leaders to debate with him. He became increasingly conscious of his powers in debate, and having wandered from the way of Quaker humility he strayed further from the Quaker faith and ideals. Returning from his tour of New England he very soon became embroiled in disputes with the Quaker preachers of Philadelphia. He accused Thomas Fitzwater of preaching that the Inner Light was "sufficient for salvation without anything else," and William Stockdale of preaching "two Christs."[4] He charged that they denied the need for the historic Christ. The denial of the efficacy of the Inner Light seems to have been the most important point of defection of Keith from Quaker tenets, and together with some deviations which held that Saturday be kept as the day of worship, and that water baptism and the Lord's Supper be practised, made up the main points of his teachings.

Disputes and counter accusations ensued and a schism developed in 1691, with Keith as the leader of a small minority in Philadelphia. Separate meetings were set up at Burlington and a few other places, none of which continued for very long, and the manuscript records of which have been lost.[5]

The controversy continued and Keith in the course of his public

---

1. Cited by Lippincott, *Keithian Separation*, p. 49.

2. Bowden, *op. cit.*, II, 102.

3. Bowden, *op. cit.*, II, 77.

4. William Sewell, *The History of the Rise, Increase, and Progress of the Christian People called Quakers*, p. 617.

5. A few relevant broadsides and pamphlets are on file at The Historical Society of Pennsylvania.

addresses and printed pamphlets attacked the character of some Quaker officials of the government, among them Thomas Lloyd the deputy governor. For this he was brought to trial in Sixth month 1692 and fined 5 pounds, which fine was never enforced. At Philadelphia Yearly Meeting in Seventh month 1692 and again at London Yearly Meeting in 1694, to which body he had appealed his case, he was soundly condemned; and in the London Yearly Meeting of 1695 he was disowned. His followers, never more than a few hundred, also left the meetings. Contentions soon arose among the Keithians, and a decline set in as early as 1696.[1]

Keith's followers were variously called "Christian Quakers," "Quaker Baptists," "Separatists," and "Keithian Quakers." In 1700 Keith returned to England and was ordained a minister in the Episcopal Church. He returned to America as the first missionary sent out by the Society for the Propagation of the Gospel in Foreign Parts and most of his Quaker following in Pennsylvania went over to that church under the influence of Keith. A quaint epitaph in the graveyard of the old Oxford Trinity Church, though now weatherbeaten and almost illegible, still bears testimony to this fact. It is on the gravestone of one Elizabeth Roberts who died in 1708.

> Here by these lines is testify'd
> No Quaker was she when she Dy'd;
> So far was she from Quakerism,
> That she desired to have Baptism
> For her own babes and children dear,
> To this these lines true witness bear;
> An furthermore, she did obtain
> That faith, that all shall rise again
> Out of the graves at the last day,
> And in this faith she passed away.

Further attestation is found in the inscription which is over the doorway of this same church; "Church of England services were held on this site AD 1696, in a log meeting house built by the Oxford Society of Friends. This church was erected AD 1711." It is very probable however that this early log meeting-house was built not by the Penn Quakers but by the Keithian Quakers after the schism took place. This view is made more tenable by the fact that Frankford Meeting, originally called Oxford Meeting, was built in 1683-84 on land given by Thomas Fairman, later the surveyor-general of the province.[2] The Present Oxford Trinity Church was on land given by Thomas Graves.[3] The two tracts are located at some distance from each other, and the present site of the Frankford Meeting at Unity and Waln Streets has been in the possession of Friends since it was given by Thomas Fairman in 1683.[4]

With Keith's return to Pennsylvania as an Episcopal minister the disturbances among Friends gradually quieted down. As his followers joined him in the establish church the Keithian meetings disappeared and no records have been preserved to locate and identify the short-lived local meetings and yearly meeting which sprang up under his able but

---

1. Bowden, op. cit., II, 102.
2. Caroline W. Smedley, "Frankford Meeting," The Friend, LXXXVIII (1915), p. 133.
3. Lippincott, Keithian Separation, p. 49.
4. See entry 107.

tempestuous leadership.

The Free Quakers

The Free Quakers came into existence as a religious organization at the time of the war for American Independence. The schism was started by a small number of Friends who had been disowned by their orthodox brethren because of their participation or implication in that war. Friends are very much opposed to war and feel that there are other means of reconciling differences outside of armed hostilities. The calling of the first Continental Congress was an act of patriotism, but it was looked upon with much disfavor by the leading members of the Society of Friends. The older members of this society retained a sense of loyalty to the British Crown, and were not inclined to support the idea of establishing a new and independent government. Under the original regime peace reigned throughout the colonies, and war to them was an overthrow of the principles of their religion.[1]

At the yearly meeting held in Philadelphia in 1774, a letter was formally approved and ordered to be sent to all meetings of Friends in America, warning all members of that Society not to depart from their peaceful principles by taking part in any of the political matters then being stirred up, reminding all Friends that under the King's government they had been favored with a peaceful and prosperous enjoyment of their rights, and strongly suggesting the propriety of disowning all members who disobeyed the orders issued by the yearly meeting. This letter was generally respected and obeyed, and most Friends took no part in the war for freedom.[2]

There is no doubt that Friends experienced a great ordeal during the period of the Revolution in their endeavor to reconcile their religious principles with what was the patriotic thought of that day. Most of them were willing to incur the odium of being called Tories rather than surrender their convictions. Some of the younger members, however, held that they owed it to their government to render active support in a time when invasion was threatened. While agreeing at the same time with their elders as to the wrongfulness of war, still they were of the firm belief that it would not be consistent to accept the protection of the Continental Congress and the armies, and refuse to aid them. Accordingly, some accepted active military duties, others served in non combatant capacities, while still others feeling no inclination to serve at all, paid the militia taxes and fines willingly. In all cases the punishment was the same, loss of membership was the ultimate result; a privilege which most of them had enjoyed as a birthright inheritance.

Some saw active service in the American army, some served on the Committee of Public Safety, while others held seats in the legislature; and those not serving in an active capacity gave freely to the cause both in money and goods. Not only did the men render services, but the women as well. Some attended their husbands to the war, and it is said that during the Battle of Trenton the wives of the Quaker soldiers helped

1. Charles Wetherill, *History of the Religious Society of Friends, called by Some the Free Quakers*, p. 10; see also Issac Sharpless, *A Quaker Experiment in Government*, II, 205, hereinafter cited as Sharpless, *Quaker Experiment*.
2. Wetherill, *op. cit.*, p. 11.

on the battlefield to bandage the wounded.[1]

As a result of such services many entries similar to the one which follows appear in the old record books of Friends' meeting:

Isaac Howell of this city who has made many years profession of the Truth with us the people called Quakers, and we believe has been convinced of that Divine principle which preserves the followers thereof from a disposition and conduct tending to promote war, has notwithstanding so far deviated therefrom as to manifest a disposition to contend for the asserting of civil rights in a manner contrary to our peaceable profession and principles, and accepted of and acted in a public station, the purpose and intention of which has tended to promote measures inconsistent therewith. It thereupon became our concern to treat with him, with desire to convince him of his error, but our labour of love not having the desired effect, and as the testimony of Truth has suffered by his means, and he doth not show a disposition to condemn the same, we are under the necessity in order to support our Christian Testimony to declare that he hath separated himself from the Unity and fellowship of our Religious Society. Yet it is our earnest desire that he may become sensible of his deviations so as to manifest a just sense of his error, and by a due concern for testimony of Truth, manifested by a suitable acknowledgement, become restored into membership.[2]

Isaac Howell had disobeyed the regulations as set forth in the letter of the yearly meeting of 1774, and also had departed from that part of the discipline of the Society of Friends as relates to peace, by serving in office under a government which at that time was not in peaceful harmony with the parent country, and by accepting service in the military forces. For these reasons he was disowned by the Philadelphia Monthly Meeting of Friends.

On June 13, 1777 the State Legislature passed a law making it compulsory for all residents to take an oath of allegiance to the State of Pennsylvania and the United States, and to renounce forever all allegiance to the King and government of Great Britain. This act required all persons to appear before justices and other officers authorized to administer judicial oaths. Friends were now confronted with a difficult problem. On one hand was a compulsory law bearing consequent punishment for treason if not complied with, while on the other hand was the letter of the yearly meeting of 1774 forbidding all members to participate in such matters, with the penalty of disownment if disobeyed. There is no doubt that some took the oath or affirmation secretly, but some young Friends, feeling no inclination to conceal the fact, appeared before the administering officers and openly and publicly obeyed the law. One of these was Samuel Wetherill, who was a minister in Friends meeting, and a grandson of Christopher Wetherill, one of the first settlers of Burlington, N. J., and one of the Council of Proprietors which originally governed that colony.[3]

---

1. Wetherill, *op. cit.*, pp. 11, 12.
2. Cited by Wetherill, *op. cit.*, p. 12.
3. *Ibid.*, pp. 15, 16.

Samuel Wetherill was born in Burlington in 1736, and as a boy he came to Philadelphia and became an apprentice to Mordecai Yarnall, a house carpenter and an eminent minister in Friends meeting. He later married his employer's daughter, and by serving honestly and faithfully became successful in business matters and was much respected by Friends. A short time before 1775 he joined with Christopher Marshall and several others in the establishment of the first cloth weaving factory in the American colonies. Cloth woven at his factory was supplied to the army during the war. Not only did Samuel Wetherill take the oath of allegiance publicly and supply the army with cloth, but his public addresses and and active pen were in constant support of the American cause. As a consequence thereof he was disowned by Friends:

Having been reared in the principles of that sect, those who were disowned would not readily be inclined to join with other denominations, and it is only natural that they missed their meetings, and the fellow-ship and associations of the same. As the war went on, others were dis-owned, and their number constantly increased. About the autumn of 1780, a small group of these disowned Friends began meeting together for wor-ship and to compare views. These meetings were held at the houses of Samuel Wetherill and Timothy Matlack. For a short time meetings for wor-ship were held in this manner, but it was finally decided that they form a meeting of their own. On the 20th day of February, 1781, the new soci-ety held its first meeting for business at the house of Samuel Wetherill. The title: "The Religious Society of Friends," called by some the "Free Quakers," was adopted, and Samuel Wetherill was appointed as the first clerk. The new organization was small, its first meeting being attended by only 8 persons, but in time its membership increased to over one hun-dred.[2]

They, and those who acted with them, felt that in forming a new re-ligious organization they ought to publicly make known their cause for so doing, and accordingly published an address. This was printed in broadside form and was the first public utterance of the Society of Free Quakers. It was addressed as follows: "To those of the people called Quakers who have been disowned for matters religious or civil," and opened with the phrase "Friends and fellow-Sufferers." It stated that the separation was not sought by them but was forced upon them, and that many had been disowned for no other cause than a faithful discharge of those duties which we owe to our country. It was agreed that as Friends and brethren, they would endeavor to support and maintain public meetings for religious worship, and that they had no new doctrines to teach, nor any design of promoting schisms in religion, and concluded with an invi-tation for those who chose to join with them.[3]

Members of the Society in other places who had suffered disownment began to organize and meet in the same manner. In Chester County in Pennsylvania, at West River in Maryland, and in Massachusetts, Free Qua-ker meetings began to spring up, and a regular correspondence between these Friends and the Philadelphia meeting seems to have existed.[4]

---

1. Wetherill, *op. cit.*, p. 16.
2. *Ibid.*, p. 18.
3. *Ibid.*, pp. 21, 47-49.
4. *Ibid.*, pp. 32, 33.

At their meetings for business, one of their first concerns was the forming of a discipline or plan of organization, and in order to obtain the assistance of all such disowned Friends who might wish to join in the formulating of the discipline, a second broadside or printed letter to "our Friends and Brethren in Pennsylvania, New Jersey and elsewhere," was issued. This was dated the 4th day of the 6th month, 1781, and contained an inv tation to join, and also solicited the advice and assistance of all who would afford their counsel. Having sent out this epistle to their friends, they continued their work on this document, and on the 6th day of 8th month, 1781, at a meeting for business, the discipline was unanimously agreed to.[1]

The new Society was very similar in many ways to the one from which it had been separated. They dressed the same, they used the plain language, and their meetings for worship and business were conducted in the same manner. They differed only in two respects. First "that no man who believed in God, in the supreme, wise and benevolent Ruler of the Universe," should be disowned for any cause whatsoever. Secondly, they differed in their belief as to the necessity of serving their country in the time of war.[2]

"Among the more conspicuous of the original members were: Timothy Matlack, who was a colonel in the army and a member of the Committee of Public Safety. Later he was a member of the State Legislature, and was a very active patriot; White Matlack, a brother of Timothy; William Crispen, who was commissary in General Washington's army; Colonel Clement Biddle, a member of the well-known family of that name, who was disowned as early as 1775 for 'studying to learn the art of war,' he having raised a company of soldiers composed largely of Quakers. He afterwards served as Quartermaster General in the Revolutionary Army under General Gates; Owen Biddle, his brother, who was a member of the State Legislature; Benjamin Say, who was a well-known physician at that time; Samuel Wetherill, Jr., who was the preacher and clerk of the meeting; Christopher Marshall, who was a well-known patriot and an active member of the Committee of Public Safety; . . Joseph Warner, who served in the army and was at the Battle of Trenton; Peter Thomson, who was employed by Congress to print the Continental money. Nathaniel Browne, Isaac Howell, Moses Bartram and Jonathan Scholfield were also prominent members."[3]

In addition to the notable men who were allied with the Free Quakers, there were also some well remembered women, among them Lydia Darragh, who warned Washington at Whitemarsh of an impending attack by the British, then stationed at Philadelphia. Betsy Ross, the designer and maker of the first flag of the Republic, became a member of this group after she was disowned by the larger body of Quakers.[4]

Some of the Friends who were disowned never joined with the Society of Free Quakers. As years went by some of those who had joined, made acknowledgement to their meetings, and were received back into member-

---

1. Wetherill, *op. cit.*, pp. 25, 26.
2. *Ibid.*, p. 27.
3. *Ibid.*, pp. 19, 20.
4. *Ibid.*, p. 20. Betsy Ross was not disowned in 1776 for making the flag. The minutes of the Northern District Monthly Meeting for Fifth Month, 1774, show that she was disowned for marrying John Ross, the son of an Episcopalian minister.

ship with the Society of Friends. The original members gradually died, and some of their ancestors joined with other denominations, until only a handful remained. By 1816 those in Maryland, Massachusetts, New York, and Ohio had passed out of existence, leaving only the meeting in Philadelphia, but despite the small number of attenders, meetings for religious worship continued each First-day.

Of the original members, Clement Biddle died in 1813, Samuel Wetherhill, Jr., in 1829, Timothy Matlack removed from the city and died in 1829, at Holmesburg. Elizabeth Claypoole (Betsy Ross) was the last survivor; she died in 1836. The families of the first members ceased to attend First-day meetings, and in the last few years of its existence as a religious organization, meetings were held but once each year. John Price Wetherill, the clerk, a descendant of Samuel Wetherill, Jr., the first clerk, worshipped almost alone for several years, and in 1836 the last meeting for religious worship was held.[1]

The organization, however, continued on as a charitable enterprise, holding meetings for business once each year. In 1928-29, it incorporated under the laws of the State of Pennsylvania, under the title of the "Free Quaker Society." Today it exists in corporate form only, its membership is small, and the business meetings continue to be held once every year. At these meetings, the main business pertains mostly to the care of property, and the appointing of committees to distribute the income from a trust fund which was derived from the proceeds of the sale of a former burial ground held by them on Fifth Street below Locust, and the rentals received from the old meeting-house at Arch and Fifth Streets. This income is distributed to the poor, mostly in coal. The administration of the same bears no expense since the members look after the work without compensation. Also at the annual meeting, all children born during the year are registered as birthright members, a custom which has been practiced since the time of the establishment of the organization.

The Great Separation of 1827-28

The "Great Separation" which took place in the Society of Friends more than one hundred years ago has long since passed its period of heated discussion and may be considered now, even by the most partisan of the two sides of the schism, in the calm perspective of history.

By way of introduction it will be well to state briefly something of the situation in which the Society of Friends found itself at the beginning of the nineteenth century, which situation became the background for the schism that developed and came to an open break in 1827.

Following the Revolutionary War, Quakerism in Pennsylvania had settled into a state of strict conformity to outward practices. The recent controversy which resulted in the Free Quakers, influenced the larger body to emphasize outward practices and customs and discouraged personal thinking. The Bible was rarely read in meeting or in the home for fear it would interfere with the activity of the Inner Light and the leading of the Spirit.[2] The ministry in the meetings had ceased to be didactic

---

1 Wetherill, *op. cit.*, p. 42.
2. Elbert Russell, *The Separation After a Century*, p. 11.

and had become mere exhortations to be faithful and "mind the Light."[1]
Another condition conducive to dissatisfaction was the dominance of the
Select Body in the local meetings and the increasing power of the Meetings for Sufferings in the yearly meeting. This latter body was almost
entirely made up of the elders of the meetings. In Philadelphia where
the stronger meetings existed, the elders controlled the meeting for Sufferings and by this indirect method also controlled the yearly meeting.[2]

This bureaucratic tendency was in definite contrast to the new
spirit of freedom and democracy which followed the war. Discerning members looked with misgiving on this growing power, particularly those in
the stronger country meetings. This feeling was no doubt aggravated and
become more defined because of the growing class distinction between the
wealthy educated city Friends and their rural brethren. These tenden-
cies and feelings, though never expressed in actual revolt, existed in
the form of an inarticulate protest against the arbitrary authority in
outward customs, personal preferment, and distinction.

Added to the foregoing conditions and causes was the great Evangelical Movement which swept England during the third-quarter of the eighteenth century, and later spread to America. It was this movement, running back to Wyclif and the Pietists, which, under John Wesley produced
the evangelical trend in the Church of England which resulted in the
"Low Church" in that denomination.[3] In America the Evangelical Movement
resulted in a revival of religious thought and activity. Its scope included revival meetings, Bible classes, foreign missions, Sunday schools,
and Bible societies. It was insistent upon personal religious experience, and it soon came to place great insistence upon definite doctrines as necessary to salvation. It was at the turn of the century that
the Movement spread to America. Yale College, under Timothy Dwight became a tower of strength for evangelicalism. In Kentucky a great revival began about 1801. The famous Haystack Prayer Meeting occurred in
1803. The American Bible Society was formed in 1807.

The Quakerism of the period was duly affected by the new religious
trends. Emphasis began to tend toward ritualistic and doctrinal conformity. The freedom of a personal inward leading was obscured. Quakers
were more and more emphasizing the plenary inspiration of the Scripture,
the deity of Christ, total depravity of man, and the necessity of a definite experience of salvation which took place at a definite moment and
which was considered the essential beginning of Christian life.

While it is true that Quakers in Pennsylvania did not adopt the extreme doctrinal and emotional emphasis of the Evangelical Movement as
did some other portions of American Quakers, they were affected by these
conceptions.

Elias Hicks was a traveling minister whose life spanned the entire
Revolutionary period. He was born in 1748 on a farm in Hempstead Township, Long Island, New York. His formal education was meagre, but he

---

1. Elbert Russell, *The Separation After A Century*, p. 11.

2. James Cockburn, *A Review of the General and Particular Causes Which Have Produced the
Late Disorders and Divisions in the Yearly Meeting of Friends Held in Philadelphia*, p. 87.

3. See forthcoming *Inventory of the Church Archives of Pennsylvania: The Episcopal
Church*.

had a keen mind and was an eager reader, which latter gave him a wider knowledge than that possessed by most Friends of his time. He grew up as a thoughtful youth, very much inclined to the youthful diversions of his time, but having overcome these desires he felt called to the Quaker ministry, and was so recorded in his home meeting in Long Island. He travelled extensively among the Quaker meetings of America, always with a minute of approval from his own meeting, as is the customary practise among Friends. From the time of his becoming a recognized minister until he was 68 years of age he labored and preached, and became a welcome and influential voice in both the meetings for business and worship in Pennsylvania and other States. Always a staunch advocate of the Quaker idea of worship and belief he was greatly concerned about the trend toward evangelical theology, and the insistence on the Scriptures as dogmatic authority for the evangelical tenets. For 150 years Quakerism had never been confined to a creed and Elias Hicks was anxiously concerned because these strict doctrinal ideas which were creeping in seemed to him to lead in that direction. It was in 1815, during a slight illness[1] that he read Mosheim's account[2] of the dissensions and struggles through which the early church creeds developed, with their accompanying hatreds, persecutions and doctrinal intolerance; and he became even more anxious lest this same spirit enter into and destroy the freedom and tolerance of the Society in which he had labored for more than forty years. Whatever Mosheim's influence may have been it is to be noted that at about this time there seems to have been a turning point in Hicks' ministry. His powers were from now on devoted to saving his church from creeds and man-made doctrines.

Hicks was a self-trained logician and his sermons abound with appeals to his hearers to reason and consider the propositions which he sets forth. Viewed in the light of present-day theology there is very little to be found in them of a controversial nature[3] but the influence of the evangelical theology of his time upon Quakerism, together with the insistence upon conformity by the recognized authority of the Society, the Elders, produced discussion, dissension, and finally separation into two bodies.

The first public disorder in connection with the controversy occurred in a monthly meeting at the Pine Street Meeting-house, in tenth month 1819, where Hicks as a travelling minister, having spoken in the men's Meeting was granted the privilege of speaking to the Women's meeting also. Upon the conclusion of his service in the Women's meeting he returned to the other side of the dividing partition only to find that the men's meeting had adjourned, although their business had not been completed.[4] This was an uncommon occurrence, and was interpreted as an act of disrespect. It is more probable however, that the meeting adjourned because of resentment by a very influential member toward Hicks who had spoken, on that occasion, concerning the sinfulness of the use of the products of slave labor.[5] Use of the products of slave labor was not the bone of contention in the controversy which followed, it was in this instance only a cause for prejudice which occasioned the first overt act

---

1. Cited by Russell, *op. cit.*, p. 29.
2. Johann Lorenz von Mosheim, *Institutes of Ecclesiastical History, Ancient and Modern.*
3. Elias Hicks, *A Series of Extemporaneous Discourses* . . . , p. 322.
4. Cockburn, *op. cit.*, p. 59.
5. *Ibid.*, p. 60.

in a situation which had a doctrinal basis in the preaching of Hicks during the previous 3 years and which had by this time developed some tenseness.

From this point the controversy developed more publicly. In 1822, in a Meeting for Sufferings, steps were taken to prevent Elias Hicks from disseminating "doctrines different from and repugnant to those held by our religious society," among the meetings of Philadelphia. This allegation appears in a letter dated twelfth month 19, 1822.[1] According to this same letter Hicks, when he arrived in Philadelphia, was waited upon by a committee which had been appointed by a private after meeting of the Meeting for Sufferings in eighth month 1822. The committee proceeded to present its charges of heterodoxy based upon the report of two elders, who had heard Hicks make certain statements inferring his disbelief in the deity of Christ.[2] Hicks refused to acknowledge their authority to question him, but later relented and discussed the points with them. He denied the charges of heresy, but apparently his questioners went away unsatisfied, for a meeting of the elders of all the monthly meetings in the city was called in order to go further into the matter with Hicks. He refused to meet them, but next day consented and suggested the following Thursday at Green Street Meeting-house for the conference. To this occasion he brought some of his own supporters as witnesses. The meeting of elders, standing on its right to a private, select opportunity with him, declined to discuss the matter, and abruptly left the building. It is worthy of notation that this group of elders were acting outside their jurisdiction in calling such a conference to pass upon the doctrinal unsoundness of a minister from another yearly meeting.

From this point in the controversy begins a movement to take sides by the members of the yearly meeting. Private meetings of groups of elders were held and the charges against Hicks were discussed. Many Friends strongly discouraged the development of partisan favor on either side. Meantime Hicks continued his preaching, promulgating his defense. Partisanship grew and became more bitter. From the writings of Hicks, his sincere effort to combat speculative theology is apparent, but it is thought by some that in his zeal in doing this he built up a system of dogma of his own which was as foreign to Quaker "experience" as the evangelical doctrines which he opposed.[3]

In the yearly meeting of 1823 there was a definite effort made by the opposers of Hicks to have the yearly meeting approve, by accepting the minutes of the Yearly Meeting for Sufferings which contained this commitment, a doctrinal statement or discipline.[4] This matter had arisen in the meeting for sufferings at this time because of the aber-

1. Cockburn, op. cit., p. 68.
2. Ibid., p. 69.
3. Rufus M. Jones, The Int... cited as Jones, Later Periods.
4. Cockburn, op. cit. Cockburn is in error in inferring that this... to have a creed approved by the yearly meeting originated at this time. The minutes of the early Meeting for Sufferings for 1805 show that an attempt was made to approve a uniform discipline for all the yearly meetings in America. See Jones, Later Periods, I, 450, and Min... of Yearly Meeting for Sufferings for 1805 (manuscript at PPFYR). The matter appears again in 817, and again in Ohio in 1821.

rations of certain statements of views held by Orthodox Friends as set forth by an anonymous writer who styled himself "Amicus." This writer had entered into a discussion in a current religious periodical with a defender of the liberal views who signed himself "Paul."[1] The opposers of Hicks took advantage of this desire in the meeting for sufferings for an official statement of Friends beliefs, which desire was occasioned by the "Paul" and "Amicus" discussion, and urged that the meeting write into its minutes such a statement. This statement was, however, rejected by the yearly meeting when the minutes of the meeting for sufferings were presented.

From the yearly meeting of 1823 to the actual separation in 1827 the controversy became an issue between Hicks and his followers versus the elders and the Yearly Meeting for Sufferings. Late in 1826 Hicks again came on a religious visit to the meetings and families of Philadelphia Yearly Meeting. Again his sympathizers flocked around him and again opposition to him flared up. There was disorder in many of the meetings he attended. The power of the city meetings was a cause of dissatisfaction among the less influential leadership of the country meetings.[2] This situation became an important factor at this stage of the controversy, and won many followers from the rural meetings to Hicks' party, since the strength of his opposition was in the city meetings.

Two men, Thomas Shillitoe and John Comly, need to be mentioned at this stage of the controversy because of their influence on the opposing sides. Shillitoe, an English Friends minister, came to America late in 1826, and despite the efforts which were made to draw him to Hicks' side of the discussion he very soon became a strong supporter of the evangelical side and one of Hicks' strongest opponents. John Comly was a minister and assistant clerk of Philadelphia Yearly Meeting. He claims in his Journal to have had a revelation "that this contest would result in a separation."[3] It was he who undertook the task of organizing the followers of Hicks[4] so as to resist more firmly the power of the elders. During the spring of 1827 he made definite plans for the crisis which he expected in the coming yearly meeting in April, and "actively promoted separation."[5] The first results of Comly's efforts are reflected in the withdrawal of Green Street Monthly Meeting from Philadelphia Quarterly Meeting, and its affiliation with Abington Quarterly Meeting.

When the yearly meeting convened in April of 1827 friction began almost immediately in the nominating committee, in the matter of the appointment of a clerk. John Comly was proposed by the followers of Hicks while the opposition wished to retain Samuel Bettle, the former clerk. In the afternoon session, when the committee made its report to the yearly meeting, it was impossible to reach a decision, so a proposal was made to continue the present clerks until the committee could unite on its recommendation. When Samuel Bettle read the minute which he had made covering this situation confusion broke forth. Gradually the meet-

---

1. For the discussion in the Wilmington, Delarare, The *Christian Repository*, known as the "Letters of Paul and Amicus," which was taken up in the Meeting for Sufferings on a basis of its own aberrations, *see* Jones, *Later Periods*, I, 462.

2. Cockburn, *op. cit.*, pp. 187, 189, 197.

3. John Comly, *Journal*, p. 309.

4. *Ibid.*, p. 310.

5. *Ibid.*, pp. 312-319.

ing case to order and John Comly was asked to take a seat beside the other clerk, Samuel Bettle. The subsequent sessions continued with occasions of disorder and dispute. The crisis came at the closing session on fourth month twenty-first, when a representative from the Women's Meeting arose and informed the group that that meeting had appointed a committee to visit the meetings throughout the yearly meeting for the purpose of restoring unity and harmony.[1] Immediately a sympathizer with Hicks arose to inform the meeting that a number of Friends there present had held a meeting at Green Street Meeting-house the previous evening and organized a separate meeting, and had prepared an address to be sent down to the quarterly and monthly meetings. He further informed the meeting that this separate session had appointed a committee to personally carry their message to the subordinate meetings. The yearly meeting was shocked into silence. Separation had at last taken place. The committee requested by the women's meeting was appointed and at the close of an impressive silence the clerk read the concluding minute.[2] The two opposing groups never met together again as a yearly meeting until in very recent years.[3]

After the split in Philadelphia Yearly Meeting four other yearly meetings, New York, Ohio, Baltimore, and Indiana separated the following year. New England and North Carolina yearly meetings never divided over this controversy, but aligned themselves with the "Orthodox" group, as did also London and Dublin yearly meetings abroad.[4]

The exact numerical basis at the time of the separation has never been determined. In Philadelphia Yearly Meeting it has been estimated[5] that about two-thirds of the membership followed Hicks, and one-third the Orthodox group, out of a membership of approximately 24,000.

Disputes arose over meeting-house property, in one or two places resulting in legal procedure. In other cases both groups continued to hold their meetings in the same building but at different times, and in some cases new meeting-houses were built by one or the other of the two branches.[6] Meeting record books and registers were divided, sometimes remaining in the hands of the dominating group in a given meeting, and sometimes divided between the two branches in cases where custodians were on opposing sides of the schism. In many cases old records were copied by the group which was deprived of them, which accounts for the now existing duplicate copies of some meeting records.

Although the liberal group very early came to be called "Hicksites" it is apparent that influences other than the doctrines and preaching of that dynamic leader entered into the final separation. Hicks died in

1. Jones, Later Periods, I, 467.

2. Cited in ibid., p. 468 as taken from a manuscript account written by one who was present.

3. In 1937 and each year since, the yearly meetings of the two branches have held jointly one or two sessions of their annual meetings. These are usually evening sessions, and are made possible by the fact that the two annual meetings are held contemporaneously.

4. It should be noted on authority of Dr. Thomas E. Drake of Haverford College, that a small group in New England Yearly Meeting, in the Nantucket meeting did separate from the main body. This group became defunct after about 10 years.

5. Russell, op. cit., p. 45.

6. See infra., entry 175.

1830 but the controversy continued in unabated form for many years after his death. In recent years the passion-quieting hand of time has laid its healing influence on both groups, and many worthy leaders in both groups are turning their minds to closer co-operation between the two branches, hoping that eventually the mistakes on both sides may be forgotten.

Progressive Friends

Near the middle of the nineteenth century there occurred in the Hicksite branch of the Society of Friends a division, which has been almost unnoticed by Quaker historians. The body which resulted from this movement called themselves the Pennsylvania Yearly Meeting of Progressive Friends. It had its origin in Western Quarterly Meeting and its center at Old Kennett Meeting-house, near Kennett Square.[1]

At a quarterly meeting held in fourth month, 1852, a report urging advance in social reforms was prepared and representatives appointed to present it to the yearly meeting to be held in Philadelphia in fifth month. This report was not read before the main body of the yearly meeting, but was referred to the representatives who met separately. This group excluded the representatives appointed by Western Quarterly Meeting to present the liberalist report, and advised the yearly meeting against reading this report.

"Entertaining no hopes of a hearing, or of having our rights acknowledged by a body, with such a manifest departure of very many of those who assume to bear rule therein from its ancient Christian democracy, its simplicity of Church order, its integrity of principle, its uncompromising testimony against the popular evils of the times, we are united in believing that the usefulness and solemnity of our religious meetings, the blessings of a free Gospel Ministry, unshackled by human authority, the preservation of our religious liberties, the advancement of our Christian testimonies, and the prosperity of truth, so far as it is connected with our labors, depend upon instituting a Yearly Meeting for ourselves of such a character as the present crisis demands."[2] This is the conclusion of the report which was returned to Western Quarterly Meeting by the representatives sent to present its concern to the yearly meeting. The liberal group took immediate action and issued the following:

> Call for a General Conference with a view to the
> establishment of a Yearly Meeting in Pennsylvania.

The various religious denominations in the land are arrayed against the progressive spirit of the age, and by their very structure, assumptions and regulations, cannot occupy a cooperative position, because they impose fetters upon freedom of speech and of conscience, by requiring a slavish conformity in matters of abstract faith and sectarian discipline. This has led and is leading to extensive secessions from such organizations in all parts of the country, leaving the seceders generally in a scattered and isolated condition, whose talents,

---

1. *Proceedings of the Pennsylvania Yearly Meeting of Progressive Friends, 1853,* p. 3, hereinafter cited as *Proceedings.*

2. *Ibid.,* p. 40.

influence and means might be profitably concentrated for the advancement of the world embracing cause of Human Brotherhood, and who are
yearning for some form of association at once simple, free and attractive.

The abuse of a good thing is not a reason for its utter rejection;
and organization, in itself considered, is not only proper, but may
be rendered powerfully efficacious as an instrument in the hand of
Reform, without impairing the liberty, detracting from the independence, or limiting the conscience of any individual; though from the
nature of things its perpetuation is not to be expected or desired,
but it is at all times to be regarded as a means to an end, and to be
discarded whenever it becomes an impediment to the progress of truth.

The Society of Friends has been a theatre of agitation for years,
growing out of ecclesiatical domination on the one hand, and the demand for practical righteousness on the other; a domination entirely
at variance with the spirit of primitive Quakerism, seeking to sup-
press free thought and to exclude from membership those whose lives
are without blemish, whose example in word and deed is as a burning
and shining light, and who are seeking to know and do the will of God
at whatever sacrifice; a domination which has been deemed so intolerable, that in the States of New York, Ohio and Michigan, Yearly Meetings have been formed, two of which have taken the name of Congregational Friends, and two others that of Progressive Friends, and which
invite to membership "all those who look to God as a Universal Father,
and who regard as one Brotherhood the whole family of man."

In view of facts like these, and believing there is an extensive
preparation of mind for such a movement, we cordially invite not only
the members of the Society of Friends, but all those who feel the
want of social and religious co-operation, and believe that a Society
may be formed, recognizing the Progressive Element which will divorce
Religion from Technical Theology, to meet with us in General Conference at Friends Meeting House, at Old Kennett, in Chester County,
Pennsylvania, on First day, the 22nd of Fifth month, 1853, to deliberate upon such plan of organization as may commend itself to the judgment of those assembled, and to take action upon such other subjects
pertaining to Human Duty and Welfare, as may appear to demand the attention of the assembly.[1]

This call was signed by 58 Friends all of them members of Western
Quarterly Meeting, Hicksite.

The cause of this division is to be found in the tendency of the
leading popular churches to claim organic communion with God and to assume authority in theological and doctrinal matters because of their
nature as a religious organization. This group of signers of the Call
emphasized the fact that the church is only a human organization. They
also believed that their own Society of Friends had become strongly
tainted with these doctrinal ideas. Despite its "professed abjurations
of all forms," its rustic garb and look of meek simplicity, all seem
deluded with the idea that the church, being made after a divine pattern,
is supernaturally preserved from error. "Even the Quaker regards the

---

1. *Proceedings, 1853,* p. 3.

decision of his Yearly Meeting with a superstitious reverence scarcely
inferior to that which the Catholic awards to the decrees of the Pope
and the Cardinals."[1]

However, these objections to the popular church's claim to organic
communion and supernatural authority served more as a background for the
action which was taken than an actual cause. More definite and immediate
reason for the division is to be found in the Society's lack of action
in needed reforms. Turning again to the Exposition of Sentiments recorded in the proceedings of the first yearly meeting session; this
statement is found. "Our terms of membership are at once simple, practical and catholic. If we may be said to have a test, it is one which
applies to the heart and the life, not to the head nor any of its spec-
ulations. Our platform is broad as Humanity, and comprehensive as Truth.
We interrogate no man as to his theological belief; we send no committees to pry into the motives of those who may desire to share the bene-
fits of our Association; but open the door to all who recognize the equal
brotherhood of the Human Family, without regard to sex, color or condition, and who acknowledge the duty of defining and illustrating their
faith in God, not by assent to a creed, but by lives of personal purity,
and works of beneficence and charity to mankind. . . . The local Associations should do more than hold weekly meetings. They should regard it
a sacred duty to provide for the visitation and help of the poor in their
respective neighborhoods, to lend their sympathy and encouragement to
such as are borne down under heavy trials, and to afford prompt and ef-,
ficient aid in every right effort for the promotion of Temperance, Peace,
Anti-Slavery, Education, the Equal Rights of Women, etc. . . ."[2]

This emphasis by the group of practical Christianity becomes the
more basic when we find that of the 58 signers of the Call more than
half of them were in some way associated with the anti-slavery movement
through the Underground Railroad? As far back as 1837 the parent yearly
meeting had recorded, "Whilst we wish affectionately to caution our members against the excitement of an untempered zeal, or joining in assoc.a-
tions founded, or conducted upon principles which may hazard the faithful maintenance of our religious testimonies, we earnestly entreat them
to cherish and dwell upon these feelings of Christian love and compas-
sion towards the afflicted class of our fellow men, which will lead them
to regard with a just abhorrence the crimes that the iniquitous systems
of slavery has introduced. . . ."[4] Although this first yearly meeting
prepared testimonies on the current reforms of temperance, equal rights
of women, use of tobacco, and capital punishment, apparently this group
in Western Quarterly Meeting were not content to merely "regard with a
just abhorrence," but urged active participation in the abolitionis*
movement. That this single reform constituted a large element in the
inception of the Progressive Friends organization is further evidenced
by the fact that of the 13 communications sent to the first yearly meeting at Old Kennett Meeting-house, more than half of them made special
issue of the anti-slavery question. The writers of these letters are
also significant. Three of them are from similar groups of Progressive

1. *Proceedings, 1853*, pp. 15, 16.
2. *Ibid.*, pp. 22, 25.
3. William H. Siebert, *The Underground Railroad, From Slavery to Freedom*, Appendix E.
4. *Discipline of Philadelphia Yearly Meeting (Hicksite) for 1837.*

Friends already organized in Ohio, New York and Massachusetts.[1] Others
are such outstanding abolitionist leaders of the time as J. G. Forman,
Samuel J. May, Theodore Parker, Cassius M. Clay, John Greenleaf Whittier,
and William Lloyd Garrison. These men were the vanguard of the abolitionist movement, the most discussed question at that time. It is also
to be noted that one of the prime movers in Western Quarterly Meeting
was Joseph Dugdale, first clerk of the Progressive Yearly Meeting, who
had come to Pennsylvania in 1851 from Salem, Ohio. He was a member of
the Progressive group at Salem which had also split off from Ohio Yearly
Meeting on the question of Negro slavery.

Among the members of the Progressive group who were active in the
Underground Railroad were Thomas Garrett, John and Hannah Cox, Isaac and
Dinah Mendinhall, and Castner Hanway who was tried for treason for refusing to help a deputy sheriff capture fugitive slaves at Christiana; and
many others.

By the time of the second meeting of the Progressive Yearly Meeting
in 1854, considerable antagonism had arisen among the more conservative
Quakers of the section. When the gathering commenced on the 21st of May,
the doors of Old Kennett Meeting-house were barred against them. The
liberals however were resourceful. Someone broke a window and a member
climbed through it and opened the door from the inside. This caused
considerable unpleasantness, and lest the quarrel over the use of the
meeting-house might lead "to an unpleasant excitement and to divert
attention from the great purpose of our organization. . . it was unanimously agreed to hold our future sessions at Hamorton Hall."[2] This hall
seemed to have been the only available meeting-place, and it proved too
small for the crowds that attended the meetings. Although the remainder
of the session of 1854 were held there, a committee was appointed to
find a new meeting-place for the following year. This was accomplished
by erecting a new building on land donated by John Cox. The cornerstone
of this building was laid on September 3, 1854, by Oliver Johnson of New
York City, with these words; "If at any future time the owners of this
temple of reform and Christian progress shall pervert it to uses of big-
otry, intolerance and despotism, and shut its doors against the messen-
gers of unpopular truths, a voice will come forth from this cornerstone
to rebuke them, and to cry shame upon them for their recreancy."[3] This
meeting-house was given the name "Longwood" after the name of the Cox
farm. It was dedicated in 1855, and Theodore Parker was invited to give
the dedicatory address. Among the things deposited in a glass jar in
the cornerstone of the meeting-house were (a) Proceedings of the Whole
World's Temperance Convention held in New York 1851: (b) Proceedings
of the Pennsylvania Peace Society at the time of its formation 1851:
(c) Platform of the American Anti-Slavery Society with the declaration
of Sentiments of 1833: (d) Proceedings of Pennsylvania Yearly Meeting
of Progressive Friends for 1853-54: (e) The Declaration and Bans of
the Ohio Yearly Meeting of Progressive Friends, and also those of the
Waterloo Yearly Meeting in New York.[4]

It was a cause of considerable annoyance to the conservative Hick-

---

site Friends that the Longwood group was able to continue its meetings.
Definite action seemed imperative to them. The minutes of the monthly
meeting held at Old Kennett on August 8, 1854 record that; "When a member has united with any other professedly religious society the meeting
ought to consider such an act to be a relinquishment of his or her right
of membership with us, and a minute recording the fact should be made."
Immediately following this action of the monthly meeting the various
meetings began to disown those members who had allied themselves with
the Progressives. As a result all of the 58 persons who had signed the
Call for the first meeting and most of those who joined the group later
were disowned. However in justice to the conservative group it should
be noted that many years later when the Civil War was over and the slaves
were freed, the various meetings invited these disowned members to come
back into membership again. All who were alive at that time returned to
their meetings with the exception of John Cox. He alone refused to return to Old Kennett Meeting. Even the gentle persuasion of his wife
Hannah could not induce him. Tradition records that on every First Day
when she was ready for meeting, her plea "John is thee not coming with
me today?" was answered by, "Not today, Hannah, not today."

The Longwood Yearly Meeting of Progressive Friends has continued on
down to the present time as an annual gathering, composed of a group of
Quakers actively interested in the needed social and religious reforms
of the day. From the beginning it brought its influence to bear on the
side of freeing the slaves. Stephan A. Foster, ardent abolitionist and
author of the Brotherhood of Thieves, A True Picture of the American
Church and Clergy, spoke in meetings of the quarterly meeting, and was
expelled from a meeting at London Grove because he was too liberal in
his anti-slavery sentiments.[1] William Lloyd Garrison printed notices of
the Longwood meetings in his The Liberator, and lent his influence to
their success. Lucretia Mott, the early proponent of women's rights
visited and took part in the sessions. Theodore Parker, J. G. Forman,
Gerritt Smith, James Belonge, and many other religious and reform leaders,
from the inception of the movement down to the present time, have given
their help and encouragement to the Progressive Yearly Meeting.

In spite of its auspicious beginning, the yearly meeting has never
attained more than an annual meeting status. Since the days immediately
following the Civil War when the schismatic members were taken back into
membership in their respective meetings, the group has become more of a
progressive reform association than a regularly organized yearly meeting
of Friends. In fact it has never at any time had regularly organized
quarterly, monthly and preparative meetings. While it is true that at
the beginning of the movement there were a few local conferences at
Kennett, Marlborough, and Kennett Square, organized meetings in these
places never developed. The Friends in these meetings who allied themselves with the Longwood annual meeting, were disowned by their meetings,
but the majority of them kept on attending the meetings which had disowned them until they were taken back into membership after the Civil

---

1. Miriam L. Griest, Notes for a History of the Progressive Friends of Longwood, p. 5
(manuscript thesis at PSC-Hi), states that when Stephen A. Foster attempted to speak on slavery
at London Grove Meeting the elders requested that he be thrown out. Foster left quietly saying
he would finish his remarks outside. The majority of the audience followed him and listened to
his speech, delivered from the stone horse-block in the yard, while the elders sat in silence
indoors.

War. The Longwood Yearly Meeting has met annually and given opportunity
for the public expression of unpopular truths by leaders in various reforms. It has held its meetings and printed their proceedings, and by
these expressions has urged its members to be active and unwearying in
their personal efforts to advance the social reforms of the day.

The present organization consists of a clerk of the association,
and a committee which arranges the yearly conferences. The present clerk
is Jesse L. Holmes, Moylan.[1]

The Wilburite Controversy

In 1845 there occurred in New England Yearly Meeting a division
which had resulted from a disaffection known as the Wilbur-Gurney Controversy. This controversy began some 10 years before, and had spread
to practically all the Orthodox yearly meetings. In Ohio Yearly Meeting
the separation occurred in 1854. In New York a small separation took
place in Dutchess County about the same time. Separations also occurred
in North Carolina, Western, Iowa, Canada, and Kansas Yearly Meetings.
There was also a division in Baltimore Yearly Meeting within Nottingham
Quarterly Meeting. This quarterly meeting, composed of three meetings,
one of which was in Pennsylvania, organized a Wilburite yearly meeting
about 1855. In 1861 this latter group joined the Primitive Friends at
Fallsington. In the remaining yearly meetings of the country the ·dis-
cussion was pursued with varying degrees of fervor but actual separations
did not follow. In the yearly meeting where actual division took place
the schismatic groups are called Wilburite or Conservative Friends.
Since there was no organic separation in the Philadelphia Yearly Meeting,
it will be unnecessary to do more than make a note of the controversy
and so place it in its historical sequence in this brief sketch.[2]

John Wilbur was born in 1774 at Hopkinton, Rhode Island. His parents were of the more strict type of Friends, both being elders in their
meeting.   John Wilbur was educated in the carefully guarded Friendly
fashion, and though limited in scope his training was thorough. Wilbur
grew up in the atmosphere of the meeting, and was recorded a minister.
In 1831 he went on a religious visit to England. It was on this visit
that he met new doctrinal ideas and methods of teaching which troubled
him greatly. He, with some who agreed with him, could not bear to depart
from the old formulas and ideas of the earlier ministers of the Society.

Joseph John Gurney, born in 1778, at Norwich, England, a minister
among English Friends, and an exponent of the more progressive ideas and
methods, aroused opposition in John Wilbur. The substance of the differences was that Wilbur objected to Gurney's position that justifica-
tion precedes sanctification. Wilbur also laid great emphasis on the
necessity for heeding the Inner Light, and he objected to definite in-
structional lectures on the teachings of the Bible, saying these were
given "in the will of the creature." Such teaching, he held, should be

---

1. Since the above sketch was written the 88th and final session of the Progressive
Friends of Longwood was held on September 7th and 8th, 1940. The Yearly Meeting was officially
discontinued on that date and the interests of the organization were gathered up in a projected
Longwood Association Lectureship, with Jesse Holmes as Director.

2. *See*, John Wilbur, *Journal*, *passim*; Allen C. and Richard H. Thomas, *A History of the
Friends in America*, pp. 143-158; Jones, *Later Periods*, I, 488-540.

directly prompted by the Spirit at the time it was spoken. In 1837 Joseph John Gurney came to America on a religious visit. The controversy grew, and factions developed. Wilbur was finally disowned by the Friends of Rhode Island because of his endeavors to injure the influence of Gurney by circulating reports about his unsoundness.

Although a split never took place in Philadelphia Yearly Meeting, yet the controversy became very heated, and there was a large number of sympathizers with the views held by John Wilbur. The yearly meeting finally, in 1857, avoided the impending split by refusing to correspond with either branch of any yearly meeting where a split had occurred; which correspondence would have constituted a recognition of the yearly meeting to which the epistle (see Explanatory note p.) was sent, and would have immediately resulted in dissension between the two factions in Philadelphia. This attitude was applied to all yearly meetings for a few years, with the result that for a period of years Philadelphia Yearly Meeting retired into isolation with regard to the other yearly meetings of the country. Correspondence was later resumed with the sister bodies, and is carried on with all yearly meetings at the present time. In an effort to avoid a separation the method employed by Philadelphia Yearly Meeting in refusing to recognize any other yearly meetings, though perhaps severe, was certainly effective. No split occurred, and the two groups continued under the same organization. The keenness of the differences has long since lost its edge, and the two factions have become indistinguishable in the body of the yearly meeting.

The Primitive Friends

The last and numerically smallest group in the Society of Friends which remains to be mentioned in this brief sketch is the group known generally as Primitive Friends. The chief interest of this group is to "maintain the ancient testimonies of the Society"[1] and to emphasize the spirituality of the Christian message rather than to propagate or proselytize. The Primitive Friends hold general and quarterly meetings, both of which are practically yearly meetings. In the past their meetings were Scipio Quarterly, in New York; Quarterly Meeting of Friends for New England, held in Rhode Island and Massachusetts; General Meeting of Friends for Pennsylvania, New Jersey, and Delaware, held at Bristol; a meeting in Iowa; and a meeting in Canada. At the present time these groups have all disintegrated and their remaining members have allied themselves with other nearby Friends meetings. There is, according to the 1936 census[2] only one meeting remaining as an organized unit. This is the Falls Meeting near Bristol, Pennsylvania.

The separation, in Pennsylvania, of Primitive Friends from the larger body may be traced directly to the Wilbur-Gurney controversy. Although the controversy never actually resulted in a separation in Pennsylvania, there was enough zeal for the old Friendly customs and ideas to cause considerable dissatisfaction.. In 1860 about 200 of the dissatisfied Friends quietly withdrew and organized a separate meeting at Fallsington. Since the organization[3] of this meeting there is little of history to note about it. It adhered to the Philadelphia Discipline

1. Thomas, Op. cit., p. 209.
2. Religious Bodies, 1936, p. 27.
3. William Hodgson, The Society of Friends in the Nineteenth Century, II, 203-225.

of 1834, and has corresponded with other yearly meetings only as "way opens." There was no fanfare or heated debate at the time of the separation, but only a move by a small group who quietly withdrew and set up another meeting, more in accord, as they felt, with the primitive teachings and customs of Friends. The first minute of the General Meeting in 1861 shows their conception of the situation which demanded their action. "This meeting issued last year an epistle to our fellow members showing that the yearly meeting at Philadelphia as controlled of late years, has not only connived at, but practically promoted the great departure from the ancient ground of our profession, connected with the unsound doctrines of Joseph John Gurney, and his adherents. Since that time, not only has that yearly meeting persisted in its course as therein represented by us, but the Quarterly and Monthly Meetings subordinate thereto have identified themselves with it by representation and otherwise, thus partaking of the responsibility of identification with schism, so that we can no longer conscientiously own them as meetings of the Religious Society of Friends. Under these circumstances and until Monthly and Quarterly meetings can again be held in a measure of the life and power of truth which is the only authority for meetings of discipline, we believe it will be right to advise Friends intending removal to make application to this meeting for its certification so that after proper inquiry has been made, and no obstruction appearing, they may rightly be joined with such meetings as may be held on the ancient foundation and clear of the deflection which so sorrowfully prevails."[1]

The General Meeting which was organized in 1861 was composed of three monthly meetings. These were Philadelphia Monthly Meeting, Falls Monthly Meeting and the Monthly Meeting of Nottingham and Little Britain. Originally the two latter meetings met quarterly at Philadelphia and joined Fallsington twice yearly in a half-years General Meeting at Fallsington. It is also to be noted that this General Meeting has for a long time been affiliated with a small meeting of Conservative Friends at Fritchley, England.

The United States Census for 1936 shows 14 members[2] belonging to the Falls Meeting. In the 80 years since its origin the group, never large, has dwindled to this small number, but the meeting is still kept up and the records preserved.

United and Independent Meetings

It is necessary to include here a brief mention of a group of Friends meetings which have come into being at various points in the country, and a few of which exist in Pennsylvania. These meetings are known as United Meetings or Independent Meetings, depending upon the local situation under which they originated.

United Meetings are those in which small meetings or groups of Friends from both the Orthodox and Hicksite branches have joined together in one meeting; which meeting has not affiliated itself with the quarterly or yearly meeting of either branch; or which meeting may have affiliated itself with the higher bodies of both branches. Independent meetings are those which have been organized in rather informal fashion

---

1. First Minute Book 1850 First Minute.
2. *Religious Bodies, 1936*, p. 27.

among groups of Friends who are isolated from local meetings and who happen to be associated together in some community. The resultant meeting however has not affiliated itself with the higher bodies of either of the main branches of Friends. These meetings are to be found in such places as college and university centers like the Bethlehem Meeting at Lehigh University or summer colonies such as the one at Buck Hill Falls. Two factors are important in the forming of the United and Independent meetings. One is the urge to worship according to the Quaker conception of group worship; and the other is the very strong desire on the part of a large number of individual Friends to weld together again the various branches of the Society caused by the separations in the past, particularly that of 1827.

There are about seventy of these meetings now existing throughout the country. Most of them meet regularly, but some meet intermittently. Twelve of the meetings are in Pennsylvania. Records are not always regularly kept, and in cases where they are, the custodians are usually non-resident and the records very difficult of access. This fact will be noted in a perusal of the entries for these meetings (entries 329-340).

The conscious tendency to form these unaffiliated meetings and to cooperate and unite in every possible way, is recognized and encouraged in both the Hicksite and Orthodox branches. This tendency has not yet developed to the proportions of a movement, but that it is important enough to be reckoned with cannot be denied. This is attested by the large number of unaffiliated meetings, and also by partial joint sessions of the two large yearly meetings which have occurred regularly during the past few years.

PRESENT ORGANIZATIONAL AFFILIATIONS OF FRIENDS IN NORTH AMERICA, BY YEARLY MEETINGS

FRIENDS WORLD COMMITTEE FOR CONSULTATION

Conservative Orthodox Independent Yearly Meetings[1]	Orthodox Independent Yearly Meetings[1]	The Five Years Meeting (Orthodox)	Friends General Conference (Hicksite)	United and Independent Groups[1] (not yearly meetings)
Primitive	Cuba	Baltimore	Baltimore	Connecticut Valley Assn. of Friends
Pennsylvania	Jamaica	California	Genesee	
	Kansas	Canada	Illinois	Pacific Coast Assn. of Friends
Wilburite	Mexico	Indiana	Indiana	
Canada	Ohio	Iowa	New York	Small Independent groups
Iowa	Oregon	Nebraska	Ohio[2]	
New England	Philadelphia	New England	Philadelphia	
New York		New York		United Monthly Meeting
North Carolina		North Carolina		
Ohio		Western		
Western		Wilmington		

1. Not interrelated
2. Suspended in 1919

II. ORGANIZATIONAL AFFILIATIONS OF FRIENDS IN NORTH AMERICA

Friends World Committee for Consultation

In recent years a definite move among the 43 yearly meetings comprising the Society of Friends throughout the world has been under way to make more articulate the belief and principles of Friends in religious and social relationships. At the present time the movement is not embodied in an organization, but a series of conferences have met for discussion and concerted thinking on various problems, and a series of studies has been prepared by Quaker groups in different parts of the world. The World Committee has no authority over its component groups.

The first of these conferences was held in 1920. Its time was given to a study and discussion of the social problems which were left as an aftermath of the World War. Since that date seven other European conferences have been held on the following topics:

> Quakerism and Modern Life and Thought (Elsinore, 1931).
> Problems of the World Crisis (Paris, 1931).
> Spiritual Values of Quakerism and Their Application in the World Today (Amsterdam, 1932).
> The Life of the Spirit and Modern Human Difficulties (Geneva, 1933).
> From Vision to Action (Prague, 1934).
> Christ and Present-Day Quaker Experience (Paris, 1935).
> Quaker Pacifism: A Realizable Ideal (Jordans, England, 1936).
> The Problems of Refugees (Valle Kilda, Denmark, 1938).
> Task and Method of Quakerism (Geneva, 1939).
> How Friends Can Help in Present World Conditions (Richmond, Ind., 1940).

A large World Conference was held at Swarthmore College in September 1937, at which the five following topics were studied on the basis of reports sent in from various countries:

> I.   The Spiritual Message of the Religious Society of Friends.
> II. The Individual Christian and the State.
> III. Methods of Achieving Economic, Racial and International Justice.
> IV. Friends' Contribution to Education.
> V.   International Co-operation of Friends.

These reports were not official pronouncements of the Society of Friends; they were to serve as directional thinking for the guidance of Friends with different national backgrounds and points of view.

The Conference has no headquarters, and operates only through a Continuation Committee and the various agencies of the Society which are already in existence in various parts of the world. Carl Heath, Friends House, Euston Road, London, England, is chairman of the committee.

33

Five Years Meeting of Friends in America

The Society of Friends in America and abroad is composed of yearly meetings, with their subordinate meetings. The bond of union is maintained by annual correspondence between these yearly meetings; by issuing and receiving credentials of ministers; by mutual transfers of membership; and by joint participation in benevolent enterprises.

Inter-yearly meeting conferences for the consideration of special concerns were held in Philadelphia in 1829 and in Baltimore in 1849. The first general conference of the yearly meetings was held at Richmond, Indiana, in 1887. This was attended by delegates from England and also all the Orthodox (not Wilburite or Primitive) yearly meetings in America except Philadelphia, which was unofficially represented. Other conferences were held in 1892 and 1897. At the meeting in 1892 it was decided to hold similar conferences of the American yearly meetings every 5 years and it was the conference of 1902 which organized under the name of the Five Years Meeting of Friends in America.[1] These meetings have been held regularly since that time with the exception of 1917, when, due to the war, the sessions were postponed to 1920. They have been held at 5-year intervals since that time.

A committee was appointed at the Richmond meeting in 1887 to draw up a Constitution and Discipline. This was adopted by 13 yearly meetings, two of which later withdrew.

While these yearly meetings which adopt the Constitution and Discipline under its provisions delegate certain authority to the Five Years Meeting, yet they retain their original independence. Most important with regard to this is the statement in the Constitution and Discipline that "each Yearly Meeting retains the authority to adopt additional disciplinary regulations," and that "such portions of this constitution and Discipline as have no application to the existing conditions of any particular Yearly Meeting shall be null therein."

There is no creed or published tenets of faith among Quakers of either the Five Years Meeting or other groups. However, the yearly meetings comprising the Five Years Meeting have, as groups, accepted as a basis of faith and practice the Richmond Declaration of Faith which was drawn up at the conference of 1887. This statement, together with the letter of George Fox to the Governor of Barbados, written in 1671, constitute the written doctrinal statements of the Five Years Meeting. Many yearly meetings have issued printed Disciplines at various times, many of which have been revised as the Society progressed, and all of which have been fairly uniform in their statements of principle and practice.

The larger cooperative work of the Five Years Meeting is carried on by boards, the members of which are appointed by the participating yearly meetings. Such interests as missions, religious education, temperance, publications, etc. are cared for by their specific boards. An executive committee acts for the Five Years Meeting ad interim. The central offices are located at 101 South 8th Street, Richmond, Indiana, and the permanent Secretary is Dr. Walter C. Woodward.

---

1. *See: Proceedings of the Conference of Friends*, 1887, 1892, 1897; also *Minutes and Proceedings of the Five Years Meeting*, 1902, 1907, 1912, 1920, 1925, 1930, 1935, 1940.

Friends General Conference

The organization designated above (entry 172), is the medium for group action of the six Hicksite yearly meetings in America. At the time of the organization, Ohio Yearly Meeting made a seventh member, but that yearly meeting was suspended in 1919. Its Representative Committee continues to function for the yearly meeting, and remains a part of the General Conference Committee. The General Conference is the result of the unification of several smaller conferences, organized for specific purposes during the period from 1868 to 1896. In 1900 at Chautauqua, New York, four special conferences namely: the First-day School, the Union for Philanthropic Labor, the Educational, and Religious conferences were united to form the Friends General Conference,[1] under the guidance of a Committee of One Hundred appointed from the component yearly meetings according to size of membership.

The sessions of the General Conference were held at various places until 1928 but since that time they have all convened at Cape May, New Jersey. This conference is one of the two national Quaker organizations in America whose constituent members are yearly meetings. The other one is the Five Years Meeting of Friends in America, whose organization and activities in the Orthodox branch are similar to those of the Friends General Conference in the Hicksite group.

In 1924 a reorganization of the agencies of the conference resulted in three sections which were charged with the various activities. These sections report to the conference at each session. In 1936 the office which the former Advancement Committee had established was changed to a General Conference Office. This office, presided over by an administrative secretary, together with the General Conference Committee, form the promotional and advisory agency of the General Conference ad interim.

Independent Yearly Meetings

This group of 15 yearly meetings are designated as "independent" because they have not allied themselves with either of the cooperative groups of yearly meetings.

Two exceptions should be made, however, those are Oregon and Kansas Yearly Meetings which allied themselves with the Five Years Meeting of Friends in America at the beginning of that organization, but withdrew in 1926, and 1937 respectively.

These yearly meetings, though grouped together here for convenience, are in no way inter-related among themselves. Each of them carries on its organization in the manner of Friends, with its various quarterly and monthly meetings, and committees for departments of church activity. They have no inter-yearly meeting organizations among themselves, neither are they affiliated with the General Conference nor the Five Years Meeting.

---

1. *See* minutes and records listed on pp. 206, 207.

United and Independent Groups

In this grouping will be found three categories of meetings which do not quite fit into either of the other classifications.

These are associations of Friends or groups, not affiliated with any organized yearly meeting, but which hold annual or semi-annual meetings. One or more local groups may constitute one of these associations.

United monthly meetings are meetings already affiliated with each of the two major branches of the Society, but which have united to form a single monthly meeting, at the same time retaining their connection with their respective superior meetings (entries 329-333).

Independent groups are local groups not officially affiliated with any superior body. (entries 334-340).

Location and Accessibility of Records

The records of the Friends meetings in Pennsylvania are for the most part deposited in two large depositories. These are the Friends Historical Library at Swarthmore College, Swarthmore, and the Friends Arch Street Center at 302 Arch Street, Philadelphia. Both these depositories have fireproof vaults. Another valuable collection, consisting of some originals and a great many verbatim transcriptions, is deposited at the Pennsylvania Historical Society, 1300 Locust Street, Philadelphia. There are also smaller collections of records at the Friends Central Bureau, 1515 Cherry Street, Philadelphia; the Haverford College Library, Haverford; the Media Friends Meeting-house, Media; the Newtown National Bank, Newtown; the Friends Library, on Coulter Street at 5400 Germantown Avenue, Germantown; the Chester County Historical Society, West Chester; The Willistown Meeting-house, ½ mile west of White Horse Village, Chester County; and various books of current records in the custody of recorders and clerks of meetings.

Many of these records are accessible to responsible persons, usually at a nominal charge to nonmembers of the two Philadelphia Yearly Meetings. Full information may be obtained by communicating with J. Henry Bartlett, Tuckerton, New Jersey, for the records deposited at 302 Arch Street, Philadelphia; and E. Virginia Walker, Swarthmore College, Swarthmore, for the records deposited in the Friends Historical Library at Swarthmore College.

PART B. MEETINGS AND THEIR RECORDS

I. PHILADELPHIA YEARLY MEETING (O)

Since the Separation of 1827-28 this branch of the Society of
Friends has been called the Orthodox Friends, or sometimes
the Arch Street Friends because the yearly meeting convenes
annually at 304 Arch Street, Philadelphia. (See Explanatory
Notes, No. 1, p.   ).

Component Quarterly Meetings

The following quarterly meetings and their subordinate meetings
lie outside the Commonwealth of Pennsylvania, and because of
the limitations which obtain in this Survey do not come within
the scope of this volume. For their history and records see
the forthcoming Inventory of the Church Archives of New Jersey,
and also the inventories of the church archives of the States of
Delaware, Maryland and Virginia.

Shrewsbury Quarterly Meeting (N.J.)	1672
Burlington Quarterly Meeting (N.J.) Merged with Bucks Quarter in 1898	1682

Salem Quarterly Meeting (N.J.)
    Merged with Haddonfield Quarter
    in 1904.
	1682

Warrington and Fairfax Quarterly Meeting
    (Md. and Va.) divided in 1787. Some
    of the subordinate meetings hereunder
    are in Pennsylvania.
	1776

Fairfax Quarterly Meeting (Va.)
    Transferred to Baltimore Yearly
    Meeting in 1790.
	1787

Warrington Quarterly Meeting (Md).
    Transferred to Baltimore Yearly
    Meeting in 1790. Some of the sub-
    ordinate meetings hereunder are in
    Pennsylvania.
	1787

Southern Quarterly Meeting (Md. and Del.)	1790
Haddonfield Quarterly Meeting (N.J.) Merged with Salem Quarter in 1904.	1794

Burlington and Bucks Quarterly Meeting (N.J.)
    Some of the subordinate meetings hereunder
    are in Pennsylvania.
	1898

Haddonfield and Salem Quarterly Meeting (N.J.)	1904

The following meetings and their constituents are
in Pennsylvania and are therefore treated in this
volume.

	Date established	Entry number
Philadelphia Quarterly Meeting	1682	2
Chester Quarterly Meeting	1683	136
Bucks Quarterly Meeting	1684	58
Western Quarterly Meeting	1758	71
Warrington and Fairfax Quarterly Meeting Only subordinate meetings in Pennsylvania included.	1776	89
Abington Quarterly Meeting	1786	92
Warrington Quarterly Meeting Only subordinate meetings in Pennsylvania included.	1787	341
Caln Quarterly Meeting	1800	116
Concord Quarterly Meeting Only subordinate meetings in Pennsylvania included.	1800	136
Burlington and Bucks Quarterly Meeting Only subordinate meetings in Pennsylvania included.	1898	161

1. PHILADELPHIA YEARLY MEETING OF FRIENDS, 1681--. 304 Arch Street
    Philadelphia.
Philadelphia Yearly Meeting of Friends is the direct successor of Burlington Yearly Meeting. Burlington was the third yearly meeting to be
established in America, and its beginning is found in the minutes of
Burlington Monthly Meeting: "At a Monthly Meeting held at Burlington,
the Second Day of the Third Month 1681, it was unanimously agreed, that
a General Meeting be yearly held in Burlington, the first of which, to
be the 28th of Sixth Month, 1681." Accordingly, the first yearly meeting was held at the house of Thomas Gardiner, in Burlington, N.J.,   on
the 28th of Sixth Month 1681. At this meeting it was mutually agreed
that a women's meeting should be established, and it was also agreed
that the next yearly meeting should be held in the Seventh month of the
following year. About the same time a yearly meeting for worship was
held in the Second month at Salem.[1] The second yearly meeting was held
at Burlington in the Seventh month, 1682. The third, in 1683, was also
held at Burlington, but this one was very heavily attended in comparison
with the earlier two; a steady migration of a large number of Friends to
Philadelphia and other parts of the Province of Pennsylvania, under the

1. Jones, *Quakers in Colonies*, Introduction, pp. XIII-XXXII; Bowden, *op. cit.*, I, 405.

patronage of William Penn, had made necessary several monthly and particular meetings, and many from these meetings attended. Penn himself,
having arrived in the colonies in November of the preceding year, became
active in the affairs of the meetings and was present at the yearly meeting of 1683, held at Burlington. A few months later one was held for
the first time at Philadelphia. This was in the third month of that year.
The records of this meeting appear to be missing but a small notice of it
being established can be found in the minutes of Bucks Quarterly Meeting
(entry). This first yearly meeting at Philadelphia, no doubt, was held
in the first meeting-house of Friends in this city, which stood at what
is now No. 122 S. Front Street; and was built of pine boards. This was
the "Boarded Meeting-house," so often referred to in the early minutes,
and was the only meeting-house in the city at that time. A temporary
meeting-shed was directed to be built at Centre Square, "with all speed,"
in 1684; to be used until the brick structure being erected at the same
location could be completed. The first Bank Meeting-house, built of
wood, and located on Front Street, north of Arch, was erected in 1685.
The same year the brick meeting-house at Centre Square was completed.
The Great Meeting-house, at the southwest corner of Second and High (now
Market) Streets, was erected in 1696; the second Bank Meeting-house
built of brick, was erected on the site of the first Bank Meeting-house,
with materials from the Centre Square house, and was in use in 1703.
With the exception of private houses, in which meetings were held, these
meeting-houses constituted the earliest places of worship of Friends in
Philadelphia, and it is a safe assumption that the early yearly meetings
held in Philadelphia were held in them.   It is definitely known that
yearly meetings were held in the Great Meeting-house, for on the 28th of
Fifth Month 1699, "it was proposed to this meeting the necessity of enlarging this meeting-house /the Great Meeting-house/ by erecting a gallery; upon which it is agreed that it be done between this time and the
time of next Yearly Meeting, and that William Harwood shall prepare the
stuff for the same." It is also found later, in 1701, after the brick
structure at Centre Square had been abandoned as a meeting-place, "that
Friends are fearful lest they should not accommodate the Friends attending the Yearly Meeting," and again looked toward the Centre Square Meeting-house. Two Friends were "desired to view, and see whether the Centre
Meeting-house be in condition to entertain a meeting, . . . but it did
not appear to be in a suitable condition, and the Yearly Meeting convened
at the Great Meeting-house."

     Early in the Seventh month of the years 1684 and 1685, the yearly
meetings for Friends of the Jerseys met at Burlington, and a short time
later in the same month, during these 2 years, Friends of Pennsylvania
held their meetings in Philadelphia. At the yearly meeting of 1685, it
was "unanimously agreed the concluded by this meeting (in Philadelphia)
that there be but one yearly and General Meeting in Pennsylvania and
West Jersey . . . one year at Burlington on the First day in the Seventh
Month, for worship, and the Fourth day to be the Men's and Women's Meeting. The next after to be at Philadelphia, on the same day of the same
month, and to continue the same time."[1]   At this session it was agreed
that the meeting should bear the title of "The General Yearly Meeting of
Friends of Pennsylvania, East and West Jersey, and the Adjacent Provin-
ces."   Some years later the title was changed to that of "The Yearly
Meeting of Pennsylvania, New Jersey, Delaware, and parts of Maryland and

---

1. Philadelphia Yearly Meeting Minutes, 1685.

Virginia." After the Separation of 1827 the Orthodox group became known as the "Arch Street Friends" to distinguish them from the "Race Street Friends," and their official title became "The Yearly Meeting of the Religious Society of Friends of Philadelphia and Vicinity." From 1686 until 1760 the yearly meeting alternated between Burlington and Philadelphia. In 1712 the question of holding all sessions in Philadelphia had been raised, but the change was ruled out. In 1760 the proposal of holding all sessions in Philadelphia was again discussed and this time approved, and Philadelphia became the permanent home of the yearly meeting. The first session at Burlington in 1681 was held in Sixth month, the second in 1682 was held in Seventh month. In 1752, when the calendar changed, the sessions were kept in September by merely changing the wording of the continuing minute to read Ninth month instead of Seventh month, as the time for the session in 1753. In 1799 the sessions were shifted to Fourth month. In 1916 they were again changed to Third month, which appointment they have kept to the present time.

Up to 1940, during the long period of 259 years of its life, there have been 19 quarterly meetings within the limits of Philadelphia Yearly Meeting of the Orthodox branch. In 1790, Warrington and Fairfax quarterly meetings were transferred to Baltimore (Maryland) Yearly Meeting, and in return the Maryland meeting transferred to Philadelphia Yearly meeting all of its meetings located in the eastern peninsula of that state. Later, in 1819, Philadelphia transferred the monthly meetings of Nottingham, Little Britain, and Deer Creek to Baltimore Yearly Meeting.

· Apparently after the erection of the Great Meeting-house, which was completed in 1696, practically all of the yearly meetings held in Philadelphia from that time until 1753, were held in that house. It is probable that during that time, one branch of it, either the men's or women's meeting, met at the second Bank Meeting-house, while the other branch convened in the Market Street house, the second Bank Meeting-house being available for the purpose during this period. In 1753, the Pine Street Meeting-house was erected, which was built expressly to accommodate the yearly meeting. From 1755, the women's meeting was held in the Great Meeting-house, for in this year this meeting-house was entirely rebuilt, and a yearly meeting convened there, as is set forth in the following reference: "The new Meeting-house (Great Meeting-house) was so far completed in the autumn of 1755, that the Yearly Meeting (then held in the Ninth month) convened in it . . . ."[1] This was the women's Yearly meeting, since the one composed of men had been settled, only 2 years prior to this, in the New Pine Street Meeting-house.

During the prevalence of the yellow fever in 1798, the men's yearly meeting assembled in the Pine Street Meeting-house on Ninth month 24th and after a time of solid deliberation, concluded to adjourn until Twelfth month. In 1802 the men's yearly meeting was removed to the meeting-house of the North Meeting. "North Meeting," was a short name given to the Northern District Monthly Meeting of Friends (entry 33), and the meeting-place of that organization in 1802 was the Key's Alley Meeting-house. This house was on the small street between Race and Vine, and Front and Second Streets, now called New Street, which at that time was called Key's Alley. Thomas Scattergood in his Journal, alludes to

---

1. "Original Objects for Which Meetings for Discipline Were Established," *The Friend*, LVIII (1885), 127.

this removal as follows: "The Meeting on consideration very unitedly agreed to adjourn to the North House, in hopes that it will accommodate the meeting better than the present place of meeting . . . the Pine Street House."[1] The first section of the present meeting-house of Philadelphia Monthly Meeting of Friends (entry 3), at Fourth and Arch (then Mulberry) Streets, was erected in 1804, and it appears that the women's yearly meeting was removed to that house upon its completion, and that the men continued to meet at the North House until 1811. In 1811 the west wing of the Arch Street Meeting-house was built, and again referring to the Journal of Thomas Scattergood, under date of Fourth month 1811, the following entry is found: "The Yearly Meeting for business was large. The two first sittings were held in the North House, where it has been held for some years; the afternoon sitting adjourned to meet in the morning of the 16th, in the East House on Mulberry Street and Fourth Street, and the women took possession of the new one just finished on the West."[2] From that time, until the . joint meetings for men and women Friends were inaugurated in 1921, all meetings of both sides of the yearly meeting have been held in the Arch Street Meeting-house, and so continue to the present.

Among the many active committees and associations of Philadelphia Yearly Meeting at the present time, the following are the most outstanding: Committee on Education; Committee on Philadelphia Yearly Meeting Schools; Committee on Religious Education; Book Committee; Friends Fiduciary Corporation, having in its care the finances and properties of 27 meetings, and various trust funds as well; Friends Mission Board; and yearly meeting representation on the following joint committees: American Friends Service Committee; Friends Peace Committee; Friends Council on Education; Friends Fellowship Council; Executive Council of Friends Temperance Association; Race Relations Committee; Social Order Committee; Indian Affairs Committee; Young Friends Movement; Friends World Committee for Consultation. The clerk of the Yearly Meeting is Harold Evans, 304 Arch Street, Philadelphia. The secretary is Edward W. Evans, at the same address.

Men's Minutes, 1681-1920, 11 vols.; Women's Minutes, 1681-1920, 6 vols.; Minutes of Joint Meetings, 1921--, 4 vols. at PPFYR.   Minutes of the Representative Meeting, 1756--, 11 vols. (called Meeting for sufferings until about 1910); Minutes of Ministers and Elders, 1686--, 6 vols. at PPFYR. Minutes of the Committee on Education and the Committee on Yearly Meeting Schools, 1875-1921, 3 vols., at PPFYR, and 1922--, 3 vols., in custody of Edna H. Vansant, 20 S. 12th Street, Philadelphia. Minutes of the Committee on Religious Education and the First-day School Association, 1922-29, 2 vols., at PPFYR, and 1929--, 1 vol., in custody of Jeanette Z. Beckenstein, 304 Arch Street, Philadelphia. Minutes of the Book Committee of the Representative Meeting, 1873--, 6 vols., at PPFYR. and 1922--, 1 vol., in custody of the chairman, Mabel B. Hoyle, 111 N. Seventh Ave., Haddon Heights, N. J. Minutes of the Peace Committee, 1891-1916, 1 vol., at PPFYR, and 1916--, 1 vol., in custody of Richard

---

1. Thomas Scattergood, *Journal of the Life and Religious Labors of Thomas Scattergood*, p. 146.

2. "The Burial Ground and Building at Arch and Fourth Streets," *The Friend*, LXIII (1890), 194, hereinafter cited as *Burial Ground*.

Wood 304 Arch Street, Philadelphia. Minutes of the Temperance Association of Friends of Philadelphia Yearly Meeting, 1881-1924, 4 vols., at
PPFYR, and 1924--, 1 vol., in custody of the chairman, Asa P. Way, 63
West Drexel Ave., Lansdowne. Minutes of the Mission Board, 1917-22,
1 vol., at PPFYR, (divided in 1923 into General Board Minutes and Executive Board Minutes); Minutes of General Board, 1923-34, 1 vol.; Minutes
of Executive Board, 1923-37, 1 vol., at PPFYR. Minutes of General Board
1934--, 1 vol., and Minutes of Executive Board, 1937--, 1 vol., both in
custody of Jeanette Z. Beckenstein. Minutes of Race Relations Committee,
1921--, 3 vols.; Minutes of Extension Committee, 1921-27, 1 vol. (contains also sub-committee No. 3 minutes); Minutes of the Social Order Committee, various dates, 1 pkg. (contains minutes and correspondence,
package not dated), at PPFYR. Treasurer's Cash Books, 1845-1916, 2 vols.
at PPFYR, and 1916--, number of vols. .not obtainable, in custody of the
treasurer Jonathan Steere, Girard Trust Co., Broad and Chestnut Streets,
Philadelphia.

PHILADELPHIA QUARTERLY MEETING (0)

COMPONENT MEETINGS

(See: Explanatory Note 3).

	Date established	Entry number
PHILADELPHIA MONTHLY MEETING	1682	3
Shackamaxon Meeting	1681	4
Haverford Preparative Meeting	1682	16
Merion Preparative Meeting	1682	17
Radnor Preparative Meeting	1682	19
Schuylkill Meeting	1683	20
The Board Meeting on the Delaware	1683	5
Centre Square Meeting	1685	6
First Bank Meeting	1685	7
High Street Meeting	1696	8
Fairhill Indulged Meeting	1702	9
Second Bank Meeting	1703	34
Pine Street Meeting	1753	38
Pottstown Indulged Meeting	1753	10
Fourth Street Meeting	1764	11
Orange Street Indulged Meeting	1872	12
West Philadelphia Indulged Meeting	1873	13
TACONY AND POETQUESINK MONTHLY MEETING	1683	14
Byberry Indulged Meeting (Poetquesink)	1683	110
Oxford Indulged Meeting (Tacony)	1683	109
Cheltenham Indulged Meeting (Abington)	1683	95
ABINGTON MONTHLY MEETING (DUBLIN)	1683	93
Byberry Indulged Meeting (Poetquesink)	1683	110
Byberry Preparative Meeting (Poetquesink)	1701	110
Oxford Indulged Meeting (Tacony)	1683	109
Oxford Preparative Meeting (Tacony)	1701	109
Cheltenham Indulged Meeting (Abington)	1683	95
Cheltenham Preparative Meeting (Abington)	1701	95
Germantown Indulged Meeting	1683	115
Germantown Preparative Meeting	1702	115
Horsham Indulged Meeting	1716	104
Horsham Preparative Meeting	1717	104
RADNOR MONTHLY MEETING	1684	15
Haverford Preparative Meeting	1682	16
Merion Preparative Meeting	1682	17
Hestonville (Merion) Preparative Meeting	1827	18
Radnor Preparative Meeting	1682	19
Schuylkill Meeting	1683	20
Newtown Indulged Meeting	1696	146
Gwynedd Preparative Meeting (North Wales)	1698	97
Valley Indulged Meeting	1698	21
Valley Preparative Meeting	1810	21
Plymouth Indulged Meeting	1703	98

Plymouth Preparative Meeting	1710	98
Schuylkill Indulged Meeting (Charlestown)	1812	22
NEWARK MONTHLY MEETING (Later KENNETT M M)	1686	79
Kennett Indulged Meeting	1707	80
Kennett Preparative Meeting	1711	80
Howell James' Indulged Meeting	1709	23
New Garden Indulged Meeting	1713	73
New Garden Preparative Meeting	1715	73
London Grove Indulged Meeting	1714	84
Bradford Indulged Meeting	1716	120
Bradford Preparative Meeting	1726	120
GWYNEDD MONTHLY MEETING	1714	96
Gwynedd Preparative Meeting	1698	97
Plymouth Indulged Meeting	1703	98
Plymouth Preparative Meeting	1710	98
Richland Indulged Meeting	1710	102
Richland Preparative Meeting	1723	102
Providence Indulged Meeting	1716	99
Providence Preparative Meeting	1733	99
Exeter (Oley) Indulged Meeting	1718	25
Exeter (Oley) Preparative Meeting	1725	25
Maiden Creek Indulged Meeting	1732	26
Maiden Creek Preparative Meeting	1735	26
Robeson Indulged Meeting	1735	135
Robeson Preparative Meeting	1741	135
EXETER MONTHLY MEETING (Formerly Oley)	1737	24
Exeter Preparative Meeting	1725	25
Maiden Creek Preparative Meeting	1735	26
Robeson Indulged Meeting	1735	135
Robeson Preparative Meeting	1741	135
Tulpehocken Indulged Meeting	1749	27
Reading Indulged Meeting	1750	28
Reading Preparative Meeting	1756	28
Pottstown Indulged Meeting	1753	10
Catawissa Indulged Meeting	1775	29
Catawissa Preparative Meeting	1794	29
Roaring Creek Indulged Meeting	1786	49
Fishing Creek Indulged Meeting	1795	42
Pottsville Indulged Meeting	1828	30
RICHLAND MONTHLY MEETING	1742	101
Richland Preparative Meeting	1723	102
Springfield Indulged Meeting	1743	31
Saucon Indulged Meeting	1744	32
NORTHERN DISTRICT MONTHLY MEETING	1772	33
Second Bank Meeting	1703	34
Key's Alley Meeting	1790	35
Green Street Indulged Meeting	1814	55
Green Street Preparative Meeting	1814	55
Tioga Indulged Meeting (Proposed)	1886	36
SOUTHERN DISTRICT MONTHLY MEETING	1772	37
Pine Street Meeting	1753	38
Fourth Street Meeting	1764	11

<u>HORSHAM MONTHLY MEETING</u>	1782	103
<u>Byberry</u> Preparative Meeting	1701	107
<u>Horsham</u> Indulged Meeting	1716	104
<u>Horsham</u> Preparative Meeting	1717	104
<u>ROBESON MONTHLY MEETING</u> (Forest Meeting)	1789	134
<u>Robeson</u> Preparative Meeting	1741	135
CATAWISSA MONTHLY MEETING	1796	39
<u>Catawissa</u> Preparative Meeting	1794	48
Roaring Creek Preparative Meeting	1796	49
<u>Muncy</u> Indulged Meeting	1788	40
Muncy Preparative Meeting	1796	40
Fishing Creek Preparative Meeting	1799	42
Greenwood Indulged Meeting	1795	43
Pine Grove Indulged Meeting	1797	44
Berwick Indulged Meeting	1799	50
MUNCY MONTHLY MEETING (Pennsdale)	1799	41
<u>Catawissa</u> Preparative Meeting	1794	48
Greenwood Indulged Meeting	1795	43
Greenwood Preparative Meeting	1836	43
Roaring Creek Preparative Meeting	1796	49
Berwick Indulged Meeting	1799	50
Fishing Creek Preparative Meeting	1799	42
Fishing Creek Indulged Meeting	1828	42
Elkland Indulged Meeting	1804	45
Elkland Preparative Meeting	1833	45
Pine Grove Preparative Meeting	1821	44
Pottsville Indulged Meeting	1828	,.
Eagles Mere Indulged Meeting	1893	46
ROARING CREEK MONTHLY MEETING	1814	47
Catawissa Preparative Meeting	1794	48
Roaring Creek Preparative Meeting	1796	49
Berwick Indulged Meeting	1799	50
WESTERN DISTRICT MONTHLY MEETING	1814	51
Hestonville (Merion) Indulged Meeting	1865	52
Haverford Indulged Meeting	1865	53
GREEN STREET MONTHLY MEETING	1816	54
Green Street Preparative Meeting	1814	55
HAVERFORD MONTHLY MEETING	1904	56
<u>RADNOR (UNITED) MONTHLY MEETING</u>	1937	333
(Controlled jointly with the Philadelphia		
Quarterly Meeting of the Race Street Friends (H)		

2. PHILADELPHIA QUARTERLY MEETING OF FRIENDS, 1682--. Fourth and
Arch Streets, Philadelphia.
The few Friends who had settled on the west side of the Delaware River
before the arrival of William Penn in 1682, attended the monthly and
quarterly business meetings of the Friends in New Jersey, crossing the
river by rowboat for this purpose. The meetings were held at various
places in West Jersey to accommodate the more distant members. The first
monthly meeting in Pennsylvania of which there is documentary record was
held at the home of Robert Wade at Chester (Upland) in Eleventh month
1681. Friends who first settled in Philadelphia and its vicinity were
concerned largely with the establishment of meetings for worship, but
meetings for discipline were set up as rapidly as need for them arose.
The first meetings for worship to be established in Philadelphia were
held in the homes of members, which in some cases were dugouts along the
Delaware River front, the only places of abode of some of the settlers at
that time. After meetings for worship were established their next concern was for the setting up of monthly meetings; where the right ordering of marriages, and the granting and receiving of certificates, and
other disciplinary business could be transacted. Quarterly meetings developed out of the emphasis placed on every third monthly meeting. This
was called a quarterly meeting without changing its functions very much
from that of the usual monthly meeting. The first quarterly meeting to
be established in the Province of Pennsylvania, was Philadelphia Quarterly Meeting. This quarter was created in 1682, shortly after the arrival
of William Penn, by the same minute which also created Philadelphia
Monthly Meeting: "Friends belonging to Philadelphia, in the province of
Pennsylvania, being met in the fear and power of the Lord at the present
meeting-place in the said city, the 9th day of the Eleventh month, the
Third-day of the week, in the year 1682, did take into consideration the
settlement of meetings therein, for the affairs and service of Truth,
and did then and there agree, that the first Third-day in the week in
every month shall thereafter be the Monthly Meeting for men's and women's
meetings for the affairs and service of Truth in this city and county;
and every third meeting shall be the Quarterly Meeting for the same."[1]

After the arrival of William Penn, Shackamaxon Preparative Meeting
which was held at the house of Thomas Fairman, was removed to Philadelphia and together with the meeting there, they formed the present Philadelphia Monthly Meeting. Thomas Fairman gave the use of his house to
Penn, and removed to Tacony (spelled Tokany, Tookany, and Tawcony, now
Frankford), where another meeting was started and kept at the house of
Sarah Seary. By a minute of Philadelphia Quarterly Meeting, dated the
5th day of Fourth month, 1683, this meeting at Tacony, the Oxford Preparative Meeting and another held at the house of John Hart in Poetquesink
(now Byberry) the Byberry Preparative Meeting, were joined to form one
monthly meeting; and the meeting at Philadelphia, together with one held
at Thomas Duckett's house, at Schuylkill (now the locality of 32nd and
Market Streets), the Schuylkill Preparative Meeting, formed another
monthly meeting. These two monthly meetings thus became the early constituents of Philadelphia Quarter. Only a short time after the meeting

---

at Philadelphia and the one at Schuylkill were united to form one monthly meeting, the membership of Schuylkill Meeting joined the meetings of
Radnor, Merion and Haverford, which three particular meetings in 1693
became Radnor Monthly Meeting of Philadelphia Quarter. Radnor Monthly
Meeting in the early days of its existence was called Haverford. The
meetings at Poetquesink and Tacony, later added Germantown, then Cheltenham (sometimes called Dublin), and eventually became the Monthly
Meeting of Abington, in the Philadelphia Quarter. In 1786, Abington
Monthly Meeting was transferred to the newly established Abington Quarterly Meeting in order to relieve the Philadelphia Quarter of some of
its increasing volume of business.

The women's meeting of Philadelphia Quarter was established in 1683,
as is evidenced by the following minute: "At the Quarterly Meeting held
the 5th day of Fourth-month, 1683. A Women's Meeting was proposed and
unanimously agreed upon. Agreed that a place be appointed for women
Friends to meet at, and that it be for the present at the house of Christopher Taylor, it being his own offer."[1] The early meetings of the men
must also have been held in private houses, as their meetings date as
far back as 1682, and the first meeting-house of Friends in Philadelphia
was not erected until 1683. This house was built of pine boards, and
was of rough and undurable construction. It stood at what is now No. 122
S. Front Street, and it seems to have been in use by the men's quarterly
meeting at the time the women's meeting was established, but evidently
it was not large enough to accommodate both. Meetings were not held in
private houses after the second meeting-house of Friends, located at
Center Square, was placed into use. This is noted by the following minutes: "Friends being met in the feare of the Lord in the Governour's
house, and waighting awhile, proceeded to business the 4th of the Ninth
month, 1684. Friends having considered about a place whear the Quarterly Meeting should be kept; and at present not knowing of a place convenient, do appoint Thomas Lloyd, Ralph Howell /and others/ to provide a
place."[2] At a monthly meeting the 4th of Third-month, 1685: "William
Frampton acquainted this meeting that he is going to divide his house,
and desires Friends that some other place be considered of and provided
against the Quarterly Meeting. The meeting appointed John Songhurst,
William Frampton /and others/ to consider of and provide a place, and
make it public to Friends against next meeting."[3] A wooden shed was
built at Centre Square in 1683-84, and meetings were held therein. In
1685 the first Bank Meeting-house on Front Street above Arch was erected.
This was a wooden structure. In the same year the brick meeting-house
at Centre Square (present site of City Hall) was completed, and the quarterly meeting convened there. Next came the Great Meeting-house, located
at the Southwest corner of Second and High (now Market) Streets, erected
in 1696, and built of brick. The second Bank Meeting-house, also a brick
structure, was completed in 1703, and erected on the site formerly occupied by the first Meeting-house. It was constructed from materials
brought from the Centre Square house. Next in order was the Pine Street
Meeting-house, another brick building, erected in 1753, and stood on the
south side of Pine Street between Front and Second. In 1755-56 the Great

---

1. Minutes of Philadelphia Quarterly Meeting, 4th month 5, 1841 (Friends Depository, 302
Arch Street, Philadelphia).

2. George Vaux, "An Account of the Centre Square and Bank Meeting Houses of Friends in
Philadelphia," *The Friend*, LXIII (1890), 99, hereinafter cited as Vaux, *Centre Square*.

3. *Ibid.*

Meeting-house was rebuilt to a structure of greater dimensions than the one which it replaced. The Fourth Street Meeting-house was next, and stood beside the Fourth Street Academy. This house was of brick and was erected in 1764. It stood on property belonging to the William Forrest Estate and was built mainly to accommodate the Youth's Quarterly Meeting, which was the meeting for worship of pupils of the school, and other young people attending quarterly meetings. In 1790 the Key's Alley Meeting-house, located on the south side of Key's Alley (now New Street), was completed and placed into use. In 1804 the first section (the present middle section) of the Fourth and Arch (then called Mulberry) Street Meeting-house was built, and from 1805 to the present time nearly all of the quarterly meetings have been held there.

Arch Street Center, erected in 1915, is under the care of the quarterly and monthly meetings which appoint a Board of Managers to look after its care and management. It stands on the east side of the meeting-house grounds, at 302-4 Arch Street, and houses the Friends Book Store; the Friends Records Depository; the offices of the Yearly Meeting Secretary, Philadelphia Monthly Meeting, the Peace Committee, Mission Board, Committee on Religious Education, The Friend, a bi-weekly publication of Friends, and several floors of rooming accommodations as well as a dining room. Among the many active committees and organizations of the quarterly meeting at the present time, the following are of the most importance: Visitation Committee, a committee that visits suburban towns and holds meetings; Friends Fiduciary Corporation, in charge of property of the various meetings as well as some trust funds; Educational Committee; Total Abstinence Committee; and the State College Committee. The present clerk of the quarterly meeting is Mary Hoxie Jones, Haverford.

Minutes of Men's Meetings, 1682-1922, 6 vols. (1711-23 missing); Minutes of Women's Meetings, 1683-1922, 2 vols. (1683-1868 missing); Minutes of Joint Meetings, 1922-31, 1 vol., at PPFYR. Minutes of Joint Meetings, 1931--, 1 vol., in custody of the clerk. Minutes of Ministers and Elders 1701--, 6 vols. (from 1701-19 called Ministers only), PPFYR. Treasurers Account Books, 1842-1922, 4 vols. (prior to 1842 missing), PPFYR, and Treasurers Account Book, 1922--, 1 vol., in custody of the treasurer, Marguerite P. Barrett, 325 Chestnut Street, Moorestown, N. J. Minutes of the Educational Committee, 1893--, 2 vols.; Record of Endorsements made by Philadelphia Quarterly Meeting on Certificates given to Ministers, 1779-95, 1 vol., PPFYR. Reports of the various committees are recorded in the general minutes of the quarterly meeting.

3. PHILADELPHIA MONTHLY MEETING, 1682--. Fourth and Arch Street, Philadelphia.

As early as 1675 Robert Wade had come over to the west bank of the Delaware River from Salem, New Jersey, and had settled at Upland (Chester). Other Quaker settlers also crossed the river from New Jersey, and settled at Shackamaxon (Kensington), Takony (Tacony), and the Falls.

The first monthly meeting in what is now Pennsylvania was held at Upland at the home of Robert Wade. This however, was a session of Burlington Monthly Meeting, held on the west side of the river for the convenience of Friends who lived on that side. A minute concerning these meetings is dated 15th of 9th month 1681, but meetings prior to this may have been held at the same place since Robert Wade had lived in Upland since 1675. We also know that there were meetings for worship held in his home at least two years earlier.

Meetings for worship were also held at Tacony and at Thomas Fairman's home at Shackamaxon. At the latter place a Six-weeks meeting was appointed to be held early in 6th month 1682. This meeting, like the one held at the home of Robert Wade at Upland, alternated with a meeting of West Jersey Friends; in this case the one held at William Cooper's at Pine Point, which was located almost directly across the river from Thomas Fairman's home at Shackamaxon. This meeting continued about a year, and a few days after the arrival of Penn a meeting was called to meet at Shackamaxon in order "to appoint other meetings where it may be thought meet." A result of this called meeting is found in the following minute, which constitutes the establishment not only of Philadelphia Monthly Meeting but also Philadelphia Quarterly Meeting: "Friends belonging to the meeting in Philadelphia, in the province of Pennsylvania, being met in the fear and power of the Lord, at the present Meeting-place in the said city, the 9th day of Eleventh Month, the Third-day of the week, in the year 1682, did take into consideration the settlement of Meetings therein, for the affairs and service of Truth, and did then and there agree, that the first Third-day in the week in every month shall hereafter be the Monthly Meeting day for the Men's and Women's meetings for the affairs and service of Truth in this city and county; and every third meeting shall be the Quarterly Meeting of the same." Soon after this action the Shackamaxon Meeting was transferred to the new city.

Another matter which demanded the attention of Friends in this meeting at Shackamaxon was locating and building a meeting-house in the newly laid-out city. Thomas Holme and three others were appointed to have the management of this, the cost to be paid by the meeting. The fruit of this committee's labor was the first Friends' meeting-house erected in Philadelphia, and possibly the first in Pennsylvania, since we have no record of a meeting-house being erected at either Upland or the Falls until a later date, although meetings were held in these places at the homes of members. According to the best historical information obtainable the location of this first Quaker meeting-house which was then often referred to as the Boarded Meeting-house on the Delaware, was at what is now 122 South Front Street, Philadelphia. This building was completed during the first months of 1683.

Following the erection of the Boarded Meeting-house other houses for worship were erected in different parts of the city as it grew and the Quaker population increased. According to the monthly meeting references in secondary historical sources the sequence of the erection of these early buildings may be given as follows: The Centre Square Meeting-house completed in 1685, toward the building of which William Penn contributed 2000 feet of boards and 3000 cedar shingles, also the stone; First Bank Meeting-house 1685; High Street Meeting-house (the Great Meeting-house) 1696; Second Bank Meeting-house 1703 (later became the first meeting-house of the Northern District Monthly Meeting); Pine Street Meeting-house 1753 (later Southern District Monthly Meeting); High Street Meeting-house rebuilt 1755; Fourth Street Meeting-house (the first meeting place of the Southern District Monthly Meeting) 1764.

The location of the meeting-place mentioned in the minute of 11th month 9, 1692 as "the present meeting place in the said city" is unfortunately not known. It is a safe assumption, however, that this meeting was held in the home of a member. That this meeting was held in Fairman's home at Shackamaxon is doubtful since this house was not "in the

said city." At any rate this occasion was the birth of Philadelphia
Monthly Meeting, and its meeting-places since that date have been the
various meeting-houses throughout the lower part of the city whose dates
of erection are noted above.

In 1701 the Center Meeting-house, which had never fulfilled the usefulness planned for it by the early Quakers because the central part of
the city did not develop as rapidly as had been expected, was sold to
Penn for 100 pounds. Shortly afterward he returned the building to the
Society as a gift and about 1702 it was dismantled and the materials used
to rebuild the Bank Meeting-house. The Great Meeting-house was enlarged
in 1755 to accomodate the quarterly and yearly meetings, but the monthly
meeting met at the Bank Meeting-house from 1703 until 1804 at which time
the center section and east wing of the Arch Street Meeting-house, located at Fourth and Arch Streets, was built. The west wing was built in
1811. In 1820 interior alterations were made in which five instead of
three raised facing-seats were placed at the front of the room. The
sessions of the quarterly and yearly meetings were early transferred to
this building and have continued to be held there to the present time.

Because of the mass of business, due to the size of the monthly
meeting, it was divided in 1772 and two new monthly meetings were created. These were the Northern District and the Southern District Monthly meetings. Again in 1814 for the same reason the monthly meeting for
the Western District was set up from part of the component meetings of
Philadelphia Monthly Meeting. This meeting was held in the meeting-house
at 20 South Twelfth Street, which was built in 1812.

One of the first concerns which arose among the early Quaker pioneers in Philadelphia was for a suitable burial place. Very soon after
their arrival they acquired an open lot for this purpose, the location
of which is unknown. In Seventh month 1683 the monthly meeting ordered
a fence placed around this lot which must have been unsatisfactory for
in the following month a committee, previously appointed to interview
William Penn with reference to a "convenient place to bury the dead," reported that the Governor had decided "that the burial place should be in
the middle of the city, in the same ground where the meeting-house was
appointed." This seems to indicate that a part of the Centre Square
Meeting-house grounds were to be used for the purpose. It is very un-
likely that this plan was carried out, for in 1687 another application
was made to Penn for "a more convenient place for a burying ground and
other uses." No evidence of conveyance for either of these plots has
been found.

The new burial plot was acquired by Friends in 1693, although the
patent executed by Penn to Edward Shippen and Samuel Carpenter was not
given until 1701, on the occasion of Penn's second visit to the colony.
The plot is located at Fourth and Arch Streets, and a part of it was used
in 1804 for the erection of the meeting-house. After the erection of
the meeting-house in 1804 burials were restricted to the southwest portion of the lot fronting Fourth Street, until 1833 when burials were discontinued there. The small plot east of the building was then opened
and burials continued there until 1851 when that portion was filled. In
1843 a strip 22' x 70' on the eastern side of the southwest burial plot
bordering Fourth Street was designated for burial purposes. Between that
date and 1880 a few interments were made there, but since 1880 no burials
have been made in any part of the ground. After 1818 members of Phila-

delphia Monthly Meeting also used the "Sassafras" burial ground, located at the present site of the Friends Select School. About 1880 they began to use the burial ground of the Western District Monthly Meeting which is located on Marshall Road, Upper Darby.

Early Friends bore testimony against the distinction indicated by the use of elaborate gravestones. For that reason the graves of the early Friends were marked only with rough stones, or not at all. A minute of the monthly meeting dated in 1731 notes that the grave digger was conniving at "the setting up of grave-stones in our burial ground, and A. Morris and J. Warder were appointed to acquaint him that unless he be more careful for the future to prevent the setting up such marks of distinction, Friends will appoint some other person to that service in his stead, that will be more careful to observe the directions of this meeting." This custom prevailed until about 1863 when, like the custom of plain dress, it gradually disappeared.

The present meeting-house is of red brick, of the plain, meeting-house style of architecture. It has a central section facing north on Arch Street and with wings at both ends flush with the front of the north side but extending beyond the south wall of the center section. It houses the weekly meetings for worship as well as the yearly, quarterly and monthly meetings. The present Clerk of the monthly meeting is Mable E. Hoyle, 304 Arch Street, Philadelphia.

See: The Friends Meeting House, Fourth and Arch Streets, Philadelphia, passim; Joseph W. Lippincott, "Some Account of the First Places of Worship of Friends in Philadelphia," The Friend, LXII (1889), 283; Burial Ground, p. 194; Vaux, Centre Square, pp. 99, 169.

Minutes of Men's Meetings, 1682-1923, 25 vols.; Minutes of Women's Meetings, 1682-1923, 14 vols. (1682-85 and 1859-90, missing); Minutes of joint Meetings, 1923-26, 1 vol., PPFYR. Minutes of Joint Meetings, 1926--, 2 vols., in custody of Edith P. MacKendrick, 304 Arch Street, Philadelphia. Minutes of Ministers and Elders, 1796-1922 6 vols., at PPFYR, and 1922--, 1 vol., in custody of Milton C. Davis, 304 Arch Street, Philadelphia. Trustees Minutes, 1882-1922, 1 vol. at PPFYR. Register of births, membership and deaths, 1688-1885, 3 vols. (1688-1826 is an abstract, also a duplicate volume for 1826-85), at PPFYR, and 1885--, 2 vols., in custody of Mary Kite, 304 Arch Street, Philadelphia. Marriage certificates, 1672-1814, 2 vols. (marriages from 1672-82 in England and in Burlington, N. J.), at PPFYR, and 1814--, 1 vol., in custody of Mary Kite. Certificates of removal (received), 1686-1927, 18 vols., at PPFYR, and 1927--, 1 vol., in custody of Mary Kite. Certificates of removal (issued), 1756-1928, 4 vols., at PPFYR, and 1928--, in custody of Mary Kite. Membership list (receptions and disownments by certificate alphabetically arranged), undated, 1 vol., PPFYR. Treasurer's cash books, 1783-1915, 6 vols., at PPFYR, and 1915--, 2 vols., in custody of Milton C. Davis. Record of interments at Fourth and Mulberry Streets burial ground, 1820-80, 1 vol.; Interment orders (same cemetery), 1785-1854, 7 vols., at PPFYR.

4. SHACKAMAXON MEETING, 1681-82. Present location would be Beach Street, a few yards north of Columbia Avenue, Philadelphia. Set up in 1681 by Burlington (N. J.) Monthly Meeting, upon approval of Burlington Quarterly Meeting. The few Friends who had settled on the west side of the Delaware River previous to the arrival of William Penn

is 16.. atten d the monthly, quarterly, and yearly meetings of Burlington. The first meetings for worship held in the county of Philadelphia were kept at Shackamaxon, in the house of Thomas Fairman and must
have preceded the recognition of the meeting by Burlington Monthly Meeting by at least a year. A six-weeks' meeting for the accommodation of
these Friends, and those of Pine Point (N. J.) was established in 1682,
as set forth by the following minute: "At a general meeting held at
Salem, in the Province of West Jersey the 11th of Second Month, 1682, it
was ordered that a six weeks' meeting of men and women Friends for the
ordering of the affairs of the church be kept the 24th day of the Third
Month at William Cooper's, /at Pine Point/ and the next six weeks at
Thomas Fairman's at Shackamaxon, and so in course." This meeting, however, did not continue long, for "Soon after the arrival of William Penn
in the fall of 1682, it was ordered that notice be given to Friends the
next First-day, that as many as can conveniently, may meet at Shackamaxon,
in order to appoint other meetings where it may be thought meet." Thomas
Fairman gave up his mansion at Shackamaxon to the use of Penn and his
family and removed to Tacony where another meeting was soon appointed.
The meeting at Shackamaxon was then merged with the one formed at the intended site of Philadelphia, and subsequently the two became Philadelphia
Monthly Meeting. Hence the meeting at Shackamaxon, the first one established within the bounds of Philadelphia County was a forerunner of the
present Philadelphia Monthly Meeting (entry 3).

Shackamaxon was the site of what is now known as Kensington. It had
been settled by Swedes, who received their titles from the Governor of
New York as early as 1665.[1] From old prints the mansion of Thomas Fairman appears to have been constructed of brick and stone, but the original
house was no doubt logs or stone. The following quotation alludes to a
replacement of the original building in 1702: "It will be seen respecting Fairman's Mansion that by a letter of Robert Fairman of London, in
1711, he speaks of the house at the Treaty Tree, built of brick in 1702,
(and taken down in 1825) as the locality of the said Thomas Fairman's
former house. . . he having been dead some time, and his widow being then
(in 1711) on the premises,"[2] The original mansion was built by Thomas
Fairman, a surveyor for William Penn, and in its time served as the official residence of three Governors. During the period when the city of
Philadelphia was being laid out and settled Fairman's house was the
center of activity. To it came William Markham, a cousin of Penn, and
his Lieutenant Governor, who preceded him to his Province. Here also lived
William Haige, one of the commissioners to lay out the city; and Thomas
Holme, the Surveyor General, and his children. Here in 1685, it is believed that William Bradford printed his "Kalendarium Pennsilvaniense,"
being an almanac for the year 1686. The title page neglects to indicate the place of publication, but mentions the location as "near Philadelphia." Bradford's press was the first set up in the middle colonies.

While William Penn was living in Fairman's mansion, awaiting completion of Pennsbury Manor, an Indian council was called to meet the new
proprietor of the Province. Tradition has it that they met beneath a
great elm, which stood near the river, and across the road from the Fairman house. The scene has been treated pictorially by the Pennsylvania
artist Benjamin West, who has entitled his composition "William Penn's

---

1. Watson, *op. cit.*, I, 10.
2. *Ibid.*, p. 141.

Treaty with the Indians."   It illustrates the meeting of Penn with the
Indians under the spreading branches of the giant "Penn Treaty Tree."
Historians have been unable to find any record of a treaty at this time
or place, but have discovered references to a meeting there with prominent Indian chieftains, and it is believed that the meeting at Shackamaxon was a peace conference between Penn and the Indians. This vener-
able treaty tree, though old when the alleged treaty took place, still
stood in 1810, when a wind storm in that year blew it down. A small in-
scribed marble marker now marks the spot where this famous tree stood.
It is located on the Beach Street front of Penn Treaty Park, just a few
feet north of Columbia Avenue. At the present time the locality is given
over to factories and other industrial plants, and a large power plant
of the Philadelphia Electric Company is located next to the park, only
a few feet distant from the' marker of the old Penn Treaty Tree. See:
Lippincott, Joseph, op. cit., p. 283; Watson, op. cit., I, 10, 140, 141;
J. Thomas Scharf and Thompson Westcott, History of Philadelphia, 1609-
1884, III, 1783.

5. THE BOARDED MEETING ON THE DELAWARE, 1683-ca. 1686. Present
site of 122 S. Front St., Philadelphia.
It is a significant fact that the Quaker immigrants who first came to
Philadelphia were among the most prominent and influential of that sect
which, for the first three-quarters of a century of the existence of the
province, gave color to its social and political life, and was the controlling force in governmental affairs. The first meetings for worship
and business held in the county of Philadelphia were kept at Shackamaxon
(now Kensington), in the house of Thomas Fairman, where they continued
for more than a year (entry 4).   A 6-weeks meeting for Friends of
Shackamaxon and Pine Point was established in 1682, at which time it was
ordered that meetings be held each alternate 6 weeks at William Cooper's
at Pine Point, and Thomas Fairman's, at Shackamaxon, and to continue so
in course. This meeting, however, did not continue long, for shortly
after the arrival of Penn a meeting was called for the purpose of appointing meetings at suitable places. This meeting met on Tuesday 11th
month 9, 1682 at some point, presumably a home, in the new city. At
this opening meeting it was ordered that "Friends of this meeting do
bring in their Certificates from the respective meeting of Friends they
belonged to in other Countries, and that they be registered according to
the time of their arrival here, in this province." Another subject considered was "a fit place to build a meeting-house in this city, as also
the manner and form of building; being taken into the consideration of
Friends, the whole was referred to the care and management of Thomas
Holme, John Songhurst, Thomas Wynne, and Griffith Jones, or any three of
them, and that the charge thereof shall be borne by this meeting, consisting of Friends belonging to the said city." The subject of a proper
place and suitable houses for worship was one that exercised the Friends
in no small degree as is evidenced by many early minutes of their meetings. At the second meeting held the 6th day of Twelfth month 1682, "The
overseers appointed for the building of the meeting-house brought their
answer, that according to order, men were already set to work in order
to that building." At the following meeting, held the 6th of First month
1683: "Certificates were brought in and read. Agreed that they would
be registered and afterward returned." The town of William Penn at that
time consisted of two little streets on the banks o. the Delaware. Main
Street, which is now Front Street, ran along the edge of a bluff overlooking the Delaware. Many of the early settlers lived in caves and dugouts along the river, small cottages of wood being built later. Richard

Townsend, a primitive settler and public Friend, writes: "Our first concern is to keep up and maintain our religious worship; and in order thereto we had several meetings in the abodes of the inhabitants, and one boarded meeting-house was set up near the Delaware." This is the meeting-house referred to in the minute cited above.

The location of the first meeting-house of Friends in Philadelphia, the, "Boarded Meeting-house" as it is so often referred to in the early minutes of Philadelphia Monthly Meeting and also in the records of the early sessions of the Pennsylvania Assembly, was not definitely known to the writers of the nineteenth century, some of them assumed that the reference was "probably to the First Bank Meeting-house," which according to the old minutes was built some years later. Early records of the transactions of William Penn and the proceedings of the city show that it was built on a small plot of ground on Front Street north of Sansom Street. Dr. Albert Cook Myers, who located this historic building, states: "It is quite clear from documents I have examined, that the location of the first Friends' meeting-house in Philadelphia, was on the plot of ground at 122 South Front Street. In the early part of 1683 a load of pine boards came over from New York. With these, Friends built a meeting-house forty feet wide and fifty feet long on the plot of ground mentioned. This little house of wood was used for Friends' Meetings, for sessions of the State Assembly, and for sittings of the Philadelphia court. William Penn preached there, and in it many of the early laws of the State were formulated. The lot of ground on which this house was built was sold originally to Christopher Taylor by Penn through his land office in George Yard in Lombard Street. Taylor, who was a London schoolmaster, came over with Penn as one of his consellers. He owned about 102 feet on Front Street and later sold the southern half of this plot to Thomas Hooton. It was on the part retained by Taylor that the meeting-house was built." The sources of information from which the knowledge of the site was gleaned include the early records of Friends at Philadelphia and the Pennsylvania land warrants at Harrisburg. The following minutes of Philadelphia Monthly Meeting support these findings. Second day of Eighth month 1683 it was: "Agreed and concluded that Thomas Lloyd, Christopher Taylor, Griffith Jones and John Goodson be the undertakers for repairing the present meeting-house of Friends, and to pay the workmen, the meeting promising to reimburse them their charges. Christopher Taylor, whose the present meeting-house is, refers himself to the discretion of Friends, as touching his satisfaction for the general use of it." At a monthly meeting held the Fourth day of Third month 1685, it is stated: "Friends taking into consideration the business of the old meeting-house by Thomas Hooton's, and seeing that it was fitted for the Assembly, it was afterward made use of for a Court; for the use and charge of fitting up thereof Christopher Taylor doth demand five pounds, of which this meeting is willing to allow forty shillings; the rest they leave for the Court to defray, and those Magistrates who are members of this meeting are desired to take notice of the same when the County assessment is laid."

It is evident that Friends were poorly accommodated in this their first meeting-house, as indicated by the minute of Seventh month 2nd 1684, when it was "Agreed that in regard of ye straightness of room in ye present meeting-house, there be a meeting at the Governour's house every fifth day of ye week in the forenoon, about the ninth hour." The construction must have been very poor, as is evidenced by the minute of Eighth month 2, 1683, quoted above, which sets forth the need of repairs

to the house so soon after its completion. The building of a new meeting-house was proposed very soon after the Boarded Meeting-house, owned
by Christopher Taylor, was placed in use. This proposal was made in a
minute of Fifth month 3rd, 1683, and after some time the new building
was erected at Centre Square. Shortly after the erection of the second
meeting house, the first one was torn down.

The building at 122 South Front Street, occupied in 1920 by J.
Bateman and Company, has since been demolished, no rebuilding having
taken place. A vacant lot now occupies the site of the old meeting house.
In 1932, The Pennsylvania Historical Commission in conjunction with the
Friends' Historical Association erected a bronze tablet on the building
which adjoins the lot on the south, and now occupied by William D.
Oelbermann Company, wool merchants. This building at No. 124 South
Front Street, stands on the land which Christopher Taylor sold to Thomas
Hooton as indicated in the early records. The inscription on the marker
reads as follows:

The First/ Friends Meeting House/ in Philadelphia/ Built in 1683/
of Pine Boards from New York/ Stood about 36 Feet/ North of this Marker/
Here William Penn worshipped/and here were held/ Early Sessions/ of the
Pennsylvania Assembly/ and of the/ Philadelphia County Courts/ **/
Marked by the Pennsylvania Historical Commission/ and the Friends' His-
torical Association./ 1832. **

See: Lippincott, Joseph, op. cit., pp. 282, 301; Albert C. Myers,
"First Friends' Meeting-house at 122 South Front Street," Philadelphia
Public Ledger, March 14, 1920.

For minutes and other records, see the record books of Philadelphia
Monthly Meeting of Friends.

6. CENTRE SQUARE MEETING, ca.1685-ca.1697. Present site of City
    Hall, Broad & Market Sts., Philadelphia.
Although meetings were held in the Bank Meeting-house a month or so before they were started at Centre Square, it cannot be said that the Bank
Meeting-house was the second to come into existence in Philadelphia.
The Centre Square house had been proposed and projected by the monthly
meeting about a year prior to the proposal of the one at the Bank. Soon
after the first meeting-house, located at what is now 122 S. Front Street,
came into use, it is found that its rough board construction and the
accomodations it provided would not be suitable for long use. Consequently the matter of building a new meeting-house was brought up at
several of the sessions of the monthly meetings during 1683, and again
in 1684, and at a meeting held the fifth day of Sixth month of that year,
it was "agreed that the said meeting-house be builded at the Centre, being the middle way betwix Delaware and Schuylkill, according as it was
already designed and pitched upon, and the building to be of brick. Its
dimensions being in length 60 feet, in breadth 40 feet, and the height
referred to further consideration. Agreed and concluded that the persons
formerly appointed for the supervising of the building of the meeting-
house should take care that with all speed a shed be built in the city,
at the centre, of the same dimensions as the meeting-house." It is
claimed that the original design of William Penn in his plan for laying
out Philadelphia, was to locate Broad Street so that it should intersect
with High Street (Market Street) midway between the Delaware and Schuylkill rivers, and to have an equal number of parallel streets both east

and was of it, numbering from one, from each river, toward the centre
of the city. (See map). In this case Twelfth instead of Fourteenth.
Street would have become Broad Street, since it is more nearly midway between the rivers. Under these circumstances the Centre Square Meeting-
house would have been located near the site now occupied by Twelfth Street
Meeting-house. This is an erroneous supposition. Penn's original plan
existed only on paper. The records of the Philadelphia Survey Department show that in the Sixth month 1683, a lot was surveyed bounded on
the east by Broad Street, and on the west by Eighth Street from the
Schuylkill which is now Fifteenth Street. This proves that as early as
that time Broad Street had already been located where it now is. Since
the decision to locate the new meeting-house at Centre Square was not
made until a year after the above mentioned survey was made, it is very
improbable that it was erected at Twelfth Street. The evidence rather
points to the southwest corner of the intersection of Broad Street and
Market Street as now located.

In 1685 Friends were eager to have the construction work on the
Centre Square Meeting-house started, and by a minute of the meeting held
the 4th day of the 4th month of that year it was agreed that building of the
meeting-house should proceed with all expedition. The structure was
of brick, 50 feet long and 36 feet wide. Andrew Griscom offered to do
the timber work and the mason and brick-work was to be done by William
Preston. It is recorded that in Fifth month 1685: "This meeting doth
appoint Thomas Duckett and John Redman to join with William Preston in
carrying on the brick-work of the meeting-house in the Centre, and also
doth appoint Samuel Carpenter /and others/ to go to the Centre with the
workmen as before said, and get the place where the meeting-house shall
stand set out, and to get bricks and stone to the place to begin work.
This meeting agrees that the meeting-house in the Centre shall be 50 foot
long, 35 foot wide and 10 /sic/ foot high." At a meeting held the 5th
of Eighth month of the same year: "It is advised that all Friends
that have subscribed towards building the meeting-house in the Centre
do answer the same, that the meeting-house may be finished before this
winter. Andrew Griscom hath undertaken to carry on and finish the carpenter work ... that is to say, the floor, roof, and to cover it." On the 2nd
of the following month: "Philip England is desired to speak to Thomas
Duckett to finish the well at the Centre, least for want of doing it,
it may be unfit for use."

In the Eleventh month 1685, a committee was appointed for the purpose of raising funds to defray the cost of building. Following this a
loan was effected to pay for putting on the roof and protecting the walls,
which had stood some time exposed to the weather. That the country
meetings were also solicited for aid appears from the following extracts
from the Merion minutes: "At our Monthly Meeting held at Hugh Roberts'
house in Merion, on ye 11th day of ye First month, 1686 it was ordered
that Friends of each particular meeting do bring into ye next meeting
their voluntary subscriptions towards ye building of ye meeting-house in
ye centre at Philadelphia," and, "Hugh Roberts for Merion, William Howell
for Harford /Haverford/ John Humphrey for Scoolkill, David Meredith for
Radnor, are ordered to bring an account of ye sd collections into ye next
meeting." At the next meeting held at John Bevan's house in Haverford,
further action was taken. "The Friends of each meeting are ordered to
bring their collections for ye building of ye meeting-house in Philadelphia to Thomas Duckett's house in Schoolkill agst ye first day of ye
Sixth month next."

Radnor Meeting, Ł 7 7s 6d.
Harford Meeting, Ł 6 0s 0d.
Merion Meeting, Ł 6 5s 0d."

The work on the building was pushed forward as rapidly as possible
for a time, but it seems to have been suspended entirely for some months.
In the second month, 1686 it was reported to the monthly meeting, that
Andrew Griscom had disappointed Friends, and had done nothing toward
completing the woodwork upon the meeting-house. He was given another opportunity, however, and it was noted that on the Sixth month 2nd "Some
Friends acquaint the meeting, that Andrew Griscom saith, that the meeting-
house will be ready to raise the Third or Fourth-day next, which shall
be appointed for the purpose; the meeting desires John Jones and others
to speak to Friends belonging to the meeting, to send help at that time,
as Andrew Griscom they shall appoint, and that the said Friends with
Andrew, consider of materials for the duly raising of the roof." On 27th
of Sixth month 1686, it was: "Agreed that the Centre Square Meeting-house
be now taken care of. Barnabas Wilcox offers to speak to work-men that
are fit to be concerned, to cover the Centre Meeting-house. Griffith
Jones offers to give credit to provide shingles, and B. Wilcox the nails,
and it is desired to speak to Thomas Duckett that he go on with the brick
work of the meeting-house." On the 29th of 8th month it is stated:
"Thomas Fitzwater hath undertaken to send a man to the Centre Meeting-
house to be an assistant to Thomas Marl (or Maul) for the carrying on the
boarding and shingling the roof." The next minute, dated Ninth month 26
states: The hipping of the roof of the Centre Square Meeting-house being in discourse how to proceed to get it done, and accordingly several
persons have subscribed to pay those workmen that undertake the same."
Tenth month 31st, 1686, "At the request of Andrew Griscom the following
Friends were pitched upon; Thomas Bradford, John Masters, John Day and
Thomas Jacques, to take a survey of the carpenter work on the Centre meeting-house, and give their judgment of the value thereof." The meeting now
turned its attentions to the wooden shed which had been ordered to be
built "with all speed" at Centre Square. This shed must have been built
and used, for now that the brick structure nears completion, the temporary one is to be removed. The monthly meeting of the First month 1687
records: "According to an order of last month, Anthony Morris hath sold
John Redman the wood of the old meeting shed for 25 shillings." The new
building was nearing completion, for the 24th of Fourth month 1687 a committee was appointed: "to agree with workmen about making forms and doors
and a seat for public Friends, at the meeting-house at the Centre." There
is no positive information as to the exact time when the first meeting
was held there. However, meetings had been held in the shed for some
time, for a minute of the quarterly meeting of 7th of Tenth month 1685
says: "it is agreed that the meeting at the Centre on First-days begin
between the hours of nine and ten." The brick meeting-house must have
been used in an uncompleted condition for almost 2 years since in the
First month 1689, funds from a legacy left by "John Jones' brother" were
used for flooring it, and the following autumn the meeting instructed
"that the windows be substantially hanged."

It appears that Friends never held a title to the lot upon which the
Centre Square Meeting-house stood. Samuel Carpenter and Robert Turner
were ordered by the meeting to make inquiry and if necessary to write to
Penn in England to secure a patent for it. Subsequent events obviated
the necessity for such inquiry, for the lot was ultimately set aside by
Penn as part of the property devoted to public purposes. Although this

meeting-house was erected in what was designed to be the centre of the
city, its location was remote from the center of population and inconvenient to reach. It appears that all the effort required to erect and pay
for it was a mistake. The city did not expand from the centre toward
both rivers, as was apparently expected. The commerce of the Delaware
gathered the population along its banks. Watson in his Annals says:
"This house was so far in the wild forest, that a Friend by the name of
Morris stated that when she used to go out to Centre Square meeting she
had often seen deer and wild turkeys cross her path." Friends evidently
found it inconvenient to attend the Centre meeting especially in winter,
for by a minute of 27th of Eighth month 1693: "It is agreed that there
be one meeting upon each First-day during the winter, or as long as the
meeting may see occasion; beginning betwix ten and eleven in the forenoon,
on the front of the Delaware." Meetings appear to have been discontinued
at Centre Square in the latter part of 1696, but were resumed in the
spring of 1697, when it was "agreed to have a meeting during the summer
following, on First and Fifth-days, whilst the High Street house is being
plastered." This seems to be the last reference in the minutes to the
matter. In 1700 the Centre Square Meeting-house had so decayed in some
of its parts as to be in danger of falling down. The monthly meeting
appointed a committee to consult with William Penn, who was then in this
country, as to the best course to be pursued in regard to it. This committee reported that it was best to sell the building and that they had
sold it to William Penn for 100 pounds. This action the meeting did "unanimously consent unto and confirm." The career of the Centre Square
Meeting-house would thus appear to be closed, but it would not be disposed of so easily. Several years had passed since the removal of the
first Bank Meeting-house and its site was still vacant. About a year
after the old building at the Centre had been sold to Penn, Friends decided to apply to him to "resign" it to the monthly meeting, "supposing
the same may be of great service to them toward building another meeting-
house." In seventh month 1701 Penn attended the monthly meeting, probably the last time before his departure for England, after his second and
final visit to the colony. At this time the question was put to him in
open meeting, as to whether he would not "resign the Centre Meeting-house
to Friends again." With characteristic generosity and nobleness of heart
he readily consented, judging that it might be an advantage to Friends to
have the materials to use toward building another meeting-house. The
building again became the property of Friends. The meeting-house was
dismantled in 1703, and the materials used in erecting the second bank
Meeting-house on the lot previously occupied by the first meeting-house
by that name.

From the time of the removal of the Centre Square Meeting house many
and varied were the uses of the Centre Square. Public handings, military
encampments, fairs, horse races, patriotic celebrations, a pump-house and
reservoir and other such uses, until in 1823 Mayor Robert Wharton forbade
the erection of booths and tents in the Square in an effort to end its
notorious reputation. In 1829 the name was changed to Penn Square, and
in 1833 its use for the erection of a city hall was authorized, which
building was not begun until 1871.

See: Lippincott, Joseph, op. cit., pp. 283, 301, 302, 307; Vaux
Centre Square, pp. 99, 100, 109; Harrison W. Fry, Philadelphia, Evening
Bulletin, December 16, 1939.

For minutes and other records, see records of Philadelphia Monthly Meeting of Friends.

7. THE FIRST BANK MEETING, 1685-ca.1696. Present site: west side of N. Front Street, above Arch St., Philadelphia.
The first Bank meeting-house was especially intended for the holding of afternoon meetings, and although there was some diversity of opinion regarding its use at the time of its completion, the quarterly meeting made the final decision that it would be used for that purpose. In the 14th of Fourth month 1865: "Some Friends proposing that some place be prepared on the front of Delaware for an afternoon meeting on First-days, the meeting did condescend that the said Friends may prepare a place accordingly." The same year a frame building was built for that purpose, and was situated on an elevation overlooking the river. Robert Turner, in a letter to William Penn, dated 1685, says: "besides the brick meeting-house at the Centre, another one 50 by 38 feet is going up, on the front of the river." The building had no cellar, and seems to have been rather hastily and poorly built. Repairs and alterations were soon needed, since we find that in the Ninth month 1684, the monthly meeting appointed a committee to make the building more comfortable. The location was on the west side of Main (Front) Street, 58 feet north of Mulberry (Arch) Street. The lot originally had a 44 foot front and was 89 feet deep. It was conveyed in 1687 by Thomas Holme, Surveyor General, to John Longhurst and others, in trust for Friends. The deed recites that it was the lot "whereon the Public Meeting-house now stands." From this and references in the minutes it appears that the title to the property was not acquired by the meeting until some 2 years after the meeting-house had been built. In 1713 the lot was increased in width to 48 feet, by the purchase of an additional strip of ground 4 feet wide from Penticost Teague.

On Seventh month 12, 1685, this record was made: "Forasmuch as a difference hath arisen, more especially about the meeting-house and burying-ground, to set it open, to the dissatisfaction of many good Friends, . . . therefore, from this meeting, for the time to come, we have considered the use of the aforesaid meeting-house on the front street of Philadelphia, to be for afternoon First-day meetings; and further, as shall be ordered from time to time by the Monthly and Quarterly Meetings. The morrow week is agreed upon as the beginning of the service at that place, the meeting to begin between the hours of two and three in the afternoon." Again this record on the fifth of Fifth month, 1686: "This meeting proposed that there be a general subscription by Friends belonging to this meeting to pay for the meeting-house ground on Delaware side; likewise for paling it in, and that Thomas Fitzwater /et al./ do go from house to house among Friends belonging to said meeting, and receive their contributions for that purpose." Sometime later this committee reported that Friends had subscribed and that they hoped to have the funds to clear the property by next meeting. Repairs were soon needed, for in Third month 1686: "The weakness and insufficiency of the meeting-house on the front of Delaware for want of supporting and bracing, was spoken of, and considering there was a present necessity for doing something about it, the meeting proposed the strengthening of it to John Parsons and Thomas Bradford." Further repairs were made in 1689 when the meeting-house had to be underpinned. There are some indications that a part of the Bank Meeting lot may have been used as a graveyard in very early times, but the references to it are vague.

It appears that both monthly and quarterly meetings were regularly
held in this house for some years, for minutes read: "At our Quarterly
Meeting, held at the meeting-house upon the front of Delaware," and "At
our Monthly Meeting on Delaware side" and "the front of Delaware, at our
usual place," until about 1694, when for some cause they were held at the
house of Robert Ewer, until 1696. In 1693 Friends found Centre Meeting
inconvenient, especially in winter when the dirt-roads were mud-holes.
A minute of 27th of Eighth month 1693, reads: "It is agreed that there
be one meeting upon each First-day during the winter, or as long as the
meeting may see occasion; beginning betwix ten and eleven in the forenoon,
on the front of the Delaware. It is desired that henceforth the Monthly
Meeting gather precisely at the eleventh hour, and that Fifth-day meetings
may begin at the same hour." And on the 24th of Second month, 1696:
'this meeting agrees that there be two meetings on First-days: one at the
Centre, and the other at the Bank meeting-house; to begin at the Centre
at the ninth hour in the morning, and at the meeting-house on the bank,
to begin at the third hour in the afternoon."

When the Market Street meeting-house was completed in 1696 and the
afternoon meetings were transferred to that place, the Bank Meeting
seems to have been abandoned. This is intimated by the following minute
of Sixth month 1698: "Whereas the Old Bank meeting-house is much decayed,
and in great danger of falling down, this meeting hath taken the same
into consideration, and is agreed that William Southerley, Anthony Morris
/et al./ do endeavor to get it sold at a public outcry, sometime between
this and the next Monthly Meeting." Two months later the committee reported that: "We have sold the old meeting-house to James Cooper for 16
pounds, 5 shillings, and he is to take it off the ground in three months."
In the Eleventh month, "John Austin proposed to this meeting that he had
a mind to rent the ground that the old meeting-house stood on; whereupon
the meeting hath this day let the said ground for three years, he to pay
30 shillings yearly. Friends promising that it shall not be a burden to
him."

See: Lippincott, Joseph, op. cit., p. 307; Vaux, Centre Square, p.
109.

For minutes and other records, see the minutes of Philadelphia
Monthly Meeting of Friends.

8. HIGH STREET MEETING (The Great Meeting-House), 1696-1809. South-
   Southwest corner of Second and Market Streets.
In spite of all their efforts to provide suitable meeting-houses early
Philadelphia Friends soon found that their problem of housing was not yet
solved. The Centre Square house was too inconvenient of access, and the
one on the bank of the Delaware above Mulberry Street was not large enough
to accommodate their needs. They, therefore, took up the matter of
erecting a new one in a central location, of a more sturdy construction;
and large enough to accommodate their growing meetings for some time to
come.

In the monthly meeting minutes of the 29th of Fourth month 1694 we
find this record: "The Meeting, considering the want of a convenient
place for a meeting-house desired Samuel Carpenter and others to inquire
after a more commodious place, as near the High Street and the Front of
the Delaware as can be conveniently got." At the meeting in the following Tenth month "the meeting requested Anthony Morris and Samuel Carpenter

to speak to Governor Markham about his lot of land that layeth in the High Street near the market-place, and inquire the length and breadth, and if it be thought convenient to erect a meeting-house thereon; and they, with Edward Shippen, are desired to agree with Governor Markham as reasonably as they can." The following month this committee reported that Governor Markham was "very ready to serve Friends therein, and Friends agree to present him with fifty pounds, and acknowledge his kindness therein." A month later the committee was ordered to pay the Governor the money and request him to make out a title to the lot for the meeting in the name of Edward Shippen, Anthony Morris and Samuel Carpenter as trustees. It was further directed that "David Lloyd is desired to draw a deed to confirm the lot of land bought of the Governor Markham, also another Deed to declare the use of it." This lot purchased in 1695 had a frontage on High Street of 90 feet, and on Second Street of 80 feet, with an additional piece adjoining it on the south, about 60 feet west of Second Street, 66 feet in length east and west with a frontage of 25 feet on Strawberry Street. About 3 years later an additional lot was granted by Lyonell Britain to the trustees. This lot joined the first lot on the south adding 45 feet to the frontage on Second Street making 125 feet on Front Street, and running through to Strawberry Street and adding 20 feet more to the frontage there, making 45 feet on that Street. Later it was discovered that both Markham and Britain held only squatters rights to these lots and hence the conveyances which they had made were worthless.[1] In 1705 the matter of title was taken up and application was made to Penn to confirm the land to the meeting. Penn agreed to present Friends with a patent for the land without charge but the meeting declined to accept since it had bought the land in good faith. Ultimately a compromise was arranged whereby Friends paid 40 pounds for the patent. The patent, dated the 3rd of Seventh month 1705, covered the lots bought from both Markham and Britain. That part of the lot having a frontage of 90 feet on High Street and 80 feet on Second Street was designated for the new meeting-house and the remainder was granted to the overseers of the public schools for school purposes. The meeting-house erected on this property was known at first as the High Street Meeting-house and later as the Great Meeting-house.

In Ninth month 1695, "the meeting taking into their consideration the necessity of a new meeting-house, the said matter is left to the consideration of the Quarterly Meeting." On the second of the Tenth month 1695, at a quarterly meeting held at the house of Robert Ewer, the matter of building a new meeting-house in Philadelphia was again brought up and unanimously agreed to, and several Friends subscribed funds for it; and it was further "recommended to the Monthly Meetings of this county for their assistance. The meeting desires John Lineham and Robert Ewer to get Friends about Philadelphia to subscribe towards the building, and desires Edward Shippen, Sam'l Carpenter, John Lineham and John Jones to provide materials and agree with workmen to build a meeting-house 60 feet long and 40 feet wide, and as high as may be convenient in proportion to the length and breadth." The following month a report was made that an agreement had been entered into with "Thomas Duckett and William Harwood for the building of the said house, which is to contain fifty

---

1. Watson, *op. cit.*, I, 355. This is not the lot which came to the Friends through a gift of George Fox. That lot was located between 3rd and 4th Streets. *See also* Scharf and Westcott, *op. cit.*, 88, footnote p. 1245.

feet square, with cellars all underneath, and the committee deem the
charge of the whole will amount to about 1,000 pounds." Although the
house was sufficiently finished in 1696 for holding meeting, it was
not completed until the ensuing year. In describing this building, one
author says, "It was built of brick and nearly square in shape; the roof
rose on each side to a central lantern, which gave light to the interior."
Another says, "It was surmounted on the centre of its four-angled roof
by a raised frame of glass work, so constructed as to pass light down
into the meeting below."

The first monthly meeting held in the new meeting-house was in
Eleventh month 1696, as set forth in the following minutes: "At our
Monthly Meeting held at the New meeting-house the 29th day of Eleventh
month 1696," and again: "at our Monthly Meeting-house in High Street
in Philadelphia, the 30th of Second month 1697, 'tis agreed by this meeting that henceforward there be two meetings at this place upon a First-
day during the summer time, the morning meeting beginning at the ninth
hour, and the other about two in the afternoon. Also it is agreed by
this meeting, at the request of Friends on Schuylkill side, that there be
a morning meeting at the Centre Meeting-house during the summer season,
beginning at the ninth hour, and that John Lineham give Friends notice
next First-day, that the Fifth and First-days' meeting following, be held
at the Centre while this place is plastering."

The next concern of Friends was to eliminate the debt, for at a
meeting held the Second month 1699 it is recorded; "Whereas several
Friends are at Salem Yearly Meeting, this meeting thinks it convenient
to defer a subscription for discharging the debt of the meeting-house
until the next Monthly Meeting, when Sam'l Carpenter and Anthony Morris
are desired to assist Pentecoast Tague and John Buzby in getting subscriptions presented for paying the debts due for building the meeting-
house." When it was necessary to hold the yearly meeting in Philadelphia,
it was found that this house did not have a sufficient seating capacity.
Friends therefore set about increasing it. This was a problem, and the
only thing that could be done in the matter it seems was to erect a gallery.   This was proposed to the monthly meeting in Fifth month 1699,
"upon which it was agreed that it be done between this and the next
Yearly Meeting, and that William Harwood shall prepare stuff for the
same." The gallery was quickly erected at a cost of about 16 pounds.

In 1738, the question of again increasing meeting-house accommodations arose. This time the suggestion was made that instead of enlarging
the Market Street house an entirely new building be erected on the Burial
Ground at Mulberry and Fourth Streets. Subscriptions were solicited for
funds for this purpose, to which Friends in Barbadoes contributed 50
pounds, but the project afterwards fell through. For many years the subject of a larger meeting-house does not appear to have been prominently
discussed; but at the close of 1754 it was revived, when it was proposed
to make an addition to the Great Meeting-house on its western side, to
accommodate meetings for business and provide room for those who attended
public meetings on occasions when they were very large. Like the former
proposal this also was not carried into effect. Two months later the
meeting decided to build a new meeting-house on the foundations of the
old one, "and to extend as far westward as our ground goes." A committee
was appointed to proceed with the work immediately following the general
meeting in the spring, and to have the new building ready for the accommodation of the yearly meeting in the fall. The new house was to contain

two apartments on the lower floor at the west end, for holding meetings for business. This plan was afterwards modified, and the new building seems to have been erected regardless of the old foundations. It was 73 feet long east and west, and 55 feet wide north and south, and was set back 8½ feet from the south line of Second Street. There was a passageway on the west side 6 feet wide. The building contained an upper room approached by a stairway, which was not finished, however, until some months after the building was occupied. A few years after its completion there were doubts as to whether the floors were strong enough, and pillars were introduced to strengthen them. The entire cost of the new building was L2,145 19s. 6d., which was mainly paid by a special subscription made by Friends for the purpose. Meetings were held in the second Bank Meeting-house and the Pine Street Meeting-house while the rebuilding at Second and Market took place.

The new Meeting-house was so far completed in the autumn of 1755, that the yearly meeting convened in it, and in Tenth Month 1755, "The Great Meeting-house having been ready for service and used at the time of our late Quarterly Meeting, it is now agreed that there be three meetings kept in it on First-days. One in the morning at the Bank, and one at Pine Street Meeting-house in the afternoon. The meeting on Third-day to be held as usual at the Bank, and the meeting on Fifth-day to be held at this house." The three First-day meetings designated to be held in the new house were arranged to be held in the morning, afternoon, and evening.

This building was built of brick. The gable faced Second Street, and the building was two stories high. There were doors with porticos on the north and east sides. The windows of the first story were provided with outside shutters. The lot around it was enclosed with a high brick wall, which was pierced with two gateways on Second Street and one on Market Street. In 1763, gates were placed in the yard "to prevent the boys running around the house," and at the same time considerable alterations were made in the interior arrangements. The stairway leading to the gallery on the women's side, was removed to the north side of the house, and continued into the upper chamber. These alterations resulted in the impairment of the acoustic qualities of the meeting-room, and it was found necessary "to fix up a suitable board for the conveyance of the voice when Friends are concerned in public testimony."

About 1796 the scheme, which had originated nearly 60 years before, for building a large meeting-house at Fourth and Arch Streets was again promoted, and at the same time the proposal was made for the sale of the Great Meeting-house. The latter suggestion was not, however, carried out until some years later, when the increased travel on the two streets made the location so noisy that it became evident that the old premises no longer possessed a value for meeting-house purposes. In 1804 the new meeting-house was built on Arch Street below Fourth, on the lot that had been used as a burial place since 1690.

By 1809 meetings at the Market Street house had been entirely discontinued, and it was decided to sell the ground in building lots of suitable size. The building was preserved, and later a part of the materials derived from it were used in connection with the erection of the present Twelfth Street Meeting-house. Giant wooden beams across the ceiling of the tea room of the Twelfth Street house may be seen at the present time. These are a part of the material that was salvaged from the old edifice when it was dismantled. The property was sold and the proceeds of the sale were mainly devoted to the following purposes: Purchase of lot and erection of meeting-house on Twelfth Street; purchase of lot and erection of meeting-house on Green Street; erection of west wing of Arch Street Meeting-house. The deeds for the sale of the lots into which the Second and Market Streets property was divided, contained covenants on the part of the purchasers that no "dram-shops" should ever be located on the premises. Thus the "Great Meeting House," so long the centre of attraction for Friends disappeared forever.

See: Lippincott, Joseph, op. cit., pp. 316, 317, 331, 332; George Vaux, "The Great Meeting house," The Friend, LXIII (1890), 147, 148.

For minutes and other records, see records of Philadelphia Monthly-Meeting of Friends.

9. FAIRHILL INDULGED MEETING, 1702-ca.1800. Southeast corner Germantown Avenue & Cambria Street, Philadelphia.
Set up in 1702 by Philadelphia Quarterly Meeting (entry 2), and attached to Philadelphia Monthly Meeting (entry 3). Friends living in the vicinity of Fairhill found it very inconvenient, especially in winter, to transport their families to either the meeting at Philadelphia or the one at Germantown, both being about the same distance from Fairhill. An appeal was made to Philadelphia Monthly Meeting for the establishment of a meeting there, which was agreed to by the monthly meeting and approved by the quarterly meeting. In 1703, 4 acres of ground were purchased from Isaac Norris who was a prime mover in the establishment of this meeting. Later 20 acres of ground were acquired which adjourned the 4 already purchased. This last addition was made by the Proprietary in the name of Penn, and in the fulfillment of a promise made by Penn to George Fox before his death. Fox's heirs were pressing Penn for 16 acres in the center of the city in fulfillment for the 16 acres of liberty lands due Fox because of his purchase of 1,000 acres. Fox, however, was not a bonefide purchaser, since the 1,000 acres had been acquired through a gift of Penn to Fox of the right to take up land. Fox, during his lifetime did not receive a patent to the land.

First meetings were held in private homes until the latter part of 1703, when the first meeting-house, a one-story, small, red and black brick building was erected on a portion of the ground allotted for this purpose. The black bricks in the rear of the building were arranged in a diamond-shaped pattern, which is a decorative design found on the Trinity Church, Oxford, built in 1709. Fairhill Meeting-house is one of the four known American examples of this borrowed English decoration. About 1800, due to the migration of a large number of its members to other parts, the meeting was abandoned. Shortly after a stone farm-house was erected to adjoin the old brick meeting-house, which then became the kitchen of this farm-house. For final disposition of this building refer to Fairhill Indulged Meeting (H), (entry 293).

See: Thompson Westcott, The Historic Mansions and Buildings of Philadelphia With Some Notice of Their Owners and Occupants, p. 76; W. C. Brenner and Henry Beck, A Brief History of Fair Hill Friends Meeting (manuscript in custody of Henry Beck, 1018 W. Cambria Street, Philadelphia); Lippincott, Joseph, op. cit., 365.

The records and register of membership will be found among the minutes and records of Philadelphia Monthly Meeting.

10. POTTSTOWN INDULGED MEETING, 1753-1935.   231 King Street, Potts-
     town, Montgomery County.
Set up 1753 as an indulged meeting by Exeter Monthly Meeting (entry 24).
This meeting was early known as "Pottsgrove." The first meeting-house
was erected about 1753 on ground donated by John Potts, the founder of
Pottstown. This structure was razed in 1785 and replaced by a second
red brick building. At the time of Separation, in 1827, Exeter Monthly
Meeting became a Hicksite meeting and this meeting was transferred to
the care of Philadelphia Monthly Meeting (entry 3). In 1875 a white frame
meeting-house was erected on the site of the second meeting-house. Due
to decreased membership, the meeting was laid down in 1935 by Philadelphia
Monthly Meeting. This is one of the few meetings which remained for such
a long time as an indulged meeting. It functioned under that status for
182 years.

     Its records and register of membership are included in the records
of the two monthly meetings of which it was a part.

11. FOURTH STREET MEETING, 1764-ca.1772.   East side of Fourth
     Street, below Chestnut, Philadelphia.
Fourth Street Meeting-house seems to have been designed largely to accommodate the "Youths' Meetings," which originated in 1696, and which were
at this time held four times a year on the second day after the quarterly
meeting. Another purpose was to afford a suitable place to hold monthly
and other business meetings, and also to provide a place of meeting for
the students in the school nearby. Although the chambers of the Great
Meeting-house (entry 8) had been fitted up for these and kindred uses,
Friends were not well satisfied in that respect. Various plans were
proposed, among others the enlargement of the accommodations of the Pine
Street Meeting (entry 38), but the conclusion to build a new meeting-
house was finally reached. At a meeting of Philadelphia Monthly Meeting,
held the 24th of Sixth month 1763: "It is generally acknowledged that a
more convenient place is wanted for holding our meetings than
we are accommodated with. It being considered, it is agreed that a building should be erected on some part of the lot belonging to this meeting,
on which the public school-house stands, and which may not only serve for
this purpose but for accommodating the meeting held Quarterly with the
scholars under the care of Friends." The lot referred to was the one on
Fourth Street below Chestnut, given the meeting by William Forrest, and
the trust which was created by this gift is known as the William Forrest
Estate (entry 412). A committee was appointed "to make out a plan of a
suitable building and to calculate the expense of erecting it." The following month the committee reported that a building could "be erected to
the northward of the schoolhouse, about nine feet from Fourth Street,
seventy-six feet front and forty-two feet deep, one story high, about
twelve feet from floor to ceiling, and the floor about twenty-one inches
above the brick pavement in the street; a cellar under the house about
8 feet deep. Probable cost about L1,200, seats and benches and outside
pavement included." The report of the committee was adopted with the
reserve that the new building should not be placed nearer the north wall
of the schoolhouse than 25 feet, since it was feared that it might interfere with the light and air. In accordance with this decision work was
started on the new building, and although one story had been decided upon,
on further consideration it was determined to raise it another story.
Eleventh month, 1763: "the Friends who undertook to solicit subscriptions
for carrying the meeting-house (now building) another story, report that
they have obtained subscriptions to the amount of 550 pounds, upon con-

sideration thereof, and the report of the workmen that materials may be
readily procured, it is agreed to carry up the wall another story between
10 and 12 feet, and to get the house covered in." It was completed the
following year.

A picture of this building appears in Joseph Jackson's Encyclopedia
of Philadelphia, and shows it was built of brick, with its longest side
parallel with Fourth Street. The gables were on the north and south sides.
The cornice was continued across all four sides. The entrances, of which
there were two, were at the ends, and there were 12 windows facing Fourth
Street, six above and six below, all equipped with outside shutters. A
high brick wall through which there were five entrance gates, enclosed
the grounds of the meeting-house and school on the front. Side by side
for many years stood the meeting-house and the Friends' School, the latter
erected in 1745, on a portion of the Forrest lot, to the south of the
meeting-house. This historic old school was very often referred to as
the "Friends' Fourth Street Academy," and in it many of the early Quaker
school-masters including Anthony Benezet, Robert Proud, John Todd, Jeremiah
Paul, and William Waring taught classes. It was a forerunner of the
present William Penn Charter School (entry 411), and the Friends' Select
School (entry 410) as well.

After the division of Philadelphia Monthly Meeting into three parts
or districts, in 1772, the first monthly meeting for the Southern District was held in this meeting house, as is shown by the following
minute: "On the 25th day of Eleventh month, being the fourth of the week,
1772, divers men and women Friends assembled in our meeting-house on
Fourth Street, being the first Monthly Meeting of Friends of Philadelphia
for the Southern District, appointed for the maintaining of the testimony
of Truth and our Christian discipline, within the limits prescribed for
the said Monthly Meeting." At this opening meeting it was ordered that
the next monthly meeting for the Southern District be held at the Pine
Street meeting-house, where the sessions continued to be held until 1832,
when they were removed to the newly constructed Orange Street meeting-
house. Just how long meetings were continued at the Fourth Street meeting-house is not certain, but with the creation of the Northern District
and Southern District Monthly Meetings in 1772, the congestion at the
Great Meeting-house was much relieved, and it seems likely that the meetings formerly held there were resumed, and probably continued there until
the erection in 1804 of the house at Fourth and Mulberry Streets.

A select school for girls was held in the second story of the Fourth
Street meeting-house for many years. Later a primary school was opened
on the first floor, after it ceased to be used as a meeting-room. These
schools were conducted in conjunction with the one for boys of advanced
grades, held in the adjoining school building, and were under the direction of the Overseers of the Public Schools. The schools were known as
the "Corporation Schools," and the board of overseers were all members
of the Society of Friends. The meeting-house structure was considerably
altered to adapt it to school purposes. A minute of the Ninth month
1807, contains the report of a joint committee appointed by the three
monthly meetings, and states? "On the subject of removing the galleries
from the Fourth Street meeting-house to the large committee-room on Mulberry Street, . . . that although as a committee we do not conceive that
the measure of placing a gallery there would be any improvement, yet
considering the Monthly Meeting of Philadelphia capable of deciding thereon, we are willing to recommend the subject being referred to them,

agreeing that such articles as they may judge necessary may be removed from the Fourth to the Mulberry Street house." From this it seems probable that the ministers gallery now in the large committee-room in the centre building of the Arch Street meeting-house, is the one which was formerly in use in the Fourth Street Meeting-house.

This house was taken down in 1859, and on its site was erected a section of the present Forrest Building; in 1867 the old Academy building was removed and another section of these business offices was erected on its site.

See: Lippincott, Joseph, op. cit., p. 365; George Vaux, "The Public School Founded by Charter in the Town and County of Philadelphia, in Pennsylvania; the Forrest Trust, and the Fourth Street Meeting and School-houses," The Friend, LXIII (189)), cf. pp. 75, 315, 316, 323, 324, 331, 332; Watson W. Dewees, "The William Forrest Estate," The Friend, LXXXIX (1916), 368, 377, 389, 401, 414; Joseph Jackson, Encyclopedia of Philadelphia, III, 705.

For minutes and other records, see the records of Philadelphia Monthly Meeting.

12. ORANGE STREET INDULGED MEETING, 1872-1909. Seventh Street between Locust and Spruce Streets, at the Southwest corner of Washington Square, Philadelphia.
Set up in 1872 by Philadelphia Monthly Meeting (entry 3), upon the approval of Philadelphia Quarterly Meeting (entry 2). When Southern District Monthly Meeting (entry 37) was laid down in 1872, its membership was transferred to Philadelphia Monthly Meeting, but for the convenience of those living in the vicinity of the Orange Street Meeting-house, meetings for worship under the oversight of the monthly meeting at Fourth and Arch Streets, continued to be held there. The Orange Street meeting-house, which was built in 1832, had been the home of Southern District Monthly Meeting for many years. Eventually, attenders of Orange Street Meeting moved to suburban Philadelphia and other places, and by 1909 the attendance had dwindled to such an extent that it was decided to discontinue the meetings. The last meeting for worship to be held there was on the fourth day of the Seventh month 1909. The few remaining Friends who still resided in that section attended the meetings held at Fourth and Arch Streets after the Orange Street house was closed. Following the laying down of this indulged meeting the property was sold to Charles F. Jenkins. Demolition of the building followed, and a short time later the present Farm Journal Building was erected on the site. The date stone of the old Orange Street Meeting-house has been preserved, and can be seen to-day, as it was built into one of the interior walls of the Journal Building. A fine picture of this meeting-house can also be seen there.

For membership and other records, see the minutes and register of Philadelphia Monthly Meeting.

13. WEST PHILADELPHIA INDULGED MEETING, 1873-1930. Northwest corner of 42nd Street and Powelton Avenue, Philadelphia.
Set up in 1873, by Philadelphia Monthly Meeting (entry 3), upon approval of the Philadelphia Quarterly Meeting (entry 2). In the early part of the last century William Hamilton owned a considerable body of land in West Philadelphia. There he laid out what he called "Hamilton Village." For the purpose of encouraging the sale of the lots, he donated plots of ground to various religious denominations as sites for churches and meeting-houses. Among these, Friends were included. The lot given to Friends

was on the north side of Chestnut Street, and it is believed it was situated between Fortieth and Forty-first Streets, but the exact spot cannot be determined. No meeting-house, however, was ever built upon this
lot. The property greatly increased in value, to such an extent in fact
that it was decided during the sixties, that if it were sold the proceeds would be sufficient to purchase another lot in a less expensive
neighborhood, and erect a meeting-house upon it. It was also apparent
that the Chestnut Street lot was very unsuitable for the purpose, since
it was situated next to a church built by another religious denomination.
The lot was therefore sold and the present location, with its grove of
ancient oaks, was purchased. Several years afterwards the present meeting-house was erected, and was enlarged and improved in 1903. In 1873
the meeting house was erected on this new plot of ground which is located
on the northwest corner of Forty-second Street and Powelton Avenue. It
is often referred to as the "Powelton Avenue Meeting-house." The building is a medium-sized and decidedly attractive building surrounded by
spacious grounds, all kept in the most commendable order. Paved walks,
clean grassplots and fine shade trees, all add to the beauty of the place.
A small row of old wagon sheds, made of wood and painted white, still
remain standing on the grounds to the west of the meeting house. The
house, a one-story red brick building trimmed in white, has a porch over
the front entrance. Supporting this are large white columns. There are
smaller covered entrances at each end of the house. The date, 1873, is
on a marble block built into the eastern gable to the left of the semi-
circle transom. The indulged meeting was established in 1873, when the
meeting-house was ready to be occupied. Meetings were held here for a
period exceeding half a century. Removal of its members from the vicinity greatly interfered with the meeting, but it was still listed in the
City Directory for 1930 as holding regularly scheduled meetings. After
that year there were no further listings. On the 28th of Tenth month 1930
Philadelphia Monthly Meeting with the approbation of Philadelphia Quarterly Meeting, officially laid down the indulged meeting at West Philadelphia. Through inquiry it was found that about 1935 the building began
to be used by a colored congregation for religious services. The colored
people continued to use the house until about the early part of 1939,
when their services at this place ceased. Since that time the meeting-
house has not been used for any purpose and at the present time stands
idle. The place, however, has not been allowed to run down, and its
former attractive appearance is still maintained. The land and building
are kept in good condition by a caretaker, who resides in the two-story,
red brick caretaker's dwelling, which was built in 1903 on the meeting-
house grounds. The property is under the care of Philadelphia Monthly
Meeting at Arch Street, under whose oversight the indulged meeting came,
during the entire period of its existence.

See: T. Chalkley Matlack, Brief Historical Sketches Concerning
Friends' Meetings . . ., I, 529 (manuscript, at PPFYR).

For membership and other records, see the minutes and register of
Philadelphia Monthly Meeting.

14. TACKONY AND POETQUESINK MONTHLY MEETING, 1683. Frankford and
     Byberry, Philadelphia.
Set up in 1683 by Philadelphia Quarterly Meeting (entry 2). In the
colonial days, Friends settling in the vicinity of Tackony (later called
Oxford and still later Frankford), and Poetquesink (later called Byberry),
held meetings for worship in each other's homes. A monthly meeting was

allowed between the two as set forth in the following minutes: "At a Quarterly Meeting held at Philadelphia the 5th day of the Fourth Month, 1683; proposed by Friends that the meetings of the county be settled. Agreed that there be a publick First-day meeting of Friends at Tackony, and a First-day publick meeting at Poquessin, /Poetquesink7,and that they both shall make one Monthly Meeting . . . and that Thomas Fairman give notice at Tackony, and Samuel Allen at Poquessin, to the Friends there of the Quarterly Meeting's resolutions for the service of Truth in those parts. . . ." This monthly meeting was held alternately at the house of Sarah Seary in Tackony and at the house of John Hart in Poetquesink. Later in 1683 a meeting for worship was kept at the house of Richard Wall at Cheltenham, this meeting was made a part of the aforesaid monthly meet- ing, and after 1686 monthly meeting sessions alternated between the three places. Later the meeting held at Germantown became a fourth constituent, and the monthly meeting became known as Cheltenham Monthly Meeting, and was sometimes alluded to as Dublin Monthly Meeting, from the name of the township at that time. In 1702 the name Abington Monthly Meeting (entry 93) was adopted, and remains to the present day. Hence the monthly meet- ing of Tackony and Poetquesink was merged into Cheltenham Monthly Meet- ing, which eventually became Abington Monthly Meeting.

See: Lippincott, Joseph, op. cit., p. 283.

For registers and other records, see minutes of Abington Monthly Meeting.

15. RADNOR MONTHLY MEETING, 1684-1865. Buck Lane, Haverford Twp., Delaware County.
This meeting, early known as Haverford Monthly Meeting was set up in 1684 by Philadelphia Quarterly Meeting (entry 2) in Ithan, Delaware County. The name was changed to Radnor Monthly Meeting in 1698. Meetings were held alternately in the homes of four original members: Thomas Duckett, of Schuylkill, William Warner of Radnor, Hugh Roberts of Merion, and John Bevan of Haverford, until 1693. In that year the first one-story gray stone meeting-house and a long multi-colored stone shed, which later was used as a schoolhouse, were erected in Ithan, as the home of the Radnor Preparative Meeting. The monthly meeting used the same house when it occurred here. At the time of the Separation in 1827, the meeting-house and the 2 acre burial ground adjoining the meeting-house, together with the larger part of the membership, passed into Hicksite supervision, and retained the name of Radnor Monthly Meeting (entry 294). After this the Orthodox Friends met in members' homes in Haverford until 1834 when they erected, at Buck Lane, Haverford Township, a one and one-half story gray stone meeting-house. In 1865 this meeting was laid down by the Philadel- phia Quarterly Meeting and the Friends were transferred to the Philadel- phia meeting of the Western District (entry 51) as an indulged meeting. When Haverford Monthly Meeting (entry 56) was again established in 1904, the meeting-house and the graveyard were deeded to this newly established meeting.

See: Michener, op. cit., pp. 59, 60.

Minutes of Mens' Meetings, 1684-1845, 2 vols. (1804-11, 1845-65 missing); Minutes of Women's Meetings, 1685-1865, 2 vols. (1741-45 miss- ing); Register of births, 1682-1730, 1 vol. (1731-1865 missing); Regis- ter of deaths, 1683-1865, 1 vol.; Certificates of removal, 1683-84, 1 vol.; Marriage register, 1683-1858, 1 vol. (1859-65 missing): all at PPFYR.

16. HAVERFORD PREPARATIVE MEETING,[1] 1682-1865. Eagle Rd., Oakmont,
     Haverford Twp., Delaware County.
Set up in 1682 by Philadelphia Monthly Meeting (entry 3). In 1684 Haverford (later Radnor) Monthly Meeting was set up and this meeting became
a part. Meetings were held from 1682-88 in the homes of members. William
Penn gave a grant of 5,000 acres to William Howell, who was one of the
early Welsh settlers, who, seeking religious and political freedom, arrived in this country on August 13, 1682 on the ship Lyon. In 1693 William
Howell deeded to the meeting 3 acres of ground and the present gray stone
meeting-house was built. This was the first meeting-house in what is
now Delaware County. An addition was erected in 1700. This Meeting was
attended sometimes by William Penn. It is noted, in the records of the
meeting, that during the Revolutionary War the leaden window casements
of the meeting-house were seized and converted into bullets. In 1800
extensive repairs and alterations were made on the meeting-house; the
partitions between the building proper and the southern extension were
removed and an additional wing was added to the northern end. At the
time of the Separation in 1827 the meeting-house and burial-ground were
acquired by Haverford Preparative Meeting, Hicksite (entry 295). Haverford Preparative Meeting, Orthodox then a part of the old Radnor Monthly
Meeting, together with the newly formed Hestonville (Meriou) Preparative
Meeting (entry 18), made up the reorganized Radnor Monthly meeting.

See: Michener, op. cit., p. 61.

     Registers and minutes are in the record books of the Radnor Monthly
Meeting.

17. MERION PREPARATIVE MEETING, 1682-1827. Montgomery Pike and
     Meeting House Lane, Lower Merion Twp., Montgomery County.
Set up in 1683 by Philadelphia Monthly Meeting, having functioned as a
meeting for worship since August 1682. In 1684, when Radnor Monthly
meeting was set up Merion became a part of it. First meetings were
held in the homes of various members until 1683, when the first log
meeting-house was erected near the site of present building. In 1695 the
old part of the present stone meeting-house was erected. An addition
was made to this in 1713. The burial ground, 413' x 310', adjoining the
meeting-house, now enclosed by a stone wall with two iron gates, was acquired in the same year the meeting was set up. In 1827 this Meeting together with Haverford Preparative Meeting formed the reorganized Radnor
Monthly Meeting. The Orthodox part of Merion, after this date, became
the Hestonville (Merion) Preparative Meeting (entry 18).

See: Michener, op. cit., p. 61.

     Minutes of Men's Meetings, 1701-5, 1 vol. (1682-1700 missing); Min-
utes of Women's Meetings, 1818-36, 1 vol. (1682-1818 missing), Registers
are in the records of the Radnor Monthly Meeting. Burial records, 1700-
1800, 1 vol. (1682-99, 1801-27 missing); at PSC-Hi Montgomery County Deed
Book, vol. 23, p. 505, vol. 302, p. 312.

---

1. The term "preparative" is used with these early meetings, although they did not have
that status until 1698, when the yearly meeting granted that privilege.

18. HESTONVILLE (Merion) PREPARATIVE MEETING, 1827-65. Present
site would be near Upland Way and 57th Street, Philadelphia.
Prior to the Separation in 1827, Radnor Monthly Meeting consisted of five
particular meetings, namely: Merion, Haverford, Radnor, the Valley, and
Charlestown (Schuylkill). At the time of the Separation the majority
party, followers of Elias Hicks, took over all meeting-houses and properties in these meetings. The members of the two meetings of Merion and
Haverford belonging to the minority group (O) were joined to form one
monthly meeting, which was called the Radnor Monthly Meeting (entry 15).
Friends of Haverford Preparative Meeting (entry 16), met in private
houses, and eventually in a meeting-house which they erected in 1834,
near Haverford College. At Merion, however, the two branches continued
to use the old Merion Meeting-house for worship. Meetings were held alternately, each in a manner after its own convictions. This situation
continued for some years, but unfortunately antagonisms increased until
the Orthodox group withdrew, leaving the meeting-house and property in
possession of the Hicksite majority. But they took with them some of
the old records of the meeting, and the treasurer's accounts. By mutual
arrangement both branches of the Friends have since had the old books in
each other's keeping copied for themselves. This branch, the seceding
(O) members in this particular case of the Merion meeting, transferred
their meetings for worship and business to a little schoolhouse at
Hestonville, which was built about 1732, and according to an old photo-
graph of it on file at the Friends' Historical Library of Swarthmore
College, it appears to be a stone building. Some historians, however, say
that it was built of logs and rough-cast with plaster in later years.
It was a very small square building, plain in construction, and one-story
high, with sloping roofs. It was located near what was then Lancaster
Turnpike, at the proposed Montgomery Avenue, just east of 57th Street.
In Baist's **Property Atlas of the City and County of Philadelphia, 1895,**
plan No. 15 shows it at this location, and it is plainly marked Friends'
Meeting-House, and a shed adjoining, indicated on the map as built of wood
is also plainly marked, and is shown to be a long narrow structure.
This no doubt was a horse shed built by Friends after they took posession
of the property. The property is shown to be on the eastern side of a
large property owned at that time by Wanamaker, et al. A copy of this
atlas is on hand at the Bureau of Surveys, City Hall Annex, Phila., also
another is to be found in the map department of the Free Library of
Philadelphia. One writer describes the present location of the site as
near where 57th and Jefferson Streets now intersect. Another says it
would now be at the intersection of Fifty-fourth Street with the present
Lancaster Avenue. Both are incorrect in their description of the present
location, as a map in the Real Estate Department of the Pennsylvania
Railroad, (Purchasers of the property) shows the present location of the
site to be covered with railroad tracks and railroad years, and if 57th
Street had been cut through, the old meeting-house would have stood approximately 50 feet south of the present Upland Way and about 150 feet
east of the present 57th Street.

The two meetings of Merion and Haverford continued on as Radnor
Monthly Meeting until 1865, when the membership dwindled to such an extent
that there were not enough members remaining to warrant a monthly meeting.
The older members died and others moved to remote sections. In this year
Philadelphia Quarterly Meeting laid down Radnor Monthly Meeting and the
remaining members were transferred to the Philadelphia Monthly Meeting
of Friends of the Western District (entry 51), on Twelfth Street, below
Market. From this time forward meetings at Merion and Haverford were

confined to meetings for worship only. These meetings at this time be-
came the Haverford Indulged Meeting, and the Merion Indulged Meeting of
Friends (entries 52, 53). They came under the oversight of the Western
District Monthly Meeting.

See: Charles H. Browning, Welsh Settlement of Pennsylvania, pp. 585-
587; Matlack, op. cit., I, 478.

Minutes and registers are included with the records of Radnor and
Western District Monthly Meetings.

19. RADNOR PREPARATIVE MEETING, ca.1683-1827.   Ithan, Delaware
     County.
Established about 1684, probably under the supervision of Philadelphia
Monthly Meeting, but originating in 1683 as a spontaneous meeting for
worship. The early history of the group of meetings which sprung up in
the 40,000 acre Welsh Tract is somewhat vague and lacking in documentary
evidences. The first of these Welsh settlers arrived in Merion about
August 26, 1682. Haverford and Radnor were settled immediately thereafter. The settlers were largely Quakers, and it appears from tradition
that the meetings for worship were set up almost immediately after their
arrival and settlement. The history of the three meetings which bear the
names of these three townships is very closely bound up with the history
of this settlement and each of the three meetings is linked very closely
to the other two, all having been founded about the same time (entries
16, 17).

Radnor Preparative Meeting came into being about 1683 in a community
located around the present village of Ithan.   In 1684 when Haverford
(later Radnor) Monthly Meeting was set up this meeting became a part of
it, and its history is an integral part of that of the monthly meeting,
and of the other two meetings which first composed it.

The members first met in homes no doubt. The first mention in the
minutes of a meeting-house is with reference to a Youth's Meeting which
was held there in 1698. However, the register of marriages mentions a
marriage held at the Radnor Meeting-house in 1693. The monthly meeting
minutes also refer, in 1717, to the building of a new meeting-house.
The first one no doubt was a temporary one of logs. The meeting continued as a preparative meeting until the Separation of 1827, at which time
there were five subordinate meetings composing Radnor Monthly Meeting.
After the division the minority membership of Haverford, Merion, and Radnor Preparative Meetings (O) continued as Radnor Monthly Meeting and were
divided into the two Preparative Meetings of Haverford and Hestonville
(Merion) (entries 16, 18).

See: Michener, op. cit., pp. 61, 62.

The registers and minutes are included in the record books of Radnor
Monthly Meeting.

20. SCHUYLKILL MEETING, (Thomas Duckett's) 1683-?. Present location
     would be about 32nd and Market Streets, Philadelphia.
Set up in 1683, by Philadelphia Quarterly Meeting (entry 2), attached to
Philadelphia Monthly Meeting (entry 3). The beginning of the Schuylkill
Meeting is described by an early minute of Philadelphia Quarterly Meet-
ing, as follows: At a Quarterly Meeting held in Philadelphia, 5th day

Fourth month, 1683 it was "Proposed by Friends that the meetings of the
county be settled. Agreed that there be a publick First-day meeting of
Friends at Tackony, and a First-day publick meeting at Poquessin, and
that they both shall make one Monthly Meeting. Agreed that there be a
First-day publick meeting at Philadelphia, and a First-day publick meeting at Schoolkill. (This is the only mention of this meeting to be found
anywhere. It probably refers to the Centre Square Meeting). Agreed that
the two meetings be continued in Philadelphia every First-day, and one
publick meeting every Fifth-day. Agreed that every other First-day there
be a publick meeting of Friends for the worship of the Lord, at the house
of Thomas Duckett, on the other side of Schoolkill, and that the meetings
in these two places make one Monthly Meeting, which quarterly, with the
other Monthly Meeting, shall make up a Quarterly Meeting. Agreed that
Thomas Duckett give notice at Schoolkill, Thomas Fairman at Tackony, and
Samuel Allen at Poquessin, to the Friends there, of the Quarterly Meeting's resolutions for the service of Truth in those parts, that all things
may be done carefully and savourily to the glory of God and welfare of
his people." The meeting at Schuylkill did not remain a part of Philadelphia Monthly Meeting for very long, for in the year 1684, it is found
by a minute of Radnor (Haverford) Monthly Meeting that the Schuylkill
meeting was merged with the latter meeting in that year. "At a meeting
held the 10th of Second month, 1684, at Thomas Duckett's house at Schuylkill," this was the first meeting of the newly formed Haverford Monthly
Meeting. Later the name was changed to Radnor Monthly Meeting (entry 15).
Other early meetings were held at John Bevan's house in Haverford, and
another at Hugh Roberts' house in Merion. These three meetings at that
time constituted Haverford (Radnor) Monthly Meeting. The house of Thomas
Duckett was located near the site of the former station of the Pennsylvania Railroad at Thirty-second and Market Streets. There is no record
of a meeting-house ever having been built at this point. Thomas Duckett
was the clerk of Schuylkill meeting. He is supposed to have arrived in
the colony of Pennsylvania before William Penn came, and he became a
member of the first Pennsylvania Assembly. His death occurred in 1699.

Suitable burial places for the dead were among the earliest neces-
sities of the first English settlers. Accordingly, it is recorded that,
"at our Monthly Meeting held at John Bevan's house at Haverford, the
ninth of the eighth month (October) 1684, it was ordered as followeth:
This meeting having taken to their consideration the necessity of a bury-
ing-place, it was ordered that Thomas Duckett and Barnaby Willcocks for
Schoolkill, Hugh Roberts and Robert David for Merion, George Painter and
William Howell for Haverford, should view and set out convenient places
for that purpose, respectively, for the meeting they belong to as aforesaid." At the next monthly meeting reports were made that burying places
had been laid out respectively for Haverford and Merion. The site thus
selected, with some enlargements since, constitute the burial grounds
attached to these meetings at the present time. There was greater difficulty in having ground laid out at Schuylkill but it was eventually effected, and its site was marked by a few crude gravestones, which could
still be seen as late as 1862. It was located on both sides of the street
that passed under the Pennsylvania Railroad west of the Schuylkill River,
which street was laid out through the burying ground. Since that date
every trace of the graveyard has disappeared. It was located on the
Schuylkill front of Thomas Duckett's farm.

A contest in relation to the title of the burying ground on the
Schuylkill, was renewed by a petition of the Society of Friends, pre-

sented to the State Legislature January 7th, 1811, asking that the legal
title to the lot of ground which had been used by them as a burying
ground might be vested in trustees for the use of the Society. The Board
of Health shortly afterward presented a petition, asking that the same
lot be vested in that body for a public burying ground. The Senate
passed a bill vesting the property in the Society of Friends. It was
lost, however, in the House and the Schuylkill burial ground became a
public one.

See: George Vaux, Bi-Centennial Anniversary of the Friends' Meeting
House at Merion, Pennsylvania, 1695-1895, pp. 13, 14; Matlack, op. cit.,
I, 478; Lippincott, Joseph, op. cit., p. 283.

For minutes and records, see early minutes of the Philadelphia
Monthly Meeting, the Philadelphia Quarterly Meeting, and the Haverford
(Radnor) meeting.

21. VALLEY PREPARATIVE MEETING, 1698-1827. West Side of Old Eagle
or Port Kennedy Road (Route 652), 1/5 mi. from Swedesford
Road, Tredyffrin Twp., Chester County.
Set up in 1810 by Radnor Monthly Meeting (entry 15) after functioning as
an indulged meeting since 1698. First meetings held in the home of Lewis
Walker, whose house was called "Rehobeth," and at the home of Joseph
Richardson. A stone meeting-house was built in 1775 and was located in
the southeast corner of the present graveyard. During the Revolutionary
War the meeting-house was near the scene of the Valley Forge encampment.
During the long, cold winter, private homes, churches, and this meeting-
house were filled with sick soldiers and its nearby graveyard became
crowded with the dead. After 1827 the meeting continued as Hicksite
(entry 300).

See: J. Smith Futhey and Gilbert Cope, History of Chester County,
Pennsylvania, p. 237; Priscilla Streets, Lewis Walker of Chester Valley
and His Descendents, pp. 20-22; Michener, op. cit., p. 62; Browning, op.
cit., pp. 504, 575; Thomas Woody, Early Quaker Education in Pennsylvania,
pp. 114, 120; "Valley Friends Meeting," West Chester Daily Local News,
Sept. 29, 1928; "Valley Friends' 200th Anniversary," West Chester Daily
Local News, Sept. 12, 1931.

Minutes of Men's Meetings, 1810-27, 1 vol.; Minutes of Women's Meetings, 1814-27, 1 vol., at PSC-Hi. For deed records, see Chester County
Deed Books.

22. SCHUYLKILL INDULGED MEETING, 1812-27. Corner Stores, (near
Phoenixville, at Intersection of Long Ford & Nutts Avenue
Rds.), Chester County.
Set up as Charlestown Indulged Meeting in 1812 by Valley Preparative
Meeting (entry 21) with the permission of Radnor Monthly Meeting (entry
15). The one story stone meeting-house, covered with light-brown plaster,
was erected in 1807 by Enoch Walker a member of the Valley Meeting, as a
Friends' school and as a place of worship for traveling Friends and those
living in the vicinity. In 1815 Enoch Walker deeded the schoolhouse and
approximately 2 acres of ground to the Charlestown meeting. It is likely
that the burial ground was started between 1814-16. In 1816 additional
wings were added to the east and west sides of the meeting-house and the
graveyard was enclosed by a post and rail fence. In 1818 a stone wall
was erected on the north side of the graveyard. The name of the meeting

was changed from Charlestown to Schuylkill in 1826. In 1827 this meeting
was laid down by the Radnor Monthly Meeting (O). The meeting-house and
burial grounds were retained by the Schuylkill Indulged Meeting (H)
(entry 301).

See: Futhey and Cope, op. cit., p. 242; Samuel W. Pennypacker, Annals
of Phoenixville and Its Vicinity, p. 189; Charles W. Heathcote, A History
of Chester County, p. 238; Wilmer W. Thomson, Chester County and Its
People, p. 345; "Visited Old Meeting House," Philadelphia Record, July 21,
1901; "Friends' Centennial at Corner Stores," West Chester Daily Local
News, Oct. 2, 1909; "Friends' Centennial Ends," West Chester Village
Record, Oct. 7, 1909; Sarah F. Pennypacker, "Schuylkill Meeting," Phoenixville Daily Republican, Dec. 3, 10, 17, 24, 31, 1938, Jan. 7, 1939.

Minutes and registers included in the records of Valley Preparative
and Radnor Monthly Meeting.

NEWARK MONTHLY MEETING (entry 79).

23. HOWELL JAMES' MEETING, 1709-17. Iron Hills, Chester Co.
In 1709, Howell James, venerated in Quaker history and a member of the
New Castle, Delaware, Preparative Meeting, requested of Newark Monthly
Meeting (entry 79, now Kenneth Monthly Meeting), the privilege of holding
a meeting at his home once a month for the convenience of the Friends
living in his vicinity. Permission was granted upon receipt of the
request. Meetings continued to be held at Howell James' home until his
death in 1717, when the meeting was laid down by the Newark Monthly
Meeting.

See: Futhey and Cope, op. cit., p. 236; Heathcote, op. cit , . 349.

24. EXETER MONTHLY MEETING, 1737-1899. 1 mi. southeast of Stonersville, Berks County.
Set up July 26, 1737 as Oley Monthly Meeting by Philadelphia Quarterly
Meeting (entry 2). Meetings were held about 8 miles from Reading in the
log meeting-house of Oley Preparative Meeting (entry 25), near the home of
George Boone, Jr., who was appointed the first clerk. The meeting continued under the name of Oley until the establishment of Exeter Township,
after which it requested Philadelphia Quarterly Meeting for permission,
since the meeting now fell into Exeter Township, to change the name to
Exeter. This request was granted Third month 3, 1742. At this time
there were five and possibly more meetings under the care of the Exeter
Monthly. Exeter (formerly Oley) Preparative Meeting (entry 25), Maidencreek Preparative Meeting (entry 26), Robeson Preparative Meeting (entry
135), Pottsville Indulged Meeting (entry 30), and Reading Preparative
Meeting (entry 28). Meetings of the Oley Monthly Meeting were held alternately at Oley and Maidencreek. The first Oley Monthly Meeting held
at Maidencreek was in Seventh month 1737. In 1759, because the Friends
increased in numbers, there was need of a larger meeting-house and a
building was erected on a plot of ground to the east and just across the
highway from its log predecessor. This is a two and a half story, limestone and red sandstone edifice, plain in design. This building was used
until the meeting was laid down, and it is still standing. A burial
ground of about half an acre was adjacent to the meeting-house grounds.
After a second tier of graves had been started an effort was made to record the names of the Friends who were interred here. All the property
is well preserved and in good condition. The Exeter Friends School was

a week-day school which was organized in 1790 and closed in 1860. It was
a one and a half story log building about a quarter of a mile from the
meeting-house. When the school was closed the site was sold to the county
school board. Dr. James Tyson of Philadelphia, a member of the Exeter
meeting, was the founder of the First-day school among the Friends. About
1815, when he was warden of the county jail, he began a First-day school
in the parlor of the jail, but kept it very quiet lest the Society might
not approve. Samuel E. Griscom, of Buck Hill Farm, encouraged him and
urged him to transfer his school to the Friends meeting-house, which he
finally did. It was from this beginning that the Friends First-day school
system developed. When the meeting was laid down in 1899, the members
were joined to Philadelphia Monthly Meeting (entry 3).

See: Michener, op. cit., p. 63; John Eshelman, "Friends in Berks
County," Historical Review of Berks County, I (1936) No. 2, pp. 1-66.

Minutes of Men's Meetings, 1737-1899. 7 vols.; Minutes of Women's
Meetings, 1737-1899, 3 vols.; Minutes of Ministers and Elders, 1751-1837,
2 vols. (1737-50, 1838-99 missing), at PPFYR. Registers of births and
deaths, 1759-1857, 2 vols. (1737-58, 1817-28 missing); Certificates of
removal, 1737-1899, 2 vols. (1840-87 missing); Membership list for 1830,
1 vol., at PPFYR. Berks County Deed Book, vol. A-1, pp. 229, 286; vol.
A-2, pp. 5, 350; vol. 9, p. 204; vol. 10, p. 167; vol. 20, p. 43; vol. 23,
p. 19; vol. 62, pp. 518, 519, 521; vol. 63, p. 754; vol. 94, p. 365; vol.
280, pp. 440, 444, 450; vol. 543, p. 415.

25. EXETER PREPARATIVE MEETING, 1718-1899.   1 mi. southeast of
Stonersville, Berks County.
Set up Fifth month 27, 1725 as Oley Preparative Meeting under Gwynedd
Monthly Meeting (entry 96), after having held meetings for worship since
1718, for a Friends' Meeting is mentioned in a petition presented to a
court of Philadelphia in 1718, which reads in part: ". . . a road from
the Lutheran Meeting-House at Tulpehocken Creek to the high road at the
Quaker Meeting house near the home of George Boone in Oley." There is
no other known record of a separate meeting-house at this point at so
early a date. It is certain, however, that meetings were held in the
homes of Anthony Lee, who was one of the first Friends to locate in the
Oley Valley and who settled there in 1713; and George Boone, who took up
a trust of 400 acres of land in Oley in 1718. Meetings continued in the
homes of these Friends until the first log meeting-house was erected in
1726. A reference is made to this Indulged meeting in the minutes of
Gwynedd Monthly Meeting of Fifth month 1724; "The Friends of Oley Meeting
paid 9 shillings being their quarter collection to ye assistance to this
Meett. to answer ye proper disbursement thereof." This was the first
Friends meeting in Berks County. In 1736 George Boone and Deborah his
wife deeded 1 acre of land near the site of the building erected 10 years
before, to Anthony Lee, John Webb, and Squire Boone (father of the famous
Daniel Boone) for a consideration of 20 shillings. These men in turn,
conveyed the land to Ellis Hughs, Thomas Ellis, and James Boone, in trust.
The conveyance set aside the tract in trust for a house of religious worship "for the meeting for the people called Quakers within the same
township of Oley and shall permit and suffer the said piece of land whereon the said Meeting stands and is erected . . . to be and remain a burying place for ye burying and interring of all such persons as the people
called Quakers within ye said township shall allow of, and to no and for
no other use and service whatsoever." The second meeting-house, also a
log building, was erected the same year on the new land and was made

large enough to accommodate the growing membership of Oley meeting. Oley Monthly Meeting was set up the following year, at which time Oley Preparative Meeting was detached from Gwynedd Monthly Meeting and attached to Oley Monthly Meeting. In 1742 when the township lines changed, the Oley meetings fell within the limits of Exeter Township and at Quarterly Meeting held at Philadelphia the 3rd of Third month it was agreed that "henceforward the Oley Meeting be called the Exeter Meeting." The third and last Exeter meeting-house was erected in 1759, just across the road from the original site. This was a two and a half story limestone and red sandstone building.

Minutes of Men's Meetings, 1813-71, 1 vol. (1725-1812, 1872-99 missing), at PPFYR. Registers from 1725-37 in the records of the Gwynedd Monthly Meeting; 1737-1899 in the records of the Exeter Monthly Meeting. Berks County, Deed Book, vol. 12, p. 411.

26. MAIDENCREEK PREPARATIVE MEETING, ca.1732--. One and a half miles east of Leesport, half mile east of Kindts Corner, Berks County, on Route #63.
Set up in 1735 by Gwynedd Monthly Meeting (entry 96) after having worshiped as an indulged meeting since about 1732. When Exeter Monthly Meeting (entry 24) was set up in 1737, this meeting became a part. Maidencreek Preparative Meeting was the second meeting in Berks County and tradition locates its first meeting-place in the home of Moses Starr. The exact date of the first meeting is not known but it is supposed to be about the time that the Indians released the land in 1732. It was about this time that the first, and a short time later, the second log buildings were erected near what used to be known as "The Stone Bridge" on the site of what is today Maidencreek Reservoir, sometimes called Take Ontelaunce. Prior to 1759 this meeting paid ground rent but in fnly of that year they secured title to their land from Benjamin Lightfoot. In the same year the Friends erected a one and a half story, gray stone building on the same site as the previous two buildings. A log schoolhouse was built in 1784 adjacent to the meeting-house. The first teacher was Thomas Pearson. This building was replaced in 1807 by a gray limestone building. After the Separation in 1827, all the property was retained by Maidencreek Preparative Meeting (H) (entry 285). The Orthodox Friends, after the Separation, met in a log cabin on the Reber Farm, located on the land upon which the Maidencreek Reservoir was constructed years later, and remained there until 1853 when they erected their last, small red brick building on the land belonging to Thomas Willitts and on First month 15, 1856 they secured title to the 72.2 perches of ground. This building, which is now being used as a summer home by Benjamin Parvin, is still standing on its original site. It is adjacent to the stone building erected in 1759, and which was moved from its original to its present location. Mordecai Parvin was the last male member of the Orthodox branch of the Maidencreek Friends. Since his death in 1934 his widow, Mrs. Carrie J. H. Parvin, and her daughter Rebecca H. Parvin, held a meeting each Sunday in the home of Mrs. Parvin at Berkley, about 2 miles South of Leesport, on Route #120.

See: Morton L. Montgomery, History of Berks County, Pennsylvania in the Revolution, from 1774 to 1783, p. 46; Cyrus T. Fox, Reading and Berks County Pennsylvania, I, 85; Eshelman, op. cit., pp. 1-66.

Minutes and Registers are in the Gwynedd Monthly Meeting records until 1737, and thereafter in the records of the Exeter (formerly Oley) Monthly Meeting.

27. TULPEHOCKEN INDULGED MEETING, 1749-50. Near the forks of Tulpehocken Creek and the Schuylkill River, 6 miles   north of
Reading, Berks County, Pennsylvania.
Established in 1749 by Exeter Monthly Meeting (entry 24). Friends belonging to Exeter Monthly Meeting came from east of the Schuylkill River into
Bern Township, Lancaster County (now Berks County), to live "in and near
the forks of the Tulpehocken Creek," (the fork of the Schuylkill and the
Tulpehocken, a few miles above Reading) shortly before 1745. They attended meetings of Exeter Monthly Meeting in Exeter Township but found it
difficult to do so during the winter months "by reason of the length of
the way and the difficulties of the waters." Permission was therefore
requested of Exeter Monthly Meeting to hold meetings in their own community during "the winter time." Eighth month 26, 1749 Exeter Monthly
Meeting agreed "that a meeting be kept at John Elleman's /in the vicinity
of what is today the Berks County Prison Farm/ the first and third days
of every month." Permission for meetings was granted them again for the
winter of 1750 but occasion for this meeting was not found again, evidently because roads had been built which brought other meetings within
easy access of the Tulpehocken Friends. As early as 1745, because of the
difficulty of reaching the burial ground of Exeter Monthly Meeting in
Exeter Township, the Tulpehocken Friends who had died during the winter
months were buried in the private burial ground belonging to Richard
Peters. He was then secretary to the Proprietaries, and of the 180 acres
he owned he deeded 2 acres, where the burials had already been made, to
John Elleman "in consideration of one shilling currency . . . for the use
of the congregation of the people called Quakers in that neighborhood."
It was probably the intention of the Friends to erect a meeting-house in
that neighborhood at some future date but there is no indication that
one was ever constructed. As travel to the east became less difficult
and attendance on the meetings in Exeter Township and the newly established Reading Indulged Meeting (entry 28) became easier, the idea of
maintaining a Tulpehocken meeting was abandoned. In the early 1750's,
about the time of Braddock's defeat at Fort Duquesne in 1755, marauding
Indians came from the direction of the Susquehanna River and also from
Kittaninny or "Blue" Mountains scalping, murdering, burning, and laying
waste entire settlements which were within a few hours march of Reading.
It is likely that Friends living further up-stream and nearer the North-
kill Creek suffered loss of property, although there is no record of
them being killed by the Indians. At any rate it appears that Friends
moved from the Tulpehocken neighborhood. They were in as great danger
from the settlers, who couldn't countenance the refusal of the Friends
to war against the savages as they were from the Indians themselves.
"When the ravages of the Indians were made . . . the panic flew to Reading and the people were disposed to pull down the houses of the Friends."
In 1758 John Elleman, after having deeded the 2 acres in Tulpehocken over
to the Exeter Monthly Meeting, moved to Virginia and was followed by his
neighbor, Samuel Wilkinson, and other neighbors, while still others moved
to Reading about the same time. The exact location of the burial ground,
on Richard Peter's property, is not known.

See: Lightfoot Papers, file box 6 (manuscripts at PHi).

Berks County, Deed Book, Book A, vol. 1, pp. 229, 286.

28. READING PREPARATIVE MEETING, 1750-1827. Washington St. between
     4th St. and Madison Ave., Reading, Berks County.
Set up in 1756 by Exeter Monthly Meeting (entry 24), after having held

meetings for worship since 1750 in a small log building, the location of which is not known. When the group was larger than the meeting-house could accommodate, the meetings were held in the courthouse. On the 30th day of Twelfth month 1756, Exeter Monthly Meeting "ordered meetings to be held in Reading every third day the year round, beginning with the eleventh hour." On Eleventh month 29, 1759 a committee reported that they had selected lots #402 and #403 in the plan of Reading as a suitable site for a new meeting-house. The committee was authorized to purchase the lots. On these lots, today known as 106-108 North 6th Street, forest trees were cut down and were used in the erection of a small building in which the meetings were held. A burial ground was also laid out on this plot. "On th 27th of Eighth month 1761, the Reading Friends asked for a First-day Meeting, and on the following month a committee reported favorably." On Twelfth month 30, 1762 Exeter Monthly Meeting was present- ed with a report that the "Friends of Reading are in need of a better house to meet in." Philadelphia Quarterly Meeting (entry 2) held Fifth month 6, 1765, recommended the erection of a "meeting-house of round logs only at present," and Exeter Meeting on the 30th day of the same month, concurred this action. The building of round logs was erected the same year on Washington Street, between 4th Street and Madison Avenue, where the Metropolitan Edison Building now stands. The meeting-house erected in 1759, which stood on the 6th Street burial ground was demolished when the meeting moved to the new building. In 1776, during the Revolutionary War the meeting-house was used as a hospital for the Hessians captured at Trenton. One wounded soldier, while convalescing, used a sharp in- strument to draw the picture of a British man-o-war upon the wainscoting of the meeting-house. In 1868, when this log meeting-house was torn down after having stood for 103 years, Rachel Griscom, who bought the house, sent that portion of the wainscoting containing the drawing of the ship to the Pennsylvania Historical Society at Philadelphia. A one-story log schoolhouse was built in 1787 near the meeting-house. After the Separa- tion this meeting was laid down and the remaining Orthodox Friends joined Exeter Preparative Meeting (entry 25), in Exeter Township. The Reading Hicksite Friends are joined to Exeter Monthly Meeting (entry 284), which retained the property of the original Reading Preparative Meeting.

See: Montgomery, *op. cit.*, I, 46; Fox, Cyrus, *op. cit.*, I, 85; William Stahle, *A Description of the Borough of Reading*, p. 19; Michener, *op. cit.*, pp. 63, 64; Eshelman, *op. cit.*, pp. 1-66.

Records are included in those of the Exeter Monthly Meeting. Ori- ginal deed in the vault of the Reading City Bank and Trust Co., Reading, Pa.

29. CATAWISSA INDULGED MEETING, ca.1775-94. Catawissa, Columbia County.
This meeting was indulged about 1775 by Exeter Monthly Meeting. Mention of it is rare in the records of the Monthly Meeting, and hence its history obscure. It was started about 1775 by Quaker settlers at Catawissa in Columbia County. Among these early settlers are the names of William Hughes, William Collins, James Watson, and John Love. In 1794 it became a preparative meeting, and in that status it passed through four different monthly meetings by transfer from one to another, namely, Exeter, Cata- wissa, Muncy, and Roaring Creek Monthly Meeting (entries 24, 39, 41, 47).

For the records of this meeting, see the minutes and registers of Exeter Monthly Meeting, Catawissa Monthly Meeting, Muncy Monthly Meeting, and Roaring Creek Monthly Meeting.

30. POTTSVILLE INDULGED MEETING, 1828-ca.1832. Pottsville, Schuyl-
     kill County.
Established in 1828 by Muncy Monthly Meeting (entry 41). The history of
this meeting is very obscure because of the absence of records and data.
However, the following item appeared in a local paper in 1926: "The Society of Friends was established early in 1828, when the records show that
John Comly of Byberry, Philadelphia County, was in Pottsville for the purpose of conducting a meeting." In his travels over the county, Comly kept
a diary in which he tells of his visit to Pottsville and what he found
there, when he returned 2 years later. He says: "Rode on to Pottsville
and lodged at Job Eldrege's. The town had increased in buildings since
I was here two years ago. Now it is a crowded business place." The
basement of an Episcopal Church was secured and they held meetings there.
There is no information as to how long the Orthodox Friends continued to
worship in the Episcopal Church. The only further information we have of
this meeting is a minute of the Muncy Monthly Meeting dated Eleventh month
12, 1832 which states: "The Monthly Meeting has transferred Pottsville
Meeting to the care of the Exeter Monthly Meeting. However, there is no
mention of a Pottsville Meeting in the minutes of the Exeter Monthly Meeting from 1833-1900.

     See: Matlack, op. cit., pp. 494-497, 536-538. "Society of Friends,"
Pottsville Evening Republican," July 28, 1926.

RICHLAND MONTHLY MEETING (entry 101).

31. SPRINGFIELD INDULGED MEETING, ca.1743-ca.1778. In homes in the
     vicinity of Pleasant Valley and Springfield, Bucks County.
Established about 1743 by Richland Monthly Meeting (entry 101). Permission was granted to hold meetings in the homes of Joseph Unthank and John
Dennis for a period of 6 months. Annually renewed until 1755 when Joseph
Unthank moved to North Carolina and this meeting was ordered held at the
home of Thomas Adamson. A committee was appointed by Richland Monthly
Meeting in 1746 or 1747 to assist the Friends of Springfield in selecting
a meeting-house site but the plan was not carried out and no building was
ever erected. Meetings were continued at the homes of John Dennis and
Thomas Adamson until 1757 and after that at Thomas Adamson's home exclusively. This meeting was discontinued during the Revolutionary War.

     See: Clarence V. Roberts and Warren S. Ely, Early Friends Families
of Upper Bucks, pp. 11-22; Elwood Roberts, Richland Families, p. 27.

     Registers and other notations are in the Richland Monthly Meeting
records.

32. SAUCON INDULGED MEETING, 1744-ca.1765, Lower Saucon, Northamp-
     ton County.
In 1744 Richland Monthly Meeting (entry 101) granted permission to this
meeting to hold a meeting for worship. Because of the absence of historical information, it cannot be established whether the meeting ever had a
meeting-house of its own. Before the change of the county line part of
Northampton was in Bucks County and it is possible that the Saucon Friends
worshiped with the Springfield Meeting (entry 31) of Bucks County. T.
Chalkley Matlack, says: "In 3rd mo., 1744, Saucon Friends were permitted
to hold meetings for worship on 1st days during the summer months for a
number of years at the following places: the Richland Meeting House, John
Dennis' residence, Robert Ashton's home, William Edwards' home, and later
at a schoolhouse near Benjamin Green's residence."

See: Matlack, op. cit., pp. 60, 61.

Registers are in the records of the Richland Monthly Meeting.

33. NORTHERN DISTRICT MONTHLY MEETING, 1772-1914. Sixth and Noble
    Streets, Philadelphia.
Set up in 1772 by Philadelphia Quarterly Meeting (entry 2), upon recommendation of the Philadelphia Monthly Meeting (entry 3). In 1770, after 88
years of activity, Philadelphia Monthly Meeting became overcrowded with
business to such a degree that it became expedient to have another monthly
meeting set off from it in order to lighten its burden. The recorded
minutes reveal that long morning and afternoon meetings were common, while
not infrequently two more sittings on another day were required to dispose
of the accumulated business. Friends had already spread in large numbers
to the northward. The monthly meeting kept the proposition of division
alive for almost a year and on the Fifth month 31, 1771, definite action
was taken: "The subject which has several times heretofore been under
consideration, of establishing one other or two more Monthly Meetings,
being now revived and many Friends apprehending it might tend to promote
the cause of Truth and contribute to lessen the weight and labor now attending the transaction of the affairs of our Religious Society in this
city through the great increase thereof, it was agreed that a committee
be appointed to take the matter under deliberate consideration and report
their sense of the manner whereby it may best be effected, so as to promote and maintain our Union and Fellowship and the comely order for the
preservation of which our Meetings for Dicipline were first instituted."
The proposition was referred to 20 Friends who were appointed as a committee to confer together and report their recommendations to the monthly
meeting. After the matter had several times been referred to further consideration, on the 25th of Tenth month 1771, a year from the time the subject was first taken up the meeting approved the following definite statement: "It appears to be the judgment of this meeting that it may tend to
the advancement of Truth that two other Monthly Meetings be established."
It is probable that some delicate property rights had to be adjusted as
well as details of procedure arranged, therefore before placing the whole
report upon the minutes, it was once more referred to the committee of
20 Friends, to which 11 others were added. The report of this enlarged
committee was before the meeting continuously in the early months of 1772.
Finally, on the 21st of Fourth month it was accepted. The section which
pertains to the area of the proposed districts seems to have been of the
most importance: "That all the members of our Religious Society now residing or who may hereafter dwell in houses bounded on the south side of
Mulberry Street, and the Northward thereof, including the township of the
Northern Liberties, or as far as the limits of the present Monthly Meeting hath usually extended, with the few families living on the west side
of the Schuylkill River (unless they are willing to be joined to Haverford
which we think most advisable), be deemed and considered members of a
'Monthly Meeting of Philadelphia for the Northern District, and that the
same be held on the Third-day of the same week in which our present
Monthly Meeting is held." The subject next appears in Philadelphia Quarterly Meeting of Fifth month 4, 1772, when a committee consisting of members of the other five monthly meetings of Philadelphia Quarter, were appointed to unite with the representatives of the Philadelphia Monthly Meeting to weigh and consider the expediency and propriety of such division.
This committee presented a signed report in the Eighth month following,
and in it manifested a cautious approval. Philadelphia Quarterly Meeting
finally agreed as set forth in the following minute of concurrence: " . . .

and being considered the meeting concurred therewith, and, as hereby two other Monthly Meetings are to be established in the city of Philadelphia . . . " The other meeting alluded to was the Southern District Monthly Meeting (entry 37), which accordingly was set up at the same time. The monthly meeting being thus established a further minute states: ". . . and it is concluded that the first Monthly Meeting for the Northern District of Friends in this city be held on the Third-day of the week preceding the last Sixth-day of the week in the next month, at the Bank Meeting-house at ten o'clock in the morning." Pursuant to this action, the first monthly meeting for the Northern District was held on the 24th day of the Eleventh month, 1772, as per the following minute of that date: "Friends assembling in their meeting-house on the Front Street, on the bank of the Delaware, being the first meeting of Friends of Philadelphia for the Northern District . . . ." It will be noted from the foregoing minutes that the Bank Meeting-house was given over to the use of the newly formed monthly meeting. The parent meeting retained the meeting-house at Second and High (now Market) Street, which was called the Great Meeting-house. This meeting-house built in 1696 and rebuilt in 1755, as well as the Second Bank Meeting-house which was erected in 1703, were both in use by Philadelphia Monthly Meeting up to this time (entries 8, 34). The new organization was commonly called the "North Meeting," but the official title adopted was the Monthly Meeting of Friends of Philadelphia for the Northern District."

The North Meeting with its constantly increasing membership, soon outgrew the accommodations afforded by the Second Bank Meeting-house, and because of the annoyance caused by the grading down of Front Street, purchased ground adjoining a lot which had been the gift of George Fox in the early times. This was located on the south side of Key's Alley (now New Street). On this lot a substantial brick meeting-house was constructed, and the first monthly meeting to convene there was held on the Ninth month, 1790 (entry 35).

Due to crowded conditions at the Key's Alley Meeting-house, a new house was erected at the southeast corner of Fourth and Green Sts., in the Fourth month 1814, and an indulged meeting under the oversight of Northern District Monthly Meeting was established there.   In Twelfth month of the same year Green Street Preparative Meeting (entry 55) was set up by the Northern District Monthly Meeting.   In 1816 Philadelphia Quarter, upon recommendation of the Northern District Monthly Meeting set up Green Street Monthly Meeting (entry 54), at the same location, and Green Street Preparative then became a part thereof. When the Separation took place in 1827, the property of the monthly meeting of Green Street was held by the majority group (Hicksite) of this meeting. Technically no actual separation took place at that time in these two meetings, for by a reciprocal agreement between the monthly meetings of the Northern District and Green Street, an almost equal number of Friends of both meetings, who desired to follow the opposite faction, were exchanged by the issuance of certificates of removal, and thereby the procedure of disownment which was the usual course pursued in most of the other meetings, was averted.

By the year 1835 the North Meeting was again considering the desirability of larger accommodations. From Fifth month of that year a minute reads: "The location of our present Meeting-house being brought into consideration, and the mind of Friends freely expressed, it appeared to be the prevailing sense that it was seasonable to appoint a committee to

look out for, and report to a future meeting, a site which might be procured on which to erect a house that would better accommodate the members
of this district." At the next monthly meeting this committee brought in
a report that "they had the offer of a lot bounded by Sixth, John (now
Marshall) and Noble Streets, which may be procured for about $28,000.,
and they are united in judgment that it is the most eligible situation
that has or is likely to present itself for the accomplishment of the
object." The meeting accepted this report, and it was left with a committee of four Friends to devise means to raise the purchase money and bring
in plans for the new house. In Sixth month 1837, a well prepared report
was presented to the meeting, proposing to erect on this same lot, "an
edifice of 118 feet by 65 feet and 30 feet perpendicular clear height to
the square; and to comprise a main meeting-room, 65 feet by 70 feet, with
side and end galleries for ·youth, and calculated to accommodate about
1,200 persons." The total cost of lot, house, enclosing wall, etc., was
$70,194.53, as noted in a minute dated Second month 1, 1839. The new
two-story meeting-house constructed of red brick was ready for occupancy
by the summer of 1838, and the first monthly meeting to be held therein
was on the 12th of Eighth month of that year. With the opening of the
new meeting-house the property on Key's Alley was sold.

    In 1861 a primary school as an adjunct of the Friend's Select School
(entry 410), was established. This was held on the second floor of the
meeting-house, under the care of Deborah Brooks. In this school, children of both sexes were educated in the elementary branches, so as to prepare them for the higher studies taught at the Select School, while their
moral and religious welfare was carefully guarded. This school was opened
twenty-five years before the Select School moved to its present location
on the Parkway, and 1886, when this removal took place, the intermediate
school of the Northern District was moved from the Sixth and Noble Sts.
meeting-house to the new Select School building. A few years later, in
1889, the historic Aimwell School (entry 417), established in 1796 by
Anne Parrish for the free education of young girls, was granted the free
use of the school rooms formerly occupied by the intermediate school, and
continued to occupy them until North Meeting was suspended.

    With the expansion of the city and the encroachment of mercantile
and manufacturing establishments, the membership of North Meeting gradually scattered to other centers. In order to meet the changed conditions
and following the practices of the early days, a proposition to establish
another meeting in the northwestern section of the city was considered.
A small group of members having moved into the Tioga district proposed
the erection of a school as well as a meeting-house there, but after
thorough consideration of the plan, it was not clear that this was likely
to become a Friendly center, and the project was abandoned (entry 36).
The complete change in the character of the neighborhood of the meeting
in the final days of its existence, elicited the concern of many Friends.
A little band of workers established a center for social settlement work
among the poor children, as well as for adult school work, and were
granted the use of the monthly meeting room for Bible classes on First-
days, and for meetings and classes at other times.

    The final sitting of the North meeting occurred on the 23rd of Sixth
month, 1914. A portion of the minutes of that meeting reads as follows:
"As the conclusion of this meeting will terminate the 'Northern District
Monthly Meeting,' and in accordance with the direction of Philadelphia
Quarterly Meeting, by minute dated Fifth month 1913, its membership and

property will be merged with the Monthly Meeting of Friends now held at Fourth and Arch Streets, from which it was set apart one hundred and forty-two years ago, ..." A few years after the closing of the meeting, the old meeting-house and its grounds were sold to the estate of Richard and Sarah A. Smith for a playground and social service center. A bronze tablet mounted on the side of the high red brick wall which encloses the meeting-house property, bears the following inscription: "Northern Liberties Playground, Established in 1918, under the wills of Richard Smith and Sarah A. Smith, in memory of their son Stanfield Smith, Fidelity Trust Company, Trustees."

See: Historical Sketch of North Meeting, Sixth and Noble Streets, Philadelphia. Lippincott, Joseph, op. cit., pp. 342, 357.

Minutes of Men's Meetings, 1772-1914, 13 vols.; Minutes of Women's Meetings, 1772-1914, 11 vols. (1875-88 missing); Minutes of Ministers and Elders, 1796-1914, 2 vols.; Green Street Monthly Meeting (Northern District), Minutes of Ministers and Elders, 1816-1824, 1 vol.; Registers of births and deaths, 1772-1885, 2 vols.; Membership list, 1797-1885, 7 vols.; Marriage certificates, 1772-1907, 2 vols.; Certificates of removal Issued, 1835-1914, 1 vol.; Certificates received, 1772-1820, 2 vols.; Certificates granted, 1773-1834, 2 vols.; Treasurer's cash books, 1920-1916: PPFYR.

34. THE SECOND BANK MEETING, 1703-90. Present site, west side of N. Front St., above Arch Street, Philadelphia.
After the discontinuance of Centre Square Meeting (entry 6), about 1697, and the subsequent purchase of the somewhat decayed meeting-house by William Penn; and upon his willingness to give Friends possession of it again about one year later, it was decided to rebuild it on the lot formerly occupied by the frame meeting-house of the First Bank Meeting (entry 7). The location was on the bank of the Delaware on Main Street (now Front), fifty-eight feet north of Mulberry Street (now Arch). Toward the close of 1701, the question of moving the Centre Square Meeting-house to the Bank lot was actively considered, and it was concluded to consult the quarterly meeting. By the quarterly meeting's minute of First month 2, 1701-2 it is noted: "Philadelphia Friends laying before this meeting, that it will be much more to the service of Truth, and Friends, to have the Centre meeting-house, which is ready to fall, taken down and set up in the city, on the lot belonging to Friends on the Front Street, where a meeting house formerly stood, this meeting gives its concurrence." At the monthly Meeting held First month 27, "a subscription toward moving the Centre Square Meeting-house and setting it up on the lot in town belonging to Friends, being begun at this meeting and many being absent, John Parsons and Anthony Morris are desired to get it perfected by going about to Friends' houses, in order to have them subscribe, and the same persons with Edward Shippen and John Kinsey, are desired to agree with the workmen to oversee the work." In the Third month 1702, a committee was appointed to collect the subscriptions towards rebuilding the meeting-house, which was to be set up at the upper end of the town, but some delay having occurred in proceeding with the work, it was thought at the close of the Fifth month too late to go on with it that summer, but directions were given to proceed the following spring. The work was pushed rapidly forward in the succeeding year, so that it was ready for occupancy about midsummer. Seventh month, 1703: "It is agreed that there be a meeting held at the new meeting-house on the Front Street every First day in the afternoon, to begin the next First Day, at or near

the Second hour." In the following month Nicholas Waln reported: "they have near finished the meeting-house, and that the land whereon it stands is conveyed to him and John Goodson for a Publique Service. Therefore it is desired that Thomas Story and David Lloyd may draw conveyances to Edward Shippen, Anthony Morris and others. It is also agreed that a meeting be held therein on First-days to begin at the Eleventh hour." Ninth month: "There being several debts due from the Monthly Meeting to people that have done work for the meeting-house on the Bank, and money falling short, Thomas Story is willing to lend the meeting twenty-five pounds on interest. It is agreed that Samuel Carpenter pay Ralph Jackson L1 6s. 4d. for glazing the meeting-house windows. The Preparative Meeting having recommended the necessity of paling the front of the Bank Meeting-house even with the street, John Parsons is desired to get it done, and get it painted." Thus in 1703 the Centre Square Meeting-house was removed and reconstructed substantially on the same general plan, on the Bank lot, and so became the Second Bank Meeting-house.

This house was built of brick, and of the same dimensions 36 by 36 feet, as the frame structure that preceded it upon the same site. It stood 14 feet back from the street. It may be added in support of the view that these two buildings were alike, that the known dimensions of each were the same, both were of brick and both had hipped roofs. Also that in reconstruction but little alteration in the frame work and other timbers were required and thus much expense saved. The street and building were upon the same level, but after the cutting down of the street, the building stood some 10 to 12 feet above it, giving it a singularly perched up appearance. Pictures of the Second Bank Meeting-house which have been preserved, show it elevated somewhat above the street, from which it stood back, and with a wall enclosing it on the front, in which there were two gates with flights of steps ascending to the level of the ground on the inside. The building is said to have been 38 feet north and south and 50 feet east and west, and the engraving shows it with a hipped roof rising to a point in the center, with windows for first and second stories. Porticoes are shown over the doors on the south and east sides, that on the east being supported by columns. It seems proper to call attention to a picture found among the papers of the late John Fanning Watson, the historian. In this picture the building is shown in the form of the letter "L", with two gables at right angles with each other. Windows for one story only are to be seen on each side of the doorways, which are under the gables, and the doors have gabled porticoes over them. The general appearance of the building does not correspond with the description of the minutes, and is so unlike the pictures of the Second Bank Meeting house just described, that it is not clear how such a representation could have become attached to the Centre Square Meeting-house. It can only be accounted for on one or two suppositions: either that the name was inadvertently placed on the picture or some other building, or that an attempt was made to represent it from descriptions which were erroneous.

In 1719, the galleries were ordered to be enlarged for the purpose of better accommodating the yearly meeting, and in 1721 a committee was appointed to get a gallery made for the women Friends. For about 20 years the minutes made no further mention of this property, but in 1739 it is stated in the minutes that the grade of the Front Street had been changed, which made it necessary to alter the steps. Originally, there was no wooden partition dividing the house, and a curtain was lowered to divide the men's and women's meetings when the preparative meetings were held. When the old meeting-house on Market and Second Streets was re-moved and a new one erected about 1755, a partition was put up in the Bank meeting-house, to adapt it for holding meetings previously held at Market Street. A delay occurring in completing the last named building, the monthly and quarterly meetings were continued in the Front Street house during the following winter, but as it appears to have been imper-fectly heated and it would be too cold in the depth of winter to sit through the whole meeting time it was provided that the women should adjourn to the School house," which was the Friends Academy, on Fourth Street below Chestnut.

As Friends became more numerous and more widely scattered over the city, and the business of the monthly meeting largely increased, it was deemed expedient to establish two other monthly meetings, to be known as the Monthly Meetings of Friends of Philadelphia for the Northern and Southern Districts respectively. The opening minute of that held at the Bank meeting-house being as follows: "On the 24th day of Eleventh month, being the third day of the week in the year of our Lord one thousand seven hundred and seventy-two, Men and Women Friends assembled in their meeting-house on the Front Street, on the Bank of the Delaware, being the first Monthly Meeting of Friends in Philadelphia for the Northern Dis-trict." The second Bank Meeting-house became inadequate to accomodate the Friends of that meeting, and it was necessary to provide larger quarters for the purpose. By a minute of First month, 1789, "T h e com-mittee appointed to procure a suitable lot of ground to build a meeting-house upon for the better accommodation of Friends, report they have lately made a contract for a lot;" later the more commodious building on Keys Alley above Front Street was erected. As funds were required to pay for the new structure, it was decided to sell the Second Bank Meeting-house together with an additional lot adjoining the north. This was ac-cordingly done, and on the 21st of Fifth month 1791, the Trustees who held the property conveyed it to James C. and Samuel W. Fisher, for the con-sideration of L1000. The stone steps with the forms and other movable property were reserved. The house was taken down and the old oaken col-umn that supported the gallery which had been brought from the Centre meeting, was preserved by James C. Fisher.

It is probable that the last meeting to ever convene in the Bank meeting-house was held on Third-day, Ninth month 14th, 1790, as Elizabeth Drinker states in her diary that she was present at that time, and "took leave of the old meeting-house, the new one is to be christened on First-day next." She also mentions that J. Pemberton, Edward Howell, A lice Needham and Samuel Emlen spoke. She was also present on the 19th, when the new meeting-house was "Christened," when William Savery opened the meeting in prayer and S. Emlen and W. S. appeared in testimony.

See: Lippincott, Joseph, op. cit., pp. 307, 308, 348; Vaux, Centre Square, pp. 109, 110.

For minutes and registers, see the minutes and records of Philadel-phia Monthly Meeting, and also those of the Northern District Monthly Meeting.

35. KEY'S ALLEY MEETING, 1790-1838. Present site is south side of New Street, between Front and Second Sts., Philadelphia.
When the Northern District Monthly Meeting (entry 33) was established in 1772, the Second Bank Meeting-house was given over to the use of this

newly formed monthly meeting. In course of time, Friends finding themselves in need of more adequate accommodations, obtained another location
as noted by the following minute of the monthly meeting of First month
1789: "The committee appointed to procure a suitable Lot of Ground to
build a meeting-house upon for the better accommodation of Friends, report they have lately made a contract with our Friend Samuel Emlen for
his lot on the square between Sassafras (Race) and Vine Street, and Front
and Second Street, contiguous to that held by our Society as the donation
of our friend George Fox, on which the school house now stands."

The erection of the meeting-house was of next consideration, and
"Friends were generally of the mind that a building would best answer
the purpose intended of about 75 feet long east and west, and not less
than 50 feet north and south, and that it would be necessary after dis-
posing of the Bank Meeting-house Lot, and the one adjoining it on the
north, to raise by subscription the sum of 2,000 pounds." In the Second
month "A plan was agreed upon to lessen the size of the new meeting-
house to 68 by 50 feet, and instead of dividing the men and women's
apartments by a sliding partition of wood, to erect an additional building of brick, 45 by 40 feet, on the north side of the building," for a
monthly meeting room. The building was erected in accordance to the
last proposed plans, on the south side of Key's Alley (New Street), and
the first meeting held therein on the 21st of Ninth month 1790. This
meeting was commonly called the "North Meeting," and very frequently
alluded to as the "Up Town Meeting."

As time passed the population in the Northern Liberties section increased, and Friends moved farther to the northward and westward, and it
became manifest that due to crowded conditions in the Key's Alley house,
another meeting-house still further up town would soon be required. A
lot was purchased at the southeast corner of Fourth and Green Streets,
and a substantial brick building was erected thereon, which was completed in the spring of 1814. As a result of the differences which culminat-
ed in the separation of 1827, the Green Street house passed into the
hands of the Hicksite branch and a small portion of its membership returned to the meeting in Key's Alley. In the year 1835, North Meeting
was again considering the desirability of larger accommodations, and in
the same year a lot bounded by Sixth, John (now Marshall), and Noble
Streets was procured, and a commodious meeting-house was erected. The
Sixth and Noble Streets Meeting-house was completed and placed into use
in the Eighth month 1838. The last meeting to be held in the Key's Alley
Meeting-house was held in the Seventh month, 1838, and the old house was
sold the same year to Controller's and Overseers of Public Schools of
Philadelphia, for the sum of $20,000. It was used as a school until de-
stroyed by fire in the Great Fire of 1850. After the fire a new school
building was erected on the site.

See: Lippincott, Joseph, op. cit., pp. 342, 357.

For minutes and other records, see the records of the Northern District Monthly Meeting.

36. TIOGA FRIENDS MEETING, (Proposed 1886). Ontario Street, be-
     tween 20th and 21st Streets, Philadelphia.
According to the minutes of Philadelphia Monthly Meeting for the Northern
District (entry 33), Eighth month 24, 1886, the subject of a meeting
for the families of Friends who resided in the vicinity of Tioga was

proposed. At a meeting held the 23rd of 11th month, 1886, a committee
was authorized to purchase a lot on the south side of Ontario Street, between Twentieth and Twenty-first Streets, running through to Belleview
Street. The purchase price was listed in the expense account, which is
full evidence that the property was actually purchased at that time.
There is no record, however, of the ground ever being used for the accommodation of Friends. A meeting-house, where meetings for worship were
to be conducted, and a Friends' school, were both to have been erected on
the site. There is no record of a meeting ever being held in that section, but a school was conducted there for a period of 4 years, 1889-93.
At one time there were 80 scholars; only two or three of them were members
of the Society of Friends. The minutes mentioned a property leased for
the school. At one time school sessions were held in one of the rooms
of a carriage house. The fact that the property was leased is proof that
the school did not stand on the meeting's lot. In 1893, the school at
Tioga was placed under the care of the Select School Committee, who discontinued it in that year. On Twelfth month 5, 1894 there was an expense
item of the Select School committee for paying the carfare of three children from Tioga who were attending the Select School. In 1897 carfare
was paid for four children to go to Select School from Tioga. The minutes
of the Select School committee are missing from 1894 to 1897. The lot
of ground in Tioga, was sold in 1905 by the monthly meeting, without
ever having been used by the Society of Friends.

For minutes referring to the proposal of this meeting, <u>see</u> the
minutes of Philadelphia Monthly Meeting for the Northern District. For
minutes concerning the temporary school in Tioga refer to minutes of the
aforesaid monthly meeting 1886-93, from 1893 refer to the minutes of
the Friends' Select School Committee.

37. SOUTHERN DISTRICT MONTHLY MEETING, 1772-1872. Seventh Street
    between Locust and Spruce Sts., at the Southwest corner of
    Washington Square, Philadelphia.
Set up in 1772 by Philadelphia Quarterly Meeting (entry 2), upon the
recommendation of Philadelphia Monthly Meeting (entry 3). Each year the
membership of Friends in Philadelphia increased in numbers, and as times
went on they settled in the surrounding sections of what at first was
the center of the city. In 1770, the Philadelphia Monthly Meeting was
still the only monthly meeting existing within the boundaries of the
city, and its business had grown to such an extent that the establishment of another monthly meeting to relieve congestion became imperative.
Extra sittings became necessary to dispose of the increasing volume of
business loaded upon it by the increase in membership. Following 1770
the matter was constantly before the monthly meeting. In Fifth month
1771 the matter of establishing another monthly meeting was revived and
a committee of 20 Friends were appointed to confer together and consider the propriety of the proposal. The report relates to the manner
in which the Northern District Monthly Meeting (entry 33), and the Southern District Monthly Meeting should be established, and outlines the
boundaries of each. The section of the report referring to the boundaries
of the Southern District is as follows: "That all members of our Religious
Society not residing or who hereafter may dwell in houses bounded on the
north side of Walnut Street, and all the southward thereof, including
Southwark, the townships of Moyamensing and Passyunk, be deemed and considered members of a Monthly Meeting of Philadelphia for the Southern
District, and that it be held on the Fourth-day of the same week in which
our present Monthly Meeting is held." The matter was referred to the

quarterly meeting for concurrence, and at their meeting on the 4th of Fifth month 1772, Friends of the other five monthly meetings that made up the Philadelphia Quarter at that time, were appointed to confer with the representatives of the Philadelphia Monthly Meeting as to the advisability of establishing the two new monthly meetings. The committee presented a signed report in the Eighth month following, and the quarterly meeting then minuted a statement of its approbation as follows: "and being considered, the meeting concurred therewith, and, as hereby two other Monthly Meetings are to be established in the city of Philadelphia . . . ." The quarterly meeting did not appoint a committee to oversee the opening of these two meetings, but the Philadelphia Monthly Meeting directed the formalities.

The official title adopted for the Southern District Monthly Meeting was, the "Monthly Meeting of Friends of Philadelphia for the Southern District," and the time and place for holding the first monthly meeting of the newly formed organization is set forth in the following minute: "On the 25th day of the Eleventh month, being the fourth of the week, 1772, divers men and women Friends assembled in our meeting-house on Fourth Street (entry 11), being the first Monthly Meeting of Friends for the Southern District, appointed for the maintaining of the testimony of Truth and our Christian discipline, within the limits prescribed for the said Monthly Meeting . . . ." At this opening meeting it was ordered that the next meeting rot the Southern District be held in the Pine Street Meeting-house (entry 38). From the time of the first meeting in the Fourth Street Meeting-house until the erection of the one on Orange Street, all meetings of the Southern District were held in the Pine Street Meeting-house. The locality surrounding this meeting-house at that time, was called "Society Hill," and the meeting was often referred to as the "Hill Meeting."

In 1774 a plot of ground containing 3 acres and about 22 perches was purchased; bounded by Spruce and Locust and Seventh and Eighth Streets and the southwest angle of Washington Square. The lot was "L" shaped, and the exterior lines of approximately equal length. The property was acquired for use as a burial ground, and was purchased from the Penn family. The price fixed being £500, and 5 shillings a year quit rent. Owing to the decease of Thomas Penn in 1775, and the difficulties incident to the American Revolution, the title was not perfected until 1785. In the Eleventh month of that year a patent for the tract was issued by the Supreme Executive Council of Pennsylvania to James Pemberton and others, the grant being "for the purposes of a burial ground and other religious uses." The consideration finally paid was £719 8s. 8d. In 1788 a portion of the ground 100 feet frontage on Seventh Street and probably at the corner of Spruce Street, was enclosed and plotted for burial purposes. The residue of the lot was rented out at 12 pounds a year, most likely for a pasture field. The first interment, and probably the only one, seems to have been that of a child, and was made about New Year's Day, 1789. It became apparent that the ground was not suitable for burial purposes, because there was an underlying bed of clay which held the water and prevented it from seeping away. It was concluded however, to attempt to remedy the difficulty by digging a well 6 feet in diameter, in the center of that part of the lot which had been enclosed. This well was walled and arched over. But the plan was not successful, and the use of the ground for burial purposes was in consequence abandoned. This seems to have been as early as 1795, and a part of the lot, probably the Seventh Street front, was sold. This left a frontage on Spruce Street of 252 feet, which the monthly meeting directed to be disposed of in 1801.

In 1814 the plan of using a portion of this lot for a meeting-house site was first suggested, and the monthly meeting for the Southern District adopted it. Upon conferring with the other three monthly meetings, the Middle and Northern Districts readily gave their consent to the plan, but the newly organized Western District Monthly Meeting (entry 51), objected and declined to approve. The whole scheme was, in consequence, indefinitely postponed. In 1817 a partition was made between the monthly meetings of a considerable part of the real estate owned by them in common. This partition was not based upon an equal division of values, but rather on the exigencies of the different estates. A part of this arrangement was the conveyance to trustees for the Southern District of a lot of ground at the northeast corner of Eighth and Orange (now Manning) Streets, "for the purpose of procuring a site and erecting a new meeting-house," with the provision that if a new meeting-house were not erected and a meeting established in it within 15 years then the whole lot should again become the joint property of all the city monthly meetings. In 1821, the subject of building a meeting-house on this site was revived, and the Southern District Monthly Meeting which now had control of the lot, decided to sell the Eighth Street front, and it was estimated that the proceeds would be sufficient to defray the cost of erecting a new building of ample size, and enclosing the grounds with a brick wall. In accordance with this decision, the front on Eighth Street was sold for about $15,000, which left a lot about 140 feet square for the meeting-house site. The committee who had charge of making the sale was then instructed to prepare a plan for a house, with estimates of the probable cost. This committee reported in the Twelfth month 1822, a plan for the building similar in size and arrangements to the old one on Pine Street, and estimated the whole cost would not exceed $14,000. The subject received the further consideration of several succeeding monthly meetings, but it was finally decided "best not to proceed any further therein at this time." For some years no steps were taken toward the erection of the proposed new building.

After the division of the Society in 1827, the members of the Southern District Monthly Meeting who chose to follow the Hicksite branch, were temporarily joined to the group which first met in Carpenter's Hall and later on Cherry Street (entry 282). The majority of the members of the Southern District, however, remained in the Orthodox branch, and continued on in the Pine Street Meeting-house. Soon after the Separation the subject of building a meeting-house again claimed attention and in the Ninth month 1829, it was decided to provide materials for the proposed structure, and to have them deposited on the Orange Street lot. The monthly meeting in Second month 1832 proceeded with the building, and so rapidly did it progress that it was ready for occupancy on the first First-day in the Twelfth month 1832. The building was a commodious two-story, red brick structure, resembling the Cherry Street Meeting-house in its general appearance. Although called Orange Street Meeting-house, the entrance was on the southwest corner of Washington Square, on Seventh Street, the rear of the building facing the small street after which it was named.

In 1832 two Select Schools, one for boys and one for girls were established. The school for girls was first opened in the meeting-house of Friends of the Western District on Twelfth Street below Market, while that of the boys was opened in the Orange Street Meeting-house. These two schools after locating at various places over a period of 54 years, eventually merged in 1886 and formed the present Friends' Select School, and in that year moved to their present location on the Parkway. The

boy's school continued to be held in the Orange Street house until the
22nd of Second month 1841, when it was moved to a new school building,
erected for the purpose and situated on the south side of Cherry Street,
between Eighth and Ninth. There is no record of the Orange Street Meeting-house being used for school purposes after this time.

With the exodus of Friends to the more inviting sections of the city
and suburbs, the membership of the Southern District Monthly Meeting was
constantly diminishing, and by 1872 was reduced to such an extent that
its remaining members were not sufficient to sustain a monthly meeting.
An extract from the final minute explains that: "On considering the important changes now proposed, the necessity for which has chiefly arisen
from the very general removal of residents from the older part of the
city," a minute of the Philadelphia Quarterly Meeting, dated the 4th of
Eleventh month 1872, officially laid down the Southern District Monthly
Meeting. Its membership and property were transferred to the Philadelphia Monthly Meeting from which it had been set apart exactly 100 years
before. The monthly meeting for the Southern District convened for the
last time on the 27th of Eleventh month 1872.

The laying down of the Southern District Monthly Meeting, however,
did not terminate the usefulness of the Orange Street Meeting-house.
When this meeting was laid down, the quarterly meeting at the same time
authorized the establishment of an indulged meeting for worship to be
kept there, under the oversight of the Philadelphia Monthly Meeting.
This was for the accommodation and convenience of those members that
still resided in the neighborhood. This indulged meeting continued until 1909, when it was discontinued and the building sold (entry 12).

See: Matlack, op. cit., I, 516; George Vaux, "Orange Street Meeting-
house," The Friend, LXIII (1890), 404.

Minutes of Men's Meetings, 1772-1872, 8 vols.; Minutes of Women's
Meetings 1772-1872, 9 vols.; Minutes of Ministers and Elders, 1796-1872,
1 vols.; Registers of Births, Marriages, and Deaths, 1772-1872, 1 vol.;
Separate record of Births, 1772-1872, 2 vols.; Separate Record of Births
and burials, 1772-1872, 2 vols. (births 1777-1872); Marriage Certificates,
1773-1872, 2 vols.; Membership Lists, 1773, 1784, 1797, 1802, 1819, 1828,
6 vols.; Record of Interments, 1815-72, 4 vols.; Certificates of Removal (received), 1772-1872, 2 vols.; Certificates of Removal (issued),
1773-1872, 2 vols.; Treasurer's Cash Books, 1797-1823, 2 vols.; Finances
are recorded in the late minutes of the Monthly Meeting, at PPFYR.

38. THE PINE STREET MEETING, 1753-1835. South side of Pine Street,
     between Front and Second Sts., Philadelphia.

The Pine Street Meeting-house, or the "Hill Meeting," as it was called in
its early days, had its origin in a will by Samuel Powel, Jr., in which
he left to Philadelphia Friends a lot on "Society Hill," as a site for a
building. At the monthly meeting held on the 30th of the Eighth month
1747, an extract from the will of this Friend was read as follows: "and
I do hereby authorize and direct my executors to grant and convey unto
such person or persons as the Monthly Meeting of the people called Quakers
in Philadelphia, shall nominate, and to their heirs and assigns for ever,
60 feet of ground on the south side of Pine Street, and as near the middle
between Front and Second Streets as may be, and the whole depth of my
ground there, to build a meeting-house upon, if the members of that meeting shall agree to build a meeting-house there, and not else." The month-

ly meeting gratefully received the gift and referred the consideration
of building a meeting-house to a future meeting. However, no active steps
were taken for the erection of the proposed building until the Eighth
month 1752, when a committee was appointed to view the ground and to
collect the sentiments of Friends in relation to proceeding. Two months
later this committee reported that they had viewed the lot and thought
it a convenient place for a meeting-house, if 40 feet more on Pine Street
of equal depth with the original lot were added to it, and that Samuel
Powel the elder had engaged to secure this additional piece for the monthly meeting, it being the property of the children of his son Samuel. By
this addition the whole front of the lot on Pine Street would be 100 feet.
The committee also prepared a plan for the erection of a house 60 feet
long and 43 feet broad, exterior measurement, which they deemed of suitable dimensions to hold the yearly meeting, to accommodate which seemed
to be the principal inducement to undertake the work at that time. It
was also thought that the members might increase in numbers in the future,
and that it would be expedient to authorize a weekly meeting there. The
estimated cost of the proposed building was about ₤800, and at the time
the committee made their report, they had obtained subscriptions to the
amount of ₤724 10s. They decided that any needful sum in addition could
easily be raised among Friends. The children of Samuel Powel, Jr., being
minors, a difficulty occurred in relation to procuring a proper conveyance
of the additional 40 feet of ground which it was esteemed essential to
have in order to make the site devised by him available for meeting-house
purposes. This was finally arranged by Samuel Powel, Sr. (father of
Samuel Powel, Jr.), giving a bond in ₤600, that his grand-children should
make conveyance when they came of age, of two lots 20 feet wide each, on
the east and west sides respectively, of the 60 feet wide lot devised by
the latter to build a meeting-house upon. The elder Samuel Powel to
further insure the meeting in acquiring the two additional pieces of
ground, enjoined in his will that the grand-children (the devisees of his
son Samuel) should convey these lots to trustees to be appointed by the
meeting. This was to be done within 30 days after they respectively came
of age. Pursuant to these directions, the grand-children granted the two
side lots to the Trustees of the monthly meeting. In 1768, an additional
piece of ground to the eastward, 20 feet front and 102 feet deep was purchased from Samuel Powel and a bond given for ₤240, by Isaac Greenleaf,
James Pemberton and Samuel Wetherill on account of the monthly meeting,
in payment of the purchase money. This bond remained unpaid for many
years, but was finally settled in full in 1783 by the payment of the
principal and unpaid interest for some 4 or 5 years, then amounting to
₤295 4s. As late as 1814 a further addition was made on the south side
of the lot, increasing its depth 22 feet, for 60 feet eastward of the
west line, this making that part 124 feet deep from Pine Street. Possession of the two side lots first named was obtained at the close of 1752,
and at the same time it was decided to proceed promptly with the building,
so as to have it ready for occupancy by yearly meeting time (then held in
the Ninth month) in the following year. This was accordingly accomplished,
and the yearly meeting convened there, though the structure was not entirely completed.

The Pine Street Meeting-house was built of brick, the dimensions
as before given and occupying the full breadth of the lot devised by
Samuel Powel, Jr. The roof sloped towards Pine Street, but was also
hipped both at the east and west ends, and in some particulars the structure resembled in appearance the old Bank Meeting-house. The building
stood back from the street about 20 feet, and underneath it were com-

modious cellars. There were porticoes on the west, north and east sides,
over corresponding entrances. The interior was provided with youth's
galleries around three sides, the approaches to which were by stairways
at the north, west and northeast angles. The ministers' galleries, over
which was a "sounding board," was on the south side, the main body of
the meeting facing south. The women sat on the east side of the house.
A brick wall with two gates in it separated the grounds from Pine Street.
Evening meetings were opened the 27th of Twelfth month 1754 but does not
appear that day meetings were regularly held there for some time, as may
be observed by these minutes: "At a Monthly Meeting held in the Chamber
of our Great meeting-house in Philadelphia, the 24th day of Sixth month
1757, it is agreed that an afternoon meeting be held in the Pine Street
meeting-house, the first First-day of each month, during the summer season, no meeting at this house (Great Meeting-house) at that time." Again
on the 30th of Third month 1759: "It being proposed that a meeting be
held at the Pine Street meeting-house on First-day mornings during the
summer season, it is agreed to." Also on the 25th of Fifth month, "It
is agreed that while the work is being carried on at the Great Meeting
House /i. e. fitting pillars under the floor, and finishing the chamber,
so as to accommodate the Quarterly and other public meetings/, the First-
day meeting both morning and afternoon be held at Pine Street meeting-
house, and the First-day evening meeting at the Bank meeting-house."
Note also on the 12th of Third month 1761: "The meeting agrees that meetings for public worship may be held at Pine Street meeting-house on First-
days, morning and evening."

The first monthly meeting of Friends of Philadelphia for the Southern District, which ultimately occupied the Pine Street Meeting-house,
convened on Fourth Street below Chestnut (the present site of the Forrest
Building) on the 25th of Eleventh month 1772. At this opening meeting it
was agreed that a meeting for public worship should be held at the Pine
Street house on the fourth day of the week at ten o'clock in the morning,
and that the next monthly meeting should also be held in the Pine Street
house. At the same meeting a committee was appointed to confer with the
overseers of the Public Schools, with reference to the use of a part of
their school house, also on Pine Street, in which to hold either the men's
or women's monthly meeting. In the Third month 1773, a committee was
appointed to consider what steps should be taken to provide a proper
place to hold the monthly meeting and the following month they were desired to form a plan for a suitable building, make an estimate of the
expense and endeavor to obtain subscriptions for as much money as would
be necessary to build it. This committee produced a plan which was approved, and authority was given to proceed with and complete the work as
early as possible. A final report was made in the Twelfth month 1773,
that the additional room had been completed, and it appears then to have
been specifically appropriated for the purposes of the women's monthly
meeting. This room was about 40 feet square, and was erected as an addition to the south side of the original building. It communicated with
it by two doorways, one of which was between the galleries for the men
and women members. There was also an entrance on the east from the outside. Some changes were subsequently made as indicated by the following
minutes: "Eleventh month 26th, 1794, Thomas Hough being present and requesting the liberty of opening two windows in the west wall of his house
adjoining the lot eastward of the meeting-house in Pine Street, it is
agreed to, provided he always keeps fixed to the said windows blinds, so
as to prevent the exposure of the ground and yard belonging to Friends."
In 1802 "the same Friend having offered us the privilege of opening two

windows in the south and of the Women's meeting-house, for the admission of light and air, Thos. Hough and others are named to have it done, and procure from Thomas a proper deed of conveyance of said privilege."

During the prevalence of the yellow fever in 1798, the men's yearly meeting assembled in the Pine Street Meeting-house, Ninth month 24th, and after the time of solid deliberation concluded to adjourn to Twelfth. Several Friends, about 13 in number, of those who came to attend the yearly meeting contracted the fever and died, among them was Warner Mifflin. The yearly meeting was held continuously in this house, until 1802, when it was removed to the North House (Key's Alley Meeting-house). Thomas Scattergood, in his journal dated Fourth month 19, 1802 refers to the change: "The meeting on consideration very unitedly agreed to adjourn to the North House, in hopes that it will accommodate the meeting better than the present place of meeting . . . the Pine Street House." He again alludes to a change of place of holding the yearly meeting, in Fourth month 1811: "The Yearly Meeting for business was large. The two first sittings were held in the North House, where it had been held for some years; the afternoon sitting adjourned to meet in the morning of the 16th in the East House on Mulberry Street and Fourth Street, and the women took posession of the new one just finished on the West"; the Fourth and Arch Streets Meeting-house.

After the erection of the meeting-house on Orange Street in 1832, meetings were discontinued in the Pine Street house, except that a weekly evening meeting was held there until 1835, when it was given up. In 1836 the old house and lot were sold, but the contract was not executed. In 1841 it was sold again, but the purchaser refused to take it because of defective title. Subsequently ejectment proceedings were brought by the heirs of the younger Samuel Powel, against Henry Cope and others, trustees, in the Supreme Court. The judge directed a verdict for plaintiffs, reserving the right to modify the judgement, or to enter judgment for plaintiffs or defendants. The case was argued before the court at the December term, 1850, and the opinion of the court was delivered the following year by Judge Lowrie, confirming the title of Friends to the property. The title having thus been fully established, a sale was effected in the summer of 1861. The old building was removed and a row of six dwelling houses erected on the site.

See: Lippincott, Joseph, op. cit., p. 357; George Vaux, "Pine Street Meeting-House," The Friend, LXIII (1890), 260, 261, 268.

For minutes and other records, consult the minutes and registers of Philadelphia Monthly Meeting, and the Southern District Monthly Meeting.

39. CATAWISSA MONTHLY MEETING, 1796-1808. South Street, Catawissa, Columbia County.
Set up in 1796 by Philadelphia Quarterly Meeting (entry 2). Meetings were held in the one-story log meeting-house, which was erected by Friends of Catawissa Preparative Meeting some years prior to the establishment of this meeting. This meeting lasted only a few years, consequently, there is very little historical reference to it. The removal of many of the members prompted the merger of Catawissa Monthly into that of Muncy Monthly Meeting (entry 41) in 1808.

See: Michener, op. cit., p. 138; Matlack, op. cit., I, 345-349, 385-387.

Minutes of Men's Meetings, 1796-1808, 1 vol.; Minutes of Women's Meetings, 1796-1808, 1 vol., at PSC-Hi; Register of Births, 1791-1879, 1 vol., and Burial Records, 1795-1901, 1 vol. (Registers of Births and Burial records after 1809 are those of the Roaring Creek Monthly Meeting); Marriage Certificates, 1796-1802, 1 vol. (1802-8 missing), at PSC-Hi.

40. MUNCY PREPARATIVE MEETING, 1788-99.   Route 642, Pennsdale , Lycoming County.

Set up in 1796 by Catawissa Monthly Meeting (entry 39), after having functioned as an indulged meeting since 1788. The first meetings were held in a log schoolhouse, on the land of Samuel Wallis, the site of which is believed to have been between the present Reading Railroad cross-ing and the Susquehanna River, now part of the farm of H. G. Grannis. The foundation walls, which are still standing, show the schoolhouse was about 20 x 30 feet. It is said to have been the oldest place of worship in Lycoming County. The first meeting-house, a log building was erected sometime between 1783 and 1796, on or near the site of the present meeting-house of Muncy Monthly Meeting (entry 41). In 1797 Joseph Carpenter conveyed three acres of land, on which this meeting-house stood, together with all buildings thereon, in trust for the "Society of Friends." This Meeting functioned until Oct. 1799, when it was laid down and the Muncy Monthly Meeting was set up.

See: Mrs. Charles E. Ecroyd, "Notes Gleaned from the Early Records of the Friends of Monthly Muncy Meeting," Williamsport Sun, March 4-8, 1929; Charles E. Ecroyd, Earlier Days of the Muncy Monthly Meeting, (manuscript stored in private safe at PWmp, property of Lycoming Historical Society) Mrs. Charles E. Ecroyd, op. cit., hereinafter cited as Ecroyd, Earlier Days; Lycoming County, Deed Book, vol. 3, p. 194

41. MUNCY MONTHLY MEETING, 1799--.   Route 642, Pennsdale, Lycoming County.

Set up in 1799 by Catawissa Monthly Meeting (entry 39) with the approval of Philadelphia Quarterly Meeting (entry 12). The present natural color limestone meeting-house, was erected in 1799. In 1854 a schoolhouse, constructed of similar material, was erected nearby the meeting-house. In the neighborhood of this meeting-house there were several stations of the Underground Railroad. This meeting is also known as Pennsdale Meeting. Present clerk, Charles E. Ecroyd, 118 S. Main St., Muncy, Pa.

See: Ecroyd, Mrs. Charles E., op. cit., Earlier Days; Charles Ecroyd, On the Underground Railway (manuscript stored in private safe at PWmp, property of Lycoming Historical Society).

Minutes of Men's Meetings, 1799-1870, 3 vols., at PPFYR, and 1870-1921, 1 vol., in custody of Charles E. Ecroyd. Minutes of Women's Meetings, 1799-1921, 3 vols., at PPFYR. Minutes of Joint Meetings (1921-30 included in Minutes of Men's Meetings, 1870-1921), 1930--, 1 vol., in custody of Charles E. Ecroyd. Register of Marriage Certificates and Certificates of Removal, 1799-1882, 1 vol., at PPFYR. Register of Births, Memberships, and Deaths, 1799--; Certificates of Marriage and Removal, 1882--, 1 vol.; Burial Records, 1882--, 1 vol. (1799-1882 missing), in custody of Charles E. Ecroyd. Lycoming County Deed Book, vol. 3, p. 194; vol. 85, p. 442.

FISHING CREEK PREPARATIVE MEETING, 1795-1836. Millville, Columbia County.
Set up as preparative meeting in 1799 by Catawissa Monthly Meeting (entry 39), after having functioned as an indulged meeting since 1795, under
the care of Exeter Monthly Meeting (entry 24) of Berks County. A meeting-
house was built in Millville about 1795 and the right of holding services
was granted by Exeter Monthly Meeting. At a monthly meeting at Catawissa
in 1796, Jessie Haines and Jacob Clayton on behalf of Fishing Creek
Friends requested the continuance of this indulged Meeting. It was granted and William Ellis, Thomas Ellis, and John Hughes were appointed to
supervise the affairs of that group. A short time after the preparative
meeting was set up a new monthly meeting was established, Muncy Monthly
Meeting (entry 41). Fishing Creek Preparative Meeting was then transferred to the care of the newly established monthly meeting. At the time
of the Separation the meeting-house and burial ground were acquired by
the Muncy Monthly Meeting, Hicksite (entry 309), later called the Fishing Creek Monthly Meeting. At this time the Orthodox Friends laid down
this meeting as a preparative Meeting, and re-established it as an indulged meeting under Muncy Monthly Meeting. In 1836 Fishing Creek Indulged Meeting and Greenwood Indulged Meeting merged to form Greenwood
Preparative Meeting (entry 43). The Greenwood Preparative Meeting later
became an indulged meeting.

See: Matlack, op. ciu., I, 349-353.

There are no records available. Registers are in the records of
the various monthly meetings under whose care this meeting came during
its existence.

43. GREENWOOD PREPARATIVE MEETING, 1836. (Indulged 1795-1831,
1833-36). Rohrsburg Rd., 2 miles Northeast, of Millville, Columbia County.
Established as an indulged meeting about 1795 by Muncy Preparative Meeting (entry 40). When Muncy Monthly Meeting (entry 41), was set up in
1799, this meeting was transferred to the newly established monthly meeting. Greenwood Friends made an unsuccessful effort to become a preparative meeting in 1824. The Separation among the Friends of Columbia County divided the meeting into two small groups. The Orthodox meeting of
Greenwood was discontinued in 1831, but was revived in 1833 as an indulged
meeting, and soon became a prosperous meeting. Due to the absence of
definite information, the meeting-places from 1795-1835 are unknown but
were no doubt private homes. A minute dated Twelfth month 23, 1835 from
Muncy Monthly states, "Fishing Creek Preparative Meeting informs this'
meeting that taking into consideration the smallness of their numbers and
the apparent weakness of the two Greenwood and Fishing Creek meetings, we
are united in the belief it would be to the benefit of each meeting as
well as the Society at large for them to be attached, and constitute but
one meeting. In pursuance of the above consideration, they have selected
and purchased a plot of ground on which to build a meeting house, it being
centered between the two neighborhoods and request of this meeting to appoint trustees to receive the title for the said plot. Upon taking the
subject into solemn consideration, this meeting is united, and herewith
appoints David Masters, and Thomas C. Mendenhall, to receive the title
and trust for the use and benefit of members of the Society of Friends
comprising this Monthly Meeting." A further minute of Muncy Monthly
Meeting, held Second month 17, 1836, states: "The Quarterly Meeting of
Friends in Philadelphia concurs with the judgment of this meeting in the

propriety of uniting the two meetings of Fishing Creek and Greenwood,
so as to compose but one meeting, to be held in a house about to be
erected for that purpose, and further have appropriated the sume of $200
in aid of said building." The one-story, log meeting-house was erected
in 1836, and in the same year one acre of land was purchased and plotted
for a burial ground. Fishing Creek and Greenwood Indulged Meetings were
merged in 1836 to form the new Greenwood Preparative Meeting. Greenwood
Preparative Meeting was eventually laid down and was re-established as an
indulged meeting. However, due to the absence of records, it cannot be
established exactly when the meeting reverted back to its original status.
Judged by the size of the meeting-house, Greenwood Meeting, even in its
most prosperous days, was never very large. Yet it has a continuity in
the Society of Friends for more than a century.

   See: Matlack, op. cit., I, 364-69.

   There are no records available. Registers and notations are in the
records of the Muncy Monthly Meeting.

   44. PINE GROVE PREPARATIVE MEETING (Loyal Sock), 1797-1829. Quaker
        Hill, one and a half miles northwest of Warrenville, State Route
        973, Lycoming County.
Set up in 1821 as a preparative meeting by Muncy Monthly Meeting (entry
41), after having been set up by Catawissa Monthly Meeting as an indulged
meeting in 1797. The meeting was first granted permission to hold meetings for worship by the Catawissa Monthly Meeting (entry 39). The first
mention we have of this meeting being under Muncy Monthly Meeting is in
a minute of Twelfth month 18, 1799: "Request being made to this meeting
for the continuation of the Meeting at Pine Grove, heretofore held under
the care of the Catawissa Monthly Meeting, it is agreed that the same be
held as in time past, at the house of Nathaniel Pierson, until their
meeting-house can be so finished as to accommodate this meeting. Henry
Widderfield, George Webb, Joseph Carpenter, and William Ellis are appointed to the oversight of said Meeting and to sit with Friends there occasionally and extend such assistance as may appear useful and report of
their care herein Quarterly." About 1799 a one-story stone meeting-house
was erected on the land of Samuel Carpenter, located on what is now known
as Quaker Hill. In 1802 Samuel Carpenter conveyed three acres of ground
adjoining the meeting-house for the sum of five shillings to Jonathan
Willson and Moses Starr, in trust for the Society of Friends. This
conveyance specified that the land be for the use of the Friends and that
a portion be used as a burial ground. The preparative meeting flourished
for a few years but by 1828, because of insufficient membership and support, it became apparent that the meeting would have to be discontinued.
However, it was not until 1829 that Muncy Monthly Meeting finally laid
it down. The meeting-house gradually deteriorated. The burial ground was
sold by the trustees of Muncy Monthly Meeting in February 1937, to the
Qua ker Hill Cemetery Co., Inc., a privately-owned corporation.

   See: Matlack, op. cit., I, 378-83; Michener, op. cit., p. 139;
Ecroyd, Mrs. Charles E., op. cit.

   Minutes of men's and women's meetings are included in the minute
books of the Muncy Monthly Meeting. Registers are in the records of the
Muncy Monthly Meeting. Lycoming County, Deed Book, vol. II, p. 49.

45. ELKLAND PREPARATIVE MEETING, 1833 (Indulged 1804-9; 1816-33).
    Route #154, about two and a half miles east of Shunk, Sullivan
    County.
Set up in 1833 as a preparative meeting by Muncy Monthly Meeting (entry
41), after having functioned as an indulged meeting since 1804. While
the Friends of Elkland were not granted the permission of an indulged
meeting until 1804, the influx of Friends in Elkland Township occurred
several years prior to the establishment of this meeting. The nearest
meeting-house was that belonging to Muncy meeting, to which the Elkland
Friends were attached in membership and to which they had to travel about
20 miles. The following is recorded in the Muncy Monthly Meeting Minutes,
Fifth month 1804. "A request from the Friends of the new settlement in
the Beachwoods, called the 'Elklands', was produced expressive of their
desire of being privileged to hold a Meeting of divine worship on the
First-day of each week at the home of Jesse Haines until a house is pro-
pared for the purpose. The meeting fully uniting with the request it is
directed accordingly to be opened on the First-day preceding our next
Monthly Meeting, and to be continued for six months, under the care
of Benjamin Warner, William Ellis, Joseph Carpenter, Moses Lukens, Reuben
Lundy, and Abel Roberts; who are desired to attend the first opening
thereof, as well as extend a general care to the subject, and to report
as occasion may require." In 1805 James Ecroyd granted a plot of land,
on which to build a meeting-house, to the Elkland Friends. This building
erected in 1805 was within three miles of Eldreds Tavery and is described
as a one-story stone building with two windows, one door and a clumsy fire
place and chimney. It was afterwards used as a Sunday School building.
The meeting continued until early in 1809, when the following minute was
recorded in the minutes of Muncy Monthly Meeting: "First-month 1809
Friends appointed to the care of the meeting at Elkland, report that part
of their number have lately visited that meeting and Friends there appear
easy to have a discontinuance; with which this meeting unites, and dis-
continues it accordingly." In 1816 the meeting was revived through the
efforts of Joel McCarty and his wife, Ellen, who in 1819 became a Friends'
minister. The meeting was changed from that of an indulged to a preparative meeting in 1833 and remained as such until it was laid down in
1938. The present one and a half acre property was donated about 1852
by Thomas McCarty, the son of Joel and Ellen, in order that a meeting-
house might be erected and a cemetery plotted thereon. However, it was
not until 1854 that the present one-story, white frame meeting-house was
erected. The meeting was laid down in 1938 by Muncy Monthly Meeting and
the members were transferred to that meeting.

   See: Matlack, op. cit., I, 358-64.

   Minutes of men's, women's, and joint meetings, as also the registers
are in the records of Muncy Monthly Meeting.

46. EAGLE'S MERE INDULGED MEETING, 1893--. Lakeside Hotel, Eagle's
    Mere, Sullivan County, Pennsylvania.
Organized in 1893 by Friends from Philadelphia and West Chester. The
meetings are held from June to September in the north room of the Lakeside Hotel for accommodation of Friends who are on vacation, away from
their regular meeting places. Miss Catherine Ecroyd Kirk of Pennsdale,
is the present correspondent for this meeting. Friends of Eagle's Mere
report yearly to the Muncy Monthly Meeting (entry 41) at Pennsdale.

47. ROARING CREEK MONTHLY MEETING, 1814-27. Slabtown, South of Roaring Creek, Columbia County.
Set up in 1814 by Philadelphia Quarterly Meeting (entry 2), after having functioned as a preparative meeting under Catawissa Monthly Meeting (entry 39) since 1796. The one-story, wooden meeting-house was erected in 1796. However, it cannot be definitely established when the burial ground adjoining the meeting house, was acquired. Due to the absence of Historical data and records very little is known about this meeting. When the Separation occurred in 1827, the meeting was laid down and the meeting-house and adjoining burial ground was retained by the Roaring Creek Monthly Meeting, Hicksite (entry 303).

See: Michener, op. cit., pp. 140, 141; Matlack, op. cit., I, 353-57, 387, 388.

Minutes of Men's Meetings, 1814-47, 1 vol.; Registers of births and deaths 1791-1901: at PSC-Hi.

48. CATAWISSA PREPARATIVE MEETING, 1775-ca.1827. South Street, Catawissa, Columbia County.
Set up as a preparative meeting in 1794 by Exeter Monthly Meeting (entry 24) of Berks County. However, prior to 1794, Catawissa was established as an indulged meeting by the same meeting, although Friends had been holding meetings for worship as early as 1775, as shown by the following minutes from Exeter Monthly Meeting Fifth month 21, 1775: "Request being made to this meeting on behalf of a few friends who reside near Catawissa Creek in Northumberland County for the privilege of holding a Meeting for worship on the First-day of the week, . . ." the meeting granted an indulged meeting. The meeting was discontinued about 1780, according to the extract of a minute from Exeter Monthly Meeting, dated Seventh month 27, 1780: "The meeting at Catawissa on the frontier hath been dropt, some of those who attended being confined in prison and others drove from their habitation by the white inhabitants." Following this action the meeting must have been set up again either as an indulged or preparative meeting between 1780 and 1794, by Exeter Monthly Meeting, since the records of Exeter point to the existence of a preparative meeting in that year. Due to the absence of further historical data and records, the date of erection of the one-story log meeting-house cannot be definitely established. Several Friends historians give conflicting dates for erection of this house. However, all are agreed it was erected between 1776 and 1786. When Catawissa Monthly Meeting (entry 39) was set up in 1796, this meeting was transferred to the newly established monthly meeting. The monthly meeting at Catawissa lasted only a few years. Consequently, in 1808, Catawissa Monthly Meeting was merged with Muncy Monthly Meeting (entry 41), and the Preparative Meeting was then transferred to the care of Muncy Monthly Meeting. In 1814 when Roaring Creek Monthly Meeting (entry 47) was set up, Catawissa Preparative Meeting was transferred to the care of this monthly meeting. The Separation among Catawissa Friends occurred sometime after 1827. Due to absence of records it cannot be ascertained if the Orthodox Friends continued to conduct meetings after this date. The meeting-house and surrounding burial ground about three quarters of an acre were retained by the Catawissa Indulged Meeting of the Hicksite Friends (entry 305).

See: Michener, op. cit., p. 138; Matlack, op. cit., I, 345-349, 385-87.

Minutes of Men's Meetings, 1801-15, 1 vol., PSC-Hi. There are no
other records available. The registers and other notations are in the
records of the various monthly meetings, under whose care this meeting
was, during its existence.

49. ROARING CREEK PREPARATIVE MEETING, 1786-1827. Slabtown, South
of Roaring Creek, Columbia County.
Established in 1786 as a meeting for worship by Exeter Monthly Meeting
(entry 24). Meetings were conducted in members' homes from 1786-96. In
the latter year, Catawissa Monthly Meeting (entry 39) set up this meeting as the Roaring Creek Preparative Meeting. In the same year a one-
story frame meeting-house was erected; and a burial ground adjoining the
meeting-house was acquired sometime later. When Catawissa Monthly Meeting was laid down in 1808, this meeting was transferred to the care of
Muncy Monthly Meeting (entry 41). In 1814 Muncy Monthly Meeting requested
the Philadelphia Quarterly Meeting (entry 2) to establish a monthly meeting at Roaring Creek. This was a virtual re-establishment of the old
Catawissa Monthly Meeting under a new name. The request was granted and
in the same year Roaring Creek Monthly Meeting (entry 47) was set up, and
this preparative meeting was then transferred to the new monthly meeting.
When the Separation occurred in 1827, this meeting was laid down and the
meeting house and burial ground were retained by Roaring Creek Preparative Meeting, Hicksite (entry 306).

See: Michener, op. cit., p. 141; Matlack, op. cit., I, 353-357, 387,
388.

There are no minutes available at this time. Registers are in the
records of the Exeter Monthly Meeting, 1786-96; Catawissa Monthly Meeting
1796-1808; Muncy Monthly Meeting, 1808-14; and Roaring Creek Monthly Meeting, 1814-27.

50. BERWICK INDULGED MEETING, 1799-1827. Second and Mulberry Sts.,
Berwick, Columbia County.
Established in 1799 by Catawissa Monthly Meeting (entry 39). Various
religious bodies were early represented in Briar Creek Township. Among
the first to erect a house of worship were the Friends of Berwick. In
1799, a plot of ground was purchased and a meeting-house was erected
thereon shortly after. When Catawissa Monthly Meeting was laid down in
1808, this meeting was transferred to the care of Muncy Monthly Meeting
(entry 41) until 1814, when Roaring Creek Monthly Meeting (entry 47) was
set up and this meeting was then transferred to the care of the new
monthly meeting. When the Separation occurred in 1827, this meeting was
laid down and the meeting-house and ground were acquired by Berwick Indulged Meeting, Hicksite (entry 304).

See: Michener, op. cit., p. 139; Matlack, op. cit., I, 343-345;
Deek Book of Columbia County, vol. 7, p. 679.

51. WESTERN DISTRICT MONTHLY MEETING OF FRIENDS, 1814--. Twelfth
Street, south of Market Street, Philadelphia.
Set up in 1814, by Philadelphia Quarterly Meeting (entry 2). The West-
ern District Monthly Meeting of Friends, more frequently called the
"Twelfth Street Meeting," although not one of the primitive meetings,
holds a prominent place at the present day.

A brief abstract of the title to the ground upon which the meeting-

house now stands is as follows: 23rd of March 1681: "William Penn, Esp.,
Proprietary and Governor, sold to George Rogers and Francis Rogers of
Ireland, each, 2,500 acres of land to be laid out in the province of
Pennsylvania." In 1683, George and Francis Rogers sold their respective
interests to George Collett, who bequeathed his lands in Pennsylvania to
his two grandsons Nathaniel and Joseph Pennock. In 1787 a Deed of Partition was executed to Joseph Pennock, for "Lot of ground in Philadelphia, laid out and surveyed in the right of Francis and George Rogers,
in the city of Philadelphia." Sixth month 15, 1794, "Deed of Joseph
Pennock to George and Isaac Pennock for lot on High (now Market) and
Chestnut," Fifth month 27, 1809, "Deed of Isaac Pennock and wife to
Samuel Bettle, Joseph Scattergood (et al.), Trustees, for all that lot or
the west side of Twelfth Street between High and Chestnut, &c."

In the second month 1809 a committee of Philadelphia Monthly Meeting (entry 3) was appointed to take into consideration the present local
situation and general circumstances of Friends of this city, who recommended "a conference of the three Monthly Meetings on the subject." The
three monthly meetings in the city at that time were Philadelphia Monthly Meeting (entry 3); Northern District Monthly Meeting (entry 33) and
Southern District Monthly Meeting (entry 37). At the next Monthly meeting of the Western District the following minute was made: "The Philadelphia Monthly Meeting, having for some time past held their meetings
for worship and discipline in the house on Mulberry Street /present 4th
and Arch Streets meeting-house/, and the High Street house being thereby
of little use, we have agreed that the lot upon which it stands be laid off
in suitable building lots, and disposed of nearly agreeable to the following terms, viz: The present buildings on the ground to be reserved
to Friends, and taken down as soon as may be practicable. The proceeds
of the sale might be properly vested as follows: one-third in the purchase of ground so situated as may be most likely to be useful to Friends
of the Meeting in each district. Twelve thousand dollars, or more if
necessary, may, with the materials of the present High Street Meeting-
house, or the proceeds from the sale of them, be appropriated to the
erection of a meeting-house on some of the ground proposed, to be in the
middle district, so far westward as to accommodate the families of Friends
who may be resident in that quarter." In the same year a lot of ground
was purchased of Isaac Pennock and wife, on the west side of Twelfth
Street, between High and Chestnut Sts., containing a frontage on Twelfth
Street of 112 feet, and a depth of 132 feet. In the Third month 1811
the attention of Friends was directed towards the establishment of another
meeting, and a committee was appointed to consider the matter, who reported in the Fifth month following: "It is desired that Friends of the
three Monthly Meetings will promote the building of a meeting-house on
the lot of Twelfth Street, between Chestnut and High Streets, agreeable
to our present conclusions." Tenth month 29, 1812: "A meeting-house
having been erected agreeably to the conclusion of this Meeting in the
Sixth month of last year, on Twelfth Street, and nearly finished," a committee was appointed to consider the subject of opening a new meeting
there. The committee reported that, "they agree to propose that meetings
for worship be held there on the morning and afternoon of the First-days
of the week, to begin on the first First-day in Fourth month next," which
was approved by a minute of the quarterly meeting. Another record, dated
Third month 25, 1813 gives the following: "The committee to prepare the
house on Twelfth Street for the accommodation of a meeting report that
they have engaged William Pugh, at the rate of eighty dollars per annum,
to open the house and attend to preserving it clean and in order." There

were horse sheds at the back of the meeting-house, which long since have been taken down. Fourth month 29, 1813: "The meeting in the meeting-house on Twelfth Street was opened and held at the time agreed upon."

This meeting-house built in 1812 is still in use. It is a two and one-half story red brick building of the usual type of plain architecture, and with sloping roofs. A date stone, bearing the date of erection, is embedded in the east wall of the building. A high red brick wall with two large entrance gates, enclose the front of the property. The massive black beams, two of which are visible in the ceiling of the tea room on the second floor, are of pine, nearly 55 feet long. They were a part of the roof of the Great Meeting-house (entry 8). The fir: heating was by a charcoal furnace under the ministers' gallery, evidence of which still remains. The heat flues and wall registers have been closed up. In a later period a brick-set furnace was the heating system, after that a tubular warm air furnace was installed. Then came a hot water heater for the extension at the back. Gas was used for street lighting in the 1850's, but previous to that the house was poorly lighted for night meetings. It will be noted that the clips for hanging kerosene lamps, first used for candles, have been left in the balcony railing at the second floor level.

A minute of 1814 states: "it is agreed to propose to the judgment of the Quarterly Meeting, that a monthly meeting be held at Twelfth Street on the Fourth-day preceding the last Sixth-day, but one in the month." The foregoing is an extract from the minutes of Philadelphia Monthly Meeting, dated 27th of First month 1814, which was sent up to, and approved by the quarterly meeting the Seventh of Second month 1814. The first monthly meeting of Friends of Philadelphia for the Western District was held in the Twelfth Street meeting-house on the 16th of Third month 1814. In the early days the neighborhood of Twelfth and Market Streets, was a suburban community. Abram Liddon Pennock resided next door to the meeting-house at No. 4, S. Twelfth Street, on land later occupied by the William Penn Charter School. His home was a center of Abolitionist activity, and many prominent persons of the time were entertained there. John Greenleaf Whittier was a guest there on the night that Pennsylvania Hall was burned in 1838. Later, Friends of the section scattered, some located on Spruce, Filbert, and Arch Streets from about 13th to 20th Streets. Exodus away from the city was not in full swing until after the turn of the century.

Friends in 1832, decided to open schools of their own. These were to be separate and apart from the "Corporation," then in operation under the supervision of the "Overseers of the Public School;" an organization composed of Friends and chartered by William Penn about the time the city of Philadelphia was chartered. A school for girls was opened in the early part of 1832 in the meeting-house of the Western District Monthly Meeting on Twelfth Street, below Market, and one for boys was opened a few weeks earlier in the meeting-house of the Southern District Monthly Meeting on Orange Street. These two schools were the first of the select schools to be opened in Philadelphia, and are the forerunner of the present Friends' Select School (entry 410). The school for girls continued at the Twelfth street meeting-house until Eleventh month 6, 1834, when it was removed to the new school building on St. James' Street and Morris's Court, situated above Market, and between Sixth and Seventh. This building was built expressly to accommodate the girl's school. In 1861, another school was conducted in the Twelfth street meeting-house, in this

year two elementary schools for children of both sexes were started as
an adjunct to the Friends' Select School, one for the Northern District
in the Sixth and Noble Streets Meeting-house, and one for the Western
District in the Twelfth Street Meeting-house. This latter school was
opened under the tutorship of Rachel E. Balderston. In 1870 this primary school was removed to the Boys' school building on the south side of
Cherry Street, between Eighth and Ninth Street. It appears that another
school operated privately was conducted at the Twelfth Street Meeting-
house for a short time, between the time it was discontinued as the
girls' school and the time the primary school was opened there. Relics
of these old schools are still in evidence at the Twelfth Street Meeting-
house in the form of old hinged-top desks, much carved with the names
and dates of youthful Quaker pupils. Twelfth Street Meeting-house was
filled with Penn Charter boys every Wednesday morning during the school
term from about 1874 till the school moved to its present location on
West School House Lane in Germantown in 1925. During these years the
William Penn Charter School (entry 411), stood beside the Twelfth Street
Meeting-house. The old building of the school was demolished in 1928.

The first Sunday School among Friends in Philadelphia, but not the
first in the Yearly Meeting (see Exeter entry 24), was started in this
building in 1834. The school was discontinued after some years, but
again started in 1860. In the latter year the Friends' Sabbath School
Association was organized with Twelfth Street Friends as a nucleus.
Since this time a First-day school has been conducted here regularly,
until a few years ago when it was discontinued.

After the division in 1827, Friends of Western District Monthly
Meeting who wished to affiliate with the Hicksite group, joined Phila-
delphia Monthly Meeting, Hicksite (entry 280), and Green Street Monthly
Meeting, Hicksite (entry 287).

Friends Institute (entry 442) organized in 1880 as something of a
Quaker Social Club, maintains reading and committee rooms in the committee
building which adjoins the meeting-house. The second floor of this building is now given over to the use of the American Friends Service Committee
(entry 455). The committee building, a two-story red brick structure,
was erected by the Friends Institute, one story in 1892 and the other in
1909. The accommodations in the institute building being limited, the
meeting, in 1936 decided to make alterations to the second floor of the
meeting-house to enlarge the office space of the American Friends Service
Committee. The old youth's gallery was used, with some modifications and
light partitions, to provide for nine offices and a store room. This
allowed also for the committees on Education and Race Relations to have
suitable quarters. This required a different method of heating, the old
heaters being worn out, and as central plant heat with steam was available, it was decided to use it. Later it was extended to include the
meeting room, committee room and tea room.

Some of the important committees and organizations which meet here
are: the Forrest Trust, jointly under the care of committee appointed by
the Philadelphia Monthly Meeting and the Western District Monthly Meeting. The Friends' Select School (entry 410) at 17th Street and the Parkway, owned and operated jointly by Philadelphia Monthly Meeting at Arch
Street and the Western District Monthly Meeting on Twelfth Street; the
annual meetings of the Friends' Freedmen's Association; the Friends'
Temperance Association; the Women's Foreign Missionary Association; the
Indian Rights Association; and the Peace Committee.

The first burial ground belonging to Friends of the Western District Monthly Meeting was located on the present site of the Friends' Select School, on the Parkway from 16th to 17th Sts., and from the Parkway to Cherry Street. This graveyard known as the Sassafras Burial Ground, was acquired at an early date. Records of interment show burials there as early as 1823. The cemetery has not been used for burial purposes for over 50 years. About the year 1888, when some of the original school buildings were erected, some of the bodies were removed to other Friends burial grounds and the remaining graves were leveled and the grounds now serve as recreation grounds for the school. This cemetery was also known as the Friends Western Burial Ground. The second and present burial ground of Friends of Twelfth Street, also called Friends' Western Burial Ground, is located at Marshall Road and Powell Lane in Upper Darby, Delaware County. It was acquired by purchase in 1863, and is owned and conducted by the Western District Monthly Meeting of Friends. The grounds cover about 13½ acres. The first interment was in 1863. A two-story, frame dwelling, painted a redish brown color, serves as the caretaker's residence and is situated on the burial grounds, near the entrance gate on Powell Lane. This cemetery is not restricted exclusively to the use of Friends, but is also open to persons of other denominations, providing, however, they accede to the requirements of Friends that the person to be intered has been of reputable character, also that there be a plain, quiet, unceremonious burial, and that the restrictions regarding tombstones be rigidly adhered to. All stones placed there must be uniform in height and similar to the plain design in use by Friends. Present clerk, Horace M. Burton, 1022 Commercial Trust Building, Philadelphia.

See: Matlack, op. cit., I, 526; "Twelfth Street Meeting 125th Anniversary," Twelfth Street Meeting Message, June 1938, p. 1; Lippincott, Joseph, op. cit., p. 375.

Minutes of Men's Meetings, 1814-1920, 10 vols.; Minutes of Women's Meetings, 1814-1920, 10 vols.; Minutes of Joint Meetings, 1920-38, 5 vols., at PPFYR. Minutes of Joint Meetings, 1938--, 1 vol., in custody of the clerk. Minutes of Ministers and Edlers, 1814-1920, 3 vols., at PPFYR, and 1920--, 1 vol., in custody of Mrs. Edward Wildman, 4331 Osage Avenue, Philadelphia. Register of Births and Burials, 1814-1914, 2 vols., at PPFYR, and 1914--, 1 vol., in custody of the Recorder Walter W. Jacob, Glenwood and Lake Streets, Moylan, Marriage Certificates, 1914--, 1 vol., in custody of registrar of marriages, Mrs. Mary B. Newkirk, 119 E. Montgomery Ave., Ardmore. Membership List, 1814-1912, 6 vols., at PPFYR, and 1912--, 1 vol., in custody of Walter W. Jacob. Certificates of Removal (granted and received), 1814-1927, 5 vols., at PPFYR, and 1927--, 1 vol., in custody of Walter W. Jacob. Interment orders, 1823-98, 9 vols., at PPFYR, and 1898--, 2 vols., in custody of treasurer, James C. Butt, Girard Trust Co., Broad and Chestnut Streets, Philadelphia. Financial Records, 1814-1925 (information not obtainable), and 1925--, 2 vols., in custody of James C. Butt. Record of Burials, 1863--, 1 vol., (contains date of death, date of burial, location of plot); also one chart of cemetery showing the layout of all lots and the burials within each lot, at the residence of the caretaker and in his custody.

52. HESTONVILLE (MERION) INDULGED MEETING, 1865-ca.1887. Present site would be at Upland Way and 57th Street, Philadelphia. Set up in 1865, by Philadelphia Quarterly Meeting (entry 2), and attached to Philadelphia Monthly Meeting of Friends of the Western District (entry 51). When the membership of Radnor Monthly Meeting (entry 15), consist-

ing of Merion Preparative Meeting and Haverford Preparative Meeting (entries 16, 17), declined in 1865, to such an extent that a monthly meeting
was no longer warranted, the same was laid down in that year by Philadelphia Quarterly Meeting and the remaining membership was transferred to
Western District Monthly Meeting on 12th Street, below Market. Thus the
two preparative meetings became indulged meetings under the oversight of
the meeting on 12th Street. Merion Indulged Meeting was held in the
little meeting-house near Hestonville, previously occupied by it when it
was a preparative meeting (entry 18). The meeting at Haverford continued
as an indulged meeting until 1904, when it was set off as a Monthly Meeting, under the name of Haverford Monthly Meeting (entry 56). Merion was
continued as an indulged meeting under Western District Monthly Meeting
until about 1887, when it was laid down. Charles H. Browning in his
Welsh Settlement of Pennsylvania, states that the "Merion Meeting or Hestonville Meeting, as the Merion seceders' Meeting was known, was laid
down after the death of Henry Morris, who was one of the last survivors
of the seceders." The exact date of laying down this meeting is not
certain, but after many years of listing it in the Philadelphia City
Directories, the last listing to appear was that in the 1887 edition.
After the meeting ceased the building was used as a school-house, as it
was before it became a friends' meeting-house. The property was ultimately sold to the Pennsylvania Railroad and was demolished in 1918.
Just previous to its disappearance, it was photographed by Watson W.
Dewees of Haverford, Pa., who called it "Blockley," after the township
in which it stood. On June 17, 1897, it was photographed by Gilbert Cope
of West Chester, who called it "Merion Orthodox Meeting-house." Whereas
some have thought the Blockley Meeting-house and the Merion Meeting-house
were different buildings, a comparison of the two photographs show the
buildings to be one and the same structure. The Merion Meeting house
stood on a little eminence and it with the surrounding ground here is absorbed by the Pennsylvania Railroad Company. Being consigned to railroad
purposes, the earth was dug away to reduce it to a needed level. The
building was finally undermined, toppled over, and the material from it
was used for firewood.

See: Browning, op. cit., pp. 585-587; Matlack, op. cit., I, 487.

53. HAVERFORD INDULGED MEETING, 1865-1904. Buck Lane just south
of Lancaster Road, Haverford.
In 1865, due to the continuous decline in membership, Radnor Monthly
Meeting (entry 15) was laid down, and Haverford Preparative Meeting (en-
try 16) which was a part thereof was discontinued as a preparative meet-
ing. Its membership was transferred to Western District Monthly Meeting
(entry 51) in Philadelphia, and its meetings for worship continued at the
meeting-house erected in 1834, and situated on Buck Lane, Haverford.
These indulged meetings came under the oversight of Western District
Monthly Meeting, and continued until 1904 when the indulged meeting of
Haverford was set off as a monthly meeting of its own. See Haverford
Monthly Meeting (1904) (entry 56).

54. GREEN STREET MONTHLY MEETING, 1816-27. Southeast corner of
Fourth and Green Streets, Philadelphia.
Set up in 1816 by Philadelphia Quarterly Meeting (entry 2), upon recommendation of the Monthly Meeting of Friends for the Northern District
(entry 33). First meeting was held Sixth month 20, 1816 in the two-story
red brick meeting-house erected in 1813 by the Monthly Meeting for the
Northern District, and occupied by the preparative meeting of Friends held

at Green Street (entry 55) since 1814. In 1817 a library was provided
in the meeting-house building. In Second month 1818 a small two-story,
red brick school building was erected at the southeast corner of the
meeting-house grounds.

The history of the Separation in 1827 is a bit more closely connected with this meeting than with some others. Green Street Monthly
Meeting took the initiative by severing its connection with Philadelphia
Quarterly Meeting and joining Abington Quarterly Meeting (entry 174).
During the yearly meeting held in Fourth month 1827, large groups of the
followers of Elias Hicks held conferences in the Green Street Meeting-
house. The minutes of the Green Street Monthly Meeting show that there
were no disownments there, as was the case at other meetings. For those
members of Green Street Monthly Meeting wishing to remain in the Orthodox branch, certificates were issued, transferring them to the Monthly
Meeting of Friends for the Northern District. However, the great majority of the members chose to remain in the Hicksite branch, and only a
very few transfers were made. At the Northern District Monthly Meeting,
the majority chose to remain in the Orthodox membership, and certificates
of transfer were issued to the few desiring to join the Hicksite Friends,
transferring them to the Green Street Monthly Meeting.

The burial ground at Fair Hill was acquired by Green Street Monthly
Meeting in 1817 when Philadelphia Monthly Meeting (entry 3) which previously held all property belonging to Friends in Philadelphia as joint
property, made distribution of the same to the five Monthly Meetings
then existing. This burial ground, however, was not placed into use for
burial purposes till after the Separation. The first interment there is
recorded in the burial records in 1843. Members of the Green Street Meeting up to the time of the Separation, are recorded as being buried in the
Mulberry Street (Arch Street) burial grounds. The first burial there of
a Green Street member, being recorded in 1816.

See: Thomas H. Shoemaker, An Historical Account of Green Street
Monthly Meeting (manuscript in custody of Mary Shoemaker, 120 W. Tulpe-
hocken Street, Germantown); "Friends Stirred by Fate of Old Meeting House,"
Philadelphia Public Ledger, April 23, 1911.

Minutes of Men's Meetings, 1816-27, 1 vol.; Minutes of Women's Meetings, 1816-27, 1 vol.; Registers of Members, 1816-27, 1 vol.; Register
of Births, Deaths, and Burials, 1816-27, 1 vol.; Register of Marriages,
1816-27, 1 vol.; Certificates of Transfer, 1816-27, 1 vol.; Financial
records are incorporated in the minutes of the Monthly Meeting; all records listed are in safe at 45 W. School House Lane, Germantown, Phila.

55. GREEN STREET PREPARATIVE MEETING, 1814-27. Southeast corner
of Fourth and Green Sts., Philadelphia.
Set up in 1814 by Philadelphia Quarterly Meeting (entry 2), upon recommendation of the Monthly Meeting of Friends for the Northern District
(entry 33). Due to migration of Friends to other sections of the city,
the meeting-house of the Northern District located in Key's Alley (between Race and Vine, and Front and Second Sts.) was no longer large enough
to accommodate Friends for First-day meetings for worship. A minute of
this meeting during the year 1812 expressed this condition as becoming
intolerable, and it was proposed to build another meeting-house to the
north of the one then in use to relieve congestion. The site selected
was at the southeast corner of Fourth and Green Streets, whereon the two-

story, red brick building, enclosed behind high brick walls, was erected in 1813. Building expense was defrayed from part of the proceeds of the sale of the Great Meeting-house at Second and High Sts. The Green Street Meeting-house was ready for occupancy early in 1814, and meetings for worship were held there regularly from Fourth month 26, 1814 under supervision of the Northern District Monthly Meeting. This arrangement was continued until 27th of Ninth month of that year, when approval was obtained from the quarterly meeting to establish a monthly meeting as well as a preparative meeting at the Green Street house. However, Green Street Monthly Meeting (entry 54) did not take form till about 2 years later. The first recorded minute of the preparative meeting is under date of Twelfth month 23, 1814. Members living north of Callowhill Street were considered members of this meeting, while those living south of this street retained their membership at the Northern District Monthly Meeting, and attended meetings at the Key's Alley Meeting-house. The preparative meeting of Green Street came under the monthly meeting of the Northern District until 1816, when the Green Street Monthly Meeting was created; it then became a part thereof, and continued so until the Separation of 1827, when the preparative meeting was temporarily suspended. (See entry 288).

See: Lippincott, Joseph, op. cit., p. 342.

Minutes of Men's Meetings, 1814-27, 1 vol.; Minutes of Women's Meetings, 1814-27, 1 vol., in safe at meeting-house, 45 W. School House Lane, Germantown, Phila.

56. HAVERFORD MONTHLY MEETING, 1904--. Buck Lane, Haverford Twp., Delaware County.
Set up in 1904 by Philadelphia Quarterly Meeting (entry 2) for the convenience of the great number of Friends living in Haverford and vicinity. One hundred and thirty-nine Friends were transferred from Philadelphia Monthly Meeting of the Western District (entry 51), 12 S. 12th Street, Philadelphia, to Haverford Monthly Meeting. The two-story brown stucco building, used by this meeting, was erected by Radnor Monthly Meeting (entry 15) in 1834. The building, and the 2½ acres of ground of which a section 30 x 75 feet is used for a burial ground, was transferred to the meeting in 1904 by Philadelphia Quarterly Meeting. In 1913 the meeting erected a two-story brown stucco school building a few feet from the Meeting-house. The burial ground is enclosed by a stone wall. The present clerk of the meeting is William W. Comfort, Haverford, Pa.

Minutes of Joint Meetings, 1904-18, 2 vols., at PPFYR and 1918--, 3 vols., at PHC. Registers of Births and Deaths, 1918--, 1 vol. (1904-17 not available); Registers of Marriages and Membership, 1918--, 1 vol. (1904-17 not available), at PHC.

Component Meetings

(See: Explanatory Note 3).

	Date established	Entry number
UPLAND MONTHLY MEETING	1681	137
Upland Indulged Meeting	1675	139
Chester Indulged Meeting (Upland)	1675	139
CHESTER MONTHLY MEETING	1681	137
Chester Indulged Meeting	1675	139
Chester Preparative Meeting	1698	139
Chichester Indulged Meeting	1682	145
Darby Indulged Meeting	1682	149
Middletown Indulged Meeting	1686	160
Middletown Preparative Meeting	1701	160
Thomas Minshall Indulged Meeting	1686	140
Thomas Minshall Preparative Meeting	1698	140
Providence Preparative Meeting (Minshall)	1700	140
Springfield Indulged Meeting	1686	138
Springfield Preparative Meeting	1696	138
Newtown Indulged Meeting	1696	146
Newtown Preparative Meeting	1706	146
Goshen Indulged Meeting	1702	151
Goshen Preparative Meeting	1703	151
Uwchlan Indulged Meeting	1712	130
Uwchlan Preparative Meeting	1714	130
CHICHESTER MONTHLY MEETING	1684	143
Chichester Indulged Meeting	1684	
Chichester Preparative Meeting	1701	
Birmingham Indulged Meeting	1690	
Birmingham Preparative Meeting	1726	
CONCORD MONTHLY MEETING	1684	143
Concord Preparative Meeting	1684	144
Chichester Preparative Meeting	1701	145
Caln Preparative Meeting	1716	118
Birmingham Preparative Meeting	1726	155
Westtown Indulged Meeting	1799	158
DARBY MONTHLY MEETING	1684	148
Darby Indulged Meeting	1684	149
Darby Preparative Meeting	1701	149
NEW GARDEN MONTHLY MEETING	1718	72
Sadsbury Indulged Meeting	1723	119
Sadsbury Preparative Meeting	1725	119
Newberry Indulged Meeting	1734	343
London Grove Preparative Meeting	1724	84

Hempfield Indulged Meeting (Wright's Ferry)	1728	124
Leacock Indulged Meeting	1728	125
Leacock Preparative Meeting	1732	125
Warrington Indulged Meeting	1730	342
Lampeter Preparative Meeting (Leacock)	1751	125
GOSHEN MONTHLY MEETING	1722	150
Goshen Preparative Meeting	1703	151
Newtown Preparative Meeting	1706	146
Uwchlan Preparative Meeting	1714	130
Nantmeal Indulged Meeting	1739	132
Pikeland Indulged Meeting	1758	131
Willistown Preparative Meeting	1794	152
NOTTINGHAM MONTHLY MEETING	1730	351
Little Britain Indulged Meeting (Balance)	1745	354
Little Britain Preparative Meeting (Balance)	1749	354
(For other subordinate meetings and also for records of the monthly meeting, see Inventory of the Church Archives of Maryland)		
BRADFORD MONTHLY MEETING	1737	117
Bradford Preparative Meeting	1726	120
West Caln Indulged Meeting	1741	121
West Caln Preparative Meeting	1756	121
SADSBURY MONTHLY MEETING	1737	123
Sadsbury Preparative Meeting	1723	119
Hampfield Indulged Meeting (Wright's Ferry)	1728	124
Warrington Indulged Meeting	1730	342
Menallen Indulged Meeting	1733	345
Newberry Preparative Meeting	1738	343
Huntingdon Indulged Meeting	1745	346
Lampeter Preparative Meeting (Leacock)	1751	125
Lancaster Indulged Meeting	1753	126
Columbia Preparative Meeting (Hempfield)	1812	124
WARRINGTON MONTHLY MEETING	1747	342
Warrington Indulged Meeting	1730	342
Newberry Preparative Meeting	1738	343
Huntingdon Indulged Meeting	1745	346
Menallen Preparative Meeting	1748	345
York Indulged Meeting	1754	90
Huntingdon Preparative Meeting	1761	346
Yellow Breeches Indulged Meeting	1775	91
DEER CREEK MONTHLY MEETING	1760	Balto. Y. M.
Fawn Preparative Meeting	1792	357
(For other subordinate meetings and also for records of the monthly meetings see Inventory of Church Archives of Maryland).		
UWCHLAN MONTHLY MEETING	1763	129
Uwchlan Preparative Meeting	1714	130
Nantmeal Indulged Meeting	1739	132

Nantmeal Preparative Meeting	1781	132
Pikeland Indulged Meeting	1758	131
Jacob Thomas' Indulged Meeting	1779	57
Downingtown Indulged Meeting	1784	133
MENALLEN MONTHLY MEETING	1780	344
Warrington Indulged Meeting	1730	342
Newberry Preparative Meeting	1738	343
Menallen Preparative Meeting	1748	345
Huntingdon Preparative Meeting	1761	346

UWCHLAN MONTHLY MEETING (entry 129).

57. JACOB THOMAS' INDULGED MEETING, 1779-82. Pigeon Creek, Coventry Twp., Chester County.
The first mention we have of this meeting is taken from the minutes of the women's meetings of Uwchlan Monthly Meeting of Sixth month 10, 1779 (entry 129): "We are informed from the preparative meeting that our friend, Jacob Thomas, requests the liberty to hold an afternoon meeting sometimes at his house, which is now allowed by Men Friends to be held on the First and Third First-days in each month during the summer season to begin the 20th instant at the fourth hour, with which we have unity." A further minute, dated Fifth month 4, 1780, states: "We are informed from the Men's Meeting that Jacob Thomas desires to have an afternoon meeting at his home during the summer season which they have allowed to be held the First and Third First-days in each month, with which we concur. Rachel Beale, Mercy Baldwin, Mary Jones, Mary Lightfoot, and Hannah Milhous are desired to attend in company with men Friends appointed for that service and make a report to a future meeting." A minute, dated Fifth month 10, 1781, states: "The Friends appointed to take an opportunity in Jacob Thomas' family report that most of them attended and that it was their sense it would be best to allow them a meeting once a month during the summer, which being considered here, we, in conjunction with men Friends have agreed to." The next mention of this meeting is from a minute, dated Fifth month 9, 1782: "Nantmeal Meeting informs that Rebecca, the wife of Jacob Thomas, requests a certificate jointly with her husband to Exeter Monthly Meeting." On Eighth month 8, 1782 a minute states: "We are informed from Nantmeal Preparative Meeting that Rebecca Thomas renews her request for a certificate to Exeter Monthly Meeting jointly with her husband." However, it was not until Ninth month 5, 1782 that the certificate was granted and signed. There is no further mention of this meeting in the minutes of Uwchlan Monthly or Nantmeal Preparative Meeting. The meeting was probably laid down after Jacob Thomas and his wife received their certificates of removal from this meeting to Exeter Monthly Meeting in Berks County.

BUCKS QUARTERLY MEETING (0)

Component Meetings

(See: Explanatory Note 3)

	Date established	Entry number
FALLS MONTHLY MEETING	1683	162
Buckingham Indulged Meeting	1701	59
Buckingham Preparative Meeting	1705	59
Bristol Indulged Meeting	1707	60
Bristol Preparative Meeting (To Middletown MM)	1715	60
Bristol Preparative Meeting (From Middletown MM)	1715	60
Falls Preparative Meeting	1715	61
Middletown Preparative Meeting	1722	163
Plumstead Indulged Meeting	1727	164
Makefield Indulged Meeting	1750	69
Makefield Preparative Meeting	1790	69
Pennsbury Indulged Meeting	1814	62
Pennsbury Preparative Meeting	1818	62
Buckingham Indulged Meeting (Buckingham MM)	1898	167
NESHAMINY MONTHLY MEETING (Middletown MM)	1683	166
Southampton Indulged Meeting	1683	63
Wrightstown Indulged Meeting	1686	64
MIDDLETOWN MONTHLY MEETING (Formerly Neshaminy)	1706	166
Southampton Indulged Meeting	1683	63
Wrightstown Indulged Meeting	1686	64
Wrightstown Preparative Meeting	1722	64
Bristol Preparative Meeting	1715	60
Middletown Preparative Meeting	1722	163
Newtown Indulged Meeting	1815	70
BUCKINGHAM MONTHLY MEETING	1720	167
Wrightstown Preparative Meeting (To Wrightstown MM)	1722	64
Wrightstown Preparative Meeting (From Wrightstown MM)	1722	64
Plumstead Preparative Meeting	1772	164
Plumstead Indulged Meeting	1827	164
Landisville Indulged Meeting (Formerly Plumstead)	1836	164
Solebury Preparative Meeting	1806	67
WRIGHTSTOWN MONTHLY MEETING	1734	65
Wrightstown Preparative Meeting	1722	64
Newtown Preparative Meeting	1817	70

111

SOLEBURY MONTHLY MEETING	1811	66
Solebury Preparative Meeting	1806	67
MAKEFIELD MONTHLY MEETING	1820	68
Makefield Preparative Meeting	1790	69
Newtown Preparative Meeting	1817	70

58. BUCKS QUARTERLY MEETING, 1684-1898. Bucks County.
Set up in 1683 by Philadelphia Yearly Meeting (entry 1). It was agreed
at Philadelphia Yearly Meeting in 1683 that Falls Monthly Meeting (entry
162) should be divided into Falls Monthly Meeting and Neshaminy Monthly
Meeting. The name of the latter meeting was changed in 1706 to Middletown Monthly Meeting (entry 166). This division was made for the "ease
and benefit of the Friends' and it was agreed that "the said meetings
should meet together once every Quarter." In 1684 meetings were held in
the home of William Biles and others. This meeting continued to meet in
the homes of William Biles, Nicholas Waln, Richard Hough, Joshua Hoopes,
and others up to the year 1690, about which time it appears that meeting-
houses were built at the Falls and Neshaminy. Meetings were then held
alternately at the meeting-houses of the two monthly meetings, later circulating to other meeting-houses. In 1722 Wrightstown Preparative Meeting (entry 64) was set up under Middletown Monthly Meeting, and thereafter the quarterly meeting was sometimes held in Wrightstown. An additional meeting place was added when Buckingham Monthly Meeting (entry
167) became a part of the quarterly meeting in 1736. Solebury Monthly
Meeting (entry 66) was set up under this quarterly meeting in 1811 and
Makefield Monthly Meeting (entry 68) in 1820. In 1898 Bucks Quarterly
Meeting was laid down by Philadelphia Yearly Meeting. In the same year
the monthly meetings under the quarterly meeting were joined to meetings
of Burlington Quarterly Meeting in N. J. to form the Burlington and Bucks
Quarterly Meeting (entry 161). (See forthcoming Inventory of Church Ar-
chives of New Jersey).

   See: Woody, op. cit., pp. 128-148; Michener, op. cit., p. 74; Bowden,
op. cit., II, 248.

   Minutes of Men's Meetings, 1684-1873, 4 vols., at NNBN, and 1827-87,
2 vols., at PPFYR. Minutes of Women's Meetings, 1685-1868, 2 vols., at
PPF, and 1827-98, 2 vols., at PPFYR. Minutes of Ministers and Elders,
1683-1891, 2 vols., at NNBN, and 1827-98, at PPFYR. Financial records
are in the minute books. Registers of births and burials, 1680-1782, 1
vol.; Certificates of marriages, 1683-94, 1 vol.; at NNBN. Bucks County
Deed Books, vol. 25, p. 29; vol. 54, p. 251; vol. 111, p. 342; vol. 229,
p. 114.

FALLS MONTHLY MEETING (entry 162).

   59. BUCKINGHAM PREPARATIVE MEETING, 1701-ca.1858. Old York Rd.,
Rt. #263, Lahaska Village, Buckingham Twp., Bucks County.
Dr. James Streator, an English physician who never came to America, purchased five hundred acres of land from William Penn in Buckingham Township in 1700. In the same year he donated ten acres of this tract to the
trustees of Falls Monthly Meeting (entry 162) to be used by Friends of

Buckingham and on which a meeting-house and school were to be erected. It was also stipulated that a portion of the ground was to serve as a graveyard. A meeting for worship was established in 1701 by Bucks Quarterly Meeting (entry 58) and in 1705 Buckingham Preparative Meeting was set up by Falls Monthly Meeting. Sometime between 1705 and 1708 a log meeting-house was erected in what is at present a corner of the graveyard. A minute in Bucks Quarterly Meeting records for Third month 30, 1706 recommends to the Buckingham Friends that a schoolhouse be built on their land. Subsequent reports indicate that this was done soon thereafter. However, little is known of the location and history of this early log school. In 1729 Edmund Kinsey, whose land adjoined that of the meeting-house, donated five acres to this meeting and a portion of the newly acquired land was added to the burial ground. Between 1729 and 1732 the meeting-house was enlarged by a 20 x 20 feet stone addition. Joseph Kinsey donated eight-tenths of a perch of land in 1753, eliminating a small wedge in the graveyard, and with funds subscribed for that purpose in 1752 a stone wall was erected, encircling three sides of the burial ground. In 1768 the meeting-house was partially destroyed by fire and until the rebuilding was completed the following year, meetings were held in the meeting-house of the Plumstead Preparative Meeting (entry 164). Buckingham Friends returned to worship in the reconstructed two-and-a-half story native stone meeting-house in 1769. A two-story native limestone, Colonial style, schoolhouse was erected on the meeting-house ground in 1793. In 1805 the burial ground was enlarged to four and one half acres and in 1807 a small plot in the corner of the graveyard was set aside for interments of colored people. At the time of Separation in 1827, Buckingham Monthly Meeting, Hicksite (entry 197) retained all property and the Orthodox Meeting was then held in private homes until 1830. The Orthodox Friends purchased three acres of land one quarter mile east of the old site. On this ground was erected in 1830 a two-story native stone meeting-house. Due to the absence of records and historical data after this date, it cannot be definitely established when this meeting was laid down. However, a list of Orthodox meetings made in 1858 and deposited at 302 Arch Street, Philadelphia, lists this meeting as being in existence as late as that year.

See: Matlack, op. cit., I, 93-96; Michener, op. cit., p. 79; Bowden, op. cit., II, 248; Henry Chapman, "Reminiscences of Buckingham," Bucks County Historical Society Papers, I (1908), 143; John Bailey, "Thomas Ross, a Minister of the Society of Friends," Bucks County Historical Society Papers, I (1908), 283.

No records of this meeting are available. Registers are in the records of Buckingham Monthly Meeting. Bucks County Deed Books, vol. 33, p. 656; vol. 46, p. 271; vol. 56, p. 292; vol. 88, p. 574; vol. 89, pp. 160, 331; vol. 173, p. 104; vol. 176, p. 306; vol. 261; p. 637; vol. 417, p. 31; vol. 594, p. 236, 422.

60. BRISTOL PREPARATIVE MEETING, 1707-1889. Corner of Wood and Market Streets, Bristol, Bucks County.
Set up in 1715 by Falls Monthly Meeting (entry 162) after having the status of an indulged meeting since 1707. Meetings were held in the homes of Friends until 1713. In 1711, the Bristol Friends were given 19 perches of ground located on what is now the southeast corner of Wood and Market Streets, on which a two-story brick meeting house was erected in 1713. The burial ground of this meeting consisted of four acres of ground on Wood Street, between Walnut and Penn Streets, and was deeded to Falls

Monthly Meeting for the benefit of Bristol Preparative Meeting as a
"burial site for all families of Friends, also the poor, without price,"
by Samuel Carpenter, of Philadelphia. Today the burial ground is somewhat reduced in size by rights-of-way. It is used by Hicksite, Orthodox
and Primitive Friends. In 1756, the meeting-house was enlarged and a
second story added for the use and accommodation of a free school which
had been held in the meeting-house for some time. In 1793 John Pemberton
of Philadelphia deeded one-half acre and 17½ perches of land, at the corner of Walnut and Cedar Streets, to the trustees of the meeting "for the
benefit of a school under the care and direction of the Bristol Preparative Meeting." However, a schoolhouse was never erected on this site
while the Orthodox Friends were in possession of the property. In 1788,
the meeting was transferred from the Falls Monthly Meeting to the Middletown Monthly Meeting (entry 166). When the Middletown Monthly Meeting
was laid down in 1827 Bristol Preparative Meeting again came under Falls
Monthly Meeting. After the Separation, Bristol Preparative Meeting,
Hicksite (entry 215), retained all the property of the meeting. In the
same year Bristol Preparative Meeting erected a one-story brick meeting-
house at Wood and Walnut Streets. The membership of Bristol Preparative
Meeting diminished rapidly and in 1887 the property of this meeting was
conveyed to Falls Monthly Meeting, Primitive (entry 318). The latter
meeting sold the property to the trustees of the Italian Christian Church,
in Bristol. Bristol Preparative Meeting was laid down in 1889 by Falls
Monthly Meeting.

See: Bowden, op. cit., II, 248; Michener, op. cit., p. 78; Doron
Green, History of Bristol Borough Anciently Known as Buckingham, p. 46-49;
W. J. Buck, History of Bucks County, pp. 114-160.

Minutes of Men's Meetings, 1777-1804, 1822-27, 11 vols. (1715-77,
1804-21, 1827-89 missing), in vault of the Bristol Trust Co., Bristol.
Minutes of Women's Meetings, missing. Registers are in the records of
Falls Monthly Meeting 1707-1788 and 1827-89, and in the records of Middletown Monthly Meeting 1788-1827. Bucks County Deed Books, vol. 54, p.
390; vol. 233, p. 406.

61.   FALLS PREPARATIVE MEETING, 1715-1827. Intersection of Bristol,
Burlington, and Pennsburg Roads, Fallsington, Bucks County.
The existence of this meeting is problematical. It was supposed to have
been set up in 1715 by Falls Monthly Meeting, at which meeting-house its
meetings were held. Due to the absence of available documentary data its
history is obscure, and it is not clear whether the meeting existed as a
bona fide preparative meeting or whether it existed as a preparative
committee, whose duty was to prepare the business for the monthly meeting
sessions. There are two books of records, which, from their nature and
contents, might be the product of either of these two possibilities.
However, since these records seem to point to both men's and women's
meetings, it appears to be the better assumption that the meeting existed
as a preparative meeting.

See: Michener, op. cit., p. 75; Bowden, op. cit., II, 248.

Minutes of Men's and Women's Meetings, 1765-1842, 3 vols., at the
Newtown National Bank, Newtown.

62. PENNSBURY PREPARATIVE MEETING, 1814-64. 2 miles south of Morris-
    ville on Bordentown Ferry Road, Penn's Manor, Bucks County.
Set up in 1818 by the Falls Monthly Meeting (entry 162), after having
been an indulged meeting since 1814. Meetings from 1814-18 were held in
the homes of John Comfort, Joseph Taylor, and others. In 1818 1 3/4 acres
of land were purchased from William Crozer and wife by trustees, John
Comfort, Stephan Woolston, David Brown, and William Firman. The same
year a ½ acre plot was set aside as a burial ground and the first interment made. In 1819 a one-story brown-stone, meeting-house was erected
adjacent to the graveyard. The cemetery was temporarily enclosed with a
wooden fence. In 1861 the wooden fence was replaced by a stone wall.
In 1823 a week-day school was established and conducted in the meeting-
house. In 1858 a second-story was added to the meeting house for the
accommodation of the week-day school. Because of the diminishing membership the meeting was laid down in 1864 and the remaining members joined Falls Monthly Meeting. In the same year the meeting-house was leased
to the Falls Township authorities for use as a public school and the
burial ground was placed in trust of Falls Monthly Meeting. On Eleventh month 13, 1925 the surviving trustees of Falls Monthly Meeting conveyed to the School District of Falls Township, in consideration of $1,500
most of the grounds of the Pennsbury meeting. They reserved the privilege
of a right-of-way over the premises to and from the graveyard located on
the remainder of the plot owned and held in trust by the Falls Monthly
Meeting. The meeting-house was used as a school until 1933, when it was
sold and converted into a private dwelling.

See: J. H. Battle, History of Bucks County, Pennsylvania, p. 386;
Michener, op. cit., p. 76.

Minutes of Men's Meetings, 1818-64, 2 vols., Minutes of Women's Meetings, 1836-64, 1 vol. (1818-36 no meetings held), in Newtown National
Bank, Newtown. Registers are in the records of Falls Monthly Meeting.
Treasurer's Account Book, 1823-64, 1 vol. (1818-23 incorporated in first
vol. of Men's Minutes), in Newtown National Bank.

MIDDLETOWN MONTHLY MEETING (entry 166).

63. SOUTHAMPTON INDULGED MEETING, 1683-sometime after 1737, South-
    ampton, Bucks County.
Established in 1683 by Neshaminy Monthly Meeting (entry 166). Soon after
the settlement of the township (Southampton), the Friends of Southampton
requested to have a meeting settled among them, which was granted April
1, 1868, and a general meeting, once a week, was ordered at the home of
James Dilworth. Previous to that, Friends had met at private homes for
worship, and as they have never been strong enough in the township to warrant the erection of a meeting-house, they attended meetings elsewhere,
generally at Middletown and Byberry. It is impossible to establish whether or not this meeting ever progressed beyond an indulged meeting, because its history is very obscure. The little that is known about it
indicates that it was a small meeting. On Third month 2, 1737 Robert
Heaton, for the sum of ten shillings, conveyed to Richard Sands, David
Wilson Carter and Cuthbert Hayhurst, a piece of land in Southampton Township, comprising 40 square for the convenience and purpose of erecting a
meeting-house for worship and a school house for the education of the
youth. However, the buildings were never erected and the Southampton
Indulged Meeting was eventually laid down and its members were transferred to either the Middletown or the Byberry Meeting.

See: Bowden, op. cit., II, 248; Battle, op. cit., p. 483; William
W. H. Davis, History of Bucks County, Pennsylvania, I, 159. Bucks County
Deed Book, vol. 2, p. 242.

BUCKINGHAM MONTHLY MEETING (entry--).

64. **WRIGHTSTOWN PREPARATIVE MEETING, 1686-1870.** Durham and Penns
     Park Rds., Wrightstown Village, Bucks County.
Set up in 1722 under Middletown Monthly Meeting (entry 166) after having
held meetings for worship under Neshaminy Monthly Meeting, from 1686 until
1706 when Middletown Monthly Meeting was established. In 1684, John
Chapman and his family settled in the wilderness of this section and lived
in a cave until the following summer when another Friend, James Radcliff,
and his family, arrived. Early meetings were held in the homes of these
two Friends and in the homes of other Friends as they moved into the
neighborhood. Burials were made in a small plot on the Harker tract in
what was familiarly called "Log Town," now Penns Park. The number of
members grew so rapidly, that by 1690 they had a flourishing indulged
meeting under Neshaminy Monthly Meeting. John Chapman, who owned 5
acres of land in this section, gave 4 acres to the indulged meeting for
the site of a burial ground and meeting-house. A log meeting-house was
erected on this site in 1721, and the old burial ground in "Log Town"
abandoned. In the same year, with the size of the meeting still growing
Bucks Quarterly Meeting (entry 58) was petitioned with the request that
the Friends of this indulged meeting be allowed the privilege of a preparative meeting of their own. This request was granted and the first
preparative meeting held early the following year. In 1724 this meeting
was detached from Middletown Monthly Meeting and attached to Buckingham
Monthly Meeting (entry 167) under which they remained until 1734, when
the meeting was transferred from Buckingham Monthly Meeting to the newly
set up Wrightstown Monthly Meeting (entry 65). By 1735, the membership
had increased so markedly that the seating accommodations of the meeting
house were inadequate and a 20 x 25 feet stone addition was made at the
north end of the old log structure. In 1787 the original old log section,
at the south end of the meeting-house, was torn down and rebuilt of stone,
and at the same time a second-story was added to the building. After the
Separation, Wrightstown Preparative Meeting, Hicksite (entry 213), retained all the property and records. The orthodox meetings were held in
the home of Dr. Isaac Chapman, across the road from the meeting-house,
and in the nearby wagon shed of Johnathan Weston, until 1828. In that
year a one-story frame meeting-house was erected on a corner of the old
meeting-house grounds, and the first meeting in it was held on Fifth month
10, 1828. Although the Hicksite meeting controlled the burial ground,
the Orthodox Friends continued to use it. When Wrightstown Monthly Meeting was laid down in 1833, this meeting was again attached to the Buckingham Monthly Meeting. Wrightstown Preparative Meeting was laid down in
1870, and the frame meeting-house was razed in the same year.

See: Michener, op. cit., p. 80; Buck, op. cit., p. 67; Bowden, op.
cit., I, 248; Ruth's Scrap Books, vol. 5, p. 168 (at the Bucks County
Historical Society, Doylestown), hereinafter cited as Scrap Books.

Minutes of Men's Meetings, 1800-1829, 1 vol. (1722-99, 1830-70 missing); Minutes of Women's Meetings, 1820-26, 1871-86, 1 vol. (1722-1819,
1827-70 missing): at NNBN. Minutes of Joint Meetings, missing. Registers
are in the records of the Middletown Monthly Meeting, 1722-24; in the
records of the Buckingham Monthly Meeting, 1725-34; in the records of the

Wrightstown Monthly Meeting, 1834-70. Bucks County Deed Books, vol. 54,
p. 351; vol. 58, pp. 499, 504, 508, 510, 512; vol. 64, p. 552; vol. 117,
p. 244; vol. 181, p. 274; vol. 277, p. 288.

65. WRIGHTSTOWN MONTHLY MEETING, 1734-1833. Durham and Penns Park
      Rds., Wrightstown Village, Bucks County.
Set up in 1734 by Bucks Quarterly Meeting (entry 58). Meetings were held
in the small log meeting-house which had been erected in 1721 by Wrightstown Preparative Meeting (entry 64) while still worshipping as an indulged
meeting. By 1735 the meeting had grown to such proportions that it was
found necessary to make a 20 x 25 feet stone addition to the north end of
the old log structure. In 1788 the original old log section of the meeting-house was torn down and rebuilt with stone, and at the same time a
second story was added to the building. After the Separation Wrightstown
Preparative Meeting, Hicksite (entry 213) retained all the property and
records. The Orthodox meeting was held in the home of Dr. Isaac Chapman,
and in the wagon shed of Johnathan Weston until 1828, when a one-story
frame meeting-house was erected on a corner of the old meeting-house
grounds. Wrightstown Monthly Meeting was laid down in 1833 and the members joined to Buckingham Monthly Meeting (entry 167).

      See: Michener, op. cit., p. 80; Bucks, op. cit., p. 67; Bowden, op.
cit., I, 248; Scrap Books, vol. 5, p. 168.

      Minutes of Men's Meetings, 1734-1829, 1 vol., at NNBN, and 1827-33,
1 vol., at PPFYR. Minutes of Women's Meetings, 1734-1833, 3 vols., at
PPFYR. Financial records are incorporated in the minute books. Registers
of Births and Burials, 1716-1899, 3 vols. (1827-33 missing), at NNBN.
Certificates of Marriages and Certificates of Removals, recorded in volume
of Men's Minutes for 1734-88 (1788-1833 missing). Bucks County Deed Books,
vol. 54, p. 351; vol. 58, pp. 499, 504, 508, 510, 512; vol. 64, p. 552;
vol. 117, p. 244; vol. 181, p. 274; vol. 277, p. 268.

66. SOLEBURY MONTHLY MEETING, 1811-ca.1858. Junction of Sugan and
      Meeting House Rds., Solebury Twp., Bucks County.
Set up in 1811 by Bucks Quarterly Meeting (entry 58). Meetings were held
in the two-story, native brown stone building erected by the Solebury
Preparative Meeting (entry 67) in 1806. This meeting-house was on the
opposite side of the road from the 220 perches of ground which comprised
the graveyard. In 1811 a one-story native limestone schoolhouse, which
was also across the road from the meeting-house, was transferred to this
meeting by Buckingham Monthly Meeting (entry 167) which had erected it in
1793. After the Separation, Solebury Monthly Meeting (H) (entry 209) retained all the property with the exception of the former Buckingham Monthly Meeting schoolhouse, which was obtained by John Blackfan, an Orthodox
Friend and remained in his possession until 1840 when the Hicksites purchased the building from him. Solebury Monthly Meeting held meetings in
Friends' homes from 1827-30, when they erected a two-story frame meeting-
house. This building is located 300 yards north of the Hicksite meeting-
house and is today used as a private dwelling. History concerning this
meeting after 1830 is dim and obscure. When it was laid down is unknown,
but that it is today inactive is certain.

      See: The Centennial Anniversary of Solebury Friends Meeting, herein-
after cited as Centennial Solebury. Michener, op. cit., pp. 82, 83; Davis
op. cit., I, 234-237.

Minutes of Men's Meetings, 1811-39, 1 vol., at Newtown National Bank, Newtown, and 1827-29, 1 vol., at PPFYR. Minutes of Women's Meetings, 1811-29, 2 vols.; Minutes of Ministers and Elders, 1811-29, 1 vol., at PPFYR. Registers of Births and Deaths, 1811--, 1 vol. (1827-29 missing); Certificates of Marriage, 1813--, 1 vol. (1811-13 missing), in custody of H. Howard Paxon, Carversville, and 1827-29, 1 vol., at PPFYR. Certificates of Removal, 1811--, 1 vol. (1827-29 missing), in custody of Mrs. Marion E. Ely, Meeting House Rd., R. D. #1, New Hope. Bucks County Deed Book, vol. 54, p. 351; vol. 58, pp. 499, 504, 508, 510, 512; vol. 64, p. 652; vol. 117, p. 244; vol. 181, p. 274; vol. 277, p. 286.

67. SOLEBURY PREPARATIVE MEETING, 1806-27. Junction of Sugan and
     Meeting House Rds., Solebury Twp., Bucks County.
Set up in 1806 by Buckingham Monthly Meeting (entry 167). Meetings were held in the two-story native brown stone building which was erected the same year. When the Solebury Monthly Meeting was set up in 1811, this preparative meeting became a part thereof. A graveyard of 220 perches was laid out south of the meeting-house on the opposite side of Sugan Road. This meeting was laid down in 1827, and all the property retained by Solebury Monthly Meeting, Hicksite (entry 209).

See: Centennial Solebury; Michener, op. cit., pp. 82, 83; Davis, op. cit., I, 234-237

Minutes of Men's Meetings, 1806-46, 1 vol.; Minutes of Women's Meetings, 1806-83, 1 vol., at NNBN.

68. MAKEFIELD MONTHLY MEETING, 1820-27. Junction of Yardley, Dol-
     ington and Mt. Ayre Rds., 1/8 mile east of Dolington, Route 632,
     Bucks County.
Set off in 1820 from Falls Monthly Meeting (entry 162) by Bucks Quarterly Meeting (entry 58). Meetings held alternately between Newtown and Makefield. At the time of the Separation in 1827 the membership of the meeting were practically all followers of the Race Street (H) Branch. Therefore the Orthodox meeting ceased to exist at that time. This fact should be borne in mind when consulting the records, since the records run continuously through the period of separation. For that reason all known records are listed here, even though they belong to Makefield Monthly Meeting, Hicksite (entry 204).

See: Michener, op. cit., p. 83; Davis, op. cit., I, 435; Battle, op. cit., I, 445.

Minutes for Men's Meetings, 1820-95, 2 vols. (1896-1927 missing); Minutes of Women's Meetings, 1820-92, 2 vols. (1893-1927 missing); Register of Births, Deaths, Marriage Certificates, and Membership, 1819-1926, 1 vol. (1927 missing); Certificates of Removal, 1820-76, 1 vol. (1877-1927 missing); Financial Records, 1821-96, 1 vol. (1820, 1897-1927 missing), at NNBN.

69. MAKEFIELD PREPARATIVE MEETING, 1750-1827. Junction of Yardley,
     Dolington and Mt. Ayre Rds., 1/8 mile East of Dolington, Route
     632, Bucks County.
Set up in 1790 by Falls Monthly Meeting (entry 162), after having functioned as an indulged meeting since 1750. Met from 1750-52 at the home of Benjamin Taylor and Benjamin Gilbert. Meeting-house erected in 1752. In 1753 an additional 1 acre and 18 perches of ground, adjoining the meet-

ing-house, was acquired for use as a burial ground. The first school house, a one-story log building, was erected about 1755. In 1787 Makefield Friends erected on the meeting grounds, a two-story stone house for the accommodation of the schoolmaster. This building still stands and is the home of the present caretaker. In 1799 a new one-story school building was erected on the west end of the meeting grounds. In 1815 the school, which had been erected about 1755, was raised and replaced by a two-story stone building. In 1820 this meeting became a part of Makefield Monthly Meeting (entry 68) by a division of Falls Monthly Meeting. After 1827 this was a Hicksite meeting (entry 205), and the Hicksites retained the meeting-house, the original burial ground, and the school buildings.

See: Michener, op. cit., p. 83; Davis, op. cit., I, 435; Battle, op. cit., I, 445.

Minutes of Men's Meetings and Minutes of Women's Meetings, missing. Registers and financial records incorporated in the records of the Makefield Monthly Meeting.

70. NEWTOWN PREPARATIVE MEETING, 1815-ca.1829. Southeast corner Court and State Streets, Newtown, Bucks County.
Set up in 1817 by Wrightstown Monthly Meeting (entry 65), after having worshipped as an indulged meeting under Middletown Monthly Meeting (entry 166) since 1815. Meetings from 1815-18 were held in what was then the County Court House, 106 S. Court Street, Newtown. The present meeting-house erected in 1818 is a two-story, native limestone building, adjacent to a 4½ acre cemetery. In 1820 this meeting was attached to the newly established Makefield Monthly Meeting (entry 68). Following the Separation in 1827, the Hicksites retained the property and the few remaining Orthodox members had a temporary organization which was short-lived. They did not build a separate meeting-house and after the meeting became defunct, probably about 1829, the members joined with either the Wrightstown or Middletown Orthodox Meetings (entries 65-166).

See: Michener, op. cit., p. 83.

The records run continuously through the period of the Separation, and after 1829 are Hicksite records. Minutes of Men's Meetings, 1817-92, 1 vol.; Minutes of Women's Meetings, 1817-92, 5 vols.; Registers of Births, Marriages, Certificates of Removal, and Deaths, 1793-1880, 1 vol., transcribed from the records of Middletown, Wrightstown, and Makefield Monthly Meetings, at NNBN. Burial records, 1817--, 1 vol., in custody of H. Griffin Miller, 124 S. State Street, Newtown.

Component Meetings

(See: Explanatory Note 3)

	Date established	Entry number
NEWARK MONTHLY MEETING	1686	79
Kennett Preparative Meeting	1711	80
New Garden Preparative Meeting	1715	73
NEW GARDEN MONTHLY MEETING	1718	72
New Garden Preparative Meeting	1715	73
London Grove Preparative Meeting	1724	84
West Grove Indulged Meeting	1787	74
West Grove Preparative Meeting	1789	74
Fallowfield Indulged Meeting	1792	85
Spencer's Indulged Meeting	1813	75
Pennsgrove Indulged Meeting	1820	76
London Britain Indulged Meeting	1834	77
London Britain Preparative Meeting	1842	77
BRADFORD MONTHLY MEETING	1737	117
Bradford Preparative Meeting	1726	120
West Caln Preparative Meeting	1756	121
Marlboro Indulged Meeting	1799	81
Marlboro Preparative Meeting	1802	81
SADSBURY MONTHLY MEETING	1737	123
Sadsbury Preparative Meeting	1725	119
Lampeter Preparative Meeting (Leacock)	1732	125
Huntingdon Indulged Meeting	1745	346
Lancaster Indulged Meeting	1753	126
York Preparative Meeting	1767	90
River Indulged Meeting	1789	73
Columbia Preparative Meeting (Hempfield)	1812	124
WARRINGTON MONTHLY MEETING	1747	342
Warrington Indulged Meeting	1730	342
Newberry Preparative Meeting	1738	343
Huntingdon Indulged Meeting	1745	346
Huntingdon Preparative Meeting	1761	346
Menallen Preparative Meeting	1748	345
York Indulged Meeting	1754	90
York Preparative Meeting	1767	90
Yellow Breeches Indulged Meeting	1775	91
KENNETT MONTHLY MEETING (formerly Newark MM)	1760	79
Kennett Preparative Meeting	1711	80
New Garden Preparative Meeting	1715	73
Marlboro Preparative Meeting	1802	81
Kennett Square Indulged Meeting	1812	82
Kennett Square Preparative Meeting	1814	82

LONDON GROVE MONTHLY MEETING	1792	83
London Grove Preparative Meeting	1724	84
Fallowfield Indulged Meeting	1792	85
Fallowfield Preparative Meeting	1796	85
Doe Run Indulged Meeting (Derry Meeting)	1805	88
Bernard's School House Indulged Meeting	1818	86

FALLOWFIELD MONTHLY MEETING	1811	87
Fallowfield Preparative Meeting	1796	85
Doe Run Preparative Meeting (Derry Meeting)	1811	88

71. WESTERN QUARTERLY MEETING, 1758--. Harmony Road, West Grove, Chester County.
Established in 1758 by Philadelphia Yearly Meeting (entry 1) as a result of a division of Chester Quarterly Meeting (entry 136). Met at London Grove until 1827 and then alternately at West Grove, London Grove, and New Garden until 1903 when West Grove Preparative Meeting (entry 74) at Harmony Road, West Grove, rebuilt its meeting-house in order to accommodate this meeting. The present clerk is Lloyd Balderston, Colora, Md.

See: Michener, op. cit., p. 92; Morris Cope, Western Quarter (manuscript in safe at meeting-house).

Minutes of Men's Meetings, 1758-1899, 4 vols., at PPFYR, and 1900--, 2 vols., in custody of Mrs. I. W. Wickersham, West Grove. Minutes of Women's Meetings, 1758-1827, 2 vols., at PSC-Hi, and 1827-1919, 2 vols., at PPFYR. Minutes of Joint Meetings, 1919--, 2 vols., in custody of Mrs. I. W. Wickersham. Minutes of Ministers and Elders Meetings, 1763-1827, 2 vols. (1758-62 missing), at PSC-Hi, 1828-82, 1 vol., at PPFYR, and 1883--, 1 vol., in custody of Charles Canby, Landenberg. Minutes of Conference Meetings, 1780-87, 3 vols. (1758-79, 1788 missing), at PSC-Hi. Financial records, 1907--, 1 vol. (1758-1906 missing), in custody of treasurer, Edgar T. Haines, West Grove.

72. NEW GARDEN MONTHLY MEETING, 1718--. Harmony Road, West Grove, Chester County.
Set up in 1718 by Chester Quarterly Meeting (entry 136). Meetings were sometimes held at Nottingham (entry 351), which was transferred to Baltimore Yearly Meeting in 1819. In 1758, New Garden Monthly Meeting was transferred to Western Quarterly Meeting (entry 71). Meetings alternated between Nottingham and London Grove until 1792; then alternately between New Garden and West Grove until 1845 when it began to circulate to Mill Creek. At present it meets in West Grove Preparative (entry 74) Meeting-house. Present clerk, W. Herbert Haines, Chatwood, West Chester.

See: Futhey and Cope, op. cit., p. 238; Thomson, op. cit., p. 746.

The minutes run continuously through the period of the Separation. Minutes of Men's Meetings, 1718-48, together with Register of Births and Deaths, 1746-1906, 12 vols., at PPFYR, and 1906--, 2 vols., in custody of assistant clerk, Miss Bertha Balderston, Colora, Maryland. Minutes of Women's Meetings, 1718-1919, 5 vols., at PPFYR. Minutes of Joint Meetings, 1919--, 2 vols., in custody of Miss Bertha Balderston. Minutes of

Ministers and Elders, 1812-99, 2 vols. (1718-1811, 1866-82, 1900--, missing), at PPFYR. Minutes of Meeting for Sufferings, 1777-87, micro-filmed at PSC-Hi. Register of Marriage Certificates, 1704-1891, 3 vols., at PPFYR, and 1891--, 1 vol., in safe at meeting-house. Register of membership, 1718-80 incorporated in Register of Births and Deaths, 1880--, 1 vol., in custody of recorder, Edgar T. Haines, West Grove. Register of Births and Deaths, 1685-1886, 3 vols., at PPFYR, 1886--, incorporated in Register of Membership. Register of Certificates of Removal, 1781-1903, 2 vols. (1718-80 missing), at PPFYR, and 1903--, 1 vol., in custody of Edgar T. Haines. Financial Records, 1877-1913, 1 vol. (1718-1876 missing), in safe at meeting-house, 1914--, 2 vols., in custody of treasurer, I. W. Wickersham, West Grove.

73. NEW GARDEN PREPARATIVE MEETING, 1713-1928. Two miles south of
     Toughkenamon on Newark Rd., New Garden Twp., Chester County.
Set up in 1715 by Newark Monthly Meeting (entry 79) after having functioned as an indulged meeting since 1713. First meetings under Kennett Preparative Meeting (entry 80), with the consent of Chester Quarterly meeting (entry 136), were held in the home of John Miller in 1713. A log meeting-house was erected in 1715. In 1743 a red brick addition at the south end was built; in 1790 a north end enlargement was added. After the Separation in 1827 this building was retained by the Hicksites and the Orthodox meeting erected a small red brick meeting-house, and laid out an adjoining 90 x 100 feet cemetery on Newark Road, about a quarter mile from the former meeting-house. This meeting was laid down in 1928. The meeting-house was sold to private owners in 1938 but the cemetery was retained. It is under the care of the New Garden Burial Association, formed in 1914, which has sufficient funds in trust to maintain it. The Association renders a yearly report to New Garden Monthly Meeting (entry 72) and this report is incorporated in the monthly meeting minutes.

See: Futhey and Cope, op. cit., p. 236.

Minutes of Men's Meetings, 1901-24, 1 vol. (1713-1900 missing), in custody of Charles Canby, Landenberg, and 1916-28, 1 vol., at PPFYR. Minutes of Women's Meetings, 1864-1914, 1 vol. (1713-1863 missing), at PPFYR. Minutes of Joint Meetings, 1914-28, incorporated in the Minutes of Men's Meetings. Minutes of Ministers and Elders, 1812-64, 1884-96, 1916-28, 6 vols. (1713-1811, 1865-83, 1897-1915 missing), at PPFYR. Registers incorporated in the records of the New Garden Monthly Meeting.

74. WEST GROVE PREPARATIVE MEETING, 1787--. Harmony Road at U. S.
     Route #1, Chester County.
Set up in September 1789 by New Garden Monthly Meeting, after having functioned as an indulged meeting since 1787. In 1787 a brick meeting-house was erected and an adjoining 3½ acre plot was set aside for a burial ground. The land had been owned by William Jackson and was "given for the benefit and use of the people called Quakers, forever, and for a place of public worship of God Almighty, and to bury their dead in." Alterations and repairs were made to this building in 1858 and 1860, and in 1903 it was replaced by the present larger two-story red brick meeting-house. This house was built in order to accommodate Western Quarterly Meeting (entry 71), made up of New Garden and London Grove Monthly Meetings, which has met there since that time.

See: Michener, op. cit., pp. 98-99; Futhey and Cope, op. cit., p. 241; Heathcote, op. cit., p. 341; "West Grove Meeting House, Orthodox Friends," West Chester Daily Local News, May 28, 1928.

Minutes of Men's Meetings, 1846-1902, 2 vols. (1787-1845 missing) at PPFYR, and 1903-19, 1 vol., in custody of Mrs. I. W. Wickersham, West Grove. Minutes of Women's Meetings, 1870-1917, 2 vols. (1787-1869 missing), in safe in meeting-house. Minutes of Joint Meetings, 1902--, 1 vol. in custody of Mrs. I. W. Wickersham, West Grove. Registers incorporated in the records of the New Garden Monthly Meeting. Financial records, 1817-60, 1879-1914, 2 vols. (1787-1816, 1861-78 missing), in safe in meeting-house and 1915--, 2 vols., in custody of treasurer, Horace A. Moore, State Road near West Grove. Burial records, 1787--, 1 chart showing names of deceased and dates of deaths, in custody of Mrs. I. W. Wickersham.

75. SPENCER'S INDULGED MEETING, 1813-27. New London Twp., Chester
      County.
Established in 1813 by New Garden Monthly Meeting (entry 72) for the convenience of Friends of West Grove Preparative Meeting (entry 74), living in the lower part of New London Township. Meetings were held in a stone schoolhouse, which was erected some years previous to the establishment of this meeting. This schoolhouse and 3 acres and 7 perches of ground were donated to the meeting by Samuel and Mary Spencer. At the time of the Separation in 1827, this meeting was laid down by New Garden Monthly Meeting. The schoolhouse and grounds were retained by Spencer Indulged Meeting, (H) (entry 254).

      See: Michener, op. cit., p. 99. Deed Book Chester County, W-3, vol.
69, pp. 206, 208.

76. PENNSGROVE INDULGED MEETING, 1820-27. Penn Twp., Chester County.
Established in 1820 as an indulged meeting by New Garden Monthly Meeting (entry 72). Meetings were held in the home of Joseph Brown, Jan. 1820-Aug. 1920, then at the home of John Hambleton. After 1827 this was a Hicksite meeting, hence the Pennsgrove meeting came to an end as an Orthodox Meeting in 1827.

      Records and registers are to be found included in the records of New Garden Monthly Meeting.

77. LONDON BRITAIN PREPARATIVE MEETING, 1834-ca.1928. Rt. 896, on
      road from Newark to New London, London Britain Twp., Strickers-
      ville, Chester County.
Set up in 1842 by New Garden Monthly Meeting (entry 72) after having functioned as an indulged meeting since 1834. First meetings were held in the home of Richard Chambers, White Clay Hundred, in 1834. Later in this year the meeting purchased 1½ acres of land, upon which was erected the meeting-house, and an adjoining cemetery laid out. This meeting was laid down sometime after 1928 by New Garden Monthly Meeting and the members transferred to West Grove Preparative Meeting (entry 74). The meeting-house and the cemetery are in possession of New Garden Monthly Meeting. The graveyard is maintained by a committee appointed by the monthly meeting. A trust fund takes care in part of the expenses of maintaining the meeting-house and graveyard, the balance is met by voluntary contributions. Since being laid down, an appointed meeting is held once a year.

      See: Futhey and Cope, op. cit., p. 242.

      Information on minutes cannot be procured. Registers incorporated in the records of New Garden Monthly Meeting.

SADSBURY MONTHLY MEETING (entry 123).

    78. RIVER INDULGED MEETING, 1789-92. Located on the Susquehanna
River in Lancaster County. The exact location of this meeting
has been entirely lost. The minutes refer to it as the "Meeting at the River," meaning, without doubt, the Susquehanna,
since we know it was located in Lancaster County. It could
have been anywhere on the eastern side of the river, from Peach
Bottom to Bainbridge.
The meeting was established in 1789 by Sadsbury Monthly Meeting (entry 123)
and placed under the care of Lampeter Preparative Meeting (entry 125).
The only available history is taken from the minutes of the Sadsbury
Monthly Meeting. The first mention of the meeting is in a minute of April
22, 1789: "This meeting being informed by Lampeter report that those few
Friends at the River are in the practice of assembling themselves weekly
together with divers other persons who have heretofore had a right amongst
Friends in order to perform religious worship in different habitations in
other neighborhoods which subject we think claims the care of this meeting, and we therefore appoint . . . . to unite with Women Friends in visiting and conferring with them on the occasion and report of their situation to our next meeting." In a minute of June 17, 1789 it is stated:
"Agreed to allow Indulged Meetings on the first First-day in each month
on trial." Meetings for worship were continued until 1792 when the meeting was laid down by the Sadsbury Monthly Meeting. The minutes of January 22, 1794 state: "The case of the Friends at the River being resumed
the committee is left to their liberty as way opens to have a public meeting amongst them on First-days." From the foregoing minute it appears
that meetings for worship were continued for some time after the meeting
was laid down. However, due to lack of any further information the date
of the last meeting is unknown. There is no mention of a meeting-house
and undoubtedly the meetings for worship were held in homes of the members.

    79. KENNETT MONTHLY MEETING, (Newark) 1686-1938. Southeast corner
of Marshall and Cypress Streets, Kennett Square, Chester County.
Set up in 1686 by Philadelphia Quarterly Meeting (entry 2). In 1760, the
name of the meeting was changed from Newark to Kennett Monthly Meeting by
Western Quarterly Meeting (entry 71). Meetings were held in the meeting-
houses of the preparative meetings under its care. In 1938 this meeting
was laid down and its members were transferred to New Garden Monthly Meeting (entry 72).

    See: Michener, op. cit., pp. 93-95; Futhey and Cope, op. cit., p.
232; Thomson, op. cit., p. 747; Albert C. Myers, Immigration of the Irish
Quakers into Pennsylvania, pp. 125, 311-346, hereinafter cited as Myers,
Immigration; Walter H. Jenkins, Bi-Centennial of Old Kennet Meeting House,
pp. 29-32.

    Minutes of Men's Meetings, 1686-1839, 5 vols., at PSC-Hi, and 1827-
1908, 1 vol. (1908-11 included in the minute book of Joint Meetings), at
PPFYR. Minutes of Women's Meetings, 1760-1821, 1 vol., at PSC-Hi, and
1821-1911, 2 vols., at PPFYR. Minutes of Joint Meetings, 1911-38, 1 vol.,
in custody of Anna Wickersham, Marshall Street, Kennett Square. Minutes
of Ministers and Elders, 1856-80, 1 vol. (1686-1855, 1881-1938 missing),
at PPFYR. Register of births, 1686-1705 are recorded in the book of
Men's Minutes, 1686 and following, 1705-1831, 2 vols. (1831-85 missing),
at PSC-Hi. Register of Deaths, 1683-1732, are in minutes of Men's Meet-

ings, and 1732-1828, 2 vols. (1828-85 missing), at PSC-Hi. Certificates
of removals, 1751-67, 1 vol. (1686-1750, 1768-1885 missing), at PSC-Hi,
and 1905--, 1 vol., at PPFYR. Register of membership (copied in 1836),
dates uncertain, 1 vol.. in custody of Mary Thomas, 118 Lacey Street,
West Chester. Marriage certificates, 1692-1821, 2 vols. (1686-91 missing)
at PSC-Hi, and 1821-27, 1 vol. (1828-85 missing), in custody of recorder,
Ruth Yeatman, 320 West State Street, Kennett Square. Register of births,
marriages and removals, 1885-1938, 1 vol., in custody of Mary Thomas.
Chester County Deed Books, X-2, vol. 46, p. 523; H-3, vol. 56, p. 402;
Y-3, vol. 71, p. 143; Z-4, vol. 97 p. 6; X-7, vol. 170, p. 327.

80. KENNETT PREPARATIVE MEETING, 1707-1931. Kennett Square, Chester
County.
Set up in 1711 by Newark Monthly Meeting (name changed to Kennett Monthly
Meeting in 1760) (entry 79), after having functioned as an indulged meeting since 1707. Meetings were held in members' homes until 1710, when
the first meeting-house, a two-story stone building, was erected. At the
time of the Separation in 1827, this meeting-house and 4 acres of ground,
part of which was used as a burial ground, was retained by Kennett Preparative Meeting, Hicksite (entry 245). This meeting, however, continued
to use the meeting-house jointly with the Hicksite Friends until 1830,
when the meeting moved to Parkersville where a meeting-house, a brown
stone structure, was erected in 1830 on ground consisting of two tracts
of property; one, 67 perches, purchased from John Parker and his wife
Rebecca; the adjoining tract, 103 perches, purchased from Isaac Bennett
and his wife, Ann, on the same day. This property was deeded to the
Friends' Fiduciary Corporation (p.   ) in 1931. The meeting-house is now
used for a yearly appointed meeting, held under the auspices of the Extension Committee of the Philadelphia Yearly Meeting. In 1836 21 perches
of ground, opposite the west side of Parkersville meeting-house, were
purchased by John and Rebecca Parker. A schoolhouse was erected and a
school conducted by the preparative meeting. This property was sold to
William N. Parker in 1866. The 1½ acre burial ground at Parkersville is
surrounded by a stone wall on three sides and by an iron fence on the
fourth side. The meetings were held in Parkersville until 1888, when the
meeting place was changed to Kennett Square. Meetings were held in the
following places: Sharpless Manor (now Colonial Apartments), Taylor Hall
on Broad Street, and the Wickersham home on Marshall Street. In 1891 the
meeting was deeded a lot on the southeast corner of Marshall and Cypress
Streets, on which a red brick building was erected. This building was
deeded to the Friends' Fiduciary Corporation, in trust for Kennett Monthly
Meeting, in 1938. It is now used as a dwelling. The meeting was laid
down in 1931 by Kennett Monthly Meeting.

See: Futhey and Cope, op. cit., pp. 236, 302; Heathcote, op. cit.,
p. 339; "Old Kennett Meeting House," Philadelphia Friends Intelligencer,
August 20, 1910; "Kennett Meeting a Hundred Years Ago," Philadelphia
Friends Intelligencer, October 8, 1910; "Kennett Meeting of Friends,"
West Chester Daily Local News, February 2, 1891; "Friendly Worship for
200 Years," West Chester Daily Local News, September 29, 1910; "Old Par-
kersville Meeting Reopened," West Chester Daily Local News, June 2, 1919;
"Old Kennett Friends," West Chester Daily Local News, January 25, 1928;
"Parkersville," West Chester Daily Local News, January 3, 1931.

Minutes of Men's Meetings, 1828-1911, 1 vol.; Minutes of Women's Meetings, 1859-1909, 1 vol. (1828-58 missing); Minutes of Joint Meetings,
1914-31, 1 vol. (1911-13 in Minute Book of Men's Meetings, 1828-1913); at

PPFYR. Registers are in the records of the Kennett Monthly Meeting. Financial Records, 1847-1931, 1 vol. (1828-46 missing), in custody of Mary Thomas, 118 Lacey Street, West Chester. Chester County Deed Books, X-2, vol. 46, pp. 98, 523; E-4, vol. 77, pp. 142, 143.

81. MARLBORO PREPARATIVE MEETING, 1799-ca.1827. Marlboro, East Marlboro Twp., Chester County.

Set up as a preparative meeting in 1802 by Bradford Monthly Meeting, (entry 117), after functioning as an indulged meeting since 1799. Although this meeting was set up by Bradford Monthly Meeting, it was soon after attached to Kennett Monthly Meeting (entry 79). Previous to the erection of the one-story red brick meeting-house in 1801, meetings were held in Richard Bernard's schoolhouse, located in Newlin Township, one-half mile north of East Marlboro. In Second month 1801 this meeting purchased from Richard Barnard 2 acres and 15 perches of ground, and from Isaac Baily, 2 acres and 30 perches of ground, on which was erected the meeting-house, and a portion of the ground was plotted for a burial ground. As soon as the meeting was established, plans were made for the education of children and in 1803 a proposal was submitted for the erection of a schoolhouse on the meeting-house grounds. By 1804 this building, of stone construction, was completed. At the time of the Separation in 1827, all property of the meeting was retained by Marlboro Preparative Meeting, Hicksite (entry 246). After the Separation the history of the meeting is very obscure, and it is not clear where it met until it was laid down, sometime after the Separation, by Kennett Monthly Meeting.

See: Futhey and Cope, op. cit., p. 241; Thomson, op. cit., p. 753; Michener, op. cit., p. 96; "Marlboro Friends' Meeting," West Chester Daily Local News, June 21, 1930; "Friendly Story of Marlboro," West Chester Daily Local News, August 28, 1931.

Minutes of Men's Meetings, 1802-39, 1 vol. (1839-- missing); Minutes of Women's Meetings, 1802-65, 1 vol.: at PSC-Hi. Registers are in the records of the Kennett Monthly Meeting.

82. KENNETT SQUARE PREPARATIVE MEETING, 1812-27. E. State Street, Kennett Square, Chester County.

Set up in 1814 by Kennett Monthly Meeting (entry 79), after having functioned as an indulged meeting from 1812-14. Meetings were held in the home of John Phillips until 1813, when a plot of ground was purchased on which a white-washed stone building was erected. Seven members of the Center Monthly Meeting (entry 360) and 52 members of New Garden Monthly Meeting (entry 72) were transferred to New Kennett Square Preparative Meeting in 1814. The meeting was laid down in 1827.

See: Michener, op. cit., p. 96; Futhey and Cope, op. cit., p. 242; Thomson, op. cit., p. 754; Heathcote, op. cit., p. 341.

Registers are in the record books of the Kennett Monthly Meeting. Chester County Deed Books, Y-3, vol. 71, p. 242.

83. LONDON GROVE MONTHLY MEETING, 1792--. Two and one-half miles north of Toughkenamon on Newark Road, West Marlboro Twp. Chester County.

Set up in 1792 by Western Quarterly Meeting (entry 71). Meetings were held in the meeting-house of London Grove Preparative Meeting (entry 84). The meeting-house became unstable with age and it was agreed to demolish

it and erect another structure in its place. In 1818 a two-story meeting-
house of native stone was erected to replace the razed one. London Grove
Monthly Meeting agreed to pay one-third of the expense and Western Quarterly Meeting the balance of the cost. At the time of the Separation in
1827, the meeting-house and the surrounding 20 acres of ground, a small
portion of which had been used for a burial ground, were retained by
London Grove Monthly Meeting, Hicksite (entry 250). Meetings were then
held in members' homes until 1834, when the present one-story red brick
meeting-house was erected. This building was located on 1 acre and 20
perches of ground, purchased from Joel and Phebe Pennock for the sum of
$300, and a part of which was used for burials. The present clerk is
Evan B. Sharpless, Kennett Square, Pa.

See: Futhey and Cope, op. cit., p. 241; Woody, op. cit., p. 140;
Michener, op. cit., p. 100; 200th Anniversary Book of London Grove Meeting, hereinafter cited as 200th Anniversary London Grove.

Minutes of Men's Meetings, 1792-1834, 2 vols., PSC-Hi, 1827-47, 1
vol., at PPFYR, 1847-89, 1 vol., in custody of S. Sharpless, Kennett
Square, and 1890--, 1 vol., in custody of clerk. Minutes of Women's Meetings, 1792-1854, 2 vols., at PSC-Hi, and 1827-1912, 3 vols., in custody of
S. Sharpless, Kennett Square. Minutes of Joint Sessions, 1912--, are in
the 1890-- vol. of Minutes of Men's Meetings. Minutes of Ministers and
Elders, 1850-81, 1 vol. (1792-1849, 1882-95 missing), at PPFYR, and 1896-
1912, 1 vol., in custody of S. Sharpless, (discontinued after 1912). Register of Membership (made in 1830), 1 vol., at PPFYR. Certificates of Removals, 1792-1871, 1 vol., in the meeting-house of the London Grove Monthly Meeting, Hicksite, and 1827-91, 1 vol., in custody of S. Sharpless.
Marriage Certificates, 1792-1844, 1 vol. (1827-30 missing), in the meeting-house of the London Grove Monthly Meeting, Hicksite, and 1830-1909, 1
vol., in custody of S. Sharpless. Register of Births and Deaths, 1792-
1895, 1 vol. (1827-30 missing), in the meeting-house of the London Grove
Monthly Meeting,Hicksite, and 1830-83, 1 vol., S.F. P. Register of Births,
Deaths, Membership, Removal, and Marriages, 1883--, 1 vol. in custody of
recorder Evan B. Sharpless. Financial Records, 1889--, 1 vol. (1792-1888
missing) in custody of treasurer, Walter Sharpless, Kennett Square. Chester County Deed Books, Y-vol. 23, p. 42; B-3 vol. 50, p. 314; C-4 vol.75,
p. 178; K-4 vol. 82, p. 250; Y-6 vol. 146, p. 341; Miscellaneous Deed
Book #2, p. 538; P-12 vol. 287, p. 308.

84. LONDON GROVE PREPARATIVE MEETING, 1714-1907. Two and one-
      quarter miles north of Toughkenamon on Street and Newark Roads,
      West Marlboro Twp., Chester County.
Set up in 1724 by New Garden Monthly Meeting (entry 72), after having
functioned as an indulged meeting since 1714 under Newark Monthly Meeting
(entry 79). Meetings were held in the homes of members until 1724, when
the first meeting-house, built of logs, was erected near the site of the
present meeting-house used by London Grove Monthly Meeting (entry 83). The
original 20 acre property was granted in two lots of 10 acres each. The
southern 10 acres were granted Third month 4, 1722 by Tobias Collett and
company. The northern 10 acres were granted for the sum of 3 pounds on
Fifth month 24, 1733 by the executors of the estate of Henry Traviller.
This had been preceded by an article of agreement Fourth month 3, 1724,
between several Friends and Henry Traviller to purchase the 10 acres. However, it was not conveyed until 1732 and then by executors of Traviller's
estate. The original log meeting-house underwent two structural changes;
in 1743 a brick wing was added and in 1775 an addition was built to ac-

commodate Western Quarterly Meeting (entry 71), which had been sharing
the use of this meeting-house since 1758. The expense of the second addition was divided between the monthly meetings under Western Quarterly
Meeting. When London Grove Monthly Meeting was established in 1792, the
London Grove Preparative became a part. The meeting-house became unstable with age and it was agreed to demolish it and erect another meeting-house on the same site. In 1818 a red brick building was erected
replacing the razed one. London Grove Monthly Meeting agreed to pay one-
third of the cost and Western Quarterly Meeting the balance. At the time
of the Separation in 1827, this meeting-house and the surrounding 20 acres
of ground, a portion of which had been used for a burial ground, were retained by London Grove Monthly Meeting, Hicksite (entry 250). Orthodox
meetings were then held in members' homes until 1834, when the present red
brick meeting-house was erected by London Grove by Monthly Meeting. The
1 acre and 20 perches of ground, on which the building was erected, were
purchased from Joel and Phebe Pennock for $300. The membership of London
Grove Monthly Meeting and this meeting became identical so this meeting
was laid down by the London Grove Monthly Meeting in 1907.

    See: Futhey and Cope, op. cit., p. 237; Michener, op. cit., p. 100;
200th Anniversary London Grove.

    Minutes of Men's Meetings, 1776-85, 1847-80, 3 vols. (1724-76, 1786-
1826, 1881-1907 missing), in custody of S. Sharpless, Kennett Square, and
1827-47, 1 vol., at PPFYR. Minutes of Women's Meetings, 1847-1907, 2
vols. (1724-1846 missing), in custody of S. Sharpless. Registers are
in the New Garden Monthly Meeting from 1724-92, and 1792-1907 are in the
records of London Grove Monthly Meeting. Financial records, 1889--, 1 vol.
(1724-1888 missing), in custody of treasurer, Walter Sharpless, Kennett
Square, (this vol. for 1907-- contains only the financial records of the
London Grove Monthly Meeting). Account book of the "William Jackson
Fund," 1849-94, 2 vols., in the meeting-house of the London Grove Monthly
Meeting. Chester County Deed Books, Y. vol. 23, p. 42; B-3 vol. 50, p.
314; C-4 vol. 75, p. 178; K-4 vol. 82, p. 250; Y-6 vol. 146, p. 371; Mis-
cellaneous Deed Book #2, p. 538; P-12 vol. 287, p. 308.

    85. FALLOWFIELD PREPARATIVE MEETING, ca.1792-1890. One-eighth mile
         north of Ercildoun, Chester County.
Set up in 1796 by London Grove Monthly Meeting (entry 83), after having
functioned as an indulged meeting from sometime prior to 1792. The indulged meeting had been under the care of New Garden Monthly Meeting
(entry 72) until London Grove Meeting was set up in 1792 by Western Quarterly Meeting (entry 71). Meetings were held in the home of George Welsh
until 1794. In that year an acre of land in Ercildoun was purchased from
James Welsh and a log meeting-house was erected thereon. In 1797 an adjoining acre of ground was purchased from Matthew Welsh; in 1814, 107
perches of ground were purchased from Thomas Welsh. Meetings were held
in the log meeting-house until 1801, when a one-story brick meeting-house
was erected. When Fallowfield Monthly Meeting (entry 87) was set up in
1811 by Western Quarterly Meeting, Fallowfield Preparative Meeting became
a part of it. At the time of the Separation in 1827, this meeting-house
and ground were retained by Fallowfield Preparative Meeting, Hicksite (entry 243). From 1327-41 Fallowfield Preparative Meeting (Orthodox) again
met in the original log meeting-house erected in 1794. In 1841 1 acre
and 25 perches of land were purchased 1/8 mile north of Ercildoun and a
red brick meeting-house was erected. The 80' x 90' burial ground, which
is at present surrounded by a substantial stone fence, was included in

this purchase. Meetings continued here until 1890, when this meeting was
laid down by London Grove Monthly Meeting. The trustees of Fallowfield
Preparative Meeting sold the property (burial ground excluded) to Samuel
Ruth in April 1911.

See: Michener, op. cit., pp. 104, 105; Futhey and Cope, op. cit.,
p. 241; One Hundredth Anniversary of Fallowfield Friends Meetings.

Minutes of Men's Meetings, 1827-90, 6 vols. (1796-1826 missing),
in the custody of Mrs. Sue Sharpless, R. F. D., Kennett Square. Minutes
of Women's Meetings, 1823-27 (1796-1822, 1828-90 missing), included in the
1823-47 vol. of Minutes of Women's Meetings of the Fallowfield Preparative
Meeting (Hicksite), at PSC-Hi. Registers are in the records of the London
Grove Monthly Meeting. Chester County Deed Books, I-3, vol. 57, p. 465;
L-2, vol. 35, p. 6; 0-2, vol. 38 p. 300; V-4, vol. 93, p. 139.

86. BERNARD'S SCHOOL HOUSE INDULGED MEETING, 1818-27. One and one-
half miles east of Doe Run, West Marlboro, Chester County.
While London Grove Monthly Meeting-house was being erected in 1818, meetings for worship were held in the London Grove and Bernard School buildings. The ground of 20 perches on which the school building was erected,
was donated by George and Susanna Bernard in 1810, to three trustees, for
the purpose of erecting a schoolhouse for members of London Grove Meeting. After the new meeting-house had been erected, the Friends, who had
been meeting in the Bernard School requested the privilege of holding indulged meetings in the schoolhouse during the winter months. The permission was granted upon receipt of the request. Meetings continued to
be held in the school building until 1827, when the meeting was laid down
by London Grove Monthly Meeting. This schoolhouse was later called "West-
stone," and an attempt was made to sell it in 1867. However, it was not
disposed of for the want of a purchaser. There is no record of this
building ever being sold, and the disposition of the building cannot be
accounted for.

87. FALLOWFIELD MONTHLY MEETING, 1811-38. One-eighth mile north
of Ercildoun, on the Coatesville and Doe Run Rds., East Fallowfield Twp., Chester County.
Set up in 1811 by Western Quarterly Meeting (entry 71). Meetings were
held in the one-story red brick meeting-house of Fallowfield Preparative
Meeting (entry 85). This meeting interred its dead in the burial ground
of Fallowfield Preparative Meeting. In 1838, because the membership had
decreased to such an extent that it could not maintain a monthly meeting,
this meeting was laid down by Western Quarterly Meeting and its members
were attached to London Grove Monthly Meeting (entry 83).

See: Michener, op. cit., p. 103.

Minutes of Men's Meetings, 1811-34, 1 vol., at PSC-Hi, and 1827-38,
1 vol., at PPFYR. Minutes of Women's Meetings, 1811-53, 1 vol., at PSC-Hi,
and 1827-38, 1 vol., at PPFYR. Minutes of Ministers and Elders, 1829-38,
1 vol. (1811-28 missing), at PPFYR. Certificates of Removal, 1811-65, 1
vol. (1827-38 missing), at PSC-Hi. Register of births and deaths, 1824-
38, 1 vol. (1811-23 missing), in custody of Mrs. Sue Sharpless, London
Grove (in the back of this volume are the names of the Separatists).

88. DOE RUN PREPARATIVE MEETING (Derry), 1805-27. Intersection of
Rd. #15053 and #15055, Londonderry Twp. Chester County.
Set up in 1811, when Fallowfield Monthly Meeting (entry 87) was established, after having meetings for worship from 1805-8, and after having functioned as an indulged meeting under Fallowfield Preparative Meeting (entry 85) from 1808 to 1811. From 1805-8 meetings were held in the schoolhouse of London Grove Monthly Meeting (entry 83). In 1808 Joshua and
Mary Jackson donated 1 acre and 28 perches of land, upon which a red
brick meeting-house was erected in the same year. A burial ground was
also plotted. At the time of the Separation in 1827, the meeting-house
and burial ground were retained by the Hicksite Friends. The Orthodox
meeting was laid down in 1827, and the Friends joined with Fallowfield.

See: Futhey and Cope, op. cit., p. 68; Michener, op. cit., p. 105.

Minutes of Men's Meetings, 1822-34, 1 vol. (1811-21 missing), at
FSC-Hi. Burial Records, 1810-30, 1 vol., in custody of George Maule,
Gum Tree, Route #3, Coatesville. Register books are in the records of the
Fallowfield Monthly Meeting.

Component Meetings

(Only Meetings within the Commonwealth of
Pennsylvania are included here. See: Inventory of Church Archives of Maryland
also that of Virginia for remaining ones).

	Date established	Entry number
WARRINGTON MONTHLY MEETING	1747	342
Warrington Indulged Meeting	1730	342
Newberry Preparative Meeting	1738	343
Huntingdon Preparative Meeting	1761	346
Menallen Preparative Meeting	1748	345
York Indulged Meeting	1754	90
York Preparative Meeting	1767	90
Yellow Breeches Indulged Meeting	1775	91
MENALLAN MONTHLY MEETING	1780	344
Warrington Indulged Meeting	1730	342
Newberry Preparative Meeting	1738	343
Menallen Preparative Meeting	1748	345
Huntingdon Preparative Meeting	1761	346
YORK MONTHLY MEETING	1786	348

89. WARRINGTON-FAIRFAX QUARTERLY MEETING, 1776-1787.   Southern
     Pennsylvania, parts of Maryland and Virginia.
Set up by Philadelphia Yearly Meeting (entry 1) in 1776, and composed of
monthly meetings in Maryland and Virginia together with Warrington Monthly
Meeting of Western Quarter, in Pennsylvania. As early as 1774 the Yearly
Meeting appointed a committee to investigate and consider the establish-
ment of this quarterly meeting. The committee reported favorably in 1775
and in 1776 the yearly meeting wrote into its minutes that Warrington-
Fairfax Quarterly Meeting was allowed. This meeting continued until 1787
at which time it was divided into two quarterly meetings; Fairfax Quarter
composed of Hopewell, Fairfax, Crooked Run, Westland, and Goose Creek
Monthly Meetings, and Warrington Quarter, composed of Pipe Creek, Menallen
Warrington and York Monthly Meetings.

The records of this meeting will be found in the record book of Warrington Quarterly Meeting deposited in the vault of Baltimore Yearly Meeting at Park Avenue and Laureus Street, Baltimore, Md.

90. York Preparative Meeting, 1754-1786. 135 Philadelphia Street,
     York, York County.
Set up in 1767 as a preparative meeting by Warrington Monthly (entry 342),
of Western Quarterly Meeting. After the formation of York County in 1749,

a number of Friends moved to the town of York. Among them was John Day, who became the first President Justice of the County Courts. In 1754 an indulged meeting was organized under the Newberry Preparative of Sadsbury Monthly Meeting (entry 123). Due to the absence of records, the meeting place from 1754 until 1766 is unknown. In 1765 the meeting purchased from Nathan Hussey and his wife a plot of ground and during the following year the eastern part of the present meeting-house was erected and a portion of the ground was plotted for a graveyard. In 1773 a plot of ground adjoining the western side of the meeting-house was donated. However, it was not until 10 years later that the western portion of the meeting-house was erected on this ground. In 1784 York Friends requested that a monthly meeting be settled amongst them. It was not until 1786 that Warrington-Fairfax Quarterly Meeting (entry 89) granted this request, and York Monthly Meeting was set up at the same time York Preparative Meeting was laid down.

See: George R. Prowell, History of York County, Pennsylvania, II, 11; Matlack, op. cit., II, 925-929.

Minutes of Men's and Women's Meetings missing. Registers are in the records of the Warrington Monthly Meeting. York County Deed Books, vol. 2-G, p. 152; vol. 2-E, p. 238; vol. 3-D, p. 42.

91. YELLOW BREECHES INDULGED MEETINGS, 1775-84. Yellow breeches, Fairview Twp., York County.
Established in 1775 by Newberry Preparative Meeting. This meeting never had a meeting-house of its own. Meetings for Worship were conducted in the home of William Maulsby. Because many Friends left the community this meeting diminished in strength and it was finally laid down by Newberry Preparative Meeting in 1784.

ABINGTON QUARTERLY MEETING (O)

Component Meetings

(See: Explanatory Note 3)

	Date established	Entry number
ABINGTON MONTHLY MEETING (DUBLIN)	1683	93
Cheltenham Friends Meeting (Abington M M)	1917	94
Byberry Preparative Meeting (Pontquesink)	1701	107
Frankford Preparative Meeting (Oxford)	1701	109
Abington Preparative Meeting (Cheltenham)	1701	96
Germantown Preparative Meeting	1702	115
Horsham Indulged Meeting	1716	104
Horsham Preparative Meeting	1717	104
Stroudsburg Preparative Meeting	1811	111
Stroudsburg Indulged Meeting	1857	111
GWYNEDD MONTHLY MEETING	1714	96
Gwynedd Preparative Meeting	1698	97
Plymouth Preparative Meeting	1710	98
Exeter Preparative Meeting (Oley)	1725	95
Providence Preparative Meeting	1733	99
Maiden Creek Preparative Meeting	1735	94
Whitemarsh Indulged Meeting	1791	100
RICHLAND MONTHLY MEETING	1742	101
Richland Preparative Meeting	1723	102
Stroudsburg Indulged Meeting	1809	111
Stroudsburg Preparative Meeting	1811	111
HORSHAM MONTHLY MEETING	1782	103
Byberry Preparative Meeting (Poetquesink)	1701	107
Horsham Preparative Meeting	1717	104
Upper Dublin Preparative Meeting	1814	105
BYBERRY MONTHLY MEETING	1810	106
Byberry Preparative Meeting (Poetquesink)	1701	107
FRANKFORD MONTHLY MEETING	1815	108
Frankford Preparative Meeting (Oxford)	1701	109
Germantown Preparative Meeting	1702	115
Byberry Indulged Meeting	1827	110
Stroudsburg Indulged Meeting	1857	111
STROUDSBURG MONTHLY MEETING	1827	112
Stroudsburg Preparative Meeting	1811	111
Friendsville Indulged Meeting	1819	113
Friendsville Preparative Meeting	1822	113
GERMANTOWN MONTHLY MEETING	1906	114
Germantown Preparative Meeting	1702	115

CHESTNUT HILL (UNITED) MONTHLY MEETING   1924   330
(Controlled jointly with the Philadelphia
Quarterly Meeting of the Hicksite Friends).

92. ABINGTON QUARTERLY MEETING, 1786--. Meeting-house of German-
      town Friends: Coulter Street, west of Germantown Avenue, German-
      town, Philadelphia.
Set off from Philadelphia Quarterly Meeting (entry 2), in 1786, by Philadelphia Yearly Meeting (entry 1), upon the request of Philadelphia Quarter. Abington Monthly Meeting suggested this division in 1785. The Quarterly Meeting of Philadelphia since its establishment in 1682, had never
been divided until 1786, when the constituent monthly meetings forming it
had become so numerous that it was decided to establish another quarter
within its limits, in order to lighten the volume of business coming before it. The action of Philadelphia Yearly Meeting in the matter is set
forth in the following extracts from the minutes of that meeting in 1786:
"The minutes of the Quarterly Meeting of Philadelphia relative to the
institution of another Quarterly Meeting within the limits of that, and
the report of their committee thereon being read, obtained the solid attention and concurrence of this meeting. To attend the opening thereof,
the following Friends are named, viz., Robert Kirkbride, Oliver Paxson,
Eli Yarnall, Thomas Lightfoot, George Churchman, Thomas Pimm, Benjamin
Clarke, John Hoskins, William Jackson, Jr., David Cope, Mark Reeve,
Benjamin Shotwell, and Joseph Stackhouse. The said Quarterly Meeting to
be composed of the Monthly Meetings of Abington, Horsham, Gwynedd, and
Richland, and to be known by the name of 'Abington Quarterly Meeting.' "
The first meeting was held Fifth month 4, 1786. Meetings for a number of
years alternated between the meeting-house of the various constituent
meetings, but in recent years the quarterly meeting has been held continuously at the meeting-house which was built by Friends of the Germantown Preparative Meeting (entry 115) in 1869, and situated on Coulter
Street, just west of Germantown Avenue. The present clerk of the meeting
is Francis R. Taylor, 910 Girard Trust Building, 1400 South Penn Square,
Philadelphia.

      See: Matlack, op. cit., I, 29, 30.

      Minutes of Men's Meetings, 1785-1920, 5 vols.; Minutes of Women's
Meetings, 1827-1920, 4 vols.: at PPFYR. Minutes of Joint Meetings,
1921--, 1 vol., in custody of the clerk. Minutes of Ministers and Elders,
1827-1926, 4 vols., at PPFYR, and 1926--, 1 vol., in meeting-house.

      93. ABINGTON MONTHLY MEETING, 1683--. Jenkintown Road, east of
            Meeting House Road, Jenkintown.
Set up originally in 1683 by Philadelphia Quarterly Meeting (entry 2).
To trace the history of Abington Monthly Meeting to its source, it is necessary to refer to the minute of Philadelphia Quarterly Meeting, dated
Sixth month 1683, which establishes a First-day meeting for worship at
Tacony (Tookany), later called Oxford and still later Frankford. At the
same time it also established another at Poetquesink (later called Byberry), the two particular meetings to constitute one monthly meeting
(entries 107-109). The monthly meeting composed of and circulating between these two particular meetings continued in this manner until at a

monthly meeting held the 3rd of Tenth month 1683: "At the request of some Friends belonging to this meeting, a meeting was settled at Cheltenham at the house of Richard Wall." (entry 95). Meetings for worship were then held at the houses of Sarah Seary at Tacony, John Hart at Poetquesink and Richard Wall at Cheltenham, while the monthly meeting continued to alternate between the two original places only. This continued until 1686, when a monthly meeting held the 30th of First month, it is stated: "It is agreed that whereas it was ordered that ye Monthly Meeting should be held at three Several places: Byberry, Oxford and Cheltenham." The reference to Cheltenham in this minute is the first mention of a monthly meeting to be held in the vicinity of Abington. The monthly meeting when held at Cheltenham convened at the house of Richard Wall, but by a minute dated 31st of First month 1687, this was changed, viz: "It is agreed that the Monthly Meeting be kept at the house of Richard Worrel Junr. henceforward, on ye last Second-day of every Month.. ." The meeting for worship at Cheltenham, however, continued to be held at the house of Richard Wall. The first mention of a fourth particular meeting to function as a part of this monthly meeting appears in this same minute of First month 31st, 1687, when the meeting at Germantown for the first time is alluded to, although meetings for worship had been held at that place as early as 1683. The minutes herein referred to are called revised minutes, and are only extracts from the original ones. It is possible that the Germantown meeting may have been mentioned earlier in the original minutes, but in compiling the abstract copy this information may have been considered nonessential at that time, and therefore was omitted in the revised copy. In the later part of 1701 and the early part of 1702 the particular meetings of Oxford, Byberry, Cheltenham, and Germantown were established as preparative meetings.

In 1691 only two minutes of this monthly meeting contain any reference to the George Keith troubles. Abington was very little troubled during this period, and very little mention is made outside of its constituent meeting at Byberry, where John Hart became a follower of the Keithian movement, and the meeting for worship formerly held at his house was transferred to that of Henry English.

No mention is made in the revised minutes regarding the place where the monthly meeting was kept from the time it was appointed to be held at the house of Richard Worrel in Cheltenham in 1687, until 1702. It is possible that it may have alternated as before, and when held in Cheltenham convened at the house of Richard Worrel; however, according to tradition, an early meeting-house built of logs was erected sometime before 1699, and located at what is now Ashbourne Road west of Old York Road. An old burial ground is still in evidence at this place. The first authentic information regarding the building of a meeting-house appears Second month 5, 1697 when John Barnes came forward with his gift of land in Abington. Upon this land the first one-story stone meeting-house of Abington Friends was erected, but no record of its completion and placement into use appears until 1702. In the same minute of 1702 it is stated that the next monthly meeting was directed to be held at Abington, and it seems to be the entry where the monthly meeting was first called Abington. The meeting was often alluded to as the "Dublin Monthly Meeting," after the township of Dublin. This might have been more proper if it had been called "Dublin Monthly Meeting held at Cheltenham," but formalities of titles in those days seemed to be unimportant.

In 1688, the first protest against slavery was submitted by Friends of the particular meeting held at Germantown, to the monthly meeting at the house of Richard Worrel in Cheltenham. The document is lengthy and is written by Francis Daniel Pastorius, founder of Germantown. It was signed by several of the prominent pioneers of Germantown meeting, including Thones Kunders (Dennis Conrad) and the Op den Graeff's. The matter was discussed at the monthly meeting, but many Friends felt that it would be impracticable to free the slaves, and the meeting passed the protest to the quarterly meeting as too weighty a matter to decide. Subsequently it was sent from the quarterly to the yearly meeting, where it was allowed to rest.

After the meeting-house at Abington was placed into use in 1702, it appears that the monthly meeting continued to alternate among the various constituent meetings. In 1709 it was directed to be held at Byberry, but in 1710, a minute of the 24th of Fourth month states; "It is concluded that the Monthly Meeting be kept at Abington until further notice."

In 1716 a meeting for worship attached to Abington Monthly Meeting was allowed the Friends at Horsham, and in the following year this meeting was established as a preparative meeting. In 1772 Byberry Preparative Meeting suggested the setting up of another monthly meeting on account of the great volume of business of the Abington Monthly Meeting. This was not approved at that time, but 10 years later the matter was given definite consideration, and Horsham Monthly Meeting (entry 103) was established in 1782. This consisted of the preparative meetings of Byberry and Horsham. The same congestion of business was being felt by Philadelphia Quarterly Meeting, and in First month 1785 Abington Monthly Meeting suggested that a new quarterly meeting be established in that territory. This was approved by the quarterly and yearly meetings, and accordingly Abington Quarterly Meeting (entry 92) was established and Abington Monthly Meeting became a part of it. The first quarterly meeting at Abington was held on Fifth month 4, 1786.

Abington Monthly Meeting now consisted of Abington, Germantown, and Oxford Preparative Meetings. In 1805 the name of Oxford Preparative Meeting was changed to Frankford. In 1815 another monthly meeting was proposed to be set off from Abington, and in that year Frankford Monthly Meeting (entry 108) was established, consisting of the preparative meetings of Germantown and Frankford. Since that time Abington's own preparative meeting has been its only subordinate.

In 1786 it was decided to rebuild the east end of the old Abington meeting-house. This was accomplished, and ready for use in the early part of 1787. Again in 1797 the old west end of the building was in need of repairs, and the committee appointed to take the matter under its consideration, reported that it was their judgment that mere repairs to the building would not be sufficient, and recommended that the west end be rebuilt. This met with the approval of both Monthly and Quarterly meetings and complete rebuilding of what the minutes call the "western apartment of this house", was begun at once. In June the monthly meeting was shifted to Oxford, and was held there until October, while the reconstruction work was carried on. By the Eleventh month the house was again ready for occupancy and the monthly meeting met there on the 27th day of that month. No further extensive building took place until 1849, when remodeling of the meeting-house took place. In 1926 the Advancement Committee suggested to the monthly Meeting held on Eleventh month 26, that a new wing adjoining the older house at the west end be constructed. The building of this, however, was not started until 1929, and in the same year this addition was completed.

There is no reference in Abington meeting minutes relative to any of the doctrinal and personal controversies that precede the Separation of 1827. The majority of members, however, favored the Hicksite group. At the monthly meeting in Ninth month 24, 1827 a few Orthodox Friends in each of the men's and women's meetings arose and stated that they had assembled for the purpose of holding Abington Monthly Meeting. If they were not permitted to do so in this building, they would be obliged to withdraw and hold the meeting at the house of Daniel Fletcher, and this they proceeded to do. There is no reference to any of this in the minutes of that day, but a committee was appointed in December to consider the status of the Friends who had withdrawn. Upon their report in February a minute was made, reciting the facts of the withdrawal, and giving it as the sense of the meeting that these Friends could no longer be regarded as members of the meeting. The yearly meeting made a request, a few months later, for a corrected account of the meeting membership and for the Friends who withdrew. This report gives the total membership of the meeting at the time of the Separation as 584, and the members who withdrew as 47. In 1836 the Orthodox group built their present meeting-house, a small one-story stone structure, situated on Jenkintown Road, east of Meeting-house Road, in Jenkintown. The present meeting is called "Little" Abington Meeting, in order to distinguish it from the Hicksite meeting of the same name, and meetings have continued in the meeting-house erected in 1836, until the present day. In 1917 a group of Friends residing in the vicinity of Cheltenham, members of Abington Monthly Meeting, started holding meetings there, and in 1921 built their present meeting-house on Ryers Avenue (entry 95). At present meetings for worship are held at both houses, while the monthly meeting is held two times each year at the Little Abington Meeting-house, and 10 times at the meeting-house in Cheltenham.

In 1722 the minutes of Abington Monthly Meeting make the first of the very few of the early references to the Abington Friends School, for the maintenance of which the gift of John Barnes was partly made. This school reverted to the control of the Hicksite Branch of Friends in the Separation of 1827 (entry 175).

An old burial ground on the meeting-house property was maintained until 1827 and was at that time a part of the property retained by the Hicksite Branch. The orthodox meeting has no burial ground of its own but its burials are made at various places.

In 1686 it had been decided to hold separate business meetings of men and women Friends, "from time to time," for greater freedom of deliberation and expression. This was the beginning of the separate meetings, which continued for 217 years until 1903 when the custom was discontinued and "Joint Meetings" were adopted. The present clerk of Abington Monthly Meeting is Willard S. Hastings, 49 E. Church Road, Elkins Park, Pa.

See: Arthur H. and Ann R. Jenkins, "A Short History of Abington Meeting," Bulletin of Friends' Historical Association, XXII(1933) No. 2, p. 115; Matlack, op. cit., I, 7-37.

Minutes of Men's Meetings, 1682-1827, 8 vols., in meeting-house, and

1827-1903, 6 vols., at PPFYR. Minutes of Women's Meetings, 1773-1827,
4 vols., in meeting-house, and 1827-1903, 3 vols., at PPFYR. Minutes of
Joint Meetings, 1903-31, 1 vol., at PPFYR, and 1931--, 2 vols., in custody
of the clerk. Registers of Births, Deaths, and Marriages, 1885--, 1 vol.
(1828-50 destroyed by fire, 1851-84 missing), in custody of the recorder,
Catherine S. Ortlip, 119 Ryers Avenue, Cheltenham. Certificates of removal, 1828--, 1 vol.; Certificates of Marriage, 1835--, 1 vol., in custody of the recorder. Financial Records, 1921--, 1 vol., in custody of
the treasurer, Howard W. Ortlip, 119 Ryers Avenue, Cheltenham.

94. CHELTENHAM FRIENDS MEETING, 1917--.   521 Ryers Avenue, Chel-
     tenham.
This meeting was established in 1917 by Abington Monthly Meeting. It is
a modern meeting in the sense of being recently organized, and is not in
the direct line of descent of the old Cheltenham Meeting (entry 95) which
originated about 2 miles away at the home of Richard Wall in 1683. The
present meeting was founded for the benefit of Friends living in and near
the village of Cheltenham. For 3 years following its origin the meeting was held in the home of Francis R. Taylor, who was largely instru-
mental in founding it. Following this it met in Cheltenham Hall until
1921 when the new meeting-house was built. The meeting is one of the
two component meetings for worship belonging to Abington Monthly meeting
at the present time, the other being Little Abington Meeting.

The Meeting-house, erected in 1921, is a one-story frame building,
painted white. The benches now in use in it were brought from the old
Horsham meeting (entry 104) which was discontinued about the time this
meeting-house was built.

Records and registers of the Meeting will be found in the minutes
and registers of Abington Monthly Meeting.

95. ABINGTON PREPARATIVE MEETING, 1683--. Jenkintown Road east of
     Meeting House Road, Jenkintown.
The official origin of this meeting followed by 4 months that of Tacony
(Oxford-Frankford, entry 109) and Poetquesink (Byberry entry 107). The
three meetings are closely associated together and the history has been
outlined under the two former meetings and need not be repeated here.

In Tenth month 1683, 4 months after Philadelphia Quarterly Meeting
had set up a monthly meeting composed of the two meetings of Tookany and
Poetquesink, a monthly meeting of this recently constituted body was held
at the home of Sarah Seary, at Tookany. A minute from this session states,
"at the request of some Friends, a meeting was established at Cheltenham
at the house of Richard Wall, where a goodly body of Friends lived." This
is the origin at the Cheltenham-Dublin Abington meetings, as they were
subsequently and respectively designated.

Richard Wall came to Pennsylvania in 1682 and took up 600 acres of
land on the upper course of Tacony Creek, where he built a stone house
on the bank of the creek near what is now the junction of Old York Road
and Church Road. Monthly meetings continued to be held alternately in
this home until 1687 when for some, as yet undetermined reason, they
were moved to the home of Richard Worral. The assumption follows that
the meetings for worship were also moved at the same time. There is
little known of the history of this Meeting from 1686 to 1697. A small
burial ground on Ashbourne Road, west of Old York Road indicates that a

meeting-house once stood there. Gravestones indicate that this burial
ground was in use during this obscure period, and the location is probably the site of a log meeting-house which was used until the new house
was built.

On second month 5, 1697, John Barnes made a gift of 120 acres of
land to "Dublin" Monthly Meeting, "for and towards the erection of a meeting-House for Friends and towards the maintenance of a School." Barnes
also contributed ₤150 in money toward the project, as noted in a minute
dated in 1808. Plans for the new meeting-house were started at once.
Although the land had been given to "Dublin," more properly Oxford Monthly
Meeting as it was called at that time, it seems that the gift was made
more directly to Cheltenham Particular Meeting. This appears in the minutes of Philadelphia Monthly Meeting for Eleventh month 1697, to which
the Cheltenham Friends had appealed for financial aid. It is here stated;
"Whereas the last meeting agreed that ₤20 should be lent out of the Meeting Stock to Cheltenham /sic/ friends to help them in building a meeting-
house. This Meeting upon further consideration agrees, that a collection
be made by way of a subscription for that service, and if it do not arise
to ₤20, then this Monthly Meeting to make it up out of the meeting stock,
and if it arises to more than ₤20 they are to have it." This house was
located at the corner of what is now east Greenwood Avenue, and Meeting
House Road, Jenkintown. Just when the new building was begun is not known
but it was slow in starting, and was probably not under way until early
1700. The first monthly meeting held in it was that of Second month 1702.
Whatever business meetings were held by the local meeting were no doubt
held in the new meeting-house after 1702.

It was not until 1698 that local meetings for business or preparative meetings were allowed by the yearly meeting. Previous to this they
were called particular meetings. No documentary evidence is available for
the exact date of the establishment of Abington Preparative Meeting, but
since the other two meetings of the Abington Monthly Meeting trilogy
(Tacony and Poetquesink) were set up as preparative meetings in 1701,
and because of the close association of these three meetings it is strongly probable that Abington Preparative Meeting was established at the same
time.   In 1785 when Abington Quarterly Meeting (entry 92) was set up
Abington Monthly and likewise Abington Preparative Meeting became a part
thereof. In 1815 Frankford Monthly Meeting was established with Germantown and Frankford Preparative meetings as its subordinate units, thus
leaving Abington Preparative Meeting as the sole subordinate meeting under
Abington Monthly Meeting. The Abington Preparative Meeting sessions continued in unbroken sequence until Ninth month 1919, when monthly sessions were
considered unnecessary. It is now incorporated and meets once or twice
a year as business demands. It is composed of two meetings for worship,
Cheltenham, and little Abington.

The original building erected in 1702 served the meeting until 1786,
when, because of the sessions of the newly established quarterly meeting
which were held here, it was necessary to enlarge the building. Accordingly committees were appointed by the four constituent monthly meetings,
who decided to extend the east end of the old meeting-house "as large as
the other part, and carried as high as to have galleries above." This
was completed in 1787. Ten years later, in 1797, the house was again too
small to comfortably accommodate the quarterly meeting. Again repairs
were made, and the entire west end of the house was pulled down and rebuilt. In 1840 a new floor was laid over the old one in the east end,

and the seats along the entire south side were raised.

At the time of the Separation in 1827 the Orthodox were the minority group. They withdrew from the monthly meeting and held their monthly business session in the home of Daniel Fletcher. It is a strong possibility that Abington Preparative Meetings of the Orthodox group were also held in private homes, until 1836 when they built the present "Little" Abington meeting-house on Greenwood Avenue, about 200 yards east of Meeting House Road, in Jenkintown. So far as can be ascertained Abington Preparative continued, from the time of the Separation to the present, as a preparative meeting under Abington Monthly. In 1917 when Cheltenham Friends established their meeting for worship it became a part of Abington Preparative, and so continues.

There is practically nothing in the early minutes referring to Friends Schools, but tradition affirms that a school has been kept in connection with the meeting continuously since the days of John Barnes gift of land. After the Revolutionary War references are more numerous, and the Abington Friends School reached a degree of popularity and efficiency.

The oldest burial ground is a small one located on what is now Ashbourne Road west of Old York Road. The earliest known interment in this cemetery was in 1694. In 1697 when John Barnes donated the large tract for the use of the meeting it is a safe assumption that a portion of it was at once set aside for a burial ground. A minute dated in 1769 notes that Abington Friends have persuaded most of the families who have marked their graves with stones, to have them removed. In 1835 the question again came up and a special committee was authorized to remove the remaining large stones or sink them level with the ground. Generally only small markers bearing names and dates were acceptable to the Friends. The extreme attitude of preference for large elaborate markers was limited to a very few. The present burial ground is a few feet to the north-west of the old meeting-house (now Hicksite), and contains about 5 acres. It is the original graveyard plotted on the Barnes tract about 1697. There is no burial ground at the Little Abington Meeting-house. Both groups use the old burial ground on the Barnes tract.

See: Jenkins, Arthur H. and Ann. R., op. cit., p. 115; Book of Meetings, pp. 5, 17, 53.

Before listing the records it is worthy of note that although Thomas Fairman was directed to get a book for keeping the minutes of the Monthly Meeting, the meeting must have been dissatisfied with their condition. In 1716 a committee of four was appointed to "view the former minutes and judge what is requisite to be transcribed." The committee was slow in accomplishing its work for it was not completed until 1719. The transcription was made by George Boone, probably the schoolmaster at Abington School, who was the brother of Squire Boone, father of Daniel Boone the famous Kentucky pioneer. George Boone noted specifically that his copy was "Transcribed from Sundry Manuscripts." The complete minutes begin with 1718. It must also be noted that many of the records of Abington Preparative Meeting are included in the records of Abington Monthly Meeting and are therefore not repeated here.

Minutes of Men's Meetings, 1786-1869, 2 vols., at PPFYR, 1800-1896, 2 vols., at PGC-Hi, and 1800-1809, 1 vol., 1683-1893, 10 vols., at Abington Meeting-house. Minutes of Women's Meeting, 1713-1875, 1 vol., at

PSC-Hi, and 1862-93, 1 vol., 1773-1893, 5 vols., at Abington Meeting-
house. Minutes of Ministers and Elders, 1713-1875, 3 vols, at PPFYR,
and 1713-1825, 1 vol., at PSC-Hi.   Membership List, 1830--, 1 vol.;
Deaths, 1720-56, 1 vol.: at PPFYR.   Births and deaths, 1683--, 2 vols.;
Marriage certificates, 1685--, 3 vols.   (1722-44 missing): at PSC-Hi.
Some of these records have been transcribed, hence the overlapping of
dates.

96. GWYNEDD MONTHLY MEETING, 1714-1936.   Swede and Pine Streets,
       Norristown, Montgomery County.
Set up in 1714 by Philadelphia Quarterly Meeting (entry 2), at the recommendation of Radnor Monthly Meeting (entry 15).   When Abington Quarterly
Meeting (entry 92) was set up in 1786 this monthly meeting became a part.
Meetings were held in the meeting-house of Gwynedd Preparative Meeting
(entry 97). When Gwynedd Preparative Meeting was laid down in 1853, the
meeting-house and burial ground were transferred to this meeting. Some
years later the small burial ground was transferred to Chestnut Hill
Monthly Meeting (entry 330), Coulter Street and Germantown Avenue, Philadelphia, under whose care it has remained until the present time. In 1890
Gwynedd Monthly Meeting erected at Swede and Pine Streets, Norristown, a
two-story brown stone meeting-house, enclosed partly by a stone wall and
partly by an iron fence. This meeting was laid down in 1936 by Abington
Quarterly Meeting. The meeting-house and grounds were sold to the "Bible
Testimony Church."

See: Michener, op. cit., p. 86.

    Minutes of Men's Meetings, 1714-1936, 13 vols., at PPFYR, and 1801-
30, 2 vols., at PSC-Hi.   Minutes of Women's Meetings, 1717-1897, 5 vols.
(1714-16 missing), PPFYR.   Minutes of Ministers and Elders, 1757-1853, 4
vols., at PPFYR, and 1793-1829, 2 vols., at PSC-Hi.   Register of Births,
1690-1899, 1 vol.; Register of Deaths, 1715-1889, 1 vol., at PPFYR. Register of Births and Deaths, 1764-1921, 2 vols., at PSC-Hi. Marriage Certificates, 1715-81, 1 vol., at PPFYR, and 1793-1917, 1 vol., at PSC-Hi.
Certificates of Removal, 1779-1856, 2 vols., at PSC-Hi. Montgomery County
Deed Books, vol. 7, p. 116; vol. 981, p. 442.

97. GWYNEDD PREPARATIVE MEETING, 1698-1853. Spring House and Penn-
       llyn Turnpike, Lower Gwynedd Twp., Montgomery County.
Set up in 1698 by Radnor Monthly Meeting (entry 15). Meetings were held
from 1689-1700 in the homes of members.   In 1700 this meeting acquired
2½ acres of ground at De Kalb Street and Sumneytown Pike, on which a small
meeting-house was erected and a burial ground was plotted. Meetings were
held here until about 1712 when the building was razed and a larger meeting-house was built on the same site. When Gwynedd Monthly Meeting (entry 96) was established in 1714, Gwynedd Preparative Meeting became a
part. In 1823 a new gray stone frame building was erected on the same
site as the two previous meeting-houses. At the time of the Separation
in 1827 the meeting-house and the 2 acre burial ground were retained by
Gwynedd Preparative Meeting, Hicksite (entry 180). Meetings were held by
the Orthodox Friends in the homes of members until 1830, at which time the
meeting moved to Pennllyn and the three-story stone meeting-house was
erected and a graveyard of 2 perches was plotted at Spring House and Pennllyn Turnpike, Pennllyn, Lower Gwynedd Twp. When this meeting was laid
down in 1853 by Gwynedd Monthly Meeting, the meeting-house and burial
ground were transferred to the care of Gwynedd Monthly Meeting.

See: Michener, op. cit., p. 89.

Minutes of Men's Meetings, 1798-1834, 4 vols. (1714-97 missing), at PSC-Hi, and 1827-52, 1 vol., at PPFYR. Meetings of Women's Meetings, 1798-1827, 2 vols. (1714-97 missing), at PPFYR, and 1810-27, 1 vol., at PSC-Hi. Registers are in the records of the Gwynedd Monthly Meeting. Montgomery County Deed Books, vol. 7, 116; vol. 981, p. 442.

98. **PLYMOUTH PREPARATIVE MEETING, 1703-1896.** Germantown Pike and Harmonville Road, Plymouth Meeting, Montgomery County. Set up in 1710 by Radnor Monthly Meeting (entry 15), after having functioned as an indulged meeting from 1703-10. First meetings were held in the homes of Hugh Jones and David Meredith. The exact date of the erection of the meeting-house cannot be determined. Various authorities give conflicting dates varying from 1709 to 1714. Plymouth Meeting-house is mentioned for the first time in connection with a June wedding at Radnor, in 1709. Edward Dawes of Plymouth, and Sarah Cassell, late of Abington, (spinster), at Plymouth meeting-house. Because this is the first recording in which the Plymouth meeting-house is mentioned, it may be assumed that the meeting-house must have been erected during the preceeding summer months of 1708. It is hardly likely that the meeting-house would have been erected during the winter of 1709. However, as late as 1714, the Plymouth Friends requested of Radnor Monthly Meeting the privilege of meeting on alternate Fourth-days in the home of David Meredith, a prominent member of the meeting. The reason advanced for meeting alternately at David Meredith's home and at the Plymouth meeting-house is that most of the Friends lived too far away from the meeting-house to travel there weekly. In 1714, when Gwynedd Monthly Meeting (entry 96) was established, Plymouth Preparative Meeting was transferred from Radnor Monthly Meeting to the newly established Gwynedd Monthly Meeting. Extensive changes were also made to the meeting-house, and a new section was constructed of brown sandstone. The northeastern part of the meeting-house was used as a school for the Friends' children and the children of other settlers. Many traveled a great distance to attend. In early days of this meeting, Plymouth enjoyed the ministrations of three noted preachers, Ellis Pugh, Rowland Ellis, and William Trotter. At the time of the Separation in 1827, the meeting-house, grounds, and a portion of the burial ground were retained by Plymouth Preparative Meeting, Hicksite (entry 181). The Orthodox meetings were held in the homes of members until the new meeting-house, a two-story stone building covered with white plaster, was erected in 1828 opposite the Hicksite meeting-house. The meeting was laid down in 1896 by Gwynedd Monthly Meeting. A few years later the meeting-house and grounds were sold and the meeting-house was remodeled and converted into a private residence. The 1½ acre burial ground was transferred to the care of Chestnut Hill Monthly Meeting (entry 330), 100 E. Mermaid Lane, Chestnut Hill, Philadelphia.

See: Michener, op. cit., p. 86; Elwood Roberts, Plymouth Meeting Passim.; 200th Anniversary Plymouth Friends' Meeting, hereinafter cited as 200th Anniversary, Plymouth.

Minutes of Men's Meetings, 1844-97, 1 vol. (1710-1843 missing); Minutes of Women's Meetings, 1827-97, 2 vols. (1710-1826 missing): at PPFYR. Registers are in the records of the Gwynedd Monthly Meeting. Financial records, 1773-1936, 4 vols. (1710-72 missing), in custody of F. C. Jones, 926 Fayette Street, Conshohocken, and 1838-70, 1 vol., at PPFYR. Montgomery County Deed Books, vol. 29, pp. 160, 167; vol. 43, p. 218; vol.

49, p. 43; vol. 73, p. 182; vol. 102, p. 98.

99. **PROVIDENCE PREPARATIVE MEETING, 1716-1827.** Black Rock Road,
    Upper Providence Twp., Montgomery County.
Set up in 1733 by Gwynedd Monthly Meeting Orthodox (entry 96) after having
functioned as an indulged meeting since 1716. The first Friends of Upper
Providence who located near the confluence of the Perkiomen and Schuylkill
Rivers, were Joseph Richardson, Robert Edwards, and John Jacobs. They
arrived in 1716 when Upper Providence was a large tract of land named
"Manor of Gilbert," in honor of William Penn's paternal grandmother, whose
maiden name was Gilbert. Meetings were first held in the home of James
Hammer until 1730, when the meeting-house, a one-story log building, was
erected on the "Manor of Gilbert." The ground for the meeting-house
and a graveyard, containing 1 acre and 9 perches, was deeded to this meeting Tenth month 15, 1743. The burial ground and meeting-house were enclosed by a wire fence and a stone wall. After the Separation in 1827,
this meeting became a Hicksite Meeting (entry 182), and the Hicksite
Friends retained the meeting-house and the burial ground.

See: Charles Major, Commemorative of Providence Meeting (Manuscript
at PNort Hi).

Minutes of Men's Meetings, 1812-66, 2 vols. (1716-1811 destroyed by
fire), at PSC-Hi. Registers are in records of Gwynedd Monthly Meeting.

100. **WHITEMARSH INDULGED MEETING, 1791-1827.** Bethlehem Pike, a-
     bout one-half mile south of Fort Washington, Whitemarsh Twp.,
     Montgomery County.
Set up in 1791 by Gwynedd Monthly Meeting (entry 96). In 1791 Joshua
Morris, donated to this meeting 2 acres and 21 perches of land. On this
land a burial ground was plotted and a meeting-house was erected in 1815.
At the time of the Separation this meeting was laid down by Gwynedd Monthly Meeting. The meeting-house and burial ground were retained by Whitemarsh Indulged Meeting, Hicksite (entry 183).

See: Michener, op. cit., p. 91. Deed Book Montgomery County, vol.
6, p. 350.

101. **RICHLAND MONTHLY MEETING, 1742-1827.** Northwest Corner Main
     Street and Mill Road, Quakertown, Bucks County.
Set off in 1742 from Gwynedd Monthly Meeting (entry 96) by Philadelphia
Quarterly Meeting (entry 2). Meetings were held in the meeting-house
which had been erected by the Richland Preparative Meeting (entry 102).
A school was established in 1742. Springfield Indulged Meeting (entry
31), which was formed about 1743 and the Saucon Indulged Meeting (entry
32), which was formed in 1744 were part of this Monthly Meeting. In 1781
11 of the leading members of Richland were read out of the meeting for
subscribing to an oath of allegiance to the Colonies but the yearly meeting failed to concur and most of them retained their membership. In 1786
the meeting was transferred to Abington Quarterly Meeting (entry 92).
Stroudsburg (entry 111) was permitted to hold an indulged meeting in 1809
and a preparative meeting in 1811. At the time of the Separation in 1827
Richland became a Hicksite Meeting (entry 190). The few remaining Orthodox Friends joined the Plumstead and Buckingham Meetings.

See: Joseph Thomas, "Reminiscences of Quakertown and Its People,"
Bucks County Historical Society Papers, III (1909), 42; Roberts and Ely,

op. cit., p. 46; Battle, op. cit., p. 762.

Minutes of Men's Meetings, 1742-1896, 7 vols.; Minutes of Women's
Meetings, 1765-1896, 8 vols.; Minutes of Ministers and Elders, 1748-1894,
4 vols.; Epistles from the yearly meeting at London, 1761-1813, 1 vol.;
Epistles from the yearly meetings of women Friends of Philadelphia, Genesee, London, and Baltimore, 1745-1845, 1 vol., at PSC-Hi. Registers of
Births and Removals, 1742-96, 1 vol., at PSC-Hi, and 1796--, 1 vol., in
custody of Miss Mabel Dick, 140 S. Main Street, Quakertown. Registers
of Marriages, 1742-1890, in List of Marriages at PSC-Hi, and 1804--, 7
vols., in meeting-house. Registers of Deaths and Burials, 1742--, 2 vols.,
in meeting-house. Treasurer's Account of Poor Fund, 1821-28, 1 vol., at
PSC-Hi. Bucks County Deed Book, vol. 39, p. 541.

102. RICHLAND PREPARATIVE MEETING, 1710-1827. Northwest corner Main
Street and Mill Roads, Quakertown, Bucks County.
Set up in 1723 by Gwynedd Monthly Meeting (entry 96) after having met in
private homes as an indulged meeting since 1710. One of these homes was
the residence of Peter Lester who was the first settler of what is now
Quakertown. In 1723 a log building was erected on a plot of land at Old
Bethlehem Pike and Station Road, by Everand Boland. A small portion of
this land, to the rear of the meeting-house, was set aside for a burial
ground. When the membership increased a frame meeting-house was erected
in 1730 at Main Street and Mill Road, on a 10-acre plot leased from Morris
Morris. Two and one-half acres at the north and northeast end of the
ground were set aside for a graveyard the same year. The first burial
recorded is that of William Roberts, son of Thomas and Alice Roberts, in
1731. At Richland the first organization for maintaining friendly relations with the Indians, called, "Ye friendly association for regaining
and preserving peace with the Indians" was formed. When Richland Monthly
Meeting (entry 101) was set up in 1742 this meeting became a part. From
1746-65 meetings for business were suspended. In 1749 a stone addition
20' x 26' was added to the north end of the meeting-house. In 1759 Morris
Morris donated the 10 acre plot to the meeting. A frame schoolhouse was
erected nearby in 1773. In 1792 a stone wall was built around the northern section of the graveyard. In 1793-95 the frame meeting-house was replaced by one of stone. At the time of the Separation in 1827 this became a Hicksite Meeting (entry 191). The few remaining Orthodox Friends
joined the Plumstead and Buckingham Meetings.

See: Thomas, op. cit., p. 42; Roberts and Ely, op. cit., p. 46;
Battle, op. cit., p. 762.

Minutes of Men's Meetings, 1725-41 in Gwynedd Monthly Minutes; 1742-
45, 1766-99 in Richland Monthly Minutes (1746-65 meetings were suspended;
1800-1827 missing). Minutes for Women's Meetings, 1765-99, in records of
Richland Monthly Minutes and 1800-1896, 5 vols., at PSC-Hi. Register of
births, removals, marriages, deaths, and burials, 1725-41 in records of
Gwynedd Monthly Meeting; 1742-1827 in records of Richland Monthly Meeting.

103. HORSHAM MONTHLY MEETING, 1782-1827. Easton and Horsham Roads,
Horsham Twp., Montgomery County.
Set up in 1782 by Philadelphia Quarterly Meeting (entry 2). Meeting were
held in the two-story native stone building erected in 1724 near the intersection of the Norristown Road and Easton Highway, by Horsham Preparative Meeting (entry 104) and in 1803 in the two-story stone building at
Easton and Horsham Roads. In 1827, after the Separation, this meeting

was laid down by Abington Quarterly Meeting. Horsham Monthly Meeting (H) retained the meeting-house and property.

See: Michener, op. cit., pp. 88-90; Theodore W. Bean, History of Montgomery County, p. 375.

Minutes of Men's Meetings, 1782-1846, 2 vols., at PSC-H1. Minutes of Women's Meetings, 1782-93, 1 vol. (1794-1818 missing), at PPFYR, and 1819-42, 1 vol., at PSC-H1. Minutes of Ministers and Elders, 1786-1874, 1 vol.; Registers of births and deaths, 1782-1889, 1 vol.; Certificates of removals, 1782-1821, 1 vol., at PSC-H1. Certificates of Marriage, 1782-1827, 1 vol., at PPFYR. Horsham School Committee Minutes, 1783-1849, 2 vols.; Treasurer's Records, 1782-1896, 1 vol., at PSC-H1. Montgomery County Deed Books, vol. 30, p. 478.

104. HORSHAM PREPARATIVE MEETING, 1717-ca.1919. Northwest corner Saw Mill Lane and Dreshertown Road, Horsham Township, Montgomery County.

Set up in 1717 by Abington Monthly Meeting (entry 93) after having been an indulged meeting since 1714. Meetings were held in private homes from about 1712 until about 1714 when a 50-acre farm including a two-story stone farmhouse, located on what is now the upper corner of the graveyard west of Easton Highway, and a barn across the road, were conveyed to trustees for the meeting by Hannah Carpenter by a deed of trust, March 27, 1719. This farm had been given by Samuel Carpenter in 1714, but could not be conveyed until trustees were appointed in 1719. The land was to be used for a meeting-house, a burial ground, and the proceeds from the farm were to be given to the poor. A small stone meeting-house was erected in 1714 or 1715 it appears. A school was also conducted according to the wish of the donor. The first school was held in the meeting-house but later a stone schoolhouse was built. The present schoolhouse, now a residence bears a date stone of 1739. Burials were made in the meeting land very early and a 3-acre cemetery was laid out in 1719. Meetings were held in small stone building until 1724, when a larger native stone addition was erected adjoining the first building, and near the intersection of the Norristown Road and Easton Highway. This double building was located on a triangular piece of ground adjoining the graveyard. A one-story native stone schoolhouse was erected in 1739 adjoining the graveyard on the Norristown Road. The barn was repaired in 1758 and rebuilt in 1772. When Horsham Monthly Meeting was set up in 1782, this preparative meeting then became a part thereof. In 1803 a two-story stone building was erected at Easton and Horsham Roads. It was partially built from stone taken from the meeting-house erected in 1724. In 1827, after the Separation, Horsham Preparative Meeting (H) (entry 187) retained the property, and the remaining Orthodox Friends held their meetings in private homes until 1830, when a one-story native brown stone building was erected, about 2 miles south of the present Hicksite building, on the east side of Welsh Road. In 1890 a small stone meeting-house was erected on the northwest corner of Saw Mill Lane and Dreshertown Road. Meetings were held here until 1907 and it is said that Richard Showmaker continued this meeting until his death in 1919. The meeting-house was sold and converted into a private dwelling in 1920.

See: Michener, op. cit., pp. 88-90; Charles H. Smith, History of Horsham Preparative Meeting House (manuscript in custody of author, Horsham).

Minutes of Men's Meetings, 1757-1827, 3 vols. (1717-56 missing) at PSC-Hi, and 1827-1907, 2 vols., at PPFYR. Minutes of Women's Meetings, 1757-1828, 3 vols. (1717-56, 1829-78 missing), at PSC-Hi, and 1879-89, 1 vol., at PPFYR. Minutes of Joint Meetings, 1889-1907 in 1869-1907 vol. of Minutes of Men's Meetings, Registers, 1717-81, 1827-ca.1919 are in the records of Abington Monthly Meeting; 1782-1826 are in records of Horsham Monthly Meeting. Montgomery County Deed Book, vol. 110, p. 1.

105. UPPER DUBLIN PREPARATIVE MEETING, 1814-27. Fort Washington
      Avenue and Limekiln Pike, Upper Dublin, Montgomery County.
Set up in 1814 by Horsham Monthly Meeting (entry 103). Meetings were held in a one-story stone building erected in 1814 on land which had been donated by Phoebe Shoemaker for a meeting-house and burial grounds. In 1827 this became a Hicksite Meeting (entry 188).

See: Michener, op. cit., p. 90.

Minutes of Men's Meetings, 1814-80, 2 vols. (1881-85 missing); Minutes of Women's Meetings, 1814-85, 2 vols., S. C.

106. BYBERRY MONTHLY MEETING OF FRIENDS, 1810-27. Byberry Road,
      at Southampton Road, Byberry, Philadelphia.
Set up in 1810, by Abington Quarterly Meeting (entry 92). From 1782 Byberry was a part of Horsham Monthly Meeting (entry 103), as a preparative meeting. In 1810 the number of members at Horsham became so large and the membership at Byberry also increased to such an extent that it was decided to separate the two and have a monthly meeting at each place. The proposal was forwarded to Abington Quarter for approval, and in the same year, a minute of concurrence was received thus creating Byberry Monthly Meeting. This meeting was comprised of its own preparative only. Sessions were held in the meeting-house, erected in 1808 by members of Byberry Preparative (entry 107). In 1811 a few friends associated for the purpose of establishing a school for girls. They provided a house which stood on a lot near the Byberry Store, which was situated in the immediate vicinity of the meeting-house. This school was very successful, it was continued in the same building, under supervision of the association until 1827. In this year the house was sold and the school was afterwards kept in the second story of the present school building on the meeting-house grounds, until 1838, at which time it was discontinued. The frame school building erected in 1789, with its addition in 1792, was no longer usable in 1823. A new building was erected in that year, and shortly after its opening the old one was removed. This school building is the one standing to-day. It occupies a site on the meeting-house grounds, some yards north of the present meeting-house; a moderate size structure, two-stories high, and built of stone, which is stuccoed a gray color. A small frame addition was added to the north end at a later date. At the time of the Separation sessions of Byberry meeting continued on without interruption but the major sympathy of the meeting was with the Hicksite group. Application was therefore, made to the newly formed Abington Quarterly Meeting Hicksite (entry 174), for permission to join as a constituent thereof. This was approved and Byberry Monthly Meeting (O) was laid down.

See: James C. Martindale, History of Byberry and Moreland Townships pp. 10-18 (Manuscript at PHi); Matlack, op. cit., I, 38; John and Isaac Comly, "Settlement and Progress of Byberry Meeting," Friends' Miscellany, VII, 100; "Byberry Meeting," The Friend, I (1827), 68, hereinafter cited as Byberry Meeting; "A Historical Excursion to Byberry," The Friend, XCIII (1920), 53, 63, hereinafter cited as Historical Excursion.

Minutes of Men's Meetings, 1810-27 were destroyed by fire sometime between 1860-70, but abstracts therefrom are preserved by the Pennsylvania Historical Society. Minutes of Women's Meetings, 1810-27, 2 vols., at PPF. For registers of membership, births, marriages, deaths, and burials, certificates of removal, disownments, financial records, and other miscellaneous records, see records of Byberry Monthly Meeting (H) (entry 177).

107. BYBERRY PREPARATIVE MEETING, 1701-1827.   Byberry Road and
      Southampton Road, Byberry, Philadelphia.
Set up in 1701, by Abington Monthly Meeting (entry 93). As early as 1675, Friends were settled in the community which is now Byberry. The four Walton brothers, Nathaniel, Thomas, Daniel, and William, whose names appear frequently in the minutes of Byberry meeting, migrated here in 1675. These brothers, all young men, came from England, and first landed at New Castle. Equipping themselves with a supply of food and tools, they set out to select a site for their new home. Following the course of the Delaware River, they finally reached the mouth of Poquessing Creek. They followed this stream until they decided upon a spot suited to their needs, and here made a temporary shelter, a cave covered with bark. The locality was first named after the creek, "Poetquesink" later called "Poquessing." The township was called "Byberry" after the native town of the Walton brothers, near Bristol, in Gloucestershire, England. The first settlers in Byberry, mostly Quakers, lived in caves dug into the ground to a depth of about 3 to 6 feet, with roofs formed of limbs of trees covered with sod or bark.

At the time of the arrival of William Penn, several families of Friends who came with him, settled at Poetquesink. At a Quarterly Meeting held the 5th day of the Fourth month 1683, the following minute was made: "Proposed by Friends that the meetings in the county be settled. Agreed that there be a publick First-day meeting of Friends at Tackony, and a First-day publick meeting at Poetquesink, and that they both shall make one Monthly meeting . . . . Agreed that Thomas Duckett give notice at Skoolkill, Thomas Fairman at Tacony, and Samuel Allen at Poetquesink, to the Friends there of the Quarterly Meetings resolutions for the service of Truth in those parts." The first public meeting for worship in Byberry was established in 1683, and the first monthly meeting in that section consisted of Byberry and Tackony. Tackony was later known as Oxford, and still later the meeting was called Frankford. The monthly meeting consisting of Byberry and Tackony, and the one consisting of Philadelphia and Schuylkill formed the first quarterly meeting of which Byberry was a part. The monthly meeting was held alternately at the house of Sarah Seary, at Tackony, and at the house of John Hart at Poetquesink. The weekly meetings for worship were held at the house of Giles Knight until the 4th month 1685, when the monthly meeting "ordered that the meeting which of late hath been held at Giles Knight's, be removed to the house of John Hart."

After the meetings for public worship were removed to John Hart's house, the distance proved too great for many Friends living in the northern part of the township, and in order to accommodate them, it was decreed in the 11th month 1686 that: "a meeting for worship be held once a month, on First-days, at the house of Henry English," so that two meet-

ings for worship were, for a time, held in Byberry.   The location of
these meetings seems to have been unsatisfactory, and frequent changes
were the result.   In the year 1686, at a quarterly meeting, it was agreed
that a new monthly meeting be set up consisting of the particular meetings of Byberry and Oxford (formerly Tackony), and the newly formed one
at Cheltenham, this to be held alternately at the houses of Sarah Seary
at Oxford, John Hart's at Byberry and Richard Wall's at Cheltenham.   This
continued until the following year, and in the First month 1687 it was
agreed to hold the monthly meeting "at the house of Richard Worrall, Jr.,
henceforth, on the last Second-day in every month, and that there shall
be a general meeting, movable at four places, Germantown, Byberry. Oxford,
and at Richard Wall's at Cheltenham." (This meeting was called "Cheltenham," and "Dublin," and afterwards became Abington Monthly Meeting).   In
1691 the Keithian Quakers (entry 169) arose through the agency of George
Keith, who then resided in Philadelphia.   In Byberry the leading follower
of Keith was John Hart, who influenced a small group of Byberry Friends,
including Nathaniel Walton, to join with the Keithian movement.   The majority of Friends in this section, however, declined the principles of
Keith, and withdrew from the meetings held at John Hart's house and assembled with those who met at the house of Henry English.   The Keithian
Meeting was not successful and after 2 or 3 years was discontinued.   After
the Keithian separation Friends continued to meet at the house of Henry
English.   On the 2nd of First month 1692, Henry English gave 1 acre of
land to John Carver and Daniel Walton, in trust for Friends.   The deed
specified that "the said one acre of ground is for the use of the people
of God called Quakers, who are and shall be and continue in unity and
religious fellowship with friends of Truth, and shall belong to the Monthly Meeting of said people, for whose use the said piece of ground is intended to be employed as a burying place, and to no other use or service
whatsoever; provided always, that it is the true intent and meaning of the
parties hereunto, that no person or persons who shall be declared by the
Members of the Monthly or Quarterly Meeting, whereunto he, she or they
shall belong, to be out of unity with them, shall have any right or interest in the said piece of ground hereby granted, while he, she or they
shall remain out of unity and church fellowship with those people to whom
he, she or they did so belong."   Although the deed states quite specifically that the ground was never to be used for any purpose except a burial
ground, a meeting-house was badly needed at that time.   Shortly after
acquisition of the land, and with the full consent of the donor, the first
meeting-house of Byberry Friends was erected thereon in 1692.   It was
built of logs, ridged and notched at the corners, chinked with mud and
covered with bark.   It stood in the northern corner of the present site
of the old graveyard, and was the original forerunner of the present
Friends meeting-house.   It served as a place of worship during the next
22 years.   In 1701, at a meeting of Abington Monthly Meeting (entry 93),
it was agreed, "that a Preparative Meeting be established at Byberry, to
be held on the weekly meeting-day that happeneth next before the Monthly
Meeting, and that those Friends that are appointed as overseers, to attend
to such service."   This was the origin of the preparative meeting at Byberry although no records of its proceedings covering the first 20 years
have been found.   The earliest minute of the preparative meeting bears the
date of 2nd month 18, 1721.   These early minutes are made up almost entirely of the pecuniary matters of the organization.   John Carver is mentioned as the clerk at that time.   He appears to have given good satisfaction, as he was continued until 1740, when he requested the meeting
to appoint someone else in his place.

In 1714, the old log meeting-house being no longer tena...., a new house was erected in that year, on the acre given by English. It was a few feet to the east of the log one, and was built of stone. It measured 35' x 50', was two-stories high, had hipped gables, arched ceilings, and double doors on the front. It had large windows without shutters, with small panes of glass set in a leaden sash attached to a wooden frame which was hung on hinges. The only means of warming this old meeting-house was by a fireplace in the west end on the outside of the building, and separated from the interior by large cast iron plates through which the heat was conveyed to the room. In order to complete this house, Friends borrowed L50 of James Cooper, which was paid off by subscription in 1723. In 1753 a collection was taken up to pay for roofing the meeting-house. Another collection was taken up the same year for making an addition to the meeting-house. The addition was 30' x 35' and one-story high, and constructed of stone. Two large fireplaces were built in it, one in each corner of the east end. Some time after this other improvements were made by introducing stoves, substituting wooden sashes for the leaden ones, and putting shutters to the windows. This building, erected in 1714, was in such condition by 1808 that Friends in that year erected a new house a few yards to the south of the old one. The old house was torn down shortly after the completion of the new one. The dimensions of the new house were 66' x 36', and the cost about $2,600. The whole of this sum was raised by subscription among the members, except about $60 which was given by Abington Meeting in consideration of a like sum formerly received from Byberry for a similar purpose. This is the present meeting-house. It is built of natural gray stone, and is a high-ceilinged one-story building, with a gallery.

In 1782 when Horsham Monthly Meeting was set off from Abington, Byberry Preparative Meeting became a part of it. By 1810 Horsham Monthly Meeting had so increased in strength that another Monthly Meeting was set off by Abington Quarterly Meeting, as Byberry Monthly Meeting (entry 106). The preparative meeting at Byberry then became a part thereof. In 1827, at the time of the Separation, the monthly and preparative meetings continued on without any interruption. The monthly meeting, with the consent of the newly formed Abington Quarterly Meeting, Hicksite (entry 174), became a part of this Quarter. The preparative meeting became Byberry Preparative Meeting, Hicksite (entry 178).

Byberry in the early days, had but one school, which was held at the meeting-house, and under the control of the preparative meeting. This was founded about 1711. In 1720 a log schoolhouse was erected near the meeting-house, and in this the school was kept until 1772, when the building was pulled down. The school was then removed to the meeting-house where it continued until after the Revolution. In 1776 John Eastburn bequeathed about L113 1s. 8d. to be applied to the school fund for the purpose of making the school free. In 1794 James Thornton bequeathed L100 for the same purpose. In 1800 John Townsend left L50, also to be applied to this use. In 1802 the free school was started. It was only free to those who were in straitened circumstances. School sessions continued up to 1789 in the meeting-house, but in this year a new schoolhouse was built on the meeting's lot. This is described as being a wooden structure and was only about 20' square, with but one-story. This building was soon found to be entirely too small to accommodate the pupils, so that an addition of the same material was built in 1792.

Soon after this meeting began a lot of ground of about 1 acre, lying a few yards north of Hart's house, was set apart as a place of burial for Friends and others. John Hart, grandson of the ancient John Hart, in 1786 bequeathed this old cemetery to the township of Byberry in the following words: "I give and devise to the Overseers of the poor in the township of Byberry, in the county of Philadelphia, who shall be such at the time of my decease, and to their successors, forever, a certain burying ground lot of one acre of land, which was conveyed to me by my grandfather, deceased, the same to be occupied as a burying ground for the poor, forever." The cemetery was used as a burying place for Friends and other settlers until the Keithian schism after which time it was used only by followers of George Keith. Among those buried here at an early time, were Aurelia, wife of William Rush, in 1683; Thomas Young, 1684; Mary Borman, 1685; Joseph English, 1686; Christopher Crowden, of Bensalem, in 1687; and William Rush, in 1688. The lot served for many years after the death of John Hart, as the township burial ground for the indigent and was commonly termed the "Potter's Field" of Byberry Township. It is located on the Red Lion Road, near the present historic Red Lion Inn. Not much care was given it and late years it has presented a forlorn appearance. In 1685 it is recorded that Byberry Friends were desirous of having a larger lot of ground for a cemetery than the one at John Hart's for in this year a minute of the monthly meeting, dated Sixth month 1685, says: "Friends did freely accept of ten acres of land given by Walter Forrest, near the Poetquesink Creek, and it is left to the trust and care of Joseph Fisher, John Hart, Samuel Ellis and Giles Knight, to get the ground conveyed, the deed of conveyance to be made from Walter Forrest to themselves, for the only use and behoof of Friends, forever, and that from henceforth it shall be made use for the service aforesaid." As no further mention of this donation has been found, it is doubtful whether it was ever applied to the service intended, and its location cannot now with certainty be known. Previous to 1780 the colored people who died in the township were generally buried in the orchards belonging to their masters, or in the woods. Accordingly, in this year, Byberry Meeting purchased a lot from Thomas Townsend for a burying place for the blacks, and the practice of burying on private grounds was discontinued. This burying ground was located about 254' from the Poquessing Creek, on the east side of Townsend Road.

See: Martindale, op. cit., (ms. at PHi); Matlack, op. cit., I, 38; Comly, John and Isaac, op. cit., p. 100; Byberry Meeting, p. 68; Historical Excursion, pp. 53, 63.

Minutes of Men's Meetings, 1721-1827, 4 vols. (1701-20 missing); Minutes of Women's Meetings, 1771-1827, 2 vols. (1701-70 missing), at PPF.

108. FRANKFORD MONTHLY MEETING OF FRIENDS, 1815--. Unity and Waln Streets and Orthodox and Penn Streets, Philadelphia.
Set up in 1815, by Abington Quarterly Meeting (entry 92). From a minute of Abington Monthly Meeting (entry 93), held Eighth month 24, 1815: "The committee appointed to consider of and report a plan for the division of the Monthly Meeting, report as their sense, that Germantown and Frankford Preparative Meetings constitute a Monthly Meeting to be known by the name of Frankford Monthly Meeting of Friends." Meetings were first held in the little brick and stone meeting-house, erected in 1775 at Unity and Waln Streets (entry 290), and continued until the Separation of 1827. After the Separation the Orthodox branch of Frankford Friends met for a time at the house of Robert Waln, at Waln Grove, near the Frankford Station of the

Pennsylvania Railroad. The old mansion, a forlorn relic of a former beautiful home is still standing. Later the meetings were held in a house which stood at the corner of what is now Frankford Avenue and Ruan Street, and still later were held at the house of James Brooks, a machinist, on the southwest side of Frankford Creek, near Frankford Avenue. In 1832, land was purchased on Smith's Lane, west of Frankford Avenue, extending from the present boundary on the rear, as far as Leiper Street on the west. The location is now the southeast corner of Orthodox and Penn Streets. The present frame meeting-house, painted gray, was erected on this site in 1832, and the first meeting held in the new meeting-house was on the first day of the First month 1833. The Friends school first was held in the upper story of the meeting-house. In 1868 the meeting-house was altered and enlarged, the second story was removed, thereby giving greater height to the meeting room, and all the interior of the meeting-house was given over to the use of the meeting. Wright's Institute of Franklin and Unity Streets, was used for meetings during the rebuilding and alterations. Except for the slight changes of papering, painting, carpeting, etc., and the addition of a social room in 1924-25, the meeting-house has remained unchanged until the present time. The social room is used during the week, by the kindergarten department of the school. The ground extending from Penn to Leiper Streets was sold when there was less need of carriage sheds than formerly. Some of the carriage sheds, constructed of wood, mounted on stone foundations, and painted the same grey color as the meeting-house, are still standing in the rear of the meeting-house grounds. From the time of organization Frankford Monthly Meeting was composed of Frankford Preparative Meeting (entry 109) and Germantown Preparative Meeting (entry 115). This affiliation continued until 1906, when the meeting at Germantown was granted permission to organize a monthly meeting of its own, by the consent of Abington Quarterly Meeting. This left only Frankford Preparative as a lone constituent of Frankford Monthly Meeting, and in the Eleventh month 1928, when this preparative meeting was laid down, Frankford Monthly Meeting of Friends became a single unit, with no subordinate meetings under its care, and it so continues until the present day.

In 1868 a new red brick schoolhouse was erected, additions being added from time to time, until the present two-story building was attained. The school is under the care of the Educational Committee of the Philadelphia Yearly Meeting (entry 1), and also under the auspices of Frankford Monthly Meeting of Friends.

The old burial ground at Unity and Waln Streets, was used by Friends of Frankford Monthly Meeting, until the Separation of 1827. After 1827 burials were made at the burial ground of Germantown Friends, Coulter Street near Germantown Avenue, and at the other places until the present burial ground was acquired. In 1877, a plot of ground, located on Bustleton Pike, north of Dark Run Lane, was purchased by the Monthly Meeting. This enclosure, oblong in shape, and containing about 1 acre of ground, is the present burial ground of the Frankford Orthodox Friends. First interment was in the year 1884. Present clerk is Howard Burtt, 1919 Packard Building, 15th and Chestnut Streets, Philadelphia.

See: Smedley, Caroline, op. cit., pp. 133-136, 147, 148; Walter Brinton, "Friends' Meetings in Frankford," Papers Read Before the Historical Society of Frankford, II (1910), No. 4, p. 135.

Minutes of Men's Meetings, 1816-1914, 5 vols.; Minutes of Women's Meetings, 1816-1914, 4 vols.; Minutes of Joint Meetings, 1915-32, 2 vols.;

at PPFYR. Minutes of Joint Meetings, 1933--, 1 vol., in custody of the
clerk. Registers: Births, 1816-1915, 2 vols.; Deaths, 1816-1915, 2 vols.;
Marriages, 1828-1906, 2 vols. (1816-27 missing); Membership, 1816-1906,
2 vols.; Certificates of removal and transfer, 1816-1906, 1 vol.; Disownments, 1816-44, 1 vol. (after 1844 in Minutes of Monthly Meeting): at
PPFYR. Register of membership, births, marriages, and deaths, 1907--, 1
vol., in custody of the recorder, Benjamin S. Thorp, 5012 Penn Street,
Frankford, Philadelphia. Certificates of removal and transfer, 1907--,
1 vol.; Certificates of marriage, 1907--, 1 vol., in custody of the registrar, Clement B. Webster, 4832 Penn Street, Frankford, Philadelphia.
Treasurer's account, 1849-1906, 2 vols. (1816-48 missing), at PPFYR, and
1907--, 2 vols., in custody of the treasurer, Franklin S. Hilles, c/o
Smedley Brothers Lumber Co., Church and Tacony Streets, Frankford, Philadelphia. Burial records, 1815-27, 1 vol., PPFYR, and 1884--, 1 vol., in
custody of the chairman of burial committee, Clement B. Webster.

109. FRANKFORD PREPARATIVE MEETING, 1701-1928. Unity and Waln-
      Streets, Frankford, Philadelphia.
The history of this meeting involves that of Tacony and Oxford. Therefore, this sketch treats these three together in order to save duplication. Shortly after the arrival of William Penn in 1682, Thomas Fairman
at the request of Governor Penn left his mansion at Shackamaxon, and went
to reside at Tookany (Tacony) in Oxford Township, "where there was also
a meeting appointed to be kept." In the Sixth month 1683, at a quarterly
meeting held in Philadelphia, a First-day meeting was established at Tookany, and one at Poetquesink, the two to form one monthly meeting of men
and women. The former met at the house of Sarah Seary at Tookany, the
latter met at the house of John Hart at Poetquesink. The first Monthly
meeting was held Seventh month 3, 1683, and Thomas Fairman was directed
to procure record books. It was agreed to build a log meeting-house on
land given by Fairman for that purpose. In Tenth month 1683, at a meeting at Sarah Seary's, "at the request of some Friends, a meeting was established at Cheltenham in the house of Richard Wall, where a goodly body
of Friends lived." This meeting was called Cheltenham and sometimes Dublin, and later became Abington Meeting. Sarah Seary, the wife of Thomas
Seary, lived on what is now Bristol Pike, just above Frankford north of
Cedar Hill Cemetery.

In 1684, the log meeting-house was built on the above mentioned
Fairman ground, which was bounded by what is now Unity, Waln and Oxford
Streets, Frankford. After Third month 1684, this new meeting-house was
used instead of Sarah Seary's house very early the name of Tookany meeting was changed to that of Oxford, probably by influence of Thomas Seary
who came from Oxford, England. In 1686 it was concluded that men and
women meet separately. Previous to this the monthly meetings must have
been held in joint session, although it is doubtful that the term "joint
meetings" was used at that time. At a monthly meeting held 29th of the
Eleventh month 1698 it is stated "Whereas Friends of Oxford Meeting,
having taken into consideration the want of having a piece of land purchased whereon the meeting-house stands, they do appoint Joseph Paul and
John Worrell to purchase it of Thomas Fairman and to get a deed in their
own name." It appears that the deed for this land which had been given
by Fairman for the log meeting-house in 1683, had never been properly
and legally transferred to the meeting until this time. The reason for
buying the land after it had been given by Fairman is not clear. A copy
of this deed is now on the walls of the Historical Society of Frankford,
the original being in care of Frankford Monthly Meeting (entry 108).

Friends of Oxford in Ninth month 1699, complained of the want of a new
meeting-house and the monthly meeting directed them to consult together
in order to make plans for this building. It is probable that a brick
meeting-house was built soon after, as we find mention in a deed, of a
brick house in 1704. "Deed of Joseph Paul and John Worrell to Edmund
Orpwood, Timothy Henson, Richard Worrell, William Buzbee, Edward Buzbee,
and Richard Buzbee, dated 12th of the Fourth month, called June, (old
calender) 1704, for 1 acre and 96 perches in Oxford Township, together
with the brick house thereon erected and all out-houses, buildings, ways
etc." On the Eleventh month 26, 1701, Oxford Preparative Meeting was
established, the records of which are complete from 1772. In 1773, a lot
adjoining the meeting was purchased for its use. By a minute of Oxford
Preparative Meeting, dated First month 25, 1774: "it is reported that the
meeting-house is much out of repair and a committee is appointed to collect money." Oxford Friends again petitioned the monthly meeting for assistance in building a new meeting-house. This was built in 1775, and
is the old Frankford meeting-house now standing which has the above date
on its outside wall. As one part of this building is decidedly older than
the other, it is believed that the new meeting-house just referred to had
an addition in 1811, according to a minute stating that in 1811 the meeting concluded to add 20 feet to the east end of the meeting-house.

Some description of this oldest of all meeting-houses still standing
within the limits of Philadelphia is worth noting. The tradition that
the bricks were brought from England as ballast in a ship is not authentic. The building has a peculiar appearance since but one end and one
side are of brick, the other end and side being of grey stone. Whether
this was due to lack of bricks, to economy, or to other cause is undetermined. Every second brick is a binder, the end being vitrified, which
gives a unique appearance. The line of demarcation between the old and
new part is plainly visible. The original portion is about two-thirds of
the present size and agrees exactly with the deed of 1773. Near the wom-
en's end stands the old horse-block, which in colonial days was of great
use to equestrienne Friends as they mounted and dismounted. Inside, the
different styles of benches indicate that they were made at different
times. In preparation for an approaching monthly meeting in 1797 to be
held at Oxford, a preparative meeting record appoints three Friends to
"get some benches made with backs on, for the better accommodation of
the meeting." At one end of the meeting room is still to be seen the
brick hearth of the old fireplace. The old lock and key, among the
largest in existence, are among the many interesting features of the interior. By a minute Tenth month 23, 1800: "it appears that some sheds
would be useful to preserve the carriages dry in stormy weather." A
committee was appointed and they were built at a cost of $88.13. Oxford
Preparative Meeting continued until 8th month 20, 1805, when the name
was changed to Frankford Preparative Meeting, the borough of Frankford
having been established in the Fifth month, 9th, of the same year. The
name "Frankford" had been used for this community in other connections,
long before the formal establishment of the borough. Frankford Preparative was at first attached to Abington Monthly Meeting (entry 93) until
1815, when Frankford Monthly Meeting was established, and Frankford Preparative then became a part thereof. When the Separation took place in
1827, the Orthodox minority removed themselves from the meeting-house
at Unity and Waln Streets, and met in private houses for several years.
In 1832 ground was purchased at what is now Orthodox and Penn Streets
and a frame meeting house was erected thereon in 1832. Meetings were
held regularly until 1907, but from this time on they were only held at

intervals, and finally were held but once a year. The last preparative meeting was held on the 21st of Eleventh month 1928, at which time Frankford Preparative Meeting was formally laid down. In early times an old school building stood on a lot containing 2 acres adjoining the meeting house. It is no longer existent; a fire which burned a row of sheds formerly surrounding the meeting on three sides, took with it the old school building. Just when the school was established is not determined, but it is presumed it was at a very early time. Date of erection of the school building, and the type of its construction is not known. Sessions of the school after the loss of the school building were held in the meeting-house, until the school was discontinued, the date of this discontinuance is also undetermined. Later the 2 acres of ground were sold, and a row of houses now occupies the site.

Back of the meeting-house is the 1-acre graveyard, for many years Frankford's only burial place. Here lie Thomas Fairman, Robert Scatten, Richard Worrall, and many other ancient worthies. The first burial was made in 1687. A few grave stones had been placed in earlier times, contrary to Friends ideas, and these were removed by order of the meeting in 1802. The burial ground at Unity and Waln Streets was in use by Orthodox Friends until the Separation in 1827. From that time until 1884 burials were mostly made at the burial ground of the Germantown Friends, Coulter Street near Germantown Avenue. From 1884 interments were made at the burial ground of Frankford Friends, on Bustleton Pike, north of Dark Run Lane, which was acquired by purchase in the year 1877.

See: Smedley, Caroline, op. cit., pp. 133-136, 147, 148; Brinton, op. cit., p. 135.

Minutes of Men's Meetings, 1771-1884, 3 vols. (1701-70 missing); Minutes of Women's Meetings, 1795-1905, 3 vols. (1701-94 missing), at PPFYR. Minutes of Joint Meetings, 1906-28, 1 vol., in custody of the clerk of the Frankford Monthly Meeting, Howard Burtt, 1919 Packard Building, 15th and Chestnut Streets, Philadelphia. (This volume contains the minutes of men's meetings, 1885-1905). Minutes of Ministers and Elders, 1816-83, 1 vol., at PPFYR.

110. BYBERRY INDULGED MEETING, 1827-59. Byberry Road, near Byberry
          and Andalusia Turnpike, Byberry, Philadelphia.
Set up in 1827, by Frankford Monthly Meeting (entry 108), with the approval of Abington Quarterly Meeting (entry 92). In 1827, when the Separation took place, there was some discussion in the monthly meeting at Byberry as to which part should retain possession of the meeting's property, and be considered the monthly meeting. The matter was finally settled by the Orthodox group withdrawing, leaving the Hicksite majority in peaceable possession. The majority group also retained the old records. Some of the original records, however, were burned in a fire which took place some time between 1860 and 1870, while they were in the custody of the clerk of that time, Watson C. Martindale. Among the most important of those destroyed were the minute books of the men's meeting from 1810-31, but abstracts therefrom are preserved by the Historical Society of Pennsylvania, in Philadelphia. A great portion of the treasurer's account books, in fact it appears to be all of them up to 1877, seem to be missing, and it is the general belief that some of the earlier ones were destroyed by this fire.

After their withdrawal the Orthodox group consisting of 39 members, organized a meeting for worship, which attached to Frankford Monthly Meeting. Meetings were first held at the house of David Comfort in Byberry, and continued there until they had time to erect a meeting-house. This they did in the latter part of 1828, on a lot then belonging to Watson Atkinson. This lot was situated about a half-mile south of the site of the old meeting-house which they had left, and about 50 yards from the Byberry and Andalusia Turnpike. The meeting-house was a very small, one-story frame building, and was unpainted. From the start the lot upon which the house stood was rented, and the consideration was a yearly rent of 1 ton of hay. In the year 1834, David Comfort, having purchased the property from Atkinson, deeded the lot to James C. Comfort and Thornton Comfort, in trust, for the use of the Orthodox portion of Friends living in Byberry, both as a meeting-house lot and a burying ground. There does not appear, however, any record of a cemetery ever having been opened there. The lot contained about 100 square perches, and was given with the proviso that if the said meeting should be discontinued, and no meeting afterwards held there, the trustees were to sow it with grass seed, and with the proceeds keep it in good order. They continued to hold their meetings there for many years, until death had removed many of the members, and others had moved from the neighborhood. In 1859 the meeting was laid down. The property was then placed under the care of the Frankford Monthly Meeting. In 1939, the clerk of the present Byberry Monthly Meeting Hicksite, Edwin K. Bonner recalls having seen this old meeting-house in his very early boyhood. He describes it as then being quite old and standing on a field a short distance off the road, and at that time was being used by a farmer to store tools and other farm implements. He described the building as being very small, and almost square. It was one story and constructed of wood, and had the appearance of never having been painted. A few years later it became quite dilapidated and was torn down. No traces of it are seen today.

See: Martindale, op. cit., p. 36; Matlack, op. cit., I, 38; Historical Excursion, pp. 53-63.

111. STROUDSBURG PREPARATIVE MEETING, 1809-83. Southwest corner 8th and Main Streets, Stroudsburg, Monroe County.
Set up as an indulged meeting in 1809 by Richland Monthly Meeting (entry 101). From 1809-11 meetings were held in the homes of members. In 1811 a small two-story stone meeting-house was erected at the southwest corner of 8th and Main Streets. Stroudsburg Indulged Meeting had its status changed in 1811 to a preparative meeting by Richland Monthly Meeting, and in the same year, a burial ground, 85' x 100' located at Eighth and Ann Streets was acquired. In 1815 when Stroudsburg Monthly Meeting (entry 112) was established, Stroudsburg Preparative Meeting was transferred from Richland Monthly Meeting to Stroudsburg Monthly Meeting. After Stroudsburg Monthly Meeting was laid down in 1839, Stroudsburg Preparative Meeting was attached to Abington Monthly Meeting (entry 93). In 1857 Stroudsburg Preparative Meeting was laid down by Abington Quarterly Meeting (entry 92). It then reverted back to its original status of an indulged meeting and functioned under the care of Horsham Preparative Meeting, until 1870, at which time it was transferred to the care of Frankford Preparative Meeting (entry 109). In 1883 Stroudsburg Indulged Meeting was laid down. The meeting-house, however, was maintained until 1932 when it was sold to the Borough of Stroudsburg and a town hall was erected on the same site. The burial ground, surrounded on three sides by a concrete wall and a picket fence enclosing the entrance, is held in trust by the Frankford Monthly Meeting (entry 108). No burials have been made in this graveyard for many years and no additional interments are permitted.

See: Michener, op. cit., p. 88; A. Mitchell Palmer, A History of
Quakers in Stroudsburg (manuscript in Monroe County Historical Society,
Stroudsburg).

Minutes of Men's Meetings, 1850-57, 1 vol., at PPFYR. Monroe County
Deed Books, vol. 31, p. 662; vol. 37, p. 36.

112. STROUDSBURG MONTHLY MEETING, 1815-39. Southwest corner of 8th
and Main Streets, Stroudsburg, Monroe County.
Set up in 1815 by Richland Monthly Meeting (entry 101) with the consent
of Abington Quarterly Meeting (entry 92). Meetings were held alternately
in the meeting-houses of Richland Monthly Meeting and Stroudsburg Preparative Meeting (entry 111). Stroudsburg Monthly Meeting was laid down
Fifth month 9, 1839 by Abington Quarterly Meeting.

See: Michener, op. cit., p. 88.

Minutes of Men's Meetings, 1815-39, 1 vol.; Minutes of Women's Meet-
ings, 1815-39, 1 vol.; Minutes of Ministers and Elders, 1815-39, 1 vol.;
Register of Births, 1809-39, 1 vol.; Register of Deaths, 1809-39, 1 vol.;
Marriages, 1818-38, 1 vol.; Certificates of Removal, 1816-27, 1 vol.,
S.F.P.

113. FRIENDSVILLE PREPARATIVE MEETING, 1819-37. On route 695, south
of Chacomet Lake, Friendsville, Susquehanna County.
Set up as a Preparative Meeting in 1822 by Stroudsburg Monthly Meeting
(entry 112), after having functioned as an indulged meeting since 1819.
Request for a preparative meeting is found in an extract of a minute of
Stroudsburg Monthly Meeting dated Sixth month 22; "Stroudsburg Monthly
Meeting of Friends appointed a committee to visit those settled at Friendsville in Susquehanna County to which service Daniel Stroud and James Bell
were appointed." Two years later this request was granted, as is evidenced by a minute of the Stroudsburg Monthly Meeting, held Fourth month
25th; "This Monthly Meeting received a request from Friends at Friendsville for the establishment of a preparative meeting to be held on the
Fifth-day of the week and 2 weeks before the time of the holding of the
Monthly Meeting. This meeting having considered the same are of the mind
their request ought to be granted. The clerk is directed to forward a
copy of this minute to our next quarterly meeting for their concurrence."
This request was granted and the preparative meeting was established
Eleventh month 21, 1822. Early meetings were held in members' homes.
It was not until 1824 that a frame meeting-house was erected on a lot
situated south of Chacomet Lake. The surrounding ½ acre of ground was
plotted for a burial ground. Members of this meeting found it exceed-
ingly difficult to communicate with their monthly meeting, because of the
distance separating them.   Consequently they appealed to Stroudsburg
Monthly Meeting to be attached to Hector Monthly Meeting of New York (see
forthcoming Inventory of the Church Archives of New York. This request
for transfer of attachment was recorded in a minute of Stroudsburg Monthly Meeting of Fourth month 27; "A communication was received from Friendsville Preparative Meeting requesting to be joined to the Hector Monthly
Meeting of the State of New York, which claiming the consideration of the
Meeting, John Z. Flagor, Daniel Stroud, James Bell, and William Pickering
were appointed to unite with a committee of Women Friends to visit the
meeting and report to our next or future Monthly Meeting." After consideration of this application, the committee's report was recorded in a
minute dated Seventh month 27, 1826; "The Committee in the 4th month last

on the application of Friendsville Preparative Meeting made the following
report, viz., 'We of your committee appointed to visit Friends of Friendsville in consequence of the proposal of that meeting to be joined to Hector Monthly Meeting. That we were with them at a meeting of worship and
afterwards had a meeting called together on the subject of our appointment. That since the proposal was made four families have removed and
five other families decided to remove quite soon. The other families,
eleven in number, of a changed mind, prefer remaining a part of Stroudsburg Monthly Meeting, and that it does not appear to us the proper time had
arrived to make a change.'".In 1830 a separation occurred in this meeting.
The Hicksite Friends retained the meeting-house and burial ground. In the
same year this meeting requested the monthly meeting to lay it down. However, the request was not granted. In 1837, because the meeting was
"greatly decreased in membership" the meeting was laid down by Stroudsburg
Monthly Meeting and its members were attached to Stroudsburg Preparative
Meeting (entry 111).

See: Emily C. Blackman, History of Susquehanna County, pp. 92, 436-
438, 440, 442, 447; Matlack, op. cit., I, 76-84.

There are no minutes or records available at the present time.

114. GERMANTOWN MONTHLY MEETING, 1906--. Coulter Street, west of
Germantown Avenue, Germantown, Philadelphia.
Set up November 8, 1906 by Abington Quarterly Meeting (entry 92). Its
only constituent meeting is Germantown Preparative Meeting (entry 115),
which was attached to Frankford Monthly Meeting (entry 108) until Germantown Monthly Meeting was set up. First session held December 27, 1906.
Meetings have always been held at the meeting-house of Germantown Preparative Meeting. The present clerk is Alfred G. Scattergood, Awbury, Germantown.

See: Horace Lippincott, An Account of the People Called Quakers,
in Germantown, Philadelphia, Passim, hereinafter cited as Lippincott,
Account.

Minutes of Joint Meetings, 1906-23, 1 vol., at PPFYR, and 1924--,
2 vols., in meeting-house. Minutes of Overseers' Meetings, 1917--, 2
vols.; Minutes of Germantown Mission Board, 1923--, 1 vol.; Register of
Members, 1906--, 1 vol., in meeting-house. Recorder's Register of Members, Births, Marriages, and Deaths, 1906--, 1 vol., in custody of recorder, Horatio C. Wood, 164 West School House Lane, Germantown, Philadelphia.

115. GERMANTOWN PREPARATIVE MEETING, 1683--. Coulter Street west of
Germantown Avenue, Germantown, Philadelphia.
William Penn, traveling in Holland and Germany accompanied by George Fox,
Robert Barclay, George Keith, and others, found that Friends of these
countries were greatly persecuted, and a few years later, he invited them
to join his province of Pennsylvania, where religious toleration would be
theirs. They gladly accepted. Under the leadership of Francis Daniel
Pastorius (founder of Germantown), who had preceded them, 33 persons from
Cresheim, Germany, arrived on October 6, 1683, at what is now Germantown.
One of the original settlers, Dennis Conrad, built a stone house at what
is now 5109 Germantown Avenue. First meetings of Friends in Germantown
were held here, and later at the homes of others. In 1683, a meeting for
worship was held, and later became attached to Abington Monthly Meeting

(entry 93). It was from this little meeting in 1688, that the first public protest against slavery, written by Pastorius, in the form of a minute, was directed to the Monthly Meeting held at Richard Worrall's. Jacob
Shoemaker, who came over from Cresheim with Pastorius, gave to the meeting, in 1690, 3 perches of land on Germantown Avenue near Coulter Street.
Here, it is believed, a log meeting-house was built in 1690. This was
the first meeting-house of Germantown Friends. A larger lot adjoining
the 3 perches was purchased in 1693. In 1705, 50 acres more, which also
adjoined the land already acquired, were purchased. A minute of Abington
Monthly Meeting of Twelfth month 26, 1704, says, "Germantown Friends laid
before the meeting, their new meeting-house to be built next summer and
subscriptions were requested by the next Monthly Meeting." Subscriptions,
partly in wheat, were received from Friends of Philadelphia, Frankford,
Abington, and Byberry. In 1705 a stone meeting-house was erected on the
lot which is now the old graveyard on the Germantown Avenue side. This
house was replaced in 1812 by another stone meeting-house, erected on
grounds adjoining the old meeting-house. There seems to have been no
records kept of the early meetings, but some of their concerns are noticed
in the minutes of Abington Monthly Meeting. In January 1816, the meeting
was transferred to Frankford Monthly Meeting (entry 108), of Abington
Quarter (entry 92). The Germantown Friends School was established in
1845 (entry 434) by a legacy left in 1841 by Isaac Jones. About the
same time a section of the present building of the Germantown Friends Free
Library (entry 435) was erected. In 1869 the present large two-story,
stone meeting-house was built. In 1900 the preparative meeting was incorporated. A two-story gray stone caretaker's residence built early
in the history of this meeting, stands upon the grounds. When Germantown
Monthly Meeting (entry 114) was established in 1906, the preparative meeting became a part thereof. It now meets but once a year, and its concerns
are mostly of the schools and the library.

There are two burial grounds on the premises, the old one on Germantown Avenue side, has long been discontinued, and the burial records appear to be missing. The second burial ground on the Greene Street side,
acquired in 1854, is in use at the present time. First burial was January 31, 1860.

See: Lippincott, Account, Passim.

Minutes of Men's Meetings, 1756-1895, 3 vols. (1683-1755 missing);
Minutes of Women's Meetings, 1784-1849, 2 vols. (1683-1783, 1850-95 missing), at PPFYR. Minutes of Joint Meetings, 1896--, 1 vol., in meeting-
house. Minutes of Ministers and Elders, 1816-24, 1 vol. (1825-1915 missing), at PPFYR, and 1916--, 1 vol., in meeting-house. Minutes of Property
Committee, 1904--, 2 vols., in meeting-house. Financial Records, 1832-
1918, 7 vols., at PPFYR, 1919-29, 6 vols., in Germantown Friends' Free
Library; and 1930--, 1 vol., in custody of treasurer, Joseph H. Haines,
130 W. Walnut Lane, Germantown, Philadelphia. Register of Interments,
1860--, 1 vol., in meeting-house.

Component Meetings

(Only Meetings within the Commonwealth of Pennsylvania are listed here. See: Inventory of Cnurch
Archives of Maryland for remaining ones).

The listing of the monthly and preparative meetings under this quarterly meeting is the same as that given under the Warrington and Fairfax
Quarterly Meeting. This quarterly meeting, organized in 1776 was divided
in 1787 into Warrington Quarterly Meeting, whose subordinate meetings lay
almost entirely in Pennsylvania; and Fairfax Quarterly Meeting, whose subordinate meetings were in Maryland and Virginia. Since this Survey is
limited to churches within the Commonwealth of Pennsylvania, and since,
after the division of the quarterly meeting in 1787, the Pennsylvania
meetings are those which come under Warrington, it is unnecessary to duplicate the listing.

CALN QUARTERLY MEETING (0)

Component Meetings

(See: Explanatory Note 3)

	Date established	Entry number
BRADFORD MONTHLY MEETING	1737	117
Caln Preparative Meeting	1716	118
Sadsbury Preparative Meeting	1725	119
Bradford Preparative Meeting	1726	120
West Caln Preparative Meeting	1756	121
Cambridge Indulged Meeting	1824	122
SADSBURY MONTHLY MEETING	1737	123
Columbia Indulged Meeting (Hempfield)	1728	124
Columbia Preparative Meeting (Hempfield)	1812	124
Lampeter Preparative Meeting (Leacock)	1732	125
Lancaster Indulged Meeting	1753	126
River Indulged Meeting	1789	78
East Sadsbury Indulged Meeting	1810	127
Bart Indulged Meeting	1820	128
UWCHLAN MONTHLY MEETING	1763	129
Uwchlan Preparative Meeting	1714	130
Uwchlan Indulged Meeting	1881	130
Pikeland Indulged Meeting	1758	131
Pikeland Preparative Meeting	1802	131
Nantmeal Preparative Meeting	1791	132
Downingtown Indulged Meeting	1784	133
Downingtown Preparative Meeting	1811	133
ROBESON MONTHLY MEETING (FOREST MEETING)	1789	134
Robeson Preparative Meeting (Forest Meeting)	1741	135

116. CALN QUARTERLY MEETING, 1800--. Sixth Avenue and Chestnut Street, Coatesville.
Set up in 1800 by Philadelphia Yearly Meeting (entry 1) by a division in Chester Quarterly Meeting (entry 136) and Western Quarterly Meeting (entry 71). Met from 1800-1911 in meeting-houses of the meetings belonging to the subordinate meetings. Since 1911 meetings have been held in the one-story gray stone meeting-house of Caln Preparative Meeting (entry 118), Sixth Avenue and Chestnut Street, Coatesville. The present clerk is Ellis Y. Brown, Jr., Downingtown.

See: Futhey and Cope, op. cit., p. 241; Michener, op. cit., p. 124.

Minutes of Men's Meetings, 1800-1842, 1896-1922, 2 vols. (1843-97

missing); Minutes of Women's Meetings, 1800-1919, 5 vols. (1 ... 22 missing), at PPFYR. Minutes of Joint Meetings, 1823--, 1 vol., in custody
of clerk. Minutes of Ministers and Elders, 1916---, 1 vol. (1800-1815
missing), in custody of Anne Windle, Downingtown.

117. BRADFORD MONTHLY MEETING, 1737--. Sixth Avenue and Chestnut
Street, Coatesville.
Set up in 1737 by Chester Quarterly Meeting (entry 136), with the consent of Newark Monthly Meeting (now Kennett Monthly Meeting) (entry 9)
and Concord Monthly Meeting (entry 143). In 1758 when Western Quarterly
Meeting (entry 71) was set up, this meeting became a part. When Caln
Quarterly Meeting (entry 116) was established in 1800 this meeting was
transferred from Western Quarterly to Caln Quarterly Meeting. The monthly meetings were held alternately in the meeting-houses of Bradford Preparative Meeting (entry 120) and Caln Preparative Meeting (entry 118)
until 1911. Since then the meetings have been held in the new meeting-
house of Caln Preparative Meeting, which was erected in Coatesville in
1911. The present clerk is Newlin L. Moore, Box 135, Coatesville.

See: Michener, op. cit., p. 124; George Smith, History of Delaware
County, p. 246; Futhey and Cope, op. cit., p. 240; Thomson, op. cit.,
p. 747.

Minutes of Men's Meetings, 1737-1922, 11 vols. (contains minutes of
Joint Meetings, 1919-22); Minutes of Women's Meetings, 1737-1918, 15
vols., at PPFYR. Minutes of Joint Meetings, 1923--, 1 vol., in custody
of clerk. Register of Births and Deaths, 1726-1834, 1 vol., at PPFYR,
and 1885--, 1 vol., in custody of recorder, Webb Holstein, 86 Pennsylvania Avenue, Coatesville. Register of Marriages, 1737-1909, 2 vols.,
at PPFYR, and 1909--, 1 vol., custody of recorder. Certificates of Removal, 1737-1907, 9 vols. (1908-- mot found), at PPFYR. Financial Records, 1923--, 1 vol. (1739-1922 missing), in custody of Arthur Yearsley,
10 South Third Avenue, Coatesville (contains financial records of Caln
Preparative Meeting, 1916-22).

118. CALN PREPARATIVE MEETING, 1716--. Sixth Avenue and Chestnut
Street, Coatesville.
Set up in 1716 by the Concord Monthly Meeting (entry 143). In the same
year, an acre of ground, part of which was used for a burial ground, and
on which a meeting-house was erected, was purchased from John Mendenhall.
The ground was located on "the Old Pim place at the foot of the hill."
The property is now owned by Joseph Edge. Meetings were held here until
1726, when 4 acres of land were purchased from Richard Pake on which a
three-room stone structure was erected. Today this building is the Old
Caln Meeting-House, located on King's Highway a short distance northeast
of Coatesville. In 1737 the meeting was transferred to the care of Bradford Monthly Meeting (entry 117). The first meeting-house was sold to
William Pim in 1743, and the burial ground was deeded back to the meeting
"for the use of Friends forever." After the Separation in 1827 the meetings were held in the homes of members in Downingtown. Caln Preparative
Meeting, Hicksite (entry 277), obtained title to this meeting-house about
1830. Plans were then made for Orthodox meetings to be held in the east
room of the meeting-house; the Hicksite Friends to hold their meetings in
the west room and the room between to be used by both branches of Caln
Quarterly Meeting (entry 116). The Orthodox Friends continued to meet here
until 1907, when permission was granted by Bradford Monthly Meeting to
meet in the home of Elizabeth B. Calley, 8 South Third Avenue, Coatesville,

where meetings were held from November 1907, until 1911. A lot, located at Sixth Avenue and Chestnut Street, Coatesville, was purchased in 1910. The same year a large building was erected with stone quarried from the ground. The meeting-house has a porch supported by large white pillars. A porte-cochere is on the Sixth Avenue side. The date stone is marked 1910. The first meeting was held here February 26, 1911. In 1919 the members of Sadsbury Preparative Meeting (entry 119) were transferred to this meeting. Since 1923 only weekly meetings for worship have been held, and all business of the preparative meeting was directed by Bradford Monthly Meeting. However, according to the minutes of Bradford Monthly Meeting, Caln Preparative Meeting has never been laid down.

A school was conducted in the Old Caln Meeting-House in 1780 for a very long time, but definite data about it is not available. Both Orthodox and Hicksite Friends of Caln used the old burial grounds until 1855 when the Orthodox Friends purchased ½ acre of land from William Windle, to be used as a burial ground. This burial ground is located on the south side of King's Highway. The first interment was that of Richard Pim, in 1856. In September 1857, an additional half-acre of ground was purchased. The chart for this burial ground is in the possession of Mrs. Annie Windle, R.F.D., Downingtown.

See: Michener, op. cit., pp. 124, 125; Smith, George, op. cit., pp. 226, 238; Futhey and Cope, op. cit., pp. 237, 238; Woody, op. cit., p. 136; "One of the Unique Churches in Chester County," Philadelphia Record, March 27, 1901; "Quaker Meeting-House is Divided," Philadelphia Record, November 8, 1908; "Many Attend Initial Service," West Chester Daily Local News, February 27, 1911; "Friends Meet at Old Caln," West Chester Daily Local News, July 24, 1914; "Caln Friends Meeting," West Chester, Daily Local News, September 13, 1930; "East Caln Meeting-House be Reopened," West Chester Daily Local News, May 29, 1937; "Caln First-day School Opens," Honeybrook Herald, June 10, 1937.

Minutes of Men's Meetings, 1842-74, 2 vols. (1716-1841, 1875-98 missing); Minutes of Women's Meetings, 1882-96, 1 vol. (1716-1881 missing); Minutes of Joint Meetings, 1897-1919, 1 vol., at PPFYR. Registers are in the records of the Concord Monthly Meeting, 1716-38; in the records of the Bradford Monthly Meeting, 1737--. Financial Records, 1842-1912, 1 vol. (1817-41, 1913-15 missing), at PPFYR, and 1916-22 in Bradford Monthly Meeting financial records. Chester County Deed Books, F-6, vol. 128, p. 498; F-6, vol. 128, p. 374.

119. SADSBURY PREPARATIVE MEETING, 1723-1919. Slokum Avenue, Christiana, Lancaster County.

Sadsbury Preparative Meeting was set up about 1725 by New Garden Monthly Meeting (entry 72), after having functioned as Sadsbury Indulged Meeting since 1723. Previous to the erection of a log meeting-house in 1725, meetings for worship were undoubtedly held in members' homes. When Sadsbury Monthly Meeting (entry 123) was set up in 1737, this meeting was transferred to the newly established monthly meeting. About 1744, 56 acres of ground located 1 mile north of Christiana, on the road to Simmontown was purchased from Richard and Thomas Penn. A few years later a burial ground was plotted and a new meeting-house was erected on a portion of this property. Later 2 additional purchases of ground were made. In 1759, 4 acres were purchased from the heirs of Andres Moore, and in 1818, 2 acres on the west side of the road were purchased from John Murry. In the minutes of Sadsbury Monthly Meeting there is evidence of schools with-

in the limits of Sadsbury Preparative Meeting. However, due to the absence of further historical data the locations and the length of time
these schools were in existence is unknown. When the Separation occurred
in 1828, the meeting-house and property were retained by the Sadsbury
Preparative Meeting, Hicksite (entry 268). However, the Orthodox Friends
continued to use the meeting-house until 1831, and the burial ground until
the Orthodox meeting was laid down years later. On August 1, 1831, 1 acre
of ground on the north side of the road in Simmontown was purchased from
Isaac Bower, and in the same year a meeting-house was erected thereon.
In 1880 this meeting purchased from Samuel Slokum a plot of ground on
which they erected a one-story red brick meeting-house in the same year.
When Sadsbury Monthly Meeting was laid down in 1907, this meeting was
transferred to Bradford Monthly Meeting (entry 117). Due to decreasing
membership Sadsbury Preparative Meeting was laid down in 1919 by Bradford
Monthly Meeting. The property in Christiana was sold in 1930 to Harry
E. Mullen.

See: Futhey and Cope, op. cit., p. 239; Michener, op. cit., p. 128;
Thomson, op. cit., p. 751; Franklin Ellis and Samuel Evans, History of
Lancaster County, p. 1036; Woody, op. cit., pp. 141, 142; Thaddeus S.
Kenderdine, "Around Sadsbury," Philadelphia Friends Intelligencer, July
10, 1909, hereinafter cited as Kenderdine, Around Sadsbury; Kenderdine,
"Landmarks of Caln Quarter," Philadelphia Friends Intelligencer, November
20, 1909, hereinafter cited as Kenderdine, Landmarks; "Sadsbury Friends
Looking Backwards," West Chester Daily Local News, June 17th, 1924; "Old
Sadsbury, 1724-1924," Philadelphia Friends Intelligencer, June 25, 1924;
Jessie W. Jackson, "Historical Sketch of Old Sadsbury," Philadelphia
Friends Intelligencer, July 5, 1924.

Minutes of Men's Meetings, 1828-50, 4 vols. (1725-1813 missing), at
PPFYR, and 1814-1919, at PSC-Hi. Minutes of Women's Meetings, missing.
Registers, 1723-37 in the records of New Garden Monthly Meeting; 1737-1906
in the records of Sadsbury Monthly Meeting; 1907-19 in the records of
Bradford Monthly Meeting. Lancaster County Deed Books, KX, p. 572; R5,
p. 369; U8, p. 367; N11, p. 370; H-10, vol. 230, p. 194; Book-E, vol. 30,
p. 504.

120. BRADFORD PREPARATIVE MEETING, 1716-1922. Junction of Strasburg
      and Northbrook Roads, Marshallton, West Bradford Twp., Ches-
      ter County.
Set up in 1726 by Newark Monthly Meeting (entry 79), after having functioned as an indulged meeting since 1716 under Kennett Preparative Meeting (entry 80). This meeting is sometimes called Marshallton Meeting.
The first meeting-house is reported to have been at or near the northeast
corner of the land of Abraham Marshall. This meeting-house soon proved
inadequate so in 1729, 2½ acres of ground was purchased from Edward Clayton
and a new meeting-house was erected thereon and a part of the land was
plotted for a burial ground. When Bradford Monthly Meeting (entry 117)
was set up in 1738, Bradford Preparative Meeting became a part of the
newly established monthly meeting. A one-story gray stone meeting-house
was erected near the second meeting-house in 1765. This house is still
standing. The graveyard was enclosed by a stone wall in 1774. The minutes of the Bradford Monthly Meeting record that from 1789-97 there were
two schools within the limits of the Bradford Preparative Meeting. One
of the schools was held in the schoolhouse, erected near the meeting-house
in 1792, on ground donated by Humphrey Marshall. The other school occupied the old stone schoolhouse, located on the road west of the boundary

of the meeting-house property. The latter school was conducted by this meeting, Birmingham Preparative Meeting (entry 155) and Goshen Monthly Meeting (entry 150). The school was discontinued about 1910 and the building was razed in 1916. Due to decreased membership the meeting was laid down by Bradford Monthly Meeting in 1922 and its members were transferred to Caln Preparative Meeting (entry 118). In the same year the trustees deeded the meeting-house and property to the Friends Fiduciary Corporation.

See: Woody, op. cit., pp. 136, 146; Thomson, op. cit., pp. 747, 750; Heathcote, op. cit., p. 340; Michener, op. cit., pp. 124, 125; Futhey and Cope, op. cit., p. 238; "Friends' Meeting, Marshalltown," West Chester Daily Local News, January 13, 1880; "Old Marshalltown Meeting, West Chester Daily Local News, October 10, 1893; "Bradford Meeting," West Chester Daily Local News, March 8, 1930; "Bradford Old Stone School House," West Chester Daily Local News, August 9, 1938.

Minutes of Men's Meetings, 1828-45, 1 vol. (1726-27, 1845-98 missing), at PPFYR, and 1899-1915, 1 vol., in custody of Miss Grace Evans, West Chester (this volume will soon be sent to PPFYR). Minutes of Women's Meetings, 1821-44, 1907-19, 2 vols. (1726-1820, 1845-1906 missing), at PPFYR. Minutes of Joint Meetings, 1916-22 included in the 1899-1915 vol. of Minutes of Men's Meetings. Registers are in the records of the Kennett Monthly Meeting, 1726-36; and in the records of Bradford Monthly Meeting, 1737-1922. Chester County Deed Books, N-6, vol. 135, p. 117; L-4, vol. 83, p. 143; X-4, vol. 95, p. 23; D-5, vol. 101, p. 203; Z-7, vol. 172, p. 293; A-16, vol. 373, p. 298.

121. WEST CALN PREPARATIVE MEETING, 1741-1908. King's Highway, 1½ miles of Wagontown Village, West Caln Twp., Chester County. Set up by Bradford Monthly Meeting (entry 117) in 1756, after having functioned as an indulged meeting since 1741. From 1741-56 meetings were held in members' homes. In 1747 the Friends purchased 2 acres of land from Evan Lewis; 3/4 acre was set aside as a burial ground. In 1756 the present brownstone meeting-house was erected. As the meeting became smaller part of the ground was sold. In 1908, when this meeting was laid down by the Bradford Monthly Meeting, there remained only about 1½ acres. After the meeting was laid down, the remaining members went to Bradford Preparative Meeting (entry 120). The meeting-house and burial ground were placed in the hands of a committee. Mr. A. N. Yearsley, treasurer of Bradford Monthly Meeting, is a sole surviving member.

See: Thomson, op. cit., p. 747; Heathcote, op. cit., p.241; Michener, op. cit., p. 126; Futhey and Cope, op. cit., p. 240. Registers of this meeting are recorded in the records of the Bradford Monthly Meeting.

122. CAMBRIDGE INDULGED MEETING, 1824-27. Close to Main Street, Cambridge, Honeybrook Twp., Chester County. Set up in 1824 by Bradford Monthly Meeting (entry 117) for the convenience of Friends who lived too far from either Bradford Monthly Meeting or Sadsbury Monthly Meeting (entry 123). In 1824 Solomon and Catherine Landas donated ½ acre of ground to the meeting. The one-story frame meeting-house was erected thereon in the same year. One-eighth of the donated land was laid out as a cemetery. Later the burial ground was enclosed by a stone wall. At the time of the Separation in 1827, this meeting was laid down by the Bradford Monthly Meeting. The meeting-house and ground were retained by Cambridge Indulged Meeting, Hicksite (entry 246).

See: Michener, op. cit., pp. 126, 127; Futhey and Cope, op. cit., p. 242.

All records are included in those of Bradford Monthly Meeting.

123. SADSBURY MONTHLY MEETING, 1737-1907. Slokum Avenue, Christiana, Sadsbury Twp., Lancaster County.
Set up in 1737 by Chester Quarterly Meeting (entry 136), upon the recommendation of the New Garden Monthly Meeting (entry 72). When the Western Quarterly Meeting (entry 71) was set up in 1758, Sadsbury Monthly Meeting was transferred to the newly established Quarterly Meeting. Meetings were held alternately in the meeting-houses of the preparative meetings, which were under the care of Sadsbury Monthly Meeting. In 1800 Caln Quarterly Meeting (entry 116) was set up and this meeting was then transferred to the newly established quarterly meeting. For many years Sadsbury Monthly Meeting was a powerful influence among the Friends in Lancaster and York Counties. Most of the indulged and preparative meetings in these counties were established by Sadsbury Monthly Meeting. Due to decreased membership the meeting was laid down in 1907 and its members joined with Bradford Monthly Meeting (entry 119).

See: Futhey and Cope, op. cit., p. 240; Thomson, op. cit., p. 751; Michener, op. cit., pp. 127, 128; Woody, op. cit., pp. 141-145; Matlack, op. cit., I, 210-213; Kenderdine, Landmarks; Kenderdine, Around Sadsbury.

Minutes of Men's Meetings, 1737-1827, 3 vols., at PSC-Hi, and 1737-52, 1828-1907, 4 vols., at PPFYR. Minutes of Women's Meetings, 1777-90, 1 vol. (1737-76, 1791-1805, 1905-7 missing), at PSC-Hi, and 1806-1904, 3 vols., at PPFYR. Registers of Marriage Certificates, 1738-1830, 1 vol., at PSC-Hi, and 1829-1901, 1 vol., at PPFYR. Registers of Births and Deaths, 1737-1835, 1 vol., at PSC-Hi, and 1830-80, 1 vol. (1881-1907 missing), at PPFYR. Certificates of Removal, 1764-1828, 1 vol. (1737-63, 1902-7 missing), at PSC-Hi, and 1828-1901, 1 vol., at PPFYR.

124. COLUMBIA PREPARATIVE MEETING, 1728-1829. 312-16 Cherry Street, Columbia, Lancaster County.
Set up in 1812 as a preparative meeting by Sadsbury Monthly Meeting (entry 123). In 1728 Robert Barber, Samuel Blumston, and John Wright, who had moved from Chester to Columbia, organized this meeting under the name of Hempfield Meeting. During its early period the meeting was not affiliated with any higher meeting. However, soon after 1751, it became an indulged meeting under the Lampeter Preparative Meeting (entry 125) and was called Wright's Ferry Meeting. Due to the absence of historical data, the meeting places from 1728-58 are unknown but were probably private homes. In 1758 a log meeting-house was erected on the south side of Union Street near Lane Avenue. This building was occupied until 1812. In that year a small, red brick, meeting-house was erected at 312-316 Cherry Street and an 80' x 162' plot of ground located on the north side of Cherry between Sixth and Bethel Streets was plotted as a graveyard. This ground was the property of William and Deborah Wright and was donated to the meeting in 1819. When the status of this meeting was changed to that of a preparative meeting in 1812, its name was changed to Columbia Preparative Meeting. At the time of the Separation in 1828 the meeting-house and burial ground were retained by Columbia Indulged Meeting, Hicksite (entry 269). However, the Orthodox Friends continued to meet in the same building until 1829, when Columbia Preparative Meeting, Orthodox, was laid down by Sadsbury Monthly Meeting.

See: Michener, op. cit., pp. 128-130; Ellis and Evans, op. cit.,
pp. 552-561; Matlack, op. cit., I, 214-217, 264; Kenderdine, Around Sadsbury; Kenderdine, Landmarks.

Minutes of Men's Meetings, 1812-29, 2 vols.; Minutes of Women's Meetings, 1819-29, 1 vol. (1812-18 missing), at PSC-Hi. Registers are in the
records of the Sadsbury Monthly Meeting. Lancaster County Deed Books,
vol. 21, p. 82; T-vol. 14, p. 40; Q-vol. 14, p. 73.

125. LAMPETER PREPARATIVE MEETING (formerly Leacock), 1728-1852.
      On Route 340, Bird-in-Hand, East Lampeter Twp., Lancaster
      County.
Set up in 1732 as Leacock Preparative Meeting by New Garden Monthly Meeting (entry 73), after having functioned since 1728 as an indulged meeting
under the care of Sadsbury Preparative Meeting (entry 119). From 1729 until 1732 meetings were held in the home of Hattil Varman (also written
Hatwell Vernon), which was located in Leacock Township. In 1732 a log
meeting-house was erected on a plot of ground called "Varman's Land."
When Sadsbury Monthly Meeting (entry 123) was set up in 1737, this preparative meeting was transferred to the newly established monthly meeting.
About 1748 Leacock Preparative Meeting requested the privilege of moving
the meeting to Bird-in-Hand. This request was granted by Sadsbury Monthly
Meeting, and in 1749 this meeting purchased from John Mcnab and Joseph
Steer, 2½ acres of ground in Bird-in-Hand. The same year the meeting
was moved to its new location and a portion of this ground was plotted
as a burial ground. In 1751 the name of this meeting was changed from
Leacock Preparative Meeting to Lampeter Preparative Meeting. There are
several references to a Friends School under the care of Lampeter Preparative Meeting in the minutes of Sadsbury Monthly Meeting. However,
due to absence of records and historical data, the number of years that
this school was in existence is unknown. In 1790 a new red brick meeting-house was erected on the site of the former log building. At the
time of the Separation, the meeting-house and burial ground was retained
by Lampeter Preparative Meeting, Hicksite (entry 367). The only information as to where the Orthodox Friends held their meetings after the Separation, is taken from a minute of Tenth month 31, 1849: "The Friends of
Lampeter believed it has been a great disadvantage to their meetings held
on the first days of the week on account of the uncomfortable and crowded
situation of the room they meet in, are about to repair it and fit it up
exclusively for holding meetings, request the monthly meeting to grant a
part of the sum in their hands for that purpose for making the necessary
alterations." Where this room was located does not appear.

Matlack, op. cit., I, 225-228; Ellis and Evans, op. cit., pp. 896,
897; Janetta W. Schoonover, A History of William Brinton, pp. 163, 164;
Futhey and Cope, op. cit., p. 239; Michener, op. cit., pp. 130, 131;
Thomson, op. cit., p. 751; Woody, op. cit., pp. 141-144; Kenderdine,
Landmarks.

Minutes of Men's Meetings, 1849-52, 1 vol. (1732-1848 missing); Minutes of Women's Meetings, 1828-52, 1 vol. (1732-1827 missing), in custody
of Gulielma Smith, 800 Second Street, Parkesburg. The registers are in
the records of the New Garden Monthly, 1732-36 and in the records of the
Sadsbury Monthly Meeting, 1737-1852.

126. LANCASTER INDULGED MEETING, 1753-1802. South Queen Street,
      between Vine and German Streets, Lancaster, Lancaster County.
Established in 1753 by Sadsbury Monthly Meeting (entry 123). Due to the

absence of historical data, the meeting places from 1753-59 are unknown.
In 1754 this meeting purchased from James Hamilton a plot of ground 64'
x 252'. However, it was not until 1759 that a brick meeting-house was
erected thereon and a burial ground plotted. Due to decreased membership
the meeting was laid down in 1802 by Sadsbury Monthly Meeting and the
members transferred to Lampeter Preparative Meeting (entry 125). The
meeting-house and property were then transferred to the care of the Sadsbury Monthly Meeting. In 1845 the meeting-house and grounds were sold
to Ellis Lewis, who in turn sold the property to the Odd Fellows. This
ground was later sold to a Roman Catholic Church but is now in the hands
of a private owner. A marble yard is now located on the lot where the
meeting-house stood. The burial ground was sold on June 12, 1874, to
Warwick Cooper by the trustees of Sadsbury Monthly Meeting.

See: Ellis and Evans, op. cit., p. 1092; Michener, op. cit., pp. 131-
133; Harry M. J. Klein, and others, A History of Lancaster County, II, 838;
Matlack, op. cit., I, 228-230; Kenderdine, Around Sadsbury; Kenderdine,
Landmarks.

Registers are in the records of the Sadsbury Monthly Meeting. Lancaster County Deed Books, vol. Z, pp. 335, 338; A-vol. 7, p. 233; Q-vol.
10, p. 64.

127. EAST SADSBURY INDULGED MEETING, 1810-13, 1819-68. One-quarter
mile south of Lincoln Highway, 2½ miles west of Sadsbury, Chester County.
Established by Sadsbury Monthly Meeting in 1810. Meetings for worship
were first held in 1809 in a schoolhouse located near Turnpike Road. In
1813 services were discontinued for reasons given in the following minute
of the monthly meeting dated April 6, 1813: "We of the committee in the
case of the indulged meeting at Sadsbury having met and had a conference
with some of the members of that meeting do agree to report that it appears to us the way is not open for them to provide themselves with better
accommodations to meet in, and under existing circumstances, we are of the
mind it would be better if the indulgence should be withdrawn and said
meeting be discontinued for the present which is submitted to the meeting."

In 1818, on behalf of 29 applicants, a request was made to Sadsbury
Monthly Meeting for the privilege of building a meeting-house on a lot
of land bargained for with Aaron and Cyrus Cooper; also while waiting
for the proposed meeting-house to be erected, that an indulged meeting be
permitted in a house lately built by Joseph Cooper. Accordingly the meeting was reestablished on June 6, 1819 by Sadsbury Monthly Meeting and remained under the latter's care until 1868, when it was laid down. An
attempt was made in 1869 to sell the property but the sale was not completed. Afterward the meeting-house was used as a dwelling which was
later destroyed by fire. In 1924 William Paroni Smith purchased 1 acre
and 14 perches of the land, the proceeds of this sale to be used for the
upkeep of the graveyard, containing 66 perches. The graveyard is now
under the care of Bradford Monthly Meeting (entry 117) which fell heir to
the property when Sadsbury Monthly Meeting was discontinued in 1907.

See: Futhey and Cope, op. cit., p. 242; Michener, op. cit., pp. 133,
134; Kenderdine, Landmarks.

Burial records, undated, 1 vol., and draft of graveyard are in the

custody of Gulielma Smith, 800 Second Avenue, Parkesburg. List of gravestones, 1833-1906, at PSC-Hi.

128. BART INDULGED MEETING, 1820-80. One-half mile west of Coopersville, on the south side of Valley Road, Sadsbury Twp., Lancaster County.
Established in 1820 by Sadsbury Monthly Meeting (entry 123). From 1820
to 1825 meetings for worship were held in the schoolhouse of Jeremiah
Cooper. In 1825 a plot of ground, located 1 mile west of Coopersville,
on the north side of Valley Road, was purchased. In the same year a one-
story stone meeting-house was erected and a burial ground plotted. When
the Separation occurred in this meeting in 1828, the meeting-house and
burial ground were retained by Bart Indulged Meeting, Hicksite (entry
226). Due to the absence of records and historical data, the place of
worship from 1828-31 is unknown. From 1831 until 1847, meetings were
held in the home of Truman Cooper. In 1847 a plot of ground was purchased
on the South side of Valley Road, from John Allen. A stone meeting-house
was erected and a burial ground was plotted therein in the same year. Due
to decreasing membership, the meeting was laid down in 1880 by Sadsbury
Monthly Meeting. The meeting-house and property were then transferred
to the care of Sadsbury Monthly Meeting. When Sadsbury Monthly Meeting
was laid down in 1907, the property was transferred to Bradford Monthly
Meeting (entry 117).

See: Matlack, op. cit., I, 203-205, 259, 260, 264-266; Michener, op.
cit., pp. 134, 135; Ellis and Evans, op. cit., p. 1036.

Registers are in the records of the Sadsbury Monthly Meeting. Lancaster County Deed Book, vol. F-5, p. 142.

129. UWCHLAN MONTHLY MEETING, 1763--. Downingtown on Lincoln Highway, East Caln Twp., Chester County.
Set up in 1763 by Chester Quarterly Meeting (entry 136). From 1763 until
1884 meetings were held in the meeting-house which, after 1827 was owned
jointly by Uwchlan Preparative Meetings Orthodox and Hicksite (entries
130-278). Meetings were held in the Nantmeal Preparative Meeting-house
(entry 132) for 6 months during 1778. From 1884-1890 meetings were held
alternately in the meeting-houses of Uwchlan Preparative Meeting and Downingtown Preparative Meeting (entry 133). Since 1900 the meetings have
been held permanently at Downingtown Meeting-house. When Clan Quarterly
Meeting (entry 116) was set up in 1800 this meeting was transferred to
the newly established quarterly meeting. This monthly meeting has in its
charge the burial grounds at Uwchlan, Nantmeal, and Downingtown. The
present clerk is Thomas Parke, Downingtown.

See: Futhey and Cope, op. cit., p. 241; Matlack, op. cit., I, 250-
254; Michener, pp. 135, 136; Thomson, op. cit., p. 751; Gilbert Cope,
Genealogy of the Smedley Family, pp. 190-191, hereinafter cited as Cope,
Genealogy.

Minutes of Men's Meetings, 1763-1903, 5 vols., at PPFYR, 1796-99,
1 vol., at PSC-Hi, and 1903-8, included in the Minutes of Joint Meetings.
Minutes of Women's Meetings, 1763-1908, 7 vols., at PPFYR, 1775-83, 1 vol.,
at PWcHi, and 1789-93, 1 vol., at PHi. Minutes of Joint Meetings, 1902--,
1 vol., in custody of assistant clerk, Mrs. 'Laura T. Edge, Wickford. Minutes of Ministers and Elders, 1782-87, 1 vol., at PSC-Hi, and 1809-57,
7 vols. (these meetings suspended in 1857), at PPFYR. Register of Births

and Deaths, 1/ -1887, 1 vol., at PSC-H; Register of Births and Burials, 1752-1894, 2 vols.; Certificates of Removal, 1763-1881, 2 vols.; at PPFYR. Registers of Births, Marriages, Removal, Deaths, and Burials, 1885--, 1 vol., in custody of recorder, Ellis Y. Brown, South Second Avenue, Downingtown. Financial Records, 1754--, 1 vol., in custody of treasurer, John R. Thomas, Whiteford.   Minutes of school committee, 1814-20, 1 vol.; School Fund Account Book, 1851-55, 1 vol., at PPFYR.

130. UWCHLAN PREPARATIVE MEETING, 1712-1894. Route #100, Village of
      Lionville, Chester County.
Set up in 1714 as a preparative meeting by Chester Monthly Meeting (entry 137), after having functioned as an indulged meeting from 1712-14 under the care of the Goshen Preparative Meeting (entry 151). When Goshen Monthly Meeting (entry 150) was established as a result of the division of Chester Monthly in 1721, Uwchlan Preparative Meeting was transferred to the care of the newly established Goshen Monthly Meeting. Meetings were held in the home of John Cadwallader from 1712 until 1756, at which time a log meeting-house was erected on a part of the 1-acre lot donated to this meeting by John Cadwallader in 1737. A portion of this ground had been previously set aside for use as a burial ground. When Uwchlan Monthly Meeting (entry 129) was set up in 1763 this meeting was transferred to the care of the newly established monthly meeting. A minute dated August 10, 1778 of the Chester Quarterly Meeting (entry 136) notes that the meeting-house was used in 1778 as a hospital for the accommodation of the wounded and sick American soldiers. During this time the Friends held their meetings in the home of George Thomas. There are records attesting to three additions of land obtained by this meeting. In 1796 Thomas Evans donated 42 perches; in 1818 and 1819 John Beitler (also written Beidler) donated 53 perches. The total amount of ground was then 1 acre and 95 perches. When Caln Quarterly Meeting (entry 116) was set up in 1800 Uwchlan preparative and monthly meetings were transferred to the newly established quarterly meeting. When the Separation occurred in this meeting in 1828 both the Orthodox and Hicksite Friends used the same meeting-house. The Orthodox Friends used the north side and the Hicksite Friends the south side. A minute of the Uwchlan Preparative Meeting, dated February 7, 1867, states: "The Hicksite Friends continue to hold meetings in part of the house and make interments in the graveyard, but the deed of trust of the property is in our possession." The log meeting-house was razed in 1875 and was replaced by a gray stone building in the same year. Due to decreased membership Uwchlan Preparative Meeting was laid down in 1881 by Uwchlan Monthly Meeting and an indulged meeting under the care of Downingtown Preparative Meeting (entry 133) was set up. Due to further decrease in membership the indulged meeting was laid down in 1894 by Downingtown Preparative Meeting and its members were attached to that meeting. During the summer of 1904 the Orthodox Friends made arrangements to rent the east side of the meeting-house to the Uwchlan Township School Board to be used as a high school. The Hicksite Friends were opposed to such an arrangement and secured an injunction until the courts could determine whether the Hicksite or Orthodox Friends owned the property. The decision was that neither could give a clear title alone, since both occupied the property. Both groups, however, granted the permission and the school has since been held in the east side of the meeting-house. On July 3, 1920, the trustees of the Orthodox and Hicksite Friends signed a deed selling 70 perches of the ground to Uwchlan Grange Patrons of Husbandry, #1298, for the sum of $1,200. The remaining property of 1 acre and 25 perches, which is the burial ground, remains in the possession of the Friends of both branches but is under the care of the Orthodox Friends.

170 SOCIETY OF FRIENDS

While the meeting-house is at present leased to the school board, the Friends have the privilege of conducting a meeting there once a year. This meeting is held in the summer.

See: Cope, Genealogy, pp. 190, 191; Michener, op. cit., p. 136; Matlack, op. cit., I, 250-254; Heathcote, op. cit., p. 749; Thomson, op. cit., p. 740; Bowden, op. cit., II, 248; Series of articles in the West Chester Daily Local News, from August 16, to August 31, 1904; "Friends' Old Minute Books," West Chester Daily Local News, February 6, 1909.

There are no minutes available at the present time. Some are thought to have been destroyed in a fire, which burned one of the members' homes where the records were stored. Registers are in the records of the Chester Monthly Meeting, 1712-20; Goshen Monthly Meeting, 1721-62; and Uwchlan Monthly Meeting, 1763-1894. Chester County Deed Books, L-11, p. 135; 2-3, pp. 266, 396; R-3, p. 528; F-15, p. 546.

131. PIKELAND PREPARATIVE MEETING (known as Kimberton), 1758-1828. Kimberton Village, East Pikeland Twp., intersection of Nutts Road, Chester County.

Set up as a preparative meeting in 1802 by Uwchlan Monthly Meeting (entry 129), after having functioned as an indulged meeting since 1758. The first mention of this meeting is taken from the minutes of Goshen Monthly Meeting (entry 150) of January 16, 1758: "Application is made by Uwchlan Preparative Meeting (entry 130), setting forth that a considerable number of Friends' families, situated on the lower end of Pikeland, are very remote from their or any other Friends' meeting, and that said friends are unanimously desirous of having a meeting established amongst them." A committee was appointed and a further minute of Goshen Monthly Meeting, April 17, 1758, states: "Committee reported they had found 11 families of Friends who live remote from any meeting and seem unanimous in desiring the privilege of having a meeting amongst them. They have also agreed upon a spot of ground which we viewed and think may answer the purpose when a title for it can be procured. We are in hopes that if their request be granted it may be advantage in a religious sense as it will greatly ease them on account of Travelling." This request was forwarded to the quarterly meeting but it was not until August 14, 1758 that it was granted by Chester Quarterly Meeting (entry 136). When Uwchlan Monthly Meeting was established in 1763 this meeting was transferred from the care of Goshen Monthly Meeting to that of the newly established monthly meeting. The first meeting-house was erected about 1758 and was located on the road from Phoenixville to Chester Springs and was used by Pikeland Friends until 1802. According to a minute dated Ninth month 25, 1792: "Two and one-half acres and twenty-four perches were given for five shillings, by Samuel Hoare of Great Britain from several divers good and benevolent purposes, on which a small meeting-house is now erected." In the same year about a half acre of this ground was plotted for a graveyard. The second meeting-house was erected in 1802 near the site of the first meeting-house and was used until 1818. In 1818 Emmor Kimber, who conducted a boarding school for girls near Kimberton donated 131 perches of land near the village of Kimberton, at the intersection of Nutts Road. In 1819 a meeting-house was constructed on this lot. After the Separation, which occurred in this meeting in 1828, the meeting became the Pikeland Preparative Meeting, Hicksite (entry 275) and the Hicksite Friends retained the meeting-house and other property. The Orthodox Friends were then transferred to Uwchlan Preparative Meeting (entry 130).

See: Matlack, op. cit., I, 234-239; Futhey and Cope, op. cit., p.
240; Thomson, op. cit., p. 752; Grace Anna Lewis, "Old Kimberton," West
Chester Daily Local News, September 28, 1890.

There are no minutes of men's or women's meetings available at the
present time. Registers are in the records of the Goshen Monthly Meeting,
1758-62, and Uwchlan Monthly Meeting, 1763-1828.

132. NANTMEAL PREPARATIVE MEETING, 1739-ca.1833. Nantmeal Village,
     Nantmeal Twp., Chester County.
Set up as a preparative meeting in 1781 by Uwchlan Monthly Meeting (entry
129), after having functioned as an indulged meeting since 1739 under the
care of Uwchlan Preparative Meeting (entry 130), with the permission of
Goshen Monthly Meeting (entry 150). The first meeting-house was erected
in the village of Nantmeal but due to the absence of records and historical data the date of erection and description of the meeting-house are
unknown. In 1773 the meeting purchased 5 acres of ground from James Pugh
and his wife Anna, for the sum of 5 pounds. A few years later a gray
stone meeting-house was erected on this land and ½ acre was plotted for
a burial ground. One history states: "In 1795, the members of Nantmeal
Preparative Meeting were excused from full proportion of contribution, on
account of having had their meeting-house burned." After the Separation
which occurred in this meeting in 1828, both the Orthodox and Hicksite
Friends continued to use the same meeting-house. This meeting was evidently greatly weakened by the Separation as both the Orthodox and the
Hicksite meetings were laid down within a few years thereafter. A minute
of Caln Quarterly Meeting for February 7, 1867, states: "the trust for our
property at Nantmeal has been transferred in Sixth month 1865, by the sole
surviving trustees to trustees named and approved by the monthly meeting;
but the meeting-house, graveyard, and lot is now and has been for several
years in the posession of the Hicksites. Probable value $500." The next
mention made of this property is in a minute of December 8, 1881 of Uwchlan Monthly Meeting: "The trustees, having charge of the property belonging to Friends in East Nantmeal Township, inform the monthly meeting
that the parties claiming ownership, and having been for some time past
in posession of said property, have, without solicitation, freely abandoned all claim, right, and title to it, and as the following deeds of
conveyance will show, have assigned all their interest to the trustees
appointed by this Monthly Meeting the Thirteenth-day of the Sixth Month
1865." In a minute of March 9, 1882 it is stated: "The trustees, holding
the title deeds to the meeting-house graveyard, and ground, mention having
informed the meeting that the graveyard and other premises are in need of
repairs and about four acres of the lot might be sold. The proceeds of
the sale be apportioned to keep the graveyard and grounds in repair. On
deliberate consideration united in authorizing and empowering the said
trustees to sell so much of the land held by them in trust as they may
think necessary and proper, to any person or persons at public or private
sales, and to give a deed therefore to the purchasers, and to hold the
proceeds of such sale in trust for the preservation and repair of said
graveyard and ground or such other purposes as may be consonant with the
purpose of said trust." In accordance with the above authority, the trustees on April 3, 1882 sold to John E. Rettew 4 acres for the sum of $110.
The remaining 1 acre, one-half of which comprises the burial ground, is
enclosed by a stone wall. After the meeting-house was razed about 50
years ago, the stones of the demolished meeting-house were used in enclosing the ground surrounding the graveyard.

See: Matlack, op. cit., I, 231-234, 264; Futhey and Cope, op. cit., p. 240; Hoathcote, op. cit., p. 340; Michener, op. cit., p. 136; Thomson, op. cit., p. 752; Chester County Collection, Minutes of Nantmeal Preparative Meeting, X, 358-361, XI, ⟨⟩-387; XII, 408-410; XIII, 426-429. Chester County Historical Society, West Chester.

Minutes of Men's Meetings and Women's Meetings are not available at the present time. Registers are in the records of the Uwchlan Monthly Meeting. Chester County Deed Books, C-5, vol. 125, p. 361; K-9, vol. 207, p. 434.

133. DOWNINGTOWN PREPARATIVE MEETING, 1784-1907. Lincoln Highway, Downingtown, East Clan Twp., Chester County.
Set up in 1811 by Uwchlan Monthly Meeting (entry 129), after having functioned as an indulged meeting since 1784. From 1784 to 1806 meetings were held in a schoolhouse, which was located on property now owned by Clara D. Fox. In 1806 John Roberts and his wife deeded to the trustees of this meeting 2 acres of land upon which a one-story gray stone meetinghouse was erected and a burial ground was plotted the same year. Joseph and Elizabeth Downing, in 1818, deeded 74 perches of ground, located about a half mile east of the meeting-house and today part of the Lincoln Highway, upon which a Friends' school was to be erected. A clause in the deed stipulated that should the school be unoccupied during the next 90 years for a period of 5 consecutive years, the school and lot should revert back to the heirs of the donor. On this ground a two-story schoolhouse was erected and was known as the Octagon Friends' School. According to a minute of the Uwchlan Monthly Meeting September 10, 1885: "Downingtown Preparative Meeting has ceased to have under its direction or control, for the last 5 successive years the Octagon Friends' School, and whereas at a meeting of Downingtown Preparative Meeting, held Eleventh month 26th, 1884, the School Committee of said Preparative Meeting reports that they think best for the meeting to advise the trustees of the school property to cancel the trust and convey the property back to the original owners or their heirs in a legal manner." This was approved by the meeting and the said trustees transferred the property to the legal heir, Richard J. Downing. The property was later willed to J. Harvard Downing, who in turn sold it to the East Caln School District on December 15, 1891. A public school was conducted there for a number of years and in 1924 the school district sold the property to Lewis R. Downing. A number of alterations were made and at present it is used as Bell's Tourist Home. In 1907 Downingtown Preparative Meeting was laid down by Uwchlan Monthly Meeting because its work and business was a duplication of that of the monthly meeting.

See: Michener, op. cit., p. 126; Matlack, op. cit., I, 217, 218; Futhey and Cope, op. cit., p. 241; Cope, Genealogy, pp. 299, 300; Heathcote, op. cit., p. 340; Thomson, op. cit., p. 752; "Downingtown Friends' Meeting," West Chester Daily Local News, September 8, 1938.

Minutes of Men's Meetings, 1807-1907, 5 vols.; Minutes of Women's Meetings, 1811-1907, 1 vol., at PPFYR. Burial Records 1870--, 2 vols., (1811-69 missing), in custody of the recorder of the Uwchlan Monthly Meeting, Ellis Y. Brown, South Second Avenue, Downingtown. Registers are in the records of the Uwchlan Monthly Meeting. Chester County Deed Books, K-3, vol. 58, p. 479; vol. 125, p. 473.

134. ROBESON MONTHLY MEETING, 1789-1872. Five and one-half miles south of Birdsboro, 1 mile above junction of Routes 82 and 33, Berks County.
Set up in 1789 by Philadelphia Quarterly Meeting (entry 2). Meetings were held in the red sandstone meeting-house which had been erected in 1788 by Robeson Preparative Meeting (entry 135). In 1800 this meeting was detached from Philadelphia Quarterly Meeting and attached to East Caln (later called Caln) Quarterly Meeting (entry 116). The meeting was laid down in 1872 and the members were attached to Bradford Monthly Meeting (entry 117).

See: Michener, op. cit., p. 136.

Minutes of Men's Meetings, 1789-1872, 4 vols.; Minutes of Women's Meetings, 1789-1872, 2 vols.; Minutes of Ministers and Elders, 1798-1847, 2 vols. (1789-97, 1848-72 missing), S.F.P. Berks County Deed Books, vol. 10, p. 167; vol. 44, pp. 225, 227, 228; vol. 68, pp. 28, 30.

135. ROBESON PREPARATIVE MEETING, 1735-1872. Five and one-half miles south of Birdsboro, 1 mile above junction of Routes 82 and 33, Berks County.
Set up in 1741 by Oley (Exeter) Monthly Meeting (entry 24), with the consent of Philadelphia Quarterly Meeting (entry 2), after having functioned as an indulged meeting under Gwynedd Monthly Meeting since 1735. The meeting at Robeson was long known as the Forest Meeting, because it was situated in the great tract of almost unbroken woodland called "The Forest," which extended from Flying Hill south beyond the Hopewell Hills. A log meeting-house was erected and was in use until the plain red sandstone meeting-house was built on the same site in 1788. Robeson Preparative became a part of Robeson Monthly Meeting upon the establishment of this monthly meeting in 1789. The Robeson Preparative Meeting was laid down in 1872 and the members were attached to the Bradford Preparative Meeting (entry 120). The property of Robeson Meeting, containing about 20 acres, was sold to Jacob Kurtz, with the exception of the graveyard, adjoining the meeting-house, which was reserved as a permanent place of interment, by the Bradford Meeting. The meeting-house is now in the hands of Mr. Clarence Bingeman, R. D., Birdsboro, and is used for farm purposes.

See: Michener, op. cit., p. 136.

Minutes of Men's Meetings, 1827-66, 1 vol. (1741-1826 missing); Minutes of Women's Meetings, 1792-1813, 1 vol. (1741-91 missing); Minutes of Ministers and Elders, 1798-1847, 3 vols. (1741-97 missing), at PPFYR. Berks County Deed Books, vol. 10, p. 167; vol. 44, pp. 225, 227, 228; vol. 68, pp. 28, 30.

Component Meetings

(See: Explanatory Note 3)

	Date established	Entry number
CHESTER MONTHLY MEETING (UPLAND MM)	1681	137
Springfield Preparative Meeting	1696	138
Chester Preparative Meeting	1698	139
Providence Preparative Meeting	1698	140
Middletown Preparative Meeting	1701	160
Media Preparative Meeting	1878	141
Media-Springfield Preparative Meeting	1903	142
CONCORD MONTHLY MEETING (CHICHESTER MM)	1684	143
Concord Preparative Meeting	1684	144
Chichester Preparative Meeting	1701	145
Newtown Preparative Meeting	1706	146
Caln Preparative Meeting	1716	118
Birmingham Preparative Meeting	1726	155
Westtown Indulged Meeting	1799	158
West Chester Indulged Meeting	1810	147
West Chester Preparative Meeting	1813	147
DARBY MONTHLY MEETING	1684	148
Darby Preparative Meeting	1701	149
GOSHEN MONTHLY MEETING	1722	150
Goshen Preparative Meeting	1703	151
Newtown Preparative Meeting	1706	146
Willistown Indulged Meeting	1753	152
Willistown Preparative Meeting	1794	152
Whiteland Indulged Meeting	1816	153
Whiteland Preparative Meeting	1822	153
NOTTINGHAM MONTHLY MEETING	1730	351
Little Britain Indulged Meeting (Balance)	1745	354
Little Britain Preparative Meeting (Balance)	1749	354
Little Elk Preparative Meeting	1794	352
(For other subordinate Meetings, see Inventory of Church Archives of Maryland)		
WILMINGTON MONTHLY MEETING	1750	Del.
(See: Inventory of Church Archives of Delaware)		
LITTLE BRITAIN MONTHLY MEETING	1804	353
Little Britain Preparative Meeting (Balance)	1749	354

Eastland Indulged Meeting	1796	355
Eastland Preparative Meeting	1803	355
Drumore Indulged Meeting	1810	356
Drumore Preparative Meeting	1818	356
BIRMINGHAM MONTHLY MEETING	1815	154
Birmingham Preparative Meeting	1726	155
LANSDOWNE MONTHLY MEETING	1904	156
WESTTOWN MONTHLY MEETING	1920	157
Westtown Indulged Meeting	1799	158
MIDDLETOWN MONTHLY MEETING	1931	159
Middletown Preparative Meeting	1701	160
CONCORD (UNITED) MONTHLY MEETING	1932	331
PROVIDENCE (UNITED) MONTHLY MEETING	1934	332

136. CONCORD QUARTERLY MEETING, 1800. Third Street near Olive, Media.
Set up in 1683 as Chester Quarterly Meeting, under Philadelphia Yearly Meeting (entry 1). Meetings were held in homes until 1701; 1702-4 at the meeting-house of Providence Preparative Meeting (entry 140); 1705-6 at the meeting-houses of Springfield and Middletown Preparative Meetings (entries 138, 160); 1707-17 at the meeting-house of Providence Preparative Meeting; 1718-19 at the meeting-house of Concord Monthly Meeting (entry 143); 1720-24 at the meeting-house of Providence Preparative Meeting; 1725-30 at the meeting-houses of Concord Monthly and Providence Preparative Meetings (entries 140, 143); 1730-1800 at the meeting-house of Concord Monthly Meeting; 1800-1885 in a brick house in Concordville; 1885 to present at the meeting-house at Third Street near Olive Street, Media. In 1758, Chester Quarter had become, both numerically and geographically, very large, consisting of 14 monthly meetings: Chester (entry 137), Goshen (entry 150), Darby (entry 148), Concord, Wilmington (see quarterly meeting list), Newark (entry 79), New Garden (entry 72), Nottingham (entry 350), Bradford (entry 117), Sadsbury (entry 123), Duck Creek (see Maryland Inventory), Hopewell (see Virginia Inventory), Fairfax (see Virginia Inventory), and Warrington (entry 342). A division was found necessary, and this Quarterly Meeting was divided into Western Quarterly Meeting (entry 71) and Chester Quarterly Meeting, which later retained Chester, Goshen, Darby, Concord, and Wilmington Monthly Meetings. In 1763, by a division of Goshen Monthly Meeting, Uwchlan Monthly Meeting (entry 129) was set up and attached to this quarterly meeting. In 1800 Uwchlan Monthly Meeting was transferred to Caln Quarterly Meeting (entry 116). In the same year Chester Quarterly Meeting adopted the name of Concord Quarterly Meeting. In 1815, by a division of Concord Monthly Meeting, Birmingham Monthly Meeting (entry 154) was set up and attached to this quarterly meeting. In 1931, by division of Chester Monthly Meeting, Middletown Monthly Meeting was set up and attached to Concord Quarterly Meeting. In 1936 Providence United Monthly Meeting (entry 332), and in 1937 Concord United Monthly Meeting, Hicksite (entry 331), became affiliated

with this quarterly meeting as a United Monthly Meeting.   The present
clerk is Ernest N. Votaw, 27 West Seventh Street, Media.

See: Bowden, op. cit. II, 248; Michener, op. cit., p. 65.

Minutes of Men's Meetings, 1683-1919, 7 vols.; Minutes of Women's
Meetings, 1695-1919, 4 vols. (1683-94 missing), at PPFYR. Minutes of
Joint Meetings, 1919-2;, contained in last volume of minutes of Women's
meetings, and 1923--, 1 vol., in custody of the clerk. Minutes of Ministers and Elders, 1701-1923, 6 vols. (1683-1700 missing), at PPFYR, and
1873--, 1 vol., in custody of clerk, James F. Walker, Westtown School,
Westtown. Membership List, 1701-1818, loose papers (1683-1700, 1819--,
missing), at PPFYP.

137.   CHESTER MONTHLY MEETING (UPLAND), 1681--.   Third Street near
       Olive Street, Media
Established in 1681 as Upland Monthly Meeting by Burlington Monthly Meeting of New Jersey (see; Inventory of the Church Archives of New Jersey);
after having functioned as a meeting for worship from 1675. The first
monthly meeting of Friends of Chester to be found on record, was held
January 10, 1681 at the house of Robert Wade and consisted of the Friends
of Chichester and Upland, or Chester. Robert Wade came with John Fenwicks
to Salem, New Jersey, in 1675, but soon crossed the Delaware and occupied
the "Essex House" on the south side of Chester Creek called Wade's Landing. Here Friends' meetings were held and here also William Penn took
lodgings on his arrival. The first Assembly of Pennsylvania held its
session here in the year 1682.   In 1711 the name of the meeting was
changed from Upland Monthly Meeting to Chester Monthly Meeting. Until
1700 meetings were held in the homes of Friends; from 1700-22, with a
few exceptions, at the Providence Meeting-house. Chester Monthly Meeting was divided in 1722 and the Goshen Monthly Meeting was set up from
the division. After the Separation from Chester Monthly Meeting, Hicksite
(entry 222), in 1827, this meeting used the meeting-house of the Springfield Preparative until 1835 and then, until 1876, alternately at the Middletown Preparative meeting-house and the Springfield Preparative meeting-
house. The present brick meeting-house was erected in 1875, and the first
meeting was held October 30, 1876. A school was established the same year
in the meeting-house and is still functioning there. In 1885, a west end
apartment was added to accommodate Concord Quarterly Meeting (entry 136),
and after 1934 the west end was used for a school and social hall. The
present clerk is Ernest N. Votaw, 27 West Seventh Street, Media.

See: Michener, op. cit. p. 64.

Minutes of Men's Meetings, 1681-1919, 9 vols., at PPFYR, and 1920-
1930, 2 vols., at Media meeting-house, Third and Olive Streets, Media.
Minutes of Women's Meeting, 1695-1779, 2 vols. (1681-94 missing), at PSC-HA
and 1780-1919, 4 vols., at Media meeting-house. Minutes of Joint Meetings,
1920-26, 1 vol., at meeting-house, and 1927--, 1 vol., in custody of clerk.
Minutes of Ministers and Elders, 1915--, 1 vol. (1681-1914 missing), in
custody of T. Barclay Whitson, Osage Lane and Manchester Avenue, Moylan.
Registers of Births and Deaths, 1677-1883, 1 vol. in meeting-house, and
1884--, 1 vol., in custody of recorder, Miss Mary Williamson. Register
of Marriage Certificates, 1692-1782, 1 vol. (1681-91 missing), in meeting-
house, and 1782--, 1 vol., in custody of Mrs. Horace Way, 297 East Lincoln
Avenue, Media. Register of Certificates of Removals, 1704-33, 1766-1925,
3 vols. (1734-65 missing), in meeting-house; 1914-24, 1 vol., in custody

of executor of the estate of former recorder, Miss Aller, and 1925--, 1
vol., in custody of recorder, Miss Mary Williamson. Members and Marriages,
1677-1882 included in vol. 1677-1883 of births and deaths. Financial
Records, 1927--, 1 vol. (1681-1926 missing), in custody of treasurer, Wray
Hoffman, Providence Road and Plush Mill Road, Wallingford. Minutes of
First-day School, 1910--, 2 vols., in meeting-house.

138. SPRINGFIELD PREPARATIVE MEETING, 1686-1903. Corner of Springfield and Chester Roads, Springfield Twp., Delaware County.
Set up in 1696 by Chester Monthly Meeting (entry 137), after having functioned as Springfield Indulged Meeting since 1686. From 1686 to 1701 this
meeting worshiped in Bartholomew Coppock's home, which adjoined the present burial grounds at the junction of the Darby and Chester Roads. The
first meeting-house, a log building was erected in 1701, on the land of
Bartholomew Coppock. This building was destroyed by fire in 1738, and
a new stone meeting-house was erected on the site of the old one in the
same year. Bartholomew Coppock, in 1755, donated and conveyed to this
meeting 2 acres of land adjoining the meeting-house for a burial ground,
although since 1700 the Friends were permitted the use of this land for
burial purposes. In 1792 the meeting erected a frame house, near the site
of the burial grounds, for use as a day school. In 1835 the day school
building was razed, and a new frame school house was erected in its stead.
An addition to the burial ground, 1 acre of land which adjoined the burial
grounds was purchased in 1840. The stone meeting-house was razed in 1850,
and a one-story gray stone meeting-house was built on the same site. An
addition to the burial ground of 62 perches of land adjoining the other
ground was purchased in 1854. In 1903 this meeting was laid down by Chester Monthly Meeting and its members were transferred to Media Preparative
Meeting (entry 141) to form the Media Springfield Preparative Meeting (entry 142). The meeting-house and the burial grounds were conveyed to Media
Springfield Preparative Meeting in 1909. The meeting-house is used occasionally for worship, and the day school building is now the home of the
caretaker of the burial grounds.

See: Michener, op. cit., p. 66; Bowden, op. cit., p. 248; Myers,
Immigration, p. 115.

Minutes of Men's Meetings, 1830-39, 1 vol.; Minutes of Women's Meetings, 1840-52, 1882-1903, 2 vols. (1853-81 missing), at Media meeting-
house, Third and Olive Streets, Media. Registers are in records of Chester Monthly Meeting. Minutes of Media Springfield Preparative Meeting are
in the 1903--, record book of Media Preparative Meeting.

139. CHESTER PREPARATIVE MEETING, 1675--. Twenty-fourth and Chestnut
Streets, Chester, Delaware County.
Set up in 1698 by Chester Monthly Meeting (entry 137), after having functioned as a meeting for worship from 1675 to 1682, and as Chester Indulged
Meeting from 1682 to 1698. In 1675 William Edmundson, on a religious
visit to America held a meeting for worship at the home of Robert Wade
at Upland (Chester). This is the first recorded meeting of Friends held
in the Province of Pennsylvania. Meetings for worship were held regularly
after 1677, when several more Friends settled in the neighborhood. Friends
met in the home of Robert Wade from 1675-1682. Robert Wade is considered
the first Friend to have settled in Pennsylvania. In 1675 he crossed the
Delaware River, having come from Salem, New Jersey, and settled on the
south side of Chester Creek at a place later called Wade's Landing.
William Penn lodged at his home, the Essex House, for a short time, upon

his arrival in Pennsylvania 1682; also the first Assembly of Pennsylvania held its session here in the same year. The Chester Indulged Meeting was authorized by Chester Monthly Meeting to worship at the Upland Court House. A lot, containing 104 perches, on the west side of Edgemont Street above Sixth Street was acquired by the Friends in 1682, and was used for a burial ground. This lot was conveyed to Friends by deed in 1712. In 1687, a lot was purchased on the east bank of the Chester Creek (now Edgemont Street, near Second Street), "upon which is to be erected a stone meeting-house, 24 feet square and 10 feet high." After worshipping at the Upland Court House from 1682-91 this meeting moved to its first meeting-house which was erected in 1691. Lydia Wade, widow of Robert Wade, bequeathed to this meeting a fund in 1701 for enlarging the meeting-house with a brick addition which was completed in the same year. The first meeting-house was sold in 1736 and a larger site on High Street (now Market Street) below Third Street, was purchased and a one-story red brick meeting-house was built. A lot 40' x 120', adjoining the meeting-house, was purchased in 1762, and the meeting-house was enlarged with a red brick addition in the same year. After the Separation in 1827 Chester Preparative Meeting, Hicksite (entry 223), retained the meeting-house and burial ground. From 1827 to 1829 meetings were held in members' homes. In 1829 2½ acres of land on 24th and Chestnut were purchased and a one-story gray stone meeting-house was erected and a burial ground plotted. Negroes and white people who are not members of the Religious Society of Friends were interred in the burial ground according to an agreement with the grantor.

See: Bowden, II, 248; Jones, Quakers in Colonies, p. 439; Myers, Immigration, pp. 110, 115; Michener, op. cit., p. 66.

Minutes for Men's Meetings, 1785-1889, 2 vols. (1686-1784 missing), at PPFYR, and 1861-1917, 1 vol., in custody of Isaac Wetherill, 314 West 24th Street, Chester. Minutes of Women's Meetings, 1788-1849, 2 vols. (1698-1787 missing), at PPFYR. Minutes of Joint Meetings, 1917--, are recorded in the 1861-1917 Book of Men's Minutes. Minutes of Ministers and Elders, 1842-1901, 3 vols. (1876 missing), at Media Meeting-house, Third and Olive Streets, Media. Registers are in the records of Chester Monthly Meeting. Financial records, 1914--, 1 vol. (1686-1913 missing), in custody of Reese L. Thomas, 1149 Potter Street, Chester.

140. PROVIDENCE PREPARATIVE MEETING, 1686-1828. Providence Road near Baltimore Pike, Media, Delaware County.
Set up in 1698 by Chester Monthly Meeting (entry 138), after having functioned as the Thomas Minshall Indulged Meeting from 1686 to 1698. A single reference in the minutes of Chester Quarterly Meeting of 1683 refers to Providence meeting. This indicates a date of origin at least 3 years earlier than the date of Thomas Minshall Meeting. In 1700 the meeting changed its name to Providence Preparative Meeting. From 1686 to 1700 meetings were held in the home of Thomas Minshall, and from 1700 until 1828 meetings were held in the stone meeting-house of Chester Monthly Meeting, Providence Road near Baltimore Pike. The 1-acre burial ground, adjoining the meeting-house, also belonged to Chester Monthly Meeting. This meeting was laid down in 1828 by Chester Monthly Meeting according to an order from Concord Quarterly Meeting, and the members were transferred to Springfield Preparative Meeting (entry 138).

See: Bowden, op. cit., II, 248; Michener, op. cit., p. 66; Myers, Immigration, p. 115.

Minutes of Men's Meetings, 1812-28 are included in the minutes of the Hicksite Meeting, 1827-66, at PSC-Hi. It is impossible to obtain any further information concerning the records of this meeting. Registers are in the records of Chester Monthly Meeting.

141. MEDIA PREPARATIVE MEETING, 1878-1903. Third Street, near Olive Street, Media, Delaware County.
Set up in 1878 by Chester Monthly Meeting (entry 137). Meetings were held in the red brick meeting-house erected in 1875 by Chester Monthly Meeting for its own use and for the accommodation of its Preparative Meeting. In 1903 this meeting merged with Springfield Preparative Meeting (entry 138) to form the Media-Springfield Preparative Meeting (entry 142).

Minutes of Media Preparative Meeting, 1878-1903, 2 vols. (the last volume is now being used for minutes of the Media-Springfield Preparative Meeting); Minutes of Women's Meetings, 1878-1900, in Media-Springfield Meeting-house, Third Street, near Olive Street, Media. Registers are in the record books of Chester Monthly Meeting.

142. MEDIA-SPRINGFIELD PREPARATIVE MEETING, 1903--. Third Street near Olive Street, Media, Delaware County.
Set up 1903 by Chester Monthly Meeting (entry 137), when the Media Preparative Meeting (entry 141) and the Springfield Preparative Meeting (entry 138) merged. Meetings were held i n the red brick meeting-house erected in 1875 by Chester Monthly Meeting for its own use and for the accommodation of its preparative meeting. The one-story gray stone meeting-house and the 3 acres and 62 perches of burial ground of Springfield Preparative Meeting were conveyed to the Media-Springfield Preparative Meeting by deed, dated May 11, 1909. This building is used occasionally for meetings for worship.

Minutes of Media-Springfield Preparative Meeting, 1903-5, incorporated in the minute book of the Media Preparative Meeting, 1886-1903, at Media Meeting-house, and 1905--, 1 vol., in custody of Wray Hoffman, Providence and Possum Hollow Roads, Wallingford. Registers are in the records of the Chester Monthly Meeting. Burial Records, 1856--, 1 vol. (1856-1903 are Springfield Preparative Meeting records), in custody of recc.·der, Dr. Clinton Starbuck, East Baltimore Avenue, Media.

143. CONCORD MONTHLY MEETING, 1684-1932. On Concord Road near Baltimore Pike, Concordville, Delaware County.
Set up in 1684 as Chichester Monthly Meeting by Chester (Concord since 1800) Quarterly Meeting (entry 136). Meetings were held in private homes until 1685. In that year Chichester Indulged Meeting (Chichester Preparative Meeting after 1701, entry 145), erected its first meeting-house and this monthly meeting met there. A minute of the Chester Quarterly Meeting, of Eighth month 2, 1686 ordered that: "ye Monthly Meeting formerly held at Chichester be from Henceforth kept one month at Chichester and one month at Concord and ye next Monthly Meeting to begin at Concord until further order." Meetings at Concord were held in Friends' homes until 1695, when Concord Monthly Meeting erected a small meeting-house on Birmingham Road in Concord Township. A minute of Chester Quarterly Meeting for November 4, 1695 states: "It was agreed that Concord Monthly Meeting which was movable, be now fixed at the new meeting-house." The 1¼ acre-lot, upon which the meeting-house and a stable had been erected, was donated to the meeting in 1697 by John Mendenhall, "for the use of Quakers to bury their dead and for a meeting-house." The second meeting-house,

a small red brick building, was erected in 1728. The meeting was known
as the Chichester-Concord Monthly Meeting, and was sometimes designated
by either one of these two names. In 1729 it was definitely named Concord
Monthly Meeting. The second meeting house was razed by fire early in 1788
and a new two-story red brick meeting-house was erected in the same year.
The greater part of the cost of the new meeting-house was met by Chester
Querterly Meeting. A minute of Concord Monthly Meeting for April 7, 1740
states: "This meeting appoints eight trustees to receive a piece of ground
adjoining the meeting-house and burial ground, conveyed and donated by
Nicholas Newlin and wife for the use of the said meeting." This new addition to the burial ground contained 1 acre and 138 perches. After the
Separation the Concord Monthly Meeting, Hicksite (entry 225), retained
posession of the property and both groups of Friends worshipped in the
same building, but on different days, until 1834, when the Orthodox group
erected a small two-story stucco-covered stone meeting-house on a piece
of ground belonging to Caster W. Sharpless, "On the hill a little east of
the old brick meeting-house." The 108 perches of ground, upon which the
new building was built, was loased to the Orthodox meeting at an annual
rent "of one dollar per year, if demanded," with a stipulation agreeing
to the renewal of the lease "every ten years as long as the meeting had
need of same for a meeting-house." In 1858, 62½ perches of ground adjoining the property which the Hicksite Friends had retained in 1827, were
donated to this meeting for use as a burial ground. In 1932 the Concord
Hicksite and Orthodox Meetings began to hold their meetings jointly; however, each group kept its original status until given official recognition
as Concord United Monthly Meeting (entry 331) in 1937 by both the Hicksite
and Orthodox Concord Quarterly Meetings. From 1934-36 meetings alternated
between the Orthodox and Hicksite meeting-houses. In 1936 the meeting-
house and burial ground of the Orthodox meeting was conveyed to the
Friends' Fiduciary Corporation. The present clerk is Bertha M. S. Webster,
Cheyney.

See: Bowden, op. cit., II, 248; Michener, op. cit., pp. 67-68; Matlack, op. cit., I, 282-285.

Minutes of Men's Meetings, 1684-1827, 1847-51, 1854-1916, 5 vols.
(1828-46, 1852-53 missing); Minutes of Women's Meetings, 1802-5, 1827-1912,
3 vols. (1684-1801, 1806-26, 1913-16 missing); Minutes of Joint Meetings,
1916-32, 1 vol., at PPFYR. Registers of births and deaths 1679-1827 are
transcribed into the register of the Hicksite Meeting for 1827-1916 which
is deposited at PSC-Hi, and 1827-1932, incorporated in membership book
of Concord United Monthly Meeting, in custody of Alma Fawcett, Station
Road, Cheyney. Certificates of Marriage, 1684-1834, 2 vols., at PSC-Hi,
and 1827-32 incorporated in membership book, in custody of Alma Fawcett.
Certificates of Removal, 1765-1864, 2 vols. (1684-1764 missing), at PPFYR,
and 1865-1932 incorporated in the membership book, in custody of Alma
Fawcett. Register of Membership, 1699-1932, 1 vol. (1684-98 missing), in
custody of Alma Fawcett. Financial Records, 1923-32, 1 vol. (1684-1922
missing), in custody of C. W. Fawcett, Glen Mills. Delaware County Deed
Books, vol. T., p. 508; vol. E-2, p. 694; 1017, p. 176; vol. 35, p. 159.

144.   CONCORD PREPARATIVE MEETING, 1684-1920. Philadelphia Road, near
        Chester Road, Concordville, Delaware County.
Set up in 1684 by Chichester Monthly Meeting (entry 143). Meetings were
held in members' homes until 1697. From that year until the meeting was
laid down in 1920 by Concord Monthly Meeting, this preparative meeting
used the meeting-houses of Concord Monthly Meeting.

See: Bowden, op. cit., II, 248; Michener, op. cit., p. 68.

Minutes of Men's Meetings, 1807-28, 1 vol. (1648-1806, 1829-1920 missing); Minutes of Women's Meetings, 1813-20. 1 vol. (1684-1812, 1821-1920 missing), at PSC-Hi. Registers are in the records of the Concord Monthly Meeting.

143. CHICHESTER PREPARATIVE MEETING, 1682-1881. Chelsea and Marcus Hook Road, east of Larkins Road, Upper Chichester Twp., Delaware County.
Set up in 1701 by Chichester Monthly Meeting (entry 143), after having functioned as an indulged meeting from 1682-84 under Upland Monthly Meeting (entry 137), and from 1684-1701 under Chichester Monthly Meeting. In 1729, the name Chichester-Concord Monthly Meeting was shortened to Concord Monthly Meeting. The first meeting-house was erected in 1685. However, the deed for the meeting-house and 2 acres of burial ground is dated 1688. In 1768 the meeting-house was destroyed by fire and a new stone meeting-house was erected in 1769. In 1772 an additional 1 acre and 153 perches were added to the original burial ground. At the time of the Separation in 1827 the meeting-house and burial ground were retained by the Chichester Preparative Meeting, Hicksite (entry 226). From 1827-29 meetings were held in the homes of various members. In 1829 Salkeld Larkins donated to this meeting 1 acre and 16 perches of ground upon which was erected a stone meeting-house and on which a burial ground was plotted. This ground remained the property of the meeting until 1881 when the meeting was laid down by Concord Monthly Meeting and the remaining members attached to Concord Preparative Meeting (entry 144). In 1894 Concord Monthly Meeting agreed to return the meeting-house and burial ground to the heirs of Salkeld Larkins, because a stipulation in the will stated," . . . Should the ground be discontinued for the use of Chichester Preparative Meeting for a place of worship and burial ground, it shall revert to the heirs of said donor . . . ."

See: Michener, op. cit., p. 68.

Minutes of Men's Meetings, 1802-23, 2 vols. (1802-13 vol., contains one page of 1852 minutes), at PPFYR. Registers are in the records of the Concord Monthly Meeting. Financial Records, 1781-1875, 1 vol., at PSC-Hi.

144. NEWTOWN PREPARATIVE MEETING, 1696-1828. Newtown and Paoli Roads, three-fourths mile west of West Chester Pike, Newtown Twp., Delaware County.
Set up in 1706 by Chester Monthly Meeting (entry 137), after having functioned as an indulged meeting under Radnor Monthly Meeting (entry 15) since 1696. As early as 1692 Chester Quarterly Meeting had given permission to Friends in this locality to hold meetings for worship. First meetings were held in the home of William Lewis. In 1708, 1 acre and 10 perches of ground were donated to the meeting. A meeting-house was erected and a graveyard plotted in 1711. About 1721 the meeting was transferred from Chester Monthly Meeting to Goshen Monthly Meeting (entry 150). In 1774 an additional 25 perches of ground, adjoining the original graveyard, were given by an unknown donor. In 1791 the meeting-house was razed and in its place, a two-story gray stone building was erected. In 1827 the majority of the Friends formed the Newtown Preparative Meeting, Hicksite (entry 232), and retained the meeting-house and burial ground. Newtown Preparative Meeting, Orthodox, became a part of Concord Monthly Meeting (entry 143), which discontinued it in 1828. The members were then transferred to Willistown Preparative Meeting (entry 152).

See: Michener, op. cit., p. 69.

No minutes of this meeting have been found. Registers, 1696-1705
in the records of Radnor Monthly Meeting; 1706-20 in the records of the
Chester Monthly Meeting; 1721-1827 in the records of Goshen Monthly Meeting. Burial records, 1805--, 1 vol., in custody of Horace M. Lewis, West
Chester Pike, Newtown Square.

147. WEST CHESTER PREPARATIVE MEETING, 1810--. Church and Chestnut
         Streets, West Chester.
Established 1813 by Concord Monthly Meeting (entry 143) with the consent
of Concord Quarterly Meeting (entry 136). From 1810-13 indulged meetings were held in the two-story stone schoolhouse on Old Goshen Street
in East Bradford Township. This building had been erected by Friends belonging to Goshen, Bradford, and Birmingham meetings. In 1812 a committee
of three, Jesse Hoopes, Joseph Taylor, and Thomas Hoopes, had purchased
1 3/4 acres of ground on a road leading from Wilmington to the Great Valley (now called High Street). In 1812-13 the Friends erected a gray stone
meeting-house. One hundred and twenty-five perches of this plot, at the
southeast corner of High and Marshall Streets, adjoining the northwest
end of the meeting-house, were set aside for a burial ground. After the
Separation, West Chester Preparative Meeting, Hicksite, retained the meeting-house and burial grounds. For several months the Orthodox meeting
occupied the meeting-house with the Hicksites and then moved to the east
room of a farm house owned by George G. Ashbridge. This farm house was
located on the site of what is now the Chester Art Center. In 1830 a
two-story red brick meeting-house was erected on the north side of Chestnut Street. In 1844 the present one-story stone meeting-house was built.
This meeting continued to use the old burial ground jointly with the Hicksites until 1849. In that year the Orthodox Friends purchased an acre
and 12 perches of ground in Cherry Hill, on West Gay Street, just within
the borough limits. In 1874, because of an ordinance prohibiting further
burials within the borough limits, the meeting purchased 6 acres and 25
perches of land from the Oakland Friends. This burial ground is about 1
mile north of West Chester on Pottstown Pike. In 1920 an addition to the
meeting-house was built and has been used for a First-day school.

     See: Futhey and Cope, op. cit., pp. 241,242; Susanna Sharpless, "His-
torical Sketch of West Chester Friends School," The Friend, CIV (1930),
27, 28; Gilbert Cope, "History of West Chester Meeting of (Orthodox)
Friends," Bulletin of Chester County Historical Society, 1908, pp. 34-56,
hereinafter cited as Cope, History; Past and Present, Centennial Souvenir
of West Chester, pp. 40, 106, 107, hereinafter cited as Past and Present;
pp. 40, 106, 107; "Ancient Friends School," West Chester Daily Local News
June 21, 1930; "Chestnut Street Friends Meeting," West Chester Daily Local
News, July 20, 1920; "Friends Re-Union a Happy Occasion," West Chester
Daily Local News, June 11, 1920.

     Minutes of Men's Meetings, 1832-44, 1 vol. (1814-31 missing), at PHi,
1844-66, 1 vol. in meeting-house; and 1866-97, 1 vol., at PPFYR. Minutes
of Women's Meetings, 1835-74, 6 vols. (1875-98 missing), at PPFYR. Minutes of Joint Meetings, 1898-1932, 2 vols., at PPFYR, and 1933-- incorporated in Birmingham Monthly Meeting records. Minutes of West Chester
Preparative School Committee, 1863-1912, 3 vols., in meeting-house. Registers are in the records of the Birmingham Monthly Meeting. Record of
grave Lot permits, 1874-1910, 2 vols., in meeting-house. Burial Records,
1874--, 1 vol., in custody of Walter Painter, 214 Price Street, West Ches-

ter. Treasurer's record of West Chester Preparative School Fund containing receipts from 1850-51, and West Chester Preparative School Committee
(Cash Book), 1863-1917, 4 vols.; Treasurer's Account of West Chester Preparative Meeting (Women's), 1863-1923; Treasurer's Accounts, 1899-1927,
1927--, 2 vols., in custody of Walter Painter. Chester County Deed Bo ks,
B-5, vol. 99, p. 269; R-11, vol. 264, p. 393; Z-15, vol. 372, p. 263;
L-5, vol. 108, p. 461; L-16, vol. 383, p. 352; I-5, vol. 106, p. 605; K-9,
vol. 207, p. 354; M-8, vol. 184, p. 403; W-11, vol. 269, p. 75; Q-19, vol.
463, p. 183.

148. DARBY MONTHLY MEETING (later Lansdowne), 1684-1849. Stewart
     and Lansdowne Avenues, Lansdowne, Delaware County.
Set up in 1684 by the Chester Quarterly Meeting (entry 136). Meetings
were first held in the home of John Blumston until 1687. The first Meeting-house, erected sometime previous to 1687, was built on what is now
Lansdowne Avenue, near McDade Boulevard. However, the deed for the meeting-house and 1 acre of ground donated by John Blumston, was not recorded
until 1687. This meeting-house was also used as a town hall until 1695.
In 1701 a new meeting-house near the site of the first one was erected.
The ground for the meeting-house and graveyard, consisting of 3¼ acres,
was purchased from John Blumston. In 1786 the meeting purchased 400
square perches of ground and in 1805 erected the third meeting-house, a
two-story gray stone building, located at what is now 1015 Main Street,
Darby. At the time of the Separation, in 1827 the meeting-house and yard
and the 4¼-acres burial ground were retained by Darby Monthly Meeting,
Hicksite (entry 143). From 1827-31 meetings were held in the homes of
members. In 1831 this meeting erected a one-story white stucco meeting-house
at Stewart and Lansdowne Aves., Lansdowne. The meeting was laid down as
a monthly meeting in 1849 by Concord Quarterly Meeting (entry 136). At
this time the meeting-house and grounds were conveyed to Chester Monthly
Meeting (entry 137), under whose care it remained until 1904. Lansdowne
Monthly Meeting (entry 156) was established in 1904 and the meeting-house
and grounds were conveyed to it by Chester Monthly Meeting.

     See: Michener, op. cit., p. 66; Centennial Anniversary of Darby Meet-
ing-house, hereinafter cited as Centennial Darby.

     Minutes of Men's Meetings, 1684-1833, 4 vols., at PSC-Hi, 1827-36,
1 vol, at PPFYR, and 1743-1801, 1 vol. (probably a copy, since 1750-95
missing), at PHi. Minutes of Women's Meetings, 1684-1840, 3 vols. (1840-
49 missing), at PSC-Hi. Minutes of Ministers and Elders, 1828-49, 1 vol.
(1664-1827 missing), at PPFYR. Register of Births and Deaths, 1682-1839,
1 vol., at meeting-house of Darby Monthly Meeting (H); and 1828-49, 1 vol.,
at Media meeting-house. Membership List (made in 1908), 1 vol. at meeting-house of Darby Monthly Meeting (H); and 1828-48, 1 vol., at Media
meeting-house. Marriage Certificates, 1684-1848, 1 vol., at meeting-
house of Darby Monthly Meeting (H); and 1828-49, 1 vol., at Media meeting-house. Certificates of Removals from England, 1682-1763 are incorporated in 1684-1763 volume of Minutes of Men's Meetings. Certificates of
Removal, 1751-1854, 3 vols., at meeting-house of Darby Monthly Meeting
(H) (1827-49 missing).

149. DARBY PREPARATIVE MEETING, 1682--. Lansdowne and Stewart Ave-
     nues, Lansdowne, Delaware County.
Set up in 1701 by Darby Monthly Meeting (entry 148), after having functioned as an indulged meeting under Chester Monthly Meeting (entry 137)
from 1682-84 and under Darby Monthly Meeting from 1684-1701. From 1701-

1827 meetings were held in the meeting-house of Darby Monthly Meeting;
from 1827-31 meetings were held in the homes of members. Since 1831 meetings have been held in the white stucco-stone meeting-house, erected by
Darby Monthly meeting in 1831. Darby Monthly Meeting was laid down in
1849 and its meeting-house and 2 acres of ground were conveyed to the
Chester Monthly Meeting by order of Concord Quarterly Meeting (entry 136).
Darby Preparative Meeting then became a part of Chester Monthly Meeting.
In 1904 the meeting-house of Darby Monthly Meeting, where Darby Prepara-
tive Meeting had met since 1831, was conveyed to Lansdowne Monthly Meet-
ing. The same year Darby Preparative Meeting was attached to Lansdowne
Monthly Meeting (entry 156).

See: Michener, op. cit., p. 67.

Minutes of Men's Meetings, 1878--, 1 vol. (1701-1877 missing), in
custody of C. Wilfred Conrad, Scotsdale Road, Lansdowne. Registers, 1701-
1903 are in the records of the Darby Monthly Meeting; 1849-1903 also in
the records of the Chester Monthly Meeting; and 1904-- in the records of
the Lansdowne Monthly Meeting.

150. GOSHEN MONTHLY MEETING, 1722--. Goshen, Uwchlan, Willistown,
      and Malvern Meeting-houses, Chester County.
Set up in 1722 by Chester Quarterly Meeting (entry 136). Later met alternately at the meeting-house of Goshen Preparative Meeting (entry 151) and
Newtown Preparative Meeting (entry 146) for 3 years. In 1736 it held
its meetings alternately at Uwchlan and Newtown. Uwchlan Monthly Meeting
(entry 129) was set off from Goshen Monthly in 1763 leaving this Preparative Meeting, Goshen Preparative Meeting (entry 151) and Newtown Preparative Meeting as sole components of the monthly meeting. When Willistown
Preparative Meeting (entry 152) was established in 1794, it became a part
of this meeting. A meeting-house was erected at Willistown in 1798 and
in 1801 Goshen Monthly Meeting moved its headquarters from Goshen to Willistown. Whiteland Preparative Meeting (entry 153) was added in 1822.
In 1827, after the Separation, the Hicksite meeting retained the Willistown meeting-house, and this meeting moved to Goshen. The present clerk
is Louella H. Nolan, Malvern.

See: Michener, op. cit., p. 68; Myers, Immigration, pp. 156, 314,
376; Smith, George, op. cit., p. 232; Futhey and Cope, op. cit., pp. 53,
58, 239, 413; Woody, op. cit., pp. 130-135.

Minutes of Men's Meetings, 1722-1877, 6 vols., 1722-70, 2 vols.
(1740-62 missing), at Malvern Meeting-house; 1722-1870, 2 vols. (1807-18
missing), at PPFYR; 1722-1841, 2 vols., at PHi; 1747-61, 1 vol., 1927-38
1 vol., in custody of the clerk. Minutes of Women's Meetings, 1795-98,
1 vol., at Malvern meeting-house, 1722-1911, 2 vols., at PPFYR, and 1822-
1911, 2 vols., in custody of clerk, and 1722-1830, 2 vols., at PHi. Minutes of Joint Meetings, 1927-38, 1 vol.; Minutes of Ministers and Elders,
1872-1905, 1 vol., in custody of clerk. Register of Births and Deaths,
1705-1805, 1 vol., at PPFYR. Register of Births, Removals, Members, and
Deaths, 1885--, 1 vol., in custody of clerk. Register of Marriages,
1722--, 2 vols., at PPFYR, and 1722-81, 1 vol., at PHi. Removal Certificates, 1722-1930, 2 vols. (1758-1827 missing), at PPFYR, 1722-57, 1 vol.
at PHi, and 1797-1901, 1 vol., at Malvern meeting-house. Treasurer'
Record, 1886--, 1 vol., in custody of Anna B. Hamilton, 118 Monument Av .,
Malvern. Minutes of Goshen School, 1829-30, 1 vol.; Day Book of Shu ;
Town School, 1831-32, 1 vol.; Day Book of Middletown School, 1833- ;, 1

vol., at PWcHi. Chester County Deed Books, vol. 60, M-3, p. 46; vol. 74, B-4, p. 6; vol. 147, Z-6, p. 323.

151. GOSHEN PREPARATIVE MEETING, 1702-1891. Corner Chester-Frazer Roads, Gosnenville, Chester County.
Established as an indulged meeting in 1702 by Chester Monthly Meeting (entry 137) and set up as a preparative meeting in 1703. First meetings were held in the home of Robert Williams, said to be the first settler of Goshen, on the north side of what was then called the Edgemont Road, about 1 mile east of Goshenville; and in the home of Thomas Jones and David Jones, in the "Great Valley" at Whiteland. In 1708, 100 perches of ground were given by Griffith Owen, for a cemetery and the erection of a meeting-house. The first meeting-house was erected in 1709. This house was constructed of logs and is supposed to have been a little to the west of the present Hicksite meeting-house. In 1736, a stone meeting-house was erected on the site of the first building. After the Separation in 1827, both branches continued to worship in the same meeting-house until 1849, when the Orthodox Friends purchased 2 lots adjoining the original property and erected a small one-story, stone, meeting-house. The Hicksites retained the old meeting-house and cemetery. The new cemetery, south of the Hicksite property, consisting of 153 perches, was acquired in 1849. The first burial was April 1, 1854. This meeting was laid down in 1891 after most of its members had moved away or died. The remaining members were transferred to Whiteland Preparative Meeting (entry 153). The meeting-house was sold in 1920 to the Goshen Grange, No. 121.

£. 9: Michener, *op. cit.*, p. 69; Thomson, *op. cit.*, pp. 746-751; Futhey and Cope, *op. cit.*, pp. 234-239, 764; Heathcote, *op. cit.*, p. 339; Wellington T. Ashbridge, The Ashbridge Book, pp. 118, 119; Cope, Genealogy, pp. 134-136; William H. Egle, History of the Commonwealth of Pennsylvania, pp. 540, 541; J. Smith Futhey, "East Goshen Township," West Chester American Republican, November 2, 1876; "Back Into the Days of the Long Ago," West Chester Daily Local News, June 7, 1916; "Friends Meeting-House," West Chester Daily Local News, December 31, 1917.

Minutes of Men's Meetings, 1813-22, 1 vol., in Willistown meeting-house. Registers incorporated in the records of Goshen Monthly Meeting. Record of Burials, 1705-1805, 1 vol., at PPFYR. Card index of gravestone inscriptions at Chester Historical Society, West Chester. Chester County Deed Books, Miscellaneous, vol. 7, pp. 34, 97; K-4, pp. 342, 346; B-7, p. 130; M-15, p. 204; U-15, p. 136.

152. WILLISTOWN PREPARATIVE MEETING, 1753-1863. Intersection of Penn Hotel and Rocky Hill Roads, Willistown, Chester County.
Set up in 1794 by Goshen Monthly Meeting (entry 150) with the consent of Concord Quarterly Meeting (entry 136). Permission was given in 1788 to hold meetings on the 1st and 5th days of the week but previous to this meetings had been held since 1753. It is believed that the early meetings were held in a stone schoolhouse erected about 1753 on an acre of land donated by Francis Smedley and his wife. In 1798 a two-story gray stone meeting-house was erected on the original acre and land was set aside for a cemetery. After 1798 the schoolhouse was used as a caretaker's residence. In 1801 Goshen Monthly Meeting started holding its meetings at Willistown. The meeting in 1815 sold the "Lower School," which had been conducted since 1797, and distributed the proceeds to its preparative meetings for each to establish a school. In 1816, 145 perches of land were purchased by the meeting for this purpose but information

concerning this school is unavailable. After the Separation in 1827 the
Willistown Preparative Meeting, Hicksite (entry 234), retained the meeting-house, the schoolhouse, and the cemetery. The Orthodox Friends moved
to the old schoolhouse erected in 1753 which since 1798 had been used as
a home for the caretaker. They worshipped here until 1863 when, due to
diminishing membership, those remaining were transferred to Goshen Preparative Meeting (entry 151) and the meeting was laid down in 1864.

See: Cope, Genealogy, pp. 168-171; Futhey and Cope, op. cit., p. 241;
Michener, op. cit., pp. 69, 70; "Communication," West Chester Daily Local
News, August 25, 1873; "Pages of History," West Chester Daily Local News,
September 12, 1898.

Minutes and registers are in the records of the Goshen Monthly Meeting.

153. WHITELAND PREPARATIVE MEETING, 1816--. Northwest corner Roberts
Lane and Woodland Avenue, Malvern, Chester County.
Set up in 1822 under Goshen Monthly Meeting (entry 150) with the approval
of Concord Quarterly Meeting (entry 136). Meetings for worship were held
from 1816-18 and in that year the meeting was set up as an indulged meeting. Meetings from 1816-80 were held in a one-story stone structure,
which adjoined a burial plot and was located just south of the Lincoln
Highway between Malvern and Frazer. At the time of the Separation both
branches continued to hold meetings together until 1828, when the Orthodox
Friends changed their meeting time but retained control of the property.
A school, last mentioned in the records in 1836, was conducted by this
meeting when it was at Whiteland. In 1879, since the majority of the
members had moved to Malvern, the present one-story green serpentine-stone
edifice was erected there on a lot containing 82 perches. The first meeting in the new building was held in 1880. In 1889 a one-story red brick
school was also erected here. In 1904 this school was converted into a
library and in 1918 it was remodeled into a dwelling house. At present
Whiteland Preparative holds business meetings for special reasons only
at the call of the clerk. Since it is the only preparative meeting in
Goshen Monthly Meeting, the monthly sessions are those of Goshen Monthly
Meeting.

See: Michener, op. cit., p. 70; Futhey and Cope, op. cit., p. 242;
Thomson, op. cit., pp. 754, 755; Heathcote, op. cit., p. 341; "A Landmark
Gone," West Chester Daily Local News, August 28, 1895; "Contracts for
Building a Friends Meeting-House," West Chester Daily Local News, May 21,
1879; "Meeting-House about Completed," West Chester Daily Local News,
March 30, 1880; "Malvern Friends," West Chester Daily Local News, November
16, 1929.

Minutes of the Whiteland Preparative Meeting, 1822-53, 1 vol. (1854-
57 missing), at PPFYR, 1858-1901, 1 vol., in custody of clerk, Louella
H. Nolan, Frazer; and 1902-- incorporated in the minutes of the Goshen
Monthly Meeting. Reports of the School Committees are incorporated in
the minutes of the monthly meeting. Attendance List of Malvern School,
1822-53, 1 vol. (1854-1937 missing), at PPFYR, and 1938--, 1 vol., at
PWc-Hi. Chester County Deed Books, vol. T3, p. 70; vol. 06, p. 182; vol.
K8, p. 484; vol. N, p. 44; vol. Miscellaneous, 17, p. 535; vol. F9, p. 352;
vol. U10, p. 249; Miscellaneous Docket 8, p. 390.

154. BIRMINGHAM MONTHLY MEETING, 1815--.   Church and Chestnut
     Streets, West Chester, Chester County.
Established in 1815 by Concord Quarterly Meeting (entry 136). This meeting was set off from Concord Monthly Meeting (entry 143) and was comprised
of Birmingham Preparative Meeting (entry 155) and West Chester Preparative
Meeting (entry 147). Meetings were held alternately at the Birmingham
and West Chester Meeting-houses and continued so through the years of Separation until 1845 when a plain stone meeting-house was erected on the
Birmingham-Dilworthtown Road. Since the sale of this meeting-house in
June 1938 meetings are held in the meeting-house of the Birmingham Preparative Meeting, Church and Chestnut Streets, West Chester. There is
no cemetery; burials are made in the plots of the Birmingham Preparative
and West Chester Preparative Meetings. The present clerk is I. Rowland
Evans, Kennett Square.

     See: "Friends' Reunion at Birmingham," West Chester Daily Local News,
June 23, 1910; "Early Memories of Old Birmingham," West Chester Daily
Local News, June 27, 1910; Jonathan, Eldridge, A History of Birmingham
Meeting (manuscript in custody of author).

     Minutes of Men's Meetings, 1815-1915, 4 vols.; Minutes of Women's
Meetings, 1815-19, 3 vols., at PPFYR. Minutes of Joint Meetings, 1916-21,
1 vol., at PPFYR, and 1922--, 2 vols., in custody of clerk. Register of
Membership, 1815-1922, 1 vol., at PPFYR, and 1828--, 1 vol., in custody
of recorder, Miss Rebecca Savery, 341 West Barnard Street, West Chester.
Register of Births, 1795-1886, 1 vol. (1781-1818, incorporated in the
Register of Marriage Certificates; 1828--, incorporated in register of
membership), in Birmingham meeting-house. Register of marriage certificates, 1816--, 1 vol., in custody of Miss Rebecca Savery. Register of
Certificates of Removal, 1828-90, 2 vols. (1815-27, 1891--, missing. Register of Deaths, 1816-84, 1 vol. (1885-- incorporated in register of membership), in meeting-house. Financial Records, 1875-1922, 1 vol., in
meeting-house and 1923--, 1 vol., in custody of treasurer, Walter Painter,
214 Price Street, West Chester. Women's Meetings Financial Records, 1858-
1928, 2 vols. (1815-54 missing; no records kept after 1928), in meeting-
house.

155. FIRMINGHAM PREPARATIVE MEETING, 1690-1938. Birmingham Twp.,
     Birmingham-Dilworthtown Road, northwest of Dilworthtown, Ches-
     ter County.
Set up in 1726 by Chicester Monthly Meeting (entry 143). First meetings were held in 1690 at the cabin of William Brinton, the first settler
of what is now Birmingham Township, one-half mile south of the present
village of Dilworthtown. Following this meetings were held irregularly
in other homes until 1704, when an indulged meeting was established.
Meetings continued in residences of members until 1721, when a red-cedar
log building was erected on Birmingham Road. The land was sold to the
meeting by Elizabeth Webb, a noted Quaker minister and widow of Richard
Webb, for the consideration of L3. A graveyard surrounded the meeting-
house on all sides except the south. In 1763, a native gray stone, meeting-house was built just east of the previous structure, which was converted into a stable and later razed. In 1815, when Birmingham Monthly
Meeting (entry 154) was set up, this meeting became a part. At the time
of the Separation in 1827, the gray stone meeting-house, erected in 1763,
and the 20 acres and 120 perches of land adjoining the meeting-house were
retained by Birmingham Preparative Meeting, Hicksite (entry 220). The
Orthodox Friends continued to use one section of the old meeting-house

until 1845. In that year David Garrett donated 1 acre of ground, situated across the road from the old meeting-house. In the same year a one-story stone meeting-house was erected and the remaining ground was plotted as a burial ground. A stone schoolhouse was erected across the road from the meeting-house in 1854. The enrollment, however, dwindled and the school was closed in 1872. The building was then converted into a private dwelling. Seventeen acres and 120 perches of land, which were retained by the Hicksite Friends in 1827, were returned to this meeting in 1874. Due to decreased membership, Birmingham Preparative Meeting was laid down in 1922 by Birmingham Monthly Meeting and its members transferred to West Chester Preparative Meeting (entry 147). Meetings for worship were continued, however, until 1938, when the meeting-house was sold and the burial ground and remaining property were transferred to the care of West Chester Preparative Meeting.

See: Futhey and Cope, op. cit., pp. 70, 73-79, 131, 163, 233, 234, 341; Schoonover, op. cit., pp. 114, 139; Thomson, op. cit., p. 748; Watson, op. cit., II, 83, 87; Egle, op. cit., p. 531; Michener, op. cit., pp. 70, 71; Matlack, op. cit., pp. 271-274; Gilbert Cope, Chester County Quakers During the Revolution (manuscript deposited at Chester County Historical Society); "Early settlers at Birmingham," West Chester Daily Local News, May 7, 1879 to February 4, 1880; Anna Forsythe, "Birmingham Meeting," West Chester Village Record, July 7, 1910; Herbert T. Worth, "Friends' Record in Birmingham," West Chester Daily Local News, December 10, 1915; Albert B. Huey, "Birmingham Meeting in early days," West Chester Daily Local News, October 14, 1921.

Minutes of Men's Meetings, 1852-98, 1916-22, 2 vol. (1726-1851, 1899-1915 missing), at PPFYR. Registers are in the records of the Birmingham Monthly Meeting. Financial Records, 1877-98, 2 vols. (1726-1876, 1899-1922 missing); Bank Books and Canceled Checks, 1893-92, 2 vols. (1893-1922 missing); Account of Educational Fund, Birmingham Preparative Meeting, 1895, 1 vol., in Chestnut Street meeting-house, West Chester. Chester County Deed Books, A-5, vol. 98, p. 378; B-6, vol. 124, p. 589; K-9, vol. 207, p. 85; K-16, vol. 382, p. 468; Z-9, vol. 222, p. 273; D-20, vol. 476, p. 84; P-8, vol. 187, p. 101; M-8, vol. 184, p. 509.

156. LANSDOWNE MONTHLY MEETING, 1904--. Northwest corner Stewart and Lansdowne Avenue, Lansdowne, Delaware County.
Set up in 1904 by Concord Quarterly Meeting (entry 136), upon request from the members of Darby Preparative Meeting (entry 149) and Chester Monthly Meeting (entry 137) who resided in Lansdowne. Meetings were held in the gray stone meeting-house, erected in 1831 by Darby Monthly Meeting (entry 148). When Darby Monthly Meeting was laid down in 1849, the meeting-house and 2 acres of ground were transferred to the care of Chester Monthly meeting (entry 137). When Lansdowne Monthly Meeting was set up, the meeting-house and grounds were transferred to this meeting by Chester Monthly Meeting. In 1902 a one-story gray stone schoolhouse was erected on the meeting-house grounds by the Lansdowne Friends' School Association. In 1904 an additional story, was added to the schoolhouse. Lansdowne Monthly Meeting assumed the care of this school in 1905. The present clerk is Judge Albert B. Maris, 554 Lansdowne Avenue, Yeadon.

Minutes of Men's Meetings, 1904-13, 1 vol.; Minutes of Women's Meetings, 1904-13, 1 vol.; Minutes of Joint Meetings, 1914--, 4 vols., in custody of clerk. Minutes of Ministers and Elders (now known as Ministry and Counsel), 1904--, 2 vols., in custody of clerk, John D. Carter, #5,

"The Knoll," Lansdowne. Register of Membership (contains births, deaths, removals, and marriages), 1904--, 1 vol.; Certificates of Removak, 1904--, 1 vol., in custody of recorder, Edith R. Maris, 554 S. Lansdowne Avenue, Yeadon. Financial Records, 1925--, 1 vol. (1904-24 missing), in custody of treasurer, Raymond T. Moore, 19 Willowbrook Avenue. Minute Book of School Committee, 1905-26, 1 vol., in schoolhouse, and 1926--, 2 vols., in custody of clerk, Mrs. Edith G. Banham, #47 "The Knoll," Lansdowne.

157. WESTTOWN MONTHLY MEETING, 1920--. Westtown, Chester County. Set up in 1920 by Concord Quarterly Meeting (entry 136). Meetings were held in the meeting-room of the Westtown Boarding School (entry 419) until 1929. In that year, a plain gray stone meeting-house was presented by Arthur and Emma Foster Perry of New England. The first session of the monthly meeting was held in the new building in May 19, 1929. Although the meeting-house was erected for the accommodation of this meeting, it is owned by the Westtown Boarding School. The present clerk is J. Russel Edgerton, Westtown.

   See: "Mrs. Herbert Hoover Enjoys Westtown," West Chester Daily Local News, May 20, 1929.

   Minutes of Joint Meetings, 1920-35, 1 vol., in the Westtown Boarding School, and 1935--, 1 vol., in custody of clerk. Minutes of Overseers, 1920--, 2 vols., in custody of clerk, Mrs. James F. Walker, Westtown. Registers of Births, Deaths, Members, and Removals, 1920--, 1 vol., Certificates of Marriages, 1924--, 1 vol., in custody of recorder, Mrs. Frank Spickler, Westtown. Financial Records, 1920--, 1 vol., in custody of treasurer, Mrs. Frederick W. Swan, Westtown.

   158. WESTTOWN INDULGED MEETING, 1799--. Westtown, Chester County. Established in 1799 by Philadelphia Yearly Meeting (entry 1) for the accommodation of the students of the Westtown Boarding School (entry 419). Meetings for worship were held in the meeting-room of the main school building until 1929, when Westtown Monthly Meeting (entry 157) erected a one-story gray stone building on the grounds of the Westtown School property. Since the erection of the meeting-house, the meeting worships in the new building. The meeting was set up originally for the convenience of students and teachers of the boarding School and has sometimes been omitted during the vacation months. The meeting seems at first to have been under the Westtown School Committee of the yearly meeting; later it was affiliated with Concord Monthly. In 1920 when Westtown Monthly was set up this indulged meeting became a part of it.

   159. MIDDLETOWN MONTHLY MEETING, 1931--. Middletown Road, near Glen
         Mills Road, Lima, Delaware County.
In 1931 this meeting was established through a division of Chester Monthly Meeting (entry 137) by Concord Quarterly Meeting (entry 136). It convenes at the meeting-house of the Middletown Preparative Meeting (entry 160). The present clerk is Herbert C. Barker, R. D., Malvern.

   See: Arthur Pennell, History of Middletown Meeting (manuscript in author's posession, Baltimore Pike, Wawa).

   Minutes of Joint Meetings, 193100, 1 vol., in custody of clerk. Minutes of Ministers and Elders, 1931--, in custody of clerk, Mrs. Elizabeth Pennell, Baltimore Pike, Wawa. Register of Births, Removal, Marriages, Membership, and Deaths, 1931--, in custody of Mrs. Elizabeth Thorpe, 24

E. Front Street, Media. Register of Marriage Certificates, 1931--, 1 vol., in custody of Miss Bertha Garratt, Providence and Willow Roads, Wallingford. Financial Records, 1931--, 1 vol., in custody of William Balderston, Tanger Road, Glen Mills.

160. **MIDDLETOWN PREPARATIVE MEETING, 1686--.** Middletown Road near Glen Mills Road, Delaware County.
Set up in 1701 by Chester Monthly Meeting (entry 137), after having functioned as an indulged meeting from 1686. Meetings were first held in the home of Bartholmew Coppock, afterward in the home of John Bowater until 1700. At this time a log meeting-house was erected on a portion of a lot containing 5 3/4 acres donated by Joshua Hastings and located on the east side of Middletown Road (then Edgemont Road), about 60 feet north of Yearley's Mill Road, Route #179. A portion of the land was used as a burial ground. Meetings were held in the log meeting-house until 1770, when a one-story gray stone meeting-house was erected. At the time of the Separation, in 1827, this meeting-house and the burial ground were retained by Middletown Preparative Meeting, Hicksite (entry 160). Both branches of Friends continued to meet here until 1828, when the Orthodox Friends purchased a schoolhouse from James Emlen, and met there until 1835. At this time Joseph Pennell donated 1 acre and 14 perches of ground on the east side of Middletown Road about 300 feet south of Yearsley's Mill Road, Route 179. On one section of this ground, the one-story gray stone meeting-house was erected and another section was set aside for a burial ground. In 1840 an adjoining half-acre of land was purchased for an addition to the burial ground. In 1836 the schoolhouse was sold back to James Emlen for $100. In 1931 this meeting was transferred to the care of Middletown Monthly Meeting (entry 159). The Middletown Preparative Meeting has never been officially laid down.

See: Bowden, op. cit., II, 248; Michener, op. cit., p. 68; Henry G. Ashmead, History of Delaware County, p. 561.

Minutes of Men's Meetings, 1696-1865, not available, reported to be in custody of Miss M. Darlington, treasurer of Middletown Preparative Meeting (H); 1866-1912, 1 vol., in custody of Mrs. William Thorpe, Concordville. Minutes of Women's Meetings, 1696-1890, not available, reported to be in the custody of Miss M. Darlington; 1891-1912 missing. Minutes of Joint Meetings, 1913-34, 1935, included in the Minute book of men's meetings 1866-1913; 1935--, included in the minute book of the Middletown Monthly Meeting. Registers, 1696-1935 are in the records of the Chester Monthly Meeting; 1935--, in records of Middletown Monthly Meeting. Burial Records, 1840-- (chart), in custody of Samuel L. Smedley, Jr., South Delchester Road, Glen Mills. Delaware County Deed Books, vol. O, p. 591.

BURLINGTON AND BUCKS QUARTERLY MEETING (0)

Component Meetings

(See: Explanatory Note 3)

	Date establishe(	Entry number
FALLS MONTHLY MEETING	1680	162
Middletown Preparative Meeting	1722	163
Landisville Indulged Meeting (Plumstead)	1836	164
Buckingham Indulged Meeting	1898	165
MIDDLETOWN MONTHLY MEETING (NESHAMINY MONTHLY MEETING)	1706	166
BUCKINGHAM MONTHLY MEETING	1720	167
Landisville Indulged Meeting (Plumstead)	1836	164

161. BURLINGTON AND BUCKS QUARTERLY MEETING, 1898--. Burlington (New Jersey) and Fallsington, Bucks County.
In 1898 due to the diminished membership in Bucks Quarter, Philadelphia Yearly Meeting (entry 1) decided to merge Bucks Quarterly Meeting (entry 58) and Burlington Quarterly Meeting of New Jersey (see forthcoming Inventory of the Church Archives of New Jersey). The following minute was recorded at the yearly meeting: "At the yearly Meeting of Friends held in Philadelphia . . . the Joint Committee under appointment to assist Bucks Quarterly Meeting produced a report . . . in which they propose the discontinuance of the Quarterly Meeting and that the minutes and members be attached to Burlington Quarterly Meeting and that the Preparative Meeting of Ministers and Elders of the Falls Monthly Meeting be joined to Burlington Quarterly Meeting of Ministers and Elders. The report is united with and it is decided that Bucks Quarter be discontinued and the union to Burlington Quarterly Meeting take place after the session of the second Quarterly Meeting, held in the Fifth month next. It was concluded that the meetings so united be named Burlington and Bucks Quarterly Meeting and the Yearly Meeting stock heretofore paid by Bucks Quarterly be assumed by Burlington and Bucks Quarterly Meeting. The Books and Papers of Bucks Quarter are to be placed in the custody of the newly established Quarterly." Meetings are held in Fallsington in February and August, and at Burlington, New Jersey, in May and November. The majority of the monthly meetings under Bucks and Burlington Quarterly Meeting are in New Jersey, therefore, only those in Pennsylvania are treated in the following entries. The present clerks are Henry H. Albertson, Oxmead Road, Burlington, New Jersey, and Jane M. Snipes, Morrisville, Pa.

Minutes of Women's Meetings, 1846-1921, 1 vol. (1846-98 are records of the Burlington Quarterly Meeting), at PPFYR. Minutes of the Burlington and Bucks Quarterly Meeting, 1898--, 2 vols., in custody of Henry H.

191

Albertson, Oxmead Road, Burlington, New Jersey. Minutes of Ministers and
Elders, 1898--, 2 vols., in custody of J. J. Edgerton, Edgemont Farm,
Langhorne.

162. FALLS MONTHLY MEETING, 1680--. Intersection of Bristol, Burlington and Pennsbury Roads, Fallsington, Bucks County.
Set up in 1683 by Burlington Quarterly Meeting of New Jersey (see forthcoming Inventory of the church Archives of New Jersey), after having met
as a meeting for worship in the homes of William Yardley, James Harrison,
Phineas Pemberton, William Biles, William Dark, Lyonel Britany, and
William Beaks since 1680. These Friends west of the Delaware attended
the business meetings of the Burlington meeting in New Jersey. Friends
had settled on the west side of the river around the Falls before William
Penn secured his grant for the lands in America. They acquired their
tracts of land from Governor Andros of New York, representative of the
Duke of York, and were under his jurisdiction until Lieutenant Governor
Markham arrived in 1681 with credentials from William Penn. At a meeting
held in the home of William Biles, on May 2, 1683, the Friends of Bucks
County thought it fit and necessary that a monthly meeting should be set
up. A petition was sent to the Burlington Quarterly Meeting acquainting
it with the desire of the Friends in Fallsington. This request was
granted the same year. In 1684 their meeting was transferred to the care
of the newly established Bucks Quarterly Meeting (entry 58). Meetings
continued to be held in the homes of members until 1689, at which time
definite steps were taken to erect a meeting-house. A committee was appointed to look for a suitable place. The site chosen lay between Randall
Blackshaw's and Samuel Burgess' land, where the Southampton and other
roads converged. A plot of 6 acres of land was donated in 1689 by Samuel
Burgess and a one-story red brick meeting-house was erected thereon in
1690. The location of this building was just southwest of the present
Hicksite meeting-house. The cemetery, plotted in 1692, included an additional 16 perches given by Daniel Burgess, and a portion of the 6 acres
originally contributed by him in 1689. A second meeting-house of stone
was erected east of the old graveyard, in 1728, and the former meeting-
house was repaired and used as a schoolhouse. Samuel Rhoads and his wife
conveyed 4 acres to the meeting in 1781. A two-story stone building was
erected on part of the land 1781-82 and used as the home of the schoolmaster. In order to accommodate the increased membership of the meeting
the first meeting-house, which was erected in 1690 and later used as a
school, was razed and a two-story gray stone meeting-house was built on
an adjacent hill in 1789. The school, which had been conducted in the
first Meeting-house, was then transferred to the building erected in 1728.
In 1801 a two-story gray stone schoolhouse was erected on part of the
original land donated by Samuel Burgess. At the time of the Separation
in 1827, Falls Monthly Meeting, Hicksite (entry 201), retained the original burial ground and the meeting-house erected in 1789. The Orthodox
Friends retained the schoolmaster's house, now used as a caretaker's residence; the schoolhouse, which was erected in 1801; and the remaining
grounds totaling 5 acres and 6 perches. Meetings were held by the Orthodox Friends in the schoolhouse until 1841, when a two-story native stone
meeting-house was built.

In 1846, 135 perches of land, adjacent to the original tract of land
contributed by Samuel Burgess, was purchased and used as a burial ground.
This cemetery is enclosed by a stone wall and is used for the interment
of Orthodox and Primitive Friends. Another burial place is that laid out
in 1685 on 10 square perches of land by Phineas Pemberton, an influential

Friend and leader in colonial affairs. This ground was platted both as
a family graveyard and for the burial of Friends. It is a small graveyard, 2 miles south of Norrisville, on the Delaware River bank, opposite
Biles Island, and was commonly known as The Point.   It was the first
Friends' burial ground in the county. Funds for its maintenance which
is still carefully attended to, were set aside by Phineas Pemberton   In
this graveyard, lie Phineas Pemberton, his wife Phoebe, and their children;
James Harrison, his wife; Ralph Pemberton; Ralph Smith; and Henry Gibbs.
In all, there were about 15 burials in this graveyard, all of them founders of Falls Monthly Meeting (entry 162). Further burials, by specifi-
cation of the endowment, are strictly prohibited. The last interment is
believed to have been in 1709. Some years ago the late Henry Pemberton
of Philadelphia, a descendant of Phineas Pemberton, restored the walls
surrounding the plot, which had been previously erected, and placed a
permanent marker as a memorial in the cemetery. This graveyard has always
been under the care of the Falls Monthly Meeting. Another burial ground
belonging to this meeting is that laid out in 1686 by Thomas Janney, a
notable Friend, on 144 square perches of land, ½ mile below Yardley on
the Yardley-Morrisville Road.   This burial ground, known as Slat Pit
Hill Graveyard, was deeded to the trustees of Falls Monthly Meeting for
the use of Friends in the vicinity.   In 1686 30 square yards of this
plot were enclosed by a wooden fence. By 1850 this plot, almost entirely
filled with graves, was the principal Friends burial ground in this vicinity although most of the burials had been made prior to 1800. After the
Separation, in 1827, the Hicksites were given permission to enter their
dead in this graveyard. The graveyard today, is enclosed by a stone wall.
There have been no burials for many years. Still another burial place of
this meeting is the Watson Graveyard. This was laid out prior to 1700
by John Rowland, a Friend, on 5 square perches of the 300 acres of land
patent to him by William Penn in 1683. Although the small burial ground
was on Rowland's land, it was near the land and home of Thomas Watson.
It is supposed that this was the reason the burial ground was called
Watson Graveyard. In 1700, John Rowland disposed of his grant of 300
acres to John Hiett, with the exception of the graveyard which had been
fenced in prior to 1700. In 1703-4, the graveyard was deeded by John
Rowland to Edmund Lovett, William Atkinson, and Nehemiah Blackshaw, trustees of Falls Monthly Meeting. William Atkinson, the surviving trustee,
in 1745-46 transferred this declaration of trust to Joseph Wharton, Joseph
Atkinson, Edmund Lovett, Jr., and Thomas Watson, newly appointed trustees.
In 1806 an additional 17 perches of land were added to this small burial
ground by a conveyance of Jessie Larrew to Moses Moon, Overseer and Elder
of Falls Monthly Meeting. This burial ground at present is surrounded by
a stone wall and has not been used for the past 50 years. The present
clerk of the Monthly Meeting, is Gertrude E. Jackson, Newtown.

See: George W. Brown, Historical Sketches Chiefly Relating to the
Early Settlement of Friends at the Falls in Bucks County, passim; Battle,
op. cit., pp. 314, 324, 381; Michener, op. cit., p. 75; Bowden, op. cit.,
II, 248; Matlack, op. cit., I, 98-102, 130; Jane M. Snipes, "The Founding
and Founders of Falls Meeting," Bulletin of Friends' Historical Association, XXII (1933), No. 1, p. 20.

Minutes of Men's Meetings, 1683-1834, 5 vols.; Minutes of Women's
Meetings, 1683-1918, 6 vols., at PPFYR. Minutes of Joint Meetings, 1918-

27, are in the last volume of Minutes of Men's Meetings, and 1928--, 1
vol., in custody of clerk. Minutes of Ministers and Elders, 1813-40, 1
vol. (1683-1812, 1841-58 missing), at NNBN, and 1859-1923, 1923--, in
custody of Joseph Edgerton, Trenton Road, Woodbourne. Register of Births,
Deaths, Marriages, and Burials, 1683-1788, 1 vol. at PPFYR, and 1788--,
1 vol., in custody of recorder, Mrs. Mary Oliver, Route #732 and Ferry
Road, Morrisville. Burials in the Pemberton Graveyard are recorded in
the Register of births, deaths, marriages and burials, 1683-1788, and also
in Will Book "A" 1683-1709, deposited in Bucks County Courthouse, Doylestown. Register of Removals from England to America, 1680-1720, 1 vol.
(also contains a few marriage records), at NNBN. Register of Removals,
1821-81, 1 vol. (1683-1820 missing), at NNBN, and 1863--, 1 vol., in custody of clerk. Financial Records, 1816-84, 1 vol. (1683-1815 missing),
at NNBN, and 1827-1925, 1 vol., at PPFYR, and 1926--, 1 vol., in custody
of treasurer, Lewis Leedom, 10 Main Street, Yardley. Bucks County Deed
Books, vol. 1, p. 316; vol. 9, p. 140, vol. 10, pp. 181-190; vol. 17, pp.
211, 213; vol. 23, pp. 254, 255; vol. 36, pp. 238, 355; vol. 53, pp. 393,
568; vol. 89, pp. 160, 331; vol. 276, pp. 248, 268; vol. 596, p. 234; vol.
635, p. 434; vol. 657, p. 140.

163. MIDDLETOWN PREPARATIVE MEETING, 1722-1911. Bellevue and Watson
     Avenues, Langhorne, Bucks County.
Set up in 1722 by Middletown Monthly Meeting (entry 166). From 1793 until
1827 meetings were held in a two and one-half story stone building which
Middletown Monthly Meeting erected in 1793 to replace the old one built in
1720. After the Separation, Middletown Monthly Meeting, Hicksite (entry
207) retained all the property of the original Middletown Monthly Meeting. The Orthodox meeting was laid down at that time. Middletown Preparative Meeting was then established under Falls Monthly Meeting (entry
162). Meetings were held in private homes until 1840, when 2 acres and
60 perches of ground were purchased at Bellevue and Watson Avenues, in
Langhorne, and a two and one-half story stone meeting-house was erected.
In 1911, because of rapidly diminishing membership, this meeting was laid
down by Falls Monthly Meeting and the property sold to Samuel C. Eastburn,
who converted the building into a private dwelling. Throughout the years
of its existence this meeting used the burial ground which belonged first
to the Orthodox and later to the Hicksite Middletown Monthly Meeting.

     See: Woody, op. cit., p. 87; Bowden, op. cit., I, 248; Michener,
op. cit., p. 77; Centennial of Newtown Friends Meetings, pp. 38-42, hereinafter cited as Centennial Newtown.

     Minutes of Men's Meetings, 1792-1904, 1 transcribed vol. (1722-91,
1905-11 missing), in meeting-house of the Middletown Monthly Meeting (H).
Minutes of Women's Meetings, 1722-1911, missing, but extracts, 1722-1827,
are in records of the Middletown Meeting. Registers are in the records
of the Middletown Monthly Meeting, 1722-1826, and in the records of the
Falls Monthly Meeting, 1827-1911. Bucks County Deed Books, vol. 64, p. 409;
vol. 176, p. 306; vol. 372, p. 6.

164. LANDISVILLE INDULGED MEETING (PLUMSTEAD), 1727--. Two miles
     north of Doylestown, at Intersection of Landisville and Street
     Roads, Bucks County.

Established in 1730 as Plumstead Indulged Meeting by permission of Falls
Monthly Meeting (entry 162), and placed under the care of Buckingham
Monthly Meeting (entry 167). Meetings for worship had been held without

authority in private homes since 1727. In March 1730 15 acres of land,
½ mile west of Gardenville village, were conveyed, in consideration of 1
shilling per acre, to the indulged meeting by Thomas Brown for "a burial
ground and other customary building." In the same year a small log building was erected and three quarters of ground near the meeting-house set
aside for burial purposes. Burials were made on this site in 1730 but the
earliest tombstone is dated 1742. Earlier markers have been destroyed.
The burial ground is still in use by both the Orthodox and the Hicksite
Friends. In 1752 the log building was replaced by a two-story native gray
stone meeting-house. A smaller building, one story high and constructed
of the same material, was attached at the same time to the west end of the
meeting-house for use as a school. During the Revolutionary War this
building was used as a hospital. Sometime later a small two-story stone
building was erected, south of the meeting-house, to be used as a schoolmaster's residence. This building is today used as the home of the caretaker of the meeting-house grounds. In 1772 this meeting was set up as
the Plumstead Preparative Meeting by Buckingham Monthly Meeting and continued as such until the Separation in 1827. After the division the meeting returned to an Indulged status. Plumstead Preparative Meeting, Hicksite (entry 199), retained posession of all the property. A minute in the
records of Buckingham Monthly Meeting for October 1, 1827, states: "Reported from Plumstead, Daniel Carlile, Jesse Jones, John Michener (Farmer), Joshua Michener, John Fell and John Rich have withdrawn themselves
from this Preparative Meeting declaring to that effect." Because of
their small number the Orthodox Friends met for worship in their homes
or attended the Buckingham Monthly Meeting at Lahaska. In 1836 John Rich
and other trustees of the Buckingham Monthly Meeting received a grant of
60 perches of land from Joseph Dyer in the village of Landisville, to be
used by the Friends of Plumstead "to build and erect a meeting-house, a
branch of Buckingham Monthly Meeting." At this time the meeting became
known as the Landisville Indulged Meeting. The same year a one-story
frame, meeting-house was erected on this land. Meetings continued until
1892 when only a few members remained. The following year the meeting-
house was torn down and the materials sold. By indenture, dated January
19, 1902, James Barclay, Sr., executor for John Dyer, conveyed the 60
perches of land to Newberry Moon, owner of the tract of land of which the
meeting-house lot was once a part, for $350, though the land had been
granted with the stipulation that "should it cease to be wanted in time
by the Religious Society of Friends . . . the meeting shall surrender
said lot to Joseph Dyer or his legal representative." When Buckingham
Monthly Meeting was laid down in 1898 this meeting along with its other
constituents was transferred to Falls Monthly Meeting.

See: 200th Anniversary of Buckingham Monthly Meeting, 1720-1923,
Buckingham Township, Bucks County, Pennsylvania, hereinafter cited as
200th Anniversary Buckingham; Michener, op. cit., p. 79; Plumstead Meeting-House, in Miscellaneous Records, vol. 114, p. 188 (manuscript at Bucks
County Historical Society, Doylestown).

Minutes of Men's Meetings, 1772-1847, 3 vols.; Minutes of Women's
Meetings, 1814-23, 1 vol. (1772-1813, 1824-27 missing), at NNBN. Registers are in the records of the Falls Monthly Meeting, 1730-71, and in
records of Buckingham Monthly Meeting, 1772-1827. Bucks County Deed Books,
vol. 31, p. 189; vol. 56, p. 504; vol. 60, p. 627; vol. 70, p. 236.

165. BUCKINGHAM INDULGED MEETING, 1898-1900. Old York Road, Lahaska
      village, Buckingham Twp., Bucks County.
When the Buckingham Monthly Meeting (entry 167) was laid down in 1898, an

indulged meeting under the care of Falls Monthly Meeting (entry 162) was
established. Meetings for worship were held in the two-story native stone
meeting-house, erected in 1830 by the Buckingham Monthly Meeting. Due to
diminishing membership, the indulged meeting was laid down in 1900 and
the members were transferred to Falls Monthly Meeting. Some years later
the meeting-house was sold and converted into an antique shop.

See: Matlack, op. cit., I, pp. 93-96.

Registers are in the records of the Falls Monthly Meeting.

166. MIDDLETOWN MONTHLY MEETING, 1680-1827. At intersection of
     Maple Avenue (Old Philadelphia Road), and Green Street, Lang-
     horne, Bucks County.
Established in 1680 as Neshaminy Indulged Meeting under Burlington (N. J.)
Quarterly Meeting (see forthcoming Inventory of the Church Archives of
New Jersey). For 3 years meetings were held in the homes of William
Biles, Nicholas Waln, John Otter, and Robert Hall. In 1683 this meeting
was set up as Neshaminy Monthly Meeting, through a division of Falls Monthly Meeting (entry 162), by Philadelphia Yearly Meeting (entry 1). Meetings were held in a small log building which was erected in the same year
about 1 mile west of the present Middletown Monthly Meeting-house. The
ground on which the meeting-house stood was the property of Nicholas Waln.
In 1706 the name of the meeting was changed to Middletown Monthly Meeting. A gift of 3 acres of land on the Old Philadelphia Road (Maple Avenue) had been received from William Hayhurst and Robert Heaton in 1704,
but it was not until 1720 that a new meeting-house 30' x 40' was erected
in 1793. This was a two-story house 38' x 78' built of Edgehill stone.
In 1793 a small, log schoolhouse, which had been standing on the meeting-
house site for some time was razed and a new two and one-half story stone
schoolhouse was erected with the material taken from the old 1720 meeting-
house. At the time of the Separation in 1827 the Orthodox Friends withdrew, and the property was retained by the Hicksite group. The Orthodox
Friends established their meeting in the homes of members, where they
were held until 1841, when another meeting-house was built by them. This
building was sold in 1903 and was converted into a private residence. The
membership gradually diminished and the meeting was laid down by Burling-
ton-Bucks Quarterly Meeting in 1900.

     Plots of ground comprising the meeting-house and cemetery site were
acquired at various times: 3 acres in February 1704, 4 acres in May
1782, 8½ acres in April 1793, 62 perches in 1792, 39 perches in 1792, 40
perches in 1810, and 1 acre in 1804. The earliest cemetery was laid out
in 1682 on ½ acre of land by Nicholas Waln, a prominent Friend, on his
own estate. This plot was near the meeting-house and the original site
of the "Neshamina" (Middletown) Monthly Meeting. It was intended for a
family graveyard and also for the use of Friends and others. This small
graveyard was also known as "The Burial Grounds of the Walns" and although
it was never deeded to "Neshamina" (Middletown) Monthly Meeting, it was
supervised by and appears in the early records of that meeting. The first
known burial was that of Richard Amon, September 1682, and the last known
burial was that of David Davis, January 23, 1686. The plot was irregularly
laid out and several of the numerous and scattered graves contained the
remains of Indians. In 1890 the portion of the Waln property comprising
this graveyard was purchased as a right-of-way by the Pennsylvania Railroad and is today completely submerged by the fill-in of an overhead bridge.

See: Woody, op. cit., p. 87; Bowden, op. cit., II, p. 248; Michener, op. cit., p. 77; Centennial Newtown, pp. 38-42.

Minutes of Men's Meetings, 1683-1837, 5 vols.; Minutes of Women's Meetings, 1683-1829, 2 vols., in meeting-house of Middletown Monthly Meeting, Hicksite. Register of births, deaths, and burials, certificates of marriages, and certificates of removals, incorporated in the minute books 1682-1887. Transcribed copies of removals, 1684-1890, 1 vol.; list of burials, 1869--, list of lots in cemetery, name of owner and persons buried therein; Burial Permits, 1906--, at PDoyB. See also: Will Books, "A", county records, Courthouse, Doylestown. Bucks County Deed Books, vol. 26, p. 630; vol. 31, pp. 153, 155; vol. 33, p. 656; vol. 46, p. 271; vol. 56, p. 292; vol. 88, p. 574; vol. 173, p. 104; vol. 176, p. 306; vol. 253, p. 162; vol. 259, pp. 523, 528; vol. 261, p. 637: vol. 417, p. 31.

167. BUCKINGHAM MONTHLY MEETING, 1720-1898. Old York Road, Lahaska Village, Buckingham Twp., Bucks County. Set up in 1720 by Bucks Quarterly Meeting (entry 58). For many years meetings were held alternately in the meeting-houses of Wrightstown Preparative Meeting (entry 64), Plumstead Preparative Meeting (entry 164), and Buckingham Preparative Meeting (entry 59). When Buckingham Preparative Meeting was laid down about 1858, Buckingham Monthly Meeting convened exclusively at the meeting-house belonging to the defunct preparative meeting. Due to diminished membership this meeting was laid down by Burlington and Bucks Quarterly Meeting (entry 161) in 1898. After the laying down of this monthly meeting Buckingham Friends were allowed an indulged meeting (entry 165) under the care of Falls Monthly Meeting.

See: Matlack, op. cit., pp. 93-96; Michener, op. cit., p. 78; Bowden, op. cit., I, 248; Chapman, op. cit., p. 143; Bailey, op. cit., p. 284.

Minutes of Men's Meetings, 1720-1832, 5 vols., at NNBN, and 1827-67, 1888-96, 3 vols. (1868-87, 1897-98 missing), at PPFYR. Minutes of Women's Meetings, 1722-1896, 6 vols. (1897-98 missing); Minutes of Ministers and Elders, 1787-1834, 3 vols. (1722-86, 1835-98 missing), at PPFYR. Register of Births, Deaths, and Marriages, 1793-1806, 1 vol.; Register of Births ister of Marriages, 1802--, 1 vol. (1827-30 missing), in custody of the recorder of Buckingham Monthly Meeting (H), Miss Miriam Broadhurst, Holicong, and 1831-94, 1 vol., at PPFYR. Register of Removals, 1720-1820, 2 vols., at NNBN; 1821--, 1 vol., in custody of Miss Miriam Broadhurst; and 1828-93, in the 1831-94 register of marriages. Financial records are in the minute books. Financial records of the School Fund, 1794-1839, 1 vol., at NNBN. All prior and subsequent financial records of the school fund are in the minutes. Bucks County Deed Books, vol. 33, p. 656; vol. 46, p. 271; vol. 56, 292; vol. 88, p. 574: vol. 89, pp. 160, 331; vol. 173, p. 104; vol. 176, p. 306; vol. 261, p. 637; vol. 471, p. 31; vol. 594, pp. 236, 422.

II. KEITHIAN OR CHRISTIAN QUAKERS

	Date established	Entry number
Philadelphia Keithian Meeting	1691	168
Oxford Keithian Meeting	1692	169
Thomas Powell Keithian Meeting	1692	170

168. PHILADELPHIA KEITHIAN MEETING, 1691-ca.1698. Present site of northwest corner Second and Filbert Streets, Philadelphia. Organized by George Keith and a group of dissident members of Philadelphia Monthly Meeting of Friends (entry 3). Among the leaders of Keith's adherents in Philadelphia were Thomas Budd, Thomas Rutter, Robert Turner and William Preston. Thomas Budd, originally a Jersey Friend, was on the ship **Kent** which brought the first settlers to Burlington in 1677. Thomas Rutter, once Bailiff of Germantown, was William Penn's blacksmith. Robert Turner, who was formerly a merchant of Dublin, came early to Pennsylvania. Penn placed great confidence in him and made him one of his commissioners to grant werrants and patents for land. During the Keithian controversy, Turner in company with William Preston entered the Bank Meeting-house (entries 7-34) of which he was a trustee, and in an act of derision pulled down the ministers gallery.

George Keith started his agitation in behalf of his schism in 1691. Meetings for a short time were held in private houses, but in 1692, a plot of ground was purchased on the west side of Second Street south of Mulberry (now Arch). The lot was 25' front and 300' deep, and was conveyed to Thomas Dudd, Thomas Peart, Ralph Ward and James Poulter in trust for the Christian Quakers, the title adopted for the organization. In the same year they erected a meeting-house on the premises. An illustration contained in Julius F. Sachse's **German Sectarians of Pennsylvania**, II, 84, gives what is believed to be a reasonably correct representation of this structure. It was constructed of wood, and could hardly have been more than 20' wide and about 40' long, indicating a seating capacity of perhaps a 100. It stood with its gable facing Second Street, was one-story high, and had a gambrel roof. The main entrance was at the gable end, through a large projecting vestibule, to the right of the building. On the north side there were five windows and an additional entrance near the front. Not many years after the erection of this building, George Keith returned to England and subsequently joined in membership with the Episcopal denomination, leaving his followers to take care of themselves. The organization became torn with internal dissentions and disputes, and rapidly disintegrated. What was left of the membership affiliated with the Baptist Church, and gave the meeting-house and lot to that denomination. The last survivor of the trustees, however, joined the Episcopal Church and they induced him to make a deed for the premises. The deed was not executed until after the death of the grantor, when it was produced. The Baptists vigorously contested the claim and finally compelled the grantees to give them a quitclaim deed upon the payment of a trifling consideration.

Keithian meetings must have terminated about 1698, for it was in this year that the First Baptist Church of Philadelphia was founded, and in this meeting-house the congregation of that church held their first services in this city. Subsequently they acquired an adjoining lot, nearly doubling the size of the ground, and in 1731 they removed the Keithian meeting-house and erected a brick church on the ground.

According to information contained in Christ Church, Philadelphia- the present site of the Keithian property is definitely established as the northwest corner of Second and Filbert Streets; just north of the historic old Christ Church. It was in this Keithian meeting-house that the pioneer Episcopal congregation of the famous Christ Church assembled for worship, while the first edifice, a wooden structure, was being erected in 1695-96. This was while the Keithian Quakers were still holding their meetings there. It is also stated that this meeting-house stood at La Grange Place, Second Street above Market. La Grange Place was a former name of the present Filbert Street in that section.

See: George Vaux, "The Keithian Meeting-house," The Friend, LXXVII (1903), 171; Lippincott, Keithian Separation, p. 49; Scharf and Wescott, op. cit., I, 123, II, 1243; William Keen, "Keithian Quaker Meeting-House, La Grange Place, Second Street above Market, 1692-1731," Bi-Centennial Celebration of the Founding of the First Baptist Church of Philadelphia, 1698-1898, p. 26; Louis C. Washbuth, Christ Church, Philadelphia, p. 96, and mr. p. 311.

A search was made for the minute books and other records of the Philadelphia Keithian Quakers, but without success. In view of the short life of this organization, and the state of disruption that prevailed during the last days of its existence, it is likely that the records were not preserved. Should they still exist they are no doubt in the possesion of some individual or form a part of some private collection.

169. OXFORD KEITHIAN MEETING, ca.1692-ca.1696. Disston Street and Oxford Avenue, Lawndale, Philadelphia.
About 1692 a meeting of Keithian Quakers was established in the township of Oxford. It was composed of former Friends who had separated from the Oxford (now Frankford), Poetquesink (now Byberry), and Lower Dublin (now Abington) meetings. George Keith in his journal states that "a meeting was in use at Frankford." Thomas Graves and John Hart seem to have been the principal supporters of Keith in that locality. Prior to his separation from the Orthodox body, John Hart was a leader among the Friends of Byberry Meeting, and it was at his house that their meetings were held up to that time. He induced a few of the members of that meeting to separate with him, among them was Nathaniel Walton, one of the four brothers that explored the territory of Byberry at a very early time. The Walton brothers were the first to settle in that vicinity. Nathaniel's three brothers retained their membership with Friends. In 1692, a meeting-house was erected on land belonging to Thomas Graves, not very much is known about this structure, only that it was small and is believed to have been built of logs.

About 1696, after Keith's return to England, his adherents at Oxford rapidly diminished in number, one by one they joined with other denomina-

tions. A large part of them joined with the Baptists, but the majority,
however, including Graves, joined the Episcopal Church and the meeting-
house and its land were conveyed to that denomination. The services of
this body continued there until 1711, when a new church building was erected. It is likely that the Keithian meeting-house stood near the present
site of Trinity Church, Oxford, and may have been the building spoken of
in the early records of the parish as the "School-house belonging to Oxford Church." The meeting-house, it is stated, was finally used as a stable for a short while before it was demolished. The church erected in
1711, was in later years enlarged by being added to and built upon, from
time to time, until the present structure was attained. Over its doorway
is inserted a large semicircular marble tablet bearing the following inscription. "Church of England services were held on this site A. D. 1696,
in a log meeting-house built by the Oxford Society of Friends. This
church was erected A. D. 1711." That part of the inscription that alludes
to the meeting-house built by the Oxford Society of Friends is very mis-
leading, and many have been led to believe it refers to the meeting-house
built in the early times by the Friends of Oxford Township. This is an
error, since there appears to have been two separate Oxford meeting-houses
existing at about the same time, and there is nothing to indicate that
they were one and the same structure. One was built on ground given to
Friends by Thomas Fairman in 1683-84, and located at Unity and Waln
Streets in Frankford. The title to this property has not changed hands
since that time. The other, believed to have been a log house, stood on
the premises now occupied by the Trinity Church, Oxford, at Disston Street
and Oxford Avenue, in Lawndale, near Fox Chase. This meeting-house was
built on land belonging to Thomas Graves. Land belonging to Thomas
Fairman in the year 1681, is shown on a map drawn by Thomas Holme, Survey-
or General to William Penn, but it does not show the land owned by Thomas
Graves. This is probably due to the fact that Graves purchased his land
a few years after the map was drawn. In comparing this map of 1681 with
one of present times, the land owned by Fairman is shown to be quite distant from that upon which the Trinity Church, Oxford, now stands. The
Friends Meeting at Unity and Waln Streets was first called "Tackony Meeting," later the name was changed to "Oxford," which accounts for the
confusion of the two buildings.

See: Smedley, Caroline, op. cit., pp. 133, 136, 147, 148; Matlack,
op. cit., I, 485; Lippincott, Keithian Separation, p. 49.

A search was made for the minutes and other records of the Oxford
Keithian Quakers, but they could not be located, and it was not definitely
known whether or not such records still exist.

170. THOMAS POWELL MEETING, 1692-1700. Sandy Bank, between Provi-
        dence and Greek Roads, Upper Providence Twp., Delaware County.
In 1692 a group of Friends, led by Thomas Powell, severed their relationship with the Friends of Upper Providence and under the influence of a
minister, Abel Noble, adhered to the doctrines of George Keith, whose followers are also called the Seventh Day Baptists. "Between 1692 and 1697
a minister by the name of Abel Noble, of the Seventh Day Baptists did join
this Thomas Powell Meeting and he began to put the design of the Seventh
Day Baptists into practice." In July 1697 and the following months there
were 19 members baptized by immersion. Their next step was to choose a
minister by vote. The first chosen minister was Thomas Martin. The congregation continued to grow until 1700, when a difference in doctrine a-
rose. This dissension left the meeting without the leadership of George

Keith, who abandoned the meeting and returned to England. Immediately after his departure the meeting disbanded. Some of the members, who still adhered to the Seventh Day Baptist, moved and settled down in Newtown, where they later erected a church which is still in existence today. Some continued to follow George Keith and when he returned to this country in 1702 as a missionary of the Church of England, contributed funds to erect St. Paul's Episcopal Church in Chester.

See: Morgan Edwards Collection, various papers, at Bucknell Library, Chester (see below).

Register of Baptisms, 1697-1700, one handwritten sheet (1692-97 no records kept), and one marriage certificate, 4-25-1694, in custody of David Price, Radnor. These foregoing registers are recorded in "Brandywine Baptist Church Minute Book," at the Baptist Historical Society, Bucknell Library, Crozer Seminary.

III. PHILADELPHIA YEARLY MEETING OF FREE QUAKERS

	Date established	Entry number
The Society of Free Quakers, Philadelphia	1781	171

171. THE SOCIETY OF FREE QUAKERS, 1781-1928. Southwest corner of
Fifth and Arch Streets, Philadelphia.
In the latter part of 1780, a few members of the Society of Friends who
had been disowned by that organization for having taken some part in the
war for American independence, met together for worship at the homes of
Samuel Wetherill and Timothy Matlack. At the conclusion of one of these
meetings, and after much discussion, they finally decided to formulate a
religious organization of their own. The first meeting for business was
held on February 20, 1781, at the house of Samuel Wetherill, who at that
time lived on Front Street between Arch and Race. At this meeting the
formal title of "The Monthly Meeting of Friends, called by some The Free
Quakers was adopted, and Samuel Wetherill was appointed the clerk, in which
capacity he served until 1808. He was also the minister of the meeting.
The first meeting was attended by only eight persons, but in time the enrollment increased to over a hundred. Meetings continued to be held at
the house of the clerk, and at the houses of other members, until a room
in the College of Philadelphia (now the University of Pennsylvania) was
obtained for the purpose. Within a short time the meeting outgrew the
accommodations afforded by this room. A formal printed letter was prepared, dated the 9th day of 7th month, 1781, and addressed: "To Those
of Our Brethren Who Have Disowned Us." This letter requested that the
Free Quakers be given the use of one of the meeting-houses held by them,
and also for permission to use their burial ground for the interment of
members of the new Society. This appeal was presented to the Philadelphia
Monthly Meeting of Friends (entry 3), by Timothy Matlack, Moses Bartram,
and White Matlack, but met with the refusal of the parent body. In the
same year a petition was sent to the State legislature, which was signed
by about 50 men, requesting that the Friends be forced by law to grant
the Free Quakers the two privileges mentioned in their letter of 7th month
9th. A reply to this petition in the form of an address and memorial was
filed by the parent body and signed in behalf of the meeting by John
Drinker, the clerk. The petition of the Free Quakers was tabled and no
action was taken at that session. The matter was revived at the next
session of the legislature by a memorial and remonstrance presented by
Isaac Howell and White Matlack, which repeated the request of the former
petition. This was presented on August 21, 1782. It was duly entered
upon the journal and was referred to a special committee. This committee,
however, failed to take action and another session adjourned without any
decision being rendered in the matter. In the following year Isaac Howell
presented a short petition signed by 37 of the disowned Friends, asking
for the consideration of the matter. Again the legislature declined to
act and the Free Quakers then realized that they would be obliged to obtain a meeting property some other way. Subscriptions were solicited
among the members and others in sympathy with them and by July 1783 enough

was collected to enable them to purchase a plot of ground on the southwest
corner of Fifth and Mulberry (now Arch) Streets. The lot was 48 feet in
width on Arch Street, and 100 feet in depth on Fifth Street. The first
trustees appointed to hold title to the property are thus named and described in the minutes: "Christopher Marshall, Sr., Gentlemen: Nathaniel
Browne, Blacksmith; Isaac Howell, Esquire; Peter Thomson, Conveyancer;
Moses Bartram, Druggist; Jonathan Schofield, Shop-keeper; Benjamin Say,
Practitioner in Physic; Joseph Warner, Last Maker; and Abraham Roberts,
Grocer."

Further subscriptions were solicited for the purpose of erecting a
new meeting-house on the lot acquired, and so popular were the Free Quakers
with the general public, that within the same year enough funds were raised
to start the construction work. It is said that George Washington and
Benjamin Franklin, were among the subscribers to this building fund. The
meeting-house was completed in the following year, and the first meeting
in the new house was held on June 13, 1784. This meeting-house, a modest
looking structure, stands to the present day, and is in a good state of
preservation. It is a colonial building, two stories high, and is constructed of plain red brick. It has an ample doorway on the Arch Street
front, and another on Fifth Street. The gable end of the building faces
Arch Street, and has built into its wall a marble tablet bearing the following inscription: "By General Subscription for the Free Quakers, erected,
In the Year of our Lord, 1783, of the Empire 8." Tradition has it, that
when the tablet was placed in position, one of the early Free Quakers was
asked the significance of the use of the word "empire" on the stone, and
his reply was, "I tell thee Friend, it is because our country is destined
to be the greatest empire over all of the world."

The organization, although prospering, was without a graveyard until
1786, when on August 26 of that year, an act was passed by the State legislature, giving certain city lots to their use for this purpose. The
Act, in part reads as follows: ". . . That the said Society of Free Quakers thus established through the necessity arising out of a great revolution, had with the assistance of their Christian fellow citizens purchased
a lot of ground and erected thereon a Meeting-house of their own to perform worship in to Almighty God, which having thus accomplished, they
nevertheless find themselves at a loss for a place to bury their dead,
and therefore prays the house for a grant for a suitable lot of land for
this religious and benevolent purpose. And whereas it is but right and
just to forward the designs of religion and benevolence, and that the
virtuous citizen of this Commonwealth who have been deprived of their
religious right and privileges on account of their attachment to the cause
to their country in the time of its utmost danger, should have the encouragement of the legislature. Therefore, be it enacted, and it is hereby enacted by the Representatives of the Freemen of the Commonwealth of
Pennsylvania in General Assembly met, and by the authority of the same:
That eight of the City Lots belonging to the Commonwealth marked in the
plan or draft of the public city lots, Nos. 34, 35, 36, 37, 38, 39, 40,
and 41, situate . . ." and continues with a lengthly description of the
location, which at the present time would be on the west side of Fifth
Street, below Locust. The total dimensions of the lots were 176' along
Fifth Street, by 198' deep. Further on the Act vests the property in
seven trustees of the Free Quakers, whose names are given, and recites
that these trustees and the survivors of them forever, shall hold the
property in trust, to and for the sole purpose of a burial ground for
the use of the Religious Society of Friends, distinguished by the name

of Free Quakers in the city of Philadelphia. This burial ground was
enclosed within a brick wall, and was in use for many years, when a
municipal law came into effect prohibiting further interments in that
ground. Sometime after this law became effective the property was sold,
and each person buried there was disinterred, as far as that was possible
and separately reinterred in a burial ground at Fatland, located on the
Schuylkill River, opposite Valley Forge. The cemetery at Fatland had
been acquired sometime before the one in Philadelphia was discontinued,
and came into the possession of the Society, by the will of Colonel John
Malcolm Wetherill, of Pottsville, who had made provision for the burial
and maintenance of the graves of Free Quakers, in the event that the burial ground in Philadelphia should ever be sold.

As time passed many of the original members of the Free Quakers died,
and a number of their descendants drifted into other religious organizations. Attendance dwindled to such an extent that meetings for worship
and business were held but once a year. Year after year the attendance
was less, and at the annual meeting held in 1836, the last meeting for
religious worship to be held, it is reported that only the clerk and one
other person were present, and that this person was Elizabeth Claypoole
(Betsy Ross). Meetings for business, however, continued to be held once
each year. Since its erection the old meeting-house, besides serving as
a place for religious worship and business meetings of the Free Quakers,
has also served as the meeting-place for a Masonic Lodge. A private school
was conducted there, and the Apprentices' Library occupied it for many
years. It has also served as the headquarters of the Home Missionary Society of Philadelphia, and is occupied at the present time by a business
establishment. At the annual meeting held in 1928, it was decided to ask
the courts to grant a charter, so that the property owned by the Society
might be vested in the name of a corporation rather than in individuals
acting as trustees, which had been the procedure since the time of organization. The charter was granted by Common Pleas Court No. 4, and the organization became incorporated under the corporate title of "The Free
Quaker Society." Though no longer having any religious existence, and
with very small membership, the Society still carries on important philanthropic work. From the income derived from an invested fund, which
was realized mostly from the sale of the old burial ground on Fifth Street
below Locust, and with additional income received as rent from the old
meeting-house at Fifth and Arch Streets, charities are carried on. The
charitable activities are confined mostly to the distribution of coal to
the poor. This work is carried on by the women members, who serve without pay, thereby eliminating administrative expense in the disbursement
of the fund each year. The annual business meeting is held in November,
and besides property matters, and the appointing of committees to look
after the charities, the yearly meeting also received reports as to new
members. There are children born to members during the year, and at this
yearly meeting they are enrolled as birthright members in accordance with
the custom followed since the establishment of the Free Quakers.

See: Wetherill, op. cit., p. 225; Sharpless, Quaker Experiment, II,
217-223; George Barton, "Little Journeys Around Philadelphia - The Fight-
ing Quaker," Philadelphia Evening Bulletin, July 6, 1926; "Men and Things
-The Society of Free Quakers," Philadelphia Evening Bulletin, January 17,
1929.

Minutes of the Free Quakers, 1781-1930, 3 vols., deposited in fire-
proof vault at the Pennsylvania Company, Fifteenth and Chestnut Streets,

Philadelphia, and 1930--, 1 vol., in custody of the secretary, Samuel
Price Wetherill, Morris Building, Philadelphia. Registers of Membership,
Births, Deaths, and Marriages, 1781-1920, number of vols. not available
deposited at the Pennsylvania Company and 1920--, 1 vol., in custody of
the treasurer and recorder, J. Lawrence Wetherill, Commercial Trust Building, South Penn Square, Philadelphia; Treasurers Account Books, 1781-1920,
deposited at the Pennsylvania Company and 1920--, 1 vol., in custody of
the treasurer, J. Lawrence Wetherill. Miscellaneous vouchers, papers,
bills, deeds, etc., are on deposit with the record books at the Pennsylvania Company, Philadelphia. (Note: Information concerning the records
as listed above was kindly supplied by Mr. J. Lawrence Wetherill. He
was not certain as to the exact number of volumes constituting the registers and treasurers account books. Access to the vault at the Pennsylvania Company could not be obtained.

IV.   FRIENDS GENERAL CONFERENCE (Hicksite)

> Baltimore Yearly Meeting
> Genesee Yearly Meeting
> Illinois Yearly Meeting
> Indiana Yearly Meeting
> New York Yearly Meeting
> Ohio Yearly Meeting (suspended)
> Philadelphia Yearly Meeting

All of these yearly meetings, with the exception of Philadelphia and a part of Baltimore, lie outside the Commonwealth of Pennsylvania, Hence, the subordinate meetings of these two yearly meetings only are treated in this Inventory, and of these only the meetings which are located in Pennsylvania.

172.   FRIENDS GENERAL CONFERENCE, 1900--. 1515 Cherry Street, Philadelphia.

The Friends General Conference is the national organization through which the Yearly Meetings of the branch of Friends called "Hicksite" or "Liberal" act on issues that concern the group as a whole. It is composed of all the Hicksite Yearly Meetings in the United States and acts in an advisory capacity in matters concerning them, and in an administrative and coordinating capacity in the larger issues which concern the life and work of the entire Hicksite group.

The present organization is an evolution from a number of earlier specialized conference. The First-day School Conference was started about 1868. The Friends Union for Philanthropic Labor was organized in 1882. These two conferences met together in 1892, and have convened biennially thereafter. In 1894 a Religious Conference was added, and in 1896 an Educational Conference was established. The organization was simplified in 1900 by the creation of a Central Committee of 100 members, whose duty was to plan the convening of a single unified conference and to coordinate its activities. Representation on the Central Committee was assigned to the component yearly meetings on basis of membership, and at present is as follows: Philadelphia Yearly Meeting 55 percent, Baltimore Yearly Meeting 15 percent, New York Yearly Meeting 15 percent, Indiana Yearly Meeting 6 percent, Illinois Yearly Meeting 5 percent, Genesee Yearly Meeting 4 percent, Ohio Yearly Meeting suspended its sessions in 1919, and while its Representative Committee is technically a part of the General Conference Committee the yearly meeting is not active.

The Conference conducts permanent work through three sections or large committees, namely: A section on Social Service, a section on Education, Religious and Secular, and a section for the Advancement of Friends Principles. Through these agencies such activities as the cultivation of new meetings, guidance in religious and secular education, promotion of Friends peace testimony, cooperation with the program of the American Friends' Service Committee, and similar activities are carried forward.

The sessions of Friends General Conference have been held every two years except in 1918. Since 1928 they have convened at Cape May, New Jersey. The Conference serves as a time for study and discussion, for fellowship, and for the training of leadership. It is not legislative. Each individual yearly meeting retains complete independence and responsibility.

No creed or doctrinal statement has been adopted. Each yearly meeting has a discipline based upon the early usage of Friends. In 1927 a Conference committee cooperated with several of the yearly meetings in a revision of the Book of Discipline, and since then the yearly meetings of Philadelphia, Baltimore, Indiana, Illinois, and Genesee have had a common form for their Book of Discipline, with latitude for local variations.

The Conference maintains a central office located at 1515 Cherry Street, Philadelphia, and the present chairman is Arthur C. Jackson. The administrative secretary is J. Barnard Walton.

Proceedings of Friends' General Conference, 1892-1904, 7 vols.; Summaries of Proceedings, 1906-26, 11 vols. Since 1926 the conference proceedings have not been published separately, but only reported in the Philadelphia **Friends' Intelligencer**. Minutes of the Central Committee of Friends' General Conference, 1896--, 2 vols.; Minutes of the Advancement Committee, 1901-33 (1903-6 missing), 6 vols.; all deposited at PSC-Hi; and 1933--, 1 vol.; at PPF. Minutes of the Joint Committee of the Seven Yearly Meetings of Friends' General Conference for Work Among Isolated Friends, 1901-14, 1 vol.; Minutes of Friends' Union for Philanthropic Labor, 1890-1900, 1 vol.; Minutes of Educational Committee, 1894-99, 1 vol.; Minutes of First-day School General Conference, First-day School Executive Committee Minutes, 1867-78, 1 vol.; First-day School Literature Committee Minutes, 1888-1900, 1 vol.; all deposited at PSC-Hi. Minutes of Religious Education Committee, 1900-1929, 1 vol., 1928--, 1 vol., at PPF. Treasurer's Accounts; Advancement Committee, 1902-10, 1 vol., at PSC-Hi.

V. PHILADELPHIA YEARLY MEETING (H).

Since the Separation of 1827-28 this branch of the Society of Friends has been called the Hicksite Friends, or sometimes the Race Street Friends because the yearly meeting convenes annually at the meeting-house at Fifteenth and Race Streets. This branch is also sometimes called the Liberal Friends. (See Explanatory Notes, No. 1, p.)

It must be borne in mind that many of the Hicksite meetings are not new meetings set up at the time of the Separation, but are continuations of the original Friends meetings under the new Hicksite affiliation. In such cases the records run back in unbroken sequence to the time of the first establishment of these meetings. For the purpose of historical record this survey assumes that the Hicksite branch began in 1827, and the entries hereunder are dated accordingly. This will account for their brevity, since it is unnecessary to duplicate the early history of the original meetings which has already been given under the entries of the Orthodox meetings. For early history of the Hicksite meetings see cross references in each meeting entry.

Component Quarterly Meetings

The following quarterly meetings and their subordinate meetings lie outside the Commonwealth of Pennsylvania, and because of the limitations which obtain in this Survey do not come within the scope of this volume. For their history and records see the forthcoming Inventory of the Church Archives of New Jersey, and also the inventories of the church archives of the States of Delaware and Maryland.

	Date established
Burlington Quarterly Meeting (N.J.)	1827-28
Haddonfield Quarterly Meeting (N.J.)	1827-28
Salem Quarterly Meeting (N.J.)	1827-28
Southern Half-Year Meeting (Md. and Del.)	1827-28

The following meetings are located in Pennsylvania and are therefore treated in this volume.

	Date established	Entry Number
Abington Quarterly Meeting	1827	174
Bucks Quarterly Meeting	1827	196
Concord Quarterly Meeting	1827	218

Western Quarterly Meeting	1827	240
Caln Quarterly Meeting	1828	261
Philadelphia Quarterly Meeting	1828	279
Fishing Creek Half-Year Meeting	1834	308
Millville Half-Year Meeting	1919	308

173. PHILADELPHIA YEARLY MEETING OF FRIENDS, 1827--. South side of
Race Street west of Fifteenth Street, Philadelphia.
Philadelphia Yearly Meeting of Friends, Hicksite, is one of the branches
of the Society which had their origin in the great Separation which took
place in the Society in 1827-28. All the yearly meetings in America were
affected by the controversy, and all of those east of the Alleghenies,
with the exception of Virginia Half Year Meeting and North Carolina Yearly Meeting, divided into two yearly meeting organizations at that time.
It is not within the scope of this entry to discuss the causes or merits
of the controversy. It is sufficient to state that the outstanding, capable leader of the faction which is the antecedent of this yearly meeting
was Elias Hicks, of Long Island, New York. Because of his leadership in the
controversy his name has become inseparably attached to the group of
Friends who formed one branch of the Society in the various Friends communities throughout the country. Hence the name Hicksite Friends (sometimes Liberal Friends) has been used colloquially since the inception of
the movement, but has never been officially accepted by any yearly meetings.

The actual division in the society occurred in Pennsylvania in 1827-
28, although the controversy had been in progress with increasing fervor
for a number of years before that date. The climax came at the yearly
meeting in Philadelphia in 1827, and was precipitated by the inability
of the representative committee to agree upon a person for clerk, and
also by a proposition in the closing session, presented by the women's
yearly meeting, to appoint a committee from the yearly meeting to visit
the subordinate meetings in order to compose the difficulties which had
arisen between members during the controversy. When this latter proposition was presented to the last session of the yearly meeting an announce-
ment was made that a meeting of the Liberal Friends had been held at the
Green Street Meeting-house the previous night and action toward disunion
had already been started. The yearly meeting, greatly burdened by the
situation, completed its business and adjourned without further action by
either faction. However, in June of the same year the Liberal Friends
assembled in the Green Street Meeting-house and decided to form a yearly
meeting of their own. This meeting was appointed to meet in the autumn
of 1827 at the Green Street Meeting-house because the great majority of
the members of this meeting were adherents of the liberal faction. Since
considerably more than half of the total membership of the original yearly meeting had identified themselves with the Hicksite faction the group
soon realized that the Green Street house, now in their control, would
not be large enough to accommodate the forthcoming yearly meeting. In
the summer of that year construction was started on a temporary frame

meeting-house for that purpose. This building was 101' x 50' and stood
on the southwest corner of Fourth and Green Streets, directly opposite
the Green Street Meeting-house. The building was completed and the first
Hicksite yearly meeting was held there in October of 1827.

Late in 1827 this temporary meeting-house was taken down and the materials were given toward the building of a new brick structure on Cherry
Street below Fifth. The new house was soon completed and the benches
that were used in the temporary frame building, and also those from a
temporary meeting room in Carpenter's Hall were used as part of the equipment. The second yearly meeting in 1828 met in this new building.

From 1829 the yearly meeting of men met in the Green Street house,
while that of the women met in the Cherry Street house. By 1855 it had
become too inconvenient to hold the men's and women's meeting at separate
places, and also the Cherry Street house no longer afforded comfortable
accommodations for the women's meeting. The first move for a new building came from the 1855 women's yearly meeting in a minute, which states:
"The Yearly Meeting of Women Friends, now sitting believe it right to call
the attention of men Friends to the very poor accommodations the Cherry
Street house affords. Although the additional ventilation has rendered
it a little more comfortable, still its crowded state, the difficulty of
hearing, and our position since the erection of the adjoining building,
being by many considered unsafe, we feel it right to present the subject
before you." This move ultimately resulted in the erection of the present
large meeting-house on Race Street west of Fifteenth Street. Construction
on this building was started in 1856 and it was completed in 1857. The
yearly meeting was first held there in that year, and so continues to the
present time. The yearly meeting having become permanently located in
this meeting-house, the Hicksite group came to be known as the Race Street
Friends in distinction from the Orthodox branch whose yearly meeting was
held at Fourth and Arch Streets, and who were likewise designated as Arch
Street Friends.

The first yearly meeting sessions met in October of 1827. At that
meeting the time for holding the sessions was changed to April, in which
month the sessions met in 1828. In 1838 the time for holding the annual
meetings was shifted to May. In 1933 the time of the annual gathering was
again shifted, this time to March, which appointment it has continued
since that date.

The official title of the yearly meeting is the Philadelphia Yearly
Meeting of Friends, held at Fifteenth and Race Streets. It is composed
of nine quarterly meetings, and two half-year meetings, which latter function practically the same as quarterly meetings. These are Abington,
Bucks, Concord, Western, Caln, and Philadelphia Quarters, and Fishing
Creek and Millville Half-Year Meetings. The subordinate meetings of these
lie within the Commonwealth of Pennsylvania. Outside of Pennsylvania,
and hence not treated in this survey are Burlington, Haddonfield, and
Salem Quarterly meetings, and Southern Half-Year Meeting.

In recent years the breach between the two branches has tended to
diminish. Each year some of the sessions of the two yearly meetings are
held together. This is possible because of the dates for holding the
sessions of the two annual gatherings overlap. In addition, united monthly meetings have been established in a few places, notably at Chestnut
Hill (entry 330), Concord (entry 331), Providence (entry 332) and Radnor

(entry 333). These united meetings have a membership affiliated with both branches of Friends, and come under the joint jurisdiction of quarterly meetings of both the Orthodox and Hicksite branch.

Among the important permanent committees of the Race Street Yearly Meeting are: The Representative Committee (which acts as an executive or ad-interim committee), Peace, Race Relations, Temperance, Education, and Social Service Committees. The present clerk is Thomas A. Foulke, the Secretary is Jane Rushmore, and assistant Marguerite Hallowell. They may be addressed at Friends Central Bureau, 1515 Cherry Street, Philadelphia.

See: Matlack, op. cit., 11, 430; Bunting, op. cit., p. 11; Michener, op. cit., p. 26.

Minutes of Men's Meetings, 1827-1917, 7 vols., at PSC-Hi, and 1917-23, 1 vol., at PPF. Minutes of Women's Meetings, 1827-1923, 7 vols., at Swarthmore College. Minutes of Joint Meetings, 1923--, 3 vols., at 1515 Cherry Street. Minutes of Ministry and Council (formerly Ministers and Elders), 1827-1913, 1 vol., at Swarthmore College, and 1913, 2 vols., at 1515 Cherry Street. Minutes of Representatives Committee (formerly called Meeting for Sufferings), 1827-1916, 4 vols. (1858-74, missing), at Swarthmore College, and 1916--, 3 vols., at 1515 Cherry Street. Minutes of Temperance Committee, 1881-1912, 3 vols., at Swarthmore College, and 1912-36 (Temperance Committee minutes consolidated with the Philanthropic Labor Committee), 2 vols., 1936-- (called Social Service Committee), 1 vol., at PPF. Minutes of Temperance Branch of Philanthropic Committee, Subcommittee on Books, 1900-1904, 1 vol.; Minutes of Committee on Improper Publications, 1892-1902, 1 vol., at PSC-Hi. Minutes of Child Welfare Committee, 1896-1922, 1 vol.; Minutes of Purity Committee, 1900-1917, 1 vol., at PPF. Minutes of Revision of Discipline, 1911-13 and 1922-27, 2 vols.; Minutes of Promotion Assn., First-day School Assn., 1868-1917, 7 vols.; Minutes of Executive Committee of First-day School Assn., 1879-94, 1 vol.; Minutes of Friends' Boarding Assn., 1890-1913, 1 vol.; Minutes of Assn. on Friends' School, 1900-1921, 1 vol.; Book of Memorials, 1752-1876, 1 vol.; Correspondence Book, Clerk of Philadelphia Meeting, 1865-93, 1 vol.; Yearly Meeting Epistles, 1827-1903, 4 vols.; Treasurer's Record Book for Relief in Virginia, 1865, 1 vol.; Women's Treasurer's Account Book, 1828-1921, 1 vol.; Account Book First-day School, Circulating Library, 1893-1901, 1 vol., at PSC-Hi. Annual Reports of the General Treasurer of the Yearly Meeting, are incorporated in the minutes of the Yearly Meeting.

ABINGTON QUARTERLY MEETING (H)

Component Meeting

(See: Explanatory Note 3)

	Date established	Entry number
ABINGTON MONTHLY MEETING	1867	175
Abington Preparative Meeting	1827	176
BYBERRY MONTHLY MEETING	1827	177
Byberry Preparative Meeting	1827	178
Philadelphia Indulged Meeting	1827	281
GREEN STREET MONTHLY MEETING	1827	287
Frankford Preparative Meeting	1827	289
Green Street Preparative Meeting	1827	288
GWYNEDD MONTHLY MEETING	1827	179
Gwynedd Preparative Meeting	1827	180
Plymouth Preparative Meeting	1827	181
Providence Preparative Meeting	1827	182
Whitemarsh Indulged Meeting	1827	183
Norristown Indulged Meeting	1852	184
Norristown Preparative Meeting	1860	184
Ambler Indulged Meeting	1897	185
HORSHAM MONTHLY MEETING	1827	186
Horsham Preparative Meeting	1827	187
Upper Dublin Preparative Meeting	1827	188
Warminister Indulged Meeting	1840	189
Warminister Preparative Meeting	1841	189
Ambler Indulged Meeting	1897	185
RICHLAND MONTHLY MEETING (QUAKERTOWN)	1827	191
Richland Preparative Meeting (Quakertown)	1827	192
Stroudsburg Preparative Meeting	1827	192
Friendsville Preparative Meeting	1830	193
NORRISTOWN MONTHLY MEETING	1936	194
PLYMOUTH MONTHLY MEETING	1936	195

174. ABINGTON QUARTERLY MEETING, 1827--. Montgomery County.
Abington Quarterly Meeting (entry 92) was originally set up by a division
of Philadelphia Quarterly Meeting in 1786. In 1827 when the Separation
occurred there were five monthly meetings composing it, namely: Abington,

Gwynedd, Horsham, Richland, and Green Street Monthly Meetings. Shortly before the division took place in 1827 the latter monthly meeting had severed its connection with Philadelphia Quarterly Meeting and had been annexed to Abington Quarterly Meeting. In the realignment which took place immediately following the Separation, Byberry Meeting asked to be set up as a monthly meeting under the Hicksite Abington Quarter. This addition made six monthly meetings affiliated with Abington Quarter at the beginning of its existence as a Hicksite quarterly meeting. Green Street Monthly Meeting (entry 287) was eventually transferred back to the Philadelphia Quarterly Meeting after the Hicksite organization was perfected. Norristown Monthly Meeting (entry 194) and Plymouth Monthly Meeting were added to Abington Quarter in 1936, by the division of Gwynedd Monthly Meeting into three monthly Meetings, thus making seven subordinate monthly meetings under this quarter at the present time.

Sessions of the quarterly meeting alternate between Plymouth, Byberry, and Gwynedd Meetings. The present clerk is Samuel L. Borton, Audubon.

Minutes of Men's Meetings, 1785-1898, 3 vols., 1875-79, 1 vol., 1825-1930, 2 vols.; Women's Minutes, 1786-1897, 3 vols.; Minutes of Joint Meetings, 1898-1930, 1 vol.; Minutes of Ministers and Elders, 1786-1863, 2 vols. (1863-96 destroyed by fire), 1896--, 1 vol., at Swarthmore College Friends Historical Library. Minutes of Abington First-day School Union, 1877-98, 1 vol.; Reports of Committees, 1881-82, 1 vol.; Treasurers Account, 1844-78, 1 vol., at Swarthmore College.

175. ABINGTON MONTHLY MEETING, 1827--. East Greenwood Avenue and Meeting-House Road, Jenkintown.
Continued as a Hicksite meeting in 1827 after the division of the original Abington Monthly Meeting (entry 93). The early history of this meeting has been briefly outlined under the above entry and need not be repeated. At the time of the Separation the division was accomplished with very little friction between the two factions, and the minutes of the monthly meeting make no reference to doctrinal or personal controversy. The liberal Friends were greatly in the majority and the small Orthodox group quietly withdrew. In the meeting on September 24, 1827 a few Friends in both the men's and women's meetings arose and stated that they proposed to hold Abington Monthly Meeting, and if not permitted to do so in the meeting-house they would go to the home of Daniel Fletcher and hold it there. This they did, leaving the Liberal Friends in possession of the property and records of the meeting. The monthly meeting continued its sessions in unbroken sequence, but as a Hicksite monthly meeting. It is, therefore, not quite correct to say that Abington Monthly Meeting, Hicksite, was set up in 1827. The procedure was in reality a division of the monthly meeting into two bodies, each bearing the same name, but belonging to each of the two branches of Friends which emerged at that time. This statement can be made in a general way concerning the actual procedure of the split in most of the monthly and preparative meetings. However, it will not be repeated, but should be borne in mind when studying the entries of all Hicksite meetings dating from 1827.

This monthly meeting continued as a part of Abington Quarterly Meeting, Hicksite (entry 174). The meeting-house, schoolhouse, graveyard, and grounds were retained by it. The meeting-house had been repaired and enlarged at various times, and probably retains very little of the form and style of the original house built in 1786. Under Hicksite ownership it

appears from a minute of 1863 that the hoods over the door ways were removed and a shed (porch) built. In 1929 a social room and rooms for the
First-day school were added. From its very early history a school has been
conducted under the auspices of the meeting.

In 1827 there was only one subordinate meeting affiliated with Abington Monthly Meeting. This was its own preparative meeting of Abington,
since Frankford Preparative Meeting had been set off as a monthly meeting in 1815. Since that time the monthly meeting had stood alone without subordinate meetings. This was true at the time of the Separation.

Separate business meetings for men and women were discontinued in
1893, and since that date the minutes of the meeting appear as one series
only. The present clerk is F. Palin Spruance, 8204 Cedar Road, Elkins
Park.

See: Michener, op. cit., p. 85; Jenkins, Arthur H. and Ann R, op.
cit., p. 115.

Men's Minutes, 1682-1893, 10 vols.; Extracts from Minutes, 1682-1746;
Women's Minutes, 1773-1893, 4 vols; Minutes of Joint sessions, 1893--;
Births and Deaths (Byberry, Oxford, Cheltenham, Abington, Dublin), 1682-
1809; Births and Deaths (same meeting), 1804--; Marriage Certificates,
1747--, at Friends Historical Library, Swarthmore College. Current records and registers are in the custody of the clerk, whose address is noted
above.

176. ABINGTON PREPARATIVE MEETING, 1827--. East Greenwood Avenue
      and Meeting-House Road, Jenkintown.
Continued as a Hicksite meeting in 1827 after division of the original
Abington Preparative Meeting (entry 95)). Like most of the Hicksite meetings Abington Preparative Meeting had its beginning as such in the Separation of 1827. After 1815 Abington Preparative Meeting was the only
subordinate meeting under the Abington Monthly Meeting. Since the activities and interests of the monthly and preparative meetings were es-
sentially identical and the same body of people constituted both organizations, it is not surprising that one meeting gradually took over the functions of both. Since the preparative meeting was the lesser in importance
it tended to release its functions to the monthly meeting. After the division in 1827 this condition was found in the resulting meetings of both
branches. At present Abington Preparative Meeting, Hicksite, meets only
once or twice a year or as business demands.

See: Michener, op. cit., p. 85; Jenkins, Arthur H. and Ann R., op.
cit., p. 115.

Men's Minutes, 1800-1896, 2 vols.; Women's Minutes, 1862-93, 1 vol;
Joint Sessions, 1893--; Births and Deaths, 1682-1804, 1809--, 2 vols; Mar-
riage Certificates, 1685-1716, 1747--, 3 vols.: all deposited at Friends
Historical Library, Swarthmore College.

177. BYBERRY MONTHLY MEETING, 1827--. Byberry Road, at Junction
      with Southampton Road, Byberry.
Continued as a Hicksite meeting in 1827, by Abington Quarterly Meeting,
(entry 174). When the division took place in 1827, Byberry Monthly Meeting with the permission of the Hicksite quarterly meeting at Abington,
joined with and became a part of the same. Meetings for worship and busi-

ness were continued without interruption in the old meeting-house built by Friends of Byberry in 1808 (entry 107). At the time of the Separation the membership numbered 504 persons. A large majority of these followed the liberal group and retained possession of all property. In 1919 Byberry Preparative Meeting (entry 178), was laid down, and since that time the monthly meeting exists as a single meeting, having no subordinate meetings under its care. Starting with 1 acre of land, acquired as a gift from Henry English in 1692, more land adjoining this was purchased from time to time until the present 3 or more acres were attained. Many wooden sheds built in the olden days to protect the horses have existed at various times, and a number of these, painted white, are still to be seen on the grounds. The meeting-house consists of only one high-ceilinged room, with a gallery. The partition which formerly separated the women's meeting from that of the men, is still in its original position. No varnishes or polishes have ever been applied to the woodwork and thereby the old and beautiful natural state of the wood is preserved. Old-fashioned coal stoves furnished the heat during the winter months. There was no lighting of any description in the meeting-house, until very recent times, when electric lights were installed. Many of its members have moved to other localities, but still maintain their memberships there. Monthly meetings in Byberry have continued at the present location without interruption, since 1810, and meetings for worship have been held continuously in this immediate vicinity since the time of its early settlement prior to 1682.

The old school building erected in 1823, still stands on its original site on the extreme northern end of the meeting-house grounds. The entire building was used by the boys school until 1827, when the girls school which was established in 1811, was removed from the house it had previously occupied, to the second story. It was so occupied until 1838, when this girls school was discontinued. The upper floor was then used as a school library, until a later date, when the collection of the Byberry Philosophical Society was moved there, and which at the present time shares the space with the books of the former school library. The lower floor was used continuously by the Byberry school from the date of the opening of the building until the school was discontinued in 1918. At the present time this lower floor is used by the First-day school.

There are two graveyards on the meeting's grounds. The Old Burial Ground, contains the original 1 acre given by Henry English in 1692. This is situated in the front of the meeting-house, about 50 yards distant. It is surrounded by a stone wall about 4 feet high, and has two entrances on the eastern side. It has been filled to capacity for many years, the last interment being in 1841. Among those first interred were two Indian squaws buried in 1692. It is estimated that not less than 4,000 sleep beneath the sod of this ancient cemetery. In the early days separate burial lots for families were not maintained. Burials were then made in layers, and in this way a great number, when laid close, could be interred in a comparatively small area. Not many headstones are found in this yard, and the few plain ones that are seen, were placed there during the last few years of its use, when by this time, the custom of placing stones of uniform size, was finally approved by Friends. Only about 15 of the stones bear any dates or inscriptions, and those marked, with few exceptions, bear only the initials and dates. When the first burial ground was nearly filled, another lot of about 1 acre a little to the south of the meeting-house was purchased from Robert Purvis. Later additional ground adjoining this was purchased. The newer lot extends to the rear of the meeting-house, and the two pieces joined gives this newer cemetery the shape of

an L. The first interment in the new section was 1832. This cemetery
was for several years the only place of interment in the township, and
a section of it was used by persons other than Friends. No formal burial
records are kept by the meeting, but the records of burial are incorporated in the register books which are kept by the recorder of the meeting,
and are listed among the registration of births, membership, and deaths.
The present clerk is Edwin K. Bonner, Torresdale, Philadelphia.

    See: Martindale, op. cit., pp. 10-18; Matlack, op. cit., I, 38; His-
torical Excursion, pp. 53, 63.

    Minutes of Men's Meetings, 1827-97, 3 vols. (1827-31, destroyed by
fire), 1831-97, 3 vols.; Minutes of Women's Meetings, 1827-97, 3 vols.;
Minutes of Joint Meetings, 1897-1918, 1 vol., at PPF, and 1918--, 2 vols.,
in custody of clerk. Minutes of Ministers and Elders, 1810-91, 2 vols.,
at PPF. Minutes of Ministry and Counsel, 1891--, 1 vol., in custody of
the clerk of Ministry and Counsel, Mrs. Clara W. Carter, Hulmeville Road,
Cornwells Heights, Bucks County. Minutes of Byberry School Committee and
Accounts, etc., 1863-66, 1 vol., at PPF (1868-1918 incorporated in the
meeting minutes). Register of Deaths, 1736-91, 1 vol., 1736-1823, 1 vol.;
Register of Marriage Certificates of Removal, 1810-52, 1 vol., at PPF.
Register of Membership, Births, Deaths, and Burials, 1879--, 1 vol.; Register of Marriages (certificates), 1886--, 1 vol.; Certificates of Removal, 1852--, 1 vol., in custody of the recorder, Alvin N. Walton, Comly
Road, Byberry, P. O., Torresdale. All treasurers' financial records prior
to 1877 are missing. Record of Cash Receipts and Disbursements, 1877--,
1 vol., in custody of treasurer, William F. Bonner, Somerton. Records
of First-day school, in annual report form, are recorded in the meeting
minutes. Miscellaneous records: Certificates and Minutes for Friends in
the Ministry, 1810-21, bound papers, 1 vol.; Disownments, Acknowledgments,
etc., 1811-38, bound papers, 1 vol.; Byberry Preparative Meeting, collection of Christian and Brotherly advices, 1 vol., 1785; bound reports
and extracts, 1827-1901, 77 vols., at PPF.

    178. BYBERRY PREPARATIVE MEETING, 1827-1919. Byberry Road, at Junc-
         tion with Southampton Road, Byberry.
Continued as a Hicksite meeting in 1827, by Byberry Monthly Meeting (entry
177), with approval of Abington Quarterly Meeting (entry 174). At the
time of the Separation in 1827, the Byberry Monthly Meeting made application to the newly formed Abington Quarter for admittance as a constituent
monthly meeting. This was approved and the meeting at Byberry became a
part of Abington Quarterly Meeting. At this time Byberry Preparative
Meeting, Orthodox (entry 107) was laid down. A new Byberry Preparative
was set up as a part of Byberry Monthly Meeting, by sanction of the quarterly meeting and became Byberry Preparative Meeting, Hicksite. Sessions
continued to be held in the old meeting-house built in 1808. Not much
of historical importance is recorded regarding the activities of this
meeting, since such records appear chronologically in the minutes of the
monthly meeting. The membership dwindled to such an extent that only a
few members remained. The functions of the preparative meeting decreased
and it was deemed advisable to discontinue it in 1919.

    See: Matlack, op. cit., I, 38.

    Minutes of Men's Meetings, 1827-97, 2 vols.; Minutes of Women's Meet-
ings, 1827-97, 3 vols.; Minutes of Joint Meetings, 1897-1919, 1 vol., at
Friends Central Bureau, Philadelphia.

179. GWYNEDD MONTHLY MEETING, 1827--.   DeKalb and Sumneytown Pike,
      Gwynedd Twp., Montgomery County.
Continued as a Hicksite meeting in 1827, by the Abington Quarterly Meeting
(entry 174), after separation from the Gwynedd Monthly Meeting (entry 96).
The meetings are held in the meeting-house of the Gwynedd Preparative
Meeting (entry 180).   The present clerk is Dorothy B. Hallowell, Fort
Washington.

    See: Michener, op. cit., p. 86; H. M. Jenkins, Historical Collec-
tions of Gwynedd (manuscript at PNortHi).

    Minutes of Men's Meetings, 1801-97, 5 vols.; Minutes of Women's Meet-
ings, 1827-96, 3 vols.; 1896-97 incorporated in the 1897-1909 vol. of
Minutes of Joint Meetings, at PSC-Hi.   Minutes of Joint Meetings, 1897-
1921, 2 vols. (1922-35 missing) and 1936--, 1 vol., in custody of clerk.
Minutes of Ministers and Elders, 1793-1898, 5 vols., at PSC-Hi.   Register
of Births, 1764-1875, and Deaths, 1811-78, incorporated in 1 vol.; Register of Births and Deaths, 1772-1921, 1 vol. (1922-35 missing); Register
of Marriages, 1793-1917, 1 vol. (1918-35missing); Certificates of Removal,
1779-1924, 5 vols. (1925-35 missing), at PSC-Hi, and 1936--, incorporated
in the 1936-- volume of Minutes of Joint Meetings.   Register Book of
Births, Deaths, Marriages and Members, 1 vol., in custody of recorder,
Edith Livezey, Spring House.   Financial Records, 1936--, 1 vol. (1827-1935
missing), in custody of J. Carroll Johnston, North Wales.   Montgomery
County Deed Books, vol. 7, p. 116; vol. 981, p. 442.

180. GWYNEDD PREPARATIVE MEETING, 1827-?. DeKalb and Sumneytown Pike,
      Gwynedd Twp., Montgomery County.
Continued as a Hicksite meeting in 1827 by Gwynedd Monthly Meeting (entry
179), after separation from the original Gwynedd Preparative Meeting (entry 97). The gray stone meeting-house and the frame building in the rear,
erected by Friends in 1823, and the adjoining 2-acre burial ground enclosed by a stone wall were retained by this meeting.   The functions of
this meeting gradually diminished and were absorbed by the monthly meeting.   The date of its discontinuance is uncertain.

    See: Michener, op. cit., p. 87; Jenkins, H. M., op. cit.

    Minutes of Men's Meetings, 1798-1890, 7 vols.; 1890-93 incorporated
in 1893-1920 volume of Minutes of Joint Meetings; Minutes of Women's Meetings, 1810-93, 3 vols.; Minutes of Joint Meetings, 1893-1920, 1 vol., at
PSC-Hi, and 1934--, 1 vol. (1921-33 missing), in custody of clerk, Mrs.
Martha Meadowcroft, 326 W. Montgomery Avenue, North Wales.   Registers are
in the records of the Gwynedd Monthly Meeting.   Financial Records, 1928-
39, 2 vols. (1827-1927 missing), in custody of J. Carroll Johnston, North
Wales, Montgomery County Deed Books, vol. 7, p. 116; vol. 981, p. 442.

181. PLYMOUTH PREPARATIVE MEETING, 1827-1936. Germantown Pike and
      Harmonville Road, Plymouth Meeting, Montgomery County.
Continued as a Hicksite meeting in 1827 by Gwynedd Monthly Meeting (entry
179). The limestone building, which had been erected by Friends about
1708 and enlarged in 1780, and the 2-acre burial ground, were retained by
this meeting.   In February 1867, the meeting-house was destroyed by fire.
The Friends met under a stable shed on the meeting-house grounds, until
the present brownstone meeting-house was erected in October 1867.   Prior
to the Civil War, the meeting-house was an important station of the Underground Railroad and many slaves were harbored here while escaping to Can-

ada. In 1889 a one-story stone schoolhouse was erected; and in 1899 an
additional story was added and the entire building was covered with brown
stucco. This meeting was laid down as a preparative.meeting by Gwynedd
Monthly Meeting in 1936 and set up in the same year as Plymouth Monthly
Meeting (entry 195).

See: Michener, op. cit., p. 85; Roberts, Plymouth Meeting; 200th
Anniversary Plymouth.

Minutes of Men's Meetings, 1827-97, 6 vols.; Minutes of Women's Meetings, 1810-97, 4 vols.; Minutes of Joint Meetings, 1897-1915 (incorporated in the Minute Book of Men's Meetings, ending 1897), 1915-36, 1 vol.,
in custody of Mrs. Elizabeth J. Christian, 225 East Fifth Avenue, Conshohocken. Registers are in the records of the Gwynedd Monthly Meeting Financial Records, 1773-1936, 4 vols., in custody of F. C. Jones, 926 Fayette
Street, Conshohocken. Women's Financial Contributions, 1828-74, 2 vols.,
at PSC-Hi; Montgomery County Deed Books, vol. 29, pp. 160, 167; vol. 43,
p. 218; vol. 49, p. 423; vol. 73, p. 182; vol. 102, p. 98.

182. PROVIDENCE PREPARATIVE MEETING, 1827-66. Black Rock Road,
       Upper Providence Twp., Montgomery County.
A continuation of the original Providence Meeting (entry 99), under Hicksite auspices and by authority of Gwynedd Monthly Meeting (entry 179).
The log meeting-house, which had been erected in 1730, and the graveyard
were retained by this meeting at the time of the Separation in 1827. In
1828 a new meeting-house, a one-story stone building was erected. It was
later covered with gray stucco. The meeting was laid down in 1866 but
occasional meetings were held there until the remaining members died. In
later years Friends have gathered semi-annually at the meeting-house.

See: Major, op. cit.,

Records run continuously through the year of separation. Minutes of
Men's Meetings, 1828-66, 2 vols., at PSC-Hi. Registers are in records of
Gwynedd Monthly Meeting.

183. WHITEMARSH INDULGED MEETING, 1827-1919. Bethlehem Pike, one-
       half mile south of Fort Washington, Whitemarsh Twp., Montgomery
       County.
Continued in 1827 as a Hicksite meeting by authority of Gwynedd Monthly
Meeting (entry 179), after separation from the original Whitemarsh Indulged Meeting (entry 100). The meeting-house, erected by Friends in 1815,
and the 2 acres and 81 perches of ground were retained by this meeting.
The meeting-house was used until 1852, when a three-story stone meeting-
house was erected. Membership in this meeting gradually diminished, and
only appointed meetings were held. On November 1, 1919, at a monthly meeting held in Norristown, the meeting was laid down by Gwynedd Monthly
Meeting (entry 179), and a committee was appointed to consider further
care and disposition of the Whitemarsh meeting-house and grounds. After
a petition to the court the property was sold April 20, 1920 and has since
been converted into a private residence. The bodies were disinterred from
the burial ground and reinterred in the graveyard of Gwynedd Monthly Meeting. The amount derived from the sale of the property was donated toward
the maintenance and improvement of the properties of the Gwynedd, Norristown, and the Plymouth Meetings.

See: Michener, op. cit., p. 91; Montgomery County Deed Book, vol. 6,
p. 350.

184. NORRISTOWN PREPARATIVE MEETING, 1852-1936. Swede and Jacoby
      Streets, Norristown, Montgomery County.
Set up in 1860 by Gwynedd Monthly Meeting (entry 179), after having functioned as an indulged meeting since 1852. Meetings were held in the plain
square brick building which was erected in 1852. Lucretia Mott, famous
Quaker preacher and leader in the Abolition Movement prior to the Civil
War, was one of the speakers at the first meeting held in the Norristown
meeting-house on April 18, 1852. The burial ground, 300' x 150' which adjoins the meeting-house, was acquired in 1852. It was only used for a few
years. Later, the Norristown Friends used the burial grounds of nearby
Friends' meetings. In 1919 Gwynedd Monthly Meeting obtained permission
from the court to remove the bodies from the burial ground and an order
to sell the property. The land is now included in the Fort Washington
Extension of Fairmount Park. In 1936 the meeting was laid down as a preparative and set up as the Norristown Monthly Meeting (entry 194) by the
Abington Quarterly Meeting (entry 174).

     See: Michener, op. cit., p. 87; "Short Historical Sketch of Norris-
town Friends' Meeting," Norristown Times Herald, July 29, 1936.

     Minutes of Men's Meetings, 1860-97, 1 vol.; Minutes of Women's Meet-
ings, 1860-97, 1 vol.; Minutes of Joint Meetings, 1897-1913, 1 vol. (1913-
36 missing) at PSC-Hi. Registers are included in the records of the
Gwynedd Monthly Meeting. Montgomery County Deed Books, vol. 66, p. 383;
vol. 152, pp. 504, 509.

185. AMBLER INDULGED MEETING, 1897-1906. 30 Main Street, Ambler, Mont-
      gomery County.
Established 1897 by Gwynedd Monthly Meeting (entry 179) and Horsham Monthly Meeting (entry 186) after having functioned as a First-day school since
1893. Meetings were held from 1893-97 on the second floor of the fire-
house located near the corner of Main and Race Streets. After 1897 meetings were held on the first floor. This meeting was laid down in 1906
as the members decided to unite in worship with the Friends at Gwynedd.

     See: Mary P. H. Hough, Religious Meetings of the Society of Friends
(manuscript in custody of author, at Ambler).

186. HORSHAM MONTHLY MEETING, 1827--. Easton and Horsham Roads,
      Horsham Twp., Montgomery County.
A continuation in 1827 of the original Horsham Monthly Meeting (entry 103)
under auspices of the Hicksite Yearly Meeting and by the authority of
Abington Quarterly Meeting (entry 174). This meeting retained the 50-
acre farm containing the two-story native stone meeting-house, erected in
1803; the 3-acre cemetery; the one-story native stone schoolhouse erected
in 1753; a two-story stone farmhouse (today used as a caretaker's home);
and a stone and frame barn. Classes were discontinued in the schoolhouse
in 1924 and the building is now used as a music studio and neighborhood
kindergarden. The present clerk is Jessie D. Penrose, Neshaminy, Pa.

     Minutes of Men's Meetings, 1824-85, 3 vols.; Minutes of Women's Meet-
ings, 1819-85, 3 vols.; Index Book of Minutes, 1846-79, 1 vol., at PSC-Hi.
Joint Minutes (1885-1905 in the 1879-1905 volume of Men's Minutes), 1905
--, 1 vol., in custody of clerk. Minutes of Ministers and Elders, 1786-
1874, 1 vol., at PSC-Hi, and 1875--, 1 vol., in custody of Mrs. Hannah P.
Williams, Hatboro. Minutes of Overseers, 1846-1910, 1 vol., at PSC-Hi,
and 1911--, 1 vol., in custody of overseer, Mrs. Ella S. Parks, Horsham.

Register of Births and Deaths, 1782-1880, ...ol.; Register of Marriage Certificates, 1827-94, 3 vols.; List of Members, 1845, 1883, 1897, 1908, at PSC-Hi. Register of Members, Births, Deaths, Marriages, Certificates of Removal, 1890--, 1 vol. in custody of recorder, Mrs. Lydia C. P. Cosand, Hatboro. Minutes of School Committee, 1816-49, 1 vol.; Treasurer's Book of School Committee, 1828-94, 1 vol.; List of Men Members with Apportionment, 1811-49, 1 vol.; Treasurer's Records, 1782-1896, 1 vol., at PSC-Hi, and 1897--, 2 vols., in custody of treasurer, Frank H. Hather, Hatboro. Montgomery County Deed Books, vol. 2, p. 460; vol. 58, p. 304.

187. HORSHAM PREPARATIVE MEETING, 1827--. Easton and Horsham Roads, Horsham Twp., Montgomery County.
Continued in 1827 as a Hicksite meeting by Horhsam Monthly Meeting (entry 186) after separation from the original Horsham Preparative Meeting (entry 103). Meetings are held in the two-story native gray stone meeting-house which was erected in 1803 and retained by the Hicksites. This meeting now meets only once a year to transact business relative to trust funds.

See: Matlack, op. cit., I, 48.

Minutes of Men's Meetings, 1795-1893, 3 vols.; Minutes of Women's Meetings, 1824-93, 3 vols., at PSC-Hi. Minutes of Joint Meetings, 1893-1909 are in the 1881-93 volume of minutes of men's meetings, and 1929--, 1 vol. (1909-29 missing), in custody of clerk, William C. Wood, 35 East Moreland Avenue, Hatboro. Registers and financial records are in the records of Horsham Monthly Meeting.

188. UPPER DUBLIN PREPARATIVE MEETING, 1827--. Fort Washington and Limekiln Pike, Upper Dublin, Montgomery County.
Continued in 1827 as a Hicksite meeting by Horsham Monthly Meeting (entry 186), having previously functioned as the original Upper Dublin Friends Meeting (entry 105). Meetings have always been held in the one-story stone meeting-house erected in 1814, which has since been stuccoed. A small cemetery, enclosed by a three-foot stone wall, adjoins the meeting-house. Meetings are now held regularly and very recently this meeting was set up as Upper Dublin United Monthly Meeting. It is now affiliated with both of the Abington Quarterly Meetings. Thomas Ambler, Grendleton, Ambler, is clerk.

Minutes of Men's Meetings, 1814-81, 2 vols. (1881-85 missing); Minutes of Women's Meetings, 1814-85, 2 vols., at PSC-Hi. Joint Minutes, 1907--, 1 vol. (1885-1907 missing), in custody of clerk.

189. WARMINISTER PREPARATIVE MEETING, 1840--. Jacksonville and Street Roads, Warminister Twp., Bucks County.
Set up in 1841 by Horsham Monthly Meeting (entry 186), after functioning as an indulged meeting since 1840. In 1840 Thomas Parry gave 1 acre of ground on which the present meeting-house, a one-story light-gray lime-stone building was erected. A portion of this lot 120' x 65' was set aside for a burial ground. The first burial was made in 1846. In 1848 a stone wall was built around three sides of the lot and the south end of the graveyard was enclosed by an ornamental iron fence. Due to the diminishing membership and the expense of heating the meeting-house in cold weather, Friends of Warminister closed the meeting-house for the winter months and worshiped with the Horsham Monthly Meeting.

See: Michener, op. cit., p. 90; Harriet Kirk, "Warminister Friends Meeting," Bucks County Historical Society Papers, I (1908), 116.

Minutes of Men's Meetings, 1841-98, 2 vols.; Minutes of Women's Meetings, 1841-81, 1 vol., at PSC-Hi, and 1899--, 2 vols., in custody of the clerk, Miss Hollowell, 7 North York Road, Hatboro. Register of Deaths and Burials, 1846--, 1 vol., in custody of the trustee of the cemetery, Howard Twining, Linden and Montgomery Avenues, Hatboro. Financial Records, Treasurer's Books, 1841-83, 1 vol., at PSC-Hi. Bucks County Deed Book, vol. 104, pp. 360, 365.

190. RICHLAND MONTHLY MEETING, 1827—. Northwest corner, Main Street and Mill Road, Quakertown, Bucks County.
Continued by Abington Quarterly Meeting (entry 174), in 1827 as a Hicksite meeting after separation from original Richland Monthly Meeting (entry 101). This meeting retained the stone meeting-house which has been erected in 1795, and the cemetery. In 1850 the frame schoolhouse, built in 1773, was torn down and classes were continued in the meeting-house. A red brick one-story schoolhouse was erected adjacent to the meeting-house, in 1860. The present white plastered, one-story native stone meeting-house was erected in 1862 on the site of the previous building. Classes were discontinued in the schoolhouse in 1884 and the building was remodeled to serve as a kitchen and a meeting-place for the First-day school. The present clerk is Henry D. Kinsey, 1320 Mill Road, Quakertown.

See: Thomas, op. cit., p. 42; Roberts and Ely, op. cit., p. 63; Battle, op. cit., p. 762.

Minutes of Men's Meetings, 1742-1896, 7 vols.; Minutes of Women's Meetings, 1765-1896, 8 vols., at PSC-Hi. Minutes of Joint Meetings, 1896-98, in 7th vol. of Men's Minutes, 1899-1933, 1 vol., in safe in meeting-house and 1933--, 1 vol., in custody of clerk. Ministers and Elders, 1748-1894, 4 vols., at PSC-Hi, and 1894--, 1 vol., in custody of clerk, Mrs. Ida Jamison, E. 9th St., Perkasie. Epistles from the Yearly Meeting of Women Friends of Philadelphia, Genesee, London, and Baltimore, 1745-1845, 1 vol., at PSC-Hi. Register of Births and Removals, 1796--, 1 vol., in custody of Miss Mabel Dick, 140 S. Main St. Register of Marriages, 1742-1890, in list of marriages, at PSC-Hi, and 1804--, 1 vol., in safe in meeting-house. Registers of Death and Burials, 1742--, 2 vols., in safe in meeting-house. Treasurer's Account of Poor Fund, 1821-28, 1 vol., at PSC-Hi. Treasurer's Record, 1870--, 1 vol. (1827-70 missing), in custody of Miss Emma Shaw, 140 S. Main St. Bucks County Deed Books, vol. 116, pp. 107, 115; vol. 266, p. 246; vol. 306, p. 204.

191. RICHLAND PREPARATIVE MEETING, 1827-1932. Northwest corner Main Street and Mill Road, Quakertown, Bucks County.
Continued as a Hicksite meeting in 1827 by Richland Monthly Meeting (entry 190) after separation from the original Richland Preparative Meeting (entry 102). Meetings were held in the meeting-house, which the Hicksites retained after the Separation, until 1862 when this house was replaced by a one-story white plastered building. This meeting was laid down in 1932 by Richland Monthly Meeting with the consent of the Abington Quarter.

See: Thomas, op. cit., p. 42; Roberts and Ely, op. cit., p. 65.

Minutes of Men's Meetings, 1845-96; Minutes of Joint Meetings, 1896-1932, both in 1 vol. (1827-44 missing), in meeting-house. Minutes of

Women's Meetings, 1800-1896, 5 vols., at PSC-Hi. Registers in records of
Richland Monthly Meeting. Bucks County Deed Books, vol. 116, pp. 107,
⌐15; vol. 266, p. 246; vol. 306, p. 204.

192. STROUDSBURG PREPARATIVE MEETING, 1827-ca.1894. Franklin and
     Sarah Streets, Stroudsburg, Monroe County.
Continued as a Hicksite meeting in 1827 by Richland Monthly Meeting (entry
190), after the division of the original Stroudsburg Preparative Meeting
(entry 111). Meetings were held in Friends' homes until 1828, when a small
plot of ground was purchased on the north side of Main Street, in the
rear of what is today the Pipher Building. A small frame meeting-house
was erected on this site and a burial ground plotted behind the building.
This cemetery still remains on what is known as Quaker Alley. In 1868
the meeting-house property was sold, and meetings were held in the newly
rected meeting-house on the Franklin and Sarah Streets site. This site
had been purchased from Jerome Williams earlier in the same year. Though
the exact date is not known, it is supposed that the preparative meeting
was laid down about 1894, by Richland Monthly Meeting. The property of
the meeting was sold in 1932 for the sum of $10,000.

     See: Michener, op. cit., p. 88; Palmer, op. cit.

     Information from reliable sources states that the minutes of Strouds-
burg Preparative Meeting were submitted to the monthly meeting (Richland)
after each session, and were possibly written into the monthly meeting
minutes. At any rate it has been impossible to locate any records of the
meeting other than references in the monthly meeting minutes. Registers,
such as memberships, births, deaths, and marriages would normally be recorded in the monthly records.

193. FRIENDSVILLE PREPARATIVE MEETING. 1830-49. Route 695, south of
     Chacomet Lake, Friendsville, Susquehanna County.
It appears that the Hicksite-Orthodox controversy did not affect this
meeting until 3 years after the Separation in Philadelphia. In 1830 there
was a division and the Liberal Friends being in the majority retained the
meeting-house and graveyard. The preparative meeting was continued as a
Hicksite meeting under Richland Monthly Meeting (entry 179) after the separation from the original Friendsville Preparative Meeting (entry 113).
The first record we have that testifies this meeting was under the Richland Monthly Meeting is the following extract: "Richland Monthly Meeting held October 30, 1835 by an extract from Friendsville Preparative
Meeting this Monthly Meeting is informed that owing to their remote situation and the consequence of the Monthly Meeting to extend care toward
them propose relinquishing their connection with us and transferring
their right and become a branch of Scipio Monthly Meeting (see forthcoming
Inventory of the Church Archives of New York), or to such other meeting
as way may open." Richland Monthly Meeting upon receiving this request
appointed a committee consisting of John Foulke, William H. Bell, and
Evan Penrose. In 1836 this committee reported: "The consideration of the
subject brought up from Friendsville, being resumed and the meeting being
informed that they still remain desirous of dissolving their connections
with this meeting and being attached to the Monthly Meeting held at Scipio
as a branch thereof. After due consideration, their proposal was concurred with and the clerk is directed to furnish Friendsville and Scipio
Meetings with a copy of this minute, also to furnish said Monthly Meeting
with a list of members of said Preparative Meeting." This meeting remained attached to the Scipio Monthly Meeting in New York until 1849, when

it was laid down by that monthly meeting. The meeting-house and grave-yard remained abandoned until 1876, in which year the meeting-house and surrounding ground was bought by the Church of Holy Spirit.

See: Blackman, op. cit., pp. 92, 436-438, 440, 442, 447; Matlack, op. cit., II, 76-84.

There are no minutes or records available at the present time since they are deposited in the archives of New York Yearly Meeting. (See: Explanatory Note 6, second paragraph).

194. NORRISTOWN MONTHLY MEETING, 1936--. Swede and Jacoby Streets, Norristown, Montgomery County.
Set up 1936 as a monthly meeting by Gwynedd Monthly Meeting, after having functioned as the Norristown Preparative Meeting from 1860-1936 (entry 184). Meetings for worship and business are held in the same meeting-house, which this meeting occupied as a preparative meeting. The present clerk is William L. Ambler, 122 W. Fornance Street, Norristown.

Minutes of Meetings, 1936--, 2 vols.; Register Books, 1936--, in custody of clerk. Financial Records, 1918--, 1 vol., in custody of treasurer, Miss Helen E. Richards, 809 Swede Street.

195. PLYMOUTH MONTHLY MEETING, 1936--. Germantown Pike and Harmon-ville Road, Plymouth Meeting, Montgomery County.
Set up in 1936 by Abington Quarterly Meeting (entry 174), after having functioned as a preparative meeting under Gwynedd Monthly Meeting (entry 179), since 1827. The brownstone meeting-house, erected by Plymouth Pre-parative Meeting in 1867, is still used. The present clerk is Elizabeth J. Christian, 225 E. Fifth Avenue, Conshohocken.

Minutes of Meetings, 1936--, 1 vol.; Minutes of Overseers and Elders, 1936--, 1 vol., in custody of clerk. Register of Births, Members, Mar-riages, and Deaths, 1936--, 1 vol.; Register of Burials, 1936--, 1 vol.; Financial Records, 1936--, 1 vol., in custody of treasurer, F. C. Jones, 926 Fayette St., Conshohocken. Montgomery County Deed Books, vol. 29. pp. 160, 167; vol. 43, p. 218; vol. 49, p. 423; vol. 73, p. 182; vol. 102, p. 198.

Component Meetings

(See: Explanatory Note)

	Date established	Entry number
BUCKINGHAM MONTHLY MEETING	1827	197
Buckingham Preparative Meeting	1827	198
Plumstead Indulged Meeting	1827	199
Doylestown Indulged Meeting	1834	200
FALLS MONTHLY MEETING (FALLSINGTON)	1827	201
Falls Preparative Meeting	1827	202
Pennsbury Indulged Meeting	1828	203
MAKEFIELD MONTHLY MEETING (YARDLEY)	1827	204
Makefield Preparative Meeting (Yardley)	1827	205
Newtown Preparative Meeting	1827	217
Bristol Preparative Meeting	1827	215
Yardley Indulged Meeting	1857	206
MIDDLETOWN MONTHLY MEETING (LANGHORNE)	1827	207
Middletown Preparative Meeting	1827	208
SOLEBURY MONTHLY MEETING	1827	209
Solebury Preparative Meeting	1827	210
New Hope Indulged Meeting	1864	211
WRIGHTSTOWN MONTHLY MEETING	1827	212
Wrightstown Preparative Meeting	1827	213
BRISTOL MONTHLY MEETING	1874	214
Bristol Preparative Meeting	1827	215
NEWTOWN MONTHLY MEETING	1926	216
Newtown Preparative Meeting	1827	217

196. BUCKS QUARTERLY MEETING, 1827--. Bucks County.
Continued as a Hicksite meeting in 1827 by Philadelphia Yearly Meeting (H) (entry 173) after separation from the original undivided Bucks Quarterly Meeting (entry 58). Immediately following the Separation the meetings under this Quarterly were: Falls Monthly Meeting (entry 201); Middletown Monthly Meeting (entry 207); Wrightstown Monthly Meeting (entry 212); Buckingham Monthly Meeting (entry 197); Solebury Monthly Meeting (entry 209); and Makefield Monthly Meeting (entry 205). In 1832 Kingwood Monthly Meeting of New Jersey, which changed its name to Quakertown in 1859 (see forthcoming Inventory of the Church Archives of New Jersey), became a part of this quarterly meeting. Previously Kingwood Monthly Meeting had been a part of Shrewsbury Quarterly Meeting of New Jersey. Quakertown Monthly Meeting was laid down in 1905 and an indulged meeting under Buckingham Monthly Meeting was set up in the same year. In 1906 this indulged meet-

ing was laid down by Buckingham Monthly Meeting. In 1874 Bristol Monthly Meeting (entry 214) was added to this quarterly and Newtown Monthly Meeting (entry 216) in 1926 by a division of Makefield Monthly Meeting. Quarterly Meetings are held alternately at Wrightstown, Buckingham, Fallsington, and Langhorne. The present clerk is John H. Wood, Langhorne.

See: Michener, op. cit., pp. 74, 75; Josiah B. Smith "Early Settlement of Newtown Township," Bucks County Historical Society Papers, III (1909), I; Woody, op. cit., pp. 128-148.

Minutes of Men's Meeting, 1805-93, 3 vols., at NNBN. Minutes of Women's Meetings, 1869-93, 1 vol., at NNBN (1827-69, 2 vols., were listed by Bunting, op. cit., p. 29, as being in the meeting-house at Fifteenth and Race Streets, Philadelphia, but a recent survey does not list same). Minutes of Joint Meetings, 1894-1912, in the 1873-93 vol. of the Minutes of Men's Meetings, 1912-38, 1 vol., at NNBN, and 1938--, 1 vol., in custody of clerk. Minutes of Ministers and Elders, 1816-1928, 2 vols., at NNBN, and 1928--, 1 vol., in custody of clerk Mrs. Emily Walton, George School. Minutes of First-day School Business Committee, 1897-1928, 1 vol., at NNBN, and 1928--, 1 vol., in custody of secretary, Mrs. Albert Mammel, Buck Road, Newtown. Minutes of First-day School Union, 1898-1935, 1 vol., at NNBN, and 1935--, 1 vol., in custody of secretary Mrs. Albert Mammel. Bucks County Deed Books, vol. 111, p. 342; vol., 229, p. 114.

197. BUCKINGHAM MONTHLY MEETING, 1827--. Old York Road, Route 263, Lahaska Village, Buckingham Twp., Bucks County.
Continued as a Hicksite meeting in 1827 by Bucks Quarterly Meeting (entry 196) after separation from the original undivided Buckingham Monthly Meeting (entry 167). This meeting retained both the 4½-acre cemetery and the adjoining two-story limestone meeting-house which had been erected in 1768-69 and the two-story limestone schoolhouse, erected in 1793. During the period 1827-34 meetings were held alternately at the Buckingham meeting-house and the Wrightstown preparative meeting-house (entry 213). From 1836-62, meetings were held alternately at the Buckingham meeting-house and the Plumstead preparative meeting-house (entry 181). Buckingham Monthly Meeting was incorporated in 1931. The present clerk is Alice A. Kirson, Holicong.

See: 200th Anniversary Buckingham; Chapman, op. cit., p. 143; Samuel F. Hotchkin, "Then and Now; or Old Times and New in Pennsylvania," Buck County Historical Society Papers, I (1908), 508; Baily, op. cit., pp. 283, 284.

Minutes of Men's Meetings, 1827-91, 3 vols.; Minutes of Women's Meetings, 1827-91, 2 vols.; Minutes of Joint Meetings, 1901-24, 1 vol. (1891-1901, included in last volume of minutes of men's meetings), at NNBN, and 1924--, 1 vol., in custody of clerk. Minutes of the House and Grounds Committee, 1879--, 1 vol. (1827-79 missing); Record Book of Burial Permits, 1827-33, 6 vols., in custody of Anna Fells, Holicong, and 1933--, 1 vol., in custody of the caretaker of grounds, George Cadwallader, Lahaska. Register of Births and Deaths, 1827--, 1 vol., Register of Marriages, 1827--, 1 vol.; Register of Removals, 1827--, 1 vol., in custody of Miriam Broadhurst, Holicong. Week-day Records, 1925--, 2 vols., and 1 envelope containing accounts, budgets, and contracts of day-schools, in custody of secretary of the Week-day School committee, Mrs. Forrest Crook, New Hope. First-day School Attendance Records and Miscellaneous Day-school accounts, 1881-88, 1 vol.; Trustees Record Book of Day-school

Fund, 1794-1839, 1 vol., at NNBN. Bucks County Deed Books, vol. 54, p. 214; vol. 55, pp. 786-788; vol. 97, pp. 312-325; vol. 149, p. 405; vol. 171, p. 354.

198. BUCKINGHAM PREPARATIVE MEETING, 1827--. Old York Road, Route 263, Lahaska, Buckingham Twp., Bucks County.

Continued as a Hicksite meeting in 1827 by Buckingham Monthly Meeting (entry 197) after separation from the original Buckingham Preparative Meeting (entry 59). This meeting together with Buckingham Monthly Meeting retained both the 4½-acre cemetery and the adjoining two-story limestone and brownstone meeting-house which had been erected in 1768-69.

See: 200th Anniversary Buckingham; Chapman, op. cit., p. 143; Hotchkin, op. cit., p. 508; Baily, op. cit., p. 284.

Minutes of Men's Meetings, 1870-97, 1 vol. (1827-69 missing); Minutes of Women's Meetings, 1846-78, 3 vols. (1327-45 missing) at NNBN. Minutes of Joint Meetings, 1897--, 2 vols. '1878-97 included in volume of Minutes of Men's Meetings), in custody of clerk, Mrs. Mary Watson, 123 Maple Avenue, Doylestown. Minutes of Ministers and Elders, 1827-1928, 2 vols., at NNBN, and 1928--, incorporated in minutes of Buckingham Monthly Meetings. Registers of this meeting are incorporated in the records of the Buckingham Monthly Meeting.

199. PLUMSTEAD INDULGED MEETING, 1827--. One-half mile west of Gardenville Village, Route 920 on Point Pleasant Road, Plumstead Twp., Bucks County.

Continued in 1827 as the Plumstead Preparative Meeting (H) by Buckingham Monthly Meeting (entry 197), after separation from the original Plumstead Preparative Meeting, now the Landisville Indulged Meeting (O) (entry 164). This meeting retained the two-story native gray stone building which the original meeting had erected in 1752; also the 3/4-acre burial ground, which had been laid out at the time of the purchase of the original 15 acres of land in 1730; and the two-story stone schoolmaster's home, which had been built a little south of the meeting-house shortly after 1730. In 1876 the meeting-house was reduced to one story when the house was rebuilt along colonial lines with the same native gray stone. Because of diminishing membership Plumstead Preparative Meeting was laid down in 1866 and Plumstead Indulged Meeting established under Buckingham Monthly Meeting. Since 1900 the membership of this meeting has been so small that the only one appointed meeting is held there each year in order that the title to the property may be retained. The meeting-house is in good condition, and the former schoolmaster's house is used as the home of the caretaker of the grounds. The burial ground is maintained and is still in use by both Hicksite and Orthodox Friends.

See: 200th Anniversary Buckingham; Michener, op. cit., p. 79; "Plumstead Township," Bucks County Historical Society Papers, I (1908), 310.

Minutes of Men's Meetings, 1921-66, 3 vols., at NNBN. All minutes of women's meetings are missing. Registers are in the records of the Buckingham Monthly Meeting. Bucks County Deed Books, vol. 31, p. 189; vol. 56, p. 504; vol. 60, p. 627; vol. 70, p. 236.

200. DOYLESTOWN INDULGED MEETING, 1834--. 95 East Oakland Avenue, Doylestown.

Established in 1834 as an indulged meeting by Buckingham Monthly Meeting (entry 197). Meetings were held in the Academy Building (today the Masonic Temple), 53 East State Street, until the present one-story red brick building on stone foundation, was completed in February 1836.

See: Davis, op. cit., I, 92; Michener, op. cit., p. 79.

Records for this meeting are incorporated with those of the Buckingham Monthly Meeting. Bucks County Deed Book, vol. 79, pp. 166-168.

201. FALLS MONTHLY MEETING, 1827--. Intersection of Bristol-Burlington and Pennsbury Roads, Fallsington, Bucks County.
Continued as a Hicksite meeting in 1827 by Bucks Quarterly Meeting (entry 196) after separation from the original Falls Monthly Meeting (entry 162). Meetings were held in two-story native meeting-houses, erected in 1789 on 6 acres of ground donated by Samuel Burges in 1689. In 1827 this meeting retained the meeting-house, along with the graveyard, laid out in 1692, the hip-roofed schoolhouse, and the stable lots. After the inception of the public-school system in this township a free school was continued in the schoolhouse until 1854. Between 1854-60 a boarding school for girls was conducted by Beulah and Hetty Lower. In 1860 it was leased as a private dwelling and one or more rooms served as a Friends' library and kindergarten. The graveyard, at the corner of Bristol and Tullytown Roads, was laid out in 1878. It is used by the Hicksite Friends exclusively, and contains 5/6 of an acre enclosed by a rail fence. In 1894 ownership of the original 6 acres of land, donated by Samuel Burges in 1689, was intrusted to trustees of both Orthodox and Hicksite Friends. In 1927 the schoolhouse and 2/3 of an acre of ground adjoining it were sold to Edgar T. Snipes and his wife, and Jane Moon Snipes. With their permission a week-day school was re-established and is still functioning. The horse block, which had been restored by former teachers and pupils of Fallsington Friends' schools, was dedicated at the 250th anniversary celebration in 1933. A historical marker given by the Friends' Historical Association, was installed on a large native stone slab provided by the Fallsington Friends in 1933. It is situated near the junction of the roads leading to both meeting-houses and east of the present Hicksite meeting-house. The present clerk is Elizabeth Palmer, Newtown.

See: Brown, op. cit.; Battle, op. cit., pp. 314, 324, 381; John H. Wood, "Quaker Imprints of Bucks County," Bulletin of Friends' Historical Association, XXII (1933), 28-34; Snipes, op. cit., p. 20; Henry Moon, Friends of Falls; Elizabeth B. Satterthwaite, Bucks County Friends' Meetings (manuscripts, Fallsington Library, Fallsington, Bucks County).

Minutes of Men's Meetings, 1816-90, 2 vols.; Minutes of Women's Meetings, 1827-90, 2 vols.; Minutes of Joint Meetings, 1890-98, in the 1834-90 vol. of men's minutes, at NNBN, and 1698—, 1 vol., in custody of clerk. Minutes of Ministers and Elders, 1813-71, 2 vols. (1872-1904 missing), at NNBN, and 1905--, 1 vol., in custody of clerk. Registers of Births, Marriages, and Deaths, 1827--, 1 vol., in custody of Miss Emily Stackhouse, Somerton. Register of Removals, 1821-81, 1 vol., at NNBN and 1881 --, 1 vol., in custody of recorder, Miss Mary Stackhouse. Financial Records, 1816-84, 1 vol. (1880-1910 destroyed by fire), at NNBN, and 1910--, 1 vol., in custody of treasurer, Miss Susanna Hibbs, Morrisville Road, Fallsington. Bucks County Deed Books, vol. 20, p. 141; vol. 53, pp. 393, 568; vol. 63, p. 604; vol. 72, p. 202; vol. 73, pp. 579, 580; vol. 78, p. 732; vol. 88, p. 574; vol. 89, pp. 160, 331; vol. 126, p. 143; vol. 178, p. 613; vol. 223, p. 175; vol. 243, pp. 126, 128; vol. 274, p. 251; vol. 276, p. 249; vol. 387, p. 550; vol. 472, p. 203; vol. 570, p. 138; vol.

594, p. 422; vol. 596, p. 234; vol. 631, p. 189; vol. 635, p. 434; vol. 637, p. 140.

202. FALLS PREPARATIVE MEETING, 1827-90. Intersection of Bristol-Burlington and Pennsbury Roads, Fallsington, Bucks County. Continued as a Hicksite meeting in 1827 by Falls Monthly Meeting (entry 61). Meetings were held in the two-story native stone meeting-house erected in 1789, which the Hicksite retained after the separation. This meeting was laid down in 1890 by Falls Monthly Meeting.

See: Brown, op. cit.; Battle, op. cit., pp. 314, 324, 381; Wood, John, op. cit., pp. 28-34.

Minutes of Men's Meetings, 1827-90, 5 vols. (first vol., 1827-42, contains Orthodox records from 1822-27), at NNBN. Registers are in the records of the Falls Monthly Meeting. Minutes of First-day School, 1828-55, 1 vol., at NNBN, and 1855-90 in the Preparative and Monthly Meeting minutes.

203. PENNSBURY INDULGED MEETING, 1828-95. Two miles south of Morris-ville on Bordentown Ferry Road, Penn's Manor, Bucks County. Continued as a Hicksite meeting in 1828 by Falls Monthly Meeting (entry 201) after separation from the original Pennsbury Preparative Meeting (entry 62). Meetings were held in private homes until 1868. In that year this meeting requested and received the permission of Falls Monthly Meeting (0) (entry 201) to hold meetings in their old meeting-house located 2 miles south of Morrisville on Bordentown Ferry Road, Penn's Manor. This meeting-house had been leased to the township authorities for a schoolhouse by the Pennsbury Preparative Meeting (Orthodox) after the meeting was laid down in 1864. The Orthodox meeting had reserved the right to have meetings on First-days. The Hicksite Friends continued to worship in this house until 1895, when due to diminishing members, the meeting was laid down. The remaining members then joined Falls Monthly Meeting.

204. MAKEFIELD MONTHLY MEETING, 1827--. Junction of Yardley, Dolington and Mount Ayre Roads, 1/8 mile east of Dolington, Route 632, Bucks County. Continued as a Hicksite meeting in 1827 by Bucks Quarterly Meeting (entry 196) after separation from the original Makefield Monthly Meeting (entry 68). The present clerk is J. Augustus Cadwallader, Yardley.

See: Michener, op. cit., p. 83; Davis, op. cit., I, 435; Battle, I, 445.

Minutes of Men's Meetings, 1820-95, 3 vols. (1892-95, incorporated in minutes of joint meetings), at NNBN. Minutes of Women's Meetings, missing. Minutes of Joint Meetings, 1895-1934, 2 vols., at NNBN, and 1934--, 1 vol., in custody of clerk. Registers of Births, Deaths, Marriage Certificates, and Membership, 1819-1926, 1 vol., at NNBN, and 1926--, 1 vol., in custody of recorder, Sara Cadwallader, Yardley. Certificates of Removal, 1820-1926, 1 vol., at NNBN, and 1926--, 1 vol., in custody of Sara Cadwallader. Financial Records, 1821-1926, 1 vol., at NNBN, and 1926--, incorporated in minutes of joint meetings.

205. MAKEFIELD PREPARATIVE MEETING, 1827-1926. Junction of Yardley, Dolington, and Mount Ayre Roads, 1/8 mile east of Dolington, Route 632, Bucks County. Continued as a Hicksite meeting in 1827 by Bucks Quarterly Meeting (entry

196) after separation from the original undivided Makefield Preparative
Meeting (entry 69). At the time of the Separation this meeting retained
the original acre and 18 perches of burial ground and also the stone meeting-house. The graveyard was first enclosed with a board fence until 1853,
at which time this was torn down and replaced by a stone wall. In 1853
and in 1925 additional ground was purchased so that today the meeting-
house ground and the graveyard cover about 3½ acres. There is also a mention of a schoolhouse, built by Samuel Buckman and Jesse Lloyd in 1830.
This school also served as a public-school and library for a time and was
located in Dolington. The school was discontinued before or at the time
of the passage of the School Law in 1854. The meeting was laid down in
1926.

See: Michener, op. cit., p. 83; Davis, op. cit., I, 435; Battle, op.
cit., I, 445.

Minutes of Men's Meetings, 1845-91, 3 vols. (1827-44, 1852-59 missing);
Minutes of Women's Meetings, 1837-92, 4 vols. (1827-36, 1875-84 missing);
Minutes of Joint Meetings, 1892-1926, 2 vols., at NNBN. Registers and
financial records are incorporated in the records of the Makefield Monthly meeting. Bucks County Deed Book, vol. 25, pp. 71, 72.

206. YARDLEY INDULGED MEETING, 1857--. Northwest corner Main Street
and College Avenue, Yardley (formerly Yardleyville).
Friends residing in Yardleyville petitioned Makefield Monthly Meeting
(entry 204) for the privilege of holding an indulged meeting of their own.
This request was granted November 5, 1857. From that year to 1863 meetings were held in the church building of the Church of the Second Advent,
on Main Street and College Avenue. In 1863, the present meeting-house,
a gray stone one-story building was erected.

See: Michener, op. cit., p. 336; Battle, op. cit., I, 336; "Account
of Yardley Friends' Meetings," in Centennial Newtown, pp. 23-25; Bucks
County Deed Book, vol. 308, p. 196.

207. MIDDLETOWN MONTHLY MEETING, 1827--. At intersection of Maple
Avenue (Old Philadelphia Road) and Green Street, near Borough
Line, Langhorne, Bucks County.
Continued as a Hicksite meeting in 1827 by Bucks Quarterly Meeting (entry
196) after separation from the original undivided Middletown Monthly Meeting (entry 166). Meetings have always been held in the two-story native
stone meeting-house which this meeting retained after the Separation, a-
long with the two-story native stone schoolhouse, and the 3½-acre burial
ground. The burial ground is enclosed by a stone wall. Both the meeting-
house and the schoolhouse were erected by the original meeting in 1793.
In 1897, 1 acre of land was added to the site of Middletown Monthly Meeting. The present clerk is Henry C. Pickering, Woodbourne.

See: Woody, op. cit., p. 87; Bowden, op. cit., II, 248; Michener,
op. cit., p. 77; Centennial Newtown, pp. 38-42.

Minutes of Men's Meetings, 1827-1921, 4 vols.; Minutes of Women's
Meetings, 1827-93, 3 vols., in meeting-house. Minutes of Joint Meetings,
1893--, 1 vol. (1893-1931 included in last volume of minutes of men's
meetings), in custody of Henry C. Pickering, Woodbourne. Minutes of Ministers and Elders, 1869--, 2 vols. (1827-69 missing), in meeting-house.
Registers of Births, 1745--, 1 vol.; Registers of Members, in volume of

men's minutes, 1837-61; Deaths and Burials, 1771--, 1 vol.; Certificates
of Removals, 1777--, 1 vol., in meeting-house. Certificates of Marriages,
1780-1938, 1 vol., in meeting-house, and 1938, 1 vol., in custody of
Miss Mary Stackhouse, 114 Richardson Avenue, Langhorne. Financial records
are incorporated in the minute books. Corporators' Records, 1917--, 1
vol., in custody of Mrs. Earnest Harvey, secretary of Corporators, 50
Maple Avenue, Langhorne. Corporators' Treasury Book, 1917--, 1 vol. in
custody of Furhman Mather, treasurer of Corporators, Bellevue and Gillan
Avenues, Langhorne Manor. Records of School and Meeting-house Committee,
1918--, 1 vol., in custody of Mrs. Earnest Harvey. Bucks County Deed Books,
vol. 26, p. 630; vol. 31, pp. 153, 155; vol. 33, p. 656; vol. 46, p. 271;
vol. 56, p. 292; vol. 88, p. 574; vol. 173, p. 104; vol. 176, p. 306; vol.
253, p. 162; vol. 259, pp. 523, 528; vol. 261, p. 637; vol. 417, p. 31,

208. MIDDLETOWN PREPARATIVE MEETING, 1827-1920. West Maple Avenue on
Borough Line, Langhorne, Bucks County.
Continued as a Hicksite meeting in 1827 by Middletown Monthly Meeting (entry 207) after separation from the original Middletown Preparative Meeting (entry 163). Held meetings in the two-story native stone meeting-
house, which the meeting retained after the Separation. This meeting also
retained in 1827 the present two-story stone schoolhouse erected in 1795
and the two-story lean-to annex, attached to the rear of the schoolhouse,
which was erected a few years after 1793. This preparative meeting was
laid down in 1920 and the school continued as a Friends' institution until 1929 when it was leased to the Langhorne borough authorities, who used
it for a public school.

See: Battle, op. cit., p. 938; Woody, op. cit., p. 87; Centennial
Newtown, pp. 38-42.

Minutes of Men's Meetings, 1793-1904, 7 vols. (1848-93 transcribed),
at the meeting-house. Minutes of Women's Meetings, 1859-93, 3 vols. (1827
-59 missing), at NNBN. Minutes of Joint Meetings, 1893-95, in the 1879-
93 vol. of men's minutes, and 1895-1913, 1 vol., in meeting-house. (No
records after 1913).

209. SOLEBURY MONTHLY MEETING, 1827--. Junction of Sugan and Meeting-House Roads, Solebury Twp., Bucks County.
Continued as a Hicksite meeting in 1827 by Bucks Quarterly Meeting (entry
196) after separation from the original Solebury Monthly Meeting (entry
66). This meeting retained the two-story brownstone meeting-house e-
rected in 1806 and the graveyard containing 220 perches located south of
the meeting-house and on the opposite side of the road. In 1830, 100
perches were added to the graveyard. In 1840 a school committee purchased
from John Blackfan the one-story native limestone schoolhouse located on
side of the road opposite the meeting-house. This building was erected
in 1793 by Buckingham Monthly Meeting 'entry 167) and transferred to Solebury Monthly Meeting in 1811. In 1848 the school opposite the meeting-
house was replaced with a two-story limestone structure. In 1851, the
school was discontinued and leased to the township authorities. In 1877,
1½ acres acquired from Merrick Reader were added to the graveyard, and in
the following year a stone wall was built around the four sides of the
entire plot. In 1900 the schoolhouse, opposite the meeting-house which
had been leased to the township authorities in 1851, was converted into
a home for the caretaker of the grounds. The present clerk is Marian
Eastburn Ely, R.F.D. 1, New Hope.

See: Michener, op. cit., p. 81; Davis, op. cit., I, 234-237; Centennial Solebury.

Minutes of Men's Meetings, 1811-86, 2 vols.; Minutes of Women's Meetings, 1811-86, 3 vols., at NNBN. Joint Minutes, 1886-1922, 1 vol., at NNBN, and 1922--, 1 vol., in custody of clerk. Registers of Births and Deaths, 1811--, 1 vol.; Certificates of Marriage, 1811--, 1 vol., in custody of H. Howard Paxon, Carversville. Certificates of Removal, 1811--, 1 vol., in custody of clerk. Financial records are incorporated in the minute books. Bucks County Deed Books, vol. 54, p. 351; vol. 58. pp. 499, 504, 508, 510, 512; vol. 64, p. 652; vol. 117, p. 244; vol. 181, p. 274; vol. 277, p. 286.

210. SOLEBURY PREPARATIVE MEETING, 1827-85. Junction of Sugan and Meeting-House Roads, Solebury Twp., Bucks County.
Continued as a Hicksite meeting in 1827, by Solebury Monthly Meeting (entry 209) after separation from the original Solebury Preparative Meeting (entry 67). This meeting retained the two-story brownstone meeting-house erected in 1806, and the graveyard of 220 perches located south of the meeting-house on the opposite side of Sugan Road. A plot of 100 perches was added to the graveyard in 1830. In 1877, 1½ acres acquired from Merrick Reeder, were added to the graveyard and in the following year a stone wall was built around the four sides of the entire 3½-acre plot. The meeting was laid down by Solebury Monthly Meeting in 1885.

See: Michener, op. cit., p. 82; Davis, op. cit., I, 237; Centennial Solebury.

Minutes of Men's Meetings, 1806-85, 2 vols.; Minutes of Women's Meetings, 1806-83, 1 vol., at NNBN. Registers are in the records of the Solebury Monthly Meeting. One small account book, extracts of preparative meetings, December 30, 1830, in custody of Henry Heaton, Solebury. Bucks County Deed Books, vol. 54, p. 351; vol. 58, pp. 499, 504, 508, 510, 512; vol. 64, p. 652; vol. 117, p. 244; vol. 181, p. 274; vol. 277, p. 286.

211. NEW HOPE INDULGED MEETING, 1864-81. Lower York Road at entrance to New Hope-Lambertville Bridge, New Hope Borough, Solebury Twp., Bucks County.
Set up in 1864 by Solebury Monthly Meeting (entry 209), at the request of a number of Friends residing in the villages of New Hope, Pa., and Lambertville, N. J. Meetings were held in a one-story frame building which was rented and situated on a lot at the entrance of the New Hope-Lambertville Bridge. This meeting never owned a meeting-house. In 1881 the meeting was discontinued and the members joined the Lambertville meeting (see forthcoming Inventory of the Church Archives of New Jersey), at York Road and George Street, Lambertville, N. J. The meeting-house and the lot on which it stood became the property of the Bridge Company after the meeting was discontinued. The meeting-house has been demolished.

See: Scrap Books, vol. 5, p. 190.

Registers are recorded in records of the Solebury Monthly Meetings.

212. WRIGHTSTOWN MONTHLY MEETING, 1827--. Durham and Penn Park Roads, Wrightstown Village, Bucks County.
Continued as a Hicksite meeting in 1827 by Bucks Quarterly Meeting (entry

196), after a division of the original Wrightstown Monthly Meeting (entry 65). The meeting-house, a two-story rectangular building of brown limestone, was erected in 1787. This meeting-house and 4 acres of burial ground are partly enclosed by a stone wall, on which is an old stone with the date 1772 cut into it. The first marker in the ancient burial ground reads, "S. Jolly, 1744," however, there were previous burials, indicated by records as early as 1720. In 1890 the Bucks County Historical Society erected a stone marker in one corner of the graveyard to commemorate the starting point of walkers in the famous Walking Purchase Treaty with the Indians in 1737. An inscription on a stone at the base of this monument reads: "To the memory of the Leni-Lenape Indians, Ancient Owners of this Region." In 1889 and in 1911 additional land comprising 4½ acres adjoining the meeting-house was purchased, and today the grounds cover 8½ acres. The present clerk is Russell E. Smith, Wycombe.

See: Michener, op. cit., p. 80; Buck, op. cit., p. 67; Scrap Books, vol. 5, p. 168.

Minutes of Men's Meetings, 1827-86, 4 vols., at NNBN. Minutes of Joint Meetings, 1886-95 are in 1864-86 vol. of Minutes of Men's Meetings, 1895-1935, 2 vols., at NNBN. Bank, and 1935--, 1vol. in custody of clerk. Register of Births and Deaths, 1811--, 1 vol.; Register of Marriages, 1811--, 1 vol., in custody of H. Howard Paxon, Carversville; Register of Burials, 1808--, 1 vol., in custody of caretaker, Henry Heaton, Solebury. Bucks County Deed Books, vol. 54, p. 351; vol. 58, pp. 499, 504, 508, 510, 512; vol. 64, p. 552; vol. 117, p. 244; vol. 181, p. 274; vol. 277, p. 268.

213. WRIGHTSTOWN PREPARATIVE MEETING, 1827-ca.1854. Durham and Penn
       Park Roads, Wrightstown Village, Bucks County.
Continued as a Hicksite meeting in 1827 by Wrightstown Monthly Meeting (entry 212), after division of the original Wrightstown Preparative Meeting (entry 64). This meeting retained all property, and meetings were held in the two-story limestone meeting-house which had been erected by the Friends in 1787. Both Hicksite and Orthodox Friends used the 4-acre burial ground which adjoined the meeting-house. Due to a diminishing membership this preparative meeting became inactive about 1854. Whether or not it was officially laid down is not known.

See: Michener, op. cit., p. 80; Buck, op. cit., p. 67; Scrap Book, vol. 5, p. 168.

Minutes of Men's Meetings, 1722-1829, 1 vol. (1827-54 missing); Minutes of Women's Meetings, 1832-54, 1 vol. (1827-32 missing), at NNBN. Newtown National Bank. Registers are in records of the Wrightstown Monthly Meeting.

214. BRISTOL MONTHLY MEETING, 1874--. Southeast corner of Wood and
       Market Streets, Bristol, Bucks County.
Set up in 1874 by Bucks Quarterly Meeting (entry 196). Meetings have always been held in the meeting-house of Bristol Preparative Meeting (entry 215). This meeting consists of its own preparative meeting as its only subordinate meeting. The present clerk is Lillie M. Rue, 434 Greenwood Avenue, Trenton, N. J.

See: Green, op. cit., pp. 46-49; Buck, op. cit., pp. 114-160.

Minutes of Men's Meetings, 1874-80, in first vol. of minutes of Joint Meetings. Minutes of Women's Meetings, 1874-80, 1 vol., in custody of clerk. Minutes of Joint Meetings, 1380-1912, 1 vol.; in Bristol Trust Co., Bristol, and 1912--, 2 vols., in custody of clerk. Minutes of Ministers and Elders, 1882-1921, 3 vols. (1874-82 missing), in Bristol Trust Co., and 1921--, 1 vol., in custody of clerk, Mrs. Earl Tomb, Bristol. Financial Records, 1874--, 2 vols.; loose-leaf records of Friends School for Boys and Girls, 1875-1937, in Bristol Trust Co. Registers of Births, membership, deaths, certificates of marriages, and certificates of removals, are recorded in the volume of minutes of Ministers and Elders for 1882-94. Bucks County Deed Books, vol. 54, p. 390; vol. 233, p. 406.

215. BRISTOL PREPARATIVE MEETING, 1827--. Southeast corner of Wood and Market Streets, Bristol, Bucks County.
Continued as a Hicksite meeting in 1827 by Middletown Monthly Meeting (entry 207) after division of the original Bristol Preparative Meeting (entry 60). All of the property was retained and meetings were held in the two-story brick meeting-house which the original meeting had erected in 1713. In 1874 this meeting was detached from Middletown Monthly Meeting and attached to the newly set up Bristol Monthly Meeting (entry 214). In the same year the northeast portion of the plot of land at the northwest corner of Walnut and Cedar Streets was sold and a one-story brownstone schoolhouse was erected on the remaining portion of the property. The lot originally consisted of 97½ perches. This building served as a Friends grade and primary school until 1937, when it was leased by the trustees of the meeting to the Bristol Travel Club. Prior to the erection of the schoolhouse the meeting conducted classes in the meeting-house. Although the 4-acre graveyard on Wood Street, between Walnut and Penn Streets became the property of this meeting after the Separation, it is also used as a burial ground by the Orthodox and Primitive Friends.

See: Green, op. cit., pp. 46-49; Buck, op. cit., pp. 114-160.

Minutes of Men's Meetings, 1827-69, 1 vol., in Bristol Trust Co., and 1869-77, in volume of Minutes of Joint Meetings, 1877-1926. Minutes of Women's Meeting, 1873-77, 1 vol. (1827-73 missing), in Bristol Trust Co.; Minutes of Joint Meetings, 1877--, 2 vols., in custody of Mrs. Lillie Rue, 434 Greenwood Avenue, Trenton, N.J. Registers are in the records of the Middletown Monthly Meeting, 1827-74; in the records of the Bristol Monthly Meeting, 1874--. Separate burial records have been kept since 1832-62, 1 vol., in Bristol Trust Co., and 1862--, 1 vol., in custody of caretaker, Lewis Wilhite, 432 Market Street, Bristol. Bucks County Deed Books, vol. 54, p. 390; vol. 233, p. 406.

216. NEWTOWN MONTHLY MEETING, 1926--. Southeast corner Court and State Streets, Newtown, Bucks County.
Set up in 1926 by Bucks Quarterly Meeting (entry 196), by a division of Makefield Monthly Meeting into two monthly meetings. Meetings have always been held in the meeting-house of Newtown Preparative Meeting (entry 217). This meeting consists of its own preparative meeting as its only subordinate meeting. Newtown Preparative Meeting, formerly a part of Makefield Monthly Meeting, was transferred to this monthly meeting at the time of its establishment in 1926. The present clerk is Joseph V. Shane, George School, Pa.

See: Centennial Newtown William Wynkoop, "Newtown-Old and New," Bucks County Historical Society Papers, III (1909), 292; Hanna E. Holcomb, "Edward Hicks, Approved Minister of Society of Friends," Bucks County Historical Society Papers, I, (1908), 385.

Minutes of the Newtown Monthly Meeting, 1926-37, 1 vol., at NNBN, and 1937--, 1 vol., in custody of clerk. Registers of Births and Deaths, 1926--, 1 vol., at NNBN. Financial records are incorporated in the minutes.

217. NEWTOWN PREPARATIVE MEETING, 1827--. Southeast corner Court and State Streets, Newtown, Bucks County.
Continued as a Hicksite meeting in 1827 by Makefield Monthly Meeting (entry 204) after division of the original Newtown Preparative Meeting (entry 70). This meeting retained both the 4/5-acre cemetery and the adjoining two-story native limestone meeting-house which was erected in 1818. In 1861 a Sabbath school was organized and classes are still held, in the meeting-house. This meeting formerly a part of Makefield Monthly Meeting, (entry 68), was placed under Newtown Monthly Meeting when that meeting was set up in 1926.

Minutes of Men's Meetings, 1817-92, 1 vol; Minutes of Women's Meetings, 1817-92, 5 vols., at NNBN. ^Minutes of Joint Meetings, 1902-37, 1 vol. (1892-1902 contained in Minutes of Men's Meetings, at NNBN, and 1937 --, 1 loose-leaf vol., in custody of clerk, Lavinia Hartley, 127 South Chancellor Street, Newtown. Minutes of Ministers and Counsel, 1926--, 1 vol. (minutes prior to 1926, incorporated in the Makefield Monthly minutes), in custody of clerk. Minutes of Trustees and Elders, 1893-1926, 2 vols. (minutes prior to 1893 are transcribed in current volume; 1913 missing), at NNBN, and 1926--, 1 vol., in custody of H. Griffin Miller, 124 State Street, Newtown. Registers of Births, Marriages, Certificates of Removal, and Deaths, 1739-1830, 1 vol. (transcribed from records of the Middletown, Wrightstown, and Makefield Monthly Meetings, 1880-1926 incorporated in the Makefield Monthly meeting register for the years (1819-1926), 1926--, 2 vols., at NNBN. Burial Records, 1817--, 1 vol., in custody of H. Griffin Miller. Minutes of First-day School Committees, 1893-1921, 1 vol. (reports prior to 1893 and after 1921 are incorporated in the minutes of the meeting), at NNBN. Bucks County Deed Books, vol. 52, p. 183; vol. 72, p. 326; vol. 118, p. 446; vol. 142, p. 122; vol. 171, p. 142; vol. 226, p. 418; vol. 267, p. 463.

CONCORD QUARTERLY MEETING (H)

Component Meetings

(See: Explanatory Note 3)

	Date established	Entry number
BIRMINGHAM MONTHLY MEETING (WEST CHESTER)	1872	219
Birmingham Preparative Meeting	1827	220
West Chester Preparative Meeting	1827	221
CHESTER MONTHLY MEETING	1827	222
Chester Preparative Meeting	1827	223
Springfield Preparative Meeting	1827	224
Middletown Preparative Meeting	1827	237
Providence Preparative Meeting	1827	238
CONCORD MONTHLY MEETING	1827	225
Chichester Preparative Meeting	1827	226
Concord Preparative Meeting	1827	227
DARBY MONTHLY MEETING	1827	228
Darby Preparative Meeting	1827	229
GOSHEN MONTHLY MEETING	1827	230
Goshen Preparative Meeting	1827	231
Newtown Preparative Meeting	1827	232
Whiteland Preparative Meeting	1827	233
Whiteland Indulged Meeting	1843	233
Willistown Preparative Meeting	1827	234
SWARTHMORE MONTHLY MEETING	1893	235
Swarthmore College Independent Meeting	1863	235
LANSDOWNE MONTHLY MEETING	1901	236
Lansdowne Independent Meeting	1898	236
CONCORD (UNITED) MONTHLY MEETING	1932	231
PROVIDENCE (UNITED) MONTHLY MEETING	1934	332
Middletown Preparative Meeting	1827	237
Providence Preparative Meeting	1827	238
WILLISTOWN MONTHLY MEETING	1939	239
WILMINGTON MONTHLY MEETING	1827	Del.
(See: Delaware Church Archives)		
ORANGE GROVE MONTHLY MEETING	1907	Cal.
(See: California Church Archives)		
NEWTOWN SQUARE MONTHLY MEETING[1]	1939	232

1. Information on this meeting was received too late to use as separate entry.

218. CONCORD QUARTERLY MEETING, 1827--. Chester and Delaware Counties.
Continued as a Hicksite meeting in 1827 under Philadelphia Yearly Meeting
(entry 173), after division of the original Concord Quarterly Meeting (entry 136). Meetings are held at the several meeting-houses in the quarterly meeting territory in Pennsylvania and at Wilmington, Delaware. The
present clerk is Roland G. Ullman, 213 Harvard Avenue, Swarthmore.

See: Nathaniel Richardson, Discussions and Anecdotes of Thomas Story,
p. 363; Michener, op. cit., p. 65.

Minutes of Concord Quarterly Meeting, 1827-1918, 2 vols., at PSC-Hi,
and 1918--, 1 vol., in custody of the clerk. Minutes of Ministers and
Elders, 1827-28, 1 vol., at PSC-Hi, and 1928--, 1 vol., in custody of
Frederick P. Supplee, 92 W. Albermarle Avenue, Lansdowne. Concord First-
day School Union Minutes, 1883--, 4 vols., in custody of clerk Charles J.
Suplee, 144 Hilldale Road, Lansdowne. Minutes of Circular Meeting Committee, 1868--, 3 vols., in custody of clerk, Arl)tta C. Palmer, 100 Delaware Avenue, Ridley Park. Financial Records, 1897--, 2 vols. (1827-96
missing), in custody of Chester Roberts, 409 College Avenue, Swarthmore.

219. BIRMINGHAM MONTHLY MEETING, 1827--. Birmingham and West Chester
Twps., Chester County.
Continued as a Hicksite meeting in 1827 by Concord Quarterly Meeting (entry 218) after the division of the original Birmingham Monthly Meeting
(entry 154). This meeting met alternately at Birmingham and West Chester
until about 1831. From 1831 until 1936 it met at West Chester. In 1936
the practice was revived of meeting at Birmingham during June, July, and
August. The present clerk is Edna N. Pusey, 228 E. Biddle Street, West
Chester.

See: Philip P. Sharpless, Birmingham Monthly Meeting and West Chester
Preparative Meeting (manuscript at Friends' Meeting-House, 423 N. High
Street, West Chester); An Epistle of Birmingham Monthly Meeting of Friends
held at West Chester, December 28, 1887 (manuscript in Chester County
Historical Society, West Chester); Futhey and Cope, op. cit., p. 70; Past
and Present, p. 106; Philip P. Sharpless, "Friends' Meetings," West Chester
Daily Local News, March 5, 1891; Harbert P. Worth, "Friends' Record in
Birmingham," West Chester Daily Local News, December 10, 1915.

Minutes of Men's Meetings, 1827-95, 2 vols.; Minutes of Women's Meetings, 1827-95, 2 vols., in Friends' meeting-house, 423 N. High Street,
West Chester. Minutes of Joint Meetings, 1895-1936, 2 vols., in Friends
meet-house; and 1937--, 1 vol., in custody of clerk. Minutes of Ministry
and Counsel, 1930--, 1 vol. (1827-1929 missing), in custody of clerk. Registers of Births, Members, Marriages, Certificates of Removal, and Deaths,
1827--, 3 vols., in Friends' meeting-house. Financial Records, 1922--,
1 vol. (1827-1921 missing), in custody of treasurer Alfred Hallowell, R.
D. 3, West Chester.

220. BIRMINGHAM PREPARATIVE MEETING, 1827--. Birmingham Road, 1/4
mile south of Street Road, Birmingham Twp., Chester County.
Continued as a Hicksite meeting in 1827 by Birmingham Monthly Meeting (entry 219), after division of the original Birmingham Preparative Meeting
(entry 155). At the time of the Separation in 1827 this meeting retained
the one-story gray stone meeting-house, which was erected in 1763, and also the 20 acres of ground adjoining the meeting-house, 1 acre of which had

been formerly used as a burial ground. In 1874, 17 acres and 120 perches
of this land were returned to Birmingham Preparative Meeting, Orthodox.
In 1922 Birmingham Preparative Meeting, Orthodox, was laid down and its
members were transferred to West Chester Preparative Meeting (entry 221).
However, the meeting-house continued to be used by the Orthodox Friends,
and from 1923 until 1938 united meetings were held alternately in the meeting-houses of the Orthodox and Hicksite Friends of Birmingham. Since 1938
the united character of the meeting has been continued by the West Chester
Orthodox Friends sending representatives to each weekly meeting of the
Hicksite Friends of Birmingham.

See: Cope, History, pp. 34-56; William T. Sharpless, "Birmingham
Meeting," Bulletin of Friends' Historical Association, XIX, No. 2 (1930),
p. 68; Thomson, op. cit., p. 748; Heathcote, op. cit., pp. 251, 339;
Futhey and Cope op. cit., pp. 9, 70, 73, 131, 163, 233, 234, 241; Watson,
op. cit., II, 83, 87; Lewis S. Shimmell, A History of Pennsylvania, pp. 33,
158; John T. Faris, Old Churches and Meeting-Houses in an Around Philadelphia, pp. 151, 152; Woody, op. cit., pp. 131, 134, 163; Egle, op. cit.,
p. 531; Myers, Immigration, pp. 117, 118, Michener, op. cit., pp. 70, 71,
Philip P. Sharpless, "Friends Meeting," West Chester Daily Local News,
March 5, 1891; Herbert P. Worth, "Friends Records in Birmingham," West
Chester Daily Local News, December 10, 1915; "Historians' Day at Birming-
ham," West Chester Daily Local News, May 24, 1930; "Friends Reunion",
West Chester Village Record, June 23, 1910; "Building Fine Monuments John
G. Taylor's," Philadelphia Press, July 17, 1904.

Minutes of Men's Meetings, 1827-1903 missing; Minutes of Women's
Meetings, 1827-1903 missing. Minutes of Joint Meetings, 1904-34, 1 vol.,
in West Chester Friends' meeting-house, 423 N. High Street, West Chester,
and 1934--, 1 vol., in custody of clerk, Alta J. Baily Bittle, R. D. 6,
West Chester. Registers are in the records of the Birmingham Monthly
Meeting. Financial Records, 1896--, 1 vol. (1827-95 missing), in custody of Emlen Darlington, Pocopson. Minutes of First-day school, 1913-
35, 3 vols. (1827-1912 missing), in West Chester meeting-house and 1936--,
2 vols., in custody of secretary, Elizabeth C. Reynolds, R. D. 6, West Chester. Financial Records of First-day school, 1928, 1 vol. (1827-1927 missing), in custody of treasurer, Edith Sheffield, R. D. #5, West Chester,
Chester County Deed Books, G-2, p. 479; I-3, p. 3; I-12, pp. 55, 439, 443;
K-12, p. 256; N-11; p. 424; P-2, pp. 250, 254; P-3, pp. 319, 543; P-8,
pp. 40, 51, 101; S-3, p. 338; V., p. 188; Z-3, p. 499.

221. WEST CHESTER PREPARATIVE MEETING, 1827--. 423 North High
Street, West Chester, Chester County.
Continued as a Hicksite meeting in 1827 by Birmingham Monthly Meeting (entry 219) after division of the original West Chester Preparative Meeting
(entry 147). This meeting retained the burial ground which had been purchased in 1812, and the two-story stone meeting-house, which had been e-
rected in 1810. In 1868, the western end of the building was razed and
replaced by a two-story red brick addition, and in 1907, a porch extending the entire length of the building was added. In 1873, because of an
ordinance forbidding any further burials within borough limits, the Friends
and Friends' Burial Company purchased in 1874, a 10-acre cemetery site on
the south side of West Rosedale Avenue. First burial, 1871.

See: Cope, History pp. 34-56; Sharpless, Susannah, op. cit., pp. 27,
28; Michener, op. cit., pp. 71-72; Past and Present, pp. 40, 72, 73, 105,
106; Futhey and Cope, op. cit., pp. 241, 242; "High Street Friends," West
Chester Daily Local News, January 12, 1929; "Friends Recall a Century of

Life," West Chester, Daily Local News, December 10, 1915; Cope Collection,
Historical Society of Pennsylvania, David Haines Carpenter's Account Book,
1803-29. Chester County, Recorder of Deeds, Corporation Book no. 1, p.
372.

Minutes of Men's Meetings, 1841-76, 2 vols. (1827-40, 1876-95 missing). Minutes of Women's Meetings, 1885-95, 1 vol. (1827-84 missing); Minutes of Joint Meetings, 1895--, 2 vols., at meeting-house. Registers incorporated in the records of the Birmingham Monthly Meeting. Financial
Records, 1864--, 1 vol. (1827-63 missing), at meeting-house. Minutes of
First-day School, 1895-1927, 3 vols., at meeting-house, and 1927--, 1 vol.,
in custody of school superintendent, Mrs. Howard Heston, 309 N. Matlack
Street, West Chester. Records of Friends Burial Company, 1871--, 2 vols.
(1827-70 missing), in custody of Miss Mary A. Sharpless, 22 Dean Street,
West Chester. Original Deeds (not recorded): 1811; 1812; December 15,
1813; May 13, 1837; August 21, 1841, at meeting-house. Chester County
Deed Book, G-2, p. 231.

222. CHESTER MONTHLY MEETING, 1827--. Twenty-fourth and Chestnut
      Street, Chester, Delaware County.
Continued as a Hicksite meeting in 1827 by Concord Quarterly Meeting (entry 218), after division of the original Chester Monthly Meeting (entry
137). In 1827 this meeting retained the stone meeting-house and burial
grounds of Providence Preparative Meeting (entry 140), and the Blue Hill,
Middletown, Springfield, and Providence schools. This meeting continued
to meet in the Providence Meeting-house until 1934; since that date to the
present, meetings have been held in the meeting-house of Chester Preparative Meeting, Orthodox (entry 139). In 1934, Chester Monthly Meeting was
divided into two monthly meetings; Chester Monthly Meeting and Providence
United Monthly Meeting (entry 332). At the same time, Chester Preparative
Meeting (entry 223) was laid down and its members transferred to Chester
Monthly Meeting. The red brick meeting-house belonging to origianl Chester Preparative Meeting was acquired by this meeting. However, no meetings have been held here since 1926. At the present time it is rented to
a non-Quaker sect, the Full Gospel Tabernacle. In 1934 Chester Monthly
Meeting conveyed the meeting-house and burial ground on Providence Road
and Baltimore Pike, Media, to Providence Monthly Meeting. The present
clerk is Newlin P. Palmer, Merchant's Trust Building, Eighth Street and
Edgemont Avenue, Chester.

See: Michener, op. cit., pp. 65, 66.

Minutes of Men's Meetings, 1827-91, 2 vols.; Minutes of Women's Meeting, 1827-91, 3 vols.; Minutes of Joint Meetings, 1891-1926, 3 vols. in
custody of Charles Palmer, Eighth Street and Edgemont Avenue, Chester and
1926-34, 1 vol., at PSC-Hi, and 1934--, 1 vol., in custody of clerk (this
volume contains minutes of Joint Meetings of Chester Preparative Meeting,
1932-34). Registers of Births, Deaths, Removals, Members, 1827 to about
1885, 1 vol. (exact date could not be determined), in custody of Charles
Palmer, and 1885-1934, 2 vols., at PSC-Hi, and 1934--, 1 vol., in custody
of recorder, Miss Dora Gilbert, 103 West Twenty-fourth Street, Chester.
Marriage Certificates, 1828-1916, 1 vol., at PSC-Hi, and 1916-34, recorded in book which is now being used by Providence Monthly Meeting (1934--,
is included in the volume of births, deaths, removals, and members, 1934--).
Financial Records, 1934--, 1 vol. (1827-1933 missing), in custody of
Charles Palmer. Minutes of Friends' Select School, 1891-1920, 2 vols.
(1898-1911 missing); Attendance and Committee Minutes of First-day School,

1934--, 1 vol., in custody of Mrs. Arletta Palmer, 100 Delaware Avenue, Ridley Park.

223. CHESTER PREPARATIVE MEETING, 1827-1934. Twenty-fourth and
      Chestnut Streets, Chester, Delaware County.
Continued as a Hicksite meeting in 1827 by Chester Monthly Meeting (entry
222), after the division of the original Chester Preparative Meeting (entry 139). At the time of the Separation in 1827 this meeting retained
the one-story red brick meeting-house erected in 1736, located on the west
side of Market Street below Third Street, and the 104 perches of burial
ground on the west side of Edgmont Avenue. In 1833 the meeting purchased
an additional 25 perches of ground adjoining the original burial ground.
The meeting-house on Market Street below Third Street was used until 1926.
From 1926-34 the meeting used the meeting-house of Chester Preparative
Meeting, Orthodox, Twenty-fourth and Chestnut Streets. When the meeting
was laid down in 1934 by Chester Monthly Meeting the meeting-house erected
in 1736 and the burial ground were transferred to the care of Chester
Monthly Meeting. At the present time, the meeting-house is rented to the
Full Gospel Tabernacle.

See: Michener, op. cit., pp. 65, 66.

Minutes of Men's Meetings, 1827-55, 1 vol. (1855-76 missing); Minutes
of Women's Meetings, 1827-76, 1 vol., in custody of Charles Palmer, Eighth
Street and Edgemont Avenue, Chester. Minutes of Joint Meetings, 1876-1917,
4 vols., in custody of Charles Palmer and 1917-28, 1 vol., in custody of
Mrs. Arletta Palmer, 100 Delaware Avenue, Ridley Park, and 1928-34, 1 vol.
in custody of Newlin P. Palmer, 304 Houston Street. Burial Records, 1919-
34, 1 vol. (1827-1918 missing), in custody of Miss Katherine Stevenson,
2600 Waterville Road. Registers are in the records of the Chester Monthly
Meeting. Financial Records, 1892-1934, 2 vols. (1827-92 missing), in custody of Charles Palmer. Minute Books of Teachers' First-day School, 1871-
1910, 3 vols., in custody of Charles Palmer, and 1910-34 1 vol., in custody of Arletta Palmer.

224. SPRINGFIELD PREPARATIVE MEETING, 1827-49. Springfield Twp.,
      Delaware County.
Continued as a Hicksite meeting in 1827 by Chester Monthly Meeting (entry
222) after division of the original Springfield Preparative Meeting (entry
138). Because this meeting was in existence for only a short time and
during its existence it was composed of a few members who did not have the
means to erect a meeting-house, the history is very obscure. The minutes
of Chester Monthly Meeting, held January 22, 1849, give evidence of the
difficult circumstances under which this meeting existed: "A request
from Springfield Preparative Meeting to lay down both it and the meeting
for worship there held-- having been submitted to this meeting. On considering the discouragements and difficulties under which they think themselves unable longer to keep up said meetings, we conclude to grant their
request." The meeting was therefore laid down January 22, 1849 by Chester
Monthly Meeting.

No records for the meeting are available, and none appear to be in
existence at the present time.

225. CONCORD MONTHLY MEETING, 1827-1932. Concord and Thornton Roads
      Concordville, Delaware County.
Continued as a Hicksite meeting in 1827 by Concord Quarterly Meeting (en-

try 218), after division of the original Concord Monthly Meeting (entry 143). The Hicksite Friends retained the two-story red brick building which was erected in 1788. The Orthodox Friends also worshiped in the same building, but on different days, until 1834, at which time they withdrew to their own newly erected meeting-house. In 1932 this meeting and Concord Monthly Meeting (Orthodox) began holding joint meetings but each monthly meeting held separate meetings for business until given official recognition in 1937 as the Concord United Monthly Meeting (entry 331) by Concord Quarterly Meeting, Hicksite (entry 218) and Concord Quarterly Meeting, Orthodox (entry 136). From 1932-35 meetings were held alternately in the Concord Orthodox and Hicksite meeting-houses and in 1936 the meetings were discontinued at the Orthodox meeting-house. The present clerk is Bertha M. S. Webster, Box 63, Cheyney.

See: Bowden, op. cit., II, 248; Michener, op. cit., pp. 67, 68; Matlack, op. cit., I, 282-285.

Minutes of Men's Meetings, 1824-75, 1 vol.; Minutes of Women's Meetings, 1813-77, 2 vols.; Minutes of Joint Meetings, 1876-1932, 2 vols., at PSC-Hi. Registers of Births and Deaths, 1827-1916, 1 vol. at PSC-Hi, and 1916-32, recorded in the 1827--, membership book, in custody of recorder, Thompson Palmer, Baltimore Pike, Concordville. Membership Book, 1827-32, 1 vol., in custody of Thompson Palmer. Marriage Records, 1809-1932, 1 vol., at PSC-Hi. Certificates of Removal, 1827-1913, 2 vols., 1913-32, loose forms in envelope, at PSC-Hi. Burial Records, 1813-1916, 1 vol., in custody of Thompson Palmer, and 1916-32, 1 vol., in custody of Gilbert Schraeder. Financial Records, 1892-1916, 1 vol. (1827-92 missing), and in custody of Thompson Palmer, and 1916-32, 2 vols., in custody of Gilbert Schraeder, Concord Road, Ward. Delaware County Deed Books, vol.-T. p. 508; vol. 35, p. 159; vol. K-2, p. 694; vol. 117, p. 176.

226. CHICHESTER PREPARATIVE MEETING, 1827-1914. Meeting-House Road 1/4 mile North of Boothwyn, Upper Chichester Twp., Delaware County.

Continued as a Hicksite meeting in 1827 by Concord Monthly Meeting (entry 225), after division of the original Chichester Preparative Meeting (entry 145). This meeting retained the one-story gray stone meeting-house, erected in 1769, and the 2-acre burial ground. In 1914 the meeting was laid down by Concord Monthly Meeting. The property and finances were taken over by Concord Monthly Meeting, and the members were attached to the same meeting. Occasional meetings are held.

See: Michener, op. cit., p. 68.

Minutes of Men's Meetings, 1827-1914 missing; Minutes of Women's Meetings, 1828-99, 3 vol. (1831-42, 1859-72 missing), at PSC-Hi. Registers are in the record books of the Concord Monthly Meeting. Financial Records, 1781-1875, 1 vol. (1875-92 missing), at PSC-Hi, and 1892-1908, 1 vol., in custody of Thompson Palmer, Baltimore Pike, Concordville, and 1908-14, 1 vol., in custody of Gilbert Schraeder, Concord Road, Ward. Burial Records, 1833-1901, 1 vol. (1827-83 missing), in custody of Thompsom Palmer, and 1901--, 1 vol., in custody of Gilbert Schraeder.

227. CONCORD PREPARATIVE MEETING, 1827-1914. Southeast intersection of Chester, Concord, and Thornton Roads, Concordville, Delaware County.

Continued as a Hicksite meeting in 1827 by Concord Monthly Meeting (entry

225), after the division of the original Concord Preparative Meeting (entry 144). This meeting never had its own meeting-house; meetings were held in the meeting-house of Concord Monthly Meeting.

See: Michener, op. cit., p. 68.

Minutes of Men's Meetings, 1827-76, 2 vols.; Minutes of Women's Meetings, 1827-76, 2 vols., at Swarthmore College Library. Minutes of Joint Sessions, 1876-92 (included in minute book of men's meetings, which ends 1876), 1892-1914, 1 vol. at Swarthmore College Library. Registers are in the records of the Concord Monthly Meeting.

228. DARBY MONTHLY MEETING, 1827--. 1015 Main Street, Darby, Delaware County.
Continued as a Hicksite meeting in 1827 by Concord Quarterly Meeting (entry 218) after division of the original Darby Monthly Meeting (entry 148). This meeting retained the 4½-acre burial ground and the present two-story gray stone meeting-house, erected in 1805. The present clerk is Stanley G. Child, 3126 Midvale Avenue, Philadelphia.

See: Michener, op. cit., pp. 66, 67; Centennial Darby.

Minutes of Men's Meetings, 1807-91, 2 vols.; Minutes of Women's Meetings, 1827-91, 2 vols., in meeting-house. Minutes of Joint Meetings, 1891-1922, 1 vol., in meeting-house and 1922--, 1 vol., in custody of clerk. Register of Births and Deaths, 1670--, 3 vols; Register of Membership, 1827--, 2 vols.; Certificates of Removal, 1827--, 2 vols.; Certificate of Marriage, 1827--, 2 vols.; Burial Records, 1864--, 1 vol. (1827-63 missing); Treasurer's Account Book, 1827-49, 1 vol.; Women's Friends' Treasury Cash Book, 1832-94, 2 vols.; Treasurer's Account Book of the Graveyard Committee, 1864--, 1 vol. (1827-63 missing); First-day School Roll Book, 1871-96, 10 vols., in the meeting-house.

229. DARBY PREPARATIVE MEETING, 1827-98. 1015 Main Street, Darby, Delaware County.
Continued as a Hicksite meeting in 1827 by Darby Monthly Meeting (entry 228), after division of the original Darby Preparative Meeting (entry 149). Meetings for worship and business were held in the meeting-house of the Darby Monthly Meeting.

See: Michener, op. cit., p. 67; Centennial Darby.

Minutes of Men's Meetings, 1827-91 missing; Minutes of Women's Meetings, 1827-91, 1 vol.; Minutes of Joint Meetings, 1891-98, 1 vol., in meeting-house of the Darby Monthly Meeting. Registers are in the records of the Darby Monthly Meeting.

230. GOSHEN MONTHLY MEETING, 1827--. East Goshen and Willistown Twps., Chester County, and Newtown, Delaware County.
Continued as a Hicksite meeting in 1827 by Concord Quarterly Meeting (entry 218), after division of the original Goshen Monthly Meeting (entry 150). Until 1914 Goshen Monthly Meeting held its sessions at all the meeting-houses of the Preparative Meetings under its jurisdiction. Since then meetings have been held in January and October at Goshen Preparative (entry 231); in April at Newtown Preparative (entry 232); and in July at Willistown Preparative (entry 234) meeting-houses. From 1782 to 1827, Goshen Monthly meeting conducted a school. Application was made to

the Monthly meeting in 1836 for its approval to rent the schoolhouse to Willistown Township for the purpose of establishing a free school, but the meeting did not give its consent. In 1862 a second-story addition was built into the original structure. The following year a frame stable "large enough to hold six head of horse was erected at the back of the barn." Due to decreasing attendance the school was closed temporarily in 1867, but was reopened and classes continued until about 1889. Goshen Monthly Meeting sold the property in 1903 to Norris W. Harkins for $1,500. Both buildings are now used as dwellings, and are located on the east side of the road through Media to Chester. The present clerk is E. William Pyle, Berwyn.

See: Michener, op. cit., pp. 68, 69; Futhey and Cope, op. cit., p. 239; Woody, op. cit., pp. 130-135.

Minutes of Men's Meetings, 1827-89, 4 vols.; Minutes of Women's Meetings, 1827-89, 3 vols.; Minutes of Joint Meetings, 1889--, 5 vols., at Willistown meeting-house. Minutes of Ministers and Elders (now called Ministry and Counsel), 1827-71, 2 vols. (1871-98 missing), at the Willistown meeting-house, and 1898--, 1 vol., in custody of clerk, Miss Anna S. Barclay, Paoli. Registers of Births, Certificates of Removal, Certificates Received, Membership, Marriages, and deaths, 1827--, 6 vols., at the Willistown meeting-house. Financial Records, 1900--, 1 vol. (1827-99 missing), in custody of treasurer, Thomas D. Smedley, West Chester. Chester County Deed Book, vol. 51, C-3, pp. 52, 83.

231. GOSHEN PREPARATIVE MEETING, 1827-1939. Intersection of Chester and Frazer Roads, West Chester, Paoli Pike, East Goshen Twp., Chester County.

Continued as a Hicksite meeting in 1827 by Goshen Monthly Meeting (entry 230), after division of the original Goshen Preparative Meeting (entry 151). The graveyard plot acquired in 1708 and the stone meeting-house erected in 1736, just west of the present meeting-house, were retained by this meeting. Several additional plots were purchased for burial purposes; today, the cemetery covers one-half of the present property. The burial ground is enclosed on the northwestern side by a stone wall; on the southeastern side by a wire fence. During the Revolutionary War, after the Battle of the Clouds, which was fought nearby, some soldiers were buried in one corner of the graveyard. Both the Orthodox and Hicksite Friends met in the meeting-house until 1849, when the Orthodox Friends erected their own building. The present meeting-house, a one-story stone building, was erected in 1855. The Friends of this meeting were active in the Underground Railroad. Because of diminished membership the meeting was laid down in 1939.

See: Thomson, op. cit., pp. 746-751; Futhey and Cope, op. cit., pp. 53, 58, 59, 234-239, 764; Ashbridge, op. cit., pp. 11-51, 118, 119; Cope, Genealogy, pp. 24, 25, 134-136; Michener, op. cit., pp. 58, 59; Woody, op. cit., pp. 130-135; R. C. Smedley, History of the Underground Railroad in Chester County and the Neighboring Counties of Pennsylvania, p. 53; "Friends Reunion at Goshenville," West Chester Daily Local News, October 11, 1909; "Goshen Friends' Meeting," West Chester Daily Local News, January 11, 1930.

Minutes of Men's Meetings, 1827-50, 1 vol. (1851-81 missing), at Willistown meeting-house. Minutes of Joint Meetings, 1882--, 2 vols., in custody of E. William Pyle, Berwyn. Registers are in records of the Goshen

Monthly Meeting. Minutes of Goshen First-day School, 1876-1935, 6 vols. (1892-1908, 1916-31 missing); Minutes of Malvern First-day School, 1908-18, 2 vols.; Goshen First-day School Roll Book, 1926-31, 2 vols.; Malvern First-day School Roll Book, 1920-26, 1 vol., at the meeting-house. Financial Records, 1929--, 1 vol. (1827-1928 missing); Records of Burials, 1827--, 1 vol., in custody of treasurer, Jesse W. Cox, 203 Channing Avenue, Malvern. Chester County Deed Book, vol. 51, C-3, pp. 52, 83.

232. NEWTOWN PREPARATIVE MEETING, 1827--. Newtown and Paoli Roads, 3/4 mile west of West Chester Pike, Newtown Twps., Delaware County.

Continued as a Hicksite meeting in 1827 by Goshen Monthly Meeting (entry 230), after division of the original Newtown Preparative Meeting (entry 146). This meeting retained the two-story gray stone meeting-house and the 1 acre and 25 perches of burial ground. In 1881 an additional 242 square feet of ground, adjoining the original graveyard, was donated to the meeting.

Note: Since the contents of this volume were arranged, data has been received that Newtown Square Preparative Meeting was set up as Newtown Square Monthly Meeting in 1939, by a division of Goshen Monthly Meeting. The clerk is Charlotte B. Dutton, West Chester Pike, Newtown Square.

See: Michener, op. cit., p. 69.

Minutes of Men's Meetings, 1840-97, 2 vols. (1827-40 missing); Minutes of Women's Meetings, 1847-97, 2 vols. (1827-47 missing), at PSC-Hi. Minutes of Joint Meetings, 1897-1909, 1 vol., at PSC-Hi, and 1909-25, 1 vol., at Willistown meeting-house, and 1925--, 2 vols., in custody of the clerk of the monthly meeting, Mrs. Charlotte B. Dutton, West Chester Pike, Newtown Square. Registers are in the records of the Goshen Monthly Meeting. Burial Records, 1805--, 1 vol., in custody of Horace M. Lewis. Treasurers' Account Book, 1912--, 1 vol. (1827-1912 missing), in custody of treasurer, Horace M. Lewis, West Chester Pike, Newtown Square.

233. WHITELAND PREPARATIVE MEETING, 1827-47. One-eighth mile south of Lincoln Highway between Malvern and Frazer, East Whiteland Twp., Chester County.

Continued as a Hicksite meeting in 1827 by Goshen Monthly Meeting (entry 230) after division of the original Whiteland Preparative Meeting (entry 153). At the time of the Separation, the Orthodox and Hicksite Friends continued to hold meetings together until 1828, when the Orthodox Friends changed the time of holding their meeting. The building was a one-story stone structure which adjoined a burial plot. After the Separation the Orthodox Friends retained control of the property. A minute, on July 27, 1831, records, "the Friends at Whiteland did not see the way open for them to hold their meeting separate at present." Both branches of Friends continued to use the same building until the meeting was laid down. In 1842 this meeting requested that it be attached to Goshen Preparative Meeting (entry 231), as an indulged meeting, but no action was taken on the request until it was made again in 1843 and was then approved by Goshen Monthly Meeting. The meeting was officially laid down in 1847.

See: Michener, op. cit., p. 70; Futhey and Cope, op. cit., p. 242; Heathcote, op. cit., p. 341; Thomson, op. cit., pp. 754, 755; "A Landmark Gone," West Chester Daily Local News, August 28, 1895.

Unable to locate minutes of the Whiteland Preparative Meeting. Registers are incorporated in the records of the Goshen Monthly Meeting.

234. WILLISTOWN PREPARATIVE MEETING, 1827-1939. Intersection of
    Rocky and Penn Hotel Roads, Willistown, Chester County.
Continued as a Hicksite meeting in 1827 by Goshen Monthly Meeting (entry
230) after division of the original Willistown Preparative Meeting (entry
152). This meeting retained the gray stone meeting-house, erected in
1798, which is still in use today; the adjoining cemetery, acquired in
1794; and the schoolhouse erected in 1816 across the road from the meeting-house. From 1896-1910 circular meetings were held at Willistown in
common with other meetings of Concord Quarterly Meeting. In 1928 an addition to the meeting-house was built. This was used as a classroom in
the First-day school. At the present time the school is held from May to
December. In 1930, additional land for the cemetery was acquired. The
cemetery now contains 3 acres. In 1938 a one-story white frame house was
erected on the meeting grounds to be used as a caretaker's home. The
meeting was laid down in 1939 and at the same time was set up as Willistown Monthly Meeting (entry 239).

    See: Cope, Genealogy, pp. 168-171; Futhey and Cope, op. cit., p. 241;
Smedley, R. C., op. cit., pp. 33, 135, 136, 286, 301, 304, 338, 343, 346;
Michener, op. cit., pp. 69, 70; Woody, op. cit., pp. 130-135; Thomson, op.
cit., p. 366; "Willistown Friends' Meeting-house," West Chester Daily
Local News, August 22, 1873; "A Visit to the Willistown Friends Meeting-
House," West Chester Daily Local News, January 27, 1875.

235. SWARTHMORE MONTHLY MEETING, 1863--. Swarthmore College Grounds,
    Swarthmore, Delaware County.
Set up in 1893 as a monthly meeting by Concord Quarterly Meeting (entry
218), after having functioned as a college meeting exclusively for Swarthmore College members since 1863. From 1863-1881 meetings were held in the
assembly hall of Swarthmore College. In 1881 the present one-story gray
stone meeting-house was erected by the college. The present clerk is
Eleanor Stabler Clarke, Whittier House, Swarthmore.

    See: Ellen H. E. Price, History of Swarthmore Meeting (manuscript
deposited in meeting-house).

    Minutes of Joint Meetings, 1893-1929, 2 vols., 1924-30, 1 loose-leaf
vol., at meeting-house, and 1930--, 1 vol., in custody of clerk. Minutes
of Ministry and Counsel (formerly known as Ministers and Elders), 1895-
1921, 1 vol. (1893-95 missing), at meeting-house; 1930--, 1 vol. (1921-
30 missing), in custody of Alice H. Paxson, 311 Cedar Lane, Swarthmore.
Register of Membership Records (containing births, deaths, marriages, and
removals), 1893--, 1 vol., in custody of recorder, Albert Buffington, Sproul
Road, Swarthmore. Marriage Certificates, 1893--, 1 file box; Certificates
of Removal, 1893--, 1 file box; Membership Record, 1893--, 1 file box, in
custody of Albert Buffington. Financial Records, 1921--, 1 vol. (1893-
1920 missing), in custody of Emma P. Walter, Swarthmore Apartments, Swarthmore.

236. LANSDOWNE MONTHLY MEETING, 1898--. Stratford and Owen Avenues,
    Lansdowne, Delaware County.
Set up in 1901 by Concord Quarterly Meeting (entry 218), after having
functioned as an independent meeting for worship from 1898-1901. Meetings
were first held in the homes of various members from 1898-1901 and at
Barker's Hall, Lansdowne Avenue and Baltimore Pike, from 1901-03. In
1903 the present two-story gray stone meeting-house was erected. The
present clerk is Boyd M. Trescott, 341 Upland Way, Drexel Hill.

See: Boyd M. Trescott, History of Lansdowne Monthly Meeting (manuscript at Swarthmore College Library).

Minutes of Joint Meetings, 1901-27, 2 vols., at Swarthmore College Library and 1927--, 1 vol., in custody of clerk. Register of Births, Marriages, Membership, and Deaths, 1901--, 1 vol., in custody of recorder, Certificates of Removal, 1901--, in envelope in custody of recorder. Financial Records, 1919--, 1 vol. (1901-17 missing) in custody of Percival M. Fogg, 112 Glenco Road, Stonehurst, Upper Darby. Minutes of First-day School, 1898-1920, 5 vols. (1904-9 missing); First-day School Attendance Records, 1904-15, 2 vols., at PSC-Hi.

PROVIDENCE (UNITED) MONTHLY MEETING (entry 332).

237. MIDDLETOWN PREPARATIVE MEETING, 1827--. Middletown (Edgemont) Road, North of Yearly's Mill Road, Delaware County.
Continued as a Hicksite meeting in 1827 by Chester Monthly Meeting (entry 222), after division of the original Middletown Preparative Meeting (entry 160). This meeting retained the one-story gray stone and white plaster meeting-house erected in 1770 on a portion of the 2 3/4 acres of ground, donated by Joshua·Hastings. The meeting also retained the burial ground adjoining the meeting-house. In 1934 the meeting was transferred to the care of Providence United Monthly Meeting (entry 332). The membership is very small at the present time and meetings are held irregularly in the same meeting-house.

See: Bowden, op. cit., II. 248; Michener, op. cit., p. 68; Ashmead, op. cit., p. 561.

Minutes of Men's Meetings (1827-1921, supposed to be in the custody of treasurer, Miss M. Darlington, Darlington, but not available). Women's Minutes, 1827-1921, are in the custody of treasurer, Miss M. Darlington. Minutes of Joint Meetings, 1921--, 1 vol., in custody of Miss Laura Broomall, Markham Road, Glen Mills. Registers, 1827-1934, are in the records of the Chester Monthly Meeting, and 1934--, are in the records of the Providence Monthly Meeting. Financial records are in the custody of the treasurer (dates of the years covered by these records are unknown). Delaware County Deed Book, vol., D. p. 591.

238. PROVIDENCE PREPARATIVE MEETING, 1827--. Providence Road near Baltimore Pike, Media, Delaware County.
Continued as a Hicksite meeting in 1827 by Chester Monthly Meeting (entry 222) after division of the original Providence Preparative Meeting (entry 140). From 1827 to date this meeting has continued to worship in the stone meeting-house, Providence Road near Baltimore Pike. The meeting-house belonged to Chester Monthly Meeting until 1934, when Chester Monthly Meeting was divided into Providence United Monthly Meeting (entry 332) and Chester Monthly Meeting. At that time the meeting-house was conveyed to Providence United Monthly Meeting. In 1885 Providence Preparative Meeting established a day school in a rented building at Gayley and Washington Streets. The school was continued until 1895, when this meeting transferred it to the care of Chester Monthly Meeting. In 1934 Providence Preparative was transferred to Providence Monthly Meeting.

See: Michener, op. cit., p. 66.

Minutes of Men's Meetings, 1812-66, 2 vols., at PSC-Hi, and 1830-91, 4 vols.; Minutes of Women's Meetings (1827-39 missing), 1839-91, 2 vols., in custody of Charles Palmer, Eighth Street and Edgemont Avenue, Chester. Minutes of Joint Meetings, 1891-1908, 1 vol., in custody of Charles Palmer, and 1908-23, 1 vol., in custody of Helen Bacon, Possum Hollow Road, Wallingford, and 1924-39, 1 vol., in custody of Miss Amy Way, 542 South Orange Street. Registers, 1827-1934, are in records of Chester Monthly Meeting, and 1934--, are in records of Providence Monthly Meeting. Financial Records 1920--, 1 vol. (1827-1920 missing), in custody of Charles Way. Day School Records, 1885-95, 2 vols., in custody of Charles Palmer.

239. WILLISTOWN MONTHLY MEETING, 1939--. Rocky Hill and White Horse Roads, Willistown Twp., Chester County.
The Willistown Monthly Meeting was set up November 8, 1939 by Concord Quarterly Meeting (entry 218), after having functioned as the Willistown Preparative Meeting (entry 234) since 1827. When Willistown Monthly Meeting was set up Willistown Preparative Meeting was laid down and the meeting-house and other property were transferred to the newly established monthly meeting. The present clerk is Anna S. Bartram, Paoli.

See: "Concord Quarterly Meeting," Philadelphia Friends Intelligencer, November 11, 1939.

Minutes of Monthly Meeting, 1939--, 1 vol.;Minutes of Ministry and Counsel, 1939--, 1 vol., in custody of clerk. Register of Membership, 1939--, 1 vol.; Certificates of Marriages, 1939--, 1 vol., in custody of recorder, M. Ella Smedley, West Chester. Financial Records, 1939--, 1 vol., in custody of treasurer, Alice C. Bartram, Malvern.

Component Meetings

(See: Explanatory Note 3)

	Date established	Entry number
CENTER MONTHLY MEETING	1827	366
FALLOWFIELD MONTHLY MEETING (ERCILDOWN)	1827	241
Doe Run Preparative Meeting (Derry)	1827	242
Fallowfield Preparative Meeting	1827	243
Oxford Indulged Meeting (Homeville)	1828	258
Oxford Preparative Meeting (Homeville)	1839	258
KENNETT MONTHLY MEETING	1827	244
Kennett Preparative Meeting	1827	245
Marlboro Preparative Meeting		
(Marlboro-Unionville)	1827	246
Kennett Square Preparative Meeting	1827	247
Kennett Square Indulged Meeting	1930	247
Unionville Indulged Meeting	1845	248
Unionville Preparative Meeting		
(Marlboro-Unionville)	1919	246
Unionville Indulged Meeting	1931	249
LONDON GROVE MONTHLY MEETING	1827	250
London Grove Preparative Meeting	1827	251
Unionville Indulged Meeting	1845	249
NEW GARDEN MONTHLY MEETING	1827	252
New Garden Preparative Meeting	1827	253
West Grove Preparative Meeting		
(New West Grove)	1827	260
Spencers Indulged Meeting	1827	254
Pennsgrove Indulged Meeting	1827	257
Pennsgrove Preparative Meeting	1829	257
Avondale Indulged Meeting	1874	255
PENNSGROVE MONTHLY MEETING	1842	256
Pennsgrove Preparative Meeting	1829	257
Oxford Preparative Meeting (Homeville)	1839	379
Homeville Preparative Meeting (Oxford)	1866	258
Oxford Indulged Meeting	1876	379
WEST GROVE MONTHLY MEETING	1919	259
West Grove Preparative Meeting		
(New West Grove)	1827	260

240. WESTERN QUARTERLY MEETING, 1827--. Kennett Twp., London Grove
Twp., London T p., Chester County.
Continued as a Hicksite meeting in 1827 by Philadelphia Yearly Meeting
(entry 173), after division of the original Western Quarterly Meeting (en-
try 71). At the present time Western Quarterly Meeting convenes in First
month at the Kennett Monthly Meeting-house (entry 244) and in Fourth,
Seventh, and Tenth Months at London Grove. The clerk is Frank M. Bartram,
Kennett Square.

See: Michener, op. cit., pp. 92, 93.

Minutes of Men's Meetings, 1827-92, 2 vols.; Minutes of Women's Meetings, 1827-97, 3 vols., at PSC-Hi. Minutes of Joint Meetings, 1892-1934,
2 vols., in meeting-house, and 1934--, 1 vol., in custody of clerk. Minutes of Ministry and Counsel (formerly known as Ministers and Elders),
1827-77, 1 vol., at PSC-Hi, and 1878--, 1 vol., in custody of clerk, Miss
Helen Corson, Avondale. Financial Records, 1933--, 1 vol. (1827-1932
missing), in custody of treasurer, Joel Walton, Kennett Square.

241. FALLOWFIELD MONTHLY MEETING, 1827--. Route #82, Ercildoun,
Chester County.
Continued as a Hicksite meeting in 1827 by Western Quarterly Meeting (entry 240), after division of the original Fallowfield Monthly Meeting (entry 87). Meetings from 1827-34 were held in the meeting-house of Fallowfield Preparative Meeting (entry 243). From 1834-1913 meetings were held
alternately in the meeting-houses of Fallowfield Preparative Meeting and
Doe Run Preparative Meeting (entry 242); from 1913--, meetings were held
exclusively in the meeting-house of Fallowfield Preparative Meeting. The
present clerk is Mary A. Maule, R. D. 3, Coatesville.

See: Michener, op. cit., pp. 103, 104; Futhey and Cope, op. cit., p.
242; John Hayes, Old Quaker Meeting Houses, pp. 63, 64; Heathcote, op.
cit., p. 340.

Minutes of Men's Meetings, 1811-93, 3 vols.; Minutes of Women's Meetings, 1811-93, 2 vols., at PSC-Hi. Minutes of Joint Meetings, 1907--,
2 vols. (1893-1906 missing), in custody of clerk. Minutes of Ministers
and Elders, 1852--, 2 vols. (1827-52 missing), in custody of clerk, Howard
Hampton, Doe Run. Registers of Births and Deaths, 1811--, 2 vols.; Marriages, 1811--, 2 vols.; Marriages, 1811--, 1 vol.; Certificates of Application and Removal, 1811--, 2 vols., in custody of treasurer, Jessie
Webster, Ercildoun. Financial Records, 1903--, 1 vol. (1827-1903 missing),
in custody of treasurer, George C. Maule, Coatesville. Burial Ground
Funds, 1925--, 1 vol. (1811-1925 missing), in custody of John Kendig,
Ercildoun. Chester County Deed Books, A-2, p. 77; B-11, vol. 249, p. 97;
L-5, vol. 108, p. 443; Q-4, vol. 88, p. 295; W-2, p. 94; vol. 72, p. 326.

242. DOE RUN PREPARATIVE MEETING (also known as Derry Meeting),
1827--. Intersection of roads #15053 and #15055, Londonderry
Twp., Chester County.
Continued as a Hicksite meeting in 1827 by Fallowfield Monthly Meeting
(entry 241). Previously functioned as the original Doe Run Preparative
Meeting (entry 88). The red brick meeting-house which had been erected
in 1808 and the burial ground were retained by the Hicksite Friends. In
1883 the old meeting-house was razed and the present red brick meeting-
house was erected on the site of the former schoolhouse of the original
London Grove Monthly Meeting (entry 83). Some of the material of the

first meeting-house was used in the construction of the present one. Since 1930 no regular meetings have been _old in the meeting-house, The preparative meeting is held only once a year in the homes of members.

See: Futhey and Cope, op. cit., p. 68; Michener, op. cit., p. 105; Matlack, op. cit., II, 733, 735, 788, 789; Heathcote, op. cit., p. 341.

Minutes of Men's Meetings, 1822-89, 2 vols. (1834-82 missing), at PSC-Hi, and 1890-93 incorporated in the volume of Minutes of Joint Meetings, 1893-95. Minutes of Women's Meetings, 1887-93, 1 vol. (1827-86 missing), at PSC-Hi. Minutes of Joint Meetings, 1893-95, 1 vol. (1895-1903 missing), in the London Grove meeting-house, and 1903--, 2 vols., in custody of Mary A. Maule, Gum Tree, Route #3, Coatesville. Register books are in the records books of the Fallowfield Monthly Meeting. Financial Records, 1913--, 2 vols. (1827-1912 missing), in custody of treasurer, Anna Hood, R. D. #3, Coatesville.

243. FALLOWFIELD PREPARATIVE MEETING, 1827-1936. Ercildoun Village, East Fallowfield Twp., Chester County.
Continued as a Hicksite meeting in 1827 by Fallowfield Monthly Meeting (entry 241), after division of the original Fallowfield Preparative Meeting (entry 85). At the time of the Separation in 1827, this meeting retained the one-story plastered stone building, erected in 1801, and 2½ acres of ground, of which 1½ acres were used as a burial ground. There is an active First-day school at Fallowfield which started about 1870, but at the present time it is under Fallowfield Monthly Meeting. Because the business of the preparative and monthly meetings were identical, Fallowfield Preparative Meeting was laid down January 9, 1936 by Fallowfield Monthly Meeting.

See: Michener, op. cit., pp. 103, 104; Heathcote, op. cit., p. 340; Hayes, op. cit., pp. 63, 64; Matlack, op. cit., pp. 735, 741, 789, 790; Futhey and Cope, op. cit., p. 242; "Fallowfield Township History," West Chester, Village Record, September 25, 1889.

Minutes of Men's Meetings, 1853-71, 1 vol. (1827-53, 1871-93 missing); Minutes of Women's Meetings, 1823-93, 3 vols.; Minutes of Joint Meetings, 1905-36, 1 vol. (discontinued in 1936), at PSC-Hi. Registers are in the records of the Fallowfield Monthly Meeting. Minutes of First-day School, 1873-1929, 7 vols. (1870-73 missing), in custody of Mary A. Maule, and 1929--, 2 vols., in custody of secretary, Donald Sullivan, Towerville. Minutes of the First-day School, 1893-1935, 7 vols. (1870-93 missing), at PSC-Hi, and 1935--, in custody of superintendent, Mary A. Maule, Coatesville. Chester County Deed Books, Z-3, vol. 72, p. 326; V-4, vol. 93, p. 139; V-5, vol. 118, p. 402; N-11, vol. 260, p. 389.

244. KENNETT MONTHLY MEETING, 1827--. East State Street, Kennett Square, Chester County.
Continued as a Hicksite meeting in 1827 by Western Quarterly Meeting (entry 240), after division of the original Kennett Monthly Meeting (entry 79). Kennett Monthly Meeting convenes alternately at the meeting-house of Kennett Square Preparative Meeting (entry 247), Marlboro Preparative Meeting (entry 246), and Unionville Indulged Meeting (entry 248). In 1875, Samuel Martin, a member of Kennett Square Preparative Meeting, purchased about an acre of ground from his meeting and established a school known as the Martin Academy. When Samuel Martin died in 1880, this property was willed to Kennett Monthly Meeting, to be used for educational

purposes. The school was then supervised by the monthly meeting, which immediately appointed trustees to conduct the school and appoint teachers. A yearly report was given to Kennett Monthly Meeting. In 1882 the subject of purchasing additional land from Kennett Square Preparative Meeting for the better accommodation to the Martin Academy was introduced. Under the monthly meeting, the first principal of Martin Academy was Lewis A. Brosius, and the first assistant teacher was Emma Way. In 1890, the trustees confided the management of the school to the principal, then J. Henry Painter, to operate the school at his own risk and cost, but at all times subject to the approval of the trustees. On August 10, 1892 Kennett Monthly Meeting purchased 13,877 square feet for the sum of $200 from Kennett Square Preparative Meeting for the enlargement of Martin Academy. In 1872 Kennett Preparative Meeting, by virtue of a special Act of the Assembly, was given authority to sell the real estate. In 1893, when J. Henry Painter, relinquished his contract, the school reverted to the control of the trustees, under whose supervision it continued until 1910. The building was then rented to the public school system of Kennett Square for several years. After this, the school was unoccupied until 1921 when the building and ground was sold to George B. Scarlett of Kennett Square. At this time it was converted into an apartment house. The building is a three-story red brick structure, east of the meeting-house. The present clerk is Elma Walker, 212 Marshall Street, Kennett Square.

See: Futhey and Cope, op. cit., pp. 230-232; Thomson, op. cit., p. 747.

Minutes of Men's Meetings, 1822-97, 3 vols.; Minutes of Women's Meetings, 1827-93, 4 vols., at PSC-Hi. Minutes of Joint Meeting, 1893-97, are in the minutes of men's meetings ending 1897, and 1898--, 3 vols., in custody of the clerk. Registers of Births and Deaths, 1825-98, 1 vol.; Certificates of Removal, 1767-1875, 1 vol., at PSC-Hi. Register of Marriages, 1692-1895, 1 vol., in the London Grove meeting-house. Certificates of Marriage, 1821--, 1 vol., in custody of recorder, Miss Ruth Yeatman, 320 West State Street, Kennett Square. Register of Members (made in 1851), 1 vol., at PSC-Hi. Births, Deaths, Membership, and Removal, 1895--, 3 vols., in the London Grove meeting-house, current volume in the custody of recorder, Miss Ruth Yeatman. Chester County Deed Books, X-2, vol. 46, p. 523; H-3, vol. 56, p. 402; Y-3, vol. 71, p. 204; E-4, vol. 77, p. 142; E-4, vol. 77, p. 143; Z-4, vol. 97, p. 6; X-7, vol. 170, p. 327.

245. KENNETT PREPARATIVE MEETING, 1827--. Kennett Twp., Route #1,
     1/2 mile east of Hamorton, Chester County.
Continued as a Hicksite meeting in 1827 by Kennett Monthly Meeting (entry 244), after division of the original Kennett Preparative meeting (entry 80). At the time of Separation the Hicksite meeting retained the two-story white stone building, erected in 1710, and 4 acres of ground adjoining the meeting-house with a burial ground thereon. During the years 1850-54 this meeting was much disturbed and weakened by the dissension which resulted in the formation of the Progressive Friends at Longwood (entry 311). From 1904-13 Kennett Preparative Meeting did not function as a preparative meeting, although it was not officially laid down. Since the period, however, the preparative meetings have been revived and are held at the call of the clerk of meeting.

See: Futhey and Cope, op. cit., pp. 236-302; Heathcote, op. cit., p. 339; Thomson, op. cit., p. 749; Michener, op. cit., p. 96; Matlack, op. cit., II, 768-771; Myers, Immigration, p. 126; "Old Kennett Meeting House,"

Philadelphia Friends Intelligencer, August 20, 1910;"... Kennett Reopened,"
Philadelphia Friends Intelligencer, September 3, 1910. "Old Kennett's
Bi-Centennial," Philadelphia Friends Intelligencer, October 1, 1910; "Ken-
nett Meeting One Hundred Years Ago," Philadelphia Friends Intelligencer,
October 8, 1910; "Kennett Meeting of Friends," West Chester Daily Local
News, February 2, 1891; "Friendly Worship For Two Hundred Years," West
Chester Daily Local News, September 29, 1910; "Old Kennett Friends," West
Chester Daily Local News, January 25, 1928.

Minutes of Men's Meetings and Minutes of Women's Meetings, (1827-79
missing). Minutes of Joint Meetings, 1879--, 1 vol., in custody of clerk,
Edward Darlington, Chadds Ford. Registers are in the records of the Kennett Monthly Meeting. Financial Records, 1874--, 1 vol. (1827-74 missing),
in custody of Florence Passmore, Mendenhall. Minutes of First-day School,
1930--, 2 vols., in custody of secretary, Lydia Passmore, Mendenhall.
Chester County Deed Books, G-2, vol. 31, p. 280; X-2, vol. 46, p. 98.

246. MARLBORO PREPARATIVE MEETING, 1827--. Marlboro, East Marlboro
        Twp., Chester County.
Continued as a Hicksite meeting in 1827 by Kennett Monthly Meeting (entry
244), after division of the original Marlboro Preparative Meeting (entry
81). At the time of Separation in 1827, this meeting retained the red
brick meeting-house erected in 1801 and the 1-acre burial ground. In 1828
an additional 6¼ adjoining land was purchased. A schoolhouse and a dwelling for the schoolmaster were erected in 1829. The dwelling was usually
rented and the income applied to the school funds. This school proving
inadequate in 1838, a new schoolhouse was erected and the old school was
razed. The school was closed in 1861 and the schoolhouse was rented to
the Marlboro Township School Board until 1890. When the school was closed,
one room in the east end of the meeting-house was equipped as a school
room. A number of members, who had withdrawn to join the Longwood Meeting of Progressive Friends (entry 311), were readmitted in 1874-75, upon
application to rejoin the meeting. In 1917 the school funds were transferred to Marlboro Preparative Meeting. According to the Minutes of Western Quarterly Meeting (entry 240) of April 22, 1919, "Marlboro Preparative
Meeting is henceforth to be drawn as the Marlboro Unionville Preparative
Meeting. Meetings are to be held alternately in the meeting-house of
Marlboro and Unionville." In 1925 the schoolhouse property was transferred to the newly incorporated Marlboro Preparative Meeting, which sold
it at that time to Leon Brown. In 1931 this meeting was laid down by
Kennett Monthly Meeting and set up as Marlboro Preparative Meeting and
Unionville Indulged Meeting.

See: Michener, op. cit., p. 96; Futhey and Cope, op. cit., p. 241;
Thomson, op. cit., p. 753; Hayes, op. cit., p. 35; Heathcote, op. cit.,
p. 340. Isaac Martin, "Fifty Years Ago", West Chester Daily Local News,
March 9, 1894; Isaac Martin, "Moore Reminiscenses," West Chester Daily
Local News, March 31, 1894; "Old Meeting House Opens Doors Again," West
Chester Daily Local News, May 6, 1931; "Friendly Story of Marlboro," West
Chester Daily Local News, August 28, 1931.

Minutes of Men's Meetings, 1802-83, 2 vols.; Minutes of Women's Meetings, 1802-65, 1 vol. (1866-83 missing), at PSC-Hi. Minutes of Joint Meetings, 1883-1912, 1 vol., at PSC-Hi., and 1913--, 1 vol., in custody of
clerk, Percy Barnard, Wawaset Road, Kennett Square. List of Members, 1827-
51, 1 vol., at PSC-Hi, and 1851-83, 1 vol., in London Grove meeting-house.
All other registers, 1827--, are in the records of the Kennett Monthly

Meeting. Financial Records of School Funds, 1804-29, 1 vol, (1829-57 missing), 1857-1909, 1 vol., at PSC-Hi, and 1909--, 1 vol., in custody of William Baily, Marlboro, Kennett Square. In 1926 the name of this fund was changed to Marlboro Preparative Meeting Funds. Burial Grounds Accounts, 1838-1912, 1 vol. (1827-38 missing), at PSC-Hi, and 1913--, 1 vol, in custody of William Baily. Chester County Deed Books, B-4, p. 590; B-17, vol. 399, p. 285; V-16, vol. 393, p. 204; Miscellaneous Docket, 12, p. 51, #4944.

247. **KENNETT SQUARE PREPARATIVE MEETING**, 1827---. East State Street, Kennett Square, Chester County.
Continued as a Hicksite Preparative meeting in 1827, by Kennett Monthly Meeting (entry 244), after division of the original Kennett Square Meeting (entry 82). At the time of Separation, this meeting retained the one-story stone meeting-house, erected in 1813, and the 3-acre meeting-house grounds, a small portion of which was used as a burial ground. The meeting also retained the number one school located 2½ miles west of Kennett meeting-house. In 1869 a First-day school was started by Samuel Martin. It was first held in the old meeting-house, and is a large flourishing school today. Meetings were held in the public school building at Broad and Cypress Streets, until 1873, when the present large red brick meeting-house was erected. In 1925 classrooms were added to the south of the building, with a kitchen and dining room beneath, and in 1928 the horse sheds were razed. This meeting was laid down in 1930, and was immediately re-established as Kennett Square Indulged Meeting. The number one school was sold to Pennock Mercer in 1857; in 1887, 11,840 square feet of ground were sold to Henry C. White; in 1892, Kennett Monthly Meeting purchased 13,877 square feet for the Martin Academy. In 1920 the remaining 64,625 square feet were deeded to the newly incorporated Kennett Monthly Meeting of Friends.

See: Heathcote, op. cit., p. 341. Thomson, op. cit., p. 754; Michener, op. cit., p. 96; Futhey and Cope, op. cit., p. 242; "Kennett Square Meeting One Hundred Years Ago," Philadelphia Friends Intelligencer, September 5, 1914; "Real Estate Matters," West Chester Daily Local News, May 6, 1892; "Kennett holds its Celebration," West Chester Daily Local News, September 12, 1914; "Hundreds Attend Kennett Meetings," West Chester Daily Local News, September 14, 1914; "Poems of Kennett," West Chester Daily Local News, September 15, 1914; "State Street Friends' Meeting," West Chester Daily Local News, December 7, 1929.

Minutes of Men's Meetings, 1871-91, 2 vols. (1827-70 missing); Minutes of Women's Meetings, 1863-92, 2 vols. (1827-62 missing); Minutes of Joint Meetings, 1892-1930, at the London Grove meeting-house. Registers are in the records of the Kennett Monthly Meeting. Minutes of First-day School, 1932-35, 1 vol. (1869-1932 missing) (no later records kept), in the Kennett Square meeting-house. Chester County Deed Books, G-2, vol. 31, p. 280; I-12, vol. 281, p. 17; K-8, vol. 182, p. 393; N-4, vol. 85, p. 180; N-4, vol. 85, p. 182; X-2, vol. 46, p. 98.

248. **UNIONVILLE INDULGED MEETING**, 1845--, Unionville Village, east Marlboro Twp., Chester County.
Established in 1845 by two committees appointed by Kennett Monthly Meeting (entry 244) and London Grove Meeting (entry 250), as is evidenced in a report the committees made to their respective meetings in 1845: "The committees of men and women Friends, respectively appointed by the monthly meetings of Kennett and London Grove report, that having generally met,

and had a full conference with the principal part of those members of the two monthly meetings which are embraced in the application, and after a time of solid consideration were much united in the belief that it would be right to grant the request; and that an indulged meeting, to be called Unionville Meeting, be accordingly held in the house already provided." The red brick meeting-house was erected in 1845. The 1/2-acre burial ground just east of the meeting-house was plotted on ground purchased in 1843. The burial ground has not been in use for the past 40 or 50 years. In a request made to the London Grove and Kennett Monthly Meeting in 1870, this meeting requested to be set up as a preparative meeting: ". . . We the undersigned members of Unionville Indulged Meeting of Friends, members in each part of your meetings, believing that the time has come to make application to our respective monthly meetings to confer on us the standing of an established meeting for worship, with the privilege of holding a preparative meeting to be called Unionville Preparative Meeting, and to be a branch of Kennett Monthly Meeting. All which we submit with the desire that you be directed by best wisdom." However, the request for a preparative meeting was refused, Kennett and London Grove Monthly Meetings giving the following reason: ". . . There was much expression of unity and feeling in favour of its establishment as a meeting for worship, but in consideration of the weakness which would thereby be entailed Marlboro Preparative Meeting and a like feeling might attend this branch when separated therefrom, way did not open in unity to recommend the holding a new preparative meeting at this time. . . . "The meeting was erratic during its existence from 1882 to 1931, having been discontinued and re-established several times during this period. At Kennett Monthly Meeting in March 1882 the clerks were instructed to inform Western Quarterly Meeting (entry 240) that the midweek meeting at Unionville had been discontinued subject to the approval of the quarterly meeting. In 1907 a minute of Kennett Monthly Meeting it is noted: "The Indulged Meeting at Unionville which was discontinued had been resumed." Further information from Kennett Monthly Meeting minutes, dated April 1919, notes: "The meetings at Marlboro and Unionville Preparative Meeting are to be held at Marlboro in the 5th, 7th and 9th months, and at Unionville in the other months." Due to diminishing membership, Marlboro-Unionville Preparative Meeting was laid down by Kennett Monthly Meeting, and this meeting reverted back to its present status of an indulged meeting. As noted in a Kennett Monthly Meeting minute for January 1931: "Marlboro-Unionville Preparative has been dissolved and they will be known by Marlboro Preparative Meeting (entry 246) and Unionville Indulged Meeting."

See: Michener, op. cit., p. 97; Matlack, op. cit., II, 782-784, 796, 797.

Registers are in the records of the Kennett and London Grove Monthly Meetings, 1845-1919, and 1931--, Kennett Monthly Meeting, 1919-31.

249. UNIONVILLE INDULGED MEETING, 1931--. Unionville Village, East Marlboro Twp., Chester County.
Set up in 1931 by Western Quarterly Meeting (entry 240), at the time of the dissolution of the Marlboro-Unionville Preparative Meeting (entry 246). When Marlboro Preparative Meeting (entry 246) and Uwchlan Indulged Meeting were combined, this meeting acquired ownership of the one-story red brick meeting-house and the adjoining 6 1/4 acres of land, part of which was used for a burial ground. These formerly belonging to Marlboro Preparative Meeting. This combined meeting also acquired the one-story, red brick meeting-house and 1/2-acre burial ground formerly belonging to Unionville In-

dulged Meeting when Unionville was added to the combination. Due to diminishing membership this combined preparative meeting was laid down by
Western Quarterly Meeting in 1931, and Marlboro and Unionville returned
to their former status, the first as a preparative and the second as an
indulged meeting. This fact is recorded in a minute of Kennett Monthly
Meeting, dated January 1931: "Marlboro-Unionville Preparative Meeting
has been dissolved and they will be known by Marlboro Preparative Meeting,
and Unionville Indulged Meeting." The property was then divided and held
by the individual meetings as before the information of this combined
meeting. Since 1931 Unionville Indulged Meeting has diminished in membership and at present only occasional meetings are held.

Minutes of Marlboro-Unionville Preparative Meeting, 1913-31 (1913-
19 are Marlboro Preparative Meeting Minutes), 1 vol., in custody of clerk,
C. Percy Barnard, Kennett Square Road. Registers are in the records of
the Kennett Monthly Meeting. Financial Records, 1909-31, 1 vol., in custody of clerk (1909-19 are Marlboro Preparative Meeting records). Since
1931 the Unionville Indulged Meeting kept no records. Chester County Deed
Books, B-4, p. 590; B-17, vol. 399, p. 285; V-16, vol. 393, p. 204.

250.   LONDON GROVE MONTHLY MEETING, 1827--. North of Toughkenamon at
       Intersection of Newark and Street Roads, West Marlboro Twp.,
       Chester County.
Continued as a Hicksite meeting in 1827 by Western Quarterly Meeting (entry 240), after division of the original London Grove Monthly Meeting (entry 83). At the time of the Separation in 1827, London Grove Monthly Meeting retained the 20 acres of ground, a portion of which was used for a
burial ground, and the two-story native stone meeting-house erected in
1818. The western end of this building belonged to Western Quarterly
Meeting. The present clerk is Elwood C. Stabley, Unionville.

See: Michener, op. cit., p. 100; Futhey and Cope, op. cit., p. 237;
Thomson, op. cit., p. 753; "The Old Grove Meeting-House," Philadelphia
North American, May 5, 1903; "Celebration Day at London Grove," West Ches-
ter Daily Local News, October 3, 1914.

Minutes of Men's Meetings, 1808-93, 3 vols.; Minutes of Women's Meetings, 1819-93, 2 vols., at PSC-Hi. Minutes of Joint Meetings, 1909-28, 1
vol. (1893-1909 are in the minutes of Men's Meetings ending 1893), at meeting-house, and 1929--, 1 vol., in custody of clerk. Minutes of Ministers
and Elders (now called Ministry and Counsel), 1852--, 1 vol. (1827-52 missing), in custody of clerk, Elizabeth Buffington, R. F. D. 3, Coatesville.
Register of Births and Deaths, 1792-1895, 2 vols., at meeting-house, and
1895--, 1 vol., in custody of recorder, Edwin Buffington, R. F. D. 3,
Coatesville. Certificates of Removal, 1792-1871, 1 vol., at meeting-house,
and 1871--, 1 vol., in custody of recorder. Marriage Certificates, 1792-
1844, 1 vol., at meeting-house, and 1844--, 1 vol., in custody of recorder
(in the back of this volume are records of marriages of members not married under the supervision of the meeting). Financial records, 1879--,
3 vols., 1 vol. is in meeting-house, last 2 vols., in custody of treasurer,
Clarence Yeatman, Avondale. Treasurer Book of First-day School, 1908--,
1 vol., in custody of treasurer, Catherine Taylor, Embrieville. Attendance Record of First-day School, 1922--, 3 vols., in meeting-house. Chester County Deed Books, Y-vol. 23, p. 42; B-3, vol. 50, p. 314; G-4, vol.
75, p. 178; K-4, vol. 82, p. 250; Y-66, vol. 146, p. 341; Miscellaneous
Deed Book No. 2, p. 538; P-12, vol. 287, p. 308.

251. LONDON GROVE PREPARATIVE MEETING, 1827-1912. North of Toughkenamon, at intersection of Street and Newark Roads, West
Marlboro Twp., Chester County.
Continued as a Hicksite meeting in 1827 by London Grove Monthly Meeting
(entry 250), after division of the original London Grove Preparative Meet-
ing (entry 84). Meetings were held in the meeting-house of London Grove
Monthly Meeting. In 1911, because the membership of London Grove Monthly
Meeting and this was identical, it was proposed to discontinue this meet-
ing. The proposal was finally granted in 1912 by London Grove Monthly
Meeting.

See: Michener, op. cit., p. 101; Futhey and Cope, op. cit., p. 237;
"London Grove Plans for Great Gathering," West Chester Daily Local News,
September 16, 1914; "Celebration Day at London Grove," West Chester Daily Local
News, October 3, 1914; "Gathering in Southern Part of County," West
Chester Daily Local News, October 1, 1934; "At London Grove," Philadelphia
Friends Intelligencer, February 16, 1907; "Friends at Meeting and at Home,"
Philadelphia Friends Intelligencer, February 3, 1901.

Minutes of Men's Meeting, 1858-1912, 2 vols. (1827-57 missing); Minutes of Women's Meetings, 1832-93, 2 vols. (1827-32, 1838-66 missing), in
meeting-house. Minutes of Joint Meetings, 1893-1912, incorporated in the
minute book of men's meetings ending 1912. Registers are in the records
of the London Grove Monthly Meeting. Financial Records, 1879-1900, 1 vol.
(1827-78, 1900-1912 missing), in meeting-house. Caretaker's Account Book,
1896-1909, 1 vol., in meeting-house.

252. NEW GARDEN MONTHLY MEETING, 1827--. Newark Road, 2 miles south
of Toughkenamon, New Garden Twp., Chester County.
Continued as a Hicksite meeting in 1827 by Western Quarterly Meeting (entry 240), after a division of the original Garden Monthly Meeting (entry
72). From 1827-1924 met at the meeting-house of New Garden Preparative
Meeting (entry 253). In 1928 the preparative meeting was laid down and
the red brick meeting-house and burial ground was deeded to the New Garden
Monthly Meeting. In 1925 and in 1934 several classrooms and a social room
were added to the meeting-house. The present clerk is Joseph D. Thomas,
Landenberg.

See: Michener, op. cit., p. 97; Futhey and Cope, op. cit., p. 238.
"New Garden Friends' Meeting," West Chester Daily Local News, November
19, 1927.

Minutes of Men's Meetings, 1827-91, 3 vols.; Minutes of Women's Meetings, 1823-91, 2 vols., at PSC-Hi. Minutes of Joint Meetings, 1891-1914,
1 vol., at PSC-Hi and 1914--, 1 vol., in custody of clerk. Minutes of
Ministers and Elders (now called Ministry and Counsel), 1851-84, 1 vol.
(1827-50, 1885-1932 missing), at PSC-Hi, and 1933--, 1 vol., in custody of
clerk, Miss Ethel Jefferis, Linden Street, Kennett Square. Register of
Marriage Certificates, 1828-92; Register of Removals, 1827-1909, both in
1 vol., at Swarthmore College Library. Register of Marriage Certificates,
1900--, 1 vol. (1803-99 missing). Register of Membership, 1863-95, 1 vol.
(1827-62 missing), in London Grove Meeting-house. Register of Births and
Deaths, 1745-1897, 1 vol., at PSC-Hi. Register of Removals, Marriages,
Membership, and Births and Deaths, 1897--, 1 vol., in custody of recorder,
Miss Mary Walton, 448 Sicle Street, Kennett Square. Financial Records,
1928--, 1 vol. (1827-1927 missing), in custody of treasurer, Lewis Schrader,
Chester Heights. Treasurer's Account Book of New Garden Monthly Meeting

of Women Friends, 1859-86, 1 vol. (includes on separate sheets records
from 1824-57), at London Grove Meeting-house. Treasurer's Book of New
Garden First-day School, 1916--, 1 vol., in custody of Ralph Sharpless,
Avondale. Burial records, 1835-67, 1 vol., at PSC-Hi, and 1867--, 3 vols.,
at home of caretaker, Howard Wollaston, New Garden.

253. NEW GARDEN PREPARATIVE MEETING, 1827-1928. Newark Road, 2 miles
south of Toughkenamon, New Garden Twp., Chester County.
Continued as a Hicksite meeting in 1827 by New Garden Monthly Meeting (entry 252), after the division of the original New Garden Preparative Meeting (entry 73). This meeting retained the red brick meeting-house erected
in 1743, to which a north wing was added in 1790; also the 6-acre grounds,
part of which was a burial ground. In 1905, 1925, and 1934 several classrooms and a social room were added to the meeting-house. In 1924 this
meeting was discontinued by New Garden Monthly Meeting and was finally
laid down in 1928. The meeting-house, burial ground, and all other property was then deeded to New Garden Monthly Meeting.

See: Michener, op. cit., p. 98; Futhey and Cope, op. cit., p. 236;
"New Garden Friends' Meeting," West Chester Daily Local News, November 19,
1927; "New Garden Friends Have Big Day," West Chester Daily Local News,
September 20, 1915; "Bi-Centennial in New Garden," West Chester Daily
Local News, September 18, 1915.

Minutes of Men's Meetings, 1827-91, 2 vols.; Minutes of Women's Meetings, 1847-55, 1 vol. (1827-46, 1856-91 missing); Minutes of Joint Meetings, 1891-1916, incorporated in 1874-91 vol. of Minutes of Men's Meetings, 1916-28, 1 vol., at PSC-Hi. Registers are in the records of the
New Garden Monthly Meeting.

254. SPENCER'S INDULGED MEETING, 1827-36. New London Twp., Chester
County.
Continued as a Hicksite meeting in 1827 by New Garden Monthly Meeting (entry 252). Previous to the Separation in 1827, the members of this meeting
had been a part of the original Spencer Indulged Meeting (entry 75). This
meeting retained the stone schoolhouse and 3 acres and 7 perches of ground,
which had been originally donated to the Friends by Samuel and Mary
Spencer in 1813. Due to decreasing membership the mid-week meeting was
discontinued in 1833. The meeting was finally laid down in 1836 by New
Garden Monthly Meeting.

See: Michener, op. cit., p. 99.

Chester County Deed Book, W-j, vol. 69, pp. 206, 208.

255. AVONDALE INDULGED MEETING, 1874-79. Avondale, Chester County.
Set up 1874 by New Garden Monthly Meeting (entry 252), at the request of
the Friends of Avondale and vicinity. This indulgence was granted for a
period of 6 months and the meetings were held in the Methodist Church,
southeast corner of Second and Chatham Streets. Permission was renewed
every 6 months during the existence of the meeting. In October 1874 the
meeting applied to New Garden Preparative Meeting (entry 253) for financial assistance. New Garden Preparative Meeting decided to assume one-
half of the expense incurred during the past summer. In 1875 New Garden
Monthly decided to defray one-half of the expenses of maintaining the indulged meeting. In 1877 meetings were discontinued in the Methodist
Church and were held in the homes of the members until 1879 when this
meeting was laid down by New Garden Monthly Meeting.

256. PENNSGROVE MONTHLY MEETING, 1842--. One mile north of Forrest-
      ville, Upper Oxford Twp., Chester County.
Set off in 1842 from New Garden Monthly Meeting (entry 252) and Fallowfield Monthly Meeting (entry 241) by Western Quarterly Meeting (entry
240). Composed of Pennsgrove (entry 257) and Homeville Preparative Meetings. Meetings have been held in the Pennsgrove Preparative Meeting-house
since the date of inception. The present clerk is J. Howard Broomell,
Bridgeport.

     See: Michener, op. cit., p. 105.

     Minutes of Men's Meetings, 1842-78, 1 vol. (1879-84 in volume later
used for Minutes of Joint Meetings); Minutes of Women's Meetings, 1842-
84, 2 vols., at the London Grove Meeting-house, Street Road, London Grove
Village. Minutes of Joint Meetings, 1884--, 2 vols.; Registers of Births,
Deaths, and Membership, 1842--, 1 vol.; Certificates of Marriages and
Certificates of Removals, 1842--, 1 vol., in custody of clerk. Finan-
cial Records, 1919--, 1 vol. (1842-1918 missing), in custody of Mrs.
Nellie Pusey, West Grove.

     257. PENNSGROVE PREPARATIVE MEETING, 1827--. One mile north of
           Forrestville, Upper Oxford Twp., Chester County.
Set up in 1829 by New Garden Monthly Meeting (entry 252) after having
been an indulged meeting under the original Friends meeting (entry 76)
since 1820 and Hicksite since 1827. Meetings were held in the home of
John Hambleton until March 1828 and then at the home of Samuel and Phebe
Hadley for about 9 months. After that, meetings were held in a small log
building on the Hadley premises until the erection of the present red
brick building in 1833. This building has since been stuccoed in natural
color. A 1/2-acre cemetery adjoins the meeting-house. In 1842 this meeting was transferred to Pennsgrove Monthly Meeting (entry 256).

     See: Futhey and Cope, op. cit., p. 242; Michener, op. cit., p. 106.

     Minutes of Men's Meetings, 1829-33, 1 vol., in custody of clerk, Mrs.
Alberta Wickershaw, Russelville. Minutes of Women's Meetings, 1829--, not
found. Minutes of Joint Meetings, 1934--, included in volume of Minutes
of Men's Meetings. Registers are incorporated in the records of the Pennsgrove Monthly Meeting. Cemetery records are incorporated in the minutes
of this meeting. Cemetery information is contained also on a chart giving
the layout of the cemetery and names and dates of burials. Treasurer's
Records, 1877-1920, 1 vol. (1829-77 missing), in custody of treasurer of
the monthly meeting, Mrs. Nellie Pusey, West Grove, and 1896--, 2 vols.,
in custody of Paul Harlem, Pennsgrove.

     258. HOMEVILLE (OXFORD) PREPARATIVE MEETING, 1828-1917. Homeville,
           Upper Oxford Twp., Chester County.
Set up in 1839 as the Oxford Preparative Meeting by Fallowfield Monthly
Meeting (entry 241) after having functioned as an indulged meeting since
1828. Meetings were held in the log schoolhouse at Asa Walton's in Cole-
rain Township, Lancaster County until 1839, when the present small red
brick building was erected. In 1842 when Pennsgrove Monthly Meeting (entry 256) was set up this meeting became a part, and in 1866 adopted its
present name. Owing to reduced membership the meeting was laid down
July 1917. To the west of the meeting-house is the original 3/4 acre
burial ground. It is enclosed by an iron fence. In 1914 it was incorporated as the Homeville Cemetery Company and is under the care of a

committee of former members, who also take care of the meeting-house and grounds.

See: Futhey and Cope, op. cit., p. 242.

Early records were not preserved and later records are not available.

259. WEST GROVE MONTHLY MEETING, 1919--. Prospect Avenue, West
      Grove, Chester County.
Set off in 1919 from New Garden Monthly Meeting (entry 252) by Western Quarterly Meeting (entry 240) at the request of West Grove Preparative Meeting (entry 260). Meetings always have been held in the meeting-house of West Grove Preparative Meeting. The present clerk is Robert Pyle, West Grove.

Monthly Meeting Minutes, 1919--, 2 vols., in custody of clerk; Minutes of the Committee of Ministry and Counsel, 1919-35, 1 vol., in custody of Mrs. Gertrude K. Walton, Avondale. Register of Births, Deaths, Marriages, Removals and Members, 1919--, 1 vol., in custody of recorder, Edith Cooper, West Grove. Financial Records, 1920--, in the financial records of the West Grove Preparative Meeting.

260. WEST GROVE PREPARATIVE MEETING, 1827--. 124 Prospect Avenue,
      West Grove, Chester County.
Continued as a Hicksite meeting in 1827 by New Garden Monthly Meeting (entry 252) with the permission of Western Quarterly Meeting (entry 240) after division of the original West Grove Preparative Meeting (entry 74). The first meeting-house, constructed of red brick, was erected in 1831, on land purchased from Halliday Jackson and Ann Halliday "to be used for a meeting-house and place of burial." It was located 1 mile southwest of West Grove on the road leading from New London to Avondale. In 1901 the present light-gray limestone meeting-house was built. From 1827 to 1901 this meeting was called the New West Grove Meeting, and thereafter by its present name. Since 1920, only one preparative meeting is held each year. The meeting was transferred to West Grove Monthly Meeting in 1919. The burial ground adjoining the old meeting-house is a part of the original land purchased. Although title remains vested in West Grove Preparative Meeting, the graveyard is under supervision of a committee appointed by West Grove Monthly Meeting. A yearly report is rendered by this committee and incorporated into the minutes of the meeting.

See: "New Meeting-House at West Grove," Philadelphia Friends Intelligencer, September 27, 1902.

Minutes of Men's Meetings, 1833-98, 2 vols.(1827-32, 1842-51 missing); Minutes of Women's Meetings, 1853-89, 1 vol. (1827-52, 1890-97 missing), at meeting-house and 1898-1911, 1 vol., in custody of clerk, Robert Pyle, West Grove. Minutes of Friends Forum, 1925--, 1 vol., in custody of secretary, Mrs. Elizabeth Carr, West Grove. Minutes of Young Friends Association, 1904-12, 1 vol., at meeting-house. Minutes of First-day School, 1880--, 11 vols. (1886-93, 1895-97, 1899-1903, 1922-25 missing), at meeting-house. Financial Records, 1830-52, 1 vol. (1827-29, 1853-1900 missing), at meeting-house, and 1901-18, 1 vol., in custody of Robert Pyle. First-day School Financial Records, 1925-35, 2 vols. (1880-1924 missing), at meeting-house, and 1935--, 1 vol., in custody of treasurer, Miss Edith Cooper, West Grove. Registers, 1827-1919, are in records of New Garden Monthly Meeting; 1919--, are in records of West Grove Monthly Meeting.

CALN QUARTERLY MEETING (H)

Component Meetings

(See: Explanatory Note 3)

	Date established	Entry number
BRADFORD MONTHLY MEETING	1828	262
West Caln Preparative Meeting	1828	263
Cambridge Indulged Meeting	1828	264
Cambridge Preparative Meeting	1830	264
Caln Preparative Meeting	1828	277
Bradford Preparative Meeting	1828	271
Romansville Preparative Meeting (Bradford)	1846	271
Cambridge Indulged Meeting	1848	264
SADSBURY MONTHLY MEETING	1828	265
Bart Indulged Meeting	1828	266
Bart Preparative Meeting	1840	266
Lampeter Preparative Meeting	1828	267
Sadsbury Preparative Meeting	1828	268
Columbia Indulged Meeting	1828	269
East Sadsbury Indulged Meeting	1828	270
Romansville Indulged Meeting (Bradford)	1890	271
Coatesville Indulged Meeting	1905	272
UWCHLAN MONTHLY MEETING	1828	273
Nantmeal Preparative Meeting	1828	274
Pikeland Preparative Meeting	1828	275
Pikeland Indulged Meeting (Kimberton)	1857	275
Uwchlan Preparative Meeting	1828	278
BRADFORD-UWCHLAN MONTHLY MEETING	1883	276
Caln Preparative Meeting	1828	277
Uwchlan Preparative Meeting	1828	278
Romansville Preparative Meeting (Bradford)	1846	271
Romansville Indulged Meeting	1890	271

261. CALN QUARTERLY MEETING, 1828---. Chester and Lancaster Counties,
Continued as a Hicksite meeting in 1828 by Philadelphia Yearly Meeting
(entry 173), after division of the original Caln Quarterly Meeting (entry
116). Meetings for business are held at Christiana, in the meeting-house
of Sadsbury Monthly Meeting (entry 265), on the Fifth day before the last
First-day of the First, Seventh, and Tenth months and at Caln in Seventh
month. The present clerk is Jessie W. Jackson, 33 Harrison Avenue, Christiana.

See: Futhey and Cope, op. cit., p. 241; Michener, op. cit., p. 124;
Thomson, op. cit., p. 753; Kenderdine, Around Sadsbury.

Minutes of Men's Meetings, 1828-94, 1 vol.; Minutes of Women's Meetings, 1828-94, 2 vols., at PSC-Hi. Minutes of Joint Meetings, 1901-36, 1
vol. (1894-1900 are in the 1828-1900 volume of Minutes of Men's Meeting
at PSC-Hi, and 1936--, 1 vol., in custody of clerk. Minutes of Ministers
and Elders, 1813-1918, 1 vol., at PSC-Hi, and 1918--, 1 vol., in custody
of clerk, Ella P. T. Brinton, Parkesburg. No formal records are kept of
finances. The present treasurer, Francis W. Brinton, Christiana, keeps
a personal ledger, to record the financial transactions of this meeting.

262. BRADFORD MONTHLY MEETING, 1828-83. Strasburg and North Brook
         Roads, Marshallton, Chester County.
Continued as a Hicksite meeting in 1828 by Caln Quarterly Meeting (entry
261), after division of the original Bradford Monthly Meeting (entry 117).
This meeting never owned a meeting-house, but met in the meeting-houses of
its subordinate meetings. From 1828-42 it alternated between the meeting-
houses of Bradford Preparative Meeting (entry 271) and Caln Preparative
Meeting (entry 277); from 1842-46 at Caln Preparative meeting-house; from
1846 until the meeting was laid down in 1883 meetings alternated between
the meeting-houses of Caln Preparative Meeting and Romansville Preparative
Meeting (entry 271), whose status was later changed to that of an indulged meeting. In 1883 Bradford Monthly Meeting merged with Uwchlan
Monthly Meeting (entry 273) to form the Bradford-Uwchlan Monthly Meeting
(entry 276).

See: Matlack, op. cit., I, 205-208; Futhey and Cope, op. cit., p.
240; Michener, op. cit., p. 124; Thomson, op. cit., p. 751; Kenderdine,
Landmarks.

Minutes of Men's Meetings, 1828-96, 1 vol. (1883-96 are minutes of
the Bradford-Uwchlan Monthly Meeting); Minutes of Women's Meetings, 1828-
1886, 1 vol (1883-86 are minutes of the Bradford-Uwchlan Monthly Meeting),
at PSC-Hi. Registers of Births and Deaths, 1828-99, 1 vol.; Marriage
Certificates, 1828-72, 1 vol. (1872-83 missing); Certificates of Removal,
1828-87, 1 vol.; Registers of Members, 1828-58, 1 vol. (1858-83 missing);
at PSC-Hi.

263. WEST CALN PREPARATIVE MEETING, 1828-46. King's Highway, about
         1/2 mile west of Wagontown, West Caln Twp., Chester County.
Continued as a Hicksite meeting in 1828 by Bradford Monthly Meeting (entry 262) after division from the original West Caln Preparative Meeting
(entry 121). After the Separation the Hicksite and Orthodox Friends continued to meet in the stone meeting-house erected by the original meeting about 1756 and retained by the Orthodox meeting in 1827. In 1846
this meeting was laid down by Bradford Monthly Meeting.

See: Thomson, op. cit., p. 747; Heathcote, op. cit., p. 341; Michener, op. cit., p. 126; Futhey and Cope, op. cit., p. 240. Registers are in the records of the Bradford Monthly Meeting.

264. **CAMBRIDGE INDULGED MEETING, 1828-52.** Near Main Street, Cambridge, Chester County.
Continued as a Hicksite meeting in 1828 by Bradford Monthly Meeting (entry 262). Previous to the Separation in 1827 the members of this meeting had been a part of the original Cambridge Indulged Meeting (entry 122). This meeting retained the one-story frame meeting-house, erected in 1824, and the 1/8-acre cemetery, adjoining the meeting-house. This cemetery was plotted in 1824. In 1830, because of increased membership, the status of the meeting was raised to a preparative meeting by Bradford Monthly Meeting. In 1848 Bradford Monthly Meeting discontinued the preparative meeting and re-established an indulged meeting under the care of Caln Preparative Meeting (entry 277). The meeting was laid down in 1852 by Bradford Monthly Meeting. The meeting-house, because of abandonment, fell into decay. By 1890, or thereabouts, not a vestige of the meeting-house remained. The manner of its ultimate destruction cannot be ascertained.

See: Michener, op. cit., p. 125; Futhey and Cope, op. cit., p. 242.

Minutes of Men's Meetings, 1831-45, 1 vol. (1830-31, 1845-48 missing); Minutes of Women's Meetings, 1831-42, 1 vol. (1830-31, 1842-48 missing), at PSC-Hi. Registers are in the records of the Bradford Monthly Meeting.

265. **SADSBURY MONTHLY MEETING, 1828--.** Perry Street, Christiana, Lancaster County.
Continued as a Hicksite meeting in 1828 by Caln Quarterly Meeting (entry 261), after division of the original Sadsbury Monthly Meeting (entry 123). From 1828-1919 meetings were held alternately in the meeting-houses of the preparative meetings which were under the care of this meeting. Since 1919 meetings have been held in the gray stone meeting-house erected in 1902 by Sadsbury Preparative Meeting (entry 268). The present clerk is Emma W. Martin, 303 Pennsylvania Avenue, Downingtown.

See: Futhey and Cope, op. cit., p. 240; Thomson, op. cit., p. 751; Michener, op. cit., pp. 127-128; Matlack, op. cit., I, 210-213; Kenderdine, Landmarks; Kenderdine, Around Sadsbury.

Minutes of Men's Meetings, 1828-86, 3 vols., incorporated in minute book of Joint Meetings; Minutes of Women's Meetings, 1806-85, 4 vols., at PSC-Hi; Minutes of Joint Meetings, 1882-86, included in last volume of Men's Minutes and 1886-1930, 2 vols., at PSC-Hi, and 1930--, 1 vol., in custody of clerk. Minutes of Ministry and Counsel, 1894-1927, 1 vol. (1828-94 missing); Certificates of Marriage, 1828-1903, 1 vol. (1903-37 destroyed by fire), at PSC-Hi, and 1937--, 1 vol., in custody of recorder, Betty E. Thomas, Parkesburg, Membership Records, 1937--, 1 vol. (1828-1937 destroyed by fire), in custody of recorder. Registers of Births, Deaths, and Removals, 1937-- (1827-1937, destroyed by fire), incorporated in membership book. Treasurer's Account Book, 1895--, 1 vol. (1828-95 missing), in custody of treasurer, D. Gilbert Eavenson, Perry Street, Christiana.

266. **BART PREPARATIVE MEETING, 1828-1925.** One mile west of Coopersville on Valley Road, Sadsbury Twp., Lancaster County.
Set up in 1840 as a preparative meeting by Sadsbury Monthly Meeting (en-

try 265), after having functioned as an indulged meeting since 1828. At
the time of the Separation in 1828, this meeting divided from the original Bart Indulged Meeting (entry 128), and retained the one-story stone
meeting-house erected in 1825 and the small adjoining burial ground. Due
to decreased membership, the meeting was laid down in 1925 by the Sadsbury
Monthly Meeting.

See: Matlack, op. cit., I, 203-205, 259, 260, 264-266; Ellis and
Evans, op. cit., p. 1036; Michener, op. cit., pp. 134, 135; Kenderdine,
Around Sadsbury; Kenderdine, Landmarks.

Minutes of Men's Meetings and Minutes of Women's Meetings missing.
Minutes of Joint Meetings, 1887-1925, 6 vols., at FSC-Hi. Registers are
in the records of the Sadsbury Monthly Meeting. Lancaster County Deed
Book, vol. F-5, p. 144.

267. LAMPETER PREPARATIVE MEETING, 1828-51. Route 340, Bird-in-
Hand, East Lampeter Twp., Lancaster County.
Continued as a Hicksite meeting in 1828 by Sadsbury Monthly Meeting (entry
265), after division of the original Lampeter Preparative Meeting (entry
125). At the time of the Separation the Hicksite Friends retained the
meeting-house erected in 1790 and the other property formerly owned by
the original meeting. There is some evidence of a school being under the
care of this meeting but due to the lack of any further information the
number of years this school was in existence is unknown. Due to decreasing membership the meeting was laid down in 1851 by Sadsbury Monthly
Meeting and the remaining members were transferred to Sadsbury Preparative (entry 268). The meeting-house and other property was then transferred to the care of the monthly meeting. About 1888 the meeting-house
was partly destroyed by fire and was partially rebuilt the following year.
In 1888 Sadsbury Monthly Meeting sold a portion of the ground to the
Pennsylvania Railroad Company and in 1910 a further sale was made to
Barton R. Morris. However, the meeting-house, which is now being used
as the headquarters of a Boy Scout troop, and the burial ground are still
under the care of Sadsbury Monthly Meeting.

See: Matlack, op. cit., I, 225-228; Ellis and Evans, op. cit., pp.
896-897; Schoonover, History, pp. 163, 164; Futhey and Cope, op. cit.,
p. 239; Michener, op. cit., pp. 130-131; Thomson, op. cit., p. 751;
Kenderdine, Around Sadsbury.

There are no Minutes of Men's or Women's Meetings available at the
present time. Registers are in the records of the Sadsbury Monthly Meeting.

268. SADSBURY PREPARATIVE MEETING, 1828-1925. Perry Street, Christiana, Lancaster County.
Continued as a Hicksite meeting in 1828 by Sadsbury Monthly Meeting (entry 265), after division of the original Sadsbury Preparative Meeting
(entry 119). Meetings were first held in the old Sadsbury meeting-house
situated 1 mile north of Christiana. In 1902 a gray stone structure was
erected on Perry Street, where preparative meetings continued until 1925,
when it was laid down and their remaining members joined to Sadsbury
Monthly Meeting.

See: Futhey and Cope, op. cit., p. 239; Michener, op. cit., p. 126;
Ellis and Evans, op. cit., p. 1036; Thomson, op. cit., p. 751; Woody, op.

cit., pp. 141, 142; Kenderdine, Landmarks; "The New Meeting-House at Chris-
tiana," Philadelphia Friends Intelligencer, December 12, 1901; Kenderdine,
Around Sadsbury; "Sadsbury Friends Looking Backward," West Chester Daily
Local News, June 17, 1924; Jesse W. Jackson, Historical Sketch of Old
Sadsbury (manuscript in custody of author, Christiana).

Minutes of Men's and Women's Meetings, 1828-91 missing. Minutes of
Joint Meetings, 1891-1925, 2 vols., at PSC-Hi. Treasurer's Account, 1891-
1925, 1 vol. (1828-91 missing), in custody of D. Gilbert Eavenson, Christiana. Lancaster County Deed Book, H, vol. 18, p. 388.

269. COLUMBIA INDULGED MEETING, 1828-86. 312 Cherry Street, Columbia, Lancaster County.
Continued as a Hicksite indulged meeting in 1828 by Sadsbury Monthly Meeting (entry 265), after division of the original Columbia Preparative Meeting (entry 124). At the time of the Separation Columbia Indulged Meeting
retained the small red brick meeting-house erected in 1812 at 312-316
Cherry Street and the 80' x 162' burial ground on the north side of Cherry
Street, between Sixth and Bethel Streets. However, the Orthodox Friends
occupied the meeting-house until their meeting was laid down in 1829. Due
to decreased membership, Columbia Indulged Meeting was laid down in 1886
by Sadsbury Monthly Meeting. The property, with the exception of the burial ground was sold to the Columbia Land Improvement Company in 1894. The
burial ground was sold 30 years later to the Bethel Cemetery Association.

See: Michener, op. cit., pp. 128-130; Ellis and Evans, op. cit., pp.
552-561; Matlack, op. cit., I, 214-217, 264; Kenderdine, Around Sadsbury;
Kenderdine, Landmarks.

Registers are in the records of the Sadsbury Monthly Meeting. Lancaster County Deed Books, vol. 21, p. 82; Q-vol. 14, p. 73; T-vol. 14, p. 40.

270. EAST SADSBURY INDULGED MEETING, 1828-58. Lincoln Highway,
3 1/2 miles west of Sadsburyville, Chester County.
Continued as a Hicksite meeting in 1828 by Sadsbury Preparative Meeting
(entry 268), after division of the original East Sadsbury Indulged Meeting
(entry 127). For a period of 3 years after the Separation the members
continued to worship in the same building occupied by East Sadsbury Indulged Meeting, Orthodox. In 1831 this meeting moved to Moscow schoolhouse, the first meeting-house being retained by the Orthodox Friends.
The following proposal is recorded in the minutes of Sadsbury Monthly
Meeting dated September 6, 1831: "The Joint Committee of Men and Women
Friends . . . were generally united in believing that an advantage might
be derived from changing the place of holding their meetings for worship
to Sadsbury Schoolhouse near Joseph and Timothy Paxton." Meetings were
held here until 1858, when due to declining membership East Sadsbury Indulged Meeting was laid down. The schoolhouse was rented in 1859 to the
Board of Directors in West Sadsbury Township for a term of 90 years, which
lease is in effect at the present time.

See: Futhey and Cope, op. cit., p. 242; Michener, op. cit., pp. 133,
134; Kenderdine, Landmarks.

271. ROMANSVILLE (BRADFORD) INDULGED MEETING, 1828--. North of Main
Road through Romansville, West Bradford Twp., Chester County.
Continued in 1828 as Bradford Preparative Meeting, Hicksite, by Bradford
Monthly Meeting (entry 262), after separation from the original Bradford

Preparative Meeting (entry 120). From 1828-33 meetings were held during
the afternoons in the meeting-house of the original Bradford Preparative
Meeting, which was located at the junction of Strasburg and North Brock
Roads, Marshallton. In 1833 the meeting erected a one-story brick meet
ing house on ground adjoining the Orthodox property. This ground, and
1 rod additional, were purchased from John Dowdell. Meetings were held in
the Marshallton meeting-house until 1846. In that year, because the center of Bradford Friends' population had shifted westward, the meeting purchased in Romansville 1 acre and 88 perches of ground from John and Lydia
Worth. On this property, in the same year, a small one-story red brick
building was erected and a graveyard was plotted. When this meeting moved
to Romansville, its name was changed to Romansville Preparative Meeting.
The property in Marshallton was sold in March 1846 to Abraham Marshall,
who in turn sold it to the trustees of the Orthodox Friends on June 16,
1846. As early in 1877, this meeting requested that it be laid down.
However, it was not until 1890 that this request was complied with by Caln
Quarterly Meeting (entry 261) and the preparative meeting discontinued.
At the same time the meeting was re-established as an indulged meeting
under the care of Bradford-Uwchlan Monthly Meeting (entry 276) and later
under Sadsbury Monthly Meeting (entry 265), under whose care it has remained until the present. Meetings are held during the summer months only.

See: Futhey and Cope, op. cit., p. 242; Heathcote, op. cit., p. 341;
Michener, op. cit., p. 127; Thomson, op. cit., p. 755; "Romansville
Friends' Meeting," West Chester Daily Local News, March 22, 1930.

Registers are in the records of the Uwchlan, Sadsbury, and Bradford
Monthly Meetings.

272. COATESVILLE INDULGED MEETING, ca.1905. Third Avenue and Chest-
      nut Street, Coatesville, Chester County.
The only history available for this meeting is taken from the minutes of
Sadsbury Monthly Meeting (entry 265). The first mention is in minutes of
April 5, 1905: "By request of Friends living in Coatesville, the subject
of establishing a meeting in that place was introduced. A committee was
appointed to further consider the matter and ascertain more fully the
feelings of Friends residing there." In the minutes of July 5, 1905 it
is stated: "The committee appointed to consider the establishing of a
Friends Meeting at Coatesville report having held a meeting there, and
quite a number were present, but the committee was not able to say what
would be done. They are continue' to further consider the subject." A
further minute dated February 7, 1906, states: "A committee . . . was not
ready to report much progress. They were continued to report at some future meeting when they felt they had some report to make and without a
call from the meeting." This is the last mention of Coatesville meeting
in the minutes of Sadsbury Monthly Meeting. Meetings for worship were
held on the second floor of the Nagle Building, Third Avenue and Chestnut
Street. No meeting-house for this meeting has ever existed.

273. UWCHLAN MONTHLY MEETING, 1828-83. Lionville Village, Uwchlan
      Twp., Chester County.
Continued as a Hicksite meeting in 1828 by Caln Quarterly Meeting (entry
261), after division of the original Uwchlan Monthly Meeting (entry 129).
From 1828 until 1856 meetings were held alternately in the meeting-houses
of Uwchlan Preparative Meeting (entry 278) and Pikeland Indulged Meeting
(entry 275). In 1856 Uwchlan Monthly Meeting decided that henceforth all
meetings would be held in the Uwchlan meeting-house. The proposal to unite

Uwchlan and Bradford Monthly Meetings was made in September 1883. A Minute, dated November 1883, states: It had been proposed and united with by men and Women's meetings to consolidate Uwchlan and Bradford Monthly Meetings under the name of Bradford and Uwchlan Monthly Meeting to be held alternately at Uwchlan and Caln the first Third-day in each month." The merger was approved by Caln Quarterly Meeting and accordingly both Monthly meetings were laid down and re-established as the Bradford Uwchlan Monthly Meeting (entry 276).

See: Futhey and Cope, op. cit., p. 241; Cope, Genealogy, pp. 190, 191; Michener, op. cit., p. 135.

Minutes of Men's Meetings, 1828-1900, 3 vols., and micro-film duplicate (1883-1900 are minutes of the Bradford-Uwchlan Monthly Meeting); Minutes of Women's Meetings, 1828-82, 1 vol. and micro-film cuplicate, at PSC-Hi. Register of Births and Deaths, 1763-1899, 1 vol. and micro-film duplicate (1883-99 are records of the Bradford-Uwchlan Monthly Meeting); Certificates of Removal, 1828-81, 1 vol. and micro-film duplicate (1881-83 missing); Certificates of Marriage (records of the Bradford-Uwchlan Monthly Meeting), 1830-99, 1 vol. and micro-film, at PSC-Hi.

274. NANTMEAL PREPARATIVE MEETING, 1828-33. Nantmeal Village, Nant-
     meal Twp., Chester County.
Continued as a Hicksite meeting in 1828 by Uwchlan Monthly Meeting (entry 273), after division of the original Nantmeal Preparative Meeting (entry 132). After the Separation the Orthodox and Hicksite Friends continued to use the meeting-house which had been erected a few years after 1773. Nantmeal Preparative Meeting was small in numbers from its inception. The meeting continued with diminishing membership until 1833, when it was laid down and the remaining members were transferred to Uwchlan Preparative Meeting (entry 278). On March 10, 1881 the trustees appointed by the Hicksite Friends deeded their interests in the property to the trustees appointed by Uwchlan Monthly Meeting, Orthodox.

See: Heathcote, op. cit., p. 340; Matlack, op. cit., I, 231-234, 264; Futhey and Cope, op. cit., p. 240; Thomson, op. cit., p. 753; Michener, op. cit., p. 136.

Minutes of Men's and Women's Meetings are not available. Registers are in the records of the Uwchlan Monthly Meeting. Chester County Deed Books, C-6, vol. 125, p. 361; K-9, vol. 207, p. 434.

275. PIKELAND INDULGED MEETING (also known as Kimberton), 1828-61.
     Nutts Road, Kimberton Village, East Pikeland Twp., Chester
     County.
Continued as a Hicksite indulged meeting in 1828 by Uwchlan Monthly Meeting(entry 273), after having functioned as the original Pikeland Preparative Meeting (entry 131) since 1758. At the time of the Separation, which occurred in the Pikeland Preparative Meeting in 1828, the Hicksite Friends retained the meeting-house erected in 1819 and the other property. For many years Pikeland was a flourishing meeting but in the early 1850's the members began to leave the community. The first request to discontinue part of the meeting is recorded in the November 1854 minutes of Uwchlan Monthly Meeting: "Pikeland proposes to dispense with their midweek meeting for worship." The next mention of this meeting is in the April 1857 minutes of Caln Quarterly Meeting (entry 261); "At Uwchlan Monthly Meeting held first of the twelfth month, 1856, the committee ap-

pointed on the subject brought up from Pikeland Preparative Meeting report they have had a conference with the members of that meeting and were united in proposing that both mid-week and preparative meetings be laid down and the members belonging thereto attached to Uwchlan Preparative Meeting (entry 278), which being considered is fully united with, and the information accordingly directed to the Quarterly Meeting." The preparative meeting, according to this minute, was laid down in 1857. At the same time it was established as an indulged meeting. A further minute of Caln Quarterly Meeting, dated May 1861, states: "Uwchlan Preparative Meeting informs that the meeting at Pikeland has been discontinued except those held once in three months, which are under the care of a committee of the Quarterly Meeting." In 1868 a deed was given to a new set of trustees covering the original site of 2 acres and 104 perches and the second site of 131 perches. The original site still remains in the possession of Sadsbury Monthly Meeting (entry 265), since it took over the business and property of Bradford-Uwchlan Monthly Meeting (entry 276) in 1900, which in turn had taken over the property of Uwchlan Monthly Meeting in 1883. In April 1870, three trustees of the Kimberton property sold the 131 perches to five persons classed in the deed as "not joint tenants but tenants in common." In 1872 one of the tenants in common sold his share, and in 1874 the remaining shares were sold to "The Minister Trustees, Elders, and Deacons of the German Lutheran Congregation called St. Peter's in Pikeland Township." The Centennial German Lutheran Church was erected on the property. In 1890 the grantees deeded the property to the Lutheran Church, in whose hands it still remains.

See: Futhey and Cope, op. cit., pp. 240, 241; Michener, op. cit., p. 136; Thomson, op. cit., p. 752; Grace A. Lewis, "Old Kimberton," West Chester Daily Local News, September 28, 1895; Kenderdine, Around Sadsbury; "Friends' Meeting-House Property," West Chester Village Record, December 7, 1869; "Church Property For Sale," ibid., November 16, 20, 23, 27, 30, 1869.

Minutes of Men's Meetings, 1838-54, 1 vol. (1828-38, 1854-57 missing), at PSC-Hi. No minutes of women's meetings available. Registers are in the records of the Uwchlan Monthly Meeting.

276. BRADFORD-UWCHLAN MONTHLY MEETING, 1883-1900. Lionville Village, King's Highway, 2 1/2 miles northeast of Coatesville, Chester County.

Set up in 1883 by Caln Quarterly Meeting (entry 261) as the result of a merger of a Bradford Monthly Meeting (entry 262) and Uwchlan Monthly Meeting (entry 273). Meetings were held alternately in the meeting-house of Uwchlan Preparative Meeting (entry 278) and Caln Preparative Meeting (entry 277) from 1883 until the Bradford-Uwchlan Monthly Meeting was laid down in 1900. After the discontinuance of the meeting the members were attached to Sadsbury Monthly Meeting (entry 265).

See: Matlack, op. cit., I, 205-208, 250-254.

Minutes of Men's Meetings, 1883-86 (recorded in 1880-83 minute book of the Bradford Monthly Meeting; Minutes of Women's Meetings, 1883-96 (recorded in 1828-83 minute book of the Bradford Monthly Meeting); Minutes of Joint Meetings, 1886-96 (recorded in 1880-83 minute book of the Bradford Monthly Meeting), 1896-1900, 1 vol., at PSC-Hi. Registers of Births and Deaths, 1883-99 (recorded in registers of the Uwchlan Monthly Meeting and the Bradford Monthly Meeting); Register of Marriages, 1883-

99 (recorded in 1830-83 volume of marriages of the Uwchlan Monthly Meeting), at PSC-Hi.

277. CALN PREPARATIVE MEETING, 1828-96. King's Highway, 2 1/2 miles
      northeast of Coatesville, Chester County.
Continued as a Hicksite meeting in 1828 by Bradford Monthly Meeting (entry
262), after division of the original Caln Preparative Meeting (entry 118).
At the time of the Separation this meeting retained the meeting-house and
the 5 1/2 acres of ground. The meeting-house, a one-story stone building,
was erected in 1726. The 2-acre burial ground located in the northeastern
section of the property is enclosed by a stone wall. The Orthodox Friends
continued to use the meeting-house until 1905, at which time they erected
their own building in Coatesville. In 1883, when Bradford Monthly Meeting
was combined with Uwchlan Monthly Meeting (entry 273), this meeting became
a part of the Bradford-Uwchlan Monthly Meeting (entry 276). Due to decreased membership, Caln Preparative Meeting was laid down in 1896 by
Bradford-Uwchlan Monthly Meeting, and its members were attached to Uwchlan
Preparative Meeting (entry 278). When Bradford-Uwchlan Monthly Meeting
was laid down in 1900, the property of Caln Preparative Meeting was then
transferred to the care of Sadsbury Monthly Meeting (entry 265). The
Chester Valley Bank of Coatesville is trustee of the funds held in trust
for the maintenance of the burial ground. The meeting-house had extensive
alterations in 1913; a new roof was added and the old building was repaired. In 1934 the meeting-house was repainted, and further repairs were
made. At the present time the building is being used for the summer meetings of Caln Quarterly Meeting (entry 261) and for the Sabbath school for
the children living in the community.

     Futhey and Cope, op. cit., pp. 237-238; Michener, op. cit., pp. 124,
125; Thomson, op. cit., p. 750; "One of the Unique Churches of Chester
County," Philadelphia Record, March 3, 1901; "Friends Meet at Old Caln,"
West Chester Daily Local News, July 24, 1914; "Caln Friends Meeting,"
ibid., September 13, 1930.

     Minutes of Men's Meetings, 1850-87, 1 vol. (1827-50, 1887-96 miss-
ing), at PSC-Hi. Registers are in the records of Bradford Monthly Meeting,
1827-83, and Bradford-Uwchlan Monthly Meeting, 1883-96. Original deeds
are at PSC-Hi. Chester County Deed Books, F-4, p. 275, 1832; F-6, p.
374, 1857; H-14, p. 39, 1883.

278. UWCHLAN PREPARATIVE MEETING, 1828-1900. Lionville Village,
      Uwchlan Twp., Chester County.
Continued as a Hicksite meeting in 1828 by Uwchlan Monthly Meeting (entry
273), after division of the original Uwchlan Preparative Meeting (entry
130). When the Separation occurred both the Hicksite and Orthodox Friends
continued to occupy the log meeting-house, which had been erected in 1756.
The Hicksite Friends used the south side and the Orthodox Friends the
north side. A minute of Uwchlan Preparative Meeting (o), dated February
2, 1867 states: "The Hicksite Friends continue to hold meetings in part
of the house and make interments in the graveyard but the deed of property
is in our possession." The old log meeting-house was razed in 1875 and
was replaced by a gray stone building the same year. In 1883 Uwchlan
Monthly Meeting was merged with Bradford Monthly Meeting (entry 262) to
form the Bradford-Uwchlan Monthly Meeting (entry 276). This preparative
meeting then became attached to the newly formed monthly meeting. According to a minute of Bradford-Uwchlan Monthly Meeting, dated June 1896:
"Bradford Preparative Meeting and Caln Preparative Meeting were laid down

and its members were attached to the Uwchlan Preparative Meeting." Due
to decreased membership, caused by the migration of members, the meeting
was laid down in 1900 by Bradford-Uwchlan Monthly Meeting.

During the summer of 1904, the Orthodox Friends made arrangements to
rent the east side of the Uwchlan Meeting-house for use as a high school
to the Uwchlan Township School Board. The Hicksite Friends opposed this
arrangement and secured an injunction until the courts could determine
whether the Hicksite or Orthodox Friends owned the property. The decision
was that neither could give a clear title since both had occupied the property. The Hicksite Friends then gave their permission and the school has
since been held in the east side of the meeting-house. On July 3, 1920,
the trustees of the Orthodox and Hicksite Friends signed a deed selling
70 perches of ground to Uwchlan Grange Patrons of Husbandry. The remaining 1 acre and 25 perches of burial ground remains in the possession of
both the Orthodox and Hicksite Friends but is under the care of the Orthodox Friends.

See: Matlack, op. cit., I, 250-254; Futhey and Cope, op. cit., pp.
236, 237; Cope, Genealogy, pp. 190, 191; Michener, op. cit., p. 136; Heath-
cote, op. cit., p. 339; Thomson, op. cit., p. 749; Sarah Oberholtzer, "A
Protest Against the Destruction of Uwchlan Meeting-House," West Chester
Daily Local News, August 20, 1904; "Friends' Old Minute Books," ibid.,
February 6, 1909.

Minutes of Men's Meetings, 1854-85, 1 vol. (1828-54, 1885-1900), at
PWc-Hi. Registers are in the records of the Uwchlan Monthly Meeting from
1828-83, and in the records of the Bradford-Uwchlan Monthly Meeting, 1883-
1900.

Component Meetings

(See: Explanatory Note 3)

	Date established	Entry number
PHILADELPHIA MONTHLY MEETING	1827	280
Philadelphia Preparative Meeting	1827	281
Cherry Street Meeting	1827	282
West Philadelphia Indulged Meeting	1837	283
Girard Avenue Indulged Meeting	1859	292
EXETER MONTHLY MEETING (READING)	1827	284
Maiden Creek Preparative Meeting	1827	285
Pottsville Indulged Meeting	1831	286
GREEN STREET MONTHLY MEETING	1827	287
Green Street Preparative Meeting	1827	288
Frankford Preparative Meeting (Germantown and Frankford)	1827	289
Frankford Indulged Meeting	1876	290
Germantown Preparative Meeting	1876	291
Girard Avenue Indulged Meeting	1859	292
Fair Hill Indulged Meeting	1880	293
MUNCY MONTHLY MEETING	1827	309
Greenwood Indulged Meeting	1827	302
RADNOR MONTHLY MEETING	1827	294
Haverford Preparative Meeting	1827	295
Merion Preparative Meeting	1827	296
Valley Preparative Meeting	1827	300
Schuylkill Indulged Meeting	1827	301
Schuylkill Preparative Meeting	1843	301
Schuylkill Indulged Meeting	1850	301
ROARING CREEK MONTHLY MEETING	1827	303
Berwick Indulged Meeting	1827	304
Catawissa Indulged Meeting	1827	305
Roaring Creek Preparative Meeting	1827	306
SPRUCE STREET MONTHLY MEETING	1832	297
Spruce Street Indulged Meeting	1832	298
Spruce Street Preparative Meeting	1832	298
VALLEY MONTHLY MEETING	1936	299
Valley Preparative Meeting	1827	300
Schuylkill Indulged Meeting	1850	301
CHESTNUT HILL (UNITED) MONTHLY MEETING	1924	330
RADNOR (UNITED) MONTHLY MEETING	1937	333

**279. THE PHILADELPHIA QUARTERLY MEETING, 1828--. Race Street west
of Fifteenth, Philadelphia.**

Continued as a Hicksite meeting in 1828 by Philadelphia Yearly Meeting
(entry 173). At the time of the Separation in 1827 there were two monthly
meetings of Friends in the city of Philadelphia which as a body were inclined to follow the Hicksite faction. One was Green Street Monthly Meeting (entry 54), which continued on in the meeting-house at the southeast
corner of Fourth and Green Streets. The other was composed of a group of
Friends who had previously been members of the meeting at Fourth and Arch
Streets (entry 3), as well as a small number who had been members of the
Southern District Monthly Meeting (entry 37) on Pine Street. This second
mentioned monthly meeting became Philadelphia Monthly Meeting of Friends
ter's Court (Carpenter's Hall), later they met at a meeting-house which
they erected on Cherry Street (entry 282), and still later at their present meeting-house on Race Street just west of Fifteenth. The group from
the Southern District at a later time increased in number and formed a
monthly meeting of their own, erecting a meeting-house on Spruce Street.

Philadelphia Quarterly Meeting of Race Street Friends came into existence as set forth by the following minutes of the Philadelphia Monthly
Meeting: "At an adjourned Monthly Meeting of Friends of Philadelphia held
in Carpenter's Court the 23rd day of First Month, 1928 . . . the following report from the joint committee of the Monthly Meeting of Friends
held at Green Street, Radnor, and this Meeting was read, and adopted and
directed to be forwarded to our ensuing Quarterly Meeting . . . viz.,
The Committee appointed by Radnor, Green Street and Philadelphia Monthly
Meetings to take into consideration the propriety of establishing a Quarterly Meeting to be composed of those three Monthly Meetings, having twice
met and deliberately considered the subject are united in recommending
that a proposition be laid before the ensuing Quarterly Meeting at Abington, that if there approved, it may be forwarded to the Yearly Meeting for
its approbation, that a Quarterly Meeting embracing those three monthly
meetings be established, to be held in Philadelphia on the Third-day following the first Second-day in the Second, Fifth, Eighth and Eleventh
Months . . . Meeting of Ministers and Elders the day preceding . . .
to be denominated Philadelphia Quarterly Meeting of Friends, and to be
opened in the Eighth Month next at ten o'clock in the morning, at the
Cherry Street house.

The proposition was approved by the yearly meeting, and the first
session of Philadelphia Quarterly Meeting convened in the Cherry Street
Meeting-house at the specified time. Quarterly meetings continued to be
held at the Cherry Street house for some time, and later at the Race
Street house after the erection of the same. The place of holding the
quarterly meetings has for a number of years alternated between several
meeting-houses. At the present time the one held in March convenes in
the meeting-house on School House Lane in Germantown. That in June meets
at the Valley, the one in September is held at a selected place jointly
with Arch Street Friends, and the one in December is held at Fifteenth
and Race Streets. Stapeley Hall (entry 448), the Friends' Boarding Home at
6300 Greene Street in Germantown is directly controlled by this meeting.
The present clerk of the Quarterly Meeting is William Plummer, Jr., Radnor.

See: Matlack, op. cit., II, 443.

Minutes of Men's Meetings, 1828-1905, 3 vols.; Minutes of Women's Meetings, 1828-1905, 4 vols., at PSC-Hi. Minutes of Joint Meetings, 1905-20, 1 vol., at PSC-Hi, and 1920--, 3 vols., at PPF. Minutes of Ministers amd Elders, 1853-1909, 3 vols., at PSC-Hi. Minutes of Ministry and Counsel, 1908--, 1 vol., in custody of the clerk, David G. Paul, 523 Pelham Road, Philadelphia. Minutes of Quarterly First-day School, 1888-1903, 1 vol.; Minutes of Quarterly First-day School Union, 1888-1902, 1 vol.; Annual Reports of Committee on Friends' Boarding House, 1899-1903, loose pamphlets bound into 1 vol.; Minutes of Committee on Home Influence, 1896-1900, 1 vol.; Unbound Reports and Epistles, 1828-82, 2 files, at PSC-Hi. Annual Reports of Committee of Friends' Boarding House, 1903--, loose pamphlets, in custody of J. Frank Gaskill, chairman of the committee, c/o Philadelphia Electric Co., Philadelphia. Minutes of the Philanthropic Committee on Home Influence, 1896-1900, 1 vol., at PSC-Hi. Minutes of the Visiting Committee of Philadelphia Quarter, 1889-1933, 2 vols. (1909-28 missing); Minutes of Frankford Committee, 1876-1923, 1 vol., at PPF. Minutes of Friends' Neighborhood Guild Committee, 1936--, 1 vol., in custody of the chairman of the committee, Katharine R. Wireman, c/o Friends' Central Bureau, 1515 Cherry Street, Philadelphia. Treasurer's Account Books, 1829-1923, 4 vols., at PPF, and 1923--, 1 vol., in custody of the treasurer, Clarence A. Wesp, 856 E. Rittenhouse Street, Germantown.

280. PHILADELPHIA MONTHLY MEETING, 1827--. Race Street west of
      Fifteenth Street, Philadelphia.
For the early history of this meeting it is necessary to refer to the original Philadelphia Monthly Meeting (entry 3). The organization of this meeting at the time of the division in the Society of Friends is recorded in the following minutes: "Abington Quarterly Meeting held the 9th of Eighth Month, 1827 . . . The following minute was received in the Report from Byberry, viz., . . . 'Friends of Philadelphia, belonging to the Monthly Meeting of Byberry, and who attend the indulged meeting in the city, have had a conference upon the subject of forwarding a request to the Monthly Meeting, for the establishment of a Meeting for Worship also a Preparative Meeting; and a Monthly Meeting for Discipline, to be called the Monthly Meeting of Friends of Philadelphia, and to be held on the fourth day of the week preceding the last sixth day of the month but one' . . . and after deliberation upon the important measure, and believing it would tend the promotion of the cause of Truth and Peace, and contribute to the benefit, and preservation of their members, they were united in the belief that it would be right to have the subject laid before the Monthly Meeting for its consideration and judgment . . . which subject claiming the deliberate attention of this meeting, a general unity therewith was expressed . . . it was therefore directed to be forwarded to the Quarterly Meeting for its consideration; . . . on solidly deliberating on the important subject, it appeared to be the general sense of this meeting. That said Meeting for Worship, also Preparative Meeting, and Monthly Meeting be established, agreeably to the request as stated in said Report."

The Philadelphia Monthly Meeting of Race Street Friends at first consisted of former members of Arch Street Meeting, former members of Pine Street Meeting (entry 38), and some of the former members of Twelfth Street Meeting (entry 51), the remainder of Twelfth Street Friends who had separated, joined with the Green Street Monthly Meeting (entry 287), and the Orange Street Meeting (entry 37). The group of Friends from Orange Street Meeting, formed a monthly meeting of their own in 1832, which was called Spruce Street Monthly Meeting (entry 297). Members who at first formed this monthly meeting had for a short time previously, held an indulged meeting for worship under the oversight of Byberry Monthly Meeting (entry 177). Prior to the establishment of their own monthly meeting, the majority of Friends of Philadelphia Monthly Meeting had maintained membership with Byberry Monthly Meeting, a few of them, however, had been members of Darby Monthly Meeting (entry 228), for the short intervening period. Early in 1828 they erected a meeting-house on Cherry Street (entry 282), between Fourth and Fifth Streets, and in the same year, when Philadelphia Quarterly Meeting (entry 279) was established, they became a part thereof.

The monthly meeting continued to use the meeting-house on Cherry Street, until the same became no longer desirable, on account of location, lack of space, and other reasons. The women's branch of the yearly meeting was held there, and it was upon the protest of members of this meeting (entry 173) that the need of better accommodations brought about the purchase of ground on Race Street just west of Fifteenth, and the building of their present meeting-house thereon. A committee appointed for this purpose reported in 1855 as follows: "The committee appointed to take into consideration the proposition of the Yearly Meeting's Committee, relative to accommodations for the Yearly Meeting, have several times met, and propose (That if the Yearly Meeting's Committee inform us of their ability to carry out their part of the proposition) the purchase by our meeting of the easternmost part of the lot referred to, being 80 feet front on Cherry Street by 176 feet in depth with a passage way into Race Street of 10 feet wide, for the sum of $13,000, also a dwelling on Fifteenth Street, lot 22 by 51 feet for $300. Provided that the Monthly Meeting of both Men and Women Friends, after serious deliberation, are satisfied with the proposed location for our meeting; and also provided that a sufficient amount, with our present property, to pay for the lot and suitable buildings, in addition to the proportion of the amount to be raised by the yearly meeting, is first secured by voluntary subscription. Leaving the proposition as to the manner of holding the title of the Yearly Meeting's portion for further consideration."

It is apparent that building was started in 1856 as the meeting-house bears that date in its front gable. The house was completed and ready for occupancy early in 1857. The date of the first meeting held in the new Race Street Meeting-house is definitely set forth in the following minute: "At a Monthly Meeting of Women Friends of Philadelphia held 4th Month, 1857 . . . our meetings on and since the 1st day of Second Month, have been held at the new house on Race Street west of Fifteenth Street."

The Friends' Central School (entry 436) which was for many years located at the Race Street Meeting, had its beginning on the grounds of the old Cherry Street house, and later moved to its present quarters in Overbrook.

The present clerk of Philadelphia Monthly Meeting held at Race Street is Thomas D. Paxson, c/o Friends' Central Bureau, 1515 Cherry Street, Philadelphia.

See: Matlack, op. cit., I, 498; Michener, op. cit., pp. 51-53; Bunting, op. cit., pp. 13-15.

Minutes of Men's Meetings, 1827-99, 10 vols.; Minutes of Women's Meetings, 1827-99, 8 vols.; Minutes of Joint Meetings, 1899-1907, 2 vols., at PSC-Hi. Minutes of Joint Meetings, 1907--, 6 vols., at PPF. Minutes of Ministers and Elders, 1828-1908, 4 vols., at PSC-Hi. Minutes of Ministry and Counsel, 1908--, 1 vol.; Minutes of Overseers Committee, Men, 1859-1904, 4 vols.; Minutes of Overseers Committee, Women, 1897-1904, 1 vol.; Minutes of Overseers Committee, Joint Meetings, 1904-35, 4 vols., at PPF, and 1935--, 1 vol., in custody of clerk Overseers Committee, Mrs. Franklin Edmunds, 6423 West Chester Road, Upper Darby. Register of Births and Burials, 1686-1903, 3 vols., at PSC-Hi. Register of Births and Burials, 1903--, 1 vol., at PPF. Register of Members, 1827-1906, 5 vols., at PSC-Hi. Register of Members, 1906--, 1 vol., Marriage Certificates, 1828-1925, 3 vols., at PSC-Hi. Marriage Certificates, 1925-37, 1 vol., and 1937-- (Photostats), 1 vol., at PPF. Marriages of Friends Out of Meeting, 1847-1917, 1 vol.; Certificates of Removals Received, 1684-1827, 2 vols., at PSC-Hi. Certificates of Removals Received, 1827--, at PPF. Certificates of Removals Issued, 1828-1925, 2 vols., at PSC-Hi. Certificates of Removal Issued, 1 vol., at PPF. Index Men's Minutes, 1827-1907, 1 copy at PSC-Hi, 1 copy at PPF. Index of Certificates Received, 1684-1827; Certificates Issued, 1828-1901; Marriage Certificates, 1828-1925, all in 1 vol., 1 copy at PSC-Hi, 1 copy at PPF. Treasurer's Account Books, 1882-1911, 1 vol., at PPF. Treasurer's Account Books, 1911--, 1 vol., in custody of the treasurer, Samuel Bunting, c/o Philadelphia National Bank, Philadelphia.

281. PHILADELPHIA PREPARATIVE MEETING, 1827-93. Race Street west of Fifteenth, Philadelphia.

Set up by Abington Quarterly Meeting (entry 174) upon recommendation of Byberry Monthly Meeting (entry 177). After the Separation a group of Friends, who had been members of the original Philadelphia Monthly Meeting (entry 3), and the original Southern District Monthly Meeting (entry 37), held meetings for worship in Carpenter's Court (Carpenter's Hall). These indulged meetings were under the oversight of Byberry Monthly Meeting of the Abington Quarter. A short time later they decided to maintain a preparative and monthly meeting of their own. The matter was laid before the monthly meeting where it was approved and forwarded to Abington Quarter for its concurrence. The quarterly meeting sanctioned the proposition by a minute dated August 9, 1827, and the monthly and preparative meetings of Philadelphia were established. Upon the setting up of Philadelphia Monthly Meeting (entry 280), this preparative meeting became a part thereof, and in 1828 when Philadelphia Quarterly Meeting (entry 279) was established it then became a constituent meeting of that quarter. Meetings were at first held in Carpenter's Court, but very soon a new meetinghouse was erected on Cherry Street (entry 282) between Fourth and Fifth Streets. Later, when the present meeting-house on Race Street west of Fifteenth was erected in 1856, meetings were held there from the time of its completion. This meeting was laid down by Philadelphia Monthly Meeting in 1893, upon the approval of Philadelphia Quarterly Meeting, and the business assumed by the Monthly Meeting.

See: Matlack, op. cit., II, 442.

Minutes of Men's Meetings, 1828-93, 3 vols.; Minutes of Women's Meetings, 1839-93, 3 vols., at PSC-Hi.

282. CHERRY STREET MEETING, 1828-57. Present site of 423 Cherry Street, Philadelphia.

Cherry Street Meeting was the beginning from which Race Street Meeting developed. After the Separation Friends who withdrew from Arch Street

Meeting (entry 3) and Pine Street Meeting (entry 38), held meetings for
worship in Carpenter's Hall, called Carpenter's Court in the minutes of
1827. Meetings continued at Carpenter's Hall for only a short time, since
an early minute of Philadelphia Monthly Meeting states: "At a Monthly
Meeting of Friends of Philadelphia held at Carpenter's Court the 19th of
Twelfth month, 1827 . . . the following report from our building committee
was read and adopted, and said committee authorized to purchase, in behalf of this meeting, the lot of ground therein recommended . . . and our
Trustees, . . . were directed to receive conveyance therefore, for the use
of the members of this meeting." a later minute says: "The committee appointed for the purchase of a lot and the erection of a Meeting-House,
reported last month that a lot on Cherry Street . . . had been purchased,
and it was with the expectation that the stables thereon erected could immediately be converted into a building suitable for a temporary meeting-
house. But as the alterations progressed it was found that the walls and
frame work were not sufficiently strong; and it was therefore thought most
prudent to erect substantial walls, so that the building could hereafter
be disposed of, if a situation should offer more favourable for the general accommodation of Friends . . . the walls were therefore made four-
teen and eighteen inches thick, the house is the whole width of the lot
by one hundred feet deep . . . it is now covered with an excellent roof,
the cellar has been dug, and the work has generally progressed with much
expedition . . . the intention of the committee is, to have the inside
of the meeting-house finished in a substantial plain manner, . . . to put
Youth's Galleries along the north, south and west walls, to have sliding
partitions for the convenience of separating the men's and women's meetings for business, and to plaster the walls. The General Committee of
the yearly meeting have given the materials of the Frame building on
Green Street erected for the accommodation of the late yearly meeting,
and those now in the meeting-house in Carpenter's Court will be used for
the new meeting-house. The committee is desirous that the monthly meeting will direct its attention towards purchasing the dwelling, stabling,
and lot of ground directly east of the meeting-house, containing 34 feet
on Cherry Street and extending in length to Race or Sassafras Street."
This building which was about 42 feet front on Cherry Street by 100 feet
deep, was commenced on November 19, 1827 and completely finished so that
meeting was held therein on February 3, 1828, a period of only 66 working
days in the most inclement season of the year. The following is from a
minute dated January 22, 1828: "It will be desirable to have the assistance of women Friends in the direction of cleaning the new house, preparing cushions, and other matters that will add to their comfort; the
committee would therefore suggest that their meeting should be requested
to appoint a committee for that purpose."

The present Friends' Central School (entry 436) had its beginning
on the site of the Cherry Street Meeting. In the summer and fall of 1835
a two-story school building was erected on the grounds, and in November
of that year a school was opened. The school was not very successful at
the start, but later developed into the large school that was situated
at Fifteenth and Race Streets, and later removed to its present location
in Overbrook.

The women's branch of the Philadelphia Yearly Meeting (entry 173)
was held at the Cherry Street meeting-house from the time of its erection until the Race Street house was opened, and that of the men convened during this period in the Green Street Meeting-house.

Meetings continued to be held in the Cherry Street house until the new meeting-house at Fifteenth and Race Streets was placed in use. The old house which had been in use 30 years became obsolete due to location and lack of room. At the women's yearly meeting of 1855 a report was received from the men's meeting giving the decision of that meeting to co-operate with the women's meeting erecting a new house. The report of the committee dealt with the finances and other matters relative to the purchase of ground and the building of a new meeting-house at Fifteenth and Race Streets.

After the meeting was removed to its new quarters at Fifteenth and Race Streets, the meeting-house property was sold. The meeting-house, however, was never actually demolished but from time to time, it was added to, built upon, over and about, until it is no longer recognizable. At the present time as No. 423 Cherry Street, it is occupied by the William H. Horstman Company, whose name and date, 1860, are on the front of the building.

See: Matlack, op. cit., II, 442.

For minutes and other records of the Cherry Street Meeting, refer to the entry for Philadelphia Monthly Meeting.

283. WEST PHILADELPHIA INDULGED MEETING, 1837--. Southwest corner
      35th Street and Lancaster Avenue, Philadelphia.
Set up in 1837 by Philadelphia Monthly Meeting of Friends (entry 280), upon approval of Philadelphia Quarterly Meeting of Friends (entry 279). The history of the West Philadelphia Friends Meeting at Lancaster Avenue, starts with a minute of Philadelphia Monthly Meeting held in March 1837, at Cherry Street meeting-house: "A committee of men and women Friends were appointed to consider the desirability of an indulged meeting in West Philadelphia." At the next monthly Meeting held April, 1837: "The joint committee of men and women Friends appointed to take into consideration the opening of an indulged meeting in West Philadelphia, having twice met and deliberated thereon, feel willing to recommend to the monthly meeting that an indulged meeting for worship, on First-days, in the morning, under the care of a committee, be opened in West Philadelphia, to commence the last First-day of the present month and continue until the last First-day of the 10th month next, inclusive, at 10 o'clock in the morning." Meetings were first held in a room of a building, which was situated at what is now the northwest corner of Thirty-second and Ludlow Streets. At a meeting held October 17, 1838: "The committee appointed to the care of the indulged meeting at West Philadelphia, reports they have generally attended to their appointment and have had a conference with some of the Friends for whose accommodation it was instituted. After a comparison of sentiments, the committee was united in judgment that the meetings had been satisfactory, and are free to recommend that the same be further continued for one year, under the care of a committee who shall, at the end of that time, report to the monthly meeting. It was also believed right to suggest the propriety of the erection of a suitable meeting-house." In October 1839, the meeting was continued for another year, and it was suggested that members belonging to the meeting at 9th and Spruce Streets, who lived west of the Schuylkill River, be invited to attend the West Philadelphia meeting. This suggestion did not, however, meet with the approval of either the men's or women's meeting. Although the building of a meeting-house was suggested as early as 1838 nothing was done about the matter until 1851. Meetings continued to be held in

the same room which was engaged in 1837. In 1851 a gray stone meeting-
house, two stories high, was erected on a plot of ground purchased for
the purpose, on the southwest corner of Thirty-fifth Street and Lancaster
Avenue. The first meeting in the new house was held in September 1851.
In 1859 the meeting was listed in McElroy's City Directory as being located at Lancaster Avenue and Pine Street. However, an old atlas of the
city of Philadelphia discloses the fact that 35th Street at the time end-
ed on the north side of Lancaster Avenue, and the section of it extending
half a block south of Lancaster Avenue, and now called 35th Street, was
designated in this atlas as L. Pine Street (probably Little Pine Street).
This accounts for the confusion as to the location of the building erected
in 1851, and identifies it with the present building. In 1853 the West
Philadelphia Friends' School was inaugurated. Sessions were first held
in the basement of the meeting-house. This school was in charge of a
committee of the West Philadelphia Meeting. It did not prosper very well,
and came near dissolution in 1857. It struggled on, however, and began
to improve and in 1863 was placed in the care of the committee which had
charge of the Race Street schools. It then had 44 pupils. In 1873 a new
schoolhouse was built adjoining the meeting-house on the east, half of the
expense of which was borne by the monthly meeting. In 1885 the enrollment
was 137. In 1901 the present schoolhouse was erected at a cost of $20,000.
It is a two-story red brick structure, constructed as an annex to the present meeting-house.

In 1901, when the new schoolhouse was built it was decided to build
a new meeting-house at the same time. This meeting-house, the one that
stands today, is a two-story red brick building of the unusual type of
plain architecture, with slanting roofs, and is built to adjoin the school
building. It has a small portico supported by wooden columns. Two date
stones have been placed in the front wall, one bearing the date of the
first meeting-house, 1851, and the other the date of the present one,
1901.

See: "One Hundredth Anniversary at West Philadelphia," Philadelphia
Friends Intelligencer, XCIV (1937), 327; Matlack, op. cit., II, 529; Ira
Bowne, Historical Record, West Philadelphia Meeting (manuscript at Swarthmore College Library); Mildred Willcox, Friends' Schools (manuscript in
custody of the author.

284. EXETER MONTHLY MEETING, 1827--. 106 North 6th Street, Reading,
Berks County.
Continued as a Hicksite meeting after division of the original Reading
Preparative Meeting (entry 28). In 1827 meetings were held alternately
in Reading and in the meeting-house of the Maidencreek Preparative Meeting (entry 285). Meetings in Reading were held in the small log building,
erected in 1765, which was retained from the original meeting along with
a cemetery lot on 6th Street and a log schoolhouse erected near the meeting house. By order of the monthly meeting the present one-story limestone building was erected in 1867-68. The Washington Street lot was
disposed of at public sale and the old log meeting-house was purchased
by Rachel Griscom, who razed the building, and saved only the antique
items. In 1920 an annex was added to the present meeting-house by the
Red Cross in recognition of the use of the meeting-house as a Red Cross
headquarters during the World War. This annex is now used by the Daniel
Boone Chapter of the Berks County Boy Scouts. The 1/8-acre burial ground
adjoins the meeting-house, though it is no longer used for burials. The
present clerk is Emily E. Boyer, 714 North 5th Street, Reading.

See: Montgomery, op. cit., I, 46; Fox, Cyrus, op. cit., I, 85; Stahle, op. cit., p. 19; Eshelman, op. cit., pp. 1-66.

Minutes of Men's Meetings, 1809-29, 1 vol., at PPFYR, and 1829-1901 2 vols., at PSC-Hi. Minutes of Women's Meetings, 1737-1880, 2 vols.; Minutes of Joint Meetings, 1895-1901, included in 1829-1901 vol. of Minutes of Men's Meetings (1902-29 missing), and 1930--, 1 vol., at meeting-house. Registers of Births, Deaths, Marriages and Removals, 1739-1883, 3 vols., at PSC-Hi. Berks County Deed Books, vol. 61, p. 502; vol. A-2, p. 5; vol. 78, p. 359.

285. MAIDENCREEK PREPARATIVE MEETING, 1827--. One and one-half miles east of Leesport, 1/2 mile east of Kindts Corner on Route #63, off Route #383, Berks County.

Continued as a Hicksite meeting in 1827 by Exeter Monthly Meeting (entry 284), after division of the original Maidencreek Preparative Meeting (entry 26). This meeting retained the one-story gray stone meeting-house erected in 1759; the one-story gray limestone schoolhouse built in 1807; and the 1-acre cemetery. All these properties were adjacent to each other and were located near what was then known as the Stone Bridge on the site of what is today the Maidencreek Reservoir, sometimes called the Lake Ontelaunee. The schoolhouse, which had been used by the original meeting for a weekday school, continued as such under the Hicksite Friends until it was closed in 1870. In 1926 the city of Reading purchased the land surrounding the meeting-house, school, and cemetery and in 1928 the land upon which these properties stood, with the agreement that, "the City of Reading shall remove the building stone for stone and rebuild it with the same material on another piece of land suitable to the Friends." The school-house and the cemetery were transferred to the present location under the same agreement. The city of Reading agreed to landscape the new 5-acre property and give it perpetual care. The present meeting-house of the Maidencreek Preparative Meeting (Orthodox) stands on an adjoining plot of ground.

See: Montgomery, op. cit., I, 46; Fox, Cyrus, op. cit., I, 85; Eshelman, op. cit., pp. 1-66.

Minutes and Registers are in the records of the Exeter Monthly Meeting.

286. POTTSVILLE INDULGED MEETING, 1831-ca.1836. Southwest corner of Ninth Street and Schuylkill Avenue, Pottsville, Schuylkill County.

Established in 1831 by Exeter Monthly Meeting (entry 284), after division of the original Pottsville Indulged Meeting (entry 30). In the early part of 1831, 1 acre of ground was purchased from Benjamin Potts. In the same year a one-story brick meeting-house was erected and a burial ground was plotted. The history of this meeting is very obscure because of absence of records and data. The meeting-house was converted into a public school during, or immediately following, the year 1836. An old history of Schuylkill County states that on May 20, 1836, it was resolved that the school in the second-story of the Friends meeting-house on Sharp Mountain should be called School number 1, and the school in the lower story of the same should be called School number 2. In 1841 Sarah Hunt paid a religious visit to Pottsville and recorded in her journal: "Our course led us to the foot of the mountains through several villages to Pottsville, where we stopped and dined at James Gillingham's. His is, I think, the only Friends' family here, and we had an opportunity with them." The old Friends' meeting-house, known as the old Bunker Hill School, was a large brick house that later became the property of Henry C. Russell, and is now a part of St. John's Roman Catholic Church. During the Civil War it was used as a hospital. The Friends' burial ground is situated several feet west of the meeting-house and is in the rear of the present St. John's Parochial School. There are 31 memorial stones of which 8 are uninscribed field stones. The family names being Evans, Griscomb, Hawley, Holme and Robertson. Only one stone is marked in strictly Quaker language and several bear the insignia of the Grand Army of the Republic. According to a minute of Philadelphia Monthly Meeting the financial care of the burial ground was transferred in part to that monthly meeting some time prior to that date.

See: Matlack, op. cit., II, 494-497, 536-538; Michener, op. cit., pp. 64, 65; W. W. Munsell, History of Schuylkill County, p. 163; "Society of Friends," Pottsville Evening Republican, July 28, 1926.

287. GREEN STREET MONTHLY MEETING, 1827--. Southeast corner of Fourth and Green Streets, Philadelphia.
In 1827 meetings of Green Street Monthly Meeting were continued without interruption after it severed its connection with the original Philadelphia Quarterly Meeting (entry 2) and joined with the newly organized Hicksite Quarterly Meeting at Abington (entry 174). Hicksite Friends of Frankford and a few from the Coulter Street meeting formed a meeting of their own and attached themselves to Green Street Monthly Meeting, with the approval of the Abington Quarter. When the Girard Avenue Meeting was first established it was under the supervision of a committee of Green Street Monthly Meeting, but later became indulged by the monthly meetings of 15th and Race Streets and Green Street jointly. When Fair Hill Meeting was re-established in 1880 it was also attached to Green Street as an indulged meeting. The Frankford and Fair Hill indulged meetings are still affiliated with Green Street Monthly Meeting.   As the city grew the Green Street neighborhood changed and members moved to more desirable sections. With the constant decrease in membership it was dscided to close the old meeting-house. In 1913 the quarterly meeting finally decided to buy it in order to keep it in the hands of Friends. The building still stands and is in a good state of preservation. Under the supervision of the quarterly meeting, a Friends' Neighborhood Guild is maintained there. The old two-story red brick school building at the southeast corner of the meeting-house grounds is now used as a part of the equipment of the Guild. After the sale of the meeting-house the monthly meetings were held at the meeting-house on School House Lane, and at the Seventeenth and Girard Avenue meeting-house. Green Street Preparative Meeting was held at the Girard Avenue house, and all further meetings at Fourth and Green Streets were suspended. Monthly meetings were continued under this alternate arrangement until 1917, when it was agreed to hold meetings at the Germantown house, and to discontinue the alternate meetings at Girard Avenue. Green Street preparative meeting and the preparative meeting held at Germantown were both laid down a short time after the monthly meeting settled there.   The present clerk is Charles F. Jenkins, 232 South 7th Street, Philadelphia.

See: Shoemaker, op. cit.; "Friends Stirred By Fate of Old Meeting House," Philadelphia Public Ledger, April 23, 1911; Lippincott, Account, passim.

Minutes of Men's Meetings, 1827-1904, 6 vols.; Minutes of Women's Meetings, 1827-1904, 5 vols.; Minutes of Joint Meetings, 1904-26, 4 vols., at meeting-house, 45 W. School House Lane, Germantown. Minutes of Joint Meetings, 1926--, 1 vol., in custody of the clerk. Minutes of Ministers and Elders, 1827-1919, 1 vol. (1827-77 missing), 1877-1919, 1 vol., at meeting-house and 1919--, incorporated in the minutes of the monthly meeting. Minutes of Overseers, 1827--, 3 vols. (1827-50 missing), 1850--, 3 vols., in safe at meeting-house. Register of Members, 1827--, 5 vols.; Register of Births, Deaths and Burials, 1827--, 1 vol.; Register of Marriages, 1827-56, 1 vol.; Marriage Certificates, 1856-1931, 1 vol.; Marriage Certificates (Photostats), 1931--, 1 vol.; Certificates of Removal and Transfer, 1827--, 2 vols.; Records of Peace and Service Committee, 1923-34, 1 vol.; all at meeting-house. Financial records are incorporated in the minutes of the Monthly Meeting.

288. GREEN STREET PREPARATIVE MEETING, 1827-1914. Southeast corner of Fourth and Green Streets, Philadelphia.
In 1827, at the time of the Separation, sessions of Green Street Preparative Meeting were resumed after a short suspension. The meeting-house which they had occupied with the original Green Street Monthly Meeting (entry 54), was again the place of their meeting. They met continuously at the Fourth and Green Streets meeting-house until it was sold to the Quarterly Meeting in 1913. The meeting was then removed to the meeting-house at Seventeenth Street and Girard Avenue. In the latter part of 1913 attendance at the meeting became very small and a request was made to the monthly meeting for permission to lay it down. This was done by the quarterly meeting of January 1914.

Minutes of Men's Meetings, 1827-1902, 4 vols., 1827-46, 2 vols. (1846-57 missing), 1857-60, 1 vol. (1860-75 missing), 1875-1902, 1 vol.; Minutes of Women's Meetings, 1827-1902, 9 vols.; Minutes of Joint Meetings, 1902-14, 1 vol.: all at meeting-house, 45 West School House Lane, Germantown.

289. FRANKFORD PREPARATIVE MEETING, 1827-76. Unity and Waln Streets, Frankford, Philadelphia.
Continued as a Hicksite meeting in 1827 by the monthly meeting of Friends held at Green Street, Philadelphia (entry 287), and by approval of Abington Quarterly Meeting (entry 174). At the time of the Separation the majority of the Frankford Friends followed the Hicksite branch of the Society. This meeting retained all property of the meeting and merged with a group of Friends from Germantown to form one meeting. The meeting was called the Frankford Preparative Meeting for Friends of Germantown and Frankford. All meetings were held at Frankford in the small one-story red brick and gray stone meeting-house formerly occupied by the original meeting. This building was erected in 1775, with an addition in 1811. In 1829 Friends of Germantown purchased a plot of ground on School House Lane, west of Germantown Avenue, on which they erected a meeting-house, and from the time of completion of this building, meetings for worship were held at each of the two meeting-houses, while business meetings alternated between the two. At a meeting of Frankford Preparative Meeting in 1876 this meeting was laid down and an indulged meeting established, and attached to Green Street meeting. The Germantown group were set up as Germantown Preparative Meeting in 1876.

The little graveyard adjoining the meeting-house was acquired about 1684, and contains slightly over 1 acre of ground. Date of first inter-

ment was 1687; burial records for the period prior to 1827 are found wit
the Orthodox records, and are stored at the depository, 302 Arch Street
Burials since 1827 are recorded in the burial record of Green Street Montl
ly Meeting. While there has been no burials in these grounds in almos
50 years, the graveyard is not closed to those still holding certificate
for burial lots and to Friends that would desire burial there. Most in
terments of the Hicksite branch of Frankford Friends within the last 5(
years have been made at Fair Hill burial grounds.

   See: Smedley, Caroline, op. cit., pp. 133, 136, 147, 148; Brinton
op. cit., p. 135.

   Minutes of Men's Meetings, 1827-76, 1 vol.; Minutes of Women's Meetings, 1827-75, 2 vols., at meeting-house of the Green Street Monthly Meeting, 45 West School Lane, Germantown. All registers of Births, Membership,
Marriages, Deaths and Removals, as well as all financial records are kept
by the Green Street Monthly Meeting.

   290. FRANKFORD INDULGED MEETING, 1876--.   Unity and Waln Streets
         Frankford, Philadelphia.
Established in 1876 by Green Street Monthly Meeting (entry 287), upon the
approval of Philadelphia Quarterly Meeting (entry 279). When Frankfor(
Preparative Meeting for Friends of Germantown and Frankford (entry 174)
was laid down in September, 1876, an indulged meeting attached to Greer
Street Monthly Meeting was established. This meeting has continued to
the present day and meeting for worship and First-day school are held in
the historic meeting-house, built in 1775.

   See: Smedley, Caroline, op. cit., pp. 133-136, 147, 148; Brinton,
op. cit., p. 135.

   291. GERMANTOWN PREPARATIVE MEETING, 1876-1913. 45 West School
         House Lane, Germantown.
Set up in 1876 by Green Street Monthly Meeting (entry 287). The title of
Frankford Preparative Meeting for Friends of Germantown and Frankford
(entry 289) was discontinued and the meeting at Frankford continued under
the name Frankford Indulged Meeting (entry 290). Meetings continued at
Germantown in the stone meeting-house, erected in 1856 by the former preparative meeting. The old building presented somewhat of a shabby appearance, and in 1910 the meeting subscribed the amount of $2,166 for repair
to it. The rebuilding was later accomplished by Green Street Monthly
Meeting, which was transferred to Germantown in 1913. After this transfer
of the monthly meeting there being no further need for a preparative meeting at Germantown, it was therefore laid down in December 1913.

   See: Lippincott, Account, passim.

   Minutes of Men's Meetings, 1876-1913, 1 vol.; Minutes of Women's Meetings, 1876-1902, 2 vols., at meeting-house. Registers of certificates
of transfer and financial records are in the records of the Green Street
Monthly Meeting.

   292. GIRARD AVENUE INDULGED MEETING, 1859. Northwest corner Girard
         Avenue and Seventeenth Street, Philadelphia.
Set up in Eleventh month 1859 by Green Street Monthly Meeting (entry 287),
and reorganized by Green Street Monthly Meeting and Philadelphia Monthly
Meeting (entry 280) in 1872. At a monthly meeting held at Green Street

in November 1859, a proposition for the establishment of a meeting for worship for Friends and others living in the northwestern section of the city was laid before the meeting. This was approved and a committee was appointed by the monthly meeting to assist in the opening of the same. A room at the northeast corner of Coates Street (now Fairmount Avenue) and West Street (now Uber Street) was engaged, where the first meeting was held on November 27, 1859, and continued there weekly under the care of the committee until 1860, when the monthly meeting at Green Street formally established it as an indulged meeting. In 1861 the meeting was removed to a room on the first floor of a building at the southeast corner of 19th and North Streets. Meetings continued at this place until 1866. Following this the meeting was held at the home of Alice Hunter, 721 West Street, until April 1867. The following First-day the meeting convened in the hall of the Mechanics Fire Engine Company, on Brown Street west of Broad, where it was continued until the 2nd of the 4th month 1871, when it was held in the second-story hall of a building at 1810 Poplar Street, continuing at this place until the present meeting-house at Girard Avenue and Seventeenth Street was erected. This house was built in 1872, and furnished by the joint efforts of the Philadelphia and Green Street Monthly Meetings under whose supervision this meeting came the same year. Prior to 1872 the indulged meeting was under the care of Green Street Monthly Meeting alone. The Girard Avenue Meeting-house is a natural gray stone structure with a large high-ceilinged meeting-room with a gallery, and a conference room at the west end.

School sessions were first held in the meeting-house in 1872, in two small rooms partitioned off for the purpose. School was continued in the meeting-house building until 1882, when a portion of the present school building was erected. Additions were added to the school from time to time until the present three-story red brick structure was attained. The three-story building is connected with the conference room of the meeting-house by a two-story red brick connecting building, which contains a school room on each of its two floors. In 1924 the school closed, and the remaining pupils of Girard Avenue School were transferred to the Friends Central School at 15th and Race Streets, which school was ultimately moved to its present location at Sixty-eighth Street and City Line, Overbrook. Membership of the meeting dwindled and in 1939 only appointed meetings were held three or four times a year. This indulged meeting is still under the care of the joint committee of oversight, appointed by Green Street Monthly Meeting and Philadelphia Monthly Meeting. In addition to holding appointed meetings for worship about four times a year, the meeting-house is used once a week, during winter months, for meetings of the Central Employment Association. This is a charitable organization, which does sewing, and helps the poor. Information has been received too late for revision, that this meeting-house has been sold.

Minutes of the School Committee of the Girard Avenue School, 1872-1924, 3 vols., at the depository of the Friends Central Bureau, 15th and Race Streets, Philadelphia. All other records kept by the two monthly meetings to which this indulged meeting is attached.

293. FAIR HILL INDULGED MEETING, 1880--. Southeast corner Germantown Avenue and Cambria Street, Philadelphia.
Set up as an indulged meeting in 1880 by Philadelphia Quarterly Meeting (entry 279), and attached to Green Street Monthly Meeting. Meetings were held in private homes 1880-83, when the present meeting-house, a one-story native gray stone building was erected, about 30 feet south of the site

of the first meeting-house (entry 9). A fire in October 1883 caused the meeting-house to close for repairs until January 1884. During this interval worship was again held in members' homes. In 1889 the old stone farmhouse, with its adjoining brick kitchen, which was the first meeting-house, was razed to make way for the opening of what is now Cambria Street. This street divides the present meeting-house grounds from the burial grounds. The present meeting-house is now used for worship and Sabbath school, and on week days is used by the American Red Cross.

The graveyard, 400' x 500' was acquired in 1703 and retained by this meeting in 1827. First burial May 12, 1843. Title transferred in 1817 to the Green Street Monthly Meeting (entry 54), by Philadelphia Monthly Meeting (entry 3). Lucretia Mott, the famous leader of Women's Rights and Anti-slavery Movements, is buried in this cemetery.

See: Westcott, op. cit., p. 76; Brenner and Beck, op. cit.; Lippincott, Joseph, op. cit., p. 365; Rules and Regulations for the Government of Friends Burial Grounds at Fair Hill - To which is Added - A Short Historical Account of the Title of Friends to the Premises.

Records of Burials, 1843--, 2 vols., in custody of William Cash, caretaker's residence on burial grounds.

294. RADNOR MONTHLY MEETING, 1827--. Conestoga Pike and Sproul
      Road, Ithan, Delaware County.
Continued as a Hicksite meeting in 1828 by Philadelphia Quarterly Meeting (entry 279) after division of the original Radnor Monthly Meeting (entry 15) in 1827. At the time of the Separation this meeting retained the one-story gray stone meeting-house, erected in 1718; the one-story stone building in which the deceased were placed before final interments; and the 2-acre burial ground, adjoining the meeting-house. The present clerk is Marian D. Grant, 112 East Marthart Avenue, South Ardmore, Upper Darby.

See: Matlack, op. cit., I, 503-506, 538; Michener, op. cit., pp. 59, 60; Bowden, op. cit., II, 247.

Minutes of Men's Meetings, 1827-87, 4 vols.; Minutes of Women's Meetings, 1827-87, 5 vols., at PSC-Hi. Minutes of Joint Meetings, 1887-1923 (included in the last volume of men's minutes, ending 1887), at PSC-Hi, and 1923--, 2 vols., in custody of clerk. Minutes of Ministers and Elders (1827-72 missing), 1872-1940, 3 vols. (1827-72 missing), at PSC-Hi, and 1940--, in custody of Samuel J. Bunting, Overbrook. Membership List, 1684-1911, 1 vol.; Register of Births and Deaths, 1685-1924, 3 vols., at PSC-Hi. Register of Births, Removal, and Deaths, 1918--, 1 vol., in custody of recorder, Mrs. R. Milton Croasdale, Bala-Cynwyd. Register of Marriages, 1763-1917, 2 vols., at PSC-Hi. Register of Membership and Marriages, 1891 --, 1 vol., in custody of recorder.

295. HAVERFORD PREPARATIVE MEETING, 1827--. Eagle Road, Oakmont,
      Haverford Twp., Delaware County.
Continued as a Hicksite meeting in 1827 by Radnor Monthly Meeting (entry 294). Previous to the Separation in 1827, this meeting had been a part of the original Haverford Preparative Meeting (entry 16). This meeting retained the one-story gray stone meeting-house and 3 acres of burial ground, which had been donated to the original meeting by William Howell in 1693. The burial ground is enclosed by a stone wall and a wire fence. In 1930, a stone addition was added to the meeting-house for the accommodation of the First-day school.

See: Michener, op. cit., p. 61.

Minutes of Men's Meetings, 1839-1918, 2 vols. (1827-39 missing), Minutes of Women's Meetings, 1872-79, 1 vol. (1827-72 1879-1918 missing), at PSC-Hi. Minutes of Joint Sessions, 1918--, 2 vols., in custody of clerk, Marion Anderson, Beverly Boulevard, Highland Park. Registers are in the records of the Radnor Monthly Meeting.

296. MERION PREPARATIVE MEETING, 1827--. Montgomery Pike and Meeting House Lane, Lower Merion Twp., Montgomery County.
Continued as a Hicksite meeting in 1827 by Radnor Monthly Meeting (entry 296), after functioning as the original Merion Preparative Meeting (entry 17) since 1682. This meeting retained the stone meeting-house erected in 1695 and the 413' x 310' burial ground which is now enclosed by a stone wall with two iron gates. This building underwent extensive repairs in 1713. Also a tablet in the right-hand corner of the meeting-house attests to a futher repairing and remodeling in 1829.

See: Michenerm op. cit., p. 61; Margaret B. Harvey, "Highlights of the Merion Meeting," Bryn Mawr News, September 27, 1895.

Minutes of Men's Meetings, 1832-85, 4 vols. (1827-31, 1835-53, 1860-61 missing); Minutes of Women's Meetings, 1819-84, 4 vols. (1837-47 missing): at PSC-Hi. Minutes of Joint Meetings, 1885-90, incorporated in 1868-90 vol. of Minutes of Men's Meetings, 1890-1929, 3 vols., at PSC-Hi, and 1930--, 1 vol., in meeting-house. Minutes of Ministers and Elders, 1907-38, 1 vol., at Swarthmore College Library. Registers are in the records of the Radnor Monthly Meeting. Financial Records, 1848-69, 1 vol., at PSC-Hi. Montgomery County Deed Books, vol. 23, p. 505; vol. 302, p. 312.

297. SPRUCE STREET MONTHLY MEETING, 1832-1903. Northeast corner of Ninth and Spruce Streets, Philadelphia.
Set up in 1833 by Philadelphia Quarterly Meeting (entry 279), upon the recommendation of Philadelphia Monthly Meeting (entry 280). At the time of the Separation in 1827 withdrawing members of Southern District Monthly Meeting (entry 37), which was then held at the Pine Street Meeting-house, temporarily joined with the Philadelphia Monthly Meeting held on Cherry Street. They subsequently purchased a lot of ground on the northeast corner of Ninth and Spruce Streets, and erected a red brick meeting-house thereon. A minute at this time states: "At a Monthly Meeting of Friends of Philadelphia held at Cherry Street, Third Month 21st, 1832 . . . a report being made that the house at the corner of Spruce and Ninth Streets will be sufficiently completed by the First-day of the Fourth Month to admit of the holding of a meeting; and the subject being now considered it was agreed to allow those Friends whose residence is now convenient to the vicinity of that meeting-house, to have an indulged meeting for worship on the first day of the week, morning and afternoon, to gather at the usual hours, and to be opened on the first First-day in next month . . .".

This indulged meeting functioned for only 3 months, when Friends of Spruce Street applied for a preparative and a monthly meeting of their own, as will be noted by the following minute: "At a Monthly Meeting of Friends of Philadelphia held at Cherry Street, Seventh Month 18th, 1832, a communication was received from the Friends who have for some time held an indulged meeting for worship on First-days of the week, at the corner of Ninth and Spruce Streets, with a request to hold meetings of worship on

First and Fifth days of the week, also a Preparative and Monthly Meeting; and latter to be held on the Fifth day of the week preceding the last Sixth-day in the month and to be called the Monthly Meeting of Friends of Philadelphia held at Spruce Street, the preparative meeting to be held the week preceding, and all at the usual hours, which, being deliberately considered was united with and the clerk is directed to forward informa- tion of the same to the Quarterly Meeting for its consideration and judg- ment . . . the meeting to be opened in the Ninth Month next." However, the monthly and preparative meetings were not established until the fol- lowing year, 1833.

With the removal of many Friends from the vicinity of Spruce Street meeting, the membership of the monthly meeting decreased to such a degree that in 1903 it was deemed advisable to discontinue the same, and accord- ingly the meeting was laid down by Philadelphia Quarterly Meeting in that year, and the remaining members were transferred to Philadelphia Monthly Meeting held at Race Street. In the same year the Spruce Street property was sold, and a short time later the meeting-house was demolished, and on its site a large manufacturing building was erected.

See: Matlack, op. cit., I, 516, 517; Michener, op. cit., pp. 54, 55, Bunting, op. cit., p. 18.

Minutes of Men's Meetings, 1833-93, 4 vols.; Minutes of Women's Meet- ings, 1833-93, 4 vols.; Rough Draft of Women's Minutes, 1833-35, 1 vol.; Minutes of Joint Meetings, 1893-1903, 1 vol.; Minutes of Ministers and Elders, 1845-97, 4 vols.; Minutes of Overseers Meetings, 1852-71, 2 vols.; Registers of Births, 1833-1903, 2 vols.; Registers of Deaths and Burials, 1833-1903, 1 vol.; Marriage Certificates, 1833-1903, 2 vols.; Certificates of Removal Issued, 1834-1903, 1 vol.; Certificates of Removal Received, 1833-1903, 2 vols.; Membership Roll, 1850-55, 1 vol.; Membership Roll, 1833-1902, 1 vol.; Treasurer's Account Book, 1834-1904, 1 vol.; Treasurer's Account Book of Women Friends, 1862-1901, 1 vol.; Trustees Account Book, Rowland Fund, 1861-66, 1 vol.; Sundry deeds, title papers, receipt books, etc., at PSC-Hi.

298. SPRUCE STREET PREPARATIVE MEETING, 1832-94. Northeast corner of Ninth and Spruce Streets, Philadelphia, Pa.
Set up in 1833 by Philadelphia Quarterly Meeting (entry 279). Friends of the Southern District Monthly Meeting (entry 37), who had withdrawn from that meeting at the time of the Separation in 1827, temporarily joined with Philadelphia Monthly Meeting (entry 280), then held on Cherry Street. In 1832 this group of Friends purchased a plot of ground at the northeast corner of Ninth and Spruce Streets, where they erected a meeting house. Upon completion of this house an indulged meeting for worship on Sundays under the oversight of the monthly meeting held at Cherry Street was allowed them. The monthly meeting a short time later, at their request, recommended to the quarterly meeting that they be allowed the privilege of a preparative and monthly meeting of their own. This was granted in 1833, and with the establishment of the Spruce Street Monthly Meeting (en- try 297), the preparative meeting was set up at the same time and became a part thereof.

In 1892 separate meetings of men and women Friends of the prepara- tive meeting were discontinued, and joint meetings were held thereafter. In 1894, there being no further use for a preparative meeting at Spruce Street, the same was laid down by the monthly meeting, upon the approval of Philadelphia Quarter.

See: Matlack, op. cit., I, 516, 517; Michener, op. cit., p. 55;
Bunting, op. cit., p. 18.

Minutes of Men's Meetings, 1833-92, 1 vol. (1833-67 missing), 1867-
92, 1 vol.; Minutes of Women's Meetings, 1833-92, 4 vols. (1833-43, missing); Minutes of Joint Meetings, 1892-94, 1 vol., at PSC-Hi.

299. VALLEY MONTHLY MEETING, 1936--. Tredyffrin and Schuylkill
     Twps., Chester County.
Previous to 1936 Valley Preparative Meeting (entry 300) had been a part
of Radnor Monthly Meeting (entry 294), but because it was so far removed
from the Radnor Monthly Meeting, it was deemed advisable that Valley Preparative Meeting set up its own monthly meeting. This was done and the
first monthly meeting was held September 13, 1936. The present clerk is
Frederick A. McCord, 401 Chestnut Lane, Wayne.

Minutes of Valley Monthly Meetings, 1936--, 1 vol., in custody of
clerk. Register of Marriages, Births, Deaths, and Membership, 1936--,
1 card file, in custody of recorder, Mrs. Lila C. C. Walker, 1331 De Kalb
Street, Norristown. Financial Records, 1938-- (1936-37 are incorporated
in the financial record book of the Valley Preparative Meeting), 1 vol.,
in custody of treasurer, Mrs. Emma E. Frorer, Wayne.

300. VALLEY PREPARATIVE MEETING, 1827-1939. Old Eagle or Port Ken-
     nedy Road (Route 652), 1/5 mile from Swedesford Road, Tredyf-
     frin Twp., Chester County.
Continued as a Hicksite meeting in 1827 by Radnor Monthly Meeting (entry
294). Previously had functioned as the original Radnor Meeting (entry
19). The stone building, which had been erected in 1775, just west of
the present meeting-house, and the graveyard were retained by this meeting. In 1869 in order to accommodate the quarterly meeting sessions, it
was decided to tear down the old meeting-house and build a new one. From
Joseph R. Walker the meeting purchased an additional plot of ground on
the eastern side of Eagle Road. On this newly acquired ground the present meeting-house, a two-story white stone building was erected in 1872,
and the ground on which the former meeting-house stood was utilized for
additional burial ground. Philadelphia Quarterly Meeting met here once a
year until 1902, when the Valley Friends asked to be relieved of the necessity of acting as their host. In 1935 the quarterly meeting again began meeting at this meeting-house. In 1936 Valley Preparative Meeting
began to consider the desirability of laying down the preparative meeting
and establishing a monthly meeting. Accordingly, Valley Monthly Meeting
was established September 3, 1936, and on January 9, 1939, Valley Preparative Meeting was laid down.

Valley Burial Ground was established long before the meeting. Lewis
Walker, during the latter part of the seventeenth century permitted the
Friends to bury in the private burial grounds on his property at "Rehobeth." In his will Lewis Walker bequeathed to the Friends of Valley a-
bout 3/4 of an acre of ground to be used for burial purposes. In a will
dated December 13, 1817, Joseph Walker bequeathed an additional 6 perches
of ground. Again in 1852, Friends purchased from Joseph Walker 1/2 of an
acre. The burial ground is enclosed by a stone wall on all sides, except
along the Eagle Road, where an iron fence, with a wide entrance is found.

See: Futhey and Cope, op. cit., p. 23 7 Streets, op. cit., pp. 20-
22; Heathcote, op. cit., p. 340; Thomson, op. cit., p. 749; Harry Wildes,

Valley Forge, p. 178; Charles H. Browning, Welsh Settlement of Pennsylvania, pp. 504, 505, 575; "Valley Meeting," West Chester Daily Local News, July 29, 1931; "Valley Meeting 200 Years Old," West Chester Daily Local News, September 14, 1931.

Minutes of Men's Meetings, 1827-1911, 2 vols.; Minutes of Woman's Meetings, 1842-96, 3 vols. (1828-42 missing), at PSC-Hi.   Minutes of Joint Meetings, 1911-39, 2 vols., in custody of J. Barclay Jones, Radnor. Financial Records, 1922-37, 1 vol. (1827-1922 missing), in custody of treasurer, Mrs. Emma E. Frorer, Wayne, and 1937-39, incorporated in the financial record book of the Valley Monthly Meeting. Registers recorded in record books of the Radnor Monthly Meeting.

    301. SCHUYLKILL INDULGED MEETING, 1927--. Corner Stores (near Phoenixville, at intersection of Long Ford and Nutts Avenue Roads), Chester County.

Continued as a Hicksite meeting in 1827 by Radnor Monthly Meeting (entry 294). From 1812-27 the Friends of this meeting were members of the original Schuylkill Indulged Meeting (entry 22). At the time of the Separation in 1827, the stone meeting-house and the 2-acre burial ground were retained by this meeting. In 1843 the meeting was set up as the Schuylkill Preparative Meeting by Radnor Monthly Meeting and remained as such until the latter part of 1850, when the preparative meeting was laid down and Schuylkill was returned to its original status as an indulged meeting. In later years the attendance of the meeting waned so noticeably that from 1933-38 no meetings were held. However, in 1938 attendance revived, and the weekly meetings were renewed.

    See: Futhey and Cope, op. cit., Chester County, p. 242; Pennypacker, op. cit., p. 189; Michener, op. cit., p. 62; Smedley, R. C., op. cit., pp. 174, 192, 206-214, 326, 340; William Still, The Underground Railroad, pp. 688-690; Heathcote, op. cit., p. 238; Thomson, op. cit., pp. 345, 346; "Visited Old Meeting House," Philadelphia Record, July 21, 1901; "Friends Centennial, at Corner Stores," West Chester Daily Local News, October 2, 1909; "Friends' Centennial Ends," West Chester Village Record, October 7, 1909; Sarah F. Pennypacker, "Schuylkill Meeting," Phoenixville Daily Republican, December 3, 10, 17, 24, 31, 1938, January 7, 1939.

FISHING CREEK HALF-YEAR MEETING (H)
(entry 308)

Component Meetings

(See: Explanatory Note 3)

	Date established	Entry number
MUNCY MONTHLY MEETING		
(Later FISHING CREEK)	1827	309
Greenwood Indulged Meeting	1827	302
ROARING CREEK MONTHLY MEETING	1827	303
Berwick Indulged Meeting	1827	304
Berwick Preparative Meeting	1850	304
Catawissa Indulged Meeting	1827	305
Roaring Creek Preparative Meeting	1827	306
Shamokin Indulged Meeting		
(Bear Gap)	1840	307
FISHING CREEK MONTHLY MEETING		
(Formerly MUNCY, later MILLVILLE)	1856	309
MILLVILLE MONTHLY MEETING		
(MUNCY, FISHING CREEK)	1893	309
Roaring Creek Indulged Meeting	1917	310

MUNCY MONTHLY MEETING (entry 309).

302. GREENWOOD INDULGED MEETING, 1827-38. Two miles northeast
     of Millville on Rohrsburg Road, Greenwood, Columbia County.
Continued as a Hicksite meeting in 1827 by Muncy Monthly Meeting (entry 309), later Fishing Creek. Due to the scarcity of historical data
and the absence of records, it is not possible to give a detailed account of this meeting. "The Separation occurred among the Friends of
Columbia and Lycoming Counties sometime between 1827 and 1828. This
meeting was never flourishing and was permanently laid down in 1838,
which is verified by a minute of the Muncy Monthly Meeting: 'At Muncy
Monthly Meeting held at Fishing Creek July 8, 1938, the time for which
Greenwood Meeting was indulged has expired and Friends composing it requested it to be discontinued for the present which is agreed upon by
this meeting.'"

     See: Matlack, op. cit., I, 364-369.

Registers are in the records of Muncy Monthly Meeting.

303. ROARING CREEK MONTHLY MEETING, 1827-1917. Slabtown, south
     of Roaring Creek, Columbia County.
Continued as a Hicksite meeting in 1827 by Philadelphia Quarterly Meeting (entry 279), after division of the original Roaring Creek Monthly
(entry 47). Meetings were held in the one-story frame meeting-house,
of the Roaring Creek Preparative Meeting (entry 306). Elias Hicks,
founder of the Hicksite movement spoke at this meeting house. In 1828
John Comly, prominent Hicksite Friend came here on a religious mission,
and before leaving the vicinity, visited his relatives, who were members of this meeting. The meeting house was the scene of many famous
visits by prominent Friends of the nineteenth century. In 1916 Fishing Creek Half-year Meeting (entry 308) reported to Philadelphia Yearly Meeting (entry 173): "Roaring Creek has discontinued all meetings,
except once a month, and these are held at Roaring Creek, except in
the Sixth-month, when they meet at Catawissa." Membership, however,
continued to decline, consequently, in 1917, the meeting was laid down,
and at the same time was established as an indulged meeting under the
care of Muncy Monthly Meeting.

     See: Michener, op. cit., pp. 140, 141; Matlack, op. cit., I, 353,
357, 387, 388.

     Minutes of Men's Meetings, 1814-1917, 2 vols.; Registers of Births
and Deaths, 1791-1901, 1 vol., at Swarthmore College Library. There
are no other minutes or registers available at the present time. Columbia County Deed Book, vol. 23, p. 717.

304. BERWICK PREPARATIVE MEETING, 1827-80. Second and Mulberry
     Streets, Briar Creek Twp., Berwick, Columbia County.
Set up as a preparative meeting in 1850 by Roaring Creek Monthly Meeting
(entry 303), after having functioned as an indulged meeting since 1827.
At the time of the Separation this meeting retained the meeting-house and
adjoining property which belonged to the original Berwick Indulged Meet-

ing (entry 50). When the status of the meeting was changed to that of a preparative meeting, the first meeting-house was razed and replaced by a red brick building. Although this meeting continued to function until 1880, there is no definite information to establish its status after 1865. From several reports to Fishing Creek Half-Year Meeting it is clear that Berwick really continued after 1865, although in a very weak condition. After the meeting was laid down the building was used as a schoolhouse until 1884. Some years later the property was sold to Judge Charles Evans. The Building was razed and on its site was erected a private dwelling.

See: Michener, op. cit., p. 139; Matlack, op. cit., I, 343-345; "Friends Meeting," Berwick Enterprise, June 26, 1936.

There are no minutes available at the present time. Registers are in the records of the Roaring Creek Monthly Meeting. Columbia County Deed Book, vol. 7, p. 679.

305. CATAWISSA INDULGED MEETING, ca.1827-ca.1870. South Street, Catawissa, Columbia County.
Continued as a Hicksite indulged meeting in 1827 by Roaring Creek Monthly Meeting (entry 303) after division of the original Catawissa Preparative Meeting (entry 48). At the time of the Separation this meeting retained 3/4 acre burial ground and the one-story log meeting-house of the original meeting. Due to the lack of definite historical data and absence of records, it is not possible to ascertain the exact year in which this meeting was laid down. About 1890 Mary Emma Walter opened the then closed meeting-house and each Sunday held a meeting for worship with herself the sole attendant. She continued this solitary meeting until her death in 1930.

The graveyard is separated by a crumbling stone wall from the meeting-house yard. The borough of Catawissa has taken responsibility for the care of the Friends meeting-house and cemetery, although the property belongs to Millville Half-Year Meeting.

See: Michener, op. cit., p. 138; Matlack, op. cit., I, 345-349, 385-387; Arabella Carter, "Old Building Long Closed She Saved from Disuse," Philadelphia North American, October 17, 1909; "A Meeting Composed of one Friend," Philadelphia Friends Intelligencer, October 30, 1909, Philadelphia Public Ledger, December 10, 1923.

Registers are in the records of the Roaring Creek Monthly Meeting.

306. ROARING CREEK PREPARATIVE MEETING, 1827-61. Slabtown, south of Roaring Creek, Columbia County.
Continued as a Hicksite meeting in 1827 by Roaring Creek Monthly Meeting (entry 303), after division of the original Roaring Creek Preparative Meeting (entry 49). At the time of the Separation, this meeting retained the one-story, frame meeting-house erected in 1796, and the adjoining burial ground. Due to the absence of historical data, very little is known about this meeting. North of the meeting-house is the spacious Roaring Creek Burial Ground, enclosed, in part, by an iron fence, and in part, by a stone wall.

See: Michener, op. cit., p. 141; Matlack, op. cit., I, 353-357, 387, 388.

There are no minutes available at the present time. Registers are
in the records of the Roaring Creek Monthly Meeting. Columbia County
Deed Book, vol. 23, p. 717.

307. SHAMOKIN INDULGED MEETING (Bear Gap), 1840-ca.1900. Bear Gap,
      Northumberland County.
Established in 1840 as an indulged meeting by Roaring Creek Monthly Meeting (entry 303). Prior to the erection of the one-story red brick building, Friends of this meeting held meetings for worship in a one-room
schoolhouse and in a gristmill, both located in Bear Gap. In the latter
part of 1840 a small plot of ground was acquired on which the meeting-house
was erected, and a portion was plotted for a burial ground. In 1894 the
name of the meeting was changed to Bear Gap Indulged Meeting. Due to the
absence of records and historical data, it is not possible to determine
how long this meeting existed and the exact date of termination. The
meeting-house was demolished about 1932. The burial ground, however, is
in excellent condition and is under the care of Millville Monthly Meeting
(entry 309).

See: Michener, op. cit., p. 141.

Registers are in the records of the Roaring Creek Monthly Meeting.

MILLVILLE HALF-YEAR MEETING (H)
(Fishing Creek)

Component Meetings

(See: Explanatory Note 3)

	Date established	Entry number
MILLVILLE MONTHLY MEETING		
(MUNCY, FISHING CREEK)	1893	309
Roaring Creek Indulged Meeting	1917	310

308. MILLVILLE HALF-YEAR MEETING, 1834--. Main and Maple Streets, Millville, Columbia County.
Set up in 1834 by Philadelphia Yearly Meeting (entry 173) under the name of Fishing Creek Half-Year Meeting. The first mention of this meeting is recorded in a minute of Roaring Creek Monthly Meeting (entry 303) in 1833: "We propose to the consideration of Muncy Friends the establishment of a Half-Year Meeting, to be held at Fishing Creek; and to be composed of that meeting and Roaring Creek." This movement claimed the attention of the yearly meeting which in 1834 granted the request of those isolated Friends in Columbia County. A minute of the yearly meeting of 1834 contains the following reference to a committee appointed to investigate the establishment of this meeting: "Most of Their number have attended said monthly meetings in Columbia County, and some of them have visited all the particular meetings constituting them since last year. On deliberate consideration . . . we unite in proposing their request be granted, and the said Half-Yearly Meeting be established at present under a committee of the yearly meeting, that it be called and known by the name of Fishing Creek Half-Year Meeting." The name Fishing Creek was retained until 1919, when the familiar name of Millville was adopted by both meetings. Since that year this section of the yearly meeting is known as the Half-Yearly Meeting of Friends at Millville. This meeting for many years held its sessions alternately in the meeting-houses of the various meetings in Columbia County. For the past 30 years meetings have been held exclusively in the meeting-house of Millville Monthly Meeting. The present clerk is Myra M. Eves, Millville.

See: Michener, op. cit., p. 137; Matlack, op. cit., I, 341-343.

Minutes of Men's Meetings, 1834-93, 1 vol., in custody of Charles Eves, Millville. Minutes of Women's Meetings, 1834-93, 1 vol., in Millville National Bank. Minutes of Joint Sessions, 1893--, in custody of Charles Eves.

309. MILLVILLE MONTHLY MEETING, 1827--. Main and Maple Streets, Millville, Columbia County.
Continued as a Hicksite meeting in 1827 by Philadelphia Quarterly Meeting (entry 279), under the name of Muncy Monthly Meeting, after division of

the original Muncy Monthly Meeting (entry 41). At the time of the Separation this meeting retained the one-story log meeting-house and the 3-acre burial ground from the original Fishing Creek Preparative Meeting (entry 42). The pioneer settlers of this community, John Eves and his wife Edith Westman are buried in this graveyard. When Fishing Creek Half-Year Meeting (entry 308) was set up in 1834, the meeting was transferred to this newly established meeting. The first meeting-house was replaced by the present one-story red brick building in 1846. In 1856 the name of this meeting was changed from Muncy Monthly Meeting to Fishing Creek Monthly Meeting, and in 1893 it was again changed to its present name. On June 19, 1856, the Millville Reading School held its first session. However, this school was short lived. The present First-day school was established a decade after the organization of the Millville Reading School. In 1900 supervision of the First-day school was taken over by Philadelphia Yearly Meeting (entry 173). The present clerk is Edith Y. Biddle, Millville.

See: Michener, op. cit., pp. 139, 140; Matlack, op. cit., I, 349-353.

Minutes of Men's Meetings, 1830-67, 1 vol. (1827-30 missing), 1834-93, 2 vols., at PSC-Hi. Minutes of Women's Meetings, 1834-93, 2 vols. (1827-34 missing), in Millville National Bank. Minutes of Joint Meetings, 1893--, 1 vol., in custody of clerk. Registers of Births, Deaths, Marriages, and Removal, 1834-94, 1 vol. (1827-34 missing), in Millville National Bank. Financial Records, 1834-94, 1 vol. (1827-34 missing), in Millville National Bank, and 1894--, 1 vol., in custody of clerk. Treasurer's Book of Ground Committee, 1898--, 1 vol., in custody of J. B. Kester, Millville. Minutes of Ground Committee, 1900--, 1 vol., in custody of clerk. Treasurer's Account Book of Peace and Service Committee, 1900, 1 vol., in custody of treasurer, Mrs. Minerva Davice, Millville. First-day Record Books, 1900--, 2 vols., in custody of secretary, William Eves, Millville.

310. ROARING CREEK INDULGED MEETING, 1917--. Slabtown, south of
        Roaring Creek, Columbia County.
Established in 1917 by Millville Monthly Meeting (entry 309). Meetings for worship are held in the one-story frame meeting-house, which was formerly occupied by Roaring Creek Monthly Meeting (entry 303). The interior is quaint; many of the benches are extremely primitive being made of heavy slab planking without backs. There is an odd three-legged clerk's table and a crude dividing partition in the room.

See: Matlack, op. cit., I, 353-357, 387, 388. Deed Book, Columbia County, vol. 23, p. 717.

This group never developed local monthly and preparative meetings. Hence, the only entry possible under this heading is that of the Yearly Meetings. (See: Historical Sketch, p. 23, for further history).

311. PENNSYLVANIA YEARLY MEETING OF PROGRESSIVE FRIENDS, 1853-1940.
Three miles east of Kennett Square, Route #1, Philadelphia-Baltimore Pike, Chester County.
Established May 22, 1853, after separating from Kennett Monthly Meeting (entry 244) and Western Quarterly Meeting (entry 240) of Hicksite Friends. From its establishment this meeting was known as the Pennsylvania Yearly Meeting of Progressive Friends, colloquially known and referred to as Longwood Yearly Meeting (see Historical Sketch, p. 26). As early as 1831 dissension arose amongst the members of the Kennett Monthly and Western Quarterly Meetings on the question of slavery. Many Friends wanted to take radical action in abolishing slavery. They were opposed by the conservative members. Many of the members with inclinations toward radical action were disowned and read out of meeting. However, an open breach did not occur until 1851, when the disowned members sought to conduct independent meetings in the Kennett Meeting-House. For 2 years Progressive Friends occupied the Kennett Monthly Meeting-house. On May 22, 1853, 58 men and women gathered in response to a "call for a General Religious Conference with a view to the establishment of a Yearly Meeting of such a character as the present crisis demands." Although practically all those assembled were members of the Society of Friends, they found the doors of the Kennett meeting-house barred against them and therefore made forcible entry. A reason for splitting with the Society of Friends is given in their Exposition of Sentiments: "It is our cherished purpose to restore the union between religion and life and to place works of goodness and mercy far above theological speculation and scholastic doctrine. Creed making is not among the objects of our association." Following meetings were held in Hamorton Hall, near Kennett Square, until 1855 when the present building was erected and dedicated on a plot of land donated by John Cope and his wife. The meeting-house, which is occasionally used today, is a spacious, white, frame building. A portico, supported by two columns, was added some years later. After President Lincoln's Proclamation of Emancipation liberated the slaves, a prominent member of the Old Kennett Meeting (Hicksite) wrote to the disowned members, and invited each to return. Most of them did so, but still maintained their interest in Longwood. The progressive Friends named their meeting-house "Longwood," after the name of John Cope's farm. Of late years no regular meeting for worship and business are held, but once a year, in June all branches of Friends, and some non-Friends interested in reform movements, have gathered at Longwood for conferences on vital topics of the day. On September 7 and 8, 1940, the Progressive Friends Yearly Meeting held its last sessions. It was officially discontinued at that time, and the property and other interests converted into a Longwood Association Lectureship on liberal and reform subjects. The present director of this lectureship is Jesse L. Holmes, Moylan.

See: Futhey and Cope, op. cit., pp. 242, 243; Emma Worrell, "Longwood, Meeting Then and Now," West Chester Daily Local News, September 4, 1903; Emma Worrell, "Memories of Longwood," Philadelphia Friends Intel-

ligencer, August 31, 1918; Jesse H. Holmes, "Longwood Yearly Meeting,"
ibid., August 29, 1936.

Minutes of the Representative Committee, 1892-1936, 3 vols. (1853-
92, 1904-18 missing); Minutes of the Financial Association, 1892-1936,
2 vols. (1853-92 missing), at PSC-Hi. In 1936 the Representative Committee and Financial Association were merged with the Trustees of Property. Minutes of the Trustees of Property, 1854--, 1 vol., in custody
of secretary, Mrs. Mabel K. Foulke, 120 Dean Street, West Chester. A
complete set of printed proceedings are on file at PSC-Hi. Chester County Deed Book, N-6, vol. 5, p. 110.

	Date established	Entry number
BALTIMORE YEARLY MEETING OF PRIMITIVE FRIENDS	1854	312
NOTTINGHAM QUARTERLY MEETING	1861	313
LITTLE BRITAIN MONTHLY MEETING	1864	314
Little Britain Particular Meeting (Ballance)	1864	328
NOTTINGHAM MONTHLY MEETING	1864	315
SALEM MONTHLY MEETING (See: Inventory of Ohio Church Archives)	(?)	Ohio
Sadsbury Particular Meeting	1854	316
FALLSINGTON GENERAL MEETING OF PRIMITIVE FRIENDS	1860	317
Falls Particular Meeting	1860	318
Horsham Particular Meeting	1860	326
Philadelphia Particular Meeting	1864	320
Bristol Particular Meeting	1860	319
Elkland Particular Meeting	1864	323
FALLS MONTHLY MEETING	1866	318
Bristol Particular Meeting	1866	319
Philadelphia Particular Meeting	1904	320
PHILADELPHIA MONTHLY MEETING	1866	321
Fallowfield Particular Meeting	1863	322
Little Britain Particular Meeting	1864	328
Elkland Particular Meeting	1866	323
Germantown Particular Meeting	1866	324
London-Britain Particular Meeting	1866	325
Horsham Particular Meeting	1866	326
Nottingham Particular Meeting	1868	Md.
NOTTINGHAM AND LITTLE BRITAIN MONTHLY MEETING	1868	327
Little Britain Particular Meeting (Ballance)	1864	328
Nottingham Particular Meeting (See: Inventory of Church Archives of Maryland)	1868	Md.

All available records for both the Baltimore Yearly Meeting and the Fallsington General Meeting, and also the subordinate meetings under them, are in the custody of Charles Henry Moon, Woodbourne, Pa.

312. BALTIMORE YEARLY MEETING, 1854-68. Five miles southwest of
        Oxford, Nottingham Village, Chester County.
Established in 1854 by dissenting members among Orthodox Friends, some
of whose meetings were in Maryland. (See forthcoming Inventory of Church
Archives of Maryland). In 1868 the meeting was laid down as the following
minutes will verify: "Baltimore Yearly Meeting of Men and Women Friends
held at Nottingham 10th month, 19th to 21st day, 1868. Report of Committee to General Meetings of Men and Women Friends held at Fallsington,
12th month last. We believe that the time has come for discontinuance
of our yearly and quarterly meetings, and for our monthly meetings to report to the General Meeting for Men and Women Friends for Pennsylvania,
New Jersey, Delaware, held at Fallsington, by adjournments from the 8th
and 9th of 9th month 1868. Report they have attended quarterly meeting
held at Little Britain in the 5th month and again the monthly meeting of
Nottingham and Little Britain, and Nottingham Quarterly Meeting held at
Nottingham in the 8th month, recommended acceptance of Nottingham Monthly
and Little Britain as a component part of our General Meeting in case the
yearly and quarterly at Nottingham shall be discontinued." Another minute states: "Fallsington, 9th month, 7th day, 1686, Solomon Lukens, Sarah
Cadwalader and committee prepared a minute to discontinue quarterly and
yearly meetings. The Treasurer is directed to pay over funds to the direction of the monthly meeting. The yearly meeting to be dissolved at
its close this year, and the quarterly meeting to be dissolved at its
close in 11th month. The Yearly Meeting of Ministers and Elders will
cease at its close in the 11th month next, and thence forth the select
Primitive Meeting is to report to the Meeting of Ministers and Elders
of the General Meeting of Men and Women Friends of Pennsylvania, New Jersey and Delaware, at Fallsington; That the Monthly Meeting after the 11 th
month report to said General Meeting as one of its subordinate branches
. . . That funds in treasurer's hands due the Yearly Meeting become subject to the direction of the monthly meeting . . . And that records and
papers of all the meetings hereby discontinued be subject to the direction of the General Meeting. Signed by committee, Joseph Ballance and
Lydia Waring."

        See: Hodgson, op. cit., II, 203-225; U. S. Bureau of the Census,
Census of Religious Bodies, 1926, Friends, pp. 29, 30, hereinafter cited
as Religious Bodies, 1926.

        Minutes of Men's Meetings, 1854-58, 1 vol.; Minutes of Women's Meet-
ings, 1854-58, 1 vol.; Minutes of Joint Meetings, 1858-68, in volume of
minutes of men's meetings; Minutes of Meetings for Sufferings, 1855-68,
1 vol.; Minutes of Ministers and Elders, 1856-68, 1 vol., in custody of
Charles Henry Moon, Woodbourne.

313. NOTTINGHAM QUARTERLY MEETING, 1861-68. Little Britain and Ful-
        ton Twp., Lancaster County.
Established in 1861 by Baltimore Yearly Meeting. Meetings were held alternately in Nottingham and Little Britain meeting-houses, located respectively in Colora, Md., and Ballance's, the latter situated partly in
Little Britain and Fulton Township, Lancaster County, Pennsylvania. This
meeting was officially laid down in 1868 when Baltimore Yearly Meeting
of Primitive Friends was dissolved.

        Records are incorporated with the minutes of the Baltimore Yearly
Meeting of Primitive Friends.

314. LITTLE BRITAIN MONTHLY MEETING, 1864-68. Route #222, Little
      Britain Village, Lancaster County.
Set up in 1864 by Nottingham Quarterly Meeting (entry 313) with the consent of the Baltimore Yearly Meeting (see forthcoming Inventory of Maryland Church Archives). The Primitive Friends obtained the one-story red
brick meeting-house, erected in 1840, and the 40' x 45' burial ground
from Little Britain Preparative Meeting, Orthodox (entry 354). When Nottingham Quarterly Meeting and Baltimore Yearly Meeting were laid down
in 1868, Little Britain Monthly Meeting was merged with Nottingham and
Little Britain Monthly Meeting (entry 327).

     The history of this meeting is obscure because of the absence of
historical data and records.

315. NOTTINGHAM MONTHLY MEETING, 1864-90. Little Britain and Ful-
      ton Twp., Lancaster County.
Established in 1864 by Baltimore Yearly Meeting (see forthcoming Inventory
of Church Archives of Maryland). Meetings were held alternately in the
Nottingham and Little Britain meeting-houses, located respectively in
Colora, Cecil County, Md., and Ballance's located in Lancaster County,
Pennsylvania. When Baltimore Yearly Meeting was dissolved in 1868, Nottingham Monthly Meeting was placed under the care of Falls General Meeting of Men and Women Friends (entry 317) within whose jurisdiction it remained until 1890, at which time it was officially laid down. The members were then transferred to Philadelphia Monthly Meeting (entry 321).

     See: Hodgson, op. cit., II, 203-225.

     No records are available at the present time.

SALEM MONTHLY MEETING (see Inventory of the Church Archives of Ohio).

316. SADSBURY PARTICULAR MEETING, 1854-66. Five miles from Fallow-
      field, Sadsbury Village, Lancaster County.
Established in 1854 by Salem Monthly Meeting (see forthcoming Inventory
of Ohio Church Archives). Meetings for worship were held in the home of
Joseph J. Hopkins, located midway between Gap and Christiana on the Gap-
Newport Road. Joseph Hopkins was a former resident of Baltimore, and it
was in his house in that city that the first session of Baltimore Yearly
Meeting (entry 312) was conducted.

     This meeting continued until 1866, when it was found to be out of
sympathy with the General Meeting and was officially laid down by Salem
Monthly Meeting, and its members joined to Fallowfield Particular Meeting (entry 322). There is some confusion concerning the history of this
meeting, and accurate data is not available.

     No records are available.

317. GENERAL MEETING OF MEN AND WOMEN PRIMITIVE FRIENDS OF PENNSYL-
      VANIA, DELAWARE, AND NEW JERSEY, 1860--. Intersection of Bris-
      tol, Pennsbury, and Burlington Roads, Fallsington Village,
      Bucks County.
Organized September 1860 at Fallsington by a small group of zealous members of the Orthodox Friends (see Historical Sketch, p.29). Solomon Lukens,
Charles Moon, Benjamin Cadwalader and Phoebe Ann Kirkbride were among the
organizers of the general meetings. The first general meeting was held

in the meeting-house of Falls Monthly Meeting, Orthodox (entry 162).
This meeting-house is now owned jointly by the Orthodox and Primitive
Friends. Interments of Primitive Friends are made in the burial ground
of Falls Monthly Meeting, Orthodox. The general meeting was originally
composed of Philadelphia Monthly Meeting (entry 321), Nottingham and Little Britain Monthly Meeting (entry 327) Salem (Ohio) Monthly Meeting,
and Falls Monthly Meeting of Men and Women Friends (entry 318). At present Falls Monthly Meeting is the only survivor. The general meeting
has been affiliated with a small meeting held at Fritchley, England, and
also with Friends at Poplar Ridgem New York, and Newport, Rhode Island.
The present clerk is Charles Henry Moon, Woodbourne.

See: **Religious Bodies, 1926, pp. 29, 30.**

Minutes of the General Meeting, 1860--, 4 vols.; Minutes of Ministers
and Elders, 1863-1921, 3 vols. (discontinued after 1921); Minutes of the
Committee on Publication, 1872-1917, 2 vols. (discontinued after 1917);
Register of Marriage Certificates, 1866-98, 1 vol. (Marriage records after 1898 kept by Falls Monthly Meeting), in custody of clerk.

318. **FALLS MONTHLY MEETING, 1866--.** Intersection of Bristol, Burlington and Pennsbury Roads, Fallsington, Bucks County.
The General meeting exercised the functions of the monthly meetings until the Primitive Friends were able to organize monthly meetings. This
meeting originated as a particular meeting at the time of the Primitive
Friends separation in 1861. It was proposed at the general meeting, in
April 1866, that Friends of Fallsington and Bristol, scattered members
in Bucks County, and Friends in Burlington County, New Jersey, should
form one monthly meeting to be called Falls Monthly Meeting of Men and
Women Friends. For many years meetings were held alternately in the Orthodox meeting-houses at Bristol and Fallsington. When the Bristol Particular Meeting (entry 319) was laid down in 1923, the monthly meeting
was then held permanently at Fallsington. The meeting-house at Fallsington is now owned jointly by Falls Monthly Meeting, Orthodox (entry 162)
and the Primitive Friends. Interments are made in the burial ground of
the Orthodox Friends.

Minutes of Joint Meetings, 1868--, 3 vols.; Minutes of Ministers and
Elders, 1870-78, 1 vol. (1866-70 in minutes of Joint Meetings), in custody of Charles Henry Moon, Woodbourne, and 1878--, in minutes of Joint
Meetings. Register of Births, Deaths, Membership, Marriages and Removals,
1866--, 1 vol., in custody of recorder, Sarah M. Otis, Woodbourne. Financial records are in the minutes of Joint Meetings.

319. **BRISTOL PARTICULAR MEETING, 1866-1923.** Northwest corner of
Wood and Walnut Streets, Bristol, Bucks County.
Established in 1866 by Falls Monthly Meeting of Men and Women Friends
(entry 318). Meetings for worship were held in the one-story brick meet-
ing-house of Bristol Preparative Meeting, Orthodox (entry 60). In 1887
Falls Monthly Meeting (P), purchased this meeting-house from the Orthodox
Friends. However, the Bristol Orthodox Friends meeting continued to meet
here until 1900 when it was laid down. Due to diminishing membership
Bristol Particular Meeting was laid down in 1923 by Falls Monthly Meeting.
The meeting-house was rezed in 1925 and the property upon which it stood
was sold in the same year to the trustees of the Italian Christian Church,
Bristol.

Records are not available.

320. PHILADELPHIA MONTHLY MEETING, 1866-1904. Coates Street (now
     Fairmount Avenue), above Eighth Street, Philadelphia.
This meeting was set up by Fallsington General Meeting of Primitive Friends
in 1866, having functioned as a particular meeting since 1864. The location of the meeting in 1864-65 was Coates Street above Eighth. Sometime
between 1865 and 1874 the place of meeting was changed to Olive Street
above Eleventh. A meeting-house existed at this address, but whether
built or bought outright by Primitive Friends, or what its syyle or material is not known. The meeting-house was sold in 1910 and a small library which it housed was moved to Bristol Meeting (entry 319). A meeting for worship was held from 1864-66 at which time this meeting was set
up as monthly meeting. From 1903 to 1906 the meeting apparently had two
meeting places, the new one being at 1218 Parrish Street, about two blocks
distant from the Olive Street house. After 1906 the Olive Street meeting
place was discontinued and the meetings were held at 1218 Parrish Street.
Meetings continued here until 1909; meantime the monthly meeting had been
laid down in 1904, and Philadelphia Particular Meeting (entry 320) set up.
This monthly meeting included as its subordinate meetings Nottingham,
Little Britain, Germantown, Horsham, London-Britain, Fallowfield, and
Elkland Particular Meetings. Philadelphia Monthly Meeting was set up by
authority of Fallsington General Meeting, which had exercised the functions
of both yearly and monthly meetings from the date of its origin in 1860 to
1866, and continued to do so with reference to a few particular meetings
which were not placed under monthly meetings at that time. The setting
up of Philadelphia and Falls Monthly Meetings in 1868 was an effort to
organize the Primitive meetings according to the usual Quaker system.

See: Register of Churches in Philadelphia City Directory, 1864-1909.

No records for this meeting are available.

321. PHILADELPHIA PARTICULAR MEETING, 1904-9. Olive Street above
     Eleventh Street, Philadelphia.
This meeting was set up as a meeting for worship in 1904, by Falls Monthly Meeting at the time Philadelphia Monthly Meeting was laid down. • It
apparently was established in place of Philadelphia Monthly Meeting (entry
321) when it became too weak to continue. This meeting was laid down in
1909 by Falls Monthly Meeting.

Records are not available.

322. FALLOWFIELD PARTICULAR MEETING, 1863-77. Route #82, East
     Fallowfield Twp., Fallowfield, Chester County.
Established in 1866 by Philadelphia Monthly Meeting (entry 321) after
having worshiped in a frame dwelling granted by Solomon Lukens for that
purpose in 1863. This house is at present occupied as a residence by
John Kendig, and is located on the east side of the Ercildoun-Doe Run
Road near Ercildoun (also called Fallowfield). Although largely attended
in early years, due to decreasing membership, this meeting was laid down
in 1877 by Philadelphia Monthly Meeting.

See: Hodgson, op. cit., II, 203-255, 307.

Records are not available.

323. ELKLAND PARTICULAR MEETING, 1866-1903. Elkland, Tioga County.
This meeting was established in 1866, and officially laid down on September 9, 1903 by Philadelphia Monthly Meeting (entry 321).

It is impossible to obtain further information concerning this meeting due to the lack of historical data and records.

324. GERMANTOWN PARTICULAR MEETING, 1866-80. Germantown, Philadelphia.

Germantown Particular Meeting was set up in 1866 by Fallsington General Meeting (entry 317) and placed under the jurisdiction of Philadelphia Monthly Meeting (entry 321) which was created at the same time. The exact location of this meeting is unknown; neither is dependable data concerning a meeting-house available, if one ever existed. The meeting was laid down in 1880 by Philadelphia Monthly Meeting.

No records are available, probably being kept by the Philadelphia Monthly Meeting.

325. LONDON-BRITAIN PARTICULAR MEETING, 1866-96. Route #896, Strickersville, London-Britain Twp., Chester County.

Established in 1866 by Philadelphia Monthly Meeting (entry 321). Primitive Friends occupied a small brick building near the meeting-house of London-Britain Preparative Meeting, Orthodox (entry 77). Services were discontinued about 1888 due to a decreasing membership, although it was not until 1896 that the meeting was officially laid down by Philadelphia Monthly Meeting.

See: Hodgson, op. cit., II, 307.

326. HORSHAM PARTICULAR MEETING, 1866-93. In the Horsham community 3 miles north of Willow Grove, in Horsham Twp., Montgomery County.

Horsham Particular Meeting was set up in 1866 by Fallsington General Meeting and placed under the jurisdiction of Philadelphia Monthly Meeting. If there was a meeting-house its exact location is not known. The membership dwindled so that in 1893 there was only one member, and the meeting was accordingly laid down in that year by Philadelphia Monthly Meeting.

No records are available.

327. NOTTINGHAM AND LITTLE BRITAIN MONTHLY MEETING, 1868-90. Route #222, Little Britain Village, Lancaster County.

Set up in 1868 by the General Meeting of Men and Women Primitive Friends of Pennsylvania, Delaware, New Jersey (entry 317), as the result of the merger of Little Britain Monthly Meeting (entry 314) and Nottingham Monthly Meeting (entry 315). The Nottingham and Little Britain Monthly Meeting retained the one-story red brick meeting-house, erected in 1840, and the 40' x 45' burial ground which had been obtained from Little Britain Preparative Meeting, Orthodox, by Little Britain Monthly Meeting. Because of decreased membership, the Nottingham and Little Britain Monthly Meeting was laid down in 1890 by the general meeting and its members were transferred to Philadelphia Monthly Meeting (entry 321). The meeting-house and burial ground is maintained by trustees appointed by the general meeting.

There are no minutes or registers available at this time.

328. LITTLE BRITAIN (BALLANCE) PARTICULAR MEETING, 1868-1890.
Little Britain Twp., Lancaster County.
Little Britain Particular Meeting, Primitive, was originally founded in
1857 as a result of the separation of Primitive Friends following the
Wilburite Controversy. It is also known as Ballance Particular Meeting.
From 1857 to 1864 the meeting was a particular meeting under Baltimore
Yearly Meeting of Primitive Friends. In 1864 that yearly meeting set
up Little Britain as a Monthly Meeting, which status it continued until
1868 when Baltimore Yearly was laid down and its constituent meetings
transferred to Fallsington General Meeting. At this time Little Britain
was again reduced to a particular meeting under the Nottingham-Little
Britain Monthly Meeting, which also became a part of Fallsington General
Meeting. The meeting continued this status until 1890 when Nottingham-
Little Britain Monthly Meeting was laid down by the general meeting and
the members attached to Philadelphia Monthly Meeting.

When this meeting was first formed as an Orthodox meeting after the
Separation in 1827 it was made up of members from Eastland and Little
Britain Meetings, who first met at the home of Joseph Ballance. In 1840
they erected a small red brick meeting-house 1/2 mile north of Wakefield,
Lancaster County. A 40' x 45' burial ground was acquired by the Little
Britain Primitive Friends. The meeting-house is still standing. This
meeting was laid down by Philadelphia Monthly Meeting in 1890 and the
members joined to that meeting.

No records are available.

The united meetings listed below and briefly described in the following four entries are the result of a definite but unorganized effort
to erase the mutual mistakes of the division which occurred in 1827. They
are treated here separately from either of the two branches because they
are the beginning of a new development in the Society of Friends which
began to take shape about 1920, although a tendency toward closer co-
operation of the two larger branches of the Society was apparent at a
much earlier date. These united meetings have combined their worship
and business meetings, and they maintain an official affiliation with
both the Hicksite and Orthodox quarterly yearly meeting.

UNITED MEETINGS

	Date established	Entry number
State College United Meeting	1909	329
Chestnut Hill United Monthly Meeting	1924	330
Concord United Monthly Meeting	1932	331
Providence United Monthly Meeting	1934	332
Radnor United Monthly Meeting	1937	333
Upper Dublin United Monthly Meeting [1]	1941	188
Harrisburg United Monthly Meeting [1]	1941	338

329. STATE COLLEGE UNITED MEETING, 1909--. South Atherton Avenue,
State College.
Meetings for worship were held as early as 1909 in private homes and in
the Foyer-Schwab Auditorium. Meetings were also held at a later date
in the parlor of the Friends Union, on the campus of The Pennsylvania
State College. In 1925, upon the request of the students, the meeting
was placed under a joint committee of the two Philadelphia Yearly Meetings
and given the status of a monthly meeting. In 1926 a frame meeting-house
was built at the above address, the expense borne largely by private subscription. There has never been a burial ground owned or controlled by
the Meeting.

---

1. Information on the transfer of these meetings to the status of united meetings
was received too late to include entries of them. This information has been added to the
entry of the Hicksite Upper Dublin Meeting in entry 188, and the Harrisburg Independent
Meeting, entry 338.

This meeting was established mainly for students attending the college, and therefore the rffices of clerk and recording clerk are filled by students. Necessarily these offices are held by many different students because of their relatively short stay in the community, so in order to have a permanent head of the meeting, a resident clerk has been selected. This clerk at present is a member of the college faculty and has permanent residence in the community, which gives continuity to the business affairs of the meeting. The present resident clerk is John H. Ferguson, 132 S. Patterson Street, State College.

Minutes of the Meeting, 1925-41, 2 vols.; List of Membership, including data on births, deaths, and marriages, 1925-41, 1 vol.: all records are in custody of the resident clerk. Centre County Deed Books, vol. 134, p. 462; vol. 140, p. 626.

330. CHESTNUT HILL UNITED MONTHLY MEETING, 1924--. 100 East Mermaid Lane, Chestnut Hill, Philadelphia.

Originated in 1924 by Abington Quarterly Meeting, Orthodox (entry 92), and Philadelphia Quarterly Meeting, Hicksite (entry 279). This was a local preliminary action, and was approved by the two yearly meetings about 1937. In the autumn of 1924, a number of Friends, both Orthodox and Hicksite, living in the vicinity of Chestnut Hill, found they shared a common concern for the establishment of a new meeting for worship. On November 9, 1924, 16 persons met at the home of D. Robert Yarnall. At this meeting it was decided that future meetings should be held in the large downstairs office of the Yarnall-Waring Manufacturing Company, 102 East Mermaid Lane. The meeting continued at this office until by membership subscription in 1931, ground was purchased at 100 East Mermaid Lane. The same year the present small one-story stone meeting-house was erected. The first meeting for worship in the new house was held September 13, 1931. In 1935 a burial ground approximately 50 by 300 feet was donated. This cemetery was formerly the property of the now defunct Gwynedd Monthly Meeting (0) (entry 96), and had been used by this meeting for many years. There have been no burials of Chestnut Hill members since date of acquisition. The present clerk is Leonidas Dodson, 213 Saint Mark's Square, Philadelphia.

See: D. Robert and Elizabeth Yarnall, "The Chestnut Hill Meeting," The Friend, CV (1931), 265; "Men and Things," Philadelphia Evening Bulletin, October 17, 1929.

Minutes of Meetings, 1924--, 2 vols.; Register of Births, Marriage Certificates, Membership, Deaths, 1924--, 1 vol.; Record of First-day School, 1924--, 1 vol., in safe at meeting-house. Record of Cash Receipts and Disbursements, 1924--, 1 vol., in custody of treasurer, Edwin A. Soast, 8025 Seminole Avenue, Chestnut Hill, Philadelphia.

331. CONCORD UNITED MONTHLY MEETING, 1932--. Concord and Thornton Roads, Concordville, Delaware County.

Although official recognition was not received from Concord Quarterly Meeting, Orthodox (entry 136) and Concord Quarterly Meeting, Hicksite (entry 218) until 1937, this meeting was functioning as the Concord United Monthly Meeting from 1932-37. A joint committee, consisting of Friends of the Orthodox and Hicksite Concord Monthly Meetings, drew up the following resolution: "(1) that for the present, and until there should be a more specific pronouncement from the two Yearly Meetings; (2) that Concord Friends do not for the present, look to any permanent union; (3) that they meet regularly for worship, with no distinction as to member-

ship or participation in the exercise of the meeting; (4) that the Monthly Meetings be held simultaneously and the clerk of the two meetings will
so arrange the business that the minutes of each meeting will record the
business, which is common to both, or which effects each alone, and will
exclude that which effects only the other meeting; (5) that at Meetings
for Discipline of both branches, the members of both branches, shall attend and take full part in all business; (6) that either branch shall be
at liberty at any time to meet separately for worship or discipline, and
that such a decision shall be considered in no sense a disrespect to the
other; (7) that each meeting shall contribute rotably /sie/ to the or-
dinary expenses of the meeting where used by both, but that contributions
and expense to a superior meeting, or organization be made separately;
(8) that trust funds be kept separate and used for the work or need of
the separate meeting; (9) that at all joint meetings, members of each
branch shall be eligible for service on Monthly Meeting Committees."
From 1932-36 meetings were held alternately at the meeting-houses of the
Hicksite and Orthodox Concord Monthly Meetings. Since then, meetings
are held exclusively in the meeting-house of the Hicksite Friends. At
the present time the Orthodox meeting-house is being rented to the Grange,
a farmer's organization.

Minutes of United Meetings, 1932-34, 1 vol., 1934--, 1 vol., in
custody of Mrs. Bertha Webster, Station Road, Cheyney. Register of
Births and Deaths, 1932--, in the membership books of the Concord Monthly Meeting, Orthodox, and the Concord Monthly Meeting, Hicksite; Marriage Records, 1932-34, marriage records of the Concord Monthly Meeting,
Orthodox, and the Concord Monthly Meeting, Hicksite; Register of Membership, 1932--, in the membership books of the Concord Monthly Meeting, Orthodox and the Concord Monthly Meeting, Hicksite; Certificates of Removal,
1932-36 loose-leaf forms in envelope, at FSC-Hi. Burial Records, 1932--,
in burial records of the Concord Monthly Meeting, Hicksite. Financial
Records, 1932--, 1 vol., in custody of Gilbert Schraeder, Concord Road,
Ward. Burial Ground Account Book, 1932--, in burial records of the Concord Monthly Meeting, Hicksite. Delaware County Deed Books, vol. 35, p.
159; vol. T, p. 508; vol. E-2, p. 694; vol. 1017, p. 176.

332. PROVIDENCE UNITED MONTHLY MEETING, 1934--. Providence Road and
            Baltimore Pike, Media, Delaware County.
In 1934 due to a division of Chester Monthly Meeting (H) (entry 222),
Concord Quarterly Meeting (H) (entry 218), set up Providence Monthly
Meeting. Meetings are held in the gray stone building erected in 1815,
which was deeded to Providence Monthly Meeting in 1935, by Chester Month-
ly Meeting. The Providence burial ground, consisting of 1 acre adjoining
the meeting-house, and Sandy Bank burial ground, on Providence Road near
State Road, and consisting of 3/4 acre were deeded to the meeting at the
same time. The Sandy Bank plot was donated by Thomas Powell in 1690.
This burial ground is no longer used. In 1937 with the approval of Concord Quarterly Meeting (H) (entry 218) and the Concord Quarterly Meeting
(O) (entry 136), this meeting became known as the Providence United
Monthly Meeting. The present clerk is Helen C. Bacon, Wallingford.

Minutes of Meetings, 1934-38, 1 vol. (includes minutes of Chester
Monthly Meeting, Hicksite, 1926-34); 1938--, 2 vols., in the custody of
clerk. Minutes of Ministry and Counsel, 1936--, 1 vol. (1934-36 missing), in custody of Mr. Ellis Bacon, Possum Hollow, Wallingford. Register of Births, Deaths, Marriages, Membership and Removal, Hicksite,
1934--, 2 vols., in custody of Miss Amy Way, 542 South Orange Street,

Media. Register of Marriage Certificates, 1934--, 1 vol. (includes marriage certificates of Chester Monthly Meeting, Hicksite, 1916-34), at
the Providence meeting-house. Financial Records, 1934--, 1 vol. (includes
financial records of Chester Monthly Meeting, Hicksite, 1910-34), in the
custody of Mr. William K. Brown, 509 Monroe Street, Media.

333. RADNOR UNITED MONTHLY MEETING, 1937--. Conestoga Road and
        Sproul Highway, Ithan, Radnor Twp., Delaware County.
Set up in 1937 with the approval of Philadelphia Quarterly Meeting (0)
(entry 2), and Philadelphia Quarterly Meeting, Hicksite (entry 279).
When the meeting was established its membership consisted in nine Friends,
five of whom belonged to Philadelphia Yearly Meeting (0), and four to
Philadelphia Yearly Meeting (H). Others were soon added and the present
membership includes 57 persons, 8 of whom hold membership in the Orthodox
group, 12 in the Hicksite group, and 37 are members of both yearly meetings; and all are members of the Radnor United Monthly Meeting. Meetings
are held in the one-story gray stone building erected by Radnor Monthly
Meeting (0) (entry 15), in 1718. The old horse shed has been remodeled
into a two-room building and is now used as a First-day School. The present clerk is Esther Magee, 306 Conestoga Road, Wayne.

Minutes of Joint Meetings, 1937--, 1 vol.; Register of Membership,
1937--, 1 vol., stored in meeting-house. Financial Records, 1937--, are
in the volume of joint minutes.

IX.   INDEPENDENT FRIENDS MEETINGS

The meetings listed below and noted in the following seven entries
are Friends meetings which have been organized in communities somewhat
isolated from other Friends meetings, and by groups of Friends consisting of members from the various branches, together with a few who have
not before been affiliated with Friends. Some of these meetings are so
situated that they have no occasion for organization. Others are similar to the United Meetings (entries 329-333) in that they also would
prefer to be affiliated with a united body of Friends. Since the way
is not clear at present for them to be set up under yearly meeting organization, two have been recognized as united monthly meetings by the
Fellowship Council of the American Friends Service Committee, and the
others are independent meetings with an informal organization. They are
responsible to no superior regional body.

	Date established	Entry number
Pittsburgh Independent Friends Meeting	1888	334
Buck Hill Falls Independent Friends Meeting	1901	335
Pocono Manor Independent Friends Meeting	1902	336
Pocono Lake Preserve Independent Friends Meeting	1905	337
Harrisburg Independent Friends Meeting	1909	338
Lehigh Valley Independent Friends Meeting	1930	339
Lake Shore Independent Friends Meeting	1936	340

334. PITTSBURGH INDEPENDENT FRIENDS MEETING, 1888--. Forbes and
      Bouquet Streets, Oakland, Pittsburgh.
Organized in 1888 by Benjamin Lightfoot and other Friends as an independent meeting. Meetings were held in the homes of members from 1888 to
1922, the home of Benjamin Lightfoot being used principally from 1888-98.
From 1922-26, meetings were held in the Y. W. C. A., 59 Chatham Street;
1926-29, in the Y. M. C. A., Wood Street; 1929-38, in an old school house,
926 South Aiken Avenue; and 1938-40, in Y. M. C. A. Community House, Forbes
and Bouquet Streets, Oakland, and 1940--, in the College Club, 141 N.
Craig Street. Meetings were held twice a month for some years, but are
now held weekly. This meeting was set up in Twelfth month 1940 as a U-
nited Monthly Meeting. It has over 50 members, drawn from several yearly meetings of all branches of Friends. It has no cemetery. Mrs. Hannah
B. Stratton of Moylan, the only living charter member of the group, states
that there were no business meetings, nor was the meeting for worship officially organized in her day. The meetings were: "parlor meeting held

in 'Auntie Lightfoot's home. Their son, Ferris Lightfoot, probably still living in Salem, Ohio, and four Stratton children filled in the family circle."

The clerk of the meeting is Winthrop M. Leeds, 256 Cascade Street, Pittsburgh.

The current minute book is in the care of the clerk. Earlier records are in the custody of Mrs. Edward Schriner, 60 Cedar Boulevard, Mount Lebanon. They are irregular, merely being notes on attendance, visitors, Friends who speak aloud, etc. There are no financial records. The few references to financial records are incorporated in the notes maintained by Mrs. Edward Schriner. No registers.

335. BUCK HILL FALLS INDEPENDENT FRIENDS MEETING, 1901--. Buck Hill Falls Inn, Buck Hill Falls, Monroe County.
Established in 1901 as an independent meeting by Friends, who desired to hold meetings during the summer months, while vacationing and were unable to attend their own meetings. While the larger part of the members of this group are Hicksite, many Orthodox Friends and persons of other denominations attend meetings for worship, which are held in the east room of the Buck Hill Falls Inn. From 1901-13, meetings were held only during the summer months. Since 1913 meetings have been held every First-day. The correspondent is Charles M. Thompson, Buck Hill Falls.

See: Matlack, op. cit., II, 939-941.

No regular records are kept.

336. POCONO MANOR INDEPENDENT FRIENDS MEETING, 1902--. Pocono Manor Hotel, Pocono Manor, Monroe County.
Established as an independant meeting in 1902 by Friends who desired to hold meetings during the summer months, while vacationing and unable to attend their own meetings. While the larger part of the members of this group are Orthodox, many Hicksite Friends and persons of other denominations attend the meetings for worship. Meetings have always been held in the recreation room of the Pocono Manor Hotel. Correspondent is the manager of the Pocono Manor Hall, Pocono Manor.

See: Matlack, op. cit., II, 974-976.

No regular records are kept.

337. POCONO LAKE PRESERVE INDEPENDENT FRIENDS MEETING, 1905--. Pocono Lake Preserve, Monroe County.
Established as an independent meeting in 1905 by Friends who desired to hold meetings during the summer months while vacationing and unable to attend their own meetings. First meetings weie held in tents of various Friends in the summer colony. Later, meetings were held in an open grove, equipped with wooden benches. During inclement weather, meetings are held in the recreation hall of the Preserve, situated on the grounds. While the larger portion of the members of this group are Orthodox, many Hicksite Friends and non-Friends attend the meetings for worship. Correspondent is the manager of Pocono Lake Preserve, Pocono Lake Preserve, Pennsylvania.

See: Matlack, op. cit., II, 974-976.

338. HARRISBURG INDEPENDENT FRIENDS' MEETING, 1909-35. Harrisburg,
      Dauphin County.
In 1909 a few members of both the Hicksite and Orthodox branches of the
Society of Friends met to establish a meeting for the Friends in Harrisburg. Meetings were held in the homes of the members until 1914, when
the meeting was discontinued. In 1921 Mr. A. Davis Jackson, a member of
Germantown Monthly Meeting, Hicksite (entry 287), re-established this
meeting. From 1921-28, meetings were held on the second floor of the
Patriot Building, 11 North 2nd Street, and from 1928-35, in the Pythian
Building, 225 State Street. Another lapse in the meeting occurred from
1935-39, when it was again revived. Meetings have been held regularly
since 1940 in the chapel of the Y.M.C.A. It was set up as a United Monthly Meeting in April 1941. The clerk is Marjorie M. Nevitt.

     Minutes of Congregational and Council Meetings, 1928-34, 1 vol.
(1909-27 missing); Treasurer's Records, 1909-14, 1921-35, 1 vol., in the
custody of Mr. A. Davis Jackson, 1618 Boas Street.

     339. LEHIGH VALLEY INDEPENDENT FRIENDS MEETING, 1930--. Bethlehem.
This meeting, sometimes called Bethlehem Friends Meeting, was organized
in 1930. Plans were first made for a Sunday afternoon meeting in the
Moravian Chapel in Bethlehem, to which the public was invited. The group
met again on Sunday afternoon, October 19th, at the home of Howard P.
Osler, Wayne Avenue, Overlook Terrace, Allentown. A few weeks later, on
the 2nd day of November, a third meeting of the Friends in the vicinity
of the Valley, was held at the home of T. L. Hazelhurst, 534 Tenth Avenue,
Allentown.

     The first general meeting of the newly formed Lehigh Valley Society
of Friends was held in the old Moravian Chapel of the Central Moravian
Church, Bethlehem, on Sunday, December 7, 1930. The chapel is located
in the rear of the Central Moravian Church. In 1934 meetings were still
held occasionally, but no meeting-house or permanent meeting place has
been established. In 1938 the Lehigh Valley Meeting, although not officially laid down became dormant. The correspondent is Hale Sutherland,
Lehigh University, Bethlehem.

     See: "Friendly News Notes," Philadelphia Friends Intelligencer,
October 18, November 10, 1930.

     No regular records have been kept.

     340. LAKE SHORE INDEPENDENT MEETING, 1936--. 324 East 27th Street,
     Erie, Erie County.
Established 1936, having neither the status of a monthly nor a preparative meeting, by William Bannister and his mother, Mrs. Florence Bannister,
who are members of Swarthmore Monthly Meeting. Meetings are held in the
homes of various members. This meeting is an independent meeting under
the guidance of the Fellowship Council of the American Friends Service
Committee, and of the Advancement Committee of Friends, General Conference, 1515 Cherry Street, Philadelphia. The correspondent is William
Bannister, 324 East 27th Street, Erie.

     Minutes and Financial Records, 1936--, 1 vol.; Membership Records,
1936--, 1 vol., in custody of clerk.

X. FRIENDS MEETINGS WITH EXTRA-STATE AFFILIATIONS

The following list of meetings and entries are those meetings which although located within the Commonwealth, are under the supervision of yearly meeting in adjoining States. These are arranged under the yearly meetings with which they are or were affiliated. Since the headquarters of these yearly meetings are not located in Pennsylvania no entries nor lists or records appear in this volume. For full information concerning these yearly meetings and the other subordinate meetings under them consult the inventories of the church archives of the States indicated in each particular case.

Because of lack of records it has been impossible to check much of the data given under these meetings. It was necessary to depend upon community tradition to a large extent and for that reason allowance must be made for error in the sources of information. This applies especially to the extra-State meetings under the two Ohio Yearly Meetings.

BALTIMORE YEARLY MEETING (O)
(See: Inventory of Church Archives of Maryland)

	Date established	Entry number
Warrington Quarterly Meeting	1787	341
Nottingham Quarterly Meeting	1819	350
Baltimore Quarterly Meeting		MD.
Dunnings Creek Quarterly Meeting	1840	359

BALTIMORE YEARLY MEETING (H)
(See: Inventory of Church Archives of Maryland)

Centre Quarterly Meeting	1835	365
Nottingham Quarterly Meeting	1827	372
Warrington Quarterly Meeting	1827	380

OHIO YEARLY MEETING (O)
(See: Inventory of Church Archives of Ohio)

Redstone Quarterly Meeting	1797	386
Salem Quarterly Meeting	(?)	Ohio

	Date established	Entry number
Middleton Quarterly Meeting	(?)	Ohio
New Garden Quarterly Meeting	(?)	Ohio

OHIO YEARLY MEETING (H)
(See: Inventory of Church Archives of Ohio)

Salem Quarterly Meeting	(?)	Ohio

Since the official headquarters of the four yearly meetings listed above are outside the limits of Pennsylvania, no entries for these bodies are given. Only entries for their subordinate meetings located within the Commonwealth of Pennsylvania appear in this volume.

WARRINGTON QUARTERLY MEETING (0)

	Date established	Entry number
WARRINGTON MONTHLY MEETING	1747	342
Newberry Preparative Meeting	1738	343
York Indulged Meeting	1754	90
York Preparative Meeting	1767	90
Centre Indulged Meeting	1797	361
Centre Preparative Meeting	1798	361
MENALLEN MONTHLY MEETING	1780	344
Menallen Preparative Meeting	1748	345
Huntingdon Preparative Meeting	1761	346
Bald Eagle Preparative Meeting		
(Half Moon)	1800	362
Dunning's Creek Preparative Meeting	1795	347
YORK MONTHLY MEETING	1786	348
CENTRE MONTHLY MEETING	1803	360
Centre Preparative Meeting	1798	361
Bald Eagle Preparative Meeting		
(Half Moon)	1800	362
West Branch Indulged Meeting		
(Clearfield)	1812	349
DUNNING'S CREEK MONTHLY MEETING	1803	363
CURWENSVILLE MONTHLY MEETING	1833	364

341. WARRINGTON QUARTERLY MEETING, 1787-1827. York and Adams Counties.

Warrington-Fairfax Quarterly meeting was set up in 1776, by Philadelphia Yearly Meeting (entry 1). In 1787 this quarterly meeting was divided into two meetings, namely, Warrington and Fairfax Quarterlies. The subordinate meetings of Fairfax Quarterly lie entirely outside Pennsylvania and are therefore not treated in this book. Both of these quarterly meetings were transferred to Baltimore in 1789 in exchange for meetings on the eastern shore of Maryland. Therefore, from 1787 to 1789 Warrington Quarter was under Philadelphia Yearly Meeting; after that date it was under Baltimore Yearly Meeting. This affiliation continued until the great Separation of 1827-28, at which time this meeting ceased as an Orthodox but continued as a Hicksite meeting. The following is a copy of the first minute of the new Warrington Quarterly Meeting at the time of the division in 1787: "Warrington Fairfax Quarterly Meeting after due deliberation on the situation and circumstances of the meetings and Friends

that composed them, both by committees appointed for that purpose and in
an elective capacity, be united in believing that it would advance their
religious improvements for that meeting to be divided and to establish
the one; to be composed of the Monthly Meetings of Hopewell, Fairfax,
Crooked Run, Westland, Goose Creek, and the Warrington Quarter of Pipe
Creek, Menallen, Warrington and York." This request was granted by Philadelphia Yearly Meeting in 1787. In 1789 this meeting was transferred to
the Baltimore Yearly Meeting. The following are minutes of the quarterly
meeting in regard to this matter: "At Warrington Quarterly Meeting held
at Pike Creek sixth month 1789, the weighty matter proposed by our meeting in Philadelphia respecting the uniting of this Quarter to the Yearly
Meeting in Maryland, now revived and considered . . . The proposal appears to have obtained the approval and united concurrence of this meeting." A second minute dated February 22, 1790 reads; "the time of holding the yearly meeting in Maryland, of which we are accounted members,
being soon after our next quarter, it is now recommended to our several
Monthly Meetings . . . ." At the time of the Separation in 1827, this
meeting was laid down as an Orthodox meeting and was continued as the
Warrington Quarterly Meeting, Hicksite (entry 380).

   See: Prowell, op. cit., I, III, 1084; Levi K. Brown, An Account of
the Meetings Constituting the Yearly Meeting of the Society of Friends,
pp. 31, 32; Matlack, op. cit., I, 906-910.

   Minutes of Men's Meetings, 1776-1888, 4 vols.; Minutes of Women's
Meetings, 1776-1870, 3 vols., at the Baltimore Yearly Meeting, Park Avenue,
Baltimore, Maryland.

   342. WARRINGTON MONTHLY MEETING, 1730-1827. Route #74, between
         Roseville and Wellsville, Warrington Twp., York County.
Set up as monthly meeting in 1747 by Chester Quarterly Meeting (entry
136), after having functioned as an indulged meeting since 1730 under Sadsbury Preparative Meeting (entry 119). Early meetings were held in the
residence of William Garretson in Warrington. The first meeting-house
was a log edifice, erected in 1745, on a plot of ground near the property
of Stephen Eyles (Ailes). When Western Quarterly Meeting (entry 71) was
set up in 1758, this meeting became a part of the new quarterly meeting.
In 1769, a new log meeting-house was erected near the site of the first.
In 1776 when Warrington-Fairfax Quarterly Meeting, was set up this meeting became a part thereof. In 1787 Warrington-Fairfax Quarterly Meeting
was separated into two bodies; Warrington Quarterly Meeting (entry 341)
and Fairfax Quarterly Meeting of Virginia, and this meeting became a part
of Warrington Quarterly Meeting. In 1782, it was found necessary to enlarge the meeting-house to almost double its size in order to accommodate
its increased membership, and the following year the older portion of the
meeting-house was remodeled. In 1789 Warrington Quarterly Meeting, with
its subordinate meetings was transferred to Baltimore Yearly Meeting
(see forthcoming Inventory of Church Archives of Maryland). The Women's
Minutes of June 1767, state: "The Monthly Meeting was held at Huntingdon"
and also the following year on the 12th and 6th months, after which it
was settled there in the 3rd, 6th, 9th and 12th months, until 1770, when
owing to the increase of York meeting it was settled again at Warrington
throughout the year. The burial ground which was of considerable size
was located near the meeting-house, but due to the absence of records it
cannot be determined when this ground was donated or purchased. When
the Separation occurred in 1827 the meeting-house and burial ground were
retained by Warrington Monthly Meeting, Hicksite (entry 381). This meeting apparently was laid down at that time.

See: Prowell, op. cit., I, 111, 1084; Brown, Levi, op. cit., pp. 31, 32; Matlack, op. cit., II, 905-910.

Minutes of Men's Meetings, 1747-1856, 4 vols.; Minutes of Women's Meetings, 1753-1857, 2 vols. (1747-52 missing); Register of Births and Deaths, 1739-1864; Marriage Certificates, 1748-1859, 2 vols.; Certificates of Removal, 1788-1859, 1 vol. (1747-88 missing); in vault of the Baltimore Yearly Meeting-house, Park Avenue and Laurens Street, Baltimore, Md.

343. NEWBERRY PREPARATIVE MEETING, ca.1734-1827. Between Newberry-town and Lewisberry, York County.

Set up by Sadsbury Monthly Meeting in 1738, having functioned as an indulged meeting since 1734. The first members of the Society of Friends settled in York County in 1734, locating in the eastern part of Manchester and Newberry Townships and in the Redland Valley, around the site of Lewisberry. They obtained permission to hold meetings for worship from Sadsbury Preparative Meeting (entry 119) of Lancaster County, and in 1738 was set up as a preparative meeting by Sadsbury Monthly Meeting (entry 123). From 1734 to 1745 meetings were held in the homes of members. In 1745, the first log meeting-house was erected in Newberrytown. The old burial ground is located in the eastern part of the lot adjoining the meeting-house. This meeting remained a part of Sadsbury Monthly Meeting until about 1770, when it was transferred to the care of the Warrington Monthly Meeting (entry 342). In 1792, a new meeting-house was erected and was sold about 1811 by a special act of legislature. The meeting was then moved to another location, 2 miles west of the town, midway between Newberrytown and Lewisberry Here, a grey stone meeting-house was erected on a 5-acre lot sold to Jesse Wickersham and George Garrettson, in trust for the Society of Friends by Samuel Garrettson and his wife. At the time of the Separation in 1827, the meeting-house erected in 1811 and burial ground adjoining were retained by Newberry Preparative Meeting, Hicksite (entry 384). This meeting was apparently laid down at that time.

See: Prowell, op. cit., I, 1030-1034; Brown, Levi, op. cit., p. 22; Matlack, op. cit., II, 872, 875. Records are in minutes of Warrington and Menallen Monthly Meetings. Registers are in the records of the Sadsbury, Menallen, and Warrington Monthly Meetings. All at Park Avenue and Laurens Street, Baltimore, Md.

344. MENALLEN MONTHLY MEETING, 1780-ca.1916. Menallen, 9 miles north of Gettysburg, Adams County.

Set up in 1780 by Warrington-Fairfax Quarterly Meeting (entry 89) of Philadelphia Yearly Meeting (entry 1), upon request from Menallen Preparative Meeting (entry 345), and Huntingdon Preparative Meeting (entry 346) to be united as a monthly meeting. The stipulation was made that monthly meetings were to alternate between Menallen and Huntingdon. This procedure continued until 1885 when Huntingdon Preparative Meeting was discontinued and from that date until 1916 there was only one monthly meeting held annually at Huntingdon and none at all after 1916. Meetings were conducted in a log meeting-house erected by Friends of Menallen Preparative Meeting in 1758. In 1838 the original log meeting-house was torn down and rebuilt in a more convenient place near Flora Dale, about 1 mile south of what is now Bendersville. However, the burial ground was retained for some time. Today meetings by appointment are held in a red brick meeting-house erected about 1890.

The present Menallen property was bought in three parcels; one in

1871, containing 79 perches, deeded by George Wright and wife to George Hewitt, Jesse Cook, Joel Wright, and Cyrus Rice, in trust for the Menallen meeting of Friends for the purpose of establishing a graveyard; another in 1871, containing 84 perches, by Josiah Griest and Hiram H. Wright, to the trustees of this meeting; and a third in 1889, containing 142 perches, deeded by Nathan Wright and wife to John Wright and George Hewitt, trustees for the Society of Friends.

At the time of the Separation in 1828, 11 men and 12 women withdrew from this meeting, and the remainder continued as a Hicksite meeting. The members who withdrew associated themselves with Baltimore Yearly Meeting of Orthodox Friends and for a time held meetings for worship at the homes of the individuals. The meetings gradually ceased. At present a Board of Trustees composed of C. Arthur Griest, Eyland H. Wright, Frederick E. Griest, Sr., Donald C. Tyson, and Edwin C. Tyson, care for the meeting property and graveyards at Menallen, Huntingdon, and Warrington, and the graveyard at Newberry, York County. Title to these properties . : been vested in this board since the decline of the meetings in this section.

See: Brown, Levi, op. cit., pp. 19-21.

For minutes and registers, see the records of Baltimore Yearly Meeting at Park Avenue and Laurens Street, Baltimore, Md.

345. MENALLEN PREPARATIVE MEETING, 1733-1827. Route #234, 3 miles east of Biglerville, Butler Twp., Adams County.

Set up as a preparative meeting in 1748, after having functioned as an indulged meeting since 1733. A minute of Sadsbury Monthly Meeting (entry 123), held in June 1746, states: "this meeting tolerates the Friends of Menallen to have meetings of worship on the First and Fifth days of each week until further orders." In 1748 Menallen became a preparative meeting under Warrington Monthly Meeting (entry 342). According to the register of marriages of Warrington Monthly Meetings, the first marriage recorded was performed in the meeting-house at Menallen in July 1751, which establishes the fact that the meeting-house was erected during or before that year. It was located on the northeast corner of the present property. It is not known when this earliest lot was purchased. In 1778 a plot of ground, consisting of 20 acres and 153 perches, on a part of which the meeting-house stood, was purchased from the Commonwealth of Pennsylvania. The burial ground was located near the meeting-house. When Menallen Monthly Meeting (entry 344) was set up in 1780, this meeting was then transferred to the newly established monthly meeting. In 1789, when Warrington Quarterly Meeting (entry 341) was transferred to Baltimore Yearly Meeting (see: Inventory of Church Archives of Maryland) this meeting then became a part of that yearly meeting. At the time of the Separation in 1827, this meeting was laid down and the log meeting-house and property were retained by Menallen Monthly Meeting, Hicksite (entry 382). Remaining Orthodox Friends of this meeting and others belonging to the defunct Huntingdon Preparative Meeting, Orthodox (entry 346), combined their numbers to establish the Bendersville Indulged Meeting (entry 358).

See: Brown, Levi, op. cit., p. 20; Matlack, op. cit., II, 864-866.

Records and registers are in the records of the various monthly meetings under which this meeting functioned, and now deposited at Park Avenue and Laurens Street, Baltimore, Md. Dauphin County Deed Book, vol. H, p. 33.

346. HINTINGDON PREPARATIVE MEETING, 1739-ca.1827. Township Road,
      Latimore Twp., 1 mile east of York Springs, Adams County.
In many instances, Friends who settled in Adams County held membership
in Sadsbury Monthly Meeting (entry 123). The first mention of a meeting
at Huntingdon is taken from a minute of this meeting of May 1739: "There
being divers families of Friends of late settled on the westside of the
Susquehanna, some of them have produced certificates to this meeting from
Kenet (Kennett), where they formerly dwelt, the Friends of that settlement being desirous of a toleration from this meeting to hold meetings
for worship every first fourth day of the week for six months time which
request is granted."

     In 1775, William Garretson was directed by Sadsbury monthly meeting
to read three papers of acknowledgment at the Huntingdon meeting. This
meeting evidently convened at the home of John Cox, where nearly all of
the early Friends' marriages in this section are known to have been performed. When Warrington Monthly Meeting (entry 342) was set up in 1747,
Huntingdon meeting became a part of the newly established monthly meeting.
There is no record as to the exact date when the first, log meeting-house
was erected. However, the first marriage to be witnessed in the Huntingdon meeting-house was June 30, 1752. In 1750 the Friends of Huntingdon
were granted permission to hold regularly established meetings for worship. In 1761 a request to hold a preparative meeting was granted and
the meeting set up under Warrington Monthly Meeting. The ground on which
the meeting-house was erected and the adjoining 5 acres were donated to
the trustees of this meeting in 1766 by William Beale. The larger part
of the adjoining ground was plotted as a graveyard in the same year.

     When Menallen Meeting (entry 344) was set up in 1780, this meeting
was then transferred to the newly established monthly meeting. The log
meeting-house was razed in 1790, and was replaced by a one-story, gray
stone edifice in the same year.

     When Menallen Monthly Meeting became a part of Baltimore Yearly Meet-
ing (see: Inventory of Church Archives of Maryland) in 1790, Huntingdon
then became a part of that yearly meeting. At the time of the Separation
in 1827, Huntingdon meeting-house and burial grounds were retained by
Huntingdon Preparative Meeting, Hicksite (entry 383). In the same year
the Orthodox Huntingdon Meeting was laid down and its members and those
of Menallen Preparative Meeting (entry 345) combined their numbers to
form the Bendersville Preparative Meeting (entry 358).

     See: Matlack, op. cit., I, 359-361.

     Records and registers are in the records of the various monthly
meetings of which this meeting was a part during its existance. See records of Baltimore Yearly Meeting at Park Avenue and Laurens Street, Baltimore, Md.

347. DUNNINGS CREEK PREPARATIVE MEETING, 1795-1803. Fishertown, East
      Street, Clair Twp., Bedford County.
Set up in 1795 as a preparative meeting by Menallen Monthly Meeting (entry
344). A small log meeting-house was erected the same year near Big Spring,
now Reynoldsdale Fish Hatchery. In 1803, the preparative meeting was laid
down and the meeting converted into a monthly meeting under Warrington
Quarterly Meeting. A small graveyard was started in 1795 but was not
kept up.

See: E. Howard Blackburn and William H. Welfley, History of Bedford and Somerset Counties, I, 323; John Mower and others, History of Bedford, Somerset, and Fulton Counties, p. 146.

Records and registers are in the minutes of Dunnings Creek Monthly Meeting.

348. YORK MONTHLY MEETING, 1786-1828. 135 Philadelphia Street, York. Set up as a monthly meeting by Warrington-Fairfax Quarterly Meeting (entry 89) after having functioned as York Preparative Meeting (entry 90) from 1767-86 and as a indulged meeting from 1754. In 1787 Warrington-Fairfax Quarterly Meeting was divided into the Warrington and Fairfax Quarterly Meetings. York Monthly Meeting was then transferred to the newly-established Warrington Quarterly Meeting (entry 341). When the Separation occurred in 1828 this meeting was continued as York Monthly Meeting, Hicksite (entry 385). The meeting-house and burial ground of the Orthodox Friends were retained by the Hicksite Friends.

See: Prowell, op. cit., pp. ; Matlack, op. cit., II, 925-929.

Minutes of Men's Meetings, 1786-1854, 1 vol; Minutes of Women's Meetings, 1786-1837, 1 vol.; Marriage Certificates, 1786-1823, 1 vol. (1823-28 missing); Certificates of Removal, 1787-1854, 1 vol., in vault of the Baltimore Yearly Meeting, Park Avenue and Laurens Street, Baltimore, Md. York County Deed Books, vol. 2-D, p. 152; vol. 2-E, p. 238; vol. 3-D, p. 42.

CENTRE MONTHLY MEETING (entry 360).

349. WEST BRANCH INDULGED MEETING, 1812-27. Grampian, Penn Twp., Clearfield County.
Established 1812 by Centre Monthly Meeting (entry 360) in Half Moon Township. After an indulged meeting was granted to the Friends of Grampian (known as Pennsville), meetings were held in the log cabin home of James A. Moore. Other members' homes were utilized as meeting-places until 1820, when a log meeting-house was erected on a tract of land owned by James A. Moore. On April 20, 1826 this 1 1/2-acre tract, on which the meeting-house was erected and a cemetery was plotted, was deeded by James A. Moore and his wife, Lydia, of Pike Township (which became Penn Township in 1834) to Jason Kirk and Jonathan Waln, trustees appointed by Centre Monthly Meeting. Meetings continued here until the Separation occured in 1827 when this meeting was laid down and the property was retained by West Branch Indulged Meeting, Hicksite (entry 370).

See: Clearfield County Deed Book, vol. C. p. 182.

	Date established	Entry number
NOTTINGHAM MONTHLY MEETING	1730	351
Little Elk Indulged Meeting	1825	352
LITTLE BRITAIN MONTHLY MEETING	1804	353
Little Britain Preparative Meeting (Balance)	1749	354
Eastland Preparative Meeting	1803	355
Drumore Preparative Meeting	1818	356
DEER CREEK MONTHLY MEETING	1760	Md.
Fawn Grove Preparative Meeting	1792	357

350. NOTTINGHAM QUARTERLY MEETING, 1819-61. Chester and Lancaster Counties.
Set up in 1819 by Baltimore Yearly Meeting with the approval of Philadelphia Yearly Meeting (entry 1). This meeting came at once under the care of Baltimore Yearly Meeting (see: Inventory of Church Archives of Maryland). Meetings alternated between the meeting-houses of the various meetings under the care of the quarterly meeting. At the time of the Separation in 1827 the larger portion of this quarterly meeting adhered to the Hicksite branch, and only a small portion remained with the Orthodox group. About 1860 the Orthodox meetings abondoned their Orthodox designation and the quarterly meeting became a part of the Primitive Friends and affiliated themselves with Falls General Meeting of Primitive Friends (entry 317).

Minutes of Men's Meetings, 1819-92, 1 vol., in the vault of the Baltimore Yearly Meeting, Park Avenue, Baltimore, Md. and 1828-65 (1861-65 are Primitive Friends' Minutes) 1 vol., at PPFYR. Minutes of Women's Meetings, 1819-93, 1 vol., in vault of Baltimore Yearly Meeting and 1828-68 1 vol. (1861-68 Primitive Friends Minutes), at 302 Arch Street. Minutes of Ministers and Elders, 1828-44, 1 vol. (1819-28, 1844-61 missing), at PPFYR.

351. NOTTINGHAM MONTHLY MEETING, 1730--. Chester County, Pennsylvania, and Cecil County, Maryland.
This monthly meeting was set up in 1730 by Chester Quarterly Meeting. Its component meetings were East Nottingham (1700), West Nottingham (1710), and Little Elk set up in 1825. The first two of these meetings are located in Maryland and hence are not treated here. The latter, Little Elk is in Pennsylvania and thus indicates the inclusion of this monthly meeting entry here. Nottingham Monthly Meeting passed from the care of Chester Quarterly Meeting to that of Concord Quarterly Meeting in 1800. In 1819 it was transferred to Baltimore Yearly Meeting along with Little Britain and Deer Creek Monthly Meetings. At the time of the Separation in 1827 the majority of the members adhered to the Hicksite branch, and the few remaining Orthodox members, after continuing in a weakened state for a while, finally affiliated with Falls General Meeting of Primitive Friends about 1860.

See: Brown, Levi, op. cit., pp. 32, 33, 35.

Records and registers up to 1860 will be found in the Records of Baltimore Yearly Meeting at Park Avenue and Laurens Street, Baltimore, Md., after 1861 in the custody of Charles Henry Moon, Woodbourne.

352. LITTLE ELK INDULGED MEETING, 1825-27. One-half mile west of Hickory Hill on road from Lewisville, Elk Twp., Chester County.

Established 1825 by East Nottingham Preparative Meeting, of Nottingham Monthly Meeting (entry 351) and Nottingham Quarterly Meeting (entry 350) after the transfer of Nottingham Monthly to Baltimore Yearly Meeting in 1819. Meetings were held in a small stone meeting-house erected in 1826 on land donated by Job and Ann Sidwell. A one and one-half-acre burial ground adjoins the meeting-house. In 1827, this became a Hicksite Meeting (entry 378) under Baltimore Yearly Meeting, Hicksite.

353. LITTLE BRITAIN MONTHLY MEETING, 1804-27. Route 222, Penn Hill, Fulton Twp., Lancaster County.

Set up in 1804 by Concord Quarterly Meeting (entry 136). Meetings were held alternately in the meeting-houses of the preparative meetings which were under the care of this monthly meeting. On February 17, 1819 this meeting was transferred from Concord Quarterly Meeting to the care of Nottingham Quarterly Meeting (entry 350), under Baltimore Yearly Meeting. At the time of the Separation in 1827 this meeting was laid down by Nottingham Quarterly Meeting and the Orthodox Friends were transferred to Little Britain Preparative Meeting (entry 377).

See: Matlack, op. cit., II, 861-863.

Minutes of Men's Meetings, 1804-38, 1 vol.; Minutes of Women's Meetings, 1804-57, 1 vol.; Register of Births and Deaths, 1775-1881, 1 vol., in vault of the Baltimore Yearly Meeting, Park Avenue and Laurens Street, Baltimore, Md. Register of Marriages, Members, and Removal, 1804--, 1 vol., in custody of Miss Cora Wood, Route 222, 1/2-mile south of New Texas, Fulton Township.

354. LITTLE BRITAIN (BALANCE) PREPARATIVE MEETING, 1749-ca. 1864. One-half mile north of Wakefield, P. O., Route 222, Lancaster County.

Set up in 1749 by Nottingham Monthly Meeting (entry 351), after having functioned as an indulged meeting from 1745. Meetings were held in the homes of members until 1758, when a stone meeting-house was erected on part of the 5-acre plot of ground donated by Michael King. In 1804 when Little Britain Monthly Meeting (entry 353) was set up by Concord Quarterly Meeting (entry 136), this meeting was transferred to the care of the newly established monthly meeting. In 1823 a red brick meeting-house, large enough to accommodate the Concord Quarterly Meeting, was built and donated to the meeting of Jeremiah Brown. At the time of the Separation in 1827, this property, together with the 190' x 290' burial ground adjoining, was retained by Little Britain Preparative Meeting, Hicksite (entry 377). The remaining Orthodox members, together with some members of Eastland Preparative Meeting (entry 355) met at the home of Joseph Balance until 1840 when the one-story red brick meeting-house (still standing) was erected. The burial ground, 40' x 45' adjoins the meeting-house on the southeast. Another division of this meeting took place in 1857, when some of the members became identified with the Primitive Friends (entry 314). As recent as 1925 an interment was made in the burial ground. This meeting was laid down about 1864 by Little Britain Monthly Meeting.

See: Brown, Levi, op. cit., pp. 39, 40; Matlack, op. cit., II, 861-863.

Minutes of Men's Meetings, 1749-1864; Minutes of Women's Meetings, 1749-1864; Registers, 1749-1803, are in the records of Nottingham Monthly Meeting, 1804-64, in the records of Little Britain Monthly Meeting; Financial Records, 1749-1864, at the Baltimore Yearly Meeting, 3107 North Charles Street, Baltimore, Md. Lancaster County Deed Books, vol. 1, bk., 5, p. 263; vol. K, p. 46; vol. T. bk. 6, p. 269; vol. T. bk., 7, p. 104.

355. EASTLAND PREPARATIVE MEETING, 1796-1827. Two and one-half miles east of New Texas, on road to Kirks Mills, Little Britain Twp., Lancaster County.

Set up in 1803 by Nottingham Monthly Meeting (entry 351), after having functioned as an indulged meeting since 1796. Meetings were first held in a log building, located on the site of ground where the present one-story white stone meeting-house was erected in 1803. In 1803 the 200' x 250' burial ground, adjoining the meeting-house, was plotted. When Little Britain Monthly Meeting was set up in 1804, this meeting became a part of that monthly meeting. At the time of the Separation in 1827, Eastland Preparative Meeting was laid down by Little Britain Monthly Meeting. The meeting-house and burial ground were retained by Eastland Preparative Meeting, Hicksite (entry 376).

Minutes of Men's Meetings, 1803-27, 3 vols., Minutes of Women's Meeting, 1807-18, 1 vol. (1803-7, 1818-27 missing), in custody of Walter Wood, Route #172, between Wrightsdale and Kirks Mills. Registers are in the records of the Nottingham Monthly Meeting from 1798-1804, in the records of the Little Monthly Meeting from 1804-27. Financial records are incorporated in the minute books. Lancaster County Deed Books, vol. E-6, p. 418; vol. 4, pp. 291-293.

356. DRUMORE PREPARATIVE MEETING, 1810-27. One-half mile south of Liberty Square, Drumore Twp., Lancaster County.

Set up in 1818 by Little Britain Monthly Meeting (entry 353), after having functioned as an indulged meeting since 1810. From 1810-16 meetings were held in a schoolhouse, 1 mile west of the meeting-house. On August 5, 1816, Jacob Shoemaker and his wife Joyce conveyed the site of the meeting-house to Joseph Stubbs, David Perry, and Samuel Smith, Trustees of the Drumore meeting. A one-story, stone and frame meeting-house was erected in the same year. The burial ground, 162' x 300', situated across the road from the meeting-house was plotted in 1816. At the time of the Separation in 1827, this meeting was laid down by Little Britain Monthly Meeting. The meeting-house and burial ground were retained by Drumore Preparative Meeting, Hicksite (entry 375).

See: Matlack, op. cit., II, 992-993; Brown, Levi, op. cit., p. 41.

Records are deposited at the Baltimore Yearly Meeting, Park Avenue and Laurens Street, Baltimore, Md. Registers are in the records of the Little Britain Monthly Meeting. Lancaster County Deed Book, vol. W. 7, p. 431.

DEER CREEK MONTHLY MEETING (See: Inventory of Church Archives of Maryland).

357. FAWN GROVE PREPARATIVE MEETING, 1763-1827. South side of intersection of Routes 851 and 124, Fawn Grove, York County. Set up as a preparative meeting in 1792 by Deer Creek Monthly Meeting of Maryland, of the Nottingham Quarterly Meeting (entry 350). This meeting was first organized in 1763 under Deer Creek Monthly Meeting. However, it was not until about 1792 that the meeting was officially established as a preparative meeting. The first meeting-house was erected about 1790. At the time of the Separation in 1827, this meeting-house was retained by Fawn Grove Preparative Meeting, Hicksite (entry 373). Due to the absence of records and historical data it cannot be established whether this meeting continued after 1827.

See: Prowell, op. cit., I, 113, 875; Matlack, op. cit., II, 840-843.

Records are not available. Registers are in the records of the Deer Creek Monthly Meeting.

	Date established	Entry number
BALTIMORE MONTHLY MEETING		MD.
Bendersville Indulged Meeting	1828	358
Bendersville Preparative Meeting	1893	358

358. BENDERSVILLE PREPARATIVE MEETING, 1828-1905. Railroad Street, Bendersville, Adams County.
Set up in 1893 as a preparative meeting by Baltimore Monthly Meeting, after having functioned as an indulged meeting since 1828. Early membership consisted of Friends formerly belonging to Huntingdon Preparative Meeting (entry 346) and Menallen Preparative Meeting (entry 345). These Friends withdrew from Menallen and Huntingdon when these meetings adhered to the Hicksite branch at the time of the Separation in 1828. Meetings were held in members' homes until 1890, when a frame structure and a plot of ground consisting of 43 perches were purchased from E. W. Munns. A minute from Baltimore Monthly Meeting, February 9, 1893, records the granting of a preparative meeting to the Bendersville Friends: "we recommend that the application of Friends at Bendersville for the establishment of a Preparative Meeting be granted." This action of the monthly meeting was approved by the quarterly meeting at Baltimore held at Ashton, Maryland 4th month 17, 1893. The meeting dwindled in number to such a extent that a request for permission to discontinue the meeting and dispose of the property was acted upon favorably by Baltimore Monthly Meeting held November 2, 1905 and the meeting was laid down. The remaining members were attached to Baltimore Monthly Meeting. The frame meetinghouse and ground were purchased by Hiram Geist, who presented the house and ground to the Borough of Bendersville, to be converted into a social centre.

Minutes of the Bendersville Preparative Meeting, 1893-1903, 1 vol. (1903-5 missing), at the Baltimore Monthly Meeting-house, 3107 North Charles Street, Baltimore Md. Registers are in the records of the Baltimore Monthly Meeting. Adams County Deed Book, vol. Q. Q. pp. 397, 398.

	Date established	Entry number
CENTRE MONTHLY MEETING	1803	360
Centre Preparative Meeting	1797	361
Bald Eagle (Half Moon) Preparative Meeting	1800	362
DUNNING CREEK MONTHLY MEETING	1803	363
CURWENSVILLE MONTHLY MEETING	1833	364

359. DUNNINGS CREEK QUARTERLY (HALF-YEAR) MEETING, 1840-1918. Fishertown, Bedford County; Bellefonte, Centre County; Curwensville, Clearfield County.
Set up in 1840 by Baltimore Yearly Meeting (see: Inventory of Church Archives of Maryland). This meeting had three subordinate meetings at whose meeting-houses it convened: Dunnings Creek Monthly Meeting (entry 363), which later became Fishertown Monthly Meeting, at Fishertown, Bedford County; Centre Monthly Meeting (entry 360) at Bellefonte, Centre County, and Curwensville Monthly Meeting (entry 364), at Curwensville, Clearfield County.

Bound up in the history of this quarterly meeting is also that of Dunnings Creek Half-Year Meeting. This latter meeting was in reality an enlarged session of the quarterly meeting, and possessed the same functions. It came into existence because of the fact that these meetings were so far removed from Baltimore, the place where the yearly meeting was held, that very few members were able to attend those gatherings. In the beginning these quarterly sessions were held four times a year. Because of bad weather and difficult travel condition the winter session was very likely discontinued. This meeting then came to be called the Four Months Meeting. Later, two sessions were stressed and were attended largely; and while these sessions retained their quarterly meeting status, they also constituted the Half-Year Meeting. This meeting began about 1880 and continued until 1918 when the quarterly meeting was laid down by Baltimore Yearly Meeting, bringing to a close the sessions of both the quarterly and half-year meetings. At that time the local meeting was subordinated to Baltimore Quarterly Meeting (see: Inventory of Church Archives of Maryland).

See: Anna Thomas, The Story of Baltimore Yearly Meeting From 1672-1938, pp. 12, 13; Catalog of Materials in the vault of Baltimore Yearly Meeting of Friends, pp. 93-96 (manuscript at Baltimore Yearly Meeting, 3107 North Charles Street, Baltimore).

Minutes of Men's Meetings, 1909-19, 2 vols.; Minutes of Women's Meetings, 1840-1905, 2 vols.; Minutes of Ministers and Elders of Quarterly Meeting, 1844-76, 1 vol., at Baltimore Yearly Meeting.

360. CENTRE MONTHLY MEETING, 1803-1918. South Spring Street, Belle-
       fonte Borough, Centre County.
Set up in 1803 by Warrington Quarterly Meeting (entry 341), under Baltimore
Yearly Meeting. This meeting was first set up as an indulged meeting in
1797 and 5 months later in the same year was set up as a preparative meeting. This meeting convened at the meeting-houses of its subordinate meetings until the Separation. In 1832 the present one-story, limestone meeting-house was erected in Bellefonte. There was a 65' x 200' burial ground,
which was plotted sometime prior in 1826. At the time of the Separation
in 1827 it appears that all the subordinate meetings under this monthly
meeting with the exception of Centre Preparative (entry 361) at Bellefonte,
adhered to the Hicksite branch. The Bellefonte meeting, which started as
a meeting for worship in 1815, continued in uncertain status until 1837
when it was set up as a monthly meeting by a special committee of Baltimore Yearly Meeting. A meeting-house was built there in 1832. About 1834
a one-story stone building, adjoining the meeting-house in Bellefonte was
erected to be used as a First-day School. For many years it has served
as the caretaker's residence. When Dunnings Creek Quarterly Meeting (entry 359) was set up in 1840, this meeting was transferred to the care of
the newly established quarterly meeting. In 1918 this meeting was permanently laid down.

       See: Matlack, op. cit., II, 988-990.

       Minutes of Men's Meetings, 1803-50, 1 vol. (1828-67 missing) in vault
at the Baltimore Yearly Meeting, Park Avenue and Laurens Street, Baltimore,
Md., and 1868-1908, 2 vols., in vault in Baltimore Yearly Meeting-house,
3107 North Charles Street, Baltimore, Md. Minutes of Women's Meetings,
1863-96, 4 vols. (1803-62, 1896-1905 missing); Minutes of Joint Meetings,
1906-18, 1 vol.; Minutes of Ministers and Elders, 1803-98, 2 vols. (1898-
1906 missing); 1906-11, 1 vol. (1911-18 missing), at Baltimore Yearly
Meeting-house, 3107 N. Charles Street. There are no registers available at
the present time. Centre County Deed Books, vol. R, p. 317; vol. 54, p.
135; vol. 141, p. 633; vol. B, p. 191; vol. 140, p. 154.

361. CENTRE PREPARATIVE MEETING, 1797-1837. Stony Batter Road and
       Pine Street, Bellefonte.
Set up in November 1798 as a preparative meeting by Warrington Monthly
Meeting (entry 342), after having functioned since June of the same year
as an indulged meeting. From the records the location of the first meeting is not clear, but references point to Stormstown in Half-Moon Township.
First meetings were held in private homes, and the first meeting-house was
built in 1803 at Stormstown. The first mention of this meeting is found
in the minutes of Warrington Quarterly Meeting of November 27, 1797, when;
"a request was made by Friends in the Warrior Mark and Half Moon settlements asking that a preparative meeting be settled there, and a committee
was appointed to make investigation . . . ." There was a graveyard in
connection with this meeting, located near the meeting-house. This house
apparently served until the time of the Separation when a new house was
built at Bellefonte, which became the center of Centre Monthly Meeting
for the Orthodox group. Meantime about 1815 Friends began to hold meetings for worship in the old Valentine Building, corner Spring and High
Streets, in Bellefonte. When the Separation occurred the majority of
Friends adhered to the Hicksite branch, and the small remaining group
of Orthodox Friends withdrew and established their branch of Centre Meeting at Bellefonte. This is the Second Centre Preparative Meeting, and
its proper dates are from 1837 when the monthly meeting was set up. This

group continued to meet in the Valentine Building until 1832. In that
year George, Reuben, Bond, and Abraham Valentine, and W. A. Thomas, erected at their own expense and their own land a one-story stone meeting-
house. In 1837 land for burial ground was purchased on top of a hill a-
bout 3/4 mile south of the meeting-house. Burials had already been made
in this plot as early as 1816. This meeting was laid down as a preparative meeting in 1837 and a monthly meeting established by Baltimore Yearly Meeting. It continued as a monthly meeting until 1918 at which time
it was laid down by Baltimore Yearly Meeting. The meeting-house, a small
dwelling, and the lot on which they stood were sold to the Bellefonte A-
cademy in 1928. The graveyard continued under the trustees of Baltimore
Yearly Meetings.

    See: Brown, Levi, op. cit., p. 47; Matlack, op. cit., II, 988; John
Linn, History of Centre and Clinton Counties, p. 239.

    Records and registers will be found in the vaults of the two Balti-
more Yearly Meetings, 3107 North Charles Street, and at Park Avenue and
Laurens Street, Baltimore, Md. Centre County Deed Books, vol. M, p. 432;
vol. 140, p. 154.

    362. BALD EAGLE (HALF MOON) PREPARATIVE MEETING, 1800-1828. Bald
        Eagle Valley, Wingate, Boggs Twp., Centre County.
Set up in 1800 by Menallen Monthly Meeting (entry 344) of Warrington Quarterly Meeting (entry 341) of Baltimore Yearly Meeting. When Centre Monthly Meeting was set up in 1803 this meeting became a part thereof. Meetings were first conducted in members' homes, but a frame meeting-house
was built about 1805, on the north side of Bald Eagle Creek, on land conveyed to the meeting by John Iddings in 1802. At the time of the Separation most of the members adhered to the Hicksite branch and the remaining
few Orthodox members joined the group in Bellefonte and helped establish
the meeting which became Centre Monthly Meeting in 1837. The property was
later sold by the Hicksite meeting (entry 362), and converted into a private dwelling. The Hicksite meeting was re-established at Unionville.

    Records and registers will be found in the records of Centre Monthly
Meeting deposited in the vaults at 3107 North Charles Street, and Park
Avenue and Laurens Street, Baltimore, Md. Centre County Deed Books, vol.
A, p. 259; vol. G-2, p. 318.

    363. DUNNINGS CREEK MONTHLY MEETING, 1803--. Fishertown, East
        Street, Clair Twp., Bedford County.
Set up 1803 as a monthly meeting by Warrington Quarterly Meeting, after
having functioned as Dunnings Creek Preparative Meeting from 1795-1803
(entry 347), under Menallen Monthly Meeting. The first meeting-house, a
small, log structure, was erected 1795, 1 mile northeast of the present
meeting-house near Big Spring, which is now Reynoldsdale Fish Hatchery.
The Quakers worshiped here until 1828. Shortly after this date the Hicksites built their second meeting-house on the west side of township road,
near Big Springs. The third and present meeting-house, a one-story, frame
building was erected in 1884. This was erected for the use of the Orthodox meeting after it had practically ceased to exist, but was later revived by Baltimore Yearly Meeting.

    A small graveyard was started in 1795, but was soon abandoned be-
cause the surface rock interfered with the grave digging. Only a few
partially marked graves are still to be found. The present graveyard is

on the site of the first meeting-house and is used jointly by the Orthodox and the Hicksite Friends.

See: Blackburn and Welfley, op. cit., I, 323; Celebration of the Centennial Anniversary of Dunning Creek Monthly Meeting of Friends, hereinafter cited as Centennial Dunning Creek.

Monthly Meeting Minutes, 1803-1924, 1 vol.; Park Avenue and Laurens Street, Baltimore, Md., and 1924--, 1 vol., in custody of E. E. Blackburn, R. D., New Paris. Sunday School Records, 1910--, 1 loose-leaf vol., at meeting-house. Bedford County Deed Book, vol. C, pp. 572, 573.

364. CURWENSVILLE MONTHLY MEETING, 1833-1928. 848 State Street, Curwensville, Clearfield County.
Set up in 1833 by Warrington Quarterly Meeting of Baltimore Yearly Meeting (entry 341). A meeting for worship was held here some year prior to this time, but the exact date was not determined. First met in the township schoolhouse on Filbert Street until 1838, when a one-story frame edifice was erected and a burial ground was plotted on adjoining ground. When Dunnings Creek Quarterly Meeting was set up in 1840, under Baltimore Yearly Meeting, this meeting was transferred to the care of the newly established quarterly meeting. In 1878 the frame meeting-house and adjoining ground were sold to the Presbyterian Church of the U. S. A. (see: Inventory of Church Archives of Pennsylvania: Presbyterian Church). The bodies in the burial ground were then removed from the old graveyard to the Curwensville Cemetery in Oak Hill and to the 60' x 105' burial ground in Pike Township, donated to this meeting by William McNaul in 1865. The former frame meeting-house was replaced by a stone edifice at 848 State Street in 1878. In 1880 Dunnings Creek Quarterly Meeting became the Dunnings Creek Half-Year Meeting (entry 359), and in 1918 Dunnings Creek Half-Year Meeting was laid down and this meeting was then transferred to the care of Baltimore Yearly Meeting. Due to decreased membership the meeting dwindled, and was finally laid down by Baltimore Yearly Meeting in 1928. Title to the property of this meeting was transferred to Baltimore Yearly Meeting in 1926, which sold it to Victor Kirk in 1928, who converted the meeting-house into a garage. The burial ground is still used today for the interment of deceased members of other denominations.

See: Lewis C. Aldrich, History of Clearfield County, p. 637.

Records and registers are in the vaults of the two yearly meetings at 3107 North Charles Street, and Park Avenue and Laurens Street, Baltimore, Md. Clearfield County Deed Book, vol. 286, p. 567.

Component Quarterly Meetings

Centre Quarterly Meeting
Nottingham Quarterly Meeting
Warrington Quarterly Meeting

Because of the State limits of the survey no entry of Baltimore Yearly Meeting appears in this volume. The entries of the Quarterly Meetings and their subordinate meetings follow immediately.

CENTRE QUARTERLY MEETING

	Date established	Entry number
CENTRE MONTHLY MEETING	1828	366
Centre Preparative Meeting	1827	367
Bald Eagle Preparative Meeting	1867	368
DUNNINGS CREEK MONTHLY MEETING	1831	369
WEST BRANCH MONTHLY MEETING	1833	370
Clearfield Preparative Meeting	1842	371

365. CENTRE QUARTERLY MEETING, 1835--. Fishertown, Bedford County; Port Matilda, Centre County; Grampian, Clearfield County. Set up in 1835 by Baltimore Yearly Meeting upon request from Dunnings Creek, West Branch, and Centre Monthly Meetings. It was called Centre Quarterly Meeting and its first meeting was held at Dunnings Creek in May 1835. Warrington Quarterly Meeting which established the first meetings in this section (entry 341) had been affiliated with Baltimore Yearly Meeting since 1789. Hence, when this quarterly meeting was set up in 1835 as a result of the Separation, it affiliated with the corresponding branch of the Baltimore Yearly Meeting. The meeting convenes at the meeting-house of its three subordinate meetings; Dunnings Creek (entry 369), Centre (entry 366), and West Branch Monthly Meeting (entry 370).

See: Brown, Levi, op. cit., pp. 45, 46; Advancement Committee, Directory of Members of Baltimore Yearly Meeting of the Religious Society of Friends, p. 46; Matlack, op. cit., II, 988.

Minutes of Men's Meetings, 1803-72, 3 vols. (1887-1917 missing); Women's Minutes, 1836-1916, 2 vols., at Park Avenue and Laurens Street, Baltimore, Md.

366. CENTRE MONTHLY MEETING, 1828--. Half Moon Twp., Centre Coun-
      ty.
Continued as a Hicksite meeting in 1827 by Baltimore Yearly Meeting after
the division of the original Centre Monthly Meeting (entry 360). In 1835
when Centre Quarterly Meeting was set up this meeting became a part thereof. Centre Monthly Meeting is composed of the preparative meetings of
Unionville (formerly Bald Eagle) and Centre, located at Port Matilda. Its
earliest history goes back to 1803 when it was established by Warrington
Quarterly Meeting. When the Separation occurred in 1827 most of the meetings in this section adhered to the Hicksite branch, and merely continued
on under the Hicksite supervision, with their yearly meeting affiliation
in Baltimore Yearly Meeting. This meeting is now held at Centre Meeting-
house.

      See: Matlack, op. cit., II, 990.

      Men's Minutes, 1803-85, 2 vols., 1885--, 1 vol.; Women's Minutes,
1803-85, 2 vols., at Park Avenue and Laurens Street, Baltimore, Md. Registers and certificates not found.

367. CENTRE PREPARATIVE MEETING, 1827--. Port Matilda, Centre
      County.
Continued as a Hicksite meeting by Centre Monthly Meeting (entry 366) in
1827, after the division of the original Centre Preparative Meeting (entry
361). Meetings were conducted in a log meeting-house erected by the
Friends in 1806. This structure served until 1833 when it was found inadequate. The log meeting-house was sold to Half Moon Grange #90. After
the sale the meetings convened at members' Homes. This arrangement was
maintained until 1843 when a hewed-log meeting-house was erected on the
west end of the same plot of ground. This structure is 36' x 50'. There
is a sliding door in the center which partitions the hall into two rooms
originally used to separate the men's and women's meetings. In 1835 a
1 1/2 acre lot was purchased and plotted for a burial ground. In 1926
1/4 acre was added. The burial ground adjoins the meeting-house. Regular
meetings were last held in 1935. Since then meetings have been held only
once a year.

      See: Brown, Levi, op. cit., pp. 45-47; Matlack, op. cit., I, 988.

      Records are deposited at Park Avenue and Laurens Street, Baltimore,
Md.

368. UNIONVILLE (BALD EAGLE) PREPARATIVE MEETING, 1867-1935. East
      Chestnut Street, Unionville, Centre County.
Set up in 1867 by Centre Monthly Meeting (entry 366) of Centre Quarterly
Meeting (entry 365) of Baltimore Yearly Meeting. Meetings were held in
the home of Ellis Way, Main Street, from 1867-70. In the latter year
William P. Fisher and wife sold to Pierce E. Peters and wife, trustees
of this meeting, the combination one-story frame and log meeting-house.
This meeting is a continuation of the old Bald Eagle meeting which gradually ceased to function after the Separation of 1827, but was later revived. This meeting had a share in a burial ground located about 3 miles
east of Unionville, donated about 1868, consisting of about 68 perches.

      In 1874 the meeting conducted the Select School Sessions which were
held in the meeting-house. This school was originally called the Quakers
Seminary School. At the turn of the century the meeting began to dwindle

in membership and by 1935 so few members remained that it was laid down
that year by Centre Monthly Meeting and the property was sold to Pierce
E. Peters in 1936, who remodeled it and converted it into a private dwelling.

No records for this meeting have been located.

369. DUNNINGS CREEK MONTHLY MEETING, 1831--.   Fishertown, East
Street, Clair Twp., Bedford County.
Continued as a Hicksite meeting in 1831 under Warrington Quarterly Meeting, after division of the original Dunnings Creek Monthly Meeting (entry
363). This meeting retained the original meeting-house, a log structure,
which had been erected in 1795. In 1835 Centre Quarterly Meeting (entry
365) was established and this meeting transferred thereto. In 1867 the
meeting-house was razed and replaced the same year by a frame building.
The present two-story red brick building was erected in 1888. A 6-acre
graveyard was started in 1795, located in Spring Meadow adjoining the
original meeting-house. It is now used jointly by Hicksite and Orthodox
Friends. The clerk is Amy Hughes, 1913 Fourth Avenue, Altoona.

See: Blackburn and Wolfley, op. cit., I, 323; Centennial Dunning
Creek.

Monthly Meeting Minutes, 1831--, 3 vols. (includes register of
membership, marriages, and deaths, and financial records), kept in meeting-house safe. Sunday School Records, 1900--, 1 vol., kept in safe in
meeting-house. Bedford County Deed Book, vol. C, pp. 572, 573; vol. 131,
p. 108; vol. S-3, p. 208.

370. WEST BRANCH MONTHLY MEETING, 1827--.   First Street, Grampian,
Penn Twp., Clearfield County.
Set up as a monthly meeting in 1833 by Nottingham Quarterly Meeting (entry
372) of Baltimore Yearly Meeting, after having functioned as the West
Branch Indulged Meeting since 1827. This meeting is a continuation of
the original West Branch Indulged Meeting. Services were conducted in
the log meeting-house erected by the original meeting in 1820. The log
building served as a meeting-house until 1847 when it was destroyed by
fire. A new frame meeting-house was constructed in the same year. In
1835, this meeting became affiliated with the newly established Centre
Quarterly Meeting (entry 365) under Baltimore Yearly Meeting. About
1895 the town of Pennsville became known as Grampian and the meeting is
sometimes called by that name. On August 20, 1878, Andrew Moore and
Nathan Moore deeded to the trustees of this meeting a tract of land, containing approximately 120 perches, bordering on the original tract. The
120 perches, located on the left side of the road leading from Grampian
to Lumber City, became an adjunct to the cemetery plotted in 1820. On
January 18, 1901, John A. Lytle sold to the trustees of this meeting lots
Nos. 121, 122, 123, and 124, which form part of the present property hold-
ings. In 1903 the present red brick meeting-house was erected. The frame
meeting-house was sold to Elisha Davis, who demolished it.

Minutes of the Men's and Women's Meetings (for records before 1833
see Centre Monthly Meetings Half Moon, Centre County), 1833-41, 1 vol.
(1842-46 destroyed by fire), 1847-1932, 1 vol., at Park Avenue and Laurens
Street, Baltimore, Md., and 1932--, 1 vol., in custody of assistant clerk,
Mrs. Harold McFadden, Grampian, R. D. #1. Financial records are incorporated in the minute books. Treasurer's and Collector's Book, 1924--,

1 vol., in custody of T. L. Wall, Curwensville, R. D. #1.   First-day
School Records, 1880-88, 1932--, 5 vols. (1865-80, 1888-1931 missing), in
meeting-house, and 1932--, 1 vol. in possession of clerk, James Cleaver,
Grampian, R. D. #1. Clearfield County Deed Books, vol. C, p. 185; vol.
115, p. 63.

    See: Thomas L. Wall, Clearfield County, Pennsylvania Present and
Past, p. 96.

    371. CLEARFIELD PREPARATIVE MEETING, ca.1842-ca.64. Route #862,
        between Rockton and Luthersburg, Brady Twp., Clearfield County.
Set up about 1842 by West Branch Monthly Meeting (entry 370). Meetings were
held in Friends homes until 1846 when John and Lydia Kirk deeded to R.
W. Moore and William Johnson, trustees of the Society of Friends, 120
perches of ground on which a frame meeting-house, 24' x 36' was erected.
A burial ground was plotted in the same year, although there is no trace
of it today. The first members of this meeting formerly belonged to West
Branch Monthly Meeting. It cannot be established exactly when this meeting was laid down, but the date indicated by tradition is 1864. The meeting-house was sold and converted into a private dwelling and occupied by
John Kirk until 1867. It was finally razed and the lumber used in the
construction of farmhouses in the vicinity.

    There are no minutes or records of this meeting to be found at the
present time. Clearfield County Deed Book, vol. K, p. 147.

	Date established	Entry number
DEER CREEK MONTHLY MEETING		
Fawn Grove Preparative Meeting	1828	373
LITTLE BRITAIN MONTHLY MEETING	1827	374
Drumore Preparative Meeting	1827	375
Eastland Preparative Meeting	1827	376
Little Britain Preparative Meeting (Penn Hill)	1827	377
NOTTINGHAM MONTHLY MEETING	1827	Md.
Little Elk Indulged Meeting	1827	378
Oxford Indulged Meeting	1876	379
Oxford Preparative Meeting	1883	379
Oxford Indulged Meeting	1927	379

372. NOTTINGHAM QUARTERLY MEETING, 1827--. Harford and Cecil Counties, Maryland; Lancaster and Chester Counties, Pennsylvania. Continued as a Hicksite meeting in 1827 by Baltimore Yearly Meeting after division of the original Nottingham Quarterly Meeting (entry 350). This meeting convened alternately in the meeting-houses of Deer Creek Monthly Meeting, Harford County, Md.; Nottingham Monthly Meeting, Cecil County, Md.; Little Britain Monthly Meeting, Lancaster County; and the Oxford Indulged Meeting (entry 379), 244-64 South Third Street, Oxford, Chester County. This meeting is the result of the 1827 Separation of Nottingham Quarterly Meeting which was set up by Baltimore and Philadelphia Yearly Meetings in 1819, when the three monthly meetings of Little Britain, Deer Creek, and Nottingham were transferred to Baltimore Yearly Meeting.

Minutes of Men's Meetings, 1819-92, 1 vol.; Minutes of Women's Meetings, 1819-93, 1 vol.; Minutes of Joint Meetings, 1892-1930, 1 vol., at the Baltimore Yearly Meeting, Park Avenue and Laurens Street, Baltimore, Md., and 1930--, 1 vol., in custody of clerk Margaret Gatchall, Peach Bottom, Lancaster County.

DEER CREEK MONTHLY MEETING (See: Inventory of Church Archives of Maryland).

373. FAWN GROVE PREPARATIVE MEETING, 1828-ca.1910. South side of intersection of Routes 851 and 124, Fawn Grove, York County. Continued as a Hicksite meeting in 1827 by Deer Creek Monthly Meeting of Maryland and Nottingham Quarterly Meeting (entry 372). At the time of the Separation in 1827, this meeting retained the meeting-house erected by the original Friends meeting in 1790. There is a burial ground adjoining the meeting-house, however, due to the absence of records, it cannot be ascertained if the Hicksite Friends plotted it or acquired it from the original Fawn Grove Preparative Meeting at the time of the Separation. In 1878 the former meeting-house was razed and was replaced by the pre-

sent one-story, gray stone edifice. The preparative meeting was laid down about 1910. However, meetings of worship are still held occasionally.

See: Matlack, op. cit., II, 840-843.

There are no records available at the present time. Registers are in the records of the Deer Creek Monthly Meeting, deposited at Park Avenue and Laurens Street, Baltimore, Md.

374. LITTLE BRITAIN MONTHLY MEETING, 1827--. Route 222, Penn Hill, Fulton Twp., Lancaster County.
Continued as a Hicksite meeting in 1827 by Nottingham Quarterly Meeting (entry 372) after division the original Little Britain Monthly Meeting (entry 353). At the time of the Separation, this meeting retained the one-story red brick meeting-house, erected in 1758, and the 190' x 290' burial ground adjoining it.

See: Matlack, op. cit., II, 861-863; Brown, Levi, op. cit., pp. 38, 39.

Minutes of Men's Meetings, 1804-1901, 3 vols.; Minutes of Women's Meetings, 1804-93, 2 vols. (1893-1901 missing); Minutes of Joint Meetings 1902-23, 1 vol., at Park Avenue and Laurens Street, Baltimore, Md., and 1923--, 1 vol., in custody of clerk, Mary Gatchall, Peach Bottom. Register of Marriages and Removals, 1804--, 1 vol., in custody of Miss Cora Wood, New Texas, Fulton Township. Register of Births, Members, and Deaths 1775-1881, 1 vol., in vault at Park Avenue and Laurens Street, and 1881--, 1 vol., in custody of Miss Cora Wood. Financial Records 1936--, 1 vol. (1827-1936 missing), in custody of Walter Wood, Route 172, between Wrightsdale and Kirks Mills. First-day School Records 1903-6, 1 vol. (1827-1903, 1906-26 missing), in custody of Miss Martha Brown, 34 North Third Street, Oxford, and 1926--, 1 vol., in custody of Clara Haines, Pleasant Grove. First-day School Financial Records, 1935--, 1 vol. (1827-1935 missing), in custody of William Kirk, Route 222, 1 mile south of Wakefield. Lancaster County Deed Books, vol. L-14, p. 569; vol. Y-3, p. 336; vol. K, p. 46; vol. E-3, p. 3.

375. DRUMORE PREPARATIVE MEETING, 1827-1936. One-half mile south of Liberty Square, Drumore Twp., Lancaster County.
Continued as a Hicksite meeting in 1827 by Little Britain Monthly Meeting (entry 374), after division of the original Drumore Preparative Meeting (entry 356). Meetings were held in the one-story stone and frame meeting-house erected in 1816 by the original Drumore Preparative Meeting. This meeting also retained the 162' x 300' burial ground directly across the road from the meeting-house. In 1928, the trustees of Drumore Preparative Meeting deeded the land and the meeting-house to the Drumore Cemetery Association, but reserved the right to occupy the meeting-house and the grounds as long as they desired to use it as a place of worship. The meeting-house is still in existence and there are three monthly meetings a year held there by Little Britain Monthly Meeting. Drumore Preparative Meeting was laid down in 1936.

Minutes of Men's Meetings, 1827-97; Minutes of Women's Meetings, 1827-97, at the Baltimore Yearly Meeting, Park Avenue and Laurens Street, Baltimore, Md. Minutes of Joint Meetings, 1897-1936, 4 vols., in custody of last clerk of Drumore Preparative Meeting, Charles L. Lamborn, 3 miles

south of Rawlinsville on the road to Liberty Square. Registers are in the
records of the Little Britain Monthly Meeting. Lancaster County Deed
Books, vol. W-7, p. 431, vol. G-29, p. 1.

376. EASTLAND PREPARATIVE MEETING, 1827--. Two and one-half miles
        east of New Texas on the road to Kirks Mills, Little Britain
        Twp., Lancaster County.
Continued as a Hicksite meeting in 1827 by Little Britain Monthly Meeting
(entry 374), after division of the original Eastland Preparative Meeting
(entry 355). Meetings are held in the one-story stone meeting-house
erected in 1803, which the Hicksite Friends retained after the Separation,
together with 200' x 250' burial ground which is adjacent to the northwest side of the meeting-house.

Minutes of Men's Meetings, 1827-92, 6 vols. (1829-38, 1857-70 missing); Minutes of Women's Meetings, 1827-92 missing; Minutes of Joint Meetings, 1892--, 4 vols., in custody of clerk, Walter Wood, Wrightsdale. Registers are in the records of Little Britain Monthly Meeting.

377. LITTLE BRITAIN (PENN HILL) PREPARATIVE MEETING, 1827--. On
        Route 222, 1/2 mile north of Wakefield, Penn Hill, Lancaster
        County.
Continued as a Hicksite meeting in 1827 by Little Britain Monthly Meeting
(entry 374) after division of the original Little Britain Preparative
Meeting (entry 354). This meeting retained the one-story, red brick meeting-house, which was erected in 1823, and the burial ground, 190' x 290',
adjoining the meeting-house. A placque on the meeting-house bears the
following inscription, "Established 1758." This meeting is commonly
known as the Penn Hill Meeting.

See: Brown, Levi, op. cit., pp. 39, 40; Matlack, op. cit., I, 61-63.

Minutes prior to 1909 are deposited at Baltimore Yearly Meeting,
Park Avenue and Laurens Streets, Baltimore, Md. Minutes of Joint Meetings,
1909-35, 1 vol., in custody of Mary Twill, Cherry Hill and 1935--, 1 vol.,
in custody of clerk, Maggie Stubbs, Fairhill. Registers are in the records of Little Britain Monthly Meeting. Financial Records, 1827-1908,
are at Baltimore Yearly Meeting, and 1908--, 1 vol., in custody of Joseph
Twill, Cherry Hill. Financial Records of Little Britain Preparative Incorporated (Trustees), 1919--, 1 vol. (1827-1918 missing), in custody of
treasurer, Mrs. Fred Brown, 34 North Third Street, Oxford. Lancaster
County Deed Books, vol. L-14, p. 569; vol. Y-3, p. 236; vol. K, p. 46;
vol. E-3, p. 3.

378. LITTLE ELK INDULGED MEETING, 1827-82. One-half mile east of
        Hickory Hill on road from Lewisville, Elk Twp., Chester County.
Continued as a Hicksite meeting in 1827, after division of the original
meeting (entry 352). This meeting is a branch of East Nottingham Preparative Meeting and Nottingham Monthly Meeting. Meetings were held in the
small stone meeting-house erected in 1826. A 1½-acre burial ground adjoins the meeting-house. This meeting was laid down in 1882. In 1886,
64½ perches were donated by Job S. Pugh in place of a small triangular
piece of land cut off for use of a public road. The meeting-house and
graveyard are under the care of trustees, who use the income of three
houses, left in trust by a former member for this purpose.

379. OXFORD INDULGED MEETING, 1876--. Between 244 and 246 South
      Third Street, Oxford, Chester County.
Set up as an indulged meeting in 1876 by Pennsgrove Monthly Meeting (entry
256). Meetings were held in members' homes until 1879. In that year two
lots, measuring 1 1/2 acres, were purchased, and a one-story red stone
meeting-house, was erected. In 1883 when the meeting was transferred
from the care of Pennsgrove Monthly Meeting to that of Nottingham Monthly
Meeting of Baltimore Yearly Meeting, it had its status changed to that
of a preparative meeting. The preparative meeting was discontinued in
1927 by Nottingham Monthly Meeting and the meeting reverted back to its
original status of an indulged meeting. Trustees of the Oxford property,
who had been appointed by the Court of Common Pleas, deeded the meeting-
house and grounds to Nottingham Monthly Meeting on July 12, 1937.

See: Futhey and Cope, op. cit., p. 242; "Opening of the New Meeting-
House in Oxford," West Chester Daily Local News, November 11, 1879; "Oxford Friends' Meeting-House," West Chester Daily Local News, November 26,
1879: "Oxford Friends," West Chester Daily Local News, August 13, 1873.

Minutes of Joint Meetings, 1876-1910, 1 vol. (1910-27 missing), deposited in vault of the Baltimore Yearly Meeting, Park Avenue and Laurens
Street, Baltimore, Md. Registers are in the record books of the Nottingham Monthly Meeting. Financial Records, 1912--, 2 vols. (1883-1911 missing), in custody of treasurer, Raymond T. Earnhart, 2 Broad Street, Oxford.

	Date established	Entry number
WARRINGTON MONTHLY MEETING	1827	381
Newberry Preparative Meeting	1827	384
Warrington Preparative Meeting	1827	381
MENALLEN MONTHLY MEETING	1827	382
Huntingdon Preparative Meeting	1827	383
Newberry Preparative Meeting (Redlands)	1827	384
Warrington Preparative Meeting	1827	381
DUNNINGS CREEK MONTHLY MEETING	1827	369
YORK MONTHLY MEETING	1828	385
BALTIMORE QUARTERLY MEETING	(?)	Md.
BALTIMORE MONTHLY MEETING	(?)	Md.
York Indulged Meeting	1857	385

380. WARRINGTON QUARTERLY MEETING, 1827--. Warrington Twp., York County.

Continued as a Hicksite meeting in 1827 by Baltimore Yearly Meeting, after the division of the original Warrington Quarterly Meeting (entry 341). Quarterly meetings were held alternately in the meeting-houses which at various times were under the care of this meeting. This quarterly meeting is the result of the division in 1827 of the original Warrington Quarterly which was set up in 1787 by a division of Warrington-Fairfax Quarterly Meeting.

See: Prowell, op. cit., I, 111, 1084; Brown, Levi, op. cit., pp. 31, 32; Matlack, op. cit., II, 905-910.

Minutes of Men's Meetings, 1787-1888, 2 vols.; Minutes of Women's Meetings, 1813-88, 2 vols.; Minutes of Joint Meetings, 1888-1938, 2 vols., at the Baltimore Yearly Meeting, Park Avenue, Baltimore, Md. The current minutes of joint meetings from 1938--, are in the custody of the clerk.

381. WARRINGTON MONTHLY MEETING, 1827-62. Route 74, between Rossville and Wellsville, Warrington Twp., York County.

Continued as a Hicksite meeting in 1827 by Warrington Quarterly Meeting (entry 380) after division of the original Warrington Monthly Meeting (entry 342). At the time of the Separation, this meeting retained the meeting-house and burial ground formerly belonging to the original meeting. The membership gradually diminished, and in 1862, the members of this meeting and Newberry Friends were transferred to Menallen Monthly Meeting of Adams County. This meeting was reduced to the status of a preparative

meeting. The meeting gradually weakened until by 1875 only occasional
meetings for worship were held. The meeting-house and burial ground were
placed in the care of a joint committee of Warrington Quarterly Meeting.

See: Prowell, op. cit., I, 111, 1084; Brown, Levi, op. cit., pp. 31,
32; Matlack, op. cit., II, 905-910.

Minutes of Men's Meetings, 1824-56, 1 vol. (1856-62 missing); Minutes of Women's Meetings, 1825-57, 1 vol. (1857-62 missing); Register of
Births and Deaths, 1739-1864, 1 vol.; Marriage Certificates, 1788-1857,
1 vol. (1857-62 missing); Certificates of Removal, 1788-1859, 1 vol. (1859-
62 missing), at Baltimore Yearly Meeting-house, Park Avenue and Laurens
Street, Baltimore, Md.

382. MENALLEN MONTHLY MEETING, 1827--. Flora Dale, Adams County.
Continued as a Hicksite meeting in 1827 by Warrington Quarterly Meeting
(entry 380) after division of the original Menallen Monthly Meeting (entry
344). At the time of the Separation this meeting retained the log meeting
house which was erected in 1758. This meeting-house was used until 1838,
when it was dismantled and its site was abandoned for a more favorable
location 3 miles to the northwest of the original place, upon which site
the log meeting-house was reconstructed. In 1884 the old log meeting-
house was replaced by the present brick building, erected at the rear of
the former one, on a plot of 84 perches which was purchased in 1871.
Across the lane is the burial ground consisting of 80 perches surrounded
on three sides by a substantial wall and on the side next to the meeting-
house by an iron fence. Date of purchase of the burial ground is not
known. The present clerk is Alice Black, Flora Dale.

See: Brown, Levi, op. cit., pp. 19-21.

Minutes of Men's Meetings, 1780--, 2 vols., in custody of Edwin C.
Tyson, Flora Dale. Register of Births, Members, Marriages, and Deaths,
1733--, 5 vols., first four volumes deposited in Baltimore Yearly Meeting
vault, Park Avenue, Baltimore, Md. and current volume, 1915--, in custody
of Edwin C. Tyson. Financial records are incorporated with the minutes
of the men's meetings.

383. HUNTINGDON PREPARATIVE MEETING, 1827-85. Township Road 1050,
Latimore Twp., 1 mile east of York Springs, Adams County.
Continued as a Hicksite meeting in 1827 by Menallen Monthly Meeting (entry
382) of Warrington Quarterly Meeting (entry 380), after division of the
original Menallen Preparative Meeting (entry 345). At the time of the
Separation in 1827, this meeting retained the meeting-house and surrounding 5 acres of ground, on which is situated a burial ground. In the report
of Menallen Monthly Meeting to Warrington Quarterly Meeting of June 1885,
it is stated that the Huntingdon Preparative Meeting has been discontinued
by mutual agreement. However, Menallen Monthly Meeting continued to meet
once each year in the meeting-house until 1916, when this arrangement was
discontinued. Since that year no regular meetings have been held at Huntingdon, except by appointment in June of each year.

See: Matlack, op. cit., II, 859-861; Brown, Levi, op. cit., p. 21.

No records have been found. Registers are in the records of the
Menallen Monthly Meeting.

384. NEWBERRY (REDLANDS) PREPARATIVE MEETING, 1827-ca.1875. Between
      Newberrytown and Lewisberry, York County.
Continued as a Hicksite meeting in 1827 by Warrington Monthly Meeting (entry 381), of Warrington Quarterly Meeting (entry 380), after division of
the original Newberry Preparative Meeting (entry 343). At the time of
the Separation this meeting retained the stone meeting-house, erected in
1811, and the adjoining burial ground. The meeting was laid down about
1875 and the members of this meeting and Warrington Monthly Meeting were
transferred to Menallen Monthly Meeting (entry 382) of Adams County. The
burial ground adjoining the meeting-house is enclosed by a high iron fence.
For many years, only Friends were interred in the cemetery, however, recently, the privilege was extended to other denominations. During recent
years, Warrington Quarterly Meeting has held some of its quarterly sessions in the Newberry meeting-house. An organ in the main room of the
meeting-house suggests that the house is used for service by congregations
of other denominations.

      See: Prowell, op. cit., I, 1030-1034; Brown, Levi, op. cit., p. 22;
Matlack, op. cit., II, 872-875.

      No records are available. Registers are in the records of the War-
rington Monthly Meeting.

385. YORK MONTHLY MEETING, 1828-ca.1857. 135 Philadelphia Street,
      York, York County.
Continued as a Hicksite meeting in 1828 by Warrington Quarterly Meeting
(entry 380), after division of the original York Monthly Meeting (entry
348). When the Separation occurred in 1828 the Hicksite Friends retained
the red brick meeting-house and the burial ground. Due to the absence of
data it cannot be exactly determined when York Monthly Meeting was laid
down, but the latest minutes now extant date to 1857. After the monthly
meeting was laid down the remaining members were attached to Baltimore
Monthly Meeting, probably as an indulged meeting since no minutes have
been found. The first meeting-house was no doubt built of logs. A better
house was built in 1766 of bricks said to have been brought from England.
Another section, was erected about 1776. The house is somewhat above
street level and back of it is the burial ground. Meetings are still held
by Friends in York, but not regularly. About 1857 the monthly meeting
was discontinued, and the status of the irregular meetings since that
date has been that of an indulged meeting, and later as an independent
meeting.

      See: Prowell, op. cit., p. 176; Matlack, op. cit., II, 925-929.

      Minutes of Men's Meetings, 1786-1857, 3 vols.; Minutes of Women's
Meetings, 1786-1857, 2 vols. (1837-51 missing); Certificates of Removal,
1787-1854, 1 vol. (1854-57 missing), at Baltimore Yearly Meeting, Park
Avenue and Laurens Street, Baltimore, Md. York County Deed Books, vol.
2-D, p. 152; vol. 2-E, p. 238; vol. 3-D, p. 42.

OHIO YEARLY MEETING (0)
(See: Inventory of Church Archives of Ohio)

Component Meetings

Redstone Quarterly Meeting
Salem Quarterly Meeting
Middletown Quarterly Meeting
New Garden Quarterly Meeting

Because of the State limits of the survey no entry of Ohio Yearly
Meeting appears in this volume. The entries of the quarterly meetings
and their subordinate meetings follow immediately.

REDSTONE QUARTERLY MEETING

	Date established	Entry number
WESTLAND MONTHLY MEETING	1780	387
Redstone Preparative Meeting	1788	392
Sandy Hill Indulged Meeting	1792	388
Sandy Hill Preparative Meeting	1795	388
Head of Wheeling Preparative Meeting	1795	389
Pike Run Meeting	(?)	39?
REDSTONE MONTHLY MEETING	1793	39?
Ridge or Muddy Creek Indulged Meeting	1766	392
Redstone Preparative Meeting	1788	393
Providence Preparative Meeting	1789	394
Centre Preparative Meeting	1796	395
Peace Hill Preparative Meeting	1799	396
Sewickly Indulged Meeting	1799	398
Stewart's Crossing Preparative Meeting	1800	397
Sewickly Preparative Meeting	1826	398
Sandy Creek Meeting (West Va.)	(?)	W. Va.
Pittsburg Friends Meeting	(?)	399
FALLOWFIELD MONTHLY MEETING	1799	400

386. REDSTONE QUARTERLY MEETING, 1797 ca.1866. Washington, Greene
    and Fayette Counties.
Exact information on the establishment of this meeting is not available.
Tradition indicates that it was set up in 1797 at the suggestion of Hope-
well (Virginia) Monthly Meeting at that time a subordinate meeting under
Fairfax Quarterly Meeting, of Baltimore Yearly Meeting (0). Westland,
Redstone, and Fallowfield Monthly Meetings were subordinate to this meet-
ing. Meetings were held in the houses of the subordinate meetings. Some-

time after it was established, presumably in 1812 when Ohio Yearly Meeting was set up by Baltimore Yearly Meeting, this Quarterly Meeting was transferred to the new yearly meeting. The Friends who settled this section, came up the mountain valleys from Virginia, hence the connection with Hopewell Monthly Meeting. Membership in the meetings in these three counties dwindled until by 1875 most of the subordinate meetings had ceased to exist. The local meetings were transferred to Salem Quarterly Meeting of Ohio Yearly and the Quarterly Meeting was laid down by Ohio Yearly Meeting about 1860.

See: Lewis C. Walkinshaw, Annals of Southwestern Pennsylvania, III, 372; Solon J. Buck, The Planting of Civilization in Western Pennsylvania, p. 410.

No records for this meeting are available. They will probably be found in the records of Ohio Yearly Meeting at Damascus, Ohio.

387. WESTLAND MONTHLY MEETING, 1780-1864. East Bethlehem Street, Centerville, Washington County.
Set up in 1780 as a preparative by Hopewell Monthly Meeting, Hopewell, Virginia. This was the first Friends meeting west of the Allegheny Mountains. First structure, a log meeting-house, was erected in 1780, 1 mile east of Centerville on the west side of Ridge Road, and burned down in 1785. The same year the Westland meeting became a monthly meeting. Second structure, a one-story limestone house was built in 1785 on the same site. This meeting was laid down in 1864 when most of the membership moved to Ohio. The property was sold in 1866 to two men who resold it to the Westland Cemetery Company. The cemetery which was directly behind the meeting-house, has been leveled out and now is the center of the Westland Cemetery.

All records are stored at Salem and Mount Pleasant (Ohio) meeting-houses: Washington County Deed Books, vol. 1-I, p. 355; vol. 1-0, p. 99; vol. 4-C, p. 66; vol. 4-C, p. 68: vol. 3-G, p. 558; vol. 3-U, p. 495; vol. 5-0, p. 435; vol. 5-V, p. 61; vol. 5-W, p. 465; vol. 5-W, p. 466; vol. 5-W, p. 468.

388. SANDY HILL PREPARATIVE MEETING, 1792-1850. On New Salem-Uniontown Road, near Uniontown, Fayette County.
In 1792, permission to worship as an indulged meeting was given by Westland Monthly Meeting. Westland minutes, March 1792 states: "Friends near Uniontown reneweth their request of holding meetings as heretofore, which being deliberately considered is concurred with and to be under the care of Redstone Preparative Meeting." In July 1792, Redstone Preparative Meeting assisted in choosing a place of worship for this indulged meeting. First structure, a log meeting-house erected at "Sandy Hill on Jennings Run." About 1795, the Sandy Hill Meeting became a preparative meeting. In 1850 the Sandy Hill Meeting was laid down and members attached to Redstone Preparative and Redstone Monthly Meetings. The log meeting-house disappeared and an edifice was erected on the same ground by a Union Church in 1887, to whom the property was sold. The graveyard which adjoined the Friends' meeting-house is still in fair condition.

See: Franklin Ellis, History of Fayette County, p. 44.

Records are deposited with Ohio Yearly Meeting, Salem, Ohio, Fayette County Deed Books, vol. L. 327; vol. 8, p. 496.

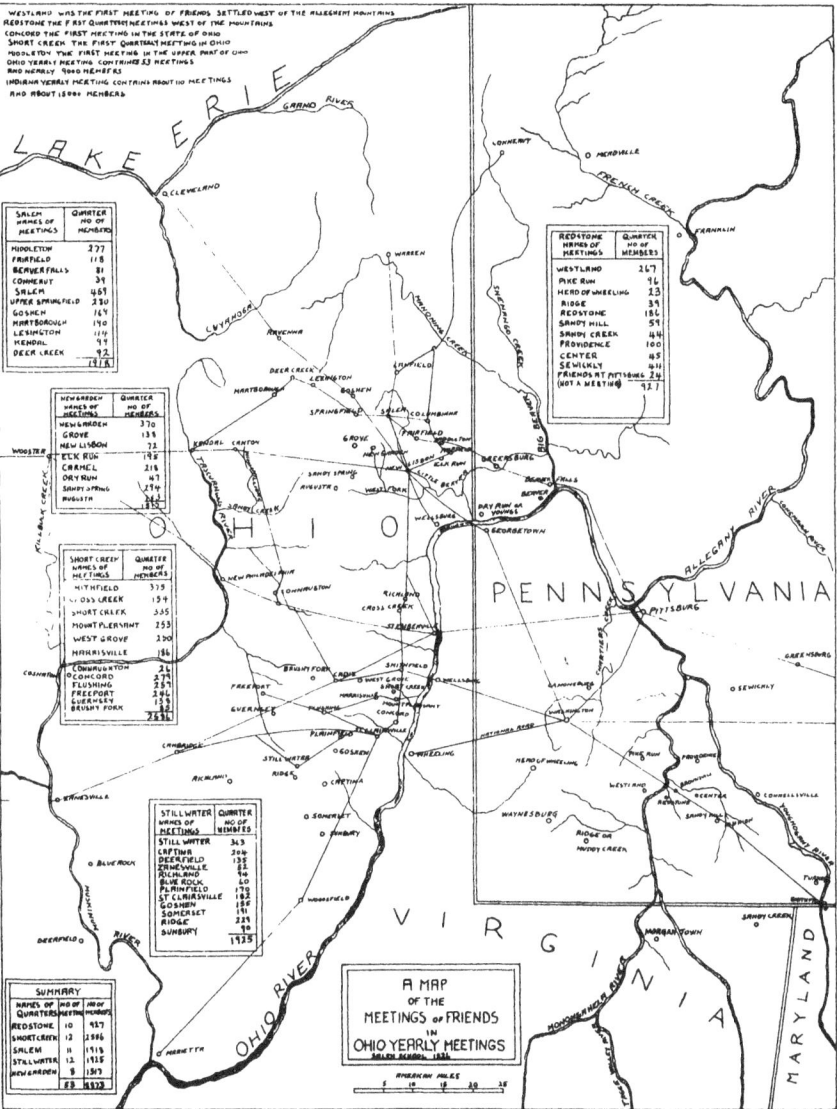

LAKE ERIE

PENNSYLVANIA

OHIO

VIRGINIA

MARYLAND

SALEM NAMES OF MEETINGS	QUARTER NO OF MEMBERS
MIDDLETON	277
FAIRFIELD	118
BEAVERFALLS	81
CONNEAUT	34
SALEM	469
UPPER SPRINGFIELD	230
GOSHEN	164
HARTBOROUGH	140
LEXINGTON	114
KENDAL	44
DEER CREEK	92
	1918

REDSTONE NAMES OF MEETINGS	QUARTER NO OF MEMBERS
WESTLAND	267
PIKE RUN	96
HERD OF MEETING	23
RIDGE	39
REDSTONE	186
SANDY HILL	59
SANDY CREEK	44
PROVIDENCE	100
CENTER	63
SEWICKLY	44
FRIENDS AT PITTSBURG (NOT A MEETING)	24
	927

NEWGARDEN NAMES OF MEETINGS	QUARTER NO OF MEMBERS
NEWGARDEN	370
GROVE	139
NEW LISBON	72
ELK RUN	195
CARMEL	216
DRY RUN	47
SANDY SPRING	294
AUGUSTA	
	1935

SHORT CREEK NAMES OF MEETINGS	QUARTER NO OF MEMBERS
SMITHFIELD	335
CROSS CREEK	154
SHORT CREEK	535
MOUNT PLEASANT	253
WEST GROVE	120
HARRISVILLE	186
CONNAUGHTON	26
CONCORD	274
FLUSHING	257
FREEPORT	246
GUERNSEY	139
BRUSHY FORK	60
	2586

STILLWATER NAMES OF MEETINGS	QUARTER NO OF MEMBERS
STILL WATER	363
CAPTINA	204
DEERFIELD	135
ZANESVILLE	82
RICHLAND	96
BLUE ROCK	60
PLAINFIELD	179
ST CLAIRSVILLE	182
GOSHEN	155
SOMERSET	191
RIDGE	229
SUNBURY	70
	1935

SUMMARY		
NAMES OF QUARTERS	NO OF MEETINGS	NO OF MEMBERS
REDSTONE	10	927
SHORTCREEK	12	2586
SALEM	11	1918
STILLWATER	12	1935
NEWGARDEN	8	1317
	53	8923

A MAP OF THE MEETINGS OF FRIENDS IN OHIO YEARLY MEETINGS

SALEM SCHOOL 1836

AMERICAN MILES
5   10   15   20   25

.

389. HEAD OF WHEELING PREPARATIVE MEETING (Old English Quaker Meet-
      ing), 1795-1841. R. D. 3, 1 mile from Pleasant Grove, Clays-
      ville, Washington County.
Set up 1797 after having met informally since 1795. First services were
held in a log house, which also was used as a schoolhouse until 1800 when
it was destroyed by fire. Meetings for worship and business were held in
private homes until completion of the second log house on the site of the
first meeting-house in 1803. Never a large one, the meeting was laid
down in 1841, after many of the members had moved to Ohio and other western states. The meeting-house was moved after 1841 and converted into a
dwelling. The burial ground used from 1798 to 1887 is still in good condition and is in care of D. M. Pressley, a retired minister.

See: Boyd Crumrine, History of Washington County, p. 76.

Minutes, 1815-41, in possession of Mrs. Emma J. E. Pressley, Washington. All other records are stored at Salem and Mount Pleasant, Ohio,
meeting-houses. Washington County Deed Book, vol. 1-X, p. 93.

390. PIKE RUN MEETING (dates unknown). Clover Hill, Pike Run Twp.,
      Washington County.
Almost nothing is known of this meeting as an Orthodox meeting. In 1827
the Separation occurred here and Pike Run Monthly Meeting, Hicksite (entry 409) was established. It is probable that the Orthodox meeting was
laid down shortly thereafter.

391. REDSTONE MONTHLY MEETING, 1793-ca.1860. Fayette County.
Set up by Hopewell (Va.) Monthly Meeting, under Fairfax Quarterly Meeting
in 1793. A minute of Fairfax Quarterly Meeting of March 1793 states: "We
the committee appointed on the request of Westland Monthly Meeting, with
respect to the request of Redstone and Providence having a monthly meeting established among them, agree to report that we visited the monthly
meeting of Westland, as also the meetings of Redstone and Providence to
a good degree of satisfaction, and are of the mind it would be best to
grant their request and that the monthly meeting be held circular between
Redstone and Providence on the Sixth-day preceeding the monthly meeting
at Westland and be called by the name of Redstone Monthly Meeting: All
of which is submitted to the Quarterly Meeting by Abel Walker, . . . (et
al.) Which being read and deliberated on is occurred with and their first
meeting to be held at Redstone the Sixth-day proceeding the monthly meeting at Westland in Fourth month next . . . ."

Subordinate meetings were added or transferred to this meeting, but
accurate information is not available. The meeting was laid down about
1860 during the general decline of Friends meetings of this section.

See: Cope Collection, Redstone Monthly Meeting Records, Historical
Society of Pennsylvania, hereinafter cited as Redstone.

392. RIDGE (MUDDY CREEK) INDULGED MEETING, 1766-1844. State Route
      30027, Garards Fort (Now Whitely) Greene County
Established in 1766 by pioneer Friends who settled in southwestern Pennsylvania. Peter Bachues, the first Quaker settler in Greene County, came
from Virginia in 1766. From 1766-70 meetings were held in members' homes
and were conducted by visiting ministers. In the latter year, a log meeting-house was erected. Reverend John Keigher, not a Friend, is recorded
as the first settled minister in that section. When the Redstone Quarterly

Meeting (entry 386) was set up this meeting came under the care of the
quarterly meeting. With the death of Peter Bachues the meeting lapsed
about 1791 and remained dormant until 1822, when it was revived. The graveyard 100' x 100', 500 feet east of the meeting-house was acquired in 1808.
In 1844 the meeting disbanded; some members joined the Cumberland Presbyterian Church at Carmichaels, and others joined the Goshen Baptist Church
of Whiteley.

393. REDSTONE PREPARATIVE MEETING, 1788-99.   Near Brownsville, Luzerne Twp.

It is believed that the first Friends' Meeting in Fayette County was set
up about 1788 in a log meeting-house on the Bull Run Road, back of the
Swan Farm in Luzerne Township, not far from the present Hopewell Church.
This building was destroyed by fire about 1799. The graveyard later became a neighborhood burying ground and is the only remaining landmark.
It is believed that this meeting was the original Redstone Preparative
Meeting set up by Westland Monthly Meeting (entry 387). In 1868 the land
was sold and the money used to help finance the erection of a yearly meeting-house for the Friends at Damascus, Ohio. This meeting was laid down
after the fire and the members organized the Peace Hill Preparative Meeting (entry 396).

See: Ellis, op. cit., p. 44.

All records are stored with Ohio Yearly Meeting at Salem, Ohio.
Fayette County Deed Books, vol. A, p. 252; vol. D, p. 3; vol. F, p. 228.

394. PROVIDENCE PREPARATIVE MEETING, 1789-ca.1870.   Rowes Run, Fay-
ette County.

Set up in 1789 as a Preparative meeting by Redstone Monthly Meeting (entry 391). The Friends met in a one-story, stone building. Date of building is unknown, but it is believed to have been occupied from date of organization to 1832. In 1895, Mrs. Mary Binns, a descendant of the early
Quakers, rebuilt the meeting-house with the materials of the original building, and it is still standing in a good state of preservation. In January 1832, the Pennsylvania General Assembly approved an act appointing
Jesse Coldron and Jesse Negrin as trustees of Providence Preparative Meeting, and further provided that in case of death or removal of one or both
of these trustees the Providence meeting could appoint new trustees.
Deaths and removals caused membership to be reduced in number and the remaining members were transferred to the Redstone meeting at Brownsville
between 1832 and 1870. Providence Preparative Meeting was laid down in
1870.

See: Ellis, op. cit., p. 76.

All records are deposited in Ohio Yearly Meeting vault at Salem,
Ohio. Fayette County Deed Books, vol. c, p. 191; vol. 1-X, p. 93.

395. CENTRE PREPARATIVE MEETING, 1796-1856.   Three miles east of
Brownsville, Redstone Twp., Fayette County.

Set up as a preparative meeting in 1796 "on a hill just beyond the farm
where George Allen lived" by Redstone Monthly Meeting (entry 391), after
holding meetings for worship in private homes, the preceding year.

First building was a log meeting-house. In 1856 "the ranks had dwindled to less than half a score, and the meeting was laid down." The only

remaining evidence of a Quaker settlement is the graveyard, which had adjoined the meeting-house and is today in poor condition.

See: Ellis, op. cit., p. 76.   Fayette County Recorder's Office Grantee's Index, vol. D, p. 80; vol. L, p. 33; vol. 26, p. 663.

396. PEACE HILL PREPARATIVE MEETING, 1799-1865. Prospect Street, Brownsville.

Set up in 1799 as a preparative meeting by Redstone Monthly Meeting (entry 391), after the destruction of Redstone Preparative Meeting-house by fire in 1799. The majority of the members were from the Redstone Preparative Meeting. Meetings for worship and business were held in private homes for several months until a stone meeting-house was erected. A burial ground was laid out on the section of Prospect Street, then known as Bridgeport Hill. This meeting-house became the seat of Redstone Quarterly Meeting for several years. After the meeting was laid down in 1865, title to the plot rested with the Ohio Yearly Meeting, which gave the Bridgeport School Directors permission to erect a school, the first in the vicinity, with the understanding that they preserve the graveyard. Later, however, the graveyard was leveled and used as a playground.

See: Ellis, op. cit., p. 78.

Records are at the Salem Monthly Meeting-house, Salem, Ohio.   Fayette County Deed Books, vol. F, p. 304; vol. S, p. 73; vol. 9, p. 501; vol. 12, p. 77; vol. 19, p. 243; vol. 19, p. 517; vol. 19, p. 606; vol. 20, p. 240; vol. 20, p. 329; vol. 20, p. 654.

397. STEWARTS CROSSING PREPARATIVE MEETING, 1800-ca.1867. Whittier Avenue and Water Street, Connellsville.

Organized 1800. First services were held in a log house owned by John Gibson, a Quaker from Chester County who lived on Water Street, near Main Street. In 1812 Gibson willed the meeting 1/4 acre of ground at Whittier Avenue and Fayette Street for a burial ground. The cemetery, completely obliterated today and the site occupied by two double houses and the Baltimore and Ohio Railroad water tanks, was enclosed by a stone wall and was popularly known as the Quaker Graveyard. It is believed the meeting was laid down in 1867.

See: Ellis, op. cit., p. 79.

All records are at the Salem Monthly Meeting-house, Salem, Ohio. Fayette County Deed Books, vol. 19, p. 433.

398. SEWICKLEY PREPARATIVE MEETING, 1799-1928. On road between Hermine and Rilton, Westmoreland County.

Set up as a preparative meeting in 1826 by Redstone Quarterly Meeting (entry 386), after having functioned as an indulged meeting since 1799. The meeting was established by pioneer Friends who migrated from Adams, Philadelphia, and Washington Counties. A deed dated December 12, 1832 records the donation of land by James McGrew: "James McGrew willed to the Society of Friends April 11, 1805, 7 acres of land in Sewickley Township for a meeting-house and burial ground." The will stated that if the Society of Friends ever discontinued meetings or abandoned the property it was to go back to James A. McGrews' children and heirs except the piece of ground used for burial ground. From 1799 until 1805 meetings were conducted in members homes. In the latter year a one-room log house was erected. Part of the surrounding 7 acres was plotted as a graveyard. The only historical reference made to this meeting is to be found in the deed books of Westmoreland County. By 1893 the meeting declined in membership to the extent that only a few members were left. A deed dated March 16, 1893 states: "The Society of Friends, Sewickley Township sold to J. M. Guffey of Pittsburgh, Allegheny County the coal under the seven acres of Ground for $628.75." Another deed, dated June 6, 1907, "The Society of Friends, Sewickley Township sold to Salem (Ohio) Monthly Meeting the Seven acres of ground in their possession." On authority of the oldest resident of the community, the meeting held its last session in 1928, and in the same year it was laid down by Salem Quarterly Meeting. The meeting-house is still standing but in poor condition. The surrounding graveyard is still in use.

Westmoreland County Deed Books, vol. 20, p. 199; vol. 221, p. 219; vol. 418, p. 242.

399. PITTSBURGH FRIENDS MEETING (dates unknown). (Location unknown). All that is known of this meeting is that it existed as a meeting for worship in 1826 under the care of Redstone Quarterly Meeting. Records are not known to exist, although possible reference to it may be made in the records of Ohio Yearly Meeting, which has been suspended.

400. FALLWFIELD MONTHLY MEETING, 1799-1840. One mile east of Roscoe, Long Branch Borough, Washington County.
Set up in 1799 as a preparative meeting by Redstone Quarterly Meeting (entry 386) after functioning for sometime as an indulged meeting. Prior to 1799 meetings were conducted in members' homes. The log meeting-house was erected in 1799 and was occupied until the dissolution of the meeting in 1840. After the meeting was laid down by Redstone Quarterly Meeting the house was abandoned until 1844, when it was occupied by John Biles as a residence. The Cemetery adjoining the meeting-house is used today and the deceased of other denominations are interred therein. In 1849 the Friends' property was sold to Cornelius McKenna, who donated a portion of the land to the Methodist congregation, who erected a church known as the Mt. Tabor Methodist Episcopal Church. When the meeting was laid down the remaining few members joined the Mt. Tabor Church and others left the county.

See: Crumrine, op. cit., pp. 16-18.

Minutes and registers are in the records of Ohio Yearly Meeting, Salem, Ohio.

SALEM QUARTERLY MEETING

	Date established	Entry number
HUGHESVILLE MONTHLY MEETING	1905	401
Opps Preparative Meeting	1915	402
MIDDLETON MONTHLY MEETING	(?)	Ohio
Beaver Falls Preparative Meeting	1824	404

401. HUGHESVILLE MONTHLY MEETING (Orthodox), 1905--. 182 East Water
Street, Hughesville, Lycoming County.
Organized January 6, 1905, in the home of B. O. Kaufman, as an Apostolic
Holiness Church. The meeting met on the second floor of the Old Post Office Building, Main Street, January 6, 1905, to April 22, 1906. The frame
church was dedicated April 26, 1906. The rear of Church was made into a
parsonage in 1910, and an addition built on the front in 1937. This meeting became a part of Ohio Yearly Meeting of Orthodox Friends in 1912 and
the present name was adopted. The first settled minister was Sarah P.
Ecroyd, who served from January 6, 1905 to September 1, 1908.

Minutes of Apostolic Holiness Church, 1905-12, 1 vol.; Minutes of
Hughesville Monthly Meeting, 1912--, 2 vols.; Register of Members, 1906--,
3 vols.; Foreign Missionary Society Records, 1905-14, 1 vol.; Ladies Mis-
sionary Auxiliary Records, 1936--, 1 vol., in pastor's study, 182 East
Water Street. Financial Records, 1919--, 1 vol., possessions of Mrs.Lillian
Shaffer, 259 East Water Street, Hughesville.

402. OPPS PREPARATIVE MEETING, 1915-31. Opps, Lycoming County.
Set up May 19, 1915, by Hughesville Monthly Meeting of Orthodox Friends
(entry 401). Held meetings in white frame church formerly occupied by
Opps Methodist congregation. The meeting-house was sold in 1939. The
cemetery, adjoining church, was not used by this meeting. The first settled clergyman, was P. B. Lindley, 1915-18, graduate Cleveland Bible Institute, Cleveland, Ohio. The meeting was laid down March 19, 1931.

Minutes, 1915-31, 1 vol. (including financial records) possession
Rev. Robert E. Mosher, 182 East Water Street, Hughesville. Register,
years not listed, 1 vol., possession Rev. Robert E. Mosher. Lycoming
County Deed Book, vol. 221, p. 148.

	Date established	Entry number
MIDDLETON MONTHLY MEETING		Ohio
Conneaut Indulged Meeting	1806	403
Beaver Falls Preparative Meeting	1824	404

403. CONNEAUT INDULGED MEETING, 1806-60. Four miles north of Lines-
ville, in Conneaut Twp., about where Conneautsville is today,
in Crawford County.
Established about 1806 under Middleton Monthly Meeting, which came under
Ohio Yearly Meeting in 1812. This monthly meeting was probably a subordinate of Salem Quarterly Meeting. Meetings were held at the home of
Cornelius Lawson until about 1840, when a log meeting-house was erected
on the northeast corner of Tract 724. A nearby 1/4-acre cemetery, which
was acquired in 1817, is still maintained. Most of the Friends in this
meeting were settled in the township by 1800, many of them having removed
from Redstone Monthly Meeting (entry 391). The membership of the meeting
dwindled greatly, until the meeting was disbanded about 1860. Isaac Paden,
who settled in the township in 1797 and received his certificate of removal from the Redstone Monthly Meeting in 1822, was a prominent friendly
figure of this neighborhood.

See: The Genealogical Catalogue (Manuscript at The Historical Society of Pennsylvania); Redstone.

404. BEAVER FALLS PREPARATIVE MEETING, 1824-49. Fallston, Bright-
boro; New Brighton, Dougherty Twp., Beaver County.
Set up in 1824 by Middleton Monthly Meeting of Salem Quarterly Meeting
of the Ohio Yearly Meeting. The meeting-house in Fallston was located on
the summit of what is now locally known as Old Quaker Hill. The building
was constructed of brick. When the Separation occurred in this meeting
in 1828, it moved to New Brighton and the meeting-house was later converted into a private residence and 40 years later it was destroyed by
fire. Afterwards the remaining hulk was torn down so that today there is
no visible evidence of the former meeting-house. The property is now owned by a railroad company. When the meeting moved to New Brighton, The
Orthodox Friends worshipped in a house, on the property of J. F. Miner,
located on the corner of what is now 15th Street and Third Avenue. In
1839 1 acre of ground situated on State Road leading from Beaver Town to
Mercer, was deeded to the Society of Friends and a burial ground was plotted thereon in the same year. Due to decreased membership, the meeting
was laid down in 1849 by the Middleton Monthly Meeting. The building was
then used as a public school until 1857 and was destroyed by fire shortly
thereafter.

Minutes of Men's Meeting, 1824-49 missing; Minutes of Women's Meetings, 1824-63, 1 vol. (1828-49 missing), at PSC-Hi. Beaver County Deed
Books, vol. 80, p. 85; vol. 114, p. 207; vol. H, pp. 106, 220; vol. L, p.
210; vol. R, p. 451; vol. 54, p. 417.

	Date established	Entry number
DRY RUN (YOUNGS) FRIENDS MEETING	(?)	405

405. DRY RUN (YOUNGS) FRIENDS MEETING (date unknown). Dry Run, near
    Ohioville in Ohio Twp., Beaver County.
No accurate data can be found on this meeting, except that it was a subordinate meeting of New Garden Quarterly Meeting of Ohio Yearly Meeting
in 1826. It must have been short-lived, since no mention of it occurs in
later records. Records are probably included in the records of New Garden
Quarterly Meeting deposited at Salem, Ohio.

SALEM QUARTERLY MEETING

	Date established	Entry number
BEAVER FALLS MONTHLY MEETING	1846	406
Beaver Falls Preparative Meeting	1828	407

406. BEAVER FALLS MONTHLY MEETING, 1846-65.   Fifth Avenue, New Brighton, Beaver County.
Set up in 1846 by the Salem Quarterly Meeting of the Ohio Yearly Meeting. Meetings were held in the one-story brick meeting-house of the Beaver Falls Preparative Meeting (entry 407). This meeting was laid down in 1865.

Minutes of Men's Meetings (1846-65 missing). Minutes of Women's Meetings, 1858-65, 1 vol. (1846-58 missing), at PSC-Hi. There are no registers available.

407. BEAVER FALLS PREPARATIVE MEETING, 1828-ca.65.   Fifth Avenue, New Brighton, Beaver County.
Convened in 1828 by Middleton Monthly Meeting of Salem Quarterly Meeting of the Ohio Yearly Meeting after division of the original Beaver Falls Preparative Meeting (entry 404). When the Separation occurred, both Hicksite and Orthodox Friends were located in Fallston. Shortly afterwards both meetings moved to New Brighton, where this meeting erected a one-story brick meeting-house. This site is now occupied by the Standard Horseshoe Nail Company which uses the building as its office. The property was surrounded by a picket fence with two large gates. A burial place was plotted at the rear of the meeting-house. Due to decreased membership the meeting was laid down about 1865. On an original deed at the office of the Standard Horseshoe Nail Company, dated April 17, 1888, is written an account on what was to be done with the property and with the bodies interred in the burial ground. After the bodies were reinterred in a suitable graveyard, the former graveyard site was sold to private individuals.

Minutes of Men's Meetings (1828-65 missing). Minutes of Women's Meetings, 1824-63, 1 vol. (1863-65 missing), at PSC-Hi. Beaver County Deed Books, vol. 80, p. 85; vol. 144, p. 207; vol. H, pp. 106, 220; vol. 1, p. 210; vol. R, p. 451; vol. 54, p. 417.

408. REDSTONE QUARTERLY MEETING, 1827--. Washington, Greene and
Fayette Counties.
Data concerning this meeting and most of the subordinate meetings under
it are not available. When the Separation occurred in 1827 most of the
meetings in this southwestern section of Pennsylvania divided. These
meetings were under Ohio Yearly Meeting at that time, and since the records are deposited at Salem, Ohio, among the yearly meeting records, it
has not been possible to obtain their history at this time.

409. PIKE MONTHLY MEETING, 1827-58. Clover Hill Pike Run Twp.,
Washington County.
Set up in 1827 by Redstone Quarterly Meeting (entry 408), after separation
from the original Westland Monthly Meeting (entry 387). This was one of
the first meetings in western Pennsylvania to divide over the Hicksite
controversy. The Orthodox Friends maintained possession of the meeting-
house. This meeting erected a brick meeting-house nearby. Both the Hicksite and Orthodox Friends used the graveyard adjoining the property of the
Orthodox Friends' meeting-house. In 1858 both meetings were discontinued.
The property belonging to both factions was sold to Samuel Price. There
was no deed attesting to the sale of this property because of the absence
of representation of the Hicksite branch. Consequently in 1863, an act of
legislature decreed that, before the sale could successfully be completed,
there would have to be equal representation from the two groups. In that
year the property was finally conveyed to Samuel Price. Today, a barn
is situated on the site where the meeting-house stood.

Minutes and registers are in the records of the Ohio Yearly Meeting,
at PSC-Hi.

XI. FRIENDS INSTITUTIONS IN PENNSYLVANIA.

The history and records of Friends institutions in the Commonwealth of Pennsylvania would fill a volume equal in size to this one; hence, space here will only permit some notations descriptive of the origin, purpose, local church affiliation, and location of those institutions which are officially connected with the Society of Friends. Those merely sponsored by Friends as individuals are not listed here. Most of the small schools have been mentioned in the entries of the meetings with which they were affiliated. Brief as the following entries are, they represent considerable research in order to establish dates of origin and other data.

For convenience of reference and in order to avoid duplication, an arrangement of the various items of data indicated by the letters (a) to (g) has been made as follows:

> NAME, (a) Present official church affiliation, if any. If marked "none" it indicates only a cooperative relationship with the church organization. The letters (H) and (O) indicate either the (Hicksite or Orthodox) branch with which an institution is affiliated. (b) Date founded. (c) Date institution became extinct, or if left blank it indicates institution still exists. (d) Present address or location, or if extinct last address or location. (e) Purpose or nature of activities. (f) Present Head. (g) Where records are deposited.

Each entry follows the same order of arrangement, and all are placed in chronological order, and given an entry number.

410. FRIENDS SELECT SCHOOL. (a) Philadelphia Monthly Meeting (O) and Western District Monthly Meeting (O); (b) 1689; (c) --; (d) Benjamin Franklin Parkway and 17th St., Philadelphia; (e) coeducational secondary school; (f) Harris G. Haviland; (g) 302 Arch St., Philadelphia and at the school.

411. WILLIAM PENN CHARTER SCHOOL. (a) none (O); (b) 1689; (c) --; (d) School House Lane and Fox St., Germantown, Philadelphia; (e) boys' secondary school; (f) Richard Knowles; (g) Provident Trust Co., 17th and Chestnut Sts., Philadelphia and at the school.

412. ABINGTON FRIENDS SCHOOL. (a) Abington Monthly Meeting (H); (b) 1697, and has had a continuous existence under Friends management since that time; (c) --; (d) Jenkintown, Montgomery County; (e) primary school for the education of the children of Friends; (f) J. Folwell Scull; (g) in the records of Abington Monthly Meeting and at the school.

413. WILLIAM FORREST ESTATE. (a) Philadelphia Monthly Meeting (O) and Western District Monthly Meeting (O); (b) 1710; (c) --; (d) Forrest Estate Buildings, east side of 4th St., below Chestnut, Philadelphia; (e) education of Friends' children; (f) Horace M. Burton, Clerk of Joint Committee; (g) 302 Arch St., and Room #53, 304 Arch St., Philadelphia.

414. FRIENDS ALMSHOUSE. (a) Philadelphia Monthly Meeting (0); (b) 1713; (c) ca. 1876; (d) Willing's Alley, Philadelphia; (e) to provide a home for destitute Friends and others; (f) --; (g) a few miscellaneous records, papers, and deeds are deposited at 302 Arch St., Philadelphia.

415. FRIENDS FOURTH STREET ACADEMY. (a) Overseers of the Public School (0); (b) 1745; (c) ca.1847; (d) east side of 4th St., below Chestnut, Philadelphia; (e) Friends' School; (f) --; (g) early minutes of Overseers of The Public School, deposited at the Provident Trust Co., 17th and Chestnut Sts., Philadelphia, and minutes of the Philadelphia Monthly Meeting (0), deposited at 302 Arch St., Philadelphia.

416. PENNSYLVANIA SOCIETY FOR PROMOTING THE ABOLITION OF SLAVERY, (a) none (0 and H); (b) 1784; (c) --; (d) 1515 Cherry St., Philadelphia; (e) title covers activities; (f) President, Charles F. Jenkins, 232 So. 7th St., Philadelphia; (g) in custody of the secretary.

417. THE BENEZET SCHOOL. (a) none (0); (b) 1882; (c) 1864; (d) Willing's Alley, Philadelphia; (e) a school conducted by Anthony Benezet for 2 years prior to his death, for the free education of poor colored children; (f) --; (g) the depository where records are kept, if any are still in existence, is not known. Benezet House Association. (a) none (0 and H); (b) 1918; (c) 1935; (d) 918 Locust St.; (e) welfare of colored children; (f) --; (g) --.

418. GOSHEN MONTHLY MEETING SCHOOL. (a) Goshen Monthly Meeting (0); (b) 1794; (c) 1815; (d) East Goshen Twp., Chester County; (e) Friends' School; (f) --; (g) 302 Arch St., Philadelphia.

419. AIMWELL SCHOOL. (a) none (0); (b) 1796; (c) 1923; (d) 869 N. Randolph St., Philadelphia; (e) for the free education of girls; (f) --; (g) a few miscellaneous records and papers are stored at 302 Arch St., Philadelphia.

420. THE PHILADELPHIA FRIENDS' MISSION TO CORNPLANTER'S VILLAGE. (a) Philadelphia Yearly Meeting (0); (b) 1798; (c) 1799; (d) Elk Twp., Warren County; (e) religious and educational work among the Indians; (f) --; (g) Philadelphia Yearly Meeting records at 302 Arch St., Philadelphia.

421. WESTTOWN BOARDING SCHOOL. (a) Philadelphia Yearly Meeting (0); (b) 1799; (c) --; (d) Westtown, Chester County; (e) coeducational secondary boarding school; (f) James F. Walker; (g) 302 Arch St., Philadelphia, and at the school.

422. THE UNDERGROUND RAILROAD. (a) none (0 and H); (b) ca.1800; (c) ca.1861; (d) this movement was active throughout the northeastern part of the United States, but its promoters in Pennsylvania, centered in Philadelphia, (e) to assist fugitive slaves to reach free states or Canada; (f) --; (g) records were destroyed in 1850.

423. OXFORD VALLEY FRIENDS' SCHOOL. (a) Falls Monthly Meeting (0); (b) 1804; (c) 1931; (d) Emile Rd., south of Lincoln Highway, Oxford Valley, Bucks County; (e) elementary Friends' School; (f) --; (g) 302 Arch St., Philadelphia.

424. THE ADELPHIA SCHOOL. (a) name (0); (b) 1808; (c) ca.1912; (d) Winslow St., between Sixth and Seventh Sts., Philadelphia; (e) for the free instruction of poor colored children; (f) --; (g) a few miscellaneous

records and papers are deposited at 302 Arch St., Philadelphia.

425. PHILADELPHIA ASSOCIATION OF FRIENDS FOR THE INSTRUCTION OF POOR CHILDREN (Adelphia School). (a) none (O and H); (b) 1808; (c) 1903; (d) 13th and Race Sts., Philadelphia; (e) day school for small colored children; (f) --; (g) unknown.

426. FRIENDS' HOSPITAL. (a) Philadelphia Yearly Meeting (O); (b) 1811; (c) --; (d) Roosevelt Boulevard and Adams Ave., Philadelphia; (e) the hospitalization of those afflicted with insanity; (f) H. T. Prentzel; (g) 302 Arch St., Philadelphia, and at the hospital. FRIENDS' HOSPITAL FARM. (a) same affiliation; (b) 1915; (c) --; (d) Bensalem Twp., Lincoln Highway, 2 1/2 miles southwest of Langhorne Borough, Bucks County; (e) to provide dairy products to the hospital, and for recreational purposes for some of the patients; (f) Henry Hull; (g) 302 Arch St., Philadelphia and at Friends Hospital.

427. FRIENDS' HOSPITAL FOR MENTAL DISEASES. (a) none (H); (b) 1813; (c) --; (d) Roosevelt Boulevard and Adams Ave., Philadelphia; (e) treatment of mental diseases; (f) Dr. Albert C. Buckley, Superintendent; (g) at hospital.

428. FEMALE SOCIETY OF PHILADELPHIA FOR THE RELIEF AND EMPLOYMENT OF THE POOR. (a) (O and H); (b) 1815; (c) --; (d) 15th and Race Sts., Philadelphia; (e) to aid women who need employment; (f) Mrs. Albert L. Hood; (g) confer with President.

429. TRACT ASSOCIATION OF FRIENDS. (a) none (O); (b) 1816; (c)--; (d) 302 Arch St., Philadelphia; (e) for the publication and distribution of Friends literature; (f) Max I. Reich, Clerk (g) records are stored at 302 Arch St., Philadelphia.

430. THE FRIEND. (a) none (O); (b) 1827; (c) --; (d) 304 Arch St., Philadelphia; (e) biweekly periodical devoted to the religious and literary interests of Friends; (f) D. Elton Trueblood, Editor; (g) records are stored at 304 Arch St., Philadelphia.

431. THE FEMALE ASSOCIATION OF PHILADELPHIA. (a) none (H); (b) 1828; (c)--; (d) Room #3,Meeting-house 15th and Race Sts., Philadelphia; (e) the relief of the sick and the infirm poor, gives out sewing for which compensation is allowed, and investigates needy cases to whom clothing is distributed; (f) Anna J. F. Hallowell, President; (g) records are in the custody of officers of the association.

432. MIDDLETOWN SCHOOL. (a) Willistown and Middletown Preparative Meetings (O); (b) 1830; (c) ca.1836; (d) East side of Delchester Rd., south of the West Chester-Philadelphia Rd., Delaware County; (e) Friends' School; (f) --; (g) 302 Arch St., Philadelphia, and Chester County Historical Society, West Chester.

433. HAVERFORD COLLEGE. (a) none (O); (b) 1833; (c)--; (d) Haverford Twp., Delaware County; (e) Friends College; (f) Felix Morley, President, (g) all stored at the college.

434. FRIENDS' COMMUNITY SCHOOL. (a) Birmingham Monthly Meeting (H); (b) 1835; (c) --; (d) 423 N. Walnut St., West Chester, Chester County (e) Friends' School; (f) James A. Morrow; (g) Birmingham Monthly Meet-

ing records at 302 Arch St., Philadelphia, at the meeting-house, and at the school.

435. FRIENDS' CHARITY FUEL ASSOCIATION. (a) none (H); (b) 1835; (c) --; (d) Meeting-house at Fifteenth and Race Sts., Philadelphia; (e) distributes coal at a reduced price to persons recommended by contributing members of the association; (f) J. Horace Alter, Clerk; (g) records are in custody of the officers.

436. WESTERN SOUP ASSOCIATION. (a) none (O); (b) 1837; (c) 1903; (d) northwest corner of 17th and Chestnut Sts., Philadelphia; (e) for the free distribution of soup and bread to the needy poor; (f) --; (g) records at 302 Arch St., Philadelphia.

437. THE GRANDOM INSTITUTION. (a) none (O and H); (b) 1841; (c) --; (d) Philadelphia; (e) supplies coal to the worthy poor at considerable reduction from prevailing retail prices; (f) Charles F. Jenkins, President; (g) records are in the custody of officers of the organization.

438. THE FRIENDS' INTELLIGENCER. (a) none (H); (b) 1844; (c) --; (d) 1515 Cherry Street, Philadelphia; (e) a weekly periodical devoted to the religious and social interests of Friends; (f) Sue C. Yerkes, Managing Editor; (g) records are stored at 1515 Cherry St., Philadelphia.

439. GERMANTOWN FRIENDS' SCHOOL. (a) Germantown Monthly Meeting (O); (b) 1845; (c) --; (d) Coulter St., near Germantown Ave., Germantown, Philadelphia; (e) Friends' School; (f) Burton P. Fowler; (g) 302 Arch St., Philadelphia, and at the school.

440. FRIENDS' FREE LIBRARY AND READING ROOM. (a) Germantown Monthly Meeting (O); (b) 1845; (c) --; (d) 5418 Germantown Ave., Germantown, Philadelphia; (e) to provide the general public with free library facilities; (f) Violet G. Gray, Librarian; (g) Germantown Friends' School, 302 Arch Street, Philadelphia, and at the library.

441. FRIENDS' CENTRAL SCHOOL. (a) Philadelphia Monthly and Green Street Monthly Meetings (H); (b) 1845; (c) --; (d) City Line Ave. and 68th St., Overbrook, Philadelphia; (e) coeducation secondary school; (f) Barclay Lincoln Jones; (g) 1515 Cherry St., Philadelphia, Swarthmore Historical Library, and at the school.

442. CENTRAL EMPLOYMENT ASSOCIATION. (a) none (H); (b) 1857; (c) ca.1925; (d) 17th St. and Girard Ave. meeting-house, Philadelphia; (e) aims to encourage the poor to help themselves by giving employment in sewing and to assist some families by the distribution of clothing; (f) Elizabeth Y. Webb; (g) records are in the custody of officers of the association.

443. BOOK ASSOCIATION OF FRIENDS. (a) none (O); (b) incorporated 1860; (c) --; (d) 302 Arch St., Philadelphia; (e) to aid Friends' schools and other institutions to purchase Friends' books; (f) Isaac P. Miller; (g) records are in the custody of the officers of the corporation.

444. SWARTHMORE COLLEGE. (a) none (H); (b) 1864; (c) --; (d) Swarthmore, Delaware County; (e) Friends' coeducational college; (f) John W. Nason, President; (g) all stored at the college.

445. FRIENDS HISTORICAL ASSOCIATION. (a) none (O and H); (b) 1873; (c) --; (d) Haverford College; (e) collects and publishes material relating to the history of the Society of Friends, and promotes interest in this field; (f) William W. Comfort; (g) all records at Haverford College.

446. FRIENDS NEIGHBORHOOD GUILD. (a) Philadelphia Quarterly Meeting (H); (b) 1879; (c) --; (d) southeast corner 4th and Green Sts., Philadelphia; (e) community social service work; (f) Herbert C. Bergstrom; (g) records of Guild Committee of Philadelphia Quarterly Meeting, deposited at 1515 Cherry St., Philadelphia.

447. FRIENDS INSTITUTE AND LYCEUM. (a) none (O); (b) 1880; (c) --; (d) 20 S. 12th St., Philadelphia; (e) to provide recreational facilities to Friends' in the central section of the city; (f) James C. Butt, Treasurer; (g) all records stored at the institute offices except treasurer's cash books which are kept at the office of the Treasurer at the Girard Trust Co., Broad and Chestnut Sts., Philadelphia.

448. FRIENDS HOME FOR CHILDREN. (a) none (H); (b) 1881; (c) --; (d) 4011 Aspen St., West Philadelphia; (e) to provide a home for destitute and neglected little children of all sects, and to secure a place for them in private homes; (f) Mary Willits Cramer, Matron; (g) stored at the home, and bound printed annual reports are in possession of the President of the Board of Directors, Franklin D. Edmunds, Real Estate Trust Building, Philadelphia.

449. HAVERFORD FRIENDS' SCHOOL. (a) Haverford Monthly Meeting (O); (b) 1885; (c) --; (d) Haverford Twp., Delaware County; (e) coeducational primary school; (f) Frances C. Ferris; (g) records are all stored at the school.

450. FRIENDS' BOARDING HOME OF CONCORD QUARTERLY MEETING. (a) Concord Quarterly Meeting (H); (b) 1892; (c) --; (d) N. Walnut St., between Marshall and Biddle Sts., West Chester, Chester County, (e) to provide a home for aged and infirm Friends in a Friendly atmosphere; (f) Stanley G. Child, President of the Board; (g) all records stored at the home.

451. GEORGE SCHOOL. (a) Philadelphia Yearly Meeting (H); (b) 1893; (c) --; (d) three miles north of Langhorne on Durham Rd., Middletown Twp., Bucks County; (e) coeducational secondary school; (f) George A. Walton, Principal; (g) all records stored at the school.

452. BARCLAY HOME. (a) none (O); (b) 1894; (c) --; (d) High and Marshall Sts., West Chester, Chester County; (e) to provide a home for aged and infirm Friends in a Friendly atmosphere; (f) Harriet Cope; Matron; (g) all records stored at the home.

453. STAPELEY HALL (FRIENDS' BOARDING HOME). (a) Philadelphia Quarterly Meeting (H); (b) 1896; (c) --;(d) 6300 Greene St., Germantown, Philadelphia; (e) to provide a home for aged and infirm Friends in a Friendly atmosphere; (f) J. Franklin Gaskill, Chairman of Committee; (g) Quarterly Meeting records at 1515 Cherry St., Philadelphia, and at the home.

454. FRIENDS BOARDING HOME OF BUCKS QUARTERLY MEETING. (a) Bucks Quarterly Meeting (H); (b) 1897; (c) --; (d) corner Center and Congress Sts., Newtown, Bucks County, (e) to provide a home for aged and infirm Friends in a Friendly atmosphere; (f) George W. Row, President of the Board; (g) Bucks Quarterly Meeting records, and at the home.

455. FRIENDS' BOARDING HOME OF WESTERN QUARTERLY MEETING. (a) Western Quarterly Meeting (H); (b) 1898; (c) --; (d) 200 block W. State St., Kennett Square, Chester County; (e) to provide a home for aged and infirm Friends in a Friendly atmosphere; (f) Edwin P. Buffington, Chairman of Committee; (g) all records stored at home.

456. PENNSBURY (FRIENDS' BOARDING HOME). (a) none (O); (b) 1908; (c) --; (d) 5431 Greene St., Germantown, Philadelphia; (e) to provide a home for aged and infirm Friends in a Friendly atmosphere; (f) Mary M. Haines, Matron; (g) records stored at the home, a few in custody of the Secretary Beulah O. Wildman, 4331 Osage Ave., Philadelphia, and a few in custody of the Treasurer, Mrs. Walter T. Moore, 121 W. Coulter St., Germantown, Philadelphia.

457. PHILADELPHIA YOUNG FRIENDS ASSOCIATION. (a) none (H); (b) 1912; (c) --; (d) 15th and Cherry Sts., Philadelphia; (e) to promote a more thorough knowledge of the history and testimonies of the Society of Friends, to assist in providing for their temporal welfare, and to establish a center for the development of these activities. The Wittier Hotel is operated by this association. (f) Charles W. Michener, Acting President; (g) records are stored at the headquarters of the association.

458. JEANES HOSPITAL. (a) none (H); (b) 1913; (c) --; (d) Central Ave. and Hartel St., Fox Chase, Philadelphia; (e) for the hospitalization of those afflicted with cancer; (f) J. Wilmer Lundy, President of the Board; (g) all records are stored at the hospital.

459. ARCH STREET CENTER. (a) Philadelphia Monthly Meeting (O); (b) 1915; (c) --; (d) 304 Arch St., Philadelphia; (e) a building erected by Friends on the Arch St. meeting-house grounds, housing the office of the Yearly Meeting, offices of the Philadelphia Monthly Meeting, other Friends' offices; also The Friends publication; Friends' Book Store, Friends Records Depository, Rooms for Friends, and a dining room; (f) Edith P. MacKendrick, Secretary of the Monthly Meeting; (g) records are stored at 304 Arch St., Philadelphia.

460. AMERICAN FRIENDS SERVICE COMMITTEE. (a) twenty-six America Yearly Meetings (all branches); (b) 1917; (c) --; (d) 20 S. Twelfth St., Philadelphia; (e) international relief and humanitarian work; (f) Clarence E. Pickett, Secretary; (g) Roberts Hall, Haverford College, and 20 S. 12th St., Philadelphia.

461. FRIENDS SOCIAL UNION. (a) Philadelphia Yearly Meeting (O and H); (b) 1924; (c) --; (d) Secretary, Friends Social Union, 1515 Cherry Street, Philadelphia; (e) social and religious fellowship; (f) M. Albert Linton, President, 4601 Market Street, Philadelphia; (g) records are in the custody of the secretary.

462. FRIENDS' CAMP ASSOCIATION (CAMP ONAS). (a) none (H); (b) 1925; (c) --; (d) Wrightstown and Northampton Twps., Bucks County (e) to provide a summer camp for children; (f) William R. Fogg, President of the Board; (g) Minute Books in custody of the Secretary, Charles Supplee, 105 S. 12th St., Philadelphia, records of finance in custody of the Treasurer, D. Hagner, 274 W. Harvey St., Germantown, Philadelphia.

463. YOUNG FRIENDS MOVEMENT. (a) Philadelphia Yearly Meetings (O and H); (b) 1930; (c) --; (d) 1515 Cherry St., Philadelphia; (e) promotes

young Friends' activities; (f) Robert C. English,Secretary; (g) records are stored at 1515 Cherry St., Philadelphia.

464. PENDLE HILL. (a) none (all branches); (b) 1930; (c) --; (d) near Wallingford, Delaware County; (e) a center for social and religious studies; (f) Howard H. and Anna C. Brinton, Directors; (g) records are in the custody of officers of the association.

465. ABINGTON FRIENDS' HOME. (a) Abington Quarterly Meeting (H); (b); (c) --; Swede and Powell Sts., Norristown, Montgomery County; (e) to provide a home for aged and infirm Friends in a Friendly atmosphere; (f) Clinton W. Morgan, Clerk of the Committee; (g) records are stored at the home.

466. CHEYNEY INSTITUTE. (a) none (0); (b) 1837; (c) --; (d) Cheyney, Chester County; (e) Negro coeducaional normal school; (f) Leslie P. Hill, Principal; (g) records are stored at the school.

467. SUNNY CREST FARM. (a) none (0); (b) 1855; (c) --; (d) Cheyney, Chester County; (e) home for destitute Negro children; (f) Mrs. William K. Brown, Secretary; (g) records are stored at the farm.

XII. GLOSSARY

ACKNOWLEDGMENTS. A formal acknowledgment in writing, by an offending member to his meeting, of having acted in a manner contrary to the rules of discipline.

ADVICES. Recommendations regarding conduct, usually originating in yearly and quarterly meetings. While failure to follow such Advices would be deplored by Friends, it would not be considered sufficient cause for disownment.

CERTIFICATES. Where certificates are mentioned, they usually refer to removal to or from a meeting. Also given to traveling ministers by their home meetings and returned to those meetings when the religious visit is completed.

CONCERN. The inner urge felt by a Friend to presistently bear testimony or act in given matter according to his spiritural leading. A strong conviction that a certain course or cause is right and that it is laid upon the person having the concern to promote it.

DENIALS. A record of persons dropped from membership in the Society of Friends for violation of discipline.

DISCIPLINE. Friends' principals of belief and practice when gathered in a volume constitutes "The Book of Discipline." This is not a creed. These disciplines are usually compiled by each yearly meeting. A uniform Discipline is now in use by the yearly meetings of the Five Years Meeting.

DISOWNMENTS. When a member of the Society of Friends commits an act contrary to the discipline, he is treated with by a committee appointed for that purpose. If, after this visitation, he fails to acknowledge the fault, he is disowned by the Society and can not be reinstaated until he has made acknowledgment of his fault.

ELDERS. A small group of men and women appointed by the monthly meetings to assist the ministers. They assist by opening and closing meetings and by giving spiritual guidance to members of their meeting, and also by encouraging the ministry of individuals of the congregation. They, with the overseers compose the meeting of Ministers and Elders, or Ministry and Counsel, as it came to be called.

EPISTLES. Letters from one yearly meeting to another or from the yearly to the quarterly and monthly meetings. Epistles usually contain greetings, state the condition of the meeting sending the Epistle, and discuss problems of the sender and of the meeting to which the letter is sent. Matters of general interest to all Friends are also discussed. Epistles may be addressed to a specific meeting or may be more general in character and sent to several yearly meetings. Epistles also constitute an official recognition of the status of fellowship with the yearly meetings to which they are sent.

INDIAN AFFAIRS. Several types of assistance were given the Indian tribes, such as peace treaties, protection from frauds, and education both religious and civic. The term is also used of the rights and physical welfare of the Indiens.

LAID DOWN. Term used to denote the official discontinuance of a meeting.

MANUMISSIONS. Documents indicating their freedom, given to slaves when freed by their owners.

MARRIAGE PAPERS. These consist of certificates of approval for marriage; a record from the respective meetings of which the contracting parties are members, stating that they are of good character and free of marriage engagements. Also parental consent for marriage; a letter from the parents of the contracting parties to their respective meetings, giving their consent for the marriage to proceed. After these preliminaries are cleared the couple appear before a regular or specially called monthly meeting and take each other in marriage by repeating to each other a pledge of marriage. No minister or any other person performs any part of the ceremony.

MEETINGS.
   Five Years Meeting. The meeting held once every five years at Richmond, Ind., for discussion of national and international questions; for advices to the lesser meetings under its jurisdiction; and for promotion of the work of its various boards. This meeting is the Orthodox branch of the Society of Friends. There is an Executive Committee with authority to act between sessions.

   General Conference Meeting. This conference assembles once every two years and serves as the national gathering in the Hicksite branch of the Society of Friends. The Central Committee is the executive body and promotes activities in the interim between sessions.

   Half-Year Meeting. A meeting held twice a year composed of monthly meetings within a convenient geographical scope, and with the duties of a quarterly meeting. These meetings are usually under the jurisdiction of a yearly meeting.

   Independent Meeting. A local meeting for worship and business having no affiliation with either the General Conference or the Five Years Meeting, or any other higher body.

   Indulged Meeting. A meeting for worship only. Set up by a monthly meeting when a preparative meeting was not practical.

   Men's and Women's Meetings. In the early years, it was customary throughout the entire organization of the Society, for the men and women to hold separate meetings for business, at the same location. Meetings for worship were held in the same room, but with the men sitting on one side and the women on the other. The meetings of the women Friends looked after the affairs of the monthly meeting which concerned that sex alone. Records, similar to those kept by the men's meeting, were kept by the women. In many cases, particularly when dealing with discipline, the clerk of the men's meeting signed records as well as the clerk of the women's meeting. Matters which were of interest to both meetings were decided by small committees from both meetings, since both assembled in separate rooms at the same place and hour. When necessary for one meeting to present a matter to the other meeting, representatives were always sent in pairs. Beginning about 1880 the custom of holding separate men's and women's meetings began to disappear, and at present all meetings are held jointly.

Ministers and Elders Meeting. An official body composed of the minis- ters, elders, and sometimes overseers of a monthly meeting. They have oversight of the spiritual welfare of a meeting, both as the quality of the ministry and also as to the spiritual moral guidance of the members.

Ministering Friends Meeting. This meeting, rarely held at the present time, is very similar to the ministers and elders meeting. It is held quarterly or monthly, or as occasion demands when visiting ministers are on visits of service to a meeting.

Monthly Meeting. This is the unit of the Friends' organization, and is the basis of their policy. The membership consists of the members of all the preparative and indulged meetings under the jurisdiction of the monthly meeting. All members have an equal right of attendance and voice. All registers of subordinate meetings are kept, and min- utes of all business recorded by the monthly meeting. The subsidiary meetings, for the most part, keep only financial records and memoranda of matters to be presented to the monthly meetings. Final decision in all questions of local administration and discipline rests with the monthly meeting, except in cases of appeal to the quarterly or yearly meeting. All members within the meeting are expected to attend its business sessions.

Particular Meeting. This term has several meanings. Generally it is used to designate the meetings for worship under a monthly meeting. In early times it was used occasionally to refer to a meeting of min- istering Friends, and sometimes to distinguish a monthly meeting from a quarterly meeting of the same name.

Preparative Meeting. Originally used to indicate meetings held by a committee appointed by the monthly meeting for the purpose of "pre- paring" matters of business to be presented to the monthly meeting. This small committee appears to be the group which later became the "overseers." The meeting of the overseers was called the "preparative meeting." When a meeting for worship was permitted, but not offici- ally set up as a monthly meeting, a committee was appointed by the monthly meeting to "oversee" its affairs When complaints or business matters were to be presented to the monthly meeting it was first given to the committee, who prepared it, in the proper form for presentation to the monthly meeting. Later the name "preparative" was applied to the entire meeting instead of the committee. Preparative meetings were officially authorized in Philadelphia Yearly Meeting in 1698. The members of these meetings are free to speak in the monthly meeting. The meetings usually keep minutes of their monthly business sessions. Their action is subject to the decision of the monthly meeting, and their minutes must be approved by that body. A few of the larger pre- parative meetings owning burial grounds, keep financial records.

Quarterly Meeting. Business meetings composed of one or more monthly meetings. While all component meetings were supposed to attend as a body they rarely did so. Monthly meetings, in the early days, some- times called every third meeting a "quarterly meeting." Later, several monthly meetings would unite at the time of the third meeting. The setting-up of new monthly meetings, combining of meetings, consideration of appeals from the decisions of monthly meetings and the giving or advice and admonition for the general good of the Society are the duties fulfilled by this meeting.

Representative Meeting. A meeting which has, in Philadelphia Yearly Meeting, developed out of the Meeting For Sufferings. It is a standing committee appointed by the yearly meeting and given administrative and executive authority to act for the yearly meeting ad interim.

Second-Day Morning Meeting. This meeting met mostly for worship but sometimes for business consultation on Monday morning. It was a meeting originating in London, and the idea brought to America by early Friends. It has been discontinued.

Select Meeting. A meeting of ministers and elders, held prior to the monthly, quarterly, or yearly meeting. Also called in later years a meeting of Ministry and Counsel.

Sufferings, Meeting for. Appointed first, as a committee, by the yearly meeting of 1756, to assist Friends and others who suffer because of Indian raids. The sum of one thousand dollars was set aside for its use at that time. After re appointment from year to year, it was permanently set up in 1771. Later, similar committees were appointed by quarterly and monthly meetings, to assist those who endured hardships due to the opposition of Friends to war and slavery. These last two factors often caused the loss of property, and much suffering. This meeting finally developed into the Representative Meeting of the Yearly Meeting.

Worship, Meeting for. The public meeting for worship is held on the principle of silent communion and waiting upon God for the leading of His Spirit. No preacher or leader is necessary, since the oral ministry may be given by any one, or no one, and in the latter instance the entire worship period is spent in silent communion. These meetings are usually held on First-days, and an additional one held sometime during the week.

Yearly Meeting. Business meetings composed of several quarterly meetings. The entire membership is supposed to attend these meetings and a large proportion do attend. Influential members of the several meetings usually attend. They are not elected nor are they in attendance as delegates, but as individual members, although certain members are usually designated to attend from the quarterly and monthly meetings in order to facilitate business.

MEMORIALS. A memorial is a written tribute, prepared by the Overseers of a meeting, or by individuals or committees specifically designated, to to commemorate the name of an outstanding member who has recently died. Memorials, as listed in Friends' records, are a collection of such tributes.

MINISTERS. Both men and women are recognized and recorded by special action of the monthly and quarterly meetings "as having a gift for the ministry." In Pennsylvania these ministers serve without pay since the two yearly meetings in Pennsylvania have never departed from this early Quaker system. In other parts of the country, however, Quaker ministers are paid a salary, and give their entire time to the work and interests of the meetings which they serve. A Friends' minister whether in Pennsylvania or elsewhere has the same legal status as an ordained minister of any other denomination.

OVERSEERS. Two or more men or women appointed by each monthly meeting to have pastoral care of the members. They report to the monthly meeting. In some meetings they meet with the ministers and elders. Records of these officials, when kept, will be found under ministers and elders.

PERMANENT BOARD. See Representative Meeting.

PUBLIC FRIENDS. A term usually applied to those who regularly took part in meetings for worship and other such services. Traveling ministers, especially distinguished ones.

REMOVALS. A certificate or record of persons who have moved to the jurisdiction of another meeting. Such persons are given removal certificates stating that they are in good standing with the meeting which they are leaving.

SET OFF. Term used when a new meeting is formed by the division of another meeting.

SET UP. Term used to designate the establishment of a new meeting by a superior meeting.

TESTIMONY. A belief or conviction of Friends in general, and the conscious promotion of the same. There are testimonies on temperance, racial equality, opposition to war and promotion of peace, abolition of slavery, opportunity for the under-privileged, international cooperation, and other modern reforms.

TRUSTEES. Individuals appointed by monthly, quarterly, and yearly meetings to have the responsibility of directing the controlling, legal and financial interests of the meetings. They hold title to the property of the meeting and act in a corporate capacity for it.

UNDERGROUND RAILROAD. A definite but unofficial organization among early Friends and a few others, whose purpose was to aid escaping slaves to reach Canada or other free territory. This activity always of uncertain legality, was, after the Fugitive Slave Act of 1850 definitely outlawed, hence the unofficial nature of the organization, and the lack of records. This aid was given quietly and the slaves who escaped from their masters in the South were secretly passed from one Quaker family to another until safe in free territory. Fugitives were not only given food and shelter but were also transported by horseback, wagon, and sometimes by boat and train from one station to another along well-defined routes. Travel was accomplished mostly by night and the slaves hidden in barns, smokehouses, and cellars during the day.

1. Since some differentiation is necessary for the sake of convenience and brevity the terms "Hicksite" and "Orthodox," where used, refer to the Yearly Meeting of Friends which meets at Fifteenth and Race Streets and the Yearly Meeting of Friends which meets at Fourth and Arch Streets respectively. Before the Separation of 1827-28 the body is known only as the Society of Friends. At the time of the split two bodies emerged and have been known since that time by the names mentioned above. It must be understood that this survey assumes no position as to which is the original body.

2. The entries for the meetings have been arranged in chronological order, or when that is not possible in alphabetical order, and grouped under their respective yearly, quarterly, and monthly meetings. Meetings affiliated with Baltimore Yearly Meeting and Ohio Yearly Meeting have been placed under these meetings and under a general heading of Meetings With Extra-State Affiliations. This has been done because the official headquarters of these yearly meetings are located outside of Pennsylvania.

3. In the list of local meetings which precedes each entry section, meetings which are underlined are not covered by entries. Many meetings have changed their affiliations at various times and, to avoid duplication, the entries of these shifting meetings have been placed under the superior body with which they are affiliated at the present time or, in cases of defunct meetings, under the superior body with which they were affiliated when they were laid down. Only the names underlined and with a cross reference to the entry are given in the lists of the component meetings of the superior bodies with which they were previously affiliated. By these lists it is therefore possible to trace the various changes of affiliation of any given meeting.

4. Friends institutions are arranged chronologically and placed together at the end of the meeting entries.

5. All meeting records which could be located have been listed. It must be borne in mind, however, that the records listed in this volume are only those pertinent to the actual business of the meetings.

6. In most cases records of Hicksite meetings are listed as beginning in 1827. In the cases where records ante-dating 1827 are listed under Hicksite meetings it should be borne in mind that the records prior to that date will be those of the original undivided Friends meeting. The terms Hicksite and Orthodox apply only after the Separation of 1827-28. This arbitrary listing is made necessary because of the present custody of some records, and also the fact that some local meeting records have been copied by either one or the other of the two bodies and it is difficult to determine the original manuscript. In many cases where there is an apparent over-lapping of the records listed under an Orthodox and Hicksite meeting bearing the same name it is to be accounted for by the copying of the records many years ago.

It should also be stated that in addition to the collections of meeting records preserved in the depositories listed on page   there are a number of small collections in the hands of private individuals who are not official custodians of meetings

7. In all cases where possible, full names, exact addresses, and complete references have been given. In addresses, the State is always Pennsylvania unless otherwise stated.

8. The Society of Friends uses the numerical designation to indicate the months and days of the week. (e.g. Eighth month 27th, 1682, or Fourth-day 9th month 8th, 1682).

In determining dates before 1752 it must be noted that England in 1751, by an act of Parliament, adopted the Gregorian Calendar, effective on September 3, 1752. This act numbered the day following September 2, 1752, as September 14, in order to account for the 11 days difference between the long used Julian Calendar (Old Style), and the newly adopted Gregorian Calendar (New Stule). Furthermore, the beginning of the calendar year was changed from March 25 to January 1, this to become effective the following January of 1753. All dates before 1752 given in this book are copied as found in the documents; therefore, if translation into terms of the New Style dating is desired it must be done by the reader.

9. The Wilburite or Wilbur-Gurney Controversy has been treated in this book only in the preliminary historical sretch, since this discussion never developed into an actual split in the Society of Friends in Pennsylvania, except a small organized group within the limits of Nottingham Quarterly Meeting. This group was short-lived and about 1860 it united with the Primitive Friends of Fallsington.

10. A few abbreviations and symbols have been used. In all cases they are as follows:

Ave.	Avenue.
(B)	meeting affiliated with Baltimore Yearly Meeting.
ca.	approximately; used with dates.
Co.	Company.
(H)	Hicksite.
ibid.	indicates reference immediately preceding.
(I)	independent meeting
(IM)	indulged meeting.
(K)	Keithian meeting.
(MM)	monthly meeting.
Ms.	manuscript.
n.d.	no date of publication.
NNBN	Newtown Nation Bank, Newtown.
No(s).	number(s).
N.	North.
(O)	Orthodox.
(OH)	meeting affiliated with Ohio Yearly Meeting.
op. cit.	in the work befor cited.
p. pp.	page, pages.
(P)	Primitive Friends Meeting.
passim.	reference to numerous passages scattered throughout the work cited.
PDoyB	Bucks County Historical Society, Doylestown. George MacReynolds, Librarian.
PHC	Haverford College Library, Haverford. Dean P. Lockwood, Librarian.

PH:	The Historical Society of Pennsylvania, 1300 Locust Street, Philadelphia. William Reitzel, librarian.
(PM)	preparative meeting.
PNortHi	The Historical Society of Montgomery County, Norristown. Emily K. Preston, librarian.
PPf	Friends Central Bureau, 1515 Cherry Street, Philadelphia. Marguerite Hallowell, custodian.
PPFYR	Department of Records of Philadelphia Yearly Meeting, 302 Arch Street, Philadelphia. J. Henry Bartlett, custodian.
PSC-Hi	Friends Historical Library, Swarthmore College, Swarthmore. E. Virginia Walker, custodian.
PWc-Hi	The Chester County Historical Society, West Chester. Bart Anderson, librarian.
PWmp	James V. Brown Library, Williamsport. O. R. H. Thomson, librarian.
(QM)	Quarterly meeting.
Rd(s).	Road(s).
So.	South.
St(s).	Street(s).
twp.	township.
(U)	United meeting.
vol(s).	volume(s).
(YM)	Yearly Meeting.
--,	following a date means up to the present time.
. . .	used in quotations to indicate an elision of words not pertinent to the reference.
[ ]	brackets are used for interpolated words or phrases.
( )	parentheses are used for modifying or explanatory words or phrases.

APPENDIX

SUBORDINATE MEETINGS OUTSIDE OF PENNSYLVANIA

The following is a list of meetings which are located outside of the boundaries of Pennsylvania and which are or have at some time been a part of one or both of the two Philadelphia Yearly Meetings. No attempt has been made to designate these meetings as Hicksite or Orthodox, since to do so would involve research outside of Pennsylvania, and the limits of this survey. For the records and history of these meetings, see the inventories of the Church Archives of the States listed.

NEW JERSEY

YEARLY MEETINGS (combined with Philadelphia in 1685).

	Date established
Shrewsbury	1681
Burlington	1681
HALF-YEAR MEETINGS	
"East Jersey"	(?)
Salem	(?)
Burlington	(?)
QUARTERLY MEETINGS	
Shrewsbury	1672
Burlington	1682
Salem	1682
Haddonfield	1794
Burlington and Bucks	1898
Haddonfield and Salem	1904
MONTHLY MEETINGS	
Shrewsbury	1670
Salem	1676
Burlington	1678
Chesterfield (Crosswicks)	1684
Great Egg Harbor	1702
Little Egg Harbor	1715
Evesham	1760
Greenwich	1770
Mount Holly	1776
Upper Springfield	1783
Woodbury	1785
Upper Evesham	1793
Westfield	1794
Woodstown (Pilesgrove)	1794
Haddonfield (Gloucester)	1795
Chester (Moorestown)	1803
Maurice River	1805
Medford (Upper Evesham)	1850

PREPARATIVE AND INDULGED MEETINGS

Shrewsbury	1670
Salem	1675
Middletown	(?)
Manesquan	(?)
Burlington	1677
Crosswicks (Chesterfield)	1677
Alloway's Creek	1678
Thompson's Bridge (Allowaystown)	(?)
Gloucester	1680
Camden (Pyne Point) (Arwamus)	1681
Rancocas	1681
Newton (Newtown)	1682
Old Springfield (Esiskunk Creek) (Copany)	1682
Freehold	1683
Mount Holly	1687
Mount Laurel (Evesham)	1694
Greenwich	1694
Woodbury	1694
Great Egg Harbor	1702
Little Egg Harbor	1704
Stony Brook	1710
Woodstown (Pilesgrove)	1715
Haddonfield	1721
Moorestown (Chester)	1721
Allentown	1727
Upper Springfield	1728
Amwell	1729
Mansfield	1731
Trenton (Trent Town)	1734
East Branch (Robbin's Meeting)	1739
Upper Freehold (Arneytown) (Woodward's) Bordentown	1740
Upper Greenwich (Mickleton) (Lippincott's)	1740
Mount (Shreve's) (Arney's Mount)	1743
Mansfield Neck (Lower Mansfield)	1753
Medford (Upper Evesham)	1760
Vincent-Town	1765
Barnegat	1767
Cropwell	1786
Upper Penn's Neck	1794
Westfield	1794
Mullica Hill (Woolwich)	1797
Easton	1803
Atlantic City (independent meeting)	1874
Rutgers (independent meeting)	1936
Cape May (Seaville)	(?)
Leeds Point	(?)
Tuckerton	(?)

MARYLAND

HALF-YEAR MEETINGS

Southern Half-Yearly Meeting	1679

MONTHLY MEETINGS
    Thirdhaven (Tredhaven)   1676
    Cecil   1698
    Deer Creek   (?)
    Nottingham   1730
    Gunpowder   1739
    Little Falls   1815
    Pike Creek   (?)

PREPARATIVE AND INDULGED MEETINGS
    Thirdhaven (Tredhaven)   (?)
    Cecil   (?)
    Chester (Chester Neck)   (?)
    Millington   (?)
    Bayside   (?)
    Bush Creek   (?)
    Monocacy   (?)
    Gunpowder   (?)
    Betty's Cove   1676
    Tuckahoe   1676
    Sassafras   1679
    Choptank   1684
    E. Nottingham   1700
    W. Nottingham   1710
    Marshy Creek   1727
    Pipe Creek   1735
    Deer Creek   1736
    Little Falls   1738
    Forest   1815
    Greensborough
        (Queen Anne's Transquaking)   1701

DELAWARE

QUARTERLY MEETINGS
    Southern Quarterly Meeting   1790

MONTHLY MEETINGS
    Duck Creek   1705
    Wilmington   1750
    Motherkill (Murderkill)   1788
    Centre   1808
    Camden (Deer Creek) (Motherkill)   1852

PREPARATIVE AND INDULGED MEETINGS
    New Castle   1684
    Centre   1687
    Duck Creek   1700
    George's Creek   1703
    Little Creek   1710
    Cool Spring (Cold Spring)   1720
    Hockessin   1737
    Wilmington   1738
    Milford (Mispillion) (Mushmellon)   1760
    Motherkill   1760
    Christiana Bridge   1772
    White Clay Creek (Christiana Bridge)   1781

DELAWARE (continued)

PREPARATIVE AND INDULGED MEETINGS (continued)
Appoquinimink	1783
Stanton (White Clay Creek)	1803
Mill Creek	1838
Camden	(?)

VIRGINIA

MONTHLY MEETINGS
Hopewell	1735
Fairfax	1745
Goose Creek	1785
Alexandria	1802

PREPARATIVE AND INDULGED MEETINGS
Fairfax	(?)
Goose Creek	(?)
Hopewell	1760
Back Creek	1777
Alexandria	(?)

NEW YORK

INDULGED MEETING
Tunesassa (Quaker Bridge)	1798

CALIFORNIA

MONTHLY MEETING
Orange Grove (Pasadena)	1907

BIBLIOGRAPHY

Much of the descriptive material included in this inventory, in addition to information on the records themselves, has been obtained at first hand. Interviews with church officials, members of local historical societies, and members of meetings have uncovered many new facts for which no documentation or bibliographical reference can be given.

A. Primary Sources

I. Manuscripts

Chester County Collection, Chester County Historical Society, West Chester.

The Gilbert Cope Historical and Genealogical Collection, The Historical Society of Pennsylvania, Philadelphia.

Lightfoot Papers, The Historical Society of Pennsylvania, Philadelphia. 21 file boxes.

Minutes of Philadelphia Quarterly Meeting, June 5, 1683. (Manuscript at Department of Records, Society of Friends of Philadelphia).

Miscellaneous Records, Bucks County Historical Society, Doylestown.

Morgan Edwards Collection, Bucknell Library, Chester.

Philadelphia Yearly Meeting Minutes, 1685. (Manuscript at Department of Records, Society of Friends of Philadelphia).

II. Newspapers

Berwick Enterprise.

Bryn Mawr News.

Honey Brook Herald.

Hughesville Independent.

Norristown Times Herald.

Philadelphia Evening Bulletin.

Philadelphia The Friend.

Philadelphia Friends Intelligencer.

Philadelphia North American.

Philadelphia Press.

Philadelphia Public Ledger.

Philadelphia Record.

Philadelphia Times.

Phoenixville Daily Republican.

Pottsville Evening Republican.

West Chester American Republican.

West Chester Daily Local News.

West Chester Village Record.

Williamsport Sun.

III. Published Sources.

Advancement Committee, Directory of Members of Baltimore Yearly Meeting
    of the Religious Society of Friends. Baltimore, 1936.

Baist, George W., Property Atlas of the City and County of Philadelphia,
    1895. Philadelphia, J. L. Smith, 1895.

The Book of Discipline of the Religious Society of Friends. Philadelphia,
    1927.

Calendar of Friends Meetings (Hicksite). Philadelphia, 1938.

Comly, John, Journal. Philadelphia, T. E. Chapman, 1853.

Constitution and Discipline for the Five Years Meeting of Friends in
    America. Richmond, Indiana, 1920.

Discipline of Philadelphia Yearly Meeting (Hicksite) for 1837. Phila-
    delphia, 1837.

Faith and Practice of the Religious Society of Friends of Philadelphia
    and Vicinity. A Book of Christian Discipline. Philadelphia,
    Friends Book Store, 1935.

Friends Meetings (Hicksite). Philadelphia, 1937.

Friends Religious and Moral Almanac. (Orthodox). Philadelphia, Tract
    Association of Friends, 1938.

Hicks, Elias, Journal of the Life and Religious Labours of Elias Hicks.
    New York, Isaac T. Hopper, 1832.

The Narrative of Sojourner Truth, Northern Slave Emancipated from Bodily
    Service by State of New York in 1828. Boston, 1850.

Philadelphia City Directory, 1864-1909. Philadelphia, 1864-1909.

Proceedings of the Pennsylvania Yearly Meeting of Progressive Friends,
    1853-54. New York, John F. Trow, 1853-54. 2 vols.

Proceedings of the Yearly Meeting of the Religious Society of Friends of Philadelphia and Vicinity, 1938. Philadelphia, Friends Book Store, 1938.

Real Estate Map of the Overbrook Section. (Surveyors map in the Real Estate Department of the Pennsylvania Railroad, 15th and Market Streets, Philadelphia).

Rules and Regulations for the Government of Friends Burial Grounds at Fair Hill - to Which is Added - A Short Historical Account of the Title of Friends to the Premises. Philadelphia, 1858.

Scattergood, Thomas, Journal of the Life and Religious Labors of Thomas Scattergood. Philadelphia, Friends Book Store, N.d.

U. S. Bureau of the Census, Census of Religious Bodies, 1926, Friends. Washington, Government Printing Office, 1926.

U. S. Bureau of the Census, Census of Religious Bodies, 1936, Friends. Washington, Government Printing Office, 1936.

Wilbur, John, Journal. New York, Piercy, 1845.

Wood, George, Report of the Trenton Trial. Philadelphia, J. Harding, 1833.

B. Secondary Works

Aldrich, Lewis C. History of Clearfield County. Syracuse, New York, D. Mason and Company, 1887.

200th Anniversary Book of London Grove Meeting. Philadelphia, Innes and Sons Press, 1914.

200th Anniversary of Buckingham Monthly Meeting, 1720-1923, Buckingham Township, Bucks County, Pennsylvania. Philadelphia, 1923.

200th Anniversary Plymouth Friends' Meeting. Norristown, Pennsylvania, 1903.

Ashbridge, Wellington T., The Ashbridge Book. Toronto, Canada, The Copp. Clark Company, 1912.

Ashmead, Henry G., History of Delaware County. Philadelphia, L. H. Everts and Company, 1884.

Bailey, John S., "Thomas Ross, a Minister of the Society of Friends," Bucks County Historical Society Papers, I (1908), 283-294.

Bancroft, George, History of the United States From the Discovery of the American Continent. Boston, Little, Brown and Company, 1834-75. 10 vols.

Barclay, John, Jaffray and His Friends in Scotland. London, Barton and Harvey, 1834.

Barclay, John, Life of Alexander Jaffray. London, Barton and Harvey, 1834.

Barclay, Robert, An Apology for the True Christian Divinity: Being an Explanation and Vindication of the Principles of the People Called Quakers. Philadelphia, Friends Book Store, 1908.

----------------, Truth Triumphant. Philadelphia, B. C. Stanton, 1831.

Battle, J. H., History of Bucks County, Pennsylvania. Philadelphia and Chicago, A. Warner and Company, 1887.

Bean, Theodore W., History of Montgomery County. Philadelphia, Everts and Peck, 1884.

Best, Mary A., Rebel Saints. New York, Harcourt, Brace Company, 1925.

Bicentennial Anniversary of the Friends Meeting House at Merion, Pennsylvania. Philadelphia, Friends Book Association, 1895.

Blackburn, E. Howard, and William H. Welfley, History of Bedford and Somerset Counties. New York and Chicago, The Lewis Publishing Company, 1906. 3 vols.

Blackman, Emily C., History of Susquehanna County. Philadelphia, Claxton, Remsen, and Haffelfinger, 1873.

Book List of Friends Records in the Fire-proof Vault of the Baltimore Yearly Meeting of the Religious Society of Friends, Park Avenue, City of Baltimore, State of Maryland, 1937. (manuscript at Friends Meeting-house, Park Avenue and Laurens St., Baltimore, Md.).

Book of Meetings. Philadelphia, Young Friends Movement, 1940.

Bowden, James, History of Friends in America. London, Charles Gilpin, 1850. 2 vols.

Bowne, Ira E., Historical Record, West Philadelphia Meeting. (Manuscript at Swarthmore College Library).

Braithwaite, William C., The Beginnings of Quakerism. London, Macmillan and Company, Limited, 1912.

----------------------, The Second Period of Quakerism. London, Macmillan and Company, Limited, 1919.

Brenner, W. C., and Henry Beck, A Brief History of Fair Hill Friends Meeting. (Manuscript in custody of Henry Beck, 1018 W. Cambria Street, Philadelphia).

Brinton, Walter, "Friends Meetings in Frankford," Papers Read Before the Historical Society of Frankford, II (1910), No. 4, 127-135.

Brookes, George S., Friend Anthony Benezet. Philadelphia, University of Pennsylvania Press, 1937.

Brown, George W., Historical Sketches Chiefly Relating to the Early Set-
    tlement of Friends at Falls in Bucks County. Philadelphia, 1882.

Brown, Levi K., An Account of the Meetings of the Society of Friends With-
    in the Limits of Baltimore Yearly Meeting, Philadelphia, T. Ellwood
    Zell, 1875.

Browning, Charles H., Welsh Settlement in Pennsylvania. Philadelphia,
    William J. Campbell, 1912.

Buck, Solon J., The Planting of Civilization in Western Pennsylvania.
    Pittsburgh, University of Pittsburgh Press, 1939.

Bucks, W. J., History of Bucks County. Willow Grove, Pennsylvania, Bucks
    County Intelligencer, 1855.

Buckmaster, Henrietta, Let My People Go, The Story of the Underground
    Railroad and the Growth of the Abolition Movement. New York, Harper
    Brothers, 1941. 398 pp.

Bunting, Morgan, A List of the Records of the Meetings Constituting the
    Yearly Meeting of the Society of Friends, Held at Fifteenth and Race
    Streets, Philadelphia. Philadelphia, 1906.

"The Burial Ground and Building at Arch and Fourth Streets," The Friend,
    LXIII (1890) 194.

"Byberry Meeting," The Friend, I (1827), 68, 74.

Cadbury, Henry J., and others, Two-and-A-Half Centuries of Quaker Educa-
    tion, Philadelphia, reprinted from The Friend, CXIII (1939), Nos. 9,
    10.

Catalog of Materials in the Vault of Baltimore Yearly Meeting of Friends.
    (Manuscript at Baltimore Yearly Meeting, 3107 N. Charles St., Bal-
    timore).

Celebration of the Centennial Anniversary of Dunning Creek Monthly Meet-
    ing of Friends. Bedford, Pennsylvania, 1903.

Centennial Anniversary of Darby Meeting-House, 1805-1905. Philadelphia,
    1905.

The Centennial Anniversary of Solebury Friends Meeting. n.p., 1906.

Centennial of Newton Friends Meetings. Doylestown, Pennsylvania, 1822.

Chapman, Henry, "Reminiscences of Buckingham," Bucks County Historical
    Society Papers, I (1908), 143-152.

Christian Discipline of the Society of Friends, Church Government. Lon-
    don, Friends Bookshop, 1917.

Cockburn, James, A Review of the General and Particular Causes Which Have
    Produced the Late Disorders and Divisions in the Yearly Meeting of
    Friends Held in Philadelphia. Philadelphia, Phillip Price, Jr.,
    1829.

Comly, John and Isaac, "Settlement and Progress of Byberry Meeting,"
Friends' Miscellany, VII (1835), 97-124.

Cope, Gilbert, Chester County Quakers During the Revolution. (Manuscript
at Chester County Historical Society, West Chester).

--------------, Genealogy of the Smedley Family. Lancaster, Pennsylvania
Wickersham Printing Company, 1901.

--------------, "History of West Chester Meeting of (Orthodox) Friends,"
Bulletin of Chester County Historical Society, 1908, 34-56.

Cope, Morris, Western Quarter. (Manuscript at meeting-house, West Grove).

Crumrine, Boyd, History of Washington County. Philadelphia, L. H. Everts
and Company, 1882.

Davis, William W. H., History of Bucks County. Doylestown, Pennsylvania,
Democrat Book and Job Office, 1876.

Dewees, Watson W., "The William Forrest Estate," The Friend, LXXXIX
(1916), 368, 377, 389, 401, 414-416.

Dobree, Bonamy, William Penn, Quaker and Pioneer. Boston and New York,
Houghton Mifflin Company, 1932.

Ecroyd, Charles E., Earlier Days of the Muncy Monthly Meeting. (Manuscript at James V. Brown Library, Williamsport).

------------------, On the Underground Railway. (Manuscript at James V.
Brown Library, Williamsport).

Egle, William H., History of the Commonwealth of Pennsylvania. Philadelphia, E. M. Gardner, 1883.

Eldridge, Jonathan, A History of Birmingham Meeting. (Manuscript in custody of author at West Chester).

Ellis, Franklin, History of Fayette County. Philadelphia, L. H. Everts
and Company, 1882.

----------- ---, and Samuel Evans, History of Lancaster County. Philadelphia Everts and Peck, 1883.

Eshelman, John, "Friends in Berks County," Historical Review of Berks
County, I (1936), No. 2, 1-66.

Fairbank, Calvin, During Slavery Times. Chicago, Patriotic Publishing
Company, 1890.

Faris, John T., Old Churches and Meeting Houses in and Around Philadelphia. Philadelphia and London, J. B. Lippincott Company, 1926.

Fisher, Sidney G., The Making of Pennsylvania. Philadelphia, J. B. Lippincott Company, 1896.

Fox, Cyrus T., Reading and Berks County Pennsylvania. New York, Lewis Historical Publishing Company, 1925. 2 vols.

Fox, George, Journal, Bicentenary Edition. London, Headley Brothers, 1902. 2 vols.

The Friends Meeting House, Fourth and Arch Streets, Philadelphia, Centennial Volume. Philadelphia, John C. Winston and Company, 1904.

Futhey, J. Smith, and Gilbert Cope, History of Chester County, Pennsylvania. Philadelphia, L. H. Everts, 1881.

The Genealogical Catalogue. (Manuscript at The Historical Society of Pennsylvania, Philadelphia).

Gibbons, William, A Review and Refutation of Some of the Opprobious Charges Against the Society of Friends, as Exhibited in a Pamphlet Called a Declaration, etc. Philadelphia, T. E. Chapman, 1847.

Green, Doron, History of Bristol Borough Anciently Known as Buckingham. Camden, New Jersey, 1911.

Griest, Mariam L., Notes for a History of the Progressive Friends of Longwood. (Manuscript thesis at Swarthmore College, 1935).

Grubb, Edward, Separations, Their Causes and Effects. London T. F. Unwin, 1914.

Gummere, Amelia M., The Journal and Essays of John Woolman. New York, Macmillan Company, 1922.

------------------, The Quakers in the Forum. Philadelphia, John C. Winston Company, 1910.

Hall, Willis H., Quaker International Work in Europe Since 1914. Savoie, France, Imprimeries Reunies de Chambery, 1938.

Harvey, Thomas E., The Rise of the Quakers. London, Unwin Brothers, Limited, 1921.

Hayes, John R., Old Quaker Meeting Houses. Philadelphia, The Biddle Press, 1911.

Heathcote, Charles W., A History of Chester County. Harrisburg, National Historical Association, Incorporated, 1932.

Hicks, Elias, A Series of Extemporaneous Discourses Delivered in the Several Meetings of Philadelphia, Germantown, Abington, Byberry, Newtown, Falls and Trenton. Philadelphia, Joseph and Edward Parker, 1825.

Hinshaw, William W., Encyclopedia of American Quaker Genealogy. Ann Arbor, Michigan, Edwards Brothers, Incorporated, 1938. 3 vols.

"Historical Excursion to Byberry," The Friend, XCIII (1920), 53, 63.

Historical Sketch of North Meeting, Sixth and Noble Streets, Philadelphia.
     Philadelphia, n.d.

Hodgson, William, The Society of Friends in the Nineteenth Century. Phil-
     adelphia, Sherman and Company, 1876. 2 vols.

Holcomb, Hanna E., "Edward Hicks, Approved Minister of Society of Friends,"
     Bucks County Historical Society Papers, I (1908), 385-392.

Holder, Charles F., The Quakers in Great Britain and America. New York,
     The Neuner Company, 1913.

Hotchkin, Samuel F., "Then and Now; or Old Times and New in Pennsylvania,"
     Bucks County Historical Society Papers, I (1908), 496-509.

Hough, Mary P. H., Religious Meetings of the Society of Friends. (Manu-
     script in custody of author, Ambler).

Hull, William I., William Penn and the Dutch Quaker Migration to Pennsyl-
     vania. Swarthmore, Pennsylvania, Swarthmore College, 1935.

----------------, William Penn, Eight First Biographies. New York and
     London, Oxford University Press, 1937.

Jackson, Jesse W., Historical Sketch of Old Sadsbury. (Manuscript in
     custody of author, Christiana).

Jackson, Joseph, Encyclopedia of Philadelphia. Harrisburg, The National
     Historical Association, 1931-33. 4 vols.

Jenkins, Arthur H. and Ann R., "A Short History of Abington Meeting,"
     Bulletin of the Friends Historical Association, XXII (1933), No. 2,
     115-135.

Jenkins, H. M., Historical Collections of Gwynedd. (Manuscript at His-
     torical Society of Montgomery County, Norristown).

Jenkins, Walter H., Bi-Centennial of Old Kennett Meeting House. Phila-
     delphia, 1910.

Jones, Rufus M., Faith and Practice of the Quakers. London, Metheun and
     Company, Limited, 1927.

----------------, Haverford College. New York, Macmillan, 1933.

----------------, The Later Periods of Quakerism. London, Macmillan Com-
     pany, 1921. 2 vols.

----------------, The Quakers in the American Colonies. London, Macmillan
     and Company, 1911.

----------------, A Service of Love in Wartime. New York, Macmillan Com-
     pany, 1920.

----------------, Spiritual Reformers in the Sixteenth and Seventeenth
     Centuries. London, Macmillan and Company, 1914.

Keen, William W., "Keithian Quaker Meeting-House, La Grange Place, Second
    Street, above Market, 1692-1731," in Bi-Centennial Celebration of
    the Founding of the First Baptist Church of Philadelphia, 1698-1898.
    Philadelphia, American Baptist Publishing Society, 1899.

Kelsey, Rayner W., Friends and the Indians. Philadelphia, Associated
    Executive Committee of Friends on Indian Affairs, 1917.

Kendall, John, The Life of Thomas Story. London, James Phillips, 1786.

Kirk, Harriet, "Warminister Friends Meeting," Bucks County Historical
    Society Papers, I (1908), 116-118.

Kite, Thomas, A Declaration of the Yearly Meeting of Friends Held in Phil-
    adelphia, Regarding the Proceedings of Those Who Have Lately Sepa-
    rated From the Society, and Also Showing the Contrast. Philadelphia,
    1828.

Klein, Harry M. J., and others, A History of Lancaster County. New York,
    The Lewis Historical Publishing Company, 1924. 4 vols.

Linn, John B., History of Centre and Clinton Counties, Philadelphia,
    L. H. Everts and Company, 1883.

Lippincott, Horace M., An Account of the People Called Quakers in German-
    town, Philadelphia. Burlington, New Jersey, Enterprise Publishing
    Company, 1923.

--------------------, "The Keithian Separation," Bulletin of the Friends
    Historical Association, XVI (1927), No. 2, 49-58.

Lippincott, Joseph W., "Some Account of the First Places of Worship of
    Friends in Philadelphia," The Friend, LXII (1889), 283, 301, 307,
    316, 331, 342, 357, 365, 373, 396.

Major, Charles, Commemorative of Providence Meeting. (Manuscript at His-
    torical Society of Montgomery County, Norristown).

Martindale, James C., History of Byberry and Moreland Townships. (Manu-
    script at The Historical Society of Pennsylvania, Philadelphia).

Matlack, T. Chalkley, Brief Historical Sketches Concerning Friends Meet-
    ings of the Past and Present, With Special Reference to Philadelphia
    Yearly Meeting. (2 vols. manuscript at Department of Records, So-
    ciety of Friends of Philadelphia).

Michener, Ezra, A Retrospect of Early Quakerism. Philadelphia, T. Ellwood
    Zell, 1860.

Miller, Joseph H., Book of Meetings. Columbus, Ohio, Traulman and Palmer,
    1884.

"Minutes of Philadelphia Monthly Meeting," The Friend, LXII (1889), 239.

Montgomery, Morton L., History of Berks County, Pennsylvania in the Rev-
    olution, From 1774 to 1783. Reading, Pennsylvania, C. F. Hoage,
    1894.

Moon, Henry, Friends of Falls.   (Manuscript at Fallsington Library).

Mosheim, Johann Lorenz, von, Institutes of Ecclesiastical History, An-
    cient and Modern. New York, Evart Duyckinck, 1764. 4 vols.

Mower, John, and others, History of Bedford, Somerset, and Fulton Coun-
    ties. Chicago, Waterman, 1884.

Munsell, W. W., History of Schuylkill County. Albany, New York, Munsell,
    1878.

Myers, Albert C., The Immigration of the Irish Quakers Into Pennsylvania,
    Swarthmore, Pennsylvania, New Era Printing Company, 1902.

One Hundredth Anniversary of Fallowfield Friends Meetings. Philadelphia,
    1911.

"Original Objects for Which Meetings for Discipline Were Established,"
    The Friend, LVIII (1885), 127.

Palmer, A. Mitchell, A History of Quakers in Stroudsburg. (Manuscript
    in Monroe County Historical Society, Stroudsburg).

Parry, Edwin C., Betsy Ross, Quaker Rebel. Philadelphia, John C. Winston
    Company, 1930.

Past and Present, Centennial Souvenir of West Chester. West Chester,
    1899.

Penn, William, The Rise, Progress, and Key of the People Called Quakers.
    Philadelphia, Friends Book Store, 1876.

Pennell, Arthur, History of Middletown Meeting. (Manuscript in author's
    possession, Baltimore Pike, Wawa).

Penny, Norman, George Fox.   Cambridge, England, Cambridge University
    Press, 1911. 2 vols.

Pennypacker, Samuel W., Annals of Phoenixville and Its Vicinity. Phila-
    delphia, Bavis and Pennypacker, 1872.

"Plumstead Township," Bucks County Historical Society Papers, I (1908),
    305-313.

Pound, Arthur, The Penns of Pennsylvania and England.   New York, The
    Macmillan Company, 1932.

Price, Ellen H. E., History of Swarthmore Meeting. (Manuscript at meet-
    ing-house, Swarthmore).

Price, Joseph H., and Stanley R. Yarnall, William Penn. Philadelphia,
    John C. Winston Company, 1932.

Prowell, George R., History of York County, Pennsylvania. Chicago, J.
    H. Beers and Company, 1905. 2 vols.

Rhode Island Historical Records Survey, Inventory of the Church Archives of Rhode Island; Society of Friends. Providence, 1940.

Richards, Helen, Organization of Friends Meeting at Norristown. (Manuscript at Historical Society of Montgomery County, Norristown).

Richardson, Nathaniel, Discussions and Anecdotes of Thomas Story. Philadelphia, T. Ellwood Zell, 1860.

Roberts, Clarence V., and Warren S. Ely, Early Friends Families of Upper Bucks. Philadelphia, 1925.

Roberts, Elwood, Plymouth Meeting. Norristown, Roberts Publishing Company, 1900.

----------------, Richland Families. Norristown, Morgan R. Wells, 1898.

Rushmore, Jane P., Testimonies and Practices. Philadelphia, Friends General Conference, 1936.

Russel, Elbert, The Separation After a Century. Philadelphia, Friends Intelligencer, 1928.

Ruth's Scrap Books, Bucks County Historical Society, Doylestown.

Sachse, Julius F., German Secterians of Pennsylvania. Philadelphia, 1899-1900. 2 vols.

Satterthwaite, Elizabeth B., Bucks County Friends' Meetings. (Manuscript at Fallsington Library).

Scharf, J. Thomas, and Thompson Westcott, History of Philadelphia, 1609-1884. Philadelphia, L. H. Everts and Company, 1884. 3 vols.

Schoonover, Janetta W., A History of William Brinton. Trenton, New Jersey, MacCrellish and Quigley, 1924.

Scripture Versus Hicks or a Line Drawn Between Elias Hicks and the Scripture of the Old and New Testaments. Philadelphia, S. Patty and Company, 1824.

Sewell, William, The History of the Rise, Increase, and Progress of the Christian People Called Quakers. Philadelphia, Friends Book Store, 1856.

Sharpless, Isaac, The Centuries of Pennsylvania History. Philadelphia, J. B. Lippincott, 1900.

----------------, Political Leaders of Provincial Pennsylvania. New York, Macmillan Company, 1919.

----------------, A Quaker Experiment in Government. Philadelphia, Ferris and Leach, 1902.

Sharpless, Philip P., Birmingham Monthly Meeting and West Chester Preparative Meeting. (Manuscript at Friends' Meeting-house, West Chester).

Sharpless, Susanna, "Historical Sketch of West Chester Friends Schools," The Friend, CIV (1930), 27, 28.

Sharpless, William T., "Birmingham Meeting," Bulletin of Friends Historical Association, XIX (1930), No. 2, 68-76.

Shimmell, Lewis S., A History of Pennsylvania. Harrisburg, R. L. Myers and Company, 1900.

Shoemaker, Thomas H., An Historical Account of Green Street Monthly Meeting. (Manuscript in custody of Mary W. Shoemaker, Germantown).

Siebert, Wilbur H., The Underground Railroad From Slavery to Freedom. New York, The Macmillan Company, 1898.

Smedley, Caroline W., "Frankford Meeting," The Friend, LXXXVIII (1914), 135, 147.

Smedley, R. C. History of the Underground Railroad in Chester County and the Neighboring Counties of Pennsylvania. Lancaster, Pennsylvania, Office of the Journal, 1883.

Smith, Charles H., History of Horsham Preparative Meeting House. (Manuscript in custody of author, Horsham).

Smith, George, History of Delaware County. Philadelphia, H. B. Ashmead, 1862.

Smith, Josiah B., "Early Settlement of Newtown Township," Bucks County Historical Society Papers, III (1909), 1-5.

Snipes, Jane M., "The Founding and Founders of Falls Meeting," Bulletin of Friends' Historical Association, XXII (1933), No. 1, 14-26.

Speakman, Thomas H., Divisions in the Society of Friends. Philadelphia, J. B. Lippincott, 1893.

Stahle, William, A Discription of the Borough of Reading. Reading, Pennsylvania, 1841.

Still, William, The Underground Railroad. Philadelphia, Peoples Publishing Company, 1879.

Streets, Priscilla W., Lewis Walker of Chester Valley and His Descendents. Philadelphia, A. J. Ferris, 1896.

Thomas, Allen C. and Richard H., A History of the Friends in America. Philadelphia, John C. Winston Company, 1930.

Thomas, Anna B., The Story of Baltimore Yearly Meeting From 1672-1938. Baltimore, The Weant Press Incorporated, 1938.

Thomas, Joseph, "Reminiscences of Quakertown and Its People," Bucks County Historical Society Papers, III (1909), 42-51.

Thomson, Wilmer W., Chester County and Its People. Chicago and New York, Union History Company, 1898.

Trescott, Boyd M., History of Lansdowne Monthly Meeting. (Manuscript at Swarthmore College Library).

"Twelfth Street Meeting 125th Anniversary," Twelfth Street Meeting Message, June 1938, 1-16.

Vaux, George, "An Account of the Centre Square and Bank Meeting Houses of Friends in Philadelphia," The Friend, LXIII (1890), 99, 109, 147, 404.

------------, Bi-Centennial Anniversary of the Friends' Meeting House at Merion, Pennsylvania, 1695-1895. Philadelphia, 1895.

------------, "The Great Meeting-house," The Friend, LXIII (1890), 147.

------------, "The Keithian Meeting-house," The Friend, LXXVII (1903), 171, 172.

------------, "Orange Street Meeting-house," The Friend, LXIII (1890), 404.

------------, "Pine Street Meeting-house," The Friend, LXIII (1890), 260, 268.

------------, "The Public School Founded by Charter in the Town and County of Philadelphia, in Pennsylvania; the Forrest Trust, and the Fourth Street Meeting and School-Houses," The Friend, LXIII (1890), 314, 323, 331.

Walkinshaw, Lewis C., Annals of Southwestern Pennsylvania. New York, Lewis Historical Publishing Company, 1939. 4 vols.

Wall, Thomas L., Clearfield County, Pennsylvania, Past and Present. Clearfield, Pennsylvania, 1925.

Washburn, Louis C., Christ Church, Philadelphia. Philadelphia, Macrae Smith Company, 1925.

Watson, John F., Annals of Philadelphia and Pennsylvania in the Olden Time. Philadelphia, Published by the author, 1854. 2 vols.

Weeks, Stephen B., Southern Quakers and Slavery. Baltimore, Johns Hopkins University Press, 1896.

Westcott, Thompson, The Historic Mansions and Buildings in Philadelphia With Some Notice of their Owners and Occupants. Philadelphia, Porter and Coates, 1877.

Wetherill, Charles, History of the Religious Society of Friends Called by Some the Free Quakers in the City of Philadelphia. Philadelphia, 1894.

Wildes, Harry E., Valley Forge. New York, The Macmillan Company, 1938.

Willcox, Mildred S., Friends' Schools. (Manuscript in custody of author at Department of Records, Society of Friends of Philadelphia).

Wood, John H., "Quaker Imprints of Bucks County," Bulletin of Friends'
    Historical Association, XXII (1933), 26-34.

Woody, Thomas, Early Quaker Education in Pennsylvania. New York, Columbia
    University Teachers College, 1920. ·

Wynkoop, William, "Newton-Old and New," Bucks County Historical Society
    Papers.   III (1909), 287-295.

Yarnall, D. Robert and Elizabeth, "The Chestnut Hill Meeting," The Friend,
    CV (1931), 265.

ALPHABETIC INDEX TO ENTRIES IN THE QUAKER VOLUME

Entry
number

Abington Friends Home 465

Abington Friends School 412

Abington Monthly Meeting (H) 175

Abington Monthly Meeting (O) 93

Abington Preparative Meeting (H) 176

Abington Preparative Meeting (O) 95

Abington Quarterly Meeting (H) 174

Abington Quarterly Meeting (O) 92

Adelphia School, The 424

Aimwell School, The 419

Ambler Indulged Meeting (H) 185

American Friends Service Committee 460

Arch Street Center 459

Avondale Indulged Meeting (H) 255

Bald Eagle (Half-Moon) Preparative Meeting (O) (B.Y.M.) 362

Baltimore Yearly Meeting (P) 312

Barclay Home 452

Bart Indulged Meeting (O) 128

Bart Preparative Meeting (H) 266

Beaver Falls Monthly Meeting (H) (O.Y.M.) 406

Beaver Falls Preparative Meeting (H) (O.Y.M.) 407

Beaver Falls Preparative Meeting (O) (O.Y.M.) 404

Bendersville Preparative Meeting (O) (B.Y.M.) 358

Benezet School, The 417

Bernard's School House Indulged Meeting (O) 86

Berwick Indulged Meeting (O) 50

Berwick Preparative Meeting (H) 304

Birmingham Monthly Meeting (H) 219

Birmingham Monthly Meeting (O) 154

Birmingham Preparative Meeting (H) 220

Birmingham Preparative Meeting (O) 155

Boarded Meeting on the Delaware, The (O)   5

Book Association of Friends 443

Bradford Monthly Meeting (H) 262

Bradford Monthly Meeting (O) 117

Bradford Preparative Meeting (O) 120

Bradford Uwchlan Monthly Meeting (H) 276

Bristol Monthly Meeting (H) 214

Bristol Particular Meeting (P) 319

Bristol Preparative Meeting (H) 215

Bristol Preparative Meeting (O) 60

Buck Hill Falls Independence Friends Meeting 335

Buckingham Indulged Meeting (O) 165

Buckingham Monthly Meeting (H) 197

Buckingham Monthly Meeting (O) 167

Buckingham Preparative Meeting (H) 198

Buckingham Preparative Meeting (O) 59

Bucks Quarterly Meeting (H) 196

Bucks Quarterly Meeting (O) 58

Burlington and Bucks Quarterly Meeting (O) 161

Byberry Indulged Meeting (O) 110

Byberry Monthly Meeting (H) 177

Byberry Monthly Meeting of Friends (O) 106

Byberry Preparative Meeting (H) 178
Byberry Preparative Meeting (O) 107

Caln Preparative Meeting (H) 277
Caln Preparative Meeting (O) 118
Caln Quarterly Meeting (H) 261
Caln Quarterly Meeting (O) 116
Cambridge Indulged Meeting (H) 264
Cambridge Indulged Meeting (O) 122
Catawissa Indulged Meeting (H) 305
Catawissa Indulged Meeting (O) 29
Catawissa Monthly Meeting (O) 39
Catawissa Preparative Meeting (O) 48
Central Employment Association 442
Centre Monthly Meeting (H) (B.Y.M.) 366
Centre Monthly Meeting (O) (B.Y.M.) 360
Centre Preparative Meeting (H) (B.Y.M.) 367
Centre Preparative Meeting (O) (B.Y.M.) 361
Centre Preparative Meeting (O) (O.Y.M.) 395
Centre Quarterly Meeting (H) (B.Y.M.) 365
Centre Square Meeting (O)   6
Cheltenham Friends Meeting (Abington) (O) 94
Cherry Street Meeting (H) 282
Chester Monthly Meeting (H) 222
Chester Monthly Meeting (O) 137
Chester Preparative Meeting (H) 223
Chester Preparative Meeting (O) 139
Chestnut Hill United Monthly Meeting 330
Cheyney Institute 466

Chichester Preparative Meeting (H) 226

Chichester Preparative Meeting (O) 145

Clearfield Preparative Meeting (H) (B.Y.M.) 371

Coatesville Indulged Meeting (H) 272

Columbia Indulged Meeting (H) 269

Columbia Preparative Meeting (O) 124

Concord Monthly Meeting (H) 225

Concord Monthly Meeting (O) 143

Concord Preparative Meeting (H) 227

Concord Preparative Meeting (O) 144

Concord Quarterly Meeting (H) 218

Concord Quarterly Meeting (O) 136

Concord United Monthly Meeting 331

Conneaut Indulged Meeting (O) (O.Y.M.) 403

Curwensville Monthly Meeting (O) (B.Y.M.) 364

Darby Monthly Meeting (H) 228

Darby Monthly Meeting (O) 148

Darby Preparative Meeting (H) 229

Darby Preparative Meeting (O) 149

Doe Run Preparative Meeting (Derry Meeting) (H) 242

Doe Run Preparative Meeting (Derry) (O) 88

Doylestown Indulged Meeting (H) 200

Downingtown Preparative Meeting (O) 133

Drumore Preparative Meeting (H) (B.Y.M.) 375

Drumore Preparative Meeting (O) (B.Y.M.) 356

Dry Run (Youngs) Friends Meeting (O) (O.Y.M.) 405

Dunnings Creek Monthly Meeting (H) (B.Y.M.) 369

Dunnings Creek Monthly Meeting (O) (B.Y.M.) 363

Dunnings Creek Preparative Meeting (O) (B.Y.M.) 347

Dunnings Creek Quarterly(Half-Year) Meeting (O) (B.Y.M.) 359

Eagles Mere Indulged Meeting (O) 46

Eastland Preparative Meeting (H) (B.Y.M.) 376

Eastland Preparative Meeting (O) (B.Y.M.) 355

East Sadsbury Indulged Meeting (H) 270

East Sadsbury Indulged Meeting (O) 127

Elkland Particular Meeting (P) 323

Elkland Preparative Meeting (O) 45

Exeter Monthly Meeting (H) 284

Exeter Monthly Meeting (O) 24

Exeter Preparative Meeting (O) 25

Fair Hill Indulged Meeting (H) 293

Fair Hill Indulged Meeting (O) 9

Fallowfield Monthly Meeting (H) 241

Fallowfield Monthly Meeting (O) 87

Fallowfield Monthly Meeting (O) (O.Y.M.) 400

Fallowfield Particular Meeting (P) 322

Fallowfield Preparative Meeting (H) 243

Fallowfield Preparative Meeting (O) 85

Falls Monthly Meeting (H) 201

Falls Monthly Meeting (O) 162

Falls Monthly Meeting (P) 318

Falls Preparative Meeting (H) 202

Falls Preparative Meeting (O) 61

Fallsington General Meeting of Primitive Friends 317

Fawn Grove Preparative Meeting (H) (B.Y.M.) 373

Fawn Grove Preparative Meeting (O) (B.Y.M.) 357

Female Association of Philadelphia, The 431

Female Society of Philadelphia for the Relief and
  Employment of the Poor 428

First Bank Meeting, The (O) 7

Fishing Creek Preparative Meeting (O) 42

Fourth Street Meeting (O) 11

Frankford Indulged Meeting (H) 290

Frankford Monthly Meeting of Friends (O) 108

Frankford Preparative Meeting (Germantown and Frankford Friends) (H) . 289

Frankford Preparative Meeting (O) 109

Friends Almshouse 414

Friends Boarding Home of Bucks Quarterly Meeting 454

Friends Boarding Home of the Concord Quarterly Meeting 450

Friends Boarding Home of the Western Quarterly Meeting 455

Friends Camp Association (Camp Onas) 462

Friends Central School 441

Friends' Charity Fuel Association 435

Friends' Community School 434

Friends Fourth Street Academy 415

Friends Free Library and Reading Room 440

Friends General Conference (H) 172

Friends Historical Association 445

Friends Home for Children 448

Friends Hospital 426

Friends Hospital For Mental Diseases 427

Friends Institute and Lyceum 447

Friends Neighborhood Guild 446

Friends Select School 410

Friends Social Union 461

Friendsville Preparative Meeting (H) 193

Friendsville Preparative Meeting (O) 113

George School 451

Germantown Friends School (O) 439

Germantown Monthly Meeting (O) 114

Germantown Particular Meeting (P) 324

Germantown Preparative Meeting (H) (School House Lane) 291

Germantown Preparative Meeting (O) (Coulter Street 115

Girard Avenue Indulged Meeting (H) 292

Goshen Monthly Meeting (H) 230

Goshen Monthly Meeting (O) 150

Goshen Monthly Meeting Schools 418

Goshen Preparative Meeting (H) 231

Goshen Preparative Meeting (O) 151

Grandom Institution, The 437

Green Street Monthly Meeting (H) 287

Green Street Monthly Meeting (O) 54

Green Street Preparative Meeting (H) 288

Green Street Preparative Meeting (O) 55

Greenwood Indulged Meeting (H) 302

Greenwood Preparative Meeting (O) 43

Gwynedd Monthly Meeting (H) 179

Gwynedd Monthly Meeting (O) 96

Gwynedd Preparative Meeting (H) 180

Gwynedd Preparative Meeting (O) 97

Harrisburg Independent Friends Meeting   338

Haverford College   433

Haverford Friends School   449

Haverford Indulged Meeting (0)   53

Haverford Monthly Meeting (0)   56

Haverford Preparative Meeting (H) . . . . . . , ...   295

Haverford Preparative Meeting (0) . . . . -   16

Head of Wheeling Preparative Meeting
    (Old English Quaker Meeting) (0) (O.Y.M.)   389

Hestonville (Merion) Indulged Meeting (0)   52

Hestonville (Merion) Preparative Meeting (0)   18

High Street Meeting (The Great Meeting House) (0)   8

Homeville (Oxford) Preparative Meeting (H)   258

Horsham Monthly Meeting (H)   186

Horsham Monthly Meeting (0)   103

Horsham Particular Meeting (P)   326

Horsham Preparative Meeting (H)   187

Horsham Preparative Meeting (0)   104

Howell James' Meeting (0)   23

Hughesville Monthly Meeting (0) (O.Y.M.)   401

Huntingdon Preparative Meeting (H) (B.Y.M.) 383

Huntingdon Preparative Meeting (0) (B.Y.M.) 346

Jacob Thomas' Indulged Meeting (0)   57

Jeanes Hospital   458

Kennett Monthly Meeting (H)   244

Kennett Monthly Meeting (0)   79

Kennett Preparative Meeting (H)   245

Kennett Preparative Meeting (O) 80

Kennett Square Preparative Meeting (H) 247

Kennett Square Preparative Meeting (O) 82

Key's Alley Meeting (O) 35

Lake Shore Independent Meeting 340

Lampetor Preparative Meeting (H) 267

Lampeter Preparative Meeting (O) 125

Lancaster Indulged Meeting (O) 126

Landisville Indulged Meeting (Plumstead (O) 164

Lansdowne Monthly Meeting (H) 236

Lansdowne Monthly Meeting (O) 156

Lehigh Valley Independent Friends Meeting 339

Little Britain Monthly Meeting (H) (B.Y.M.) 374

Little Britain Monthly Meeting (O) (B.Y.M.) 353

Little Britain Monthly Meeting (P) 314

Little Britain (Ballance) Particular Meeting (P) 328

Little Britain (Penn Hill) Preparative Meeting (H) (B.Y.M.) 377

Little Britain (Ballance) Preparative Meeting (O) (B.Y.M.) 354

Little Elk Indulged Meeting (H) (B.Y.M.) 378

Little Elk Indulged Meeting (O) (B.Y.M.) 352

London-Britain Particular Meeting (P) 325

London Britain Preparative Meeting (O) 77

London Grove Monthly Meeting (H) 250

London Grove Monthly Meeting (O) 83

London Grove Preparative Meeting (H) 251

London Grove Preparative Meeting (O) 84

Maiden Creek Preparative Meeting (H) 285

Maiden Creek Preparative Meeting (O) 26

Makefield Monthly Meeting (H) 204

Makefield Monthly Meeting (O) 68

Makefield Preparative Meeting (H) 205

Makefield Preparative Meeting (O) 69

Marlboro Preparative Meeting (Marlboro-Unionville) (H) 246

Marlboro Preparative Meeting (O) 81

Media Preparative Meeting (O) 141

Media-Springfield Preparative Meeting (O) 142

Menallen Monthly Meeting (H) (B.Y.M.) 382

Menallen Monthly Meeting (O) (B.Y.M.) 344

Menallen Preparative Meeting (O) (B.Y.M.) 345

Merion Preparative Meeting (H) 296

Merion Preparative Meeting (O) 17

Middletown Monthly Meeting (H) (Bucks County) 207

Middletown Monthly Meeting (O) (Bucks County) 166

Middletown Monthly Meeting (O) (Delaware County) 159

Middletown Preparative Meeting (H) (Bucks County) 208

Middletown Preparative Meeting (H) (Delaware County) 237

Middletown Preparative Meeting (O) (Bucks County) 163

Middletown Preparative Meeting (O) (Delaware County) 160

Middletown School 432

Millville Half-Yearly Meeting (Fishing Creek) (H) 308

Millville Monthly Meeting (Muncy) (Fishing Creek) (H) 309

Muncy Monthly Meeting (O) 41

Muncy Preparative Meeting (O) 40

Nantmeal Preparative Meeting (H) 274

Nantmeal Preparative Meeting (O) 132

Newberry (Redlands) Preparative Meeting (H) (B.Y.M.)   384

Newberry Preparative Meeting (O) (B.Y.M.)   343

New Garden Monthly Meeting (H)   252

New Garden Monthly Meeting (O)   72

New Garden Preparative Meeting (H)   253

New Garden Preparative Meeting (O)   73

New Hope Indulged Meeting (H)   211

Newtown Monthly Meeting (H) (Bucks County)   216

Newtown Preparative Meeting (H) (Bucks County)   217

Newtown Preparative Meeting (H) (Delaware County)   232

Newtown Preparative Meeting (O) (Bucks County)   70

Newtown Preparative Meeting (O) (Delaware County)   146

Norristown Monthly Meeting (H)   194

Norristown Preparative Meeting (H)   184

Northern District Monthly Meeting (O)   33

Nottingham Monthly Meeting (O) (B.Y.M.)   351

Nottingham Monthly Meeting (P)   315

Nottingham Quarterly Meeting (H) (B.Y.M.)   372

Nottingham Quarterly Meeting (O) (B.Y.M.)   350

Nottingham Quarterly Meeting (P)   313

Nottingham and Little Britain Monthly Meeting (P)   327

Opps Preparative Meeting (O) (O.Y.M.)   402

Orange Street Indulged Meeting (O)   12

Oxford Indulged Meeting (H) (B.Y.M.)   379

Oxford Keithian Meeting (K)   169

Oxford Valley Friends School   423

Peace Hill Preparative Meeting (O) (O.Y.M.)   396

Pendle Hill 464

Pennsbury (Friends Boarding Home) 456

Pennsbury Indulged Meeting (H) 203

Pennsbury Preparative Meeting (O) 62

Pennsgrove Indulged Meeting (O) 76

Pennsgrove Monthly Meeting (H) 256

Pennsgrove Preparative Meeting (H) 257

Pennsylvania Society for Promoting the Abolition of Slavery 416

Pennsylvania Yearly Meeting of Progressive Friends (Pr) 311

Philadelphia Association of Friends for the Instruction
    of Poor Children (Adelphia School) 425

Philadelphia Friends Mission to Cornplanter's Village 420

Philadelphia Keithian Meeting (K) 168

Philadelphia Monthly Meeting (H) 280

Philadelphia Monthly Meeting (O) 3

Philadelphia Monthly Meeting (P) 320

Philadelphia Particular Meeting (P) 321

Philadelphia Preparative Meeting (H) 281

Philadelphia Quarterly Meeting (H) 279

Philadelphia Quarterly Meeting of Friends (O) 2

Philadelphia Yearly Meeting of Friends (H) 173

Philadelphia Yearly Meeting of Friends (O) 1

Philadelphia Young Friends Association 457

Pikeland Indulged Meeting (H) 275

Pikeland Preparative Meeting (O) 131

Pike Run Monthly Meeting (H) (O.Y.M.) 409

Pike Run Meeting (O) (O.Y.M.) 390

Pine Grove Preparative Meeting (Loyal Sock) (O) 44

Pine Street Meeting, The (O) 38

Pittsburgh Friends Meeting (O) (O.Y.M.) 399

Pittsburgh Independent Friends Meeting 334

Plumstead Indulged Meeting (H) 199

Plymouth Monthly Meeting (H) 195

Plymouth Preparative Meeting (H) 181

Plymouth Preparative Meeting (O) 98

Pocono Lake Preserve Independent Friends Meeting 337

Pocono Manor Independent Friends Meeting 336

Pottstown Indulged Meeting (O) 10

Pottsville Indulged Meeting (H) 286

Pottsville Indulged Meeting (O) 30

Providence Preparative Meeting (H) (Delaware County) 238

Providence Preparative Meeting (H) (Montgomery County) 182

Providence Preparative Meeting (O) (Delaware County) 140

Providence Preparative Meeting (O) (Montgomery County) 99

Providence Preparative Meeting (O) (O.Y.M.) 394

Providence United Monthly Meeting 332

Radnor Monthly Meeting (H) 294

Radnor Monthly Meeting (O) 15

Radnor Preparative Meeting (O) 19

Radnor United Monthly Meeting 333

Reading Preparative Meeting (O) 28

Redstone Monthly Meeting (O) (O.Y.M.) 391

Redstone Preparative Meeting (O) (O.Y.M.) 393

Redstone Quarterly Meeting (H) (O.Y.M.) 408

Redstone Quarterly Meeting (O) (O.Y.M.) 386

Richland Monthly Meeting (H) (Quakertown) 190

Richland Monthly Meeting (O) 101

Richland Preparative Meeting (H) (Quakertown) 191

Richland Preparative Meeting (O) 102

Ridge (Muddy Creek) Indulged Meeting (O) (O.Y.M.) 392

River Indulged Meeting (O) 78

Roaring Creek Indulged Meeting (H) 310

Roaring Creek Monthly Meeting (H) 303

Roaring Creek Monthly Meeting (O) 47

Roaring Creek Preparative Meeting (H) 306

Roaring Creek Preparative Meeting (O) 49

Robeson Monthly Meeting (O) 134

Robeson Preparative Meeting (O) 135

Romansville (Bradford) Indulged Meeting (H) 271

Sadsbury Monthly Meeting (H) 265

Sadsbury Monthly Meeting (O) 123

Sadsbury Particular Meeting (P) 316

Sadsbury Preparative Meeting (H) 268

Sadsbury Preparative Meeting (O) 119

Sandy Hill Preparative Meeting (O) (O.Y.M.) 388

Saucon Indulged Meeting (O) 32

Schuylkill Indulged Meeting (H) 301

Schuylkill Indulged Meeting (O) (Charlestown) 22

Schuylkill Meeting (O) (Thomas Duckett's) 20

Second Bank Meeting, The (O) 34

Sewickley Preparative Meeting (O) (O.Y.M.) 398

Shackamaxon Meeting (O) 4

Shamokin Indulged Meeting (H) (Bear Gap) 307

Society of Free Quakers, The (F) 171

Solebury Monthly Meeting (H) 209

Solebury Monthly Meeting (O) 66

Solebury Preparative Meeting (H) 210

Solebury Preparative Meeting (O) 67

Southampton Indulged Meeting (O) 63

Southern District Monthly Meeting (O) 37

Spencer's Indulged Meeting (H) 254

Spencer's Indulged Meeting (O) 75

Springfield Indulged Meeting (O) 31

Springfield Preparative Meeting (H) 224

Springfield Preparative Meeting (O) 138

Spruce Street Monthly Meeting (H) 297

Spruce Street Preparative Meeting (H) 298

Stapeley Hall (Friends Boarding Home) 453

State College United Meeting 329

Stewarts Crossing Preparative Meeting (O) (O.Y.M.) 397

Stroudsburg Monthly Meeting (O) 112

Stroudsburg Preparative Meeting (H) 192

Stroudsburg Preparative Meeting (O) 111

Sunny Crest Farm 467

Swarthmore College 444

Swarthmore Monthly Meeting (H) 235

Tackony and Poetquesink Monthly Meeting (O) 14

The Friend 430

The Friends Intelligencer 438

Thomas Powell Meeting (K) 170

Tioga Friends Meeting (O) (Proposed 1886) 36

Tract Association of Friends 429

Tulpehocken Indulged Meeting (O) 27

Underground Railroad, The 422

Unionville Indulged Meeting (H) (1845) 248

Unionville Indulged Meeting (H) (1931) 249

Unionville (Bald Eagle) Preparative Meeting (H) (B.Y.M.) 368

Upper Dublin Preparative Meeting (H) 188

Upper Dublin Preparative Meeting (O) 105

Uwchlan Monthly Meeting (H) 273

Uwchlan Monthly Meeting (O) 129

Uwchlan Preparative Meeting (H) 278

Uwchlan Preparative Meeting (O) 130

Valley Monthly Meeting (H) 299

Valley Preparative Meeting (H) 300

Valley Preparative Meeting (O) 21

Warminster Preparative Meeting (H) 189

Warrington Monthly Meeting (H) (B.Y.M.) 381

Warrington Monthly Meeting (O) (B.Y.M.) 342

Warrington Quarterly Meeting (H) (B.Y.M.) 380

Warrington Quarterly Meeting (O) (B.Y.M.) 341

Warrington-Fairfax Quarterly Meeting (O) 89

West Branch Indulged Meeting (O) (B.Y.M.) 349

West Branch Monthly Meeting (H) (B.Y.M.) 370

West Caln Preparative Meeting (H) 263

West Caln Preparative Meeting (O) 121

West Chester Preparative Meeting (H) 221

West Chester Preparative Meeting (O) 147

Western District Monthly Meeting of Friends (O) 51

Western Quarterly Meeting (H) 240

Western Quarterly Meeting (O) 71

Western Soup Association 436

West Grove Monthly Meeting (H) 259

West Grove Preparative Meeting (H) 260

West Grove Preparative Meeting (0) 74

Westland Monthly Meeting (0) (O.Y.M.) 387

West Philadelphia Indulged Meeting (H) 283

West Philadelphia Indulged Meeting (0) 13

Westtown Boarding School 421

Westtown Indulged Meeting (0) 158

Westtown Monthly Meeting (0) 157

Whiteland Preparative Meeting (H) 233

Whiteland Preparative Meeting (0) 153

Whitemarsh Indulged Meeting (H) 183

Whitemarsh Indulged Meeting (0) 100

William Forrest Estate 413

William Penn Charter School 411

Willistown Monthly Meeting (H) 239

Willistown Preparative Meeting (H) 234

Willistown Preparative Meeting (0) 152

Wrightstown Monthly Meeting (H) 212

Wrightstown Monthly Meeting (0) 65

Wrightstown Preparative Meeting (H) 213

Wrightstown Preparative Meeting (0) 64

Yardley Indulged Meeting (H) 206

Yellow Breeches Indulged Meeting (0) 91

York Monthly Meeting (H) (B.Y.M.) 385

York Monthly Meeting (0) (B.Y.M.) 348

York Preparative Meeting (0) 90

Young Friends Movement 463